Innovation and Institutional Policy

D. N. Gupta · Sushil

Innovation and Institutional Development for Public Policy

Complexity Theory, Design Thinking and System Dynamics Application

Springer

D. N. Gupta
National Institute of Advanced Studies
(NIAS)
Bengaluru, Karnataka, India

Sushil
Department of Management Studies
Indian Institute of Technology Delhi
New Delhi, Delhi, India

ISBN 978-981-97-3662-1   ISBN 978-981-97-3663-8 (eBook)
https://doi.org/10.1007/978-981-97-3663-8

© The Editor(s) (if applicable) and The Author(s), under exclusive license to Springer Nature Singapore Pte Ltd. 2024

This work is subject to copyright. All rights are solely and exclusively licensed by the Publisher, whether the whole or part of the material is concerned, specifically the rights of translation, reprinting, reuse of illustrations, recitation, broadcasting, reproduction on microfilms or in any other physical way, and transmission or information storage and retrieval, electronic adaptation, computer software, or by similar or dissimilar methodology now known or hereafter developed.
The use of general descriptive names, registered names, trademarks, service marks, etc. in this publication does not imply, even in the absence of a specific statement, that such names are exempt from the relevant protective laws and regulations and therefore free for general use.
The publisher, the authors and the editors are safe to assume that the advice and information in this book are believed to be true and accurate at the date of publication. Neither the publisher nor the authors or the editors give a warranty, expressed or implied, with respect to the material contained herein or for any errors or omissions that may have been made. The publisher remains neutral with regard to jurisdictional claims in published maps and institutional affiliations.

This Springer imprint is published by the registered company Springer Nature Singapore Pte Ltd.
The registered company address is: 152 Beach Road, #21-01/04 Gateway East, Singapore 189721, Singapore

If disposing of this product, please recycle the paper.

Dedicated to the memory of my parents, Late Sharda Devi Gupta and Late R. N. S. Gupta, for their inspirations.

D. N. Gupta

Foreword

There are stories of policymaking that I now take for granted or describe as truisms. For example, policymakers need to make choices based on limited information and limited understanding of that information. They draw on cognitive and emotional shortcuts to make sense of their world and make policy choices. They act within a complex policymaking system that is out of their full understanding and control. As a result, focusing solely on their choices tells us very little about what will happen next. Maybe they will produce a profound impact on policymaking practices and outcomes, or maybe their choices will have no impact at all. In each case, an understanding of system dynamics helps to explain how the choices and interactions between a huge number of policy actors become greater than the sum of their parts.

This kind of story gives us a remarkably useful starting point, and is abstract enough to apply to a huge amount and wide range of experiences across space and time. However, we also have two main limitations to address. First, we need more concrete and in-depth accounts of how these policy dynamics play out in the real world. We have made a lot of progress in this respect, but mainstream studies of policymaking still rely disproportionately on evidence from studies of the US and Western Europe. Second, while detailed studies of policymaking are interesting to policy scholars, policymakers and potential influencers want to know what to do. How would greater insights on policymaking complexity help them understand their role and act accordingly?

In that context, this book provides two key functions. *First*, it examines policy problems and policy processes in India. India's population is greater than North America and the EU combined, but the number of books dedicated to its policy processes is remarkably small. *Second*, it combines academic and practitioner insights to show how to see policymaking complexity through the eyes of policymakers, planners, designers, advocates, stakeholders, and citizens.

This combination of policymaking research and policy analysis is crucial to understand and engage with policy problems and solutions. Without policymaking research, it is too tempting to conclude that politicians and lobbyists are to blame for all policy failures or the lack of implementation of necessary policy aims.

Rather, research helps us separate—at least analytically—the dynamics of poor policymaking from the dynamics that would exist in any system regardless of the people involved. Without policy analysis and application, we would not be able to understand how people make sense of complexity in different contexts. In each case, we would be doomed to repeat the same mistakes without learning from them. Rather, this book offers hope that we can combine policy theory and practice to understand policymaking and operate effectively within policy processes.

Paul Cairney
Professor of Politics and Public Policy
University of Stirling
Stirling, UK

Preface

Public policy has been of significance for centuries and instrumental in driving various social, economic, and technological changes. In the present dynamic and evolving world, it matters more than ever before, despite the growing debate about limiting the role of government. The success of developed countries and fast-emerging economies in East Asia is largely due to good public policies and institutions and effective policy implementation. Many critical problems in the world are a result of policy deficit. The future is more assured if the right policies are formulated.

The policy studies in the past several decades have shown a quest to understand the theories behind policymaking, how the decisions are made and implemented, and how better policies can be designed. Policies relate to every sphere of life and have a far-reaching impact on the way citizens live, the economy functions, and the country performs globally. They are expected to deal with a wide spectrum of problems—simple, complicated, and complex. Depending on the nature, these range from manageable to recurring to intractable.

While endeavoring to write the book, many issues were under consideration. Given the persistent and growing problems, it has examined vital questions, such as:

- why understanding policy system is fundamental to development and economy;
- how the policy process can be robust to understand the insights from the citizens to formulate policies that relate to them;
- how multiple complex problems, which are beyond the conventional approaches, can be addressed; and
- what institutional mechanism is called for sound policy design and efficient implementation.

Motivation to Write This Book

When there are multiple problems and diverse opportunities, what is lacking that should be addressed by way of public policy? It is this idea that demands exploring answers. From the importance attributed to policy management, the motivation to write the book has been the following:

- *First, to examine the efficacy of policy system—characteristics and process.* It includes studying the system's features and how the process considers different stages of policymaking, specifically, how the problems are conceptualized, the analyses are carried out, the decision-making takes place to identify policy options, and the implementation structure is put in place.
- *Second, to understand vast policy issues.* India is resource-rich but has many intractable problems. On the social front, improving the quality of public services needs to be a priority. Regarding economic problems, at both national and local levels, there are issues of unemployment, improving agriculture and industrial economy, energy management, R&D and technology readiness, inequalities, and so on. There are difficulties with last-mile connectivity for delivery mechanisms to ensure access to health services, primary education, food and nutrition, road communication, and safe drinking water. Reaching out to remote areas remains a question. Such critical development concerns ask what it will require to make a difference in policies. Climate change, changing demographics, social security, infrastructure investment, budget management, etc. deserve special consideration. The major challenge is formulating sound policies for enormous problems covering large geographical regions and diverse sectors such as human resource development, public service provisioning in rural and urban areas, rural economy, urban development, and advanced technologies and management of disruptions of existing businesses and jobs.
- *Third, to comprehend evolving challenges and opportunities.* Due to rapid globalization, a few technological trends need examination. Innovation and advanced manufacturing in a combined form are defining the future of the economy at an unprecedented scale. In the Industrial Era 4.0, multiple technologies, like ICT, nanotechnology, human science, biotechnology, energy, and smart materials, converge. These have got exponential potential for manufacturing. At the global level, the value of e-commerce, including online retail, has been $26 trillion in 2021 and will increase multifold in the next decade. By one estimate, the networked economy could have an economic value of $90 trillion by 2030. The potential from artificial intelligence (AI), 5G, the App economy, and the Internet of Things (IoT) could be about $40 trillion by 2030. These are shaping the world's future and contributing to opportunities through innovative solutions, improved efficiency, and productivity. Simultaneously, these cause disruptions and bring uncertainties.

With regard to investment needs, the estimated infrastructure investment to support global economic growth is $94 trillion by 2040, together with $5–7 trillion annually to meet the UN sustainable development goals (SDGs) by 2030. Likewise, for India, the total investment required for infrastructure will be $4.5 trillion by 2040. To meet the requirements of net-zero emissions by 2050, the projected annual global investment is about $5 trillion by 2030 and then $4.5 trillion till 2050 (by International Energy Agency). And India requires a $10 trillion investment to achieve net zero by 2070. To realize development needs in their respective countries, the governments are spending through their budgets, and the annual budgets reached $35 trillion globally and $1 trillion in India in 2019–20. In light of these figures, there are policy issues like: how to leverage the vast economic potential of the innovation economy, manage the staggering amount of investments effectively for both social development and economic growth, and utilize huge budget spending by the governments optimally.

- *Fourth, to discern new concepts and phenomena.* Nonlinearity, higher-order effects, feedback loops, circular causality, interactive effects, emergent behavior, evolution, complexity dimension, nonlinear thinking, institutional and behavioral issues, etc. need appreciation for future policymaking and theories, as brought out by various research studies.
- *Fifth, to explore alternative paradigm.* While dealing with social and economic systems, there are practical limitations. There are limits to certainty, stability, dominating approach, and growth. There are problems of high proportion concerning diverse population groups, running the economy, and managing global trends. In addition, these systems are inherently complex. It is difficult to articulate the problems and establish cause-effect relationships due to multidimensional and interconnected variables. The policy formulation, implementation, performance measurement, and monitoring are demanding as a result of complexity. A few significant points that merit study are how large persisting problems can be solved, multiple relevant factors can be comprehended and considered, and complex issues can be addressed by following current methodologies in public policy. The research underscores the shortcomings of conventional methods in defining complex problems, comprehending systems, and identifying policy options. The uncertainties and dynamics make policymaking a challenging task. These underlying reasons call for a different perspective to approach problems.

The book has been organized into seven chapters.

Chapter 1 accentuates the essentiality of public policy. Government affects all aspects of lives. Every citizen has a stake in the policies shaping the governance. It traces the evolution of policy theories by covering approaches like policy sciences, system approach, complexity theory, complexity and economics, and behavioral approach. It presents critical twenty-first century challenges and how they contribute to complexity in the system and recommends creative methods to deal with complex problems. It underscores why the system matters and how its understanding is a prerequisite for realizing intended objectives.

Chapter 2 emphasizes that if policies are examined systemically and systematically, specific measures for improvement can be introduced. Understanding them can enable stakeholders to research, critique, monitor, and evaluate the content and outcome and contribute to policymaking. Policies have the potential to improve the well-being of society, create opportunities, and enhance the sustainability of the development process. It identifies the need for a systemic approach or an integrated view for a holistic understanding of the system. It arises from the viewpoint that the system is composed of interrelated development sectors, and ignoring or inadequate knowledge of one or more sectors may give an incomplete assessment.

In every facet of life, policies have a role. Their better formulation requires investigating critical issues in various development sectors. To draw learnings, it systemically analyzes the performance in sectors such as education, health and nutrition, urban development, renewable energy, manufacturing, R&D, skill development, labor reforms, government budget, social security, and economic growth. The studies have brought to the fore relevant insights. It brings out how the outcomes in India differ from those of developed and fast-emerging countries. It attempts to understand the virtuous cycle of investment in human resources, government expenditure on social security, technology readiness, flexible labor laws, greater disposable income, and higher per capita GDP. It shows how these factors are intricately linked. The impact of linkages among sectoral policies on economic growth and quality of life is explicitly made out. For human development and the economy to grow, good policies are necessary to navigate the desired path.

Chapter 3 recognizes complexity in the social and economic systems in which the policies are formulated, the economy is run, and businesses and organizations function. The world that has been accustomed to certainty and orderliness has the challenge of dealing with complexity. A large number of interacting stakeholders, issues, and system variables make a system complex. In addition, the twenty-first century, driven by global network effects, adds to the complexity. Such systems are marked with nonlinearity in interactions, dynamic nature, and causality. At the basic level, the understanding and implications of complexity come from the 'interactive' behavior of elements and feedback loops leading to emergence. Such a phenomenon was not cognized before. It has given rise to characteristics like emergence, self-organization, adaptation, complex adaptive system (CAS), evolution, and path dependency. These were not adequately appreciated until the beginning of 1990, and they were not factored in for public policies, economic theories, or the management of organizations. Now, these have got more prominence due to the research work by many scholars. The complexity can undermine performance if not analyzed and addressed.

Why understanding complexity is essential in public system. The current approaches of assuming the system as static or government department as a standalone entity, working on linear relationships between system variables are not consistent with the concepts such as interactive effects of elements (like individuals and system variables), feedback loops, nonlinearity, emergence, and self-organizing property, as put forth by complexity science. The new concepts call for examining the problems and systems with a fresh complexity perspective.

Why economic system needs to factor in complexity. Over several decades, economic theories have been subject to criticism because of their assumptions of the rational behavior of economic agents, perfect information, and the equilibrium state of the economy. In contrast to these theories, the growing body of experts hypothesize about the non-equilibrium state and postulate that it remains in a dynamic state and evolves due to the interactive effects of economic agents and technological innovations. There are nonlinear and dynamic relationships between economic entities, institutional factors, and behavioral issues, and so there is uncertainty about the results. Such factors contribute to complexity in the economic system.

Why business needs to take into account complexity. The complexity is observed due to interactive and dynamic linkages between numerous business entities, mergers and acquisitions (M&A) at an increasing rate, entry of new products, increasing government regulations, changes in taxation, and a competitive environment.

Why organizations need to learn complexity. Organizations deal with nonlinear and dynamic interactions between individuals, structures, departments, and the environment. Such relations are uncertain and keep changing. These features make organizations complex systems.

Comprehending complexity is essential to develop better policy and economic theories and management models and design appropriate policies.

Chapter 4 presents the fundamentals of and critical challenges in the policy-making process. It covers policy theories, examines constraints, and highlights the essentiality of institutions, values, power, structure, and contexts. It stresses that the institutions are central to sustainable development and economic growth. The determinant of variations in the development outcomes across the countries in the global context and the States within the country is differences in the capacity of the institutions to deliver. While covering various approaches, theories, and models that have evolved with time, it underlines that they have considered several issues related to policymaking. As such, the 'what' part of policymaking has been in focus. But the 'how (causal linkages)' part of the policy process has not got enough recognition.

It includes case studies and field surveys. These indicate that much less attention is paid to the process required for data collection and analysis, examining grassroots realities, understanding problems and causes, and informed decision-making. The policy analyses are not adequately attempted, and the environment in which the system works is not examined. The lack of rigor leads to oversimplification of problems and the loss of substantive issues. The studies reflect that policy management is affected due to infirmities in the delivery mechanism. It is beset with low process efficiency (of service delivery) and involves considerable time and cost in availing services. The requisite technical and performance standards are inadequate. Particular emphasis is needed for a citizen focus. It identifies key determinants of successful implementation. The success of a policy depends on the efficacy of the policy process and delivery mechanism.

Chapter 5 addresses the complexity dimension. In the past, public and economic theories and management models were developed keeping in view the certainty of system behavior, stability, rational individuals, aggregate system, equilibrium state, and steady environment as the fundamental basis. They did not consider the individuals' interactive tendencies in the system, institutional factors, behavioral needs, and psychological preferences. The approaches based on Newtonian thinking, scientific management, and classical theories of the economics of the twentieth century have fallen short of dealing with dynamic and complex systems. The evolving understanding of socio-economic systems questions the existing tools and methodologies. The knowledge from complexity science opens up a new method of inquiry.

The complexity theory framework is set forth to find ways to manage them. It has two constituents—*first*, complexity theory and, *second*, framework. The theory embraces concepts such as emergence, self-organization, adaptation, and evolution to define behavior of complex systems. It explains that there is a need to shift the analysis from individual parts to the system as a whole, as a network of elements that interact to generate order, pattern, and behavior through the feedback mechanism. It highlights the need to zoom in to study the elements (at nanolevel) and simultaneously zoom out to get a holistic view. The framework covers the methodology to resolve complex problems.

In addition, for comprehending contexts of systems in the real world, it includes a strategic framework that provides a conceptual frame to diagnose the contexts, examine the complexity, and explore strategies to manage. Based on the contexts and features, it recommends four types of systems—simple, complicated, complex, and disorder. Simple and complicated systems will demand different approaches than complex systems. The scientific management tools and practices hold good for simple and complicated problems. Handling complex problems will entail systems thinking, design thinking, complexity thinking, scenario building, and pattern recognition, involving transdisciplinary studies. There is a need to develop abilities to visualize pattern or future state and synthesize various phenomena.

The study of the evolution of Silicon Valleys in Bengaluru and San Francisco Bay (USA) is a case in point. The case studies present a method for learning about complex phenomena and drawing lessons to formulate economic policies. Also, the studies stress why economic theories should factor in complexity theory.

The concepts contained in complexity theory are distinct. Still, due to multiple dimensions in the policy system, it calls for understanding causal relations between several system variables—contextual, sectoral, and outcome. Despite useful inputs from various theories, there is no single theory for public policy. It asks for a more comprehensive approach by unifying relevant transdisciplinary perspectives. The future policy theory should cover the 'causality' aspect, the underlying factors that determine policy formulation, and the theory of implementation.

Chapter 6 underlines that citizens are usually concerned about how numerous unresolved problems, which abound, can be solved. It is more challenging to address complex issues. These question the capacity of the policy system and ask what needs to be done. It emphasizes comprehending three interlinked aspects: what should be the policy process that can capture the ever-increasing issues facing the citizenry; which policies are to be formulated that can improve the quality of life and meet the challenges of the economy; and what institutional mechanism is needed.

The touchstone of rigorous policymaking is that it should match the ground reality, provide a holistic solution, and fulfill the public purpose. It requires new ways of working in the policy domain and introduces innovative approaches. Some are the system approach, adaptive policies, creative citizen engagement, and deliberative dialogue. It underscores the need to reinforce different modes of thinking, such as systems thinking, design thinking, complexity thinking, and nonlinear thinking. It articulates systemic understanding.

The conceptual understanding of core issues—assumptions, concepts, principles, and approaches—matters. Their clarity will provide a good foundation to identify the method of inquiry and interventions correctly. The chapter presents a policy design framework covering fundamental issues and methodology. The framework is like a reference document for policymakers and stakeholders.

Policy formulation should be seen beyond the prism of annual budgets, investments, and allocative efficiency, though important. It suggests going beyond notable ideas and targets and policy prescriptions. The successful deployment of resources will depend on context-specific studies and interdisciplinary inputs. Gaining specific knowledge from the micro level is critical. It can help identify hidden potential and leverage points. It calls for systemic analyses of grassroots-level conditions and problems; stakeholders' needs; micro-macro linkages; institutional, behavioral, complexity, and technical issues; and implementation mechanism. It recommends that the 'process' deserves priority. The focus of policymaking should be on: *first*, eliciting realities from the ground, end-users, and last mile; *second*, end-users-centric policy analysis; and *third*, using the 'design' approach. Simultaneously, a robust implementation structure should be put in place.

Future policymaking should consider the strategies like: while working on today's problems, preparing for the future; simultaneous to managing immediate concerns, working on the complexity dimension as a long-term strategy; and keeping an eye on the ground together with solving big problems.

The chapter has utilized the system approach, interpretive structural modeling (ISM), and system dynamics (SD) to aid decision-making and policy design for complex problems. The unique advantage has been the identification of the structure of interlinked factors within a system. The models question the basic premise of how the simplified approach does not yield expected results. They added value by revisiting existing assumptions, gaining understanding from the ground, and improving confidence level in the policy analysis.

Chapter 7 escalates the challenges that the governments are expected to resolve. It recognizes the need for institutional development for sustainability. The current organizations rooted in the twentieth century should be congruent with the changing times in the twenty-first century. The premise is that, so far, the governments have worked in a relatively homogeneous, predictable, and stable environment, which is markedly different from a dynamic and complex environment.

It demands distinct philosophy, theory, and approach for managing dynamics and uncertainty. It argues for a shift from the Weberian classical model and scientific management. It stresses designing new, efficiently performing public organizations to deliver quality services, settle local-specific problems, and manage global challenges. These should focus on building human capital with skill sets and embrace strategic planning, quality management, citizen-centric system, performance management system (PMS), and collaborative approach to manage complex issues. It concludes with the indispensability of innovation in the process of design of policy as well as for policy options.

Policymaking—A Critique

Examination of specific sectoral policies and the policy process has made several findings conspicuous. There are inadequacies in capturing local needs and end-users' requirements. It makes it difficult to conceptualize the problem and system, inform discussions, and identify policy options. While covering field studies, it underlines the need for evidence-based policy. But, the policy system lacks the requisite capacity—in terms of framework, information infrastructure, policy tools, manpower, and capabilities. Often, due to the need to deliver results in a short time, the process becomes an exercise to elicit good ideas and, often, intuitive. Making policies with less attention to analyses undermine the development process.

The studies reveal that traditional methods have fundamental limitations in formulating desired policies. As a result, the policies are not able to address the problems that citizens seek to resolve. If any program fails to succeed, it is usually attributed to the inability of the public department to deliver. But, the main reason is the inadequacies in policies and their implementation. Essentially, how they are formulated and implemented needs more effort.

The deficient policies have been a source of many problems. More often, they respond to short-term objectives and address the symptoms rather than the causes. They serve a few goals than holistic solutions and outcomes. At the conceptual level, some concerns are: lack of systemic view of the problem and system in question, mismatch between micro-level realities and macro-level requirements, and inadequate understanding of qualitative aspects (institutional and behavioral) and complexity. There are deficits in the delineation and institutionalization of the policy process. These pose questions for policymakers and ask whether the policy system has the capacity to manage big and complex problems. It underscores that if policies are not formulated correctly, the concerned sector may miss out on some crucial aspects and it may even lead to a particular sector lagging behind by several years until the correction is introduced.

Critique of Current Methods of Inquiry

From the 1950s onward, optimization techniques, mathematical models, and statistical tools were applied to decision-making. These have been suitable for physical, engineering, and business problems with easily quantifiable variables. But, they were subsequently employed in social and economic systems. These methods mainly use linear thinking and are appropriate for learning first-order effects but cannot deal with higher-order effects and feedback loops. They cannot adequately consider qualitative variables.

In the case of the economy, the experts such as Jay R. Forrester, Alan Kirman, and Brian Arthur have highlighted the inability of the economic models and theories and econometrics to examine interactions between elements and entities, multiple feedbacks, and the structures that form economic systems, besides behavioral issues. The theories deal with the economy in an aggregate form without examining the interactive behavior. The emergence and evolutionary nature of the economy are not recognized.

Quantitative analyses are of importance under specific assumptions and conditions. But, they have practical limitations in conceptualizing socio-economic problems and systems, given the presence of numerous elements and qualitative variables. Moreover, there is a limitation of aggregate data as they cannot capture the diversity, segmented data, and behavioral and cognitive issues, while both policy and economic theories have banked on aggregate data and have offered their reasoning based on that.

Predominantly, the current methods assume that the systems are steady, remain in equilibrium, and work in a stable environment. In addition, they tend to examine the issues and system in parts, without a holistic view and by not considering the effect of the environment. The studies indicate their limitations in solving problems by diagnosing the factors (variables) independently without examining their interrelationship. Besides, the context-specific examination is not sufficiently carried out. They rely on a top-down approach and tend to apply best practices or solutions taken from one setting and then use them in other contexts. As a result, the generalization of problems and their simplification becomes the basis for policy analysis.

Complexity is another dimension. The studies show how scientific approaches, including mathematical models, have limitations and are unable to analyze the interactive effects of elements, feedback, nonlinearity, and dynamic behavior. Thus, they have constraints in examining complex systems. If difficult and complex problems are examined by methods with linear thinking and using consolidated data without factoring in details (of gender, demographic, sections, sectors and subsectors, etc.), the comprehension of problems will be insufficient, leading to deficiencies in policymaking. Similarly, if the system is managed majorly through interventions worked for steady and known conditions, the results thereof will not be desirable. These necessitate revisiting whether the current conventional methods can address complexity.

Scholarly research has amply highlighted that the current approaches to public policies, particularly economic policies, are detached from the understanding of the complexity and, thus, anachronous with time. Traditional mathematical and scientific tools are primarily apt for non-organic or mechanical systems. Their applicability is not compatible with the realities in the social systems. They are away from considering the evolutionary property of social systems and the economy.

Alternate Methods of Inquiry

The socio-economic systems dealing with a large number of elements are nonlinear, dynamic, and complex. In the twenty-first century, the speed, scale, and impact of change are much higher due to globalization and the instant exchange of ideas and resources. These result in higher-order effects and uncertainty, causing complexity. These systems are more complex as compared to engineering and physical systems. These are counterintuitive, unlike simpler linear systems. In complex systems, the 'beginning and end' points of problems are not discernible. The problems keep changing and growing with time. The deterministic models and theories have limitations in dealing with dynamic and uncertain behavior, and top-down approach or macro-level interventions alone may not work for complex development problems, including economic. In complex systems, it is demanding to visualize which factors have significant influence and which policy options will be the determiner of success.

In light of the above, the new methods of inquiry need to embrace *emerging issues*—the dynamic behavior of systems, uncertainty, and evolving nature of problems; the *phenomena*—emergence, self-organization, adaptation, and evolution; the *assumptions*—interactions between elements and feedback loops determine the system's behavior; and the *concepts*—system structure, nonlinearity, higher-order consequences, behavioral and institutional dimensions, and path dependency. The policy system is expected to deal with these underlying features to provide a realistic approach to inquiry. These have implications for both social and economic policies.

Emerging Theory—Complexity Theory

The phenomenon of complexity, studied gradually through scholarly research in the last several decades, has brought to the fore unique concepts that were not realized before. It can be an advantage for the system if the complexity is understood and addressed. The system may benefit due to synergy created by multiple interactions, leveraging diversity, and unlocking hidden potential in the network. The complexity may add more cost and difficulty in decision-making due to want of understanding.

A complexity theory has been set forth as a result of, *first*, increased complexity and uncertainty of larger scale, and, *second*, generation of new knowledge about characteristics of complex systems and policy processes. Drawing on perspectives from multiple disciplines, the theory has emerged. It has opened better ways of comprehending problems. At a conceptual level, it is envisaged to provide a set of generally regarded assumptions, principles, and propositions that constitute a way to give a logical explanation for addressing the complexity in the system in the real world. The theory has relevance for complex social and economic systems. It states that the interactions between elements take place at a local level through feedback loops, not through central control, and result in the emergence of a pattern of behavior or structure. It implies that there is a possibility of unknown effects of elements. Thus, policies that encourage interactive effects are essential to bringing desired changes in the system. This characteristic is fundamental to the theory. It needs recognition and should form the basis for future policies.

In the specific context of the economy, in addition to the above, there are two key features. *First*, the economy is not just a 'monolith—a single homogeneous entity' in the real world. Rather, it is a result of interactions between thousands or even millions of elements (enterprises or economic agents). Each element matters in the complex system. The invisible role of interactive elements can have multiplier effect, and, thus, can influence the future state of economy. *Second*, the economy remains in a dynamic mode and evolves with time. The current theories are not consistent with the reality of interacting heterogeneous elements and the emergent behavior of the economic system. The complexity theory has postulated a distinct way to understand the economy that has not been a part of mainstream economics. Moreover, the knowledge economy driven by individuals, networks, information flows, creativity, and technology advancements has evolutionary features. These should form the basis for future economic theories.

For dynamic and complex systems, the business-as-usual (BAU) approach will not serve the intended purpose. The book attempts to provide the know-how to comprehend and address complexity. Complex problems demand a different mindset and method. The idea of complexity may be overwhelming, but it is an enriching subject once understood, as it allows to think about and deal with complex real-world issues and explore how to solve them.

The essence of the complexity theory is that the grassroots (nanolevel) determines the future state of any system. And values, norms, and interactions matter and influence the system. The physical world (medicine, agriculture, and engineering) has benefited immensely by working at the nanolevel—atomic and cell—through nanotechnologies. It has vast potential prospects that were unthinkable earlier. It offers a way forward for managing complex systems, and the social innovations at the community level and the application of complexity theory hold promise. It is time to work at the grassroots level and appreciate the interactive effects of elements—individuals, skills, institutions, and policies.

So far, the problem-solving world has been conditioned to solve problems with certainty and in an equilibrium state. The systems were assumed as single and uniform structures while using aggregate data. For examining and theorizing real-world socioeconomic problems, assuming the social system or economy as a single composite structure is not reasoned. Such assumptions formed the basis of thinking for research and shaped theories in the twentieth century.

These are at variance with the understanding and implications of complexity theory. It recognizes the uncertainty and dynamic nature of complex systems. It articulates that every element is vital, and the interrelationships between variables and the interactive effect define the behavior of the system or economy. The disaggregated data is essential as it brings diversity and details. The study of complexity opens up a system of examination and the possibility of solutions that are not perceptible through existing conventional approaches. It will add value to formulating the correct policies and their better implementation. This theory is fundamental to public policy, the economy, business, and organizations.

Way Ahead

How policies are vital and shape the country's future is well elaborated in the book. It has utilized the inputs from research under the Ph.D. program at IIT (Delhi). It examines both micro-level and macro-level issues and provides a comprehensive view of public policy. Striking a balance between the theoretical and practical aspects is a challenge in policy studies. It combines both researcher's analysis and the practitioner's perspective, covering international strands. It attempts to bring out in-depth knowledge about policy formulation and implementation, relying on extensive literature survey, field-level research, and case studies. Specifically, it examines several theories and approaches.

It presents a primary document or template that can be an easy aid to all stakeholders with diverse backgrounds who can have a shared vocabulary. It strives to demystify the postulates behind the complexity theory and its application. It brings a global perspective and caters to the needs of academic programs in public policy, public administration, and business management. It will help better understand policy management and serve the requirements of policymakers, students, researchers, academics, and economists. Though there has been an effort to include various pertinent aspects, all issues still need to be covered. The authors will look forward to suggestions from the readers.

Key message. The world is witnessing wide-ranging problems, challenges, and prospects. These, in a combined form, are shaping the functioning of the government. Public policies should be in anticipation of the future, based on trends and likely scenarios. They need to explore creative ways to utilize government budgets, infrastructure investments, and natural resources. More than the financial resources, the rigorous policy process should be a central point. It deserves serious thought and involves tedious exercise. It justifies a specialized and institutionalized approach. It is requisite to develop knowledge about complex problems and systems. It calls for new thinking.

Defining assumptions and principles requires priority consideration for dealing with policy issues. If the assumptions are realistic, the conclusions drawn will likely be correct. And if the principles are well-constructed and followed, the policy success will be higher. A proper theory and framework can guide toward better policies. Understanding their linkages is imperative. It suggests a complexity theory framework and a policy design framework. The first framework provides how to diagnose complexity and formulate strategies. The design framework contains the science of policymaking by relying on organized knowledge of theories, approaches, and methods based on time-tested research as a scientific basis.

There are a few interlinked questions, like why different regions or countries have varying levels of human resources—education, skills, and health; variations in poverty and family income; and differences in technology adoption, industrialization, and national income. The current policy and economic theories have yet to address them. The missing threads merit probing for answers.

Recognizing why public policy is of consequence and the appreciation of emerging knowledge of concepts and phenomena in the social and economic systems can make a distinction. It will change the thinking and perspective about policymaking and thus will bring different approaches, methods, and tools, leading to the emergence of a new policy system. Essentially, it should be able to elicit insights from the end-users and design policies that concern them; raise process efficiency and reduce transaction costs of public services, and thus release time and energy for people for more productive usage; set in motion for the innovation to explore solutions that can provide better policy options; and, through them, find ways to change productivity curve to raise it for improved economic well-being.

A new paradigm is necessitated to bring a fundamental difference. It enunciates mainstreaming the value of innovative policy processes, alternative approaches—adaptive policies and policy design, and alternative theory—complexity theory. Institutional development will shape success. The book makes a purposive effort toward this cause.

Sound policies are a driver of quality of life and economic growth. Countries need to make the right policy choices today to steer ahead.

Bengaluru, India D. N. Gupta
New Delhi, India Sushil

Acknowledgments

The completion of the book is a result of the support from several academics, researchers, officials, and individuals. I have tried to identify them to acknowledge their support and express my gratitude. A few words are of recognition toward all those who have helped during this journey.

I sincerely thank Prof. Sushil, Prof. M. P. Gupta, and Prof. V. K. Vijay of the Indian Institute of Technology (IIT) (Delhi) for their technical support during the research work. I want to thank Dr. N. C. Saxena, former Secretary Ministry of Rural Development; Mr. B. N. Yugandhar, former member Planning Commission; and the officials of the Ministries of New and Renewable Energy (MNRE), Health and Family Welfare, Rural Development, Human Resource Development, and Housing and Urban Affairs. I thank Mr. Tarun Kapoor, former Joint Secretary, and Mr. B. S. Negi and Mr. S. K. Singh Scientists of the Ministry of New and Renewable Energy (MNRE); Dr. G. J. Gyani, former Secretary General of the Quality Council of India (QCI); and Dr. K. V. Sundaram, former Adviser Planning Commission.

I am thankful for senior academics from various eminent Universities and Institutes, especially Prof. Arun Kumar, Prof. Santosh Mehrotra, and Prof. Sudha Pai of Jawaharlal Nehru University (JNU), New Delhi; Prof. Rumki Basu from Jamia Millia Islamia University; Prof. Rathin Roy former Director National Institute of Public Finance and Policy (NIPFP); Prof. Manoj Panda, former Director Institute of Economic Growth (IEG); Prof. Kirit S. Parikh, former Director Indira Gandhi Institute of Development Research (IGIDR), Mumbai; Prof. V. V. N. Kishore of The Energy and Resources Institute (TERI); and Prof. M. Sekhar and Prof. P. Ramarao of Indian Institute of Science (IISc) Bangalore.

It requires expressing thanks to the Maharashtra Energy Development Agency (MEDA) and officials of District Wardha for sharing information. I want to thank the research colleagues at IIT (Delhi) who have helped during the research work, and Vimal Kumar for his timely help in editing work. I thank my family and son Amit for the motivation to do the writing work. Special thanks are due to the team of Springer Publisher for their support.

D. N. Gupta

Contents

Part I Understanding Public Policy and Complexity

1 Introduction: Primacy of Public Policy 3
   1.1 Fundamental Issues 4
      1.1.1 Essentiality of Public Policy 4
      1.1.2 Evolution of Study of Public Policy 6
      1.1.3 Why System Matters? 15
      1.1.4 Public Policy System: Why Policymaking is Complex? 16
      1.1.5 Innovation in Public Policy 18
      1.1.6 Twenty-First Century Challenges: Complexity Dimension 20
   1.2 Policy Implementation: Importance of Institutional Development (ID) 23
   1.3 Framework of Book 25
   References 28

2 Public Policy Issues: Key Pointers 37
   2.1 Imperative of Understanding Public Policy 38
   2.2 Sectoral Analysis: Notability of Policymaking 45
      2.2.1 Education 45
      2.2.2 Health and Nutrition 48
      2.2.3 Urban Management 50
      2.2.4 Economic Growth 55
      2.2.5 Manufacturing 56
      2.2.6 Advanced Manufacturing, General Automation, and Future of Jobs 63
      2.2.7 Strategic Materials 67
      2.2.8 Innovation and Entrepreneurship 68
      2.2.9 Infrastructure Development and Public–Private Partnership (PPP) 70

		2.2.10	Labor Reforms	71
	References			75
3	**Unraveling Complexity in Policy System, Economy, Business, and Organizations**			85
	3.1	What Constitutes Complexity: Characteristics of a Complex System		88
	3.2	Complexity in Socio-Economic Systems: An Overview		104
	3.3	Complexity in Policy System		107
	3.4	Complexity in Economy		110
	3.5	Complexity in Business		113
	3.6	Complexity in Public and Business Organizations		114
	References			116
4	**Public Policy: Theories, Process, and Challenges**			123
	4.1	Policy Environment: Understanding Fundamentals of Policymaking Process		124
		4.1.1	Institutions	125
		4.1.2	Structures, Organizational Culture, and Values	126
		4.1.3	Ideas, Politics, and Power	130
		4.1.4	Multidisciplinary Perspective	133
		4.1.5	Policy Contexts	134
		4.1.6	Role of Stakeholders	137
	4.2	Key Challenges		138
		4.2.1	Complexity in Policymaking and Implementation: Operational Complexity	138
		4.2.2	Constraints	141
		4.2.3	Behavioral Aspect	143
		4.2.4	Decision-Making: Complexity and Ethical Issues	144
	4.3	Theories and Models of Public Policy		146
		4.3.1	Evolution of Approaches for Public Policy	147
		4.3.2	Evolution of Theories and Models for Public Policy	152
		4.3.3	Public Policy Theories	153
	4.4	Critique of Public Policy in India		166
		4.4.1	Policymaking in India: Select Case Studies	166
		4.4.2	Policy Implementation Issues	182
		4.4.3	Public Policymaking and Implementation: A Summary	190
	4.5	Managing Twenty-First Century Big Trends, Challenges, and Drivers		196
	References			197

Contents

Part II Way Ahead: Complexity Theory Framework, Policy Design Framework, and Institutional Development

5 Complexity Theory Framework 211
  5.1 New Paradigm: Complexity Theory 212
      5.1.1 Evolution of Complexity Theory 214
      5.1.2 Complexity Theory 215
      5.1.3 Understanding Complexity Dimensions 224
  5.2 Complexity Theory Framework 229
  5.3 Relevance of Complexity Theory 235
      5.3.1 Case Studies: Evolution of Silicon Valleys in Bengaluru (India) and San Francisco Bay (USA) 239
      5.3.2 Relevance for Public Policy 246
      5.3.3 Relevance for Economy and Business 248
      5.3.4 Relevance for Public and Business Organizations 252
  5.4 Strategic Framework: Preparing for Future 253
      5.4.1 VUCA, TUNA, and CYNEFIN Frameworks: An Overview 254
      5.4.2 Strategic Framework for Different System Contexts 255
  5.5 Future Research in Policy Theory 273
  References 275

6 Innovation in Public Policy and Policy Design Framework 283
  6.1 Understanding System: Key Thinking Modes 285
      6.1.1 Systems Thinking 287
      6.1.2 Design Thinking 288
      6.1.3 Critical Thinking 289
      6.1.4 Divergent Thinking 289
      6.1.5 Strategic Thinking 289
      6.1.6 Complexity Thinking 290
  6.2 Innovative Approaches 292
      6.2.1 Creative Problem Solving (CPS) 293
      6.2.2 Creative Citizen Engagement 293
      6.2.3 Deliberative Dialogue 294
      6.2.4 Creating Adaptive Policies 294
      6.2.5 Innovative Indicators 295
      6.2.6 Policy Design 297
  6.3 System Approach 297
      6.3.1 Interpretive Structural Modeling (ISM) 299
      6.3.2 System Dynamics Modeling 301
  6.4 Policy Design Framework 319
      6.4.1 Good Policy System Imperatives 319
      6.4.2 Framework 325
  6.5 Case Study: Policymaking for Renewable Energy 344
      6.5.1 Overview of Energy Scenario in the Country 344

		6.5.2	Systems Thinking and Design Thinking Application	346
		6.5.3	Research Design	347
		6.5.4	Application of Interpretive Structural Modeling (ISM)	351
		6.5.5	Application of System Dynamics (SD) Modeling	359
	Appendix 1: Basic Renewable Energy Data			382
	Appendix 2: Interpretive Structural Modeling (ISM)			383
	Appendix 3: System Dynamics (SD) Modeling			390
	References			415
7	**Institutional Development and Design of New Public Organizations**			423
	7.1	Institutional Development: An Overview		424
		7.1.1	Institutional Development of Policy System	426
	7.2	New Public Organizations		429
		7.2.1	Vital Public Policy Issues	430
		7.2.2	Mainstreaming Innovative Approaches	440
		7.2.3	Human Capital and Skill Sets	445
		7.2.4	Looking Beyond Resources: Primacy of Innovation in Process of Policy Design and for Policy Options	447
	Epilogue			453
		Future Ahead		456
		Summing Up		460
	References			461
Glossary				467
Index				473

About the Authors

D. N. Gupta is Adjunct Professor, National Institute of Advanced Studies (NIAS), Bengaluru. He has worked in senior positions in Government for policymaking and implementation. His research areas include system dynamics; complexity theory for public policy, economy, and business; renewable energy and climate change; public policies on advanced technologies, biotechnology, advanced manufacturing, and semiconductor; and innovation in public governance. He has contributed articles and books on development issues, technologies, public policy, and economy.

Sushil is Emeritus Professor, Department of Management Studies, Indian Institute of Technology (IIT) Delhi, India. He has served as Deputy Director (Operations) and Dean (Faculty) at IIT Delhi. He has pioneered the area of "flexible systems management" and made original contributions to the field of knowledge in the form of interpretive approaches in management. He is founder Editor-in-Chief of the journal *Global Journal of Flexible Systems Management* and of the Springer series 'Flexible Systems Management'; and serves on the editorial boards of leading international journals. His area of research includes strategic management, system dynamics, and flexible management. He has extensive research and academic experience and has written several scholarly articles and books on management.

Abbreviations

ACF	Advocacy Coalition Framework
ACTAGRCO	Actual Cotton Agro-residue Collection
BCR	Bank Credit
BPL	Below Poverty Line
BPR	Business Process Reengineering
CAGR	Compound Annual Growth Rate (CAGR)
CAPP	Capacity of Agro-residue Power Plant
CAPR	Capital Requirement
CBOs	Community-Based Organizations
CER	Certified Emission Reduction
CERC	Central Electricity Regulatory Commission
CERV	Certified Emission Reduction Value
CHE	Catastrophic Health Expenditure
CLD	Causal Loop Diagram
COELGN	Cost of Electricity Generation Consumption
CPMS	Comprehensive Performance Management System
CSOs	Civil Society Organizations
DISTANCE	Average Distance of Agro-residue Power Plant from Fields
ELUNITS	Total Electricity Units
FCTAGRCO	Feasible Cotton Agro-residue Collection
FGD	Focus Group Discussion
FLCOELGN	Final Cost of Electricity Generation
FRAGRCEF	Fraction of Total Cotton Agro-residue Collection Efficiency
FRFCTAGRCO	Feasible Fraction of Possible Cotton Agro-residue Collection
FRHHCONSAGR	Fraction of Total Cotton Agro-residue as Household
FRPCTAGRCO	Fraction of Surplus Cotton Agro-residue Collection
GCM	Garbage Can Model
GDP	Gross Domestic Product
GHG	Greenhouse Gas
HDI	Human Development Index
HHE	Household Health Expenditure

HRC	Human Resource Capital
HRD	Human Resource Development
ICT	Information and Communication Technology
IMR	Infant Mortality Rate
INCERFR	Income for Farmers from CER
INCFR	Income of Farmer
INVAPP	Investment in Agro-residue Power Plant
IPCC	Inter-governmental Panel on Climate Change
ISM	Interpretive Structural Modeling
LPVS	Loan from Private Sources
M&E	Monitoring and Evaluation
MEDA	Maharashtra Energy Development Agency
MGNREGS	Mahatma Gandhi National Rural Employment Guarantee Scheme
MIS	Management Information System
MKWhr	Million KWhr
MMR	Maternal Mortality Rate
MNRE	Ministry of New and Renewable Energy
MSF	Multi-stream Framework
MTOE	Million Tons of Oil Equivalents
MUs	Million Units
MW	Mega Watt
NAPCC	National Action Plan for Climate Change
NEP	New Education Policy
NGOs	Non-governmental Organizations
OOPE	Out-of-pocket expenditure
PCTAGR	Price of Cotton Agro-residue
PCTAGRCO	Possible Cotton Agro-residue Collection
PEST	Political, Economic, Social and Technology
PET	Punctuated Equilibrium Theory
PLF	Plant Load Factor
PMS	Performance Management System
PPP	Purchasing Power Parity
PPREL	Purchase Price of Electricity
PPT	People, Process, and Technology
QMS	Quality Management System
ROI	Return on Investment
RPR	Residue-to-Product Ratio
RTE	Right to Education
RTI	Right to Information
SD	System Dynamics
SDGs	Sustainable Development Goals
SERC	State Electricity Regulatory Commission
SLPCT	Sale Price of Cotton
SURPLUS	Surplus from the Plant

Abbreviations

THE	Total Health Expenditure
TOE	Tons of Oil Equivalents
TPES	Total Primary Energy Supply
TRHCCTAGR	Transport and Handling Cost of Cotton Agro-residue
ULBs	Urban Local Bodies
UN	United Nations
UNFCCC	United Nations Framework Convention on Climate Change

List of Figures

Fig. 1.1	Framework of book	27
Fig. 2.1	ISM model for urban development and economic growth	54
Fig. 3.1	Interactions of elements in a network in two subsystems	91
Fig. 3.2	Interactions between elements and subsystems in the network	92
Fig. 3.3	Subsystems' linkages	105
Fig. 3.4	A representative view of interactions of policies	110
Fig. 4.1	Complexity in decision-making process	146
Fig. 4.2	Progression in key approaches for social and economic systems	151
Fig. 4.3	Model of political system for policymaking	156
Fig. 5.1	General network model for a complex system	216
Fig. 5.2	Circular causality model	217
Fig. 5.3	Social system emergence model: systemic perspective	220
Fig. 5.4	Interactions and emergence dynamics	227
Fig. 5.5	Micro-level and system-level linkage—feedback loop	228
Fig. 5.6	Complex system transformation: emergence and self-organization	235
Fig. 5.7	Sample causal loop reinforcing positive feedback model: network and interaction effects	237
Fig. 5.8	System contexts based on uncertainty and dynamics	260
Fig. 5.9	Dynamics of system context	266
Fig. 5.10	Emerging knowledge and dynamic navigation	272
Fig. 6.1	Hierarchy of system conceptualization	287
Fig. 6.2	Feedback and reinforcing and balancing effects. **a** Software industry (reinforcing effects). **b** Renewable energy (RE) plants (reinforcing and balancing effects). **c** Urban development (reinforcing and balancing effects)	305
Fig. 6.3	Mental model and real-world interaction. **a** Basic mental model. **b** Improved mental model: feedback, learnings, and decisions	307

Fig. 6.4	Linear thinking approach	307
Fig. 6.5	Nonlinear thinking approach (with feedback)	308
Fig. 6.6	Building blocks of system dynamics (SD)	315
Fig. 6.7	Steps in system dynamics methodology	317
Fig. 6.8	Institutional conceptual model for public policy system	322
Fig. 6.9	Policy design framework	339
Fig. 6.10	Schematic view of policy design. **a** Schematic view of process. **b** Schematic view: basic features	341
Fig. 6.11	Flow chart of research methodology	349
Fig. 6.12	Preliminary ISM: driver power and dependence graph	355
Fig. 6.13	Final ISM: driver power and dependence graph	357
Fig. 6.14	Final ISM model	357
Fig. 6.15	Subsystem diagram	361
Fig. 6.16	Interactions between components of subsystems	362
Fig. 6.17	Policy structure diagram for agro-residue power system with policy linkage	364
Fig. 6.18	Causal loop diagram for agro-residue power system	365
Fig. 6.19	System dynamics model with STELLA software	366
Fig. 6.20	Simulation: variation in values of COELGN and FLCOELGN over years for most favorable conditions	369
Fig. 6.21	Simulation: variation in values of COELGN and FLCOELGN over years for most unfavorable conditions	370
Fig. 6.22	Performance factors under optimistic Scenario (using STELLA Software)	372
Fig. 6.23	Variation in values of COELGN and FLCOELGN under different scenarios	372
Fig. 6.24	Factors of equations for component 1 (Available resources)	398
Fig. 6.25	Factors of equations for component 2 (Resource deployment)	399
Fig. 6.26	Factors of equations for component 3 (Cotton production)	400
Fig. 6.27	Factors of equations for component 4 (Agro-residue surplus)	401
Fig. 6.28	Factors of equations for Component 5 (Price and collection of Agro-residue)	402
Fig. 6.29	Factors of equations for Component 6 (Investment, capacity, and electricity generation)	403
Fig. 6.30	Factors of equations for Component 7 (Cost of electricity generation)	405
Fig. 6.31	Factors of equations for Component 8 (Incentive and net capital)	406
Fig. 6.32	Factors of equations for Component 9 (Requirement of Agro-residue)	407
Fig. 6.33	Factors of equations for Component 10 (Purchase by state utility and surplus)	408

Fig. 6.34	Factors of equations for Component 11 (Income of farmers) ...	410
Fig. 6.35	System dynamics model with STELLA software	412
Fig. 6.36	a Performance factors under optimistic scenario. b Performance factors under normal scenario. c Performance factors under pessimistic scenario (using STELLA software)	413
Fig. 7.1	Public policy system: a conceptual macro model	452

List of Tables

Table 1.1	Important theories and approaches for public policy	7
Table 2.1	GDP growth rate, agriculture growth rate, and poverty ratio	41
Table 2.2	Basic human development indicators, poverty, and per capita GDP	44
Table 2.3	Macro-level view of health sector	49
Table 2.4	Per capita spending on capital expenditure (CapEx) and operation expenditure (OpEx)	51
Table 2.5	Requirements of investment for urban infrastructure	51
Table 2.6	Per capita GDP—a comparison	55
Table 2.7	Labor productivity and TFP growth rates	55
Table 2.8	Comparison of key HR and R&D indicators with competitiveness and per capita GDP	57
Table 2.9	World exports (2017)	58
Table 2.10	Key performance indicators of manufacturing) (India)	59
Table 2.11	Manufacturing value added and global manufacturing and exports	59
Table 2.12	CAGR for manufacturing and GDP (India)	60
Table 2.13	Exports of manufactured products	61
Table 2.14	Exports ranking of countries for manufacturing	61
Table 2.15	Peak manufacturing employment share and GDP per capita	62
Table 2.16	Labor costs, labor productivity, and disposal income	62
Table 2.17	Likely job losses due to automation	65
Table 2.18	Technical potential for automation for select sectors	65
Table 2.19	Likely employment growth rate in select sectors	66
Table 2.20	Status of Unicorns and VC investment	69
Table 2.21	Number of startups and VC investment in India	69
Table 2.22	Percentage of startups and investment in India (average of 2015, 2016, 2017)	69

Table 2.23	Year of introduction of various social security schemes in select countries	73
Table 2.24	Social sector expenditure as a percentage of GDP and per capita GDP	73
Table 2.25	Comparative study of labor laws of select countries	74
Table 3.1	Matrix of characteristics of complex systems	89
Table 3.2	Different system effects and their examples (coevolution)	99
Table 4.1	Policymaking process: operational complexity	139
Table 4.2	Institutional structures for public policy at various levels (India)	167
Table 4.3	Case studies of public policies: tools, theories, thinking, and approaches	169
Table 4.4	Implementation of central and state budgets at district level	183
Table 4.5	Key indicators of survey of delivery system and public services at grassroots level	187
Table 4.6	Coverage of and access to delivery system	188
Table 4.7	Major shortcomings in policy system	194
Table 4.8	Key human resource and economic indicators	195
Table 4.9	Key institutional indicators concerning business services	196
Table 5.1	Evolution of silicon valleys in Bengaluru and San Francisco Bay	241
Table 5.2	Strategic framework: preparing for future	261
Table 6.1	Summary of different modes of thinking	291
Table 6.2	Stages and steps in system dynamics model development	317
Table 6.3	Institutional dimensions for public policy system	322
Table 6.4	Quality dimensions in policymaking process	325
Table 6.5	Policy design framework	327
Table 6.6	Different system conditions: approaches, thinking modes, and policy analysis tools	336
Table 6.7	Policy design: approaches, thinking modes, and policy analysis tools	337
Table 6.8	Comparison of key energy indicators (India vs. World) (in 2009 and 2017)	344
Table 6.9	CO_2 emissions: comparison of key indicators (India vs. World) (in 2009 and 2017)	345
Table 6.10	Installed power capacity by source in India (grid connected)	345
Table 6.11	Installed capacity by renewable energy source in India (2010 and 2018)	346
Table 6.12	Policy research tools applied in the research study for ISM and SD modeling	350
Table 6.13	List of factors for preliminary ISM	354
Table 6.14	List of factors for final ISM	356
Table 6.15	Parameter values for simulation	368

Table 6.16	Simulation: values of performance factors over time for most favorable conditions	369
Table 6.17	Simulation: values of performance factors over time for most unfavorable conditions	370
Table 6.18	Parameter values for scenario building	371
Table 6.19	Summary of results for different scenarios	371
Table 6.20	Sensitivity analysis: impact on performance factors by the most adverse values of individual parameters	373
Table 6.21	Synthesis of results (both ISM and SD): summary of policy options	380
Table 6.22	Investment in renewable energy (RE) (in 2017)	382
Table 6.23	Global installed capacity (GW) by renewable energy source (2010 and 2019)	382
Table 6.24	Renewable power capacity in world (2017)	383
Table 6.25	Electricity generation by source in India (grid connected) (2010 and 2018)	383
Table 6.26	Identification of the stakeholders and criticality	384
Table 6.27	Feedback from stakeholders about key factors of the agro-residue electricity system	385
Table 6.28	Definitions of selected factors for preliminary ISM	386
Table 6.29	Definitions of factors for final ISM	388
Table 6.30	Structural self-interaction matrix (SSIM) (for final ISM)	389
Table 6.31	Definitions of key factors for system dynamics (SD) modeling (component-wise)	390
Table 6.32	Dimensions of factors	393
Table 6.33	Dimensions of parameters	396
Table 6.34	Sensitivity analysis: values of performance factors for different values of FRAGRCEF	414
Table 6.35	Sensitivity analysis: values of performance factors for different values of PCTAGR	414
Table 6.36	Sensitivity analysis: values of performance factors for different values of PLF	415
Table 6.37	Sensitivity analysis: values of performance factors for different values of Me	415
Table 6.38	Sensitivity analysis: values of performance factors for different values of DISTANCE	415
Table 7.1	Institutional determinants	428
Table 7.2	Basic socio-economic indicators	432
Table 7.3	Key economic output indicators	432
Table 7.4	Public sector employment in total population	433
Table 7.5	Physicians and pupils per teacher	434
Table 7.6	Government employment (as percentage of total employment)	434
Table 7.7	Process efficiency of delivery system	435
Table 7.8	Institutional issues for business and industry	435

Table 7.9	Global rank: infrastructure and business environment (rank)	436
Table 7.10	Key budgetary indicators for human resource development (HRD)	436
Table 7.11	Government budget: revenue and expenditure	437
Table 7.12	General government and social sector expenditure as a percentage of GDP	437
Table 7.13	Tax revenue indicators	438
Table 7.14	Knowledge and skill sets for policy design	446
Table 7.15	Public policy system: components and elements	452

List of Boxes

Box 2.1:	Benefits from education	45
Box 2.2:	Key factors for urban development and economic growth	53
Box 3.1.	Elements in a system	90
Box 3.2:	Emergent Property: How it happens	92
Box 3.3:	Complex adaptive system (CAS) features	95
Box 5.1:	Elements in subsystems and environment	216
Box 6.1	Interactions between elements in the system	342

Part I
Understanding Public Policy and Complexity

Chapter 1
Introduction: Primacy of Public Policy

The best public policy is made when you are listening to people who are going to be impacted.
Elizabeth Dole, Former US Secretary of Labor and Author

Abstract Public policies play a pivotal role in shaping the future of the country. The chapter emphasizes the primacy of public policy. Despite vast resources, the rising problems raise questions about—what it will take to bring a significant difference in the lives of citizens. While covering the study of the evolution of policy theories, it broadly covers policy sciences, policy analysis, system approach, complexity theory, evidence-based approach, complexity economics, and behavioral approach. It highlights how the twenty-first century challenges in the form of significant socio-economic trends, globalization, climate change, and sustainable development will determine the future of the world. Advanced technologies and an interconnected world are transforming the world. Such changes result in a marked increase in complexity in the social system and economy. It underscores a need for a cogent policymaking process and sound implementation mechanism to achieve intended objectives while addressing complexity. It lays stress on innovation and institutional development as a determinant of success.

Keywords Evolution of public policy · Policy sciences · Evidence-based policymaking · Behavioral approach · Complexity · Twenty-first century challenges · Innovation · Policy implementation · Institutional development

World over, the twenty-first century has brought numerous challenges to the fore for policymakers, who have the enviable task of formulating public policies. Policymaking is a challenging process in the social system, which is more often marked with complexity. Complexity is on account of myriad socio-economic problems, multiple stakeholders, interconnected systems and elements with nonlinearity, uncertainty, feedback loops, and counterintuitive behavior (Forrester 1971; Gigch 1974; Rihani 2005). Governments are increasingly under stress to respond to the demands of their citizens. They are required to address a number of complex social and economic issues, including poverty alleviation, employment creation, improving quality of education, provisioning of health services, environmental degradation, and so on. In addition, in the public system, there are numerous persuasive issues, which keep emerging and redefine the role of the government.

The principal issues that are taking center stage are: demographic changes, resulting in rising expectations; increasing unemployment; rapid increase in urbanization; challenges of climate change; rising income, with inequality; growing cyber-dependency, without adequately secured infrastructure; the advent of rapidly growing advanced technologies unfolding new opportunities but causing disruptions in traditional industries; and mounting public debt, limiting the scope of governments to govern in a range of development areas (NIC 2012; KPMG 2014). How these issues are addressed systemically is a test for the public policy system.

This chapter provides an overview of underlying issues pertinent to the policy system, evolution of study of public policy, institutional development, the twenty-first century challenges, complexity dimension, and innovation in policymaking.

1.1 Fundamental Issues

1.1.1 Essentiality of Public Policy

Government has multifarious roles and responsibilities. It has a vital role in public service provisioning and management of public order. Managing the delivery of various services efficiently, addressing the increasing concerns of citizens, and handling the pressure of ever-expanding newer demands are some of the primary functions that the government of the day is expected to perform. Running the economy involves augmenting user charges and taxes to fund programs and projects; increasing dependency on the government budget; necessitating newer regulations; and managing challenges of new technologies, international trade, and foreign exchange management. Mitigating shocks of natural calamities on a regular basis is a major responsibility. In an interconnected globalized world, in order to respond to emerging problems, the government has to assume evolving roles and responsibilities. Such are some illustrative examples of how the government has an important and ubiquitous role in the public system (McCool 1995; Peters 1999; Jann and Wegrichi 2007; Sapru 2012).

Some of the key attributes of public policy are discerned as follows: policy is made in response to a problem that requires handling by the government; policy is made on behalf of citizens and for the public good; policy is what the government makes choices under a given social, political, and economic environment; policy is oriented toward an objective, such as the solution of a problem; and policy is implemented by government institutions, citizens, non-governmental organizations (NGOs), academics, business organizations, and individuals who have different interpretations of problems and solutions, based on their perceptions and interests. Such

1.1 Fundamental Issues

policymaking can be at all levels, viz., Center, State, and local government (Jenkins 1978; Durlauf 2012; Chakravarty and Chand 2016).

How public policy is essential can be understood better from the definition itself, and it is elaborately discussed below:

Defining public policy. Policy is an expression of aspirations. It reflects principles, norms, and philosophy, an expression of intent, or a way of causing something. Policies are linked with the overall direction and prioritization of areas of importance for achieving long-term objectives. These are needed at both macro (for economy or sectoral development at the National level) and micro (for functional or operational needs during implementation) levels. In the context of government, a policy is defined in the New Oxford Dictionary of English as 'a course or principle of action adopted or proposed by a government, political party, business, or individual' (oxforddictionaries.com/definition/policy). Though there are various ways to define policy, there is a general consensus that the policy provides the direction for future action to achieve the desired objectives. Government formulates policies to deliver the intended benefits to citizens and bring change in the social system (Curtain 2000; Parag 2005; Banks 2009).

Government matters, and so in all walks of life. The citizens expect government to deliver, matching their expectations. The government exercises the instrument of policy to achieve public purpose. Public policy is vital because the scope of the State touches almost all aspects of citizens' lives. The definition of public policy has multiple strands. It can also lead to considerably differing views and contesting positions (Dye 1992; Fischer et al. 2007; Birkland 2011). Drawing on different aspects of the policy process and the roles of different stakeholders in policymaking, it offers multiple perspectives. For some, looking from the point of view of 'outcome', the policy reflects what government should be doing. And, viewing from the standpoint of 'process and decision-making', it refers to how government delivers on its intents. For organizations, defining public policy may help them define their role in policymaking or the role of personnel in the organization they work for.

Birkland (2011) states that public policies are the instruments through which the government achieves various objectives ranging from reforms to development, providing public services, and maintaining law and order. Public policies can also play a fundamental role in instituting changes in societies and in reshaping individual and collective behavior. Policies address issues concerning social, economic, and security sectors. Government policy reflects theoretical or experiential assumptions about what is required to resolve a particular issue or problem (Outreach 2005; Gerston 2010; Cairney 2012). Based on the values and norms, the policy can be defined as a 'choice' that government makes in response to a political issue or public problem. The policies are aimed at linking the set values and norms with problems and issues on the ground (Dunn 1981; Moran et al. 2008; Sapru 2012). For instance, norms for service standards for education, health, or environmental management and the conviction in quality standards will determine the choice of the government during policymaking.

Experts (Dye 1992; Cochran and Malone 1995; Peters 1999) on public policy believe that the definitions of public policy contain the threads of 'action by government', 'public interest', and 'direction to achieve the purpose'. To respond to exchanges between people and governments, Gerston (2010) opines that public policy is defined as the combination of basic decisions, commitments, and actions made by those who hold government positions of authority.

From the perspective of public policy framework, it can be described as the overall underlying structure within which processes for analyses and decision-making are designed and instituted for policy formulation, implementation, and evaluation to achieve public good (Easton 1965; Lasswell 1971; Cochran and Malone 1995). Such framework may include a combination of both: *first*, a socio-scientific framework that deals with policy cycle analysis, socio-economic and political analysis, understanding of complexity of systems, and so on; and *second*, a techno-managerial framework that emphasizes the technical analyses, scenario building, pattern recognition, choice of solutions, and design of policies and institutions. It may employ analytical, management, and behavioral skills necessary to effectively engage in analysis and policy formulation. Or, from the point of view of the policy process, within the public policy framework, public policy can be defined as taking decisions for allocating resources and adopting principles of actions that reflect the vision, values, or public service standards, adopted by the government (Fischer et al. 2007; Geurts 2010). It may apply analytical models in the policy process and empirical research methods to study, analyze, and explain the impact of public action on the ground.

In addition to the above, public policy can be seen from the standpoint of an instrument of change. It can bring about transformation in the economy. For example, the studies (Deloitte 2016; MGI 2017) suggest how robust public policy support has a salutary impact on manufacturing in general and the economy in particular. More specifically, in the area of advanced technologies and manufacturing, many developed countries, like the USA, Germany, and Japan, to name a few, and China, South Korea, and Taiwan, among emerging economies, have sound policies in support of science education, technology, innovation, and technology transfer for providing a strong competitive advantage for advanced manufacturing. By building state-of-the-art research facilities underpinned by policy support, they have incentivized the creation of a robust innovation ecosystem in developed and fast-emerging economies. The high-end research has resulted in new inventions and advanced technologies leading to new frontiers of manufacturing, increased employment opportunities, and innovative products with much higher economic values (DSU 2018).

1.1.2 Evolution of Study of Public Policy

Under the dispensation of public governance, the discussion on the study of the public policy evokes considerable interest among scholars of all fields. The history of public policy dates back to the beginning of civilization. The study of government policy has been studied and organized at least since the eighteenth century B.C. (Dunn 1981;

1.1 Fundamental Issues

Raymond et al. 1994; Jann and Wegrichi 2007). Birkland (2011) opines that the systematic study of public policy—scientific or technical—has been a recent discipline. Based on the studies by various scholars in social sciences, the key phases of the evolution of public policy have been categorized as follows: early developments, policy sciences, policy analysis, policy cycle, systems theory and system approach, complexity theory, evidence-based policymaking, complexity economics, behavioral approach in public policy, and innovative approaches in policymaking. The study of public policy has influenced the evolution of various theories and approaches over a period of time. Under the social and economic systems since the 1940s, some of the theories and approaches that have evolved are captured in Table 1.1.

Early developments. The study of politics has a long history, but public policy analysis gained momentum during the progressive era (1890–1920). However, the policy

Table 1.1 Important theories and approaches for public policy

S. No.	Years	Names of theories/approaches
1	1940s–50s	• Systems science • General systems theory • Systems theory • Cybernetics • Policy sciences
2	60s	• System approach • Dynamic system theory • Artificial intelligence • Cognitive science • Complex system theory • Behavioral economics
3	70s	• Complex living systems • Chaos theory • Complex adaptive system • New institutional economics
4	80s	• Social system theory • Network science • Complexity economics
5	90s	• Data mining • Computational modeling • Evidence-based policymaking • Complexity and public policy • Agent-based modeling
6	2000s	• Global network society • Behavioral approach in public policy
7	2010s	• Applied complexity • Spatial geographical complexity

Note The above list is illustrative
Sources Forrester (1971), Menard and Shirley (2011), OECD (2017a), World Bank (2019a), https://www.art-sciencefactory.com/complexity-map_feb09.html, http://www.nwlink.com/~donclark/history_isd/bertalanffy.html

analysis lacked the requisite rigor (Raymond et al. 1994; Fried 1998; Leonard 2009). It began with the examination and exploration of characteristics of the progressive era. It focused on the need for improving governance, reducing corruption, modernization, family and education, prohibition, women's suffrage, addressing the lack of proper industrial working conditions and poor urban living conditions, and unfair business practices. Such studies of this era provided the early motivation for the behavioral approach, a multidisciplinary approach to policy studies. It became the theoretical basis for policy studies in the future. In America, empirical research got more attention, and it was as much a tool for control as a tool for reform. In the USA, the Bureau of the Census, established in 1909, through surveys and statistical analysis, helped in empirical studies of government spending (Cochran et al. 1999; Fischer et al. 2007; Moran et al. 2008).

The research inquiry in public policy got thrust in the 1920s, when political scientists like Charles Merriam, Dewey, and Robert Lynd sought to connect the theory and practice of politics to understand the actual work of government (Dewey 1927; McCool 1995; Curtain 2000). Until the 1920s, due to low public spending by the National governments, the discourse on public policies was limited. The debate on government roles and responsibilities gained momentum from the 1930s onward. In the USA, on account of the great depression in the 1930s, there was the Social Security Act of 1935 under the New Deal of President Franklin Roosevelt. And thereafter, government spending in the USA rose in the social sector, which was previously viewed as private or personal affairs. The US government spending expanded and grew from a meager 3.4% of GDP in 1930 to 42% in 1945 (Cohen 1984; Gerston 2010; Gagnon 2017). It led to an increased focus on public policy due to increase in scrutiny of government decisions and actions.

From the 1920s to 40s, it was recognized that traditional analyses of government decisions were incomplete. With the emergence of complicated problems in the public sphere and the complex relationships between public institutions and the development concerns of people, the necessity emerged for a more detailed assessment of how governments make decisions, how some policy alternatives are chosen over others, and how the decisions are put into practice (Dror 1968; Howlett and Ramesh 1995; Gerston 2010). The researchers made efforts to apply both empirical tools and scientific methods to improve the analytical rigor in policy studies. It was felt that rational scientific methods could be used to improve decision-making and policies for the welfare of society. It gave rise to the quantitative approach in policymaking (Potucek and LeLoup 2003; Sapru 2012).

The social sciences emerged as a separate set of disciplines in the nineteenth century. The study of public policy has roots in social sciences. There had been a general consensus that public policy was a relatively new field of research. The studies of public policy have evolved as a multidisciplinary subject with less defined boundaries. In the 1950s, public policy emerged as a field of research encompassing political science, sociology, economics, and public administration (Lasswel 1971; Dye 1992; Cairney 2012). Also, the policy studies emerged from the concerns about the impact of government actions on society (Portney 1986; Kahan 2001; Gerston 2010). Several studies examined the causal determinants of public policies together

1.1 Fundamental Issues

with how the politics and various stakeholders influenced decision-making. The studies of government actions led to defining public policy as a course of action (or inaction). And a public policy could take the form of a law, a rule, a welfare program, a regulation, an order, an accord with regional groups, or an international agreement. The literature on public policy (Lasswel 1971; Forrester 1968; Potucek and LeLoup 2003) reflects that the researchers have drawn their strengths from various disciplines such as political science, public administration, economics, sociology, history, anthropology, cybernetics, systems theory, complexity theory, management, and behavioral science.

In India, the interest in studies of public policy increased in the 1960s, with the opening of various social sciences departments in Universities. It mainly focused on the role of government institutions in policymaking and evaluation or impact studies (De 2012; Sapru 2012; Chakravarty and Chand 2016).

Policy Sciences

Among social scientists in the 1920s and 30s, there was a felt need for a more rigorous and scientific way of studying public policy. During this period, the work of Dewey and Lynd lent support to the work on the scientific approach to policymaking (deLeon and Vogenbeck 2007). Besides, the 1930s and 40s were filled with uncertainty and concerns for National security and the economy in the USA. There was a growing realization that decision-making in the government should be more rational, based on knowledge and facts. Lasswell felt the need for a comprehensive understanding of process and knowledge in policymaking. Lasswell (1951, 1971) formalized his vision through the twofold orientation of the policy sciences: *first*, the development of a 'science' of policy forming and execution, and *second*, improving the 'concrete content' of the information and the interpretations available to policymakers.

It was later rephrased as 'the policy sciences', concerned with knowledge *of* and *in* the decision processes of the 'public and civic order' (Fischer et al. 2007). The knowledge *of* the decision process is achieved by systematic empirical studies of how policies are formulated and put into action, and whereas knowledge *in* the decision process draws upon various disciplines to increase the body of knowledge necessary for public policy (Lasswell 1971). The policy sciences emerged as an overarching social-scientific discipline with a multidisciplinary approach. It included political science, sociology, anthropology, psychology, statistics, mathematics, and natural sciences and employed both quantitative and qualitative techniques to provide a more scientific basis for policy studies.

Policy Analysis

With the acceptance of policy sciences as an approach, the policy analysts applied various quantitative techniques like cost–benefit analysis, systems analysis, and quantitative modeling. It gave momentum to policy analysis while analyzing policy options for formulating policies. From its inception in the 1950s, the field of policy analysis has been a part of the policy cycle. The policy analysis is about determining which one of the alternative policies is more likely to achieve the goal. The emphasis of the policy analysis is on policy formulation. Policy analysis has continued to get support from public administration and political science. The roots of modern policy analysis lie in various social science disciplines such as economics, political science, behavioral science, and so on (Dunn 1981, Collins 2005, Chakravarty and Chand 2016).

Policy Cycle

Lasswell was among the first to define the policy cycle in terms of stages for policymaking. To bring a multidisciplinary approach with rigor, Lasswell introduced a model comprising seven stages: intelligence, promotion, prescription, invocation, application, termination, and appraisal. The process of policymaking was conceived as a policy cycle framework. It served as a basic template for policymaking. It got acceptance among policy analysts. Further, various experts have worked on stages for the policy cycle and outlined five stages, viz., agenda-setting, policy analysis, decision-making for policy formulation, implementation, and evaluation (Jenkins 1978; Jann and Wegrich 2007; Birkland 2011).

System Perspective—Systems Theory and System Approach

Mental models have been mainly utilized for public policymaking in the past. Mental models are visual images that are created by individuals while dealing with issues of real life (Senge and Sterman 1992; Sushil 1993). Usually, individuals interact with real life through mental models. Traditional management uses mental models as the primary tools. Despite the role of mental models in policymaking, these are good for making first-order and linear relationships between two factors (Miller 1956; Forrester 1971; Mohapatra et al. 1994; Jackson 2006). These have limitations while handling dimensions more than two at a time and working on nonlinear and higher-order relationships or feedback. The mental models are often logically incomplete, and the resulting analysis is likely to be contrary to the study of the actual behavior of the system (Keeney et al. 1990; Warfield 1990).

Public policies play a key role in introducing changes in societies and altering individual and collective behavior. Focus on the public policy process has become increasingly important with the emergence of modern society, technological innovation, and burgeoning international transactions (Gerston 2010). For social systems, Forrester (1968) and Sterman (2000) suggest that good policymaking should address the complexity, nonlinearity, and dynamic nature of issues. Given the enormous leverage policies have on the system, the process and the methodology of policymaking need to be properly understood and rightly placed. Besides, policymaking requires applying new approaches to capture the reality of the system. Social scientists have derived motivation from the systems theory and have used the concepts like feedback, causal loops, and control to analyze problems arising in societal systems (Mohapatra et al. 1994; Gregoriades and Karakostas 2000; Fuentes 2006).

The limitations in the then existing approaches gave rise to systems theory and system approach in policymaking. A system approach supports learning about systems and changes in the mental models of decision makers. Gigch (1974) and Kelly 1998 have explained that the system approach is an outgrowth of the concepts of the systems theory. In reality, a system approach is not a theory but a way of thinking and a practical philosophy of solving problems in societal systems. The approach suggests a systemic approach in defining the problem and objectives of the system, designing for change, and evaluating the design. Specifically, the approach has evolved into the application of interpretive structural modeling (ISM) and system dynamics (SD) modeling in capturing the real-world situation and in utilizing both qualitative and quantitative techniques for policymaking for social systems (Coyle 1977; Morecroft 1983; Sushil 2005).

Complexity Theory

In the 1960s, various scholars (Grobman 2005; Dafermos 2014; Ismael 2019) examined the complex nature of the public system, dealt elaborately with the factors that have contributed to complexity, and studied how complexity may impact the formulation of public policy. For a long period, the dominating perspective of scientific inquiry has been based on the lens of reductionism and Newtonian philosophy (mechanistic approach). The reductionism approach emphasizes that for understanding a system, breaking the system or problem down into parts can independently determine the system's behavior. It is based on the assumption that the knowledge of parts of a system or underlying issues in a problem is sufficient to understand the system (Cohen 1999; Boulton et al. 2015). Gradually, from the middle of the twentieth century, it was increasingly realized that the behavior of the system could not always be answered from the knowledge of the behavior of its constituent parts.

It became the underlying reason for understanding a complex system (Cohen 1999; Stacey 2002; Grobman 2005). The growing body of literature suggests that public systems are complex due to multiple interconnected parts or elements and feedback loops, signifying that different parts were not independent and the total output is not the linear sum of the parts of the system. Also, cause-and-effect linkages are not discernible in the complex system, and the system is far from equilibrium. There are conditions of nonlinearity and uncertainty. The studies (Anderson 1999; Cilliers 2000; OECD 2016a) reflect that a complex system is characterized by the nonlinear interactions between elements, uncertain behavior, emergent behavior, self-organization, and adaptive behavior.

Complexity theory, as emerged from systems theory, is defined as a new approach in which systems or processes that lack order and stability are identified and studied. Due to dynamics, the system does not follow rules of linear behavior and predictable outcomes. It underscores that analysis should not be on the individual parts of a system but on the 'whole' system, which is defined as a network of elements that interact to produce system behavior (Morcol 2012; Colander and Kupers 2016; Cairney et al. 2019). Thus, there has been a realization that public systems necessitate a different approach in a departure from the reductionist approach, and the complexity theory offers a way forward.

Evidence-Based Policymaking

Governments have daunting responsibilities of managing the economy, determining priorities for different sections and development sectors, providing services to citizens, ensuring high economic growth, handling international affairs, and so on. Such a task can hardly be successfully performed by not giving enough attention to informed decision-making.

World over, governments are more occupied with increasing efficiency, effectiveness, transparency, and accountability. They are actively engaged in issues related to the economy, investments, climate change, technology management, etc. But much less attention has been given to the information, knowledge, and rationale that inform the policies and policymaking process (Banks 2009; Geurts 2010; Productivity Commission 2010). It assumes more importance in an increasingly complex and uncertain world. There is a need for a newer way of examining the problems and exploring the solutions. A new robust system is required, with an emphasis on an information infrastructure that can provide real-time information, analytical tools to analyze, and future scenarios under varying conditions. The concept of using evidence-based policy (EBP) making is not new. The current literature on evidence-based policy indicates that its origin can be traced back to the fourteenth century. But in modern times, EBP got momentum in the 1990s, especially in the UK and Australia (Marston and Watts 2003; Sutcliffe and Court 2005).

EBP calls for a combination of facts-based information and knowledge, scientific inquiry, field knowledge, values and norms, and analytical tools (Ehrenberg 1999; Flyvbjerg 2001; Productivity Commission 2010). While attempting EBP, one of the key concerns is to understand and address the underlying issues in the policy system. It will require examining multiple contexts in which the policymaking takes place, complex nature of public system, and complex policymaking process (Forrester 1971; Baron 2018). It requires comprehending complexity to conceptualize the problem and system. There cannot be a universal prescription of the policy process. It necessitates examining ground situations, socio-economic-political contexts, and the gravity of the problem. There is a need to understand diversities—linguistic, ethnic, regional, religious, and cultural. Also, traditional ways of working in society should be discerned during policymaking.

Complexity Economics

Economic theories have a bearing on public policymaking for investments, trade, macro-economic management, and economic growth. The policymakers work on these theories and rely on the assumptions underlying the theories. So under what conditions the theories are evolved and which assumptions are behind theories become essential to understand the full implications of theories. Of importance is to examine the constraints in applying the existing economic theories and to understand to what extent the theories can serve the economic purpose by contributing to policymaking. And what more is required in terms of theory to address pressing concerns of policymaking under the given state of the complexity in the economic system (Beinhocker 2006; Kirman 2011; Arthur 2013). These are some fundamental issues that need consideration for economic policies.

Over several decades, economic theories, including classical theory, neo-classical theory, growth models, and dynamic stochastic general equilibrium (DSGE) model, have been subject to criticism. It has been because of the assumptions that underlay as the basis for the respective propositions in theories or models. In addition, the

1.1 Fundamental Issues

said theories or models are not in a position to provide a satisfactory explanation for the economic crises of 2008 or the problem of a slow rate of growth in many least-developed countries (LDCs), the high incidence of poverty in developing countries, or the lack of adoption of technologies to raise the productivity and quality of life in several developing countries (Acemoglu and Robinson 2010; Kirman 2011; Kapoor 2017; OECD 2017a).

For example, take the case of neo-classical economics. It relates supply and demand to an individual's rationality and ability to maximize utility or profit. It also states that people have rational preferences, try to maximize utility, and, similarly, firms maximize profits. They act independently on the basis of perfect information, and the decisions are consistence with rational choice theory. Several experts have critiqued such assumptions and logic. They emphasize other essential aspects such as bounded rationality, behavioral issues in economic decision-making, and the interplay of multiple factors beyond the comprehension of any individual. And so, the neo-classical theory cannot be applied to most economic situations in the real world (Simon 1991; Arthur 2013; Schasfoort 2017; OECD 2017a).

Arthur (2013) has argued about the non-equilibrium state of the economy and that the economy is always in a state of flux and evolving due to fundamental uncertainty and technological innovation. These two factors keep bringing changes in the state of the economy through multiple interventions by various stakeholders. This economic world is closer to the economy that is always evolutionary and in the process of change, contrary to neo-classical theory, which focuses on market equilibrium through supply and demand. In addition, despite the inherent weaknesses of neo-classical theory, growth models, and the DSGE model, such paradigms are neither validated by empirical evidence nor have sound theoretical foundations, as explained by Kirman (2016).

In the past, economy has been considered a complicated system where simplified models were developed without factoring in the economy as a complex system in the real world. A complex system is equivalent to a network of numerous variables and their interlinkages, which may be linear or nonlinear. Such linkages are dynamic in nature (Forrester 1968; Kirman 2016; Beinhocker 2017). The economic system exhibits nonlinear dynamic nature and emergent characteristics. The resulting economy is not a well-ordered static system but a complex evolving system continuously constructing itself anew. It is more akin to evolutionary economics. One should focus not on static allocative efficiency but on adaptive efficiency, which is concerned with the rules that shape how an economy evolves over time (Arthur et al. 1997; Atkinson 2017).

Against the above backdrop, a shift is called for applying complexity science to economics and for better public policy design in the complex economic environment (Solow 2010; Kirman 2011; OECD 2016a). Complexity economics is based on the proposition that the economy is not necessarily in equilibrium. It examines the emergence of economic structures and the resulting behavior of the economy. It studies the economy as a complex system consisting of interacting economic agents and entities that modify their strategies and actions in response to emerging outcomes.

It calls for examining interactions between elements, the emergence of patterns, and likely economic scenarios (Battiston et al. 2016; Schasfoort 2017).

Behavioral Approach in Public Policy

Social norms, beliefs, attitudes, and values determine the individual's behavior and action, which impact the society as a collective behavior of individuals. Public policymaking needs to understand human behavior better and promote behavioral change through a more scientific approach. It lays stress on the use of behavioral ideas to improve policymaking. Bringing desired change in behavior can facilitate achieving the objectives of policies. There is a need to factor in behavioral aspects in decision-making to design the policies (Swanson and Bhadwal 2009; Lunn 2014; World Bank 2019a).

There are some behavioral tendencies that prevent people from doing certain things, while they may help them improve their conditions and, in turn, society. By using a behavioral approach in public policy, policymakers can help people avoid biases and make better decisions. It can lead to better implementation of policies. Applied behavioral science in public policy is particularly useful in acknowledging the cognitive biases that people have and the effect of social norms. These issues have often been overlooked by traditional approaches, which were based on incentives. This behavioral approach can help the government communicate how choices are to be offered to citizens for acceptance by them (Pottenger and Martin 2014; OECD 2016b).

Policymakers have been working on how to use insights from the study of human behavior to formulate better policies. While understanding behavior and its application in public decision-making has been for many decades, its application has got more acceptance in solving public problems and improving the quality of public services (Oliver 2013; John 2015). It is the underlying reason why the behavioral approach in public policy has emerged as a new approach to decision-making. Behavioral insights, derived through research, are increasingly contributing to shaping the design and implementation of public policies (Marsh 2010; OECD 2017b; Phillips 2018).

The behavioral science application for public policy has got acceptance in the policy system. It can potentially inform and influence all the stages of the public policy lifecycle. Interest in applying behavioral science to public policy has expanded globally, with an increasing number of countries like Australia, Canada, Germany, Netherlands, Singapore, and the USA applying and testing behavioral insights (Solek 2014; World Bank 2019a). For India, this approach has importance for policies related to sanitation, cleanliness, controlling school dropout rates, reducing IMR and MMR in the health sector, etc.

In sum, for shaping the evolution of public policy study, initially, various disciplines, like political science, sociology, economics, public administration, philosophy, management, and natural sciences, have played crucial roles. And subsequently, it is underpinned by systems theory, behavioral science, and complexity theory. Over time there has been a contribution by many scholars and researchers in

1.1 Fundamental Issues

the field of public policy. Several approaches, theories, and models have been evolved by social scientists in the last many decades, especially since the 1930s. Some of the approaches and theories are group theory, rational choice, incremental approach, advocacy coalition framework (ACF), punctuated equilibrium, system approach, system dynamics, policy design, etc. These are covered in detail in Chaps. 4 and 6.

1.1.3 Why System Matters?

A system is like a body of integrated subsystems, components, or elements to accomplish a specific purpose. The system is governed by a set of rules, values, and methods to address problems or perform a task. There are numerous types of systems. For example, biological system, ecological system, social system, organization, administrative system, etc. There are certain distinct features of a system. *Firstly*, it is a structure regarded as a whole. *Secondly*, it consists of interrelated and interdependent components, which continually affect each other to perform their functions and maintain the existence of the system to achieve the objectives. *Thirdly*, the system as a whole exhibits properties that are specific to the behavior of the 'whole', but are distinct from those of individual components or elements. The essence of these three features is that the system as a 'whole' can perform and achieve its 'purpose' if 'all' the 'components' are put in 'place fully' and 'perform individually' (Boulding 1956; Ackoff 1971; Checkland 1985). For efficiency and consistency of results, the right system is a prerequisite.

If properly designed, the system can play a significant role in realizing the strategies and achieving the organizational goals. It can be an essential building block (Senge 1990; Parag 2005). It can enable better HR management and healthy interactions among personnel and plan operational strategies. It can result in enhanced staff creativity. Systems are what make organizations perform and deliver. A sound system, in the context of a public policy system, will have a better impact on improving consistency of the implementability of the policy and will result in better employees' performance, quality of service delivery, higher output, citizen management, and the scope for future course correction (Eglin 2017; Breslins 2019; Edwards 2019; Gatty 2019).

A systemic approach is about having a system-wide view of the subsystems or elements and their interactions to have a holistic understanding of the system. Such an approach is required within a social system or for the entire economy. This approach is essential for the integration of programs and activities to create synergy. It arises from the point of view that all systems are composed of interrelated subsystems. A whole or the system can be described as a totality or in entirety, not as individual subsystems. Ignoring or inadequate understanding of one or more subsystems may have adverse consequences (Pigdon and Woolley 1992; Koskinen 2013).

For example, under urban development, the issues that need to be systemically taken into account are land use planning and management (LUPM), infrastructure creation, management of urban service delivery, internal resource mobilization, government budgetary allocation, ability to mobilize resources from financial institutions, digital governance, educational institutions, and presence of innovation hubs, to name a few. Each one of these subsystems contributes independently and in conjunction with others. Each subsystem affects others and needs to be addressed squarely. Similarly, for developing human capital, an integrated view of health, education, drinking water, sanitation, skill development, and social security is requisite.

In addition, it calls for a multidisciplinary approach to have a comprehensive understanding of a sector or development area. It is so necessary as solving complex problems and quality implementation of programs demand a collaborative, cohesive, and effective multidisciplinary team, which are critical for success (Verhulst 2013; van der Wal Zeger 2017). It involves drawing experts appropriately from diverse disciplines to analyze from multiple perspectives outside of normal boundaries and reach solutions based on a better understanding of issues. It demands team members from different fields to work collaboratively with a common objective, set goals, design processes, set standards, make decisions, and take responsibilities.

For example, in health service management system, the issues that need to be understood comprehensively are microbial study, psychological needs, individual behavior, family behavior, cognitive understanding, etc. In a similar way, the economy is to be understood from various perspectives such as institutional role, social dimension, development policy, public governance, networks of economic nodes (economic agents and entities), and so on. In the urban development context, improving the quality of urban places means working on the relationships between people, traditions, and cultural identity; understanding the complexity of urban phenomena; and meeting social, cultural, economic, and environmental needs. An interdisciplinary approach is needed to encourage innovation, urban service management, and resource mobilization. It calls for a team composed of development analysts, financial experts, planners, architects, and designers to deal with issues holistically.

In the same vein, from a system point of view, within an organization, various subsystems, such as HR management, behavioral aspects, training, finance, and performance management system, are to be designed in an integrated way. And as for delivery system, manpower, logistics, and infrastructure support to reach out to people; training unit and monitoring and evaluation (M&E) unit; quality management system (QMS); and processes and procedures of service delivery are to be factored into providing a robust mechanism for policy implementation. At the organizational level, from the operational point of view, the elements are leadership, a citizen-centric approach, teamwork, work culture management, management information system (MIS), and good communication to address issues systemically.

1.1.4 Public Policy System: Why Policymaking is Complex?

In the real world, the government functions in a social system. The social system is about interrelationships between stakeholders and social, cultural, political, and economic institutions—both public and private. The system dealing with public policy is referred to as the public policy system and works within the public system. The studies (Forrester 1971; Gigch 1974; Kelly 1998; Christiansen and Bun 2012) indicate that the public policy system is marked by an inherently complex and multi-faceted nature. It is a result of interactions of multiple problems and issues about many stakeholders and variables. It is much more complex in nature as compared to a physical system. This complexity is a result of many factors, including a large number of components, interactions, nonlinearity in interactions, dynamic nature of the behavior, causality, and feedback loops. Such systems represent difficulty in tracking policy implementation, measuring performance, and monitoring cause-effect relationships (Jones 2011; Eppel and Rhodes 2018).

There are other dimensions in complex public systems. Due to the ubiquitous role or presence of government in public affairs, public policy has an all-encompassing role in the public sphere, be it education, health, economy, agriculture, technology, business, or industry. Many of these areas have overlaps and define the state of development in a combined form, not as a standalone sector. It is difficult to identify and articulate causal relationships where causes are multidimensional and nonlinear. Besides, deciphering many problems requires a behavioral approach, as understanding the causes is difficult. For example, there are complex health, behavioral, and emotional issues concerning old and differentially abled people. For such problems, due to the difficulty in identifying causality, it demands empathy and personal attention for problem identification and then in designing policies and practices to respond to the specific needs of beneficiaries. The public policy systems or government systems, being a part of social systems, include the following characteristics (Forrester 1968; Senge and Sterman 1992; Morcol 2012; University of Groningen 2017):

- *Numerous elements, individuals, and variables.* Numerous stakeholders, including government agencies, citizens, NGOs, associations, and businesses, their interconnected problems, and diverse activities in socio-cultural-economic spheres play their roles. These, in a combined form, bring complexity. They impact the thinking and functioning of the policy system concerning problem identification, policymaking, and implementation.
- *Nonlinear and dynamic behavior.* The relationships in social systems are seldom linear, or the relations between factors are not constant or directly proportional (mathematically) to the inputs. Instead, they are nonlinear and dynamic. The values of the factors and system behavior change over time. The dynamic interactions by exchanging information or resources are propagated throughout the system.
- *Feedback, closed loop, and multiple loops.* The dynamic behavior of these systems, to a great extent, is governed by their structure, which is composed of multiple causal relationships and feedbacks. The feedbacks drive the system. For a given system, the causal lines of relationships between factors form a closed loop, i.e., the lines begin from a point and, through feedback, return to the original

point. In some cases, the factors have linkages in more than one loop, resulting in multiple loops in the system (Senge and Sterman 1992).
- *Uncertainty.* As a result of nonlinearity, dynamic behavior, feedback loops, and unknown causal relations between factors, the system behavior is uncertain. The behavior cannot be defined with certainty and can only be observed as time passes. For example, how the innovation system will develop or the industrial clusters will evolve cannot be predicted. Likewise, the behavior of the economy is not certain due to numerous interactive economic agents, entities, and factors.
- *Bounded rationality.* The complex problems, limited time, and inadequate mental computational power reduce the decision makers to a state of bounded rationality. It results in sub-optimal choices (Morecroft 1983). Simon (1957) opines that the capacity of the human mind for formulating and solving complex problems is very small compared to the size of the problems, which require detailed analysis and an objective approach.
- *Counterintuitive behavior.* The managerial and social systems exhibit behavior, which is unexpected and counterintuitive. There is a general practice to take decisions by intuition, which may not capture the real situation. The decisions taken about these systems based on intuition may prove to be counterproductive.
- *Emergent behavior, self-organizing property, and path dependency.* The *emergent behavior* is a property of a system that does not depend on its individual parts but results from the interactions between elements at a local level. It implies that collective action matters as a result of interactions. *Self-organization is* referred to as spontaneous new behavior, which emerges from local interactions between parts or elements without external control. *Path dependency* is due to a lock-in state or resistance to interventions. Such features determine the state of a system in which public policies are to be designed (Boulton et al. 2015; OECD 2017a).

Because of the aforementioned characteristics, delineating the problem, understanding the issues and concerns of stakeholders, and defining policy objectives become difficult tasks. More often, public policy issues are complex and fuzzy and so are indeterminate. And as a result, in a large and complex public system in which governments function, formulating policies becomes a complex phenomenon (Rihani 2005; Ozer and Şeker 2013; Mueller 2020).

1.1.5 Innovation in Public Policy

In the social system, public policy issues are not well-structured. Instead, these are fuzzy and amorphous. The issues in social systems are too interwoven and complex to be captured by a conventional approach, linear thinking, or a set of mathematical equations. At the conceptual and application levels, the complexity in policymaking emanates mainly from two factors. *First*, there are multiple interconnected variables and decisions, which feed back into each other. It makes the conceptualization of

1.1 Fundamental Issues

the problem a difficult proposition. *Second*, in the social system, collating data, data quality, and data usage for analysis are complicated matters.

In large and complex societal systems, conceptualization, problem definition, and design of policies are onerous tasks. The conventional mental models or scientific models have been found to lack the capacity to handle complex social issues such as economic growth or recession, the performance of stock markets, climate change, or organizational change (Forrester 1987; Sterman 2000; Gharajedaghi 2011; Arthur 2014). It becomes more critical in evolving and complex public systems with ever-increasing aspirations of population and decreasing resources. It gets more compounded in an uncertain policy environment.

In addition, the underlying problems in health care, water crisis, food shortage, malnutrition, climate change, urban management, housing, and infrastructure management have underscored the interlinkages between them. The problems in one sector cannot be addressed in isolation without studying inter-sectoral linkages. These issues continuously question the existing ways through which governments formulate policies. It raises one crucial question: are current approaches, public institutions, and decision-making processes in coherence with new realities and challenges (Swanson and Bhadwal 2009; Marsh 2010)?

Innovation is seen as an imperative in response to meeting challenges of complexity and the twenty-first century big trends. It can make significant contributions to the instruments of public policy and governance and can be construed as an answer to evolving problems (Geurts 2010; Christiansen and Bunt 2012). There is a need for bringing creative processes into policymaking and focusing more on creating valuable outcomes for citizens than just on projected targets and program outputs. It underscores new ways of working on problems and introducing innovative and comprehensive approaches for policymaking (Stacey 2002; Geurts 2010; Marsh 2010; Colander and Kupers 2016).

It demands that policymakers consider new approaches to bring stakeholders and citizens into a discussion forum for analyzing problems and exploring creative solutions, which may push traditional boundaries of decision-making and policy implementation to a better level of acceptance. It emphasizes innovation as an approach that can help improve the capacity of the public system to deal efficiently, qualitatively, productively, and consistently with problems. Innovative and comprehensive approaches are called for to address issues in the public policy system holistically, and the system-based approach is one of them. It underscores for application of systems thinking to solve systemic problems; complexity thinking to examine complex systems, working on the evolutionary potential of the system; critical thinking for a deeper understanding of issues; divergent thinking for ascertaining different solutions and then to choosing the best one; and strategic thinking for taking competitive advantage (Coyle 1977; Checkland 1985; Jackson 2006; Sanders 2010; John 2015).

Public policymaking in the social system, with multiple competing problems, requires new and right ideas. Among others, to develop intelligent and creative policy alternatives, some of the innovative approaches are adaptive policies, creative citizen engagement, deliberative dialogue (thinking together), and application of design thinking (IISD and TERI 2006; Lenihan 2009; Swanson and Bhadwal 2009; OECD 2017c).

1.1.6 Twenty-First Century Challenges: Complexity Dimension

Complexity dimension. The world, which has been familiar with linear thinking, certainty, and stability, finds it difficult to deal with the emerging understanding and implications of complexity that tends to create an uncertain and perplexing environment. It is so recognized as social, economic, environmental, and development problems are global, nonlinear, and dynamic. It is at the core of the future for public policy, the economy, and organizations. The current world is characterized by complexity and, more so, the public system. Governments operate in public space and must face and solve complexities. It is essential to understand that there is a distinction between complex and complicated systems. The complicated systems are predictable when cause-effect relations are known, while the complex systems are uncertain, with unknown cause-effect relationships, and dynamic in nature (Senge 1990; Grobman 2005; Blignaut 2019; Net Objectives 2019).

In the social system, dealing with humans and their activities, complexity is a natural phenomenon (Warfield 1990; Anderson 1999; Cilliers 2000). The fundamental basis of complexity is interconnected multiple elements and stakeholders, with nonlinear and dynamic relationships and feedback, as a response to some activity. There is an absence of perfect information, and the degree and nature of the relationships are imperfectly known. Examples of complex systems include global climate, big infrastructure such as power grid and transportation systems, cyber-systems, social and economic organizations, and ecosystem, to name a few.

Because of dynamic interactions between elements, components, or subsystems together with feedback loops, it is difficult to predict the emergent behavior of the system, even if the properties of components or subsystems are predictable. In such systems, small changes in system parameters may produce large changes or no effect on system behavior or output (Cairney 2012; University of Groningen 2017). Also, in the complex system, cause-and-effect linkages are not discernible, and the system remains in a far-from-equilibrium state. Such systems display emergent and self-organizing property and adaptive behavior. There is a path dependency, implying that the present decisions or interventions are limited by past decisions or events (Lenihan 2009; Cecere et al. 2014).

In the public system, complexity is observed due to innumerable problems at multiple levels, rising expectations, various stakeholders' demands, disconnect between macro-level requirements and micro-level needs, and capacity deficit at the policy formulation and implementation levels, to cite a few examples. The government is expected to handle a wide range of issues. With the increase in interactions between people, multiple needs, priorities, or expectations come to the fore.

These may be aligned with one another, have competing interests, or work at cross purposes. Such interactions are multitude and beyond the comprehension of a human mind. Because of the multiplicity of actors, problems, and elements, the resulting behavior or performance of the system is not accurately foreseeable. For such reasons, policymaking is a complex phenomenon (Gharajedaghi 2011; Walton 2015; Colander and Kupers 2016; University of Groningen 2017). Likewise, a government or public organization has to work for millions of citizens, with varied problems at multiple levels—local, regional, and National. It has a role in every walk of life in the public domain. These features contribute to complexity.

In the real world, the economy is a complex system due to multiple interacting social, economic, behavioral, and institutional factors (Helbing and Kirman 2013; Arthur 2014; Atkinson 2017). These factors impact the economic system. In contrast, in the economic growth model, the labor supply and capital flow remain the fundamental ingredients. The economic activities depend on the role of public institutions in speedy business transactions and adjudication, public governance for business service delivery, R&D, technology readiness, patent laws, skill sets, labor laws, cost of production, and the logistics support, among others (Durlauf 2012; Battiston et al. 2016; OECD 2017a). Further, several other economic factors add complexity. These are monetary policy, fiscal discipline, measures for savings and consumption, domestic investment, foreign investment, international trade, and foreign exchange management.

In a globalized world, businesses have to deal with technology disruption, production in multi-locations, global supply chain management, competition from firms, customers' expectations, and governments' regulations in multiple countries, besides a host of issues linked to mergers and acquisitions (M&A), investments, and financial markets. These factors contribute to complexity in business, more so for large multinational corporations (Heywood et al. 2007; Mckinsey 2010; Gharajedaghi 2011; EIU 2015).

In sum, the public system, public organizations, economy, and business entities have predominantly one common aspect, which is complexity. The study of the complexity dimension can help explain various phenomena in socio-economic systems.

Challenges of globalization. The rapid pace of globalization, accentuated by new and advanced technologies and social media, will transform the world in a significant way in the decades to come. More specifically, communication technologies are connecting people within and across National boundaries and impacting existing social and business paradigms. Automation in the manufacturing sector provides both challenges in the form of loss of jobs and opportunities in terms of enhanced productivity and new jobs (Brynjolfsson and McAfee 2011; Jaimovich and Siu 2012; WEF 2018b). Economic growth and technological innovations have opened enormous opportunities, but these have resulted in income inequality in most countries (NIC 2012; KPMG 2014; Chancel and Piketty 2017). In comparison to the first industrial revolution, the speed, scale, and impact of change are of much higher magnitude, resulting in higher-order effects (Dobbs et al. 2015). Schumpeter's concept of creative destruction stresses encouraging creativity and calls for imaginative management of destruction and minimizing potential negative effects by the governments.

In the emerging globalized world, understanding the twenty-first century challenges should set in motion what the governments should do to manage them. The traditional approaches will not work, and it calls for an innovative and systemic comprehensive approach. The governments will be required to work on various fronts—policy, program, regulation, organizational, and at multiple levels—National, State, and local. The depth of the problem areas and the resulting complexity will demand holistic solutions. The solutions should leverage shared vision, cooperation, collaborative tools, and technologies to steer the future in a sustainable manner (Walby 2003; KPMG 2014; PWC 2016).

Another impending challenge is climate change. The available evidence reveals that climate change will increase the fear of rising temperature and the frequency and magnitude of extreme weather conditions like excessive rains, flash floods, storms, or droughts. Under the current climatic conditions, the events and decisions in one part of the world can influence lives in other parts. It will have significant implications for agriculture and food security. By the middle of the twenty-first century, it is likely to affect crop and livestock production and fisheries. At the global level, the average crop yields of cereals could decrease by 3–10% per degree of warming. The link between climate change and nutrition is an important one.

The decrease in the concentration of micronutrients in many cereal crops, and so a climate-change-induced reduction in the nutritional quality of crops, can negatively affect the global nutritional outcome (Maslin 2014; FAO 2018). On account of the likely reduction of crop productivity and subsequent difficulty in the availability of food grains in rural areas, the higher prices can impact the savings of people at the lower rung of the economy. Thus, it may exacerbate existing inequalities. Besides, due to the higher cost of staple food like cereals, crop diversification to fruits and vegetables may be difficult. And it may impact the nutritional content in food as well. Due to lower disposal income, the dependence on staple food like cereals, with high-calorific content, is likely to continue as such, and the consumption of costly dairy, vegetable, and protein-rich crop products may remain low. Such underlying states will remain in the decades to come and pose policy concerns (Walby 2003; UNCTAD 2014).

The aforementioned descriptions have got policy implications and give rise to the following questions:

- with the emerging changes of multiple nature, at various levels and in numerous locations, leading to an increase in the complexity in the system, the question is how the public policy system should prepare for this task of addressing complexity;
- with the prospects of advanced technologies and high growth of knowledge capital, and the likely disruptions in areas such as manufacturing, jobs, energy, and transportation, how governments need to prepare to take advantage of opportunities while managing risks;

- with the challenge of climate change and associated adverse impact on agriculture, food, nutrition, and health, which policy initiatives are required at various levels; and
- with the emerging global challenges, which policies are to be introduced, and what kind of collaboration is required among countries worldwide.

1.2 Policy Implementation: Importance of Institutional Development (ID)

The success of a policy depends on how good is the implementation of the policy. It will determine to what degree the outputs and outcomes are close to the intended objectives. A good policy requires a mechanism by which the policy intents are converted into expected results for citizens. The main determinant of disparities in the development outcomes across the States in the country is the differences in the effectiveness of governance and the capacity of the delivery system or the institutions to deliver (Kalirajan et al. 2007; Subramanian 2007; NIPFP 2012; Chakravarty and Chand 2016).

The Constitution of India established a federal structure in the country—underlining specifically the Union of States. Part XI of the Indian constitution specifies the distribution of powers between the Union (Central) government and the States of India. The subjects under the Union list are implemented by the Union government. While under the State list, the policies related to public services and programs are implemented by States through State-level and district-level agencies. As for the Concurrent List, it includes the power to be considered by both the Union and State governments.

The policy implementation depends mainly on the concerned Ministry or department and its associated agencies. It begins with drafting rules, guidelines, and procedures and assigning work to appropriate agencies. During implementation, other institutions and stakeholders, viz., *panchayats* (local bodies in the rural areas) in districts, urban local bodies in cities, NGOs, and other public organizations, also play their roles. When any new program is started, in the beginning, for the implementation of any program or policy, a body or an organization is created. When the program is expanded, an organization evolves into a delivery system with the necessary support to implement projects and deliver services. Such a delivery system evolves into an institution over time by imbibing values and norms, for example, a health institution or an educational institution.

Due to inadequacies in policy implementation (Jones 2011; Sapru 2012; ASER 2016; Hudson et al. 2019), service delivery to people and outcomes of programs suffer. In specific terms, in the health sector, the dearth of the capacity of health system results in high IMR and MMR, large out-of-pocket expenses, difficulty in access to health treatment in many cases, etc. In the education sector, there is a high pupil-teacher ratio and inadequate attention to quality education. Likewise, in the agriculture sector, there is a deficiency in inputs management and a lack of marketing support leading to a loss of income for farmers. These are some illustrative examples of how policies are not able to deliver on the ground. Such a state of affairs exists in many cases of policy implementation. These assume more importance when some developing countries like Sri Lanka, Bangladesh, and Malaysia have performed better in human development, and new emerging economies like China, South Korea, and Taiwan have surged ahead at a rapid pace (UNDP 2018).

The studies (Gupta 2000; Rao 2009; De 2012; NIPFP 2012) indicate that the policy implementation is beset with many infirmities. From the lack of staff to limited infrastructure, inadequate logistics support, want of training, the inadequacy of resources, and lack of citizen focus, these are some prominent causes for much less than the desired level of performance of the implementation. Invariably, all the policies are meant for the welfare of citizens directly or indirectly. In comparison, a close examination will reveal that citizens do not get the desired attention at both the policy formulation and implementation levels.

Key policy implementation issues at the cutting-edge level. Good policies require a good system to implement them efficiently and effectively (Senge 1990; Parag 2005; UN 2015; WEF 2017). Having the right system in place will provide a good idea of reliability and predictability in general and likely outputs and results. It will help policymakers to visualize to what extent the policies and programs can be implemented and to what degree the implementation will be successful. At the district or cutting-edge level, a good delivery system should include essential supporting units to implement programs.

India has complex and myriad problems. The enormity of the problem can be appreciated if one looks at numbers such as: there are about 900 million people living in over six lakh villages separated by several kilometers. Government agencies are generally large, have multiple objectives, and face increasing demands from citizens to deliver more services at a lower cost, generally with a low revenue base. In addition, the agencies have significant operational responsibilities (Weiss 2000; UN 2006; Rizvi 2008; NSW 2015). They are responsible for delivering a range of services to citizens in large geographical areas. The challenge is enormous in terms of reaching out to citizens. Specifically, if a good infrastructure is developed, its efficient use will depend on how well is the management of the infrastructure. Similarly, the large allocation of funds does not necessarily mean that these are utilized for an intended purpose and optimally. In the development cycle, the implementation of policies is vital. It is where a good implementation framework can make a difference. There is a need to focus on the capacity of the delivery system.

Institutional development for policy implementation: Studies on economic growth have stressed that development and growth are not only the result of the application of human capital, financial capital, infrastructure, and technology but also of institutions (North 2003). While making the cross-country comparison, the marked variation in poverty reduction and development outcomes is due to a difference in the institutional capacity to perform (Acemoglu and Robinson 2010; UN 2015). The institution represents some enduring values and ethos, which act as a change agent for the betterment of society. The internal structures and processes help an institution promote social ideals and values (Moore et al. 1994).

Policy implementation is a crucial issue, and institutions have a vital role to play. The institutions facilitate in delivering the services which stimulate and sustain development. The growth and prosperity are unlikely to be maintained if the institutions are dysfunctional or work at a sub-optimal level. It is widely recognized that the impairment to economic prosperity and the risk to human welfare are the result of a lack of institutional development (ID) (Rodrik et al. 2004; Ferrini 2012). ID is the creation or reinforcement of the capacity of an organization to generate and utilize human and financial resources to achieve development objectives. It includes not only building but also strengthening institutions (Israel 1989; McGill 1996). The public sector delivery system is the single most important instrument for the State. How it is managed is critical for development outcomes, including service delivery, social protection, and business promotion and regulation. Public policy reform involves institutional development, i.e., improving the rules, norms, and the capacity governing public sector activities. How policymakers can drive institutional development for policymaking and implementation is a crucial matter.

1.3 Framework of Book

The principal reason for writing the book has emanated from the study and analysis of some basic development issues, which are briefly encapsulated below:

India is endowed with vast human and natural resources. For realizing the full potential of the country, there is ample scope. To achieve higher growth, over the years, several good initiatives have been undertaken for infrastructure development, skill development, energy security, investment, and so on. However, a close look at some of the socio-economic parameters reflects areas of concern. For example, lack of access to quality education (ASER 2016; Patel 2017) and health services for the majority of the population (WHO 2015; MHFW 2016); high incidence of IMR (34) and MMR (174) (HDR 2016; RBI 2019); high incidence of malnourished children (Niti Aayog 2018); lack of skilled manpower, with only 4.96% of the workforce formally skilled (KPMG and FICCI 2016); low per capita income (IMF 2019); and so on are some of the pressing problems.

Likewise, in the globalized world, there is a need to make a deeper assessment. On various development parameters like the human development index (HDI) (130th rank) (UNDP 2018), starting a business (137th rank) (World Bank 2019b), infrastructure development (66th rank), quality of electricity supply (80th rank), institutional development (163rd rank in enforcing contracts), technology readiness (110th rank) as per WEF (2018a) report, per capita income (119th rank globally on PPP basis) (IMF 2019), India's position is not encouraging, and these have an adverse impact on competitiveness and the ability to attract investment. Furthermore, the twenty-first century is dealing with challenges and the transformation process because of globalization, climate change, digital connectivity, advanced technologies, demographic transition, likely job losses as a consequence of automation, etc. Such transformation is marked with much higher speed, scale, and scope and gives rise to complexity (Jaimovich and Siu 2012; NIC 2012; KPMG 2014; Dobbs et al. 2015; WEF 2018b).

The aforementioned issues lead to a search for questions on the efficacy of public policymaking and implementation for improving the basic needs of people on the one hand and raising global standing on vital parameters such as technology readiness and competitiveness on the other. It underscores the need to understand: the public policy system; the process of policymaking; how the decisions are made behind the formulation of policies; how the policies are implemented to achieve the intended plan; and what it will take to comprehend the complexity and emerging issues of the twenty-first century, and additionally to make policymaking process an evidence-based systemic approach and institutionalize the public policy system.

In the above context, the book critically analyzes the ideas, mechanisms, processes, and development indicators and outcomes that shape the problems, programs, and policies. It examines micro-level as well as macro-level issues. Some of the micro-level topics covered are issues in the policymaking process, capturing grassroots-level concerns, implementation of policies and programs at the grassroots level, and institutional matters in rural or urban areas. It covers case studies and field surveys. It includes a perspective on policy implementation. At the macro level, various policy issues at National and international levels are studied. Some of the sectors examined are education, health, skill development, manufacturing, advanced technologies, R&D and innovation, labor reforms, urban management, agriculture, energy, and economic growth—covering key development indicators. It underlines the challenges of automation due to advanced technologies, labor reforms for spurring industrial activities and growth, social security, and climate change.

Framework. The main objective of the framework is to present the broad contours of the public policy system and determinants of policy design and management. It delineates challenges, constraints, and opportunities in policymaking. The framework of the book comprises ideas, research issues, analyses, key findings, and the way ahead. The details are summarized as follows:

The conceptual foundation of the book is to comprehend the essence of public policy—system, process, and content. It entails three significant aspects, as depicted in Fig. 1.1. *First, comprehending the public policy system*—understanding the characteristics of the public system, complexity, information infrastructure, institutional development, and sustainability. *Second, informed, fair, and transparent decision-making process*: whether ground realities are factored in during analyses, how socio-economic-cultural issues are examined, how the decisions are made, and whether the decision-making is fair and transparent and gives confidence to stakeholders are the issues that need to be examined during the process of policymaking. *Third, examining outcomes and public value creation*—how policies create public values. Specific issues are: understanding the parameters such as meeting expectations of citizens, how the public policies address basic needs and how citizens are engaged in the policymaking process; quality of public services, including primary education, health services, drinking water, or prevention of health hazards from air pollution, etc.; efficiency of service delivery and the effectiveness of the implementation;

1.3 Framework of Book

Conceptual Foundation
- Comprehending public policy system
- Informed, fair, and transparent decision-making process
- Examining outcomes and public value creation

Policy System Diagnosis

| Understanding essentiality of public policy and key policy issues (Chapters 1 and 2) | Diagnosing policy system and complexity (Chapters 3 and 4) | Studying policy theories, models, and policymaking process (Chapters 1 and 4) |

Way Ahead
- Complexity theory framework
- Innovation in public policy and policy design framework
- Institutional development (ID) for policy design and management
- New public organizations and skill sets for 21st Century roles
(Chapters 5, 6, 7)

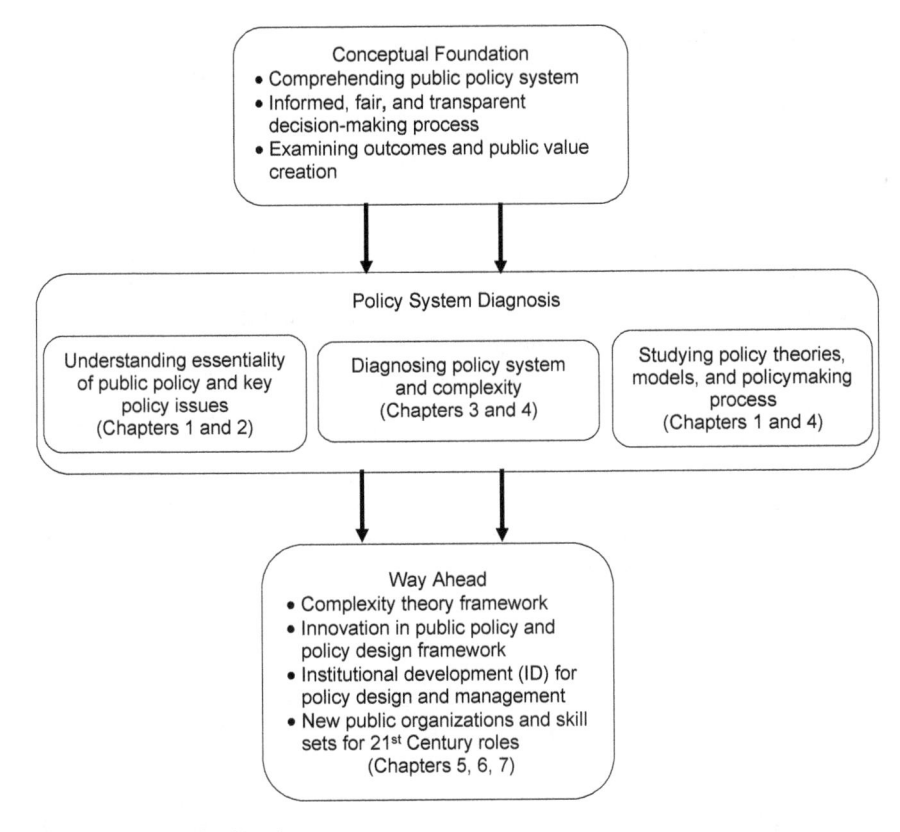

Fig. 1.1 Framework of book

sustainability of programs; how policies address issues of investment, infrastructure development, and economic growth; whether the outputs and outcomes inspire trust among the citizens; and whether there is accountability of decision-making.

As for the diagnosis of the policy system, it consists of three sections. *Firstly*, it delves into understanding the essentiality of public policy and key policy issues in socio-economic sectors. The issues are dealt with in this chapter and Chap. 2. It underscores the need for studying public policy objectively and comprehensively. It presents the issues that are essential for the progress of the country and contribute to the well-being of citizens. It stresses learnings from the correlation between education attainment, health conditions, and skill development on one hand and poverty reduction on the other. Similarly, the positive relationship between R&D, technology readiness, and skilled workforce on one side and competitiveness in manufacturing and per capita income on the other is examined. Interlinkages among air and river water pollution, health problems, urban development, innovation, future investment, and economic growth are highlighted, which provide useful pointers for future policymaking. It analyzes development indicators and outcomes that impact the quality of life. It covers policy issues of different sectors within the country as well as of other countries, with a view to obtaining a comparative perspective. The institutional issues and their correlation with development outcomes and economic growth have also been studied.

Secondly, it diagnoses policy system and complexity, as covered in Chaps. 3 and 4. It analyzes the characteristics of complex systems and elucidates how policymaking is a complex phenomenon. It examines concepts such as nonlinearity in interactions, dynamic nature, causality and feedback, emergent behavior, and self-organization. *Thirdly*, it studies underlying policy theories and models, included in this chapter and Chap. 4. The theories and models provide the basis for the policy process, decision-making, and evaluation for better policy outcomes. The study of the evolution of public policy is essential to learn how various disciplines and scholars have contributed to providing new approaches and methodologies for better policymaking. While examining the policymaking process, the issues covered are how data is collected and analyzed; how local, National, and global factors are taken into account; and how policy decisions are made in complex conditions. It analyzes the role of institutional capacity in the implementation of policies. It underscores the linkage between public policymaking and economic development, or how institutional development and a good policy system can contribute to better socio-economic outcomes.

It presents way ahead by entailing complexity theory framework, innovation in policymaking, policy design framework, institutional development (ID) for policy design and implementation, and new public organizations and skill sets for the twenty-first century roles. Chapters 5–7 are dedicated to this purpose. As a research case study, it illustrates a comprehensive application of the system approach, interpretive structural modeling (ISM), and system dynamics (SD) for policy design. To make the public policy system function successfully, it underscores the need for institutional development (ID). It argues that public organizations should encourage a value-driven and system-based perspective for policymaking.

References

Acemoglu D, Robinson J. The role of institutions in growth and development. Rev Econ Instit. 2010;1(2). https://doi.org/10.5202/rei.v1i2.1.
Ackoff RL. Towards a system of system concepts. Manage Sci. 1971;17(11):83–90.
Annual Status of Education Report (ASER); 2016. http://img.asercentre.org/docs/Publications/ASER%20Reports/ASER%202016/aser2016_nationalpressrelease.pdf.
Anderson P. Complexity theory and organization science. Organ Sci. 1999;10:217–32.
Arthur WB, Durlauf SN, Lane DA, editors. Economy as an evolving complex system. Redwood City: Addison-Wesley; 1997.
Arthur WB. Complexity economics: a different framework for economic thought; 2013. http://www2.econ.iastate.edu/tesfatsi/ComplexityEconomics.WBrianArthur.SFIWP2013.pdf.
Arthur WB. Complexity and the economy. Oxford University Press; 2014.

References

Atkinson RD. Complexity theory and evolutionary economics, in debate the issues: complexity and policy making. OECD Publications; 2017. https://www.oecd.org/naec/complexity_and_policy making.pdf.

Banks G. Challenges of evidence-based policy-making, commonwealth of Australia; 2009. http://www.apsc.gov.au/publications09/evidencebasedpolicy.pdf.

Baron J. A brief history of evidence-based policy. Am Acad Polit Soc Sci. 2018;678(1):2018.

Battiston S, Farmer JD, Flache A, Garlaschelli D, Haldane AG, Heesterbeek H, Scheffer M. Complexity theory and financial regulation. Science. 2016;351(6275):818–9.

Beinhocker ED. The origin of wealth: evolution, complexity, and the radical remaking of economics. Harvard Business School Press; 2006.

Beinhocker E. A new narrative for a complex age in debate the issues: complexity and policymaking. OECD Publications; 2017. www.oecd.org/about/publishing/corrigenda.htm.

Birkland TA. An introduction to policy process. PHI Learning Pvt. Ltd.; 2011.

Blignaut S. 7 differences between complex and complicated; 2019. https://blog.usejournal.com/7-differences-between-complex-and-complicated-fa44e0844606.

Boulding KE. General systems theory: the skeleton of science. Manage Sci. 1956;2(3):197–208.

Boulton JG, Allen PM, Bowman C. Embracing complexity: strategic perspectives for an age of turbulence. Oxford University Press; 2015.

Breslins. A successful business is about having the right systems; 2019. https://www.breslins.co.uk/business-is-about-systems-not-people/#:~:text.

Brynjolfsson E, McAfee A. Race against the machine: how the digital revolution is accelerating innovation, driving productivity, and irreversibly transforming employment and the economy. Digital Frontier Press Lexington; 2011.

Cairney P. Understanding public policy: theories and issues. Palgrave Macmillan: Textbooks in Policy Studies; 2012.

Cairney P, Heikkila T, Wood M. Making policy in a complex world (elements in public policy). Cambridge University Press; 2019.

Cecere G, Corrocher N, Gossart C, Ozman M. Lock-in and path dependence: an evolutionary approach to eco-innovations. J Evol Econ. 2014. https://muge.wp.imt.fr/files/2014/03/lock_in.pdf.

Chakravarty B, Chand P. Public policy: concept, theory and practice paperback. Sage Publications India; 2016

Chancel L, Piketty T. Indian income inequality, 1922–2014: from British Raj to Billionaire Raj? World inequality lab working paper series; 2017. https://wid.world/document/chancelpiketty2017widworld/.

Checkland PB. From optimizing to learning: a development of systems thinking for the 1990s. J Oper Res Soc. 1985;36(9):757–67.

Christiansen J, Bunt L. Innovation in policy: allowing for creativity, social complexity and uncertainty in public governance. NESTA; 2012

Cilliers P. What can we learn from complexity. Emergence? 2000. https://doi.org/10.1207/S15327000EM0201_03

Cochran CE, Mayer LC, Carr TR, Cayer NJ. American public policy: an introduction. St. Martin's Press; 1999.

Cochran CL, Malone EF. Public policy: perspectives and choices. McGraw Hill; 1995

Cohen M. Commentary on the organizational science special issue on complexity. Org Sci. 1999;10:373–6.

Cohen WJ. The development of the social security act of 1935: reflections some fifty years later. Minnesota Law Rev. 1984. https://core.ac.uk/download/pdf/217208529.pdf.

Colander D, Kupers R. Complexity and the art of public policy—solving society's problems from the bottom up. Princeton University Press; 2016.

Collins T. Health policy analysis: a simple tool. Publ Health. 2005;119:192–6.

Coyle RG. Management system dynamics. Wiley; 1977.

Curtain R. Good public policy making: how Australia fares, agenda. J Policy Anal Reform. 2000;8(1):33–46. http://www.curtain-consulting.net.au/download_controlled/Public%20policy/agenda.pdf.
Dafermos M. Chapter: reductionism In: Teo T, editor. Encyclopedia of critical psychology. Springer-Verlag Berlin Heidelberg; 2014. Downloads/ReductionismFV.pdf.
deLeon P, Vogenbeck DM. The policy sciences at the crossroads. Chapter 1. In: Fischer F, Miller GJ, Sidney MS, editors. Handbook of public policy analysis theory, politics, and methods. CRC Press; 2007.
Deloitte. Global manufacturing competitiveness index; 2016.
Deloitte and Singularity University (DSU). Exponential technologies in manufacturing transforming the future of manufacturing through technology, talent, and the innovation ecosystem; 2018
De PK. Public policy and systems. Pearson; 2012.
Dewey J. The public and its problems. New York: Henry Holt and Company; 1927.
Dobbs R, Manyika J, Woetzel J. No ordinary disruption: the four global forces breaking all the trends. Public Affairs; 2015
Dror Y. Public policy making re-examined. San Francisco: Chandler; 1968.
Dunn W. Public policy: an introduction. New Jersey: Prentice Hall; 1981.
Durlauf SN. Complexity, economics, and public policy. Polit Philos Econ. 2012;11(1):45–75.
Dye TR. Understanding public policy. Prentice Hall; 1992.
Easton D. A framework for political analysis. Prentice Hall; 1965.
Economist Intelligence Unit (EIU) Limited. Taming organisational complexity: start at the top. Economist. 2015.
Edwards R. System does matter; 2019. http://www.indie-rpgs.com/_articles/system_does_matter.html.
Eglin D. Why systems matter; 2017. https://www.productivityhub.com.au/2017/06/why-systems-matter/.
Ehrenberg J. Civil society: the critical history of an idea. New York University Press; 1999.
Eppel E, Rhodes ML. Complexity theory and public management: a 'becoming' field. Publ Manage Rev. 2018;20(7):949–59. https://doi.org/10.1080/14719037.2017.1364414.
Fischer F, Miller GJ, Sidney MS. Handbook of public policy analysis theory, politics, and methods. CRC Press; 2007.
FAO. The state of agricultural commodity markets; 2018. http://www.fao.org/3/I9542EN/i9542en.pdf.
Ferrini L. The importance of institutions to economic development; 2012. https://www.e-ir.info/2012/09/19/the-importance-of-institutions-to-economic-development/.
Flyvbjerg, B. Making social science matter: why social inquiry fails and how it can succeed again. University Press Cambridge; 2001.
Forrester JW. Principles of systems. Cambridge, Massachusetts: MIT Press; 1968.
Forrester JW. Counterintuitive behaviour of social systems. Technol Rev. 1971;53–68
Forrester JW. Lessons from system dynamics modelling. Syst Dyn Rev. 1987;3(2):136–49.
Fried B. The progressive assault on Laissez-Faire: Robert Hale and the first law and economics movement. Harvard University Press; 1998.
Fuentes HCT. Systemic methodologies in regional sustainable development. Syst Res Sci. 2006;23(5):659–66.
Gatty A. Business systems: five reasons every business owner needs to develop and follow them; 2019. https://www.allbusiness.com/business-systems-5-important-reason-you-need-to-develop-and-follow-them-104090-1.html.
Gagnon J. The redistributive properties of the social security act of 1935. J Undergraduate Res. 2017;22. http://digitalcommons.iwu.edu/respublica/vol22/iss1/10.
Gerston LN. Public policy making: process and principles. M.E. Sharpe Inc.; 2010.
Geurts T. Public policy making: the 21st century perspective; 2010. http://www.lulu.com/shop/theigeurts/public-policy-making-the-21st-century-perspective/ebook/product-21759876.html.

References

Gharajedaghi J. Systems thinking: managing chaos and complexity: a platform for designing business architecture. Morgan Kaufmann; 2011.

Gigch JPV. Applied general systems theory. Harper and Row Publishers; 1974.

Gregoriades A, Karakostas V. A simulation methodology unifying system dynamics and business objects. Int Syst Dyn Conf. 2000. http://www.systemdynamics.org/conferences/2000/PDFs/gregoria.pdf.

Grobman GM. Complexity theory: a new way to look at organizational change. Publ Admin Quart. 2005;29(3).

Gupta DN. Rural development system: policy issues, institutional development and management of rural development. New Delhi: Books India International; 2000.

Helbing D, Kirman A. Rethinking economics using complexity theory. Real-World Econ Rev. 2013;64. https://papers.ssrn.com/sol3/papers.cfm?abstract_id=2292370.

Heywood S, Spungin J, Turnbull D. Cracking the complexity code. McKinsey Quart. 2007.

Howlett M, Ramesh M. Studying public policy: policy cycles and policy subsystems. Oxford University Press; 1995.

Hudson B, Hunter D, Peckham S. Policy failure and the policy-implementation gap: can policy support programs help? Policy Des Pract. 2019;2(1):1–14. https://doi.org/10.1080/25741292.2018.1540378.

Human Development Report (HDR). UNDP;2016.

International Institute for Sustainable Development (IISD) and The Energy and Resources Institute (TERI). Designing policies in a world of uncertainty, change, and surprise; 2006. https://www.iisd.org/system/files/publications/climate_designing_policies.pdf.

International Monetary Fund (IMF). World economic outlook database (April 2019); 2019.

Ismael J. Determinism, counterpredictive devices, and the impossibility of laplacean intelligences. Monist. 2019;102(4). https://doi.org/10.1093/monist/onz021.

Israel A. Institutional development. John Hopkins University Press; 1989.

Jackson MC. Creative holism: a critical system approaches to complex problem situation. Syst Res Behav Sci. 2006;23(5):647–58.

Jaimovich N, Siu HE. The trend is the cycle: job polarization and jobless recoveries. Tech. Rep., NBER Working Paper No. 18334, National Bureau of Economic Research; 2012.

Jann W, Wegrich K. Theories of the policy cycle. In: Fischer F, Miller GJ, Sidney MS, editors. Handbook of public policy analysis theory, politics, and methods. CRC Press; 2007.

Jenkins WI. Policy-analysis. A political and organisational perspective. London: Martin Robertsen; 1978.

John P. Complexity and policy: behavioural approaches: how nudges lead to more intelligent policy design. In: Philippe Z and Guy Peters B, editors. Contemporary approaches to public policy. Palgrave Macmillan; 2015.

Jones H. Taking responsibility for complexity how implementation can achieve results in the face of complex problems working paper 330. Overseas Development Institute; 2011. https://www.odi.org/sites/odi.org.uk/files/odi-assets/publications-opinion-files/6485.pdf.

Kahan JP. Focus groups as a tool for policy analysis. Analyses of social issues and public policy, 129–146; 2001. http://www.psicopolis.com/GruppoNew/focgrpol.pdf.

Kalirajan K, Bhide S, Singh K. Development performance across Indian states and the role of the governments; 2007. https://crawford.anu.edu.au/acde/asarc/pdf/papers/2009/WP2009_05.pdf.

Kapoor S. The rising complexity of the global economy. In Debate the issues: complexity and policy making. OECD Publications; 2017. https://www.oecd.org/naec/complexity_and_policy making.pdf.

Keeney RL, von Winterfeldt D, Eppel T. Eliciting public values for complex policy decisions. Manage Sci. 1990;36:1011–30.

Kelly KL. A systems approach to identifying decisive information for sustainable development. Eur J Oper Res. 1998;109:452–64.

Kirman A. Complex economics: individual and collective rationality. Routledge; 2011.

Kirman A. Complexity and economic policy, in new approaches to economic challenge: insights into complexity and policy; 2016. https://www.oecd.org/naec/Insights%20into%20Complexity%20and%20Policy.pdf.

Koskinen KU. Systemic view and systems thinking. In: Knowledge Production in organizations book; 2013. https://doi.org/10.1007/978-3-319-00104-3_3.

KPMG. Future state 2030: the global megatrends shaping governments; 2014

KPMG and FICCI. Re-engineering the skill ecosystem; 2016. http://ficci.in/spdocument/20762/Re-engineering-the-skill-ecosystem.pdf.

Lasswell HD. A pre-view of policy sciences. American Elsevier Publishing; 1971

Lasswell HD. The policy orientation. In: Lerner D, Lasswell HD, editors. The policy sciences. Stanford University Press; 1951.

Leonard TC. American economic reform in the progressive era. Its foundational beliefs and their relation to eugenics. Hist Polit Econ. 2009;41(1).

Lenihan D. Rethinking the public policy process: a public engagement framework; 2009. https://canada2020.ca/wp-content/uploads/2015/05/FRAMEWORK-PAPER-.pdf.

Lunn P. Regulatory policy and behavioural economics. Paris: OECD Publishing; 2014. https://doi.org/10.1787/9789264207851-en.

Marsh I. Innovation and public policy: the challenge of an emerging paradigm, AIRC working paper series, WP/0710, Australian Innovation Research Centre, University of Tasmania; 2010.

Marston G, Watts R. Tampering with the evidence: a critical appraisal of evidence-based policy-making; 2003 (marston_watts.pdf). https://www.researchgate.net/publication/241578701_Tampering_With_the_Evidence_A_Critical_Appraisal_of_Evidence-Based_PolicyMaking.

Maslin M. Climate change: a very short introduction. Oxford, UK: Oxford Publication; 2014.

McCool DC. Public policy theories, models, and concepts: an anthology. Englewood Cliffs, NJ: Prentice Hall; 1995.

McGill R. Institutional development (ID). Springer; 1996. https://doi.org/10.1007/978-1-349-25071-4_1.pdf.

Mckinsey. How do I manage the complexity in my organization? In: Heywood S, Hillar R, Turnbull D, editors; 2010.

McKinsey Global Institute (MGI). Jobs lost, jobs gained: workforce transitions in a time of automation; 2017. https://www.mckinsey.com/~/media/mckinsey/featured%20insights/report-december-62017.ashx.

Menard C, Shirley MM. The contribution of douglass north to new institutional economics; 2011. https://halshs.archives-ouvertes.fr/halshs-00624297/document.

Miller G. Magical number seven plus or minus two: some limits on our capacity for processing information. Psychol Rev. 1956;63(2).

Ministry of Health and Family Welfare (MHFW), Government of India. Household health expenditures in India; 2016. https://mohfw.gov.in/sites/default/files/38300411751489562625.pdf.

Moore M, Sheelagh S, Hudock A. Institution building as a development assistance method. Brightom, UK: The Institute of Development Studies at the University of Sussex; 1994.

Mohapatra PK, Mandal P, Bora MC. Introduction to system dynamics modelling. Hyderabad, India: Universities Press Ltd.; 1994.

Morcol G. A complexity theory for public policy routledge research in public administration and public policy). Routledge; 2012. p. 2012.

Morecroft JDW. System dynamics: portraying bounded rationality. Omega. 1983;11(2):131–42.

Moran M, Rein M, Goodin, RE. The oxford handbook of public policy. Oxford Handbooks; 2008.

Mueller B. Why public policies fail: policymaking under complexity. EconomiA. 2020;21(2):311–23. https://doi.org/10.1016/j.econ.2019.11.002.

National Institute of Public Finance and Policy (NIPFP). The quality of governance: how have indian states performed? In: Mundle S, Chakraborty P, Chowdhury S, Sikdar S, editors, working paper no. 2012-104 July 2012.

National Intelligence Council (NIC). Global trends 2030: alternative worlds; 2012.

References

Net Objectives. The systems thinking view of simple, complicated, chaotic, and complex; 2019. https://portal.netobjectives.com/pages/flex/systems-thinking-view-of-simple-complicated-chaotic-complex%20complicated.

Niti Aayog. National nutrition strategy. New Delhi: Govt of India; 2018. http://niti.gov.in/writereaddata/files/document_publication/Nutrition_Strategy_Booklet.pdf.

North DC. The role of institutions in economic development, UNECE discussion papers series no. 2003.2; 2003. https://www.unece.org/fileadmin/DAM/oes/disc_papers/ECE_DP_2003-2.pdf.

NSW Public Service Commission. State of the NSW public sector report 2015: to the next level; 2015. https://www.psc.nsw.gov.au/sites/default/files/2020-11/NSW_PSC_-_State_of_the_Sector_Report_2015.pdf.

OECD. New approaches to economic challenge: insights into complexity and policy; 2016a. https://www.oecd.org/naec/Insights%20into%20Complexity%20and%20Policy.pdf.

OECD. Use of behavioural insights in consumer policy. OECD; 2016b. http://www.oecd.org/officialdocuments/?c(2016)3/FINAL&docLanguage=En.

OECD. Debate the issues: complexity and policy making. OECD Publications; 2017a. https://www.oecd.org/naec/complexity_and_policymaking.pdf.

OECD. Behavioral insights and public policy: lessons from around the world. Paris: OECD Publishing; 2017b. https://doi.org/10.1787/9789264270480-en.

OECD. OECD observatory of public sector innovation: working with change, systems approaches to public sector challenges; 2017c.

Oliver A, editor. Behavioural public policy. Cambridge University Press; 2013.

Outreach. Best practice brief, how governmental policy is made, number, 34; 2005. http://outreach.msu.edu/bpbriefs/issues/brief34.pdf.

Ozer B, Şeker G. Complexity theory and public policy: a new way to put new public management and governance in perspective, Suleyman Demirel University. J Fac Econ Administr Sci. 2013;18(1).

Patel V. Our best investment: to improve educational outcomes, policy must address deprivations in early years of children's lives; 2017. http://indianexpress.com/article/opinion/columns/our-best-investment-right-of-children-to-free-and-compulsory-education-in-india/.

Parag Y. A System perspective for policy analysis and understanding: the policy process networks; 2005. www.eci.ox.ac.uk/publications/downloads/parag06.pdf.

Peters GB. American public policy: promise and performance. Chatham House, Seven Rivers; 1999.

Phillips K. Applying behavioral science upstream in the policy design process; 2018. https://behavioralscientist.org/applying-behavioral-science-upstream-in-the-policy-design-process/.

Pigdon K, Woolley M. The big picture: integrating children's learning. Eleanor Curtain Pub; 1992.

Portney K. Approaching public policy analysis: an introduction to policy and program research. New Jersey: Prentice Hall; 1986.

Pottenger M, Martin A. Insights into behavioural public policy issues paper series No. 06/14. Melborne School of Government; 2014

Potucek M, LeLoup L. Approaches to public policy in central and Eastern Europe; 2003. Downloads/approaches-pp.pdf.

Productivity Commission. Strengthening evidence-based policy in the Australian Federation, volume 1: proceedings, roundtable proceedings, Canberra: Productivity Commission; 2010.

PWC. Five megatrends and their implications for global defense & security; 2016. https://www.pwc.com/gx/en/government-public-services/assets/five-megatrends-implications.pdf.

Rao VM. Policy making in india for rural development: the contextual limits to quantitative approaches (Rao). In: IGIDR proceedings/project reports series PP-062-07; 2009. http://www.igidr.ac.in/pdf/publication/PP-062-07.pdf.

Raymond WC, Susan JB, Morgan BN. Public administration in theory and practice. Pearson; 1994.

Reserve Bank of India (RBI). Handbook of statistics on Indian States; 2019. https://www.rbi.org.in/Scripts/AnnualPublications.aspx?head=Handbook+of+Statistics+on+Indian+States.

Rihani S. Complexity theory: a new framework for development is in the offing. Prog Dev Stud. 2005;5(1):54–61.

Rizvi G. Innovations in government, innovative governance in the 21st century. Washington: Brookings Institution Press; 2008.

Rodrik D, Subramanian A, Trebbi F. Institutions rule: the primacy of institutions over geography and integration in economic development. J Econ Growth. 2004;9(2).

Sanders TI. Strategic thinking and the new science: planning in the midst of chaos complexity and chan paperback. Free Press; 2010.

Sapru RK. Public policy: formulation, implementation and evaluation paperback. Sterling Publishers; 2012.

Schasfoort J. Complexity economics; 2017. https://www.exploring-economics.org/en/orientation/complexity-economics/.

Senge P. The fifth discipline: the art and practice of the learning organization. New York: Doubleday Currency; 1990.

Senge PM, Sterman JD. Systems thinking and organizational learning: acting locally and thinking globally in the organization of the future. Euro J Oper Res. 1992;59.

Simon HA. Models of man: social and rational. New York: Wiley; 1957.

Simon HA. Organizations and markets. J Econ Perspect. 1991;5(2):1991.

Solek A. Behavioral economics approaches to public policy. J Int Stud. 2014;7(2):2014. https://doi.org/10.14254/2071-8330.2014/7-2/3.

Solow R. Building a science of economics for the real world. prepared statement to the House Committee on Science and Technology, subcommittee on investigations and oversight; 2010. https://web.archive.org/web/20110204034313/http://democrats.science.house.gov/Media/file/Commdocs/hearings/2010/Oversight/20july/Solow_Testimony.pdf.

Stacey RD. Strategic management and organizational dynamics: the challenge of complexity. Prentice Hall; 2002.

Sterman JD. Business dynamics: systems thinking and modelling for a complex world. Irwin & McGraw-Hil; 2000.

Subramanian A. The evolution of institutions in India and its relationship with economic growth; 2007. https://www.piie.com/publications/papers/subramanian0407b.pdf.

Sushil. System dynamics: a practical approach for managerial problems. New Delhi: Wiley Eastern Limited; 1993.

Sushil. Interpretive matrix: a tool to aid interpretation of management and social research. Glob J Flex Syst Manag. 2005;6(2):27–30.

Sutcliffe S, Court J. Evidence-based policymaking: what is it? How does it work? What relevance for developing countries? Overseas Development Institute (ODI); 2005.

Swanson D, Bhadwal S, editors. Creating adaptive policies guide for policy-making in an uncertain world. Sage Publication; 2009.

United Nations (UN). Innovations in governance and public administration: replicating what works. New York: Department of Economic and Social Affairs; 2006.

UN. World public sector report 2015: responsive and accountable public governance; 2015

UNCTAD. World investment report; 2014.

UNDP. Human development report (HDR); 2018.

University of Groningen. A review of common characteristics of complex system; 2017. https://www.futurelearn.com/courses/complexity-and-uncertainty/0/steps/1836.

Van der Wal Zeger. The 21st century public manager (the public management and leadership series). Palgrave; 2017.

Verhulst S. The 21st century public servant in GovLab. Blog; 2013. http://thegovlab.org/the-21st-century-public-servant/.

Walby S. Complexity theory, globalisation and diversity; 2003. https://www.lancaster.ac.uk/fass/resources/sociology-online-papers/papers/walby-complexityglobalisationdiversity.pdf.

Walton M. Using complexity theory in policy work; 2015. https://cdn.auckland.ac.nz/assets/arts/documents/compass_seminars_2016_using_complexity_theory_in_policy_work.pdf.

Warfield JN. A science of generic design managing complexity through system design, vols. I and II. USA: Inter Publication; 1990.

References

Weiss TG. Governance, good governance and global governance: conceptual and actual challenges. Third World Quart. 2000;21(5). https://www.jstor.org/stable/3993619?seq=1#page_scan_tab_contents.

World Economic Forum (WEF). The global risks report 2017. 12th ed.; 2017.

World Economic Forum (WEF). The global competitiveness report, 2017–2018; 2018a.

World Economic Forum (WEF). The future of jobs report; 2018b.

World Bank. World bank blogs: behavioral science in public policy: future of government? In: Sanchez-Paramo C, Vakis R, Afif Z, editors; 2019a. http://blogs.worldbank.org/developmenttalk/behavioral-science-public-policy-future-government.

World Bank. Doing business report; 2019b.

World Health Organization (WHO). World health statistics; 2015.

Chapter 2
Public Policy Issues: Key Pointers

There's a tremendous gap between public opinion and public policy.
Noam Chomsky, Author, Philosopher and Social Essayist

Abstract Public policies have a universal presence in a country. There is an essentiality to understanding their impact and outcomes. Their study can provide insights into the future direction of development. For enhanced understanding, the policy issues and performance are studied under key sectors such as education, health and nutrition, urban management, economic growth, manufacturing, advanced manufacturing and future of jobs, advanced materials, government spending, innovation and entrepreneurship, infrastructure development, and labor laws. Examining issues in such sectors has brought to the fore the necessity of making policies comprehensively by factoring in multiple perspectives. For a better appreciation of the value of public policy, there is a need to understand both the perspectives—country-specific and international context. In the chapter, the learnings have been drawn from the international comparison of various development indicators and the policies that have put developed and fast-emerging countries on the path of human resource development, higher growth, and quality of life.

Keywords Policymaking process · Education · Health · Urban development · Advanced manufacturing · Industry 4.0 · Strategic materials · Innovation · Labor reforms

Government has a vast role in the public realm. Public policy concerns every citizen. Policies can play a vital role in determining the future course of a society and a country. Formulating good policies is seen as a big challenge for sustainable growth and the future. The policies are formulated by Central and State governments and entail statutes, legislations, rules, and programs that steer the lives of citizens. If policies are not developed correctly, the concerned sector may miss out on some crucial aspects, or a particular sector may lag behind by several years till correction is introduced. Thus, it places value on meticulous study of policy as a prerequisite.

The governments at various levels are put to several questions by a host of concerns of citizens. It calls for sound policymaking, which is possible once the existing policies are examined, and the lessons are drawn. The study of policies is central to the policy process.

2.1 Imperative of Understanding Public Policy

At the heart of all issues in a country are government policies and, thus, the indispensability of public policy. It is guided by the vision of the government. While the vision of the good future may not be fully realizable, it guides policy efforts. And it provides a way forward for continuous calibrated improvement in policies by way of feedback from experts and citizens. The reasons why studying policy are numerous. The need to study arises from its definition—the intent, vision, and content. Good policymaking will require an informed discussion, analysis, and research. The critical analysis of policies enables policymakers, citizens, and experts to monitor and evaluate the achievements. If policy is studied and examined, specific measures for improvement can be introduced. To get insights into policy content and implementation, it necessitates studying the policy from different perspectives, as presented below:

- *From the perspective of a citizen and engagement with public policy.* As a citizen, it is both an opportunity and the responsibility to engage in community or civic affairs. The objective is to improve the quality of life in the community. Such engagement is needed at various stages, viz., appreciating public concerns, understanding government policies and implementation of programs, and contributing to improving policy outcomes. Understanding policy analysis helps to appreciate the causes of success and failures. Knowing how policy works can improve the ability to deal with development issues better. By acquiring analytical, ethical, and practical skills, if citizens are aware of government policies and their outcomes and impacts, they may contribute by giving better ideas and developing more creative solutions. For example, the engagement of people regarding air pollution in cities, river pollution, or soil erosion in hilly areas assumes high importance as all these impact citizens, including children.

It is equally important from the point of view of the rising influence of social media and aspirations. The citizens are becoming more inquisitive and demanding. They expect responsive government. It makes the study of public policy essential for healthy participation in the democratic process in general and contributing to improving the policy content in particular. From the scale and scope of the development, the responsibilities of governments are rising in multiple ways, which calls for significant interventions in villages, towns, and cities. A large number of services are delivered in various socio-economic sectors. The amount of spending by government at all levels, viz., village, district, State, and Central, is quite staggering. Such

2.1 Imperative of Understanding Public Policy

an enormous role of government necessitates for the citizens to actively engage with the government, thereby making it imperative to learn more about policy.

- *Humane perspective.* Citizens and other stakeholders are constantly concerned about certain policies impacting livelihood and human development and the basis of specific decision-making by the government. There are specific examples that highlight why these are important. The view that there is an increase in the gap between high-income and low-income groups is widely shared (Chancel and Piketty 2017). Similarly, there is a disparity in service delivery in different regions. Some regions in a particular State or many areas within a city or district do not get the same level of services compared to what other parts receive from the government. The citizens have several concerns related to primary education, scholarships for children, health expenses, pension, and employment, to name a few. It leads many to question how public policies are formulated (Cochran and Malone 2005; Gerston 2010; Sapru 2012).

The report of the National Statistical Commission (NSC 2012) suggests that at the aggregate level, the share of labor input by the unorganized sector has been staggering 93% against the share of 53.9% in total gross value added (GVA). While the formal sector, with 7% of labor contribution, is contributing 46.1% of GVA, and thus GVA per unit labor is disproportionately higher by a factor of 13.5. It is true for all sectors, viz., agriculture, industry, and service. Thus, it gives rise to inequality. And such skewed contribution in GVA gets reflected in per capita income and rate of growth of income in the formal sector, which are much higher than that of the informal sector. It is a reason for income inequality. In the case of agriculture, how farmers can benefit from technologies and marketing support to enhance crop productivity and income are issues of policy concern.

Some illustrations in health education, water sectors, nutrition, and air pollution are summarized here. The figures for IMR and MMR stood at 37 and 174, respectively, for India (HDR 2016; RBI 2019). It reflects about less than satisfactory state of primary and secondary health services. These figures are high. And how the IMR and MMR can be reduced is a major health policy concern. How the out-of-pocket health expenses can be minimized is getting the attention of policymakers (WHO 2015; Rao 2017). Similarly, for HDI (UNDP 2018), India's position has been 130, while some South Asian countries like Bangladesh, Nepal, and Sri Lanka had better performance. The quality of education at various levels, viz., primary, middle, and higher, is questioned by citizens and several experts. It requires education departments to take a fresh look at the problems.

Likewise, for water supply, there are issues of supply of desired quantity and quality of water. In most places in the country, potable drinking water, with BIS-approved and tested quality tap water, is not supplied directly to households, resulting in health problems for many. It requires the installation of purification devices by many households, which can afford them. The nutrition intake by children is linked to individual growth—both mental and physical—which in turn leads to knowledge and skill attainments, then to productivity to the ability to earn, and then finally, at the aggregate level, to the economic growth of the country. It requires revisiting policies (World Bank 2008).

There is another pressing case of air and river water pollution. Air pollution in urban areas impacts the health of citizens, especially children. There are concerns about air quality in many cities and industrial towns in the country. It has a direct impact on health and quality of life (World Bank 1998). It impacts more people living in slums or low-income people settled near water bodies and construction sites (WHO 2018; ORF 2019). A World Health Organization (WHO) study has indicated that 14 of the 20 world's most polluted cities were in India in 2016 (HINDU 2018), and 4 out of every 10 children in Delhi suffer from lung problems. These have wider implications for health, urban development, prospects for investment, and economic growth.

The above examples reflect the gravity of the problems for citizens and underscore more firmly the need for the study and examination of public policy that determines the future of people in many ways. In every facet of life, right from health to education to employment, public policy has its impact on the lives of citizens. It requires a humane perspective in policymaking. Public policy should serve societal causes more than anything.

- *Perspective of policy impact assessment—understanding ramifications of policies.* The study of public policy is specifically essential from the point of view of understanding the trend and behavior of socio-economic indicators over time, comprehending the linkages between policy direction and outcomes, exploring linkages among different policies, and thereby drawing lessons for future course correction. It necessitates evidence-based policy impact assessments to assess household, social, economic, and environmental implications of public policy. It will serve the objectives of improving decision-making, clarifying how public policy has achieved its vision and objectives, and, thus, contributing to continuous learning and improvement in policy formulation by identifying causalities that underpin ex-post review of policy (Birkland 2011; Chakravarty and Chand 2016). In this context, the example of the agriculture and rural development sector is summed up below. It rightly highlights the necessity of understanding the policy implications.

For decades, agricultural growth has remained low, as presented in Table 2.1. It has been much lower than the GDP growth rate. From 1950 till 2012, the average growth rate in agriculture was 2.8%, while the same was 5.25% for GDP. The low growth rate in agriculture had an adverse impact on poverty, as a large population depends upon agriculture (Panagariya and Bhagwati 2014; Planning Commission 2014; Mohan and Kapur 2015; Dev 2016). To understand issues, it requires both a systemic and systematic approach to policy analysis, formulation, implementation, and evaluation of all the major activities under agriculture and rural economy. A fragmented approach may not work. Specifically, in the agriculture sector, the policies for timely inputs supply and management, credit, money-lending, irrigation management, crop yield, marketing of produce, trade policies, market support price, implementation system at the grassroots, etc. have to be linked to one another as a system.

The policy issues are quite deep-rooted. The problem of the agriculture sector cannot be solved unless a detailed analysis of underlying issues is done and the complexity of interlinked issues in both agriculture and rural development is appreciated before making decisions for policy formulation and implementation. Agriculture and rural development are dependent on various interlinked factors. The studies have indicated that the farmers have faced both private debt and poverty, and the rural areas lack basic facilities like quality school education, health centers, sanitation, and agriculture marketing system, to name a few (Rao 2009; Economic Survey 2013). These, in a combined form, impact poverty and agriculture growth.

- *Technical perspective.* The technical aspect of policymaking entails problem definition, situation analysis, policy analysis, and identification of policy options. It will include both the policymaking process as well the technical inputs. Regarding the policymaking process, the study of policy theories provides differing analyses and perspectives. These are due to the varying perceptions, beliefs, knowledge of the subject, and analytical skills of stakeholders.

Various scholars have underscored the need for analyses related to complexity, institutional aspects, and behavioral issues. As for complexity, it will be necessary to understand interacting elements, individuals, and economic agents in the public system and comprehend their relationships, including nonlinearity, feedback loops, and uncertain responses (Forrester 1968; Kirman 2011; Arthur 2014). The institutional aspects include processes, procedures, and rules; interest groups, who exert pressure to effect change; and socio-political-economic context, which influences the approach of decision makers. These require study in order to understand how the policies are formulated. The behavioral issues involve understanding the social culture, beliefs, and practices of individuals as well as families.

Table 2.1 GDP growth rate, agriculture growth rate, and poverty ratio

S. No.	Indicators	Periods			
		1950–73	1973–1998	2000–2009	2009–2012
1	GDP growth rates (%)	3.54	5.07	6.66	7.8
2	Agriculture growth rate (%)	2.7	2.4 (1973–80) 3.5 (1981–98)	4.2	3.5
3	Poverty ratio (%)	55 (1973–74)	45.3 (1993–94)	− 37 (2004–5) − 29.8 (2009–10*)	21.9 (2011–12*)

Source Panagariya and Bhagwati (2014), Planning Commission (2014), Mohan and Kapur (2015), Dev (2016)
*Based on expert group Tendulkar methodology

In addition, in the public system, there are various entities, which work concurrently. These entities are the State, public institutions, technical experts, NGOs, the community, and the market. They may work in unison or conflict depending upon their positions on a particular subject. The challenge is how to engage them constructively and elicit information and evidence to arrive at acceptable policy options. Policymakers need to organize the technical knowledge in a usable form. It requires a good understanding of existing policy. Policymakers and other stakeholders like citizens, NGOs, and interest groups should have good knowledge of the policymaking processes. It demands good to expert knowledge. More and better knowledge of the technical issues about the policy will make it easier to collect and collate knowledge and then do policy analyses. The experts (Simon 1957; Lasswell, 1971; Hoppe 1999) have highlighted the need for eliciting the maximum inputs from all the stakeholders involved in policymaking.

A good policymaking process requires a policy framework including, *firstly*, policy tools, stakeholders' analysis, evidence-based approach, technical analysis, selecting policy options, analyzing implementation mechanism, etc., and, *secondly*, self-correcting mechanisms. It calls for rigorous analysis along with an understanding of the tools to elicit innovative or new ideas and then convert them into policy options, thus advancing the call for learning about the policy process as well as content (Raymond et al. 1994; Cochran and Malone 2005).

- *Understanding complex interplay of different development issues.* The impact of policies needs to be studied for the interlinked sectors to get a better perspective. It is essential as many issues depend upon one another, and ignoring them will limit the understanding of the policies. The following illustration highlights this viewpoint. To understand the policy issues about economic growth and its impact, there is a need to understand the complex interplay of growth, poverty reduction, human resource development (HRD), inequality, and per capita GDP.

Economic growth is one of the instruments for reducing poverty and improving the quality of life (DFID 2008; Panagariya and Bhagwati 2014). The empirical studies have provided evidence that sustained growth is critical to faster progress toward poverty reduction and achievement of the sustainable development goals (SDGs). The growth can generate a virtuous cycle of employment, higher income, lower poverty, prosperity, and opportunity. In the context of India, Table 2.1 indicates that higher economic growth coupled with a better agricultural growth rate is associated with a faster reduction in poverty.

There are two fundamental links between economic growth and development, including a drop in poverty (Squire 1993; World Bank 2005. *First*, at the macro level, on the back of higher growth, government augments tax collection, which is primarily utilized for public services and infrastructure creation. The *second* link is at the micro level, in which growth leads to improved income, enabling people to participate in the development process through increased opportunities. In both cases, all people, including the poor, benefit from higher growth. Essentially, economic growth is necessary if the twin objectives of enhancing individual income and poverty reduction are to be addressed.

2.1 Imperative of Understanding Public Policy

Based on 14 cross-country study (World Bank 2005), it shows that a 10% increase in average income is likely to reduce the poverty rate by 20–30% (Squire 1993; Adams 2004; World Bank 2003). Though since the 1980s and especially from the 1990s, growth in the developing world picked up considerably, resulting in a decline in the poverty rate (World Bank 2006a). It has been supported by various studies (Kakwani 1993; World Bank 2005) that the contribution of both distributional effects and growth has an impact on poverty reduction.

But the importance of income distribution or inequality in poverty reduction has been recognized (World Bank 2006b). The poverty rate decline may vary despite similar growth rates, as reflected by various studies (Forsyth 2000; World Bank 2003) based on conditions within a country. The conditions include state of income inequality (or distribution of income), pattern of growth, and participation by the poor in the growth process. The pattern of growth can impact the employment opportunities for the poor, human development, and poverty differently. Even if there is economic growth, the income distribution does not change in the short term and so does not impact inequality much, as evidenced by low change in the Gini coefficient (Deininger and Squire 1996). It highlights that income inequality tends to remain stable over time, thus, economic growth can alleviate poverty only to a limited extent (OECD 2010). So, both the rate and pattern of growth matter for poverty reduction.

Some studies (Forsyth 2000) show evidence that economic growth is capital intensive, driven by technologies, and influenced by globalization. It accentuates the income disparity. It is observed (Kapsos 2005) that there has been a drop in employment at the global level between the period of 1995–99 and 1999–2003, when the employment rate dropped from 0.38 to 0.30%. Such a drop is likely to have an unfavorable impact on diminishing poverty. The growth elasticity of poverty decreases with inequality, implying that the rate of poverty reduction is higher if there is less inequality (Ravallion 1997; Adams 2004). Ali and Thorbecke (2000) have analyzed that poverty is more sensitive to income inequality than it is to the level of income. So it underlines the need for addressing the income and asset inequalities in low-income countries.

In addition, for a deeper understanding, there is a need to utilize the learnings from the correlation between government expenditure on education and health in a country on one hand and human development index (HDI), infant mortality rate (IMR), poverty reduction, and per capita gross domestic product (GDP) on the other (Table 2.2). It shows higher the expenditure on education and health, the better the performance of a country on human indicators, poverty reduction, and per capita GDP.

Table 2.2 Basic human development indicators, poverty, and per capita GDP

S. No.	Countries	Govt. per capita expenditure on education PPP$ (2017) (total % of GDP)*	Govt. healthcare expenditure as percentage of GDP (2012)**	HDI(rank)***	IMR***	Poverty population below $1.25 a day (%) (2010)****	Per capita GDP (PPP$) (2017)*****
1	India	299 (3.8)	1.15	130	34.6	32.7 (21.9%******)	7,874
2	China	724 (4.0)	3.14	86	8.5	11.8	18,110
3	Japan	1,591 (3.6)	8.50	19	2.0	<1%	44,227
4	South Korea	2,109 (5.1)	4.10	22	2.9	<2%	41,351
5	USA	3,150 (5.0)	8.00	13	5.6	<1%	62,606
6	World	805 (4.8)	4.40	–	29.9	–	16,779

Source *UNDP (2018); **WHO (2015); ***UNDP (2018); ****WDI (2014); *****IMF (2019); ******Planning Commission (2014)
Govt.: Government

2.2 Sectoral Analysis: Notability of Policymaking

For a better appreciation of the policy in development sectors, there is a need to understand the perspective of both country and international contexts. Examining critical issues and performance indicators can provide valuable pointers for understanding sectoral policies. Findings of some of the key development sectors are summarized below.

2.2.1 Education

Quality of life and economic growth strongly correlate to quality education (UNDP 1992; Hanushek and Wobmann 2010). In the knowledge economy, if the growth has to pick up, education needs to be improved at all levels—primary, middle, and higher—and for all. All developed nations and fast-emerging economies have successfully demonstrated so. Studies (UNICEF 2011; NPTEL 2017) reflect that the lack of education costs individuals and National and global economy. Illiterate people earn 30–42% less than their literate counterparts and do not have the literacy skills required to undertake further vocational education or training to improve their earning capacity. Or more years of education can help in raising the income of individuals. The studies highlight that every additional year of primary school enhances women's wages by 7–15%. And an extra year of secondary school raises the income by 15–25%, and a one percentage point increase in female education raises the GDP by 0.37 percentage points (Duflo 2001; Duraisamy 2002; UNICEF 2011).

The cost of illiteracy to the global economy is estimated (WLF 2015) at $1.20 trillion. The same study calculates the cost of illiteracy at 1.2% of GDP for India due to lost earnings and productivity, missed sustained earnings, and inadequate high-skilled and tech jobs. And it puts the opportunity cost of illiteracy at $ 27b ($ 58b at PPP). Some research papers suggest that for both growth and employability, the need is to enhance the number of years of education as well as the quality of education represented by learning outcomes and skills. Hanushek and Woessmann (2008, 2010) show that cognitive skills correlate more strongly with economic growth for most economies.

Box 2.1: Benefits from Education

- Better technology transfer with education: In agriculture, if a farmer had completed elementary education, his productivity was, on average, 8.5%, higher than that of a farmer who had no education.
- In case of India, there is evidence that the adoption and spread of the 'green revolution' in the early years was faster among the educated farmers.

- In industry, most evidence suggests that at the enterprise level, educated workers are more productive.
- The developing countries get much higher rates of return than the developed countries from investing in education.
- In the case of India, as per one study, the private rate of return of education increases as the level of education increases up to the secondary level.

Source: Lucas (1988), UNDP (1992), Mankiw et al. (1992), Hanushek and Wobmann (2010), WLF (2015).

The research findings (Mankiw et al. 1992; WLF 2015) indicate that education can enhance human capital and labor productivity. Also, education can raise the innovative capacity of the economy (Lucas 1988). It can facilitate the diffusion and transmission of knowledge and successfully implement new technologies, further promoting economic growth (Nelson and Phelps 1966; Benhabib and Spiegel 1994). Faster reforms will have a significant impact on the economy, with a more literate and qualified workforce. Investments in education are essential for aggregate economic growth and enable citizens to participate in the growth process through improved wages and employment. Likewise, lack of education is associated with multiple problems at both individual and National levels. For individuals, a low level of education is synonymous with fewer employment opportunities, low wages, poverty, poor health conditions, etc., leading to a debt trap and poverty trap. At the National level, it is associated with low productivity, a low knowledge economy, and low National income, resulting in a low revenue base for the government to deliver in the future (Box 2.1).

Quality of education and right to education (RTE). Various studies have shown concerns about the learning outcomes of school education. Annual Status of Education Report (ASER) report (2016) finds that nationally, the proportion of children in standard III who could read at least standard I level text was 42.5% in 2016. The same report reveals that less than 50% of children enrolled in the fifth standard could read a simple paragraph of the book at the second-standard level (Patel 2017). And less than 55% of children enrolled in the fifth standard could solve a subtraction problem. Over the years, the ASER data suggest that not only are the levels of learnings low, but they are also not improving much. Equally important is that the expenditure on primary education has not been sufficient for school performance, including quality of teaching, improvement in pedagogy, monitoring of quality teaching, and children's learning. At the international level, India's rank in the Programme for International Student Assessment (PISA) test has not been encouraging (PISA Report 2012, Muralidharan 2013).

Despite enhancement in outlay for infrastructure, science education suffers from the lack of science teachers and the inadequacy of science labs. Of the total secondary schools in the country, 42% of schools had science laboratories, and out of them, only 70% of the schools had adequate science laboratories. Likewise, for higher secondary schools, about 60% had science laboratories, and out of those schools,

57% had adequate lab facilities (NCERT 2016). Thus, access to quality infrastructure and teaching is critical for children, especially in remote rural areas and urban slums. The combination of the above factors reflects that the necessary measures were not in commensuration with the requirement of good learning outcomes (PISA 2012; NCERT 2016; Tripathi 2016).

Together with economic and social barriers felt by the parents due to a large number of malnutrition cases, what is equally alarming about undernourishment is its adverse effect on cognitive development and intellectual capabilities (PISA 2012; Niti Aayog 2018; OPHI 2018). Besides, there is a case of inadequacies in intellectually and emotionally nurturing environments. These cause initial handicaps in children for learning.

Higher education and employability. There are issues of quality of education in higher education, and the majority of college graduates are not 'employable' due to a lack of skills commensurate with job requirements. One study (ISR 2018) shows that nearly 46% of graduates in India are employable, or less than 50% are employable. Among engineering graduates, 56% are employable, excluding graduates from IITs and NITs, and other premier institutes of the country. It is mainly due to the lack of quality control, qualified faculty members, and infrastructure. Another study (as per National Employability Report 2015–16, Hindu Businessline 2018) highlights that less than 20% of engineering graduates are employable for technical jobs.

In the knowledge economy, the critical policy questions that emerge from the above discussion are as follows:

For school education

- how school education should be rightly positioned in economic policymaking to spur growth;
- how the quality infrastructure and teaching aids should be provided to ensure a good learning environment and teaching;
- how the nutritional supplement, preschool learning, and parents' skills (for responding to the needs of the child's education) be addressed;
- how the ecosystem of the school be nurtured to meet the psychological and emotional needs of children; and
- how the teacher's training, innovative pedagogy, learning outcomes, and school governance be mainstreamed for quality education.

For higher secondary and higher education

- which policy variables are to be pursued as drivers of quality education;
- how education and skill development should move in tandem with the requirement of industry and high-skill areas, enhancing employability;
- how the dearth of science labs and lack of science teachers can be addressed; and
- how education should be tailored to the requirement of new frontiers in technologies, especially advanced technologies.

2.2.2 Health and Nutrition

Health for well-being and economic growth. It is a widely held view that human capital is a clear determinant of economic growth (WHO 2001; World Bank 2008). Improving the health of citizens can directly result in economic growth because there will be more people in the workforce to contribute productively to economic activities. Healthier the citizens of a country, the more effective the workforce (WHO 2001; Lopez-casasnova et al. 2007). The paradigm that the performance in the health sector of any country is linked to economic performance has gained momentum in all the developed and fast-emerging economies. And health is considered one of the 'economic engines'. Various theoretical and empirical studies have shown that improved health increases economic growth through multiple micro- and macro-socio-economic factors (WHO 2004; Mirvis et al. 2008). Extending the coverage of health services will reduce poverty and spur economic development and growth.

Good health is a cause for good income and economic growth. The World Bank reports that 50% of the economic growth differentials between developing and developed nations are attributed to poor health and low life expectancy (Mookerjee and Bohra 2017). The good health of citizens is not only a consequence but also a cause of high income. Empirical evidence shows that high levels of health go hand in hand with high levels of National income. Likewise, higher incomes promote better health through improved education, skills, and nutrition, better access to clean water and sanitation, and increased capacity to access quality health care. Specifically, an increase in life expectancy from 50 to 70 years (a 40% increase) would raise the growth rate by 1.4% points per year. Another study shows that a 10% decrease in malaria is associated with increased annual growth of 0.3%, and malnutrition causes a decrease in the annual GDP per capita growth between 0.23 and 4.7% worldwide (WHO 2004).

Good health can impact in four distinct ways. The *first* is the role of health in enhancing labor productivity. Healthy workers lose less time from work and are more productive while working. The *second* is the effect of health on education. Good childhood health can have a direct effect on cognitive skills and the ability to learn. The *third* is the effect of health on enhanced savings through both more earnings and lesser expenditure on health-related expenses. And the *fourth* is the enhancement of individual creativity, innovation, and adoption of new technologies. The combination of all these has a high potential to raise the productive capacity of a country and, in turn, higher economic growth (World Bank 2008; Mookerjee and Bohra 2017).

Health and poverty trap. Because of direct and indirect effects, health is one of the vital determinants of the incidence of poverty and the households falling into poverty traps. Various studies and reports have reflected serious concerns about the impact of poor health on poverty. Poverty leads to a rise in health problems, which, in turn, leads to high expenses and drives people into a poverty trap. It is also true for non-BPL (below poverty line) families with a low-income base (WHO 2004;

2.2 Sectoral Analysis: Notability of Policymaking

Garg and Karan 2005; Joumard and Kumar 2015). The fundamental reason for such a problem is exorbitant household health expenditure (HHE), mainly resulting from very high out-of-pocket expenditure (OOPE). In India, in 2013–14, the HHE was estimated to be Rs. 3.06 lakh crore or 2.72% of GDP and is 67.74% of total health expenditure (THE) (including both public and private). HHE mainly includes out-of-pocket expenditures (OOPE), which is 94.79% of total HHE, 2.58% of GDP, 64.21% of THE, and about Rs. 2340 per capita. Broadly, of the total OOPE on health care, 54.84% was spent on outpatient care and 31.96% was on inpatient care (MHFW 2014, 2016; WHO 2015).

Some macro-level health indicators are captured in Table 2.3. As per a report by WHO (2015), in India, the general government expenditure on health as a percentage of total expenditure on health has been 30.5%, or the private expenditure on health as a percentage of total expenditure on health was 69.5%, reflecting that the private expenditure far exceeds that of government. The government expenditure on health care in India is low at 1.15% of GDP as compared to both developing and developed countries. Thus, the per capita government expenditure on health remains lower than the world average. The WHO (2015) report highlights that among various countries, out-of-pocket expenditure as percentage of total expenditure on health is very high at 61%, while the world average has been 22%. These put high stress on individual families to meet health expenses. As regards the numbers of physicians and nursing and midwifery personnel, these are quite low in comparison to other countries.

Education, nutrition, water, sanitation, and health linkages. Malnutrition is an area of concern. It is the underlying cause of 33% of child casualties. 35% of under-5

Table 2.3 Macro-level view of health sector

S. No.	Name of the country	Total expenditure on health as % of GDP	Government expenditure on health as % of GDP (and as % of total expenditure)	Physicians (per 10,000 population)	Nursing and midwifery personnel (per 10,000 population)	Out-of-pocket expenditure as % of total expenditure on health
1	Brazil	9.5	4.50 (47.5)	18.9	76.0	30.0
2	China	5.4	3.14 (56.0)	14.9	16.6	34.0
3	India	3.8	1.15 (30.5)	7.0	17.1	61.0
4	Japan	10.3	8.50 (82.1)	23.0	114.9	14.5
5	South Korea	7.6	4.10 (54.5)	77.4	118.7	34.0
6	USA	17.0	8.00 (47.0)	24.5	…	11.7
7	World level	7.7	4.40 (57.6)	13.9	28.6	22.0

Source WHO (2015)

children are underweight, 38% are stunted, and 15.1% are acutely malnourished (wasted) (Ministry of Health 2016; Niti Aayog 2018). There are economic costs related to malnutrition. For adults, the losses are estimated to be more than 10% of lifetime earnings, besides loss of gross domestic product (GDP) (World Bank 2006c; One Goal 2014). It has adverse implications for the attainment of education. With economic and social barriers felt by the parents due to a considerable number of cases, what is equally alarming about undernourishment is its adverse effect on cognitive development and then on intellectual capabilities (PISA 2012; Niti Aayog 2018; OPHI 2018).

Besides, there is a case of inadequacies in intellectually and emotionally nurturing environments. These cause initial handicaps in children for learning. There are problems related to the availability of water in sufficient quantity and of good quality. The absence of one or both has wider implications for health, especially for children. Many diseases spread due to a lack of cleanliness, leading to diseases like diarrhea, a leading cause for children under five, globally and also in India. The problem does not end here. It is a chief cause of malnourishment, leading to stunting and long-term cognitive problems (World Bank 1998; Spears et al. 2013; Reinhardt and Fanzo 2014). It has economic consequences as well. It impacts the poorest quintile (lowest 20% on the economic ladder) the most and leads to economic loss for the country (WSP 2010). The above discussion underscores the necessity of appreciation of integrated policies that will combine sectors such as education, skill development, health, nutrition, water supply, and sanitation for building human resource capital (HRC), poverty reduction, higher income, and economic growth.

2.2.3 Urban Management

India is urbanizing fast, and from an urban population of 440 million (32%) in 2017, it will reach 600 (38%) million by 2030 and 815 million (50%) by 2050. The need for expanding cities is due to land pressure on the existing cities and rising aspirations, coupled with migration from rural areas. It demands bringing urban development and city management to the center stage. On the other side, India's slum population touched 62 million in 2017, about 14% of the urban population (HPEC 2011, Mohanty 2016; ICRIER 2019).

It becomes all the more important in the context of economic dominance that cities will display in the times to come. It was estimated that, in 2010, nearly 60% of the GDP was contributed by the urban areas (Planning Commission 2011; MGI 2010) and is likely to go up to 70% by 2020 (Business-Standard 2014). There is a clear need to focus attention on the urban sector. Urban development is critical not just for economic growth but also for inclusive growth due to the interconnectedness of rural and urban> economic activities. China, in 2008, generated about 75% of its GDP from urban centers and is likely to go up to 90% by 2025 (MGI 2009).

India has not invested much in cities compared to other cities worldwide. Over the years, the plan outlays for urban sector have been far less. For example, in 2018–19,

2.2 Sectoral Analysis: Notability of Policymaking

for rural development, the outlay was about 3 lakh crore, while the same was Rs. 41,765 crore for the urban sector (Union Budget, 2018–19). Likewise, India spent 0.7% of its GDP on urban infrastructure in 2011, while China spent about 2.7% on urban infrastructure, which peaked at 3.6% in 2009 (Tong et al. 2018). In Europe, the average percentage has been 2.0% during 2009–15 (EPRS 2014). Low expenditure figures point toward the limitation of the creation of urban infrastructure and service provisioning in India (HPEC 2011; Planning Commission 2011).

A look at the per capita spending on capital expenditure (CapEx) and operation expenditure (OpEx) in 2007–08 shows that these have been relatively low at $17 and $33, respectively (MGI 2010) (Table 2.4). These are much lower than that of the UK, South Africa, and China. As a result of much less investment, the requirement for urban infrastructure is vast, as shown in Table 2.5. It requires policies to augment investment in urban areas.

Local taxes. On the one hand, internal own revenue collection by urban local bodies (ULBs) has been significantly low, at about 0.43% of GDP. On the other hand, the possibility of the collection is not encouraging if the trend of revenue collection is examined (NIPFP 2011; Mohanty 2016; FFC 2020). The revenue collected is much less than the actual maintenance cost for services like municipal solid waste (MSW) management, water supply, sewage treatment, sanitation, etc. It is estimated that the collection charges are less than 30% of the maintenance cost and less than 5% of the infrastructure cost. In addition, the total revenue, including the grants and

Table 2.4 Per capita spending on capital expenditure (CapEx) and operation expenditure (OpEx)

S. No.	Country	CapEx ($)	OpEx ($)	Total ($)
1	United Kingdom	391	1,381	1,772
2	South Africa	127	381	508
3	China	116	246	362
4	India	17	33	50

Source MGI (2010). (Urban services include water, sewage, city roads, stormwater drains, mass transit system, solid waste, and low-income housing)

Table 2.5 Requirements of investment for urban infrastructure

S. No.	Investment	HPEC (2012–2032)	MGI (2010–2030)
1	CapEx	Rs. 39.2 lakh crore, or, $650 billion Per capita per annum: Rs. 4,300 ($70)	Rs. 72 lakh crore, or $1.2 trillion ($1,200 billion) Per capita per annum: Rs. 8,100 ($134)
2	OpEx	Rs. 19.9 lakh crore, or, $345 billion Per capita per annum: Rs. 2,100 ($36)	Rs. 60 lakh crore, or $1.0 trillion Per capita per annum: Rs. 6,500 ($110)

Source MGI (2010), HPEC (2011)

investments, is about 1.0% of GDP (including 0.1% borrowings), much lower than the minimum requirement of 3% of GDP.

Lack of capacity for urban service management. As for urban service delivery, there are significant challenges. The prominent urban services include water supply, municipal solid waste (MSW) management, sewage management, wastewater treatment, sanitation, stormwater drains, and civic amenities. Regarding household water supply (in 2014), about 38% of urban households have been without access to tap water from a treated source. Besides, the tap connections into toilets have been much less (less than 30%), especially in low-cost housing and slums. The per capita supply of water in Indian cities is significantly low in comparison to major cities globally (IIHS 2014; RIS 2018; MoUA 2021).

With regard to water and sanitation in urban areas, as per available data, during 2015–2016, there are three major issues: *first*, insufficient quantity, lack of quality and potable water, and water supply only for a few hours through piped water; *second*, about 21% of wastewater is treated; and *third*, about 31% of sewage is treated through a sewage treatment plant (STP) (RIS 2018), with less than 30% of households connected to the treatment system. In many cases, untreated water and sewage are left near the water bodies like ponds, lakes, or rivers. The compliance capacity as per prescribed norms of pollution control boards of STPs is about 55%, thus implying that only 16% of sewage treatment is done by meeting technical standards (CPCB 2021). The processing of municipal solid waste is just 9% of the collection (RIS 2018; MoUA 2021).

Urban governance issues. There is a lack of ability for land use planning and management. It results in the problem of availability of land for housing and planned growth, infrastructure creation for sewage treatment plants and roads, and free spaces and stormwater disposal. Due to a lack of urban infrastructure management, about 20–25% of the road network is inundated by stormwater, making urban areas vulnerable to flash floods. The water utilities are normally able to recover only 30–35% of the operation and maintenance (O&M) cost (HPEC 2011; IIHS 2014; RIS 2018), raising concerns about the governance of urban services. The studies have highlighted air and water pollution, which adversely impacts the quality of life. Many cities in the country have high incidents of air pollution. It is detrimental to health, especially children and older people (World Bank 1998; WaterAid 2018; WHO 2018; ORF 2019).

Lack of manpower with urban local bodies (ULBs). The local city bodies in the country have much less than the desired number of manpower. For example, in terms of numbers, it is about 30% of cities like New York and Durban (Janaagraha 2014). Besides, there is a high staff vacancy of 35%. The manpower is much less for technical, managerial, and high-skill roles, and it is much less for the twenty-first century roles of infrastructure planning and management, innovation, and technology applications.

Right policies for urban governance. The interlinkages among factors like quality of life, innovation, future investment, and economic growth need to be discerned

2.2 Sectoral Analysis: Notability of Policymaking

for future policymaking. The Global Cities Outlook has ranked Delhi, Mumbai, and Bangalore 79, 80, and 90, respectively, for 2016–17, based on criteria of knowledge capital, innovation, technology readiness, transportation and urban infrastructure, and quality of life. In terms of quality of life, innovation, technology, and infrastructure, these cities have yet to perform better (ATKearney 2017). Some studies (MGI 2010; Anjum 2014; World Bank 2018e) suggest that globally it is expected that, in the future, over 80% of GDP and over 85% of world technological innovations will come from cities. The cities with intellectual capital, innovation and technology readiness, transportation and infrastructure, and good quality of life will have an advantage in attracting investment and enhancing economic growth. For a higher GDP growth rate, the cities will compete for investments, knowledge, technology, and talent, which will largely depend on the quality of infrastructure and quality of life in the cities (Anjum 2014; ATKearney 2017).

Box 2.2: Key Factors for Urban Development and Economic Growth

1. Land use planning and governance (LUPG).
2. Capacity of delivery system
3. Quality of services.
4. HR and skills.
5. Policies on incentives, wages, and savings.
6. Budget support.
7. Ease of doing business.
8. Innovation culture
9. Family income.
10. User charges
11. Quality of life
12. Investment
13. Quality infrastructure development.
14. Urban development.
15. Urban economic growth
16. Internal resources.

Level 1: Policies on incentives, wages, and savings; budget support, HR, and skills; capacity of delivery system
Level 2: Family income, ease of doing business, LUPG.
Level 3: User charges, quality of services.
Level 4: Internal resources, quality of life
Level 5: Investment, quality infrastructure development, innovation and technology.
Level 6: Urban development.
Level 7: Urban economic growth

The urban sector will play a critical role in the structural transformation of the Indian economy and in sustaining the high rates of economic growth. It needs to be examined in the context of the 70% contribution to GDP by the cities in the country. Given the importance of urbanization, the cost will be high if the right policies are not formulated and implemented. The inadequacies in policies will impact the creation of infrastructure and deteriorate the quality of services to inhabitants. It may further impact the investment, and the combination of various factors may lead to lower economic growth. To raise economic growth and achieve inclusive growth, the urbanization needs to be a priority for public policy and governance.

Case study applying ISM for urban development. Against the backdrop of the above discussion, the interpretive structural model (ISM) is developed for urban development and economic growth, as shown in Fig. 2.1. The key factors that influence the model are shown in Box 2.2. It depicts the factors in a hierarchical manner. The factors at the bottom are the drivers (levels 1 and 2) to achieve the objective of investment for urban development and economic growth. It highlights that for economic growth, the factors at levels 1 and 2 should get high priority for policy interventions.

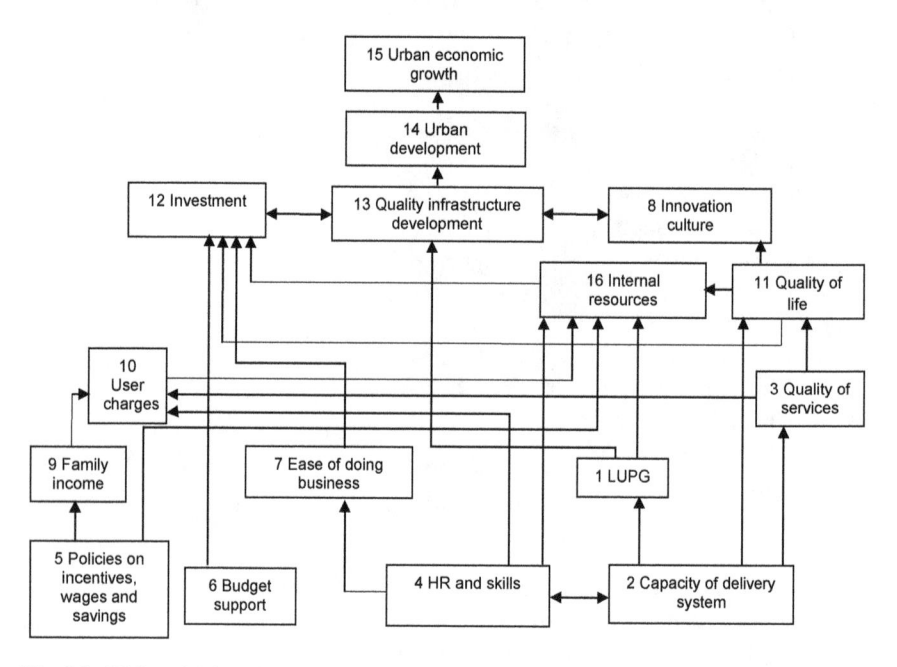

Fig. 2.1 ISM model for urban development and economic growth (*Source* Own analysis)

2.2.4 Economic Growth

Economic growth matters. Based on studies in developing economies, growth has wider ramifications (Fernald 1999; Aschauer 2000; DFID 2008). It leads to higher investment, more economic activities, employment generation, enhanced income, and poverty reduction. Growth is essential to improve the government's finances. As defined by the Solow growth model, at a fundamental level, three basic inputs are essential for higher growth. These are the level of labor, capital investment, and total factor productivity (TFP). TFP reflects the efficiency of the utilization of labor and capital. A further examination of research studies reflects that TFP depends (Acharya et al. 2003; Mohan and Kapur 2015; APO 2015) on technology application, research & development (R&D), skilled workforce, innovation, technical expertise, and experience. Some trends in GDP and TFP growth rates for India and some other countries are presented in Tables 2.6 and 2.7.

TFP and labor productivity are key. Table 2.6 reflects the increase in per capita GDP. It shows less rise for India and a rapid increase for China and South Korea, while the rise is low for Japan due to the initial high per capita base. Table 2.7 indicates growth rates in labor productivity and TFP. It shows lower rates for India vis-à-vis China and South Korea during 1970–80 and 1990–2000; subsequently, the figures have improved for India during 2000–13.

Table 2.6 Per capita GDP—a comparison

S. No.	Countries	Per capita GDP 1990*	1998*	2014**
1	India	1,309	1,746	5,400
2	China	1,858	3,117	12,100
3	Japan	18,789	20,410	38,200
4	South Korea	8,704	12,152	33,800

Source *Maddison (2006) (The World Economy (values in 1990 international $); **APO (2015) (GDP at constant market price, using 2011 PPP)

Table 2.7 Labor productivity and TFP growth rates

S. No.	Countries	1970–90 Labor productivity	TFP	1990–2000 Labor productivity	TFP	2000–2013 Labor productivity	TFP
1	India	1.4	0.65	3.1	1.8	5.3	2.8
2	China	4.3	1.7	8.9	5.15	8.8	3.4
3	Japan	3.9	0.9	2.1	-0.1	1.4	0.7
4	South Korea	7.7	1.5	5.8	1.8	4.1	1.6

Source APO (2015)

Lower GDP growth rate for India is attributed to both lower labor productivity and TFP (APO 2015). As regards Japan, it outperformed several countries during 1950–73 by registering 8–9% growth rates, and the main reason has been higher labor productivity as well as TFP (APO 2015). It reflects that TFP plays an essential role in raising growth.

There is a positive relationship between human capital, skilled workforce, and R&D on one side and competitiveness and per capita GDP on the other, as reflected in Table 2.8. The R&D expenditure directly impacts technology readiness.

Policy issues. The above discussion highlights a good scope for increasing economic growth by enhancing labor productivity and TFP, which will call for interventions in human capital (education, skill development, and health), R&D, and technology adoption.

2.2.5 Manufacturing

Historically, manufacturing has been a driver of economic growth due to its propensity to enhance productivity by attracting innovation and technology and by multiplier effect on employment, investment, and service sector. One study (EPRS 2014) shows that one job in manufacturing creates 2.5 jobs in other sectors of the economy. The National Association of Manufacturing, USA (NAM 2017; Brown 2018) estimates that for every $1.00 spent in manufacturing, another $1.40 is added to the economy, reflecting the multiplier effect. Manufacturing provides high-paying jobs for the educated, skilled, and diverse workforce. Thus, it creates a middle class, which is essential for an upward movement of the population on the economic ladder and also for raising the aggregate demand in the economy. The essentiality of industrialization was well-studied by Kaldor's law. The economist Nicholas Kaldor (1967) proposed that economic growth and quality of life have been positively correlated with National industrial activity. Further, he suggested that growth in GDP was positively related to an increase in the manufacturing sector. Thus for the future well-being of the country, the growth of the manufacturing sector has been essential (World Bank 2018a).

Industrialization, including manufacturing, has been synonymous with development and an engine of growth in developed as well as fast-emerging economies. It has been able to absorb both skilled and unskilled workers and provide a space for engaging workers from the agriculture sector (UNIDO 2018; World Bank 2018a; Mehrotra 2019a, b). All developed and fast-emerging economies have been able to reduce poverty and raise the quality of life on the back of success in manufacturing. It has been able to integrate technological advancements and provide forward and backward linkages with other sectors of the economy. Manufactured goods are crucial for the service and agriculture sectors. Though the service sector contributes more than 65% to the economy, this sector, including the transport and e-commerce industry, depends upon manufactured goods such as electronic items and telecommunication equipments.

2.2 Sectoral Analysis: Notability of Policymaking

Table 2.8 Comparison of key HR and R&D indicators with competitiveness and per capita GDP

S. No.	Countries	Expenditure on education as % of GDP*	Skill development (formally skilled as % of total workforce)**	Human capital rank (2017)****	R&D expenditure as % of GDP*****	Competitiveness******	Per capita GDP (PPP$) (2017)*******
1	India	3.8	2 (4.96% in 2016)***	103	0.82	40	7,874
2	China	4.0	40	34	2.08	27	18,110
3	Brazil	5.9	NA	77	1.23	80	14,652
4	South Korea	5.1	96	27	4.15	26	41,351
5	Japan	3.6	80	17	3.47	9	44,227
6	USA	5.0	NA	4	2.81	2	62,606

*UNDP (2018); **Planning Commission (2012); ***NCEE (2018a, b), KPMG and FICCI (2016); ****WEF (2017a); *****UNESCO (2015); ******WEF (2017b); *******IMF (2019)
NA not available

Another good reason is that manufacturing provides a strong foundation for R&D and innovation. As a result of innovative design, process, or product, it gives rise to setting up new manufacturing units, besides raising productivity. For example, manufacturing in the USA contributes to more than three-quarters of all private sector research and development (R&D) and drives capital investment and innovation compared to other sectors. It raises productivity level by employing technology, a skilled workforce, and economies of scale (Shih 2012; Deloitte 2016).

Most high-income countries (HICs) like the USA, Germany, France, and the UK, to name a few, have achieved prosperity through manufacturing and R&D investment. Since the industrial revolution in the eighteenth century, manufacturing reached its peak, accounting for 25–35% of gross domestic product (GDP). And simultaneously, their economies reached high levels. Likewise, during 1990–2010, East Asian countries like China, Taiwan, Thailand, and South Korea reached a higher trajectory of development through a focused strategy on export-led manufacturing, which peaked at 19–34% of GDP (GPS 2016). It laid a good foundation for industrialization in their respective countries (Rodrik 2015; World Bank 2018a).

There is one more underlying reason. Manufacturing is essential for trade and, thus, for earning foreign exchange, which is critical for meeting domestic requirements and improving prospects for foreign investment. According to the World Trade Organization (WTO 2018), manufactured goods accounted for 70% (or $12.24 trillion) of all merchandise exports in 2017 and 53% of total exports—goods and services together (UNCTAD 2017) (Table 2.9).

Overview of manufacturing in India. Though globally, India emerged as the 6th largest manufacturing producer in 2015 (West and Lansang 2018), the country has not been able to realize its potential. For India, Table 2.10 gives a summary of MVA and employment creation since the 1970s. The average manufacturing value added (MVA) as percentage of GDP since 1970 has been 14.8%. Subsequently, it increased and stagnated at around 16%. In contrast, fast-emerging economies like China, Taiwan, South Korea, and Thailand have seen rapid strides in manufacturing, with MVA upward of 27% (Table 2.11). India peaked at 17.8% (of GDP) in 1979 and

Table 2.9 World exports (2017)

S. No.	Items	Value ($ billion)	Percent
1	Total merchandise	17,730	100
1.a	Agricultural products	1,800	10
1.b	Fuels and mining products	2,700	15
1.c	Manufacturing	12,240	70
1.d	Others	890	5
2	Total commercial services	5,279	100
3	Grand total (merchandise and services)	23,009	

Source WTO (2018), UNCTAD (2017)

2.2 Sectoral Analysis: Notability of Policymaking

1995. China reached a high of 32.5% in 2006. And consistently, it has had values in the vicinity of 30% for over two decades, since 1990 (Planning Commission 2011; Chaudhuri 2015; World Bank 2018b).

At the global level, India's share in manufacturing output was about 3% in 2015, and its share in exports was 1.83% in 2017 (WTO 2018), while that of China was 28.7% and 17.8%, respectively (Table 2.11).

From 1951 till 1980, the CAGR for manufacturing (5.3%) has been higher than the GDP growth rate (3.4%). During 1980–2002, the manufacturing growth rate has been marginally higher than the GDP. Likewise, during 2003–2007, the growth rate in manufacturing (9%) has been higher than the GDP (8.2%). From 2008 onward, manufacturing growth (6.5%) is lagging behind the GDP growth rate (6.8%) (Table 2.12). It implies that manufacturing growth should increase at a higher rate to drive a higher GDP growth rate.

During 2nd industrial revolution (IR), India tried to maintain momentum in manufacturing but could not take much advantage. The 3rd industrial revolution started in the 1970s, mainly leveraging electronics and information technology (IT) to promote innovation and enhance the automation of manufacturing production lines. It was technology and capital intensive, and the manufacturing sector could not perform

Table 2.10 Key performance indicators of manufacturing) (India)

S. No.	Year	Manufacturing value added (MVA) (% of GDP) (average)	% of total employment (average)
1	1970s	13.5	10.5
2	1980s	14.8	10.9
3	1990s	14.9	10.8
4	2000s	15.9	12.1
5	2010s	15.2 (till 2018)	11.5 (till 2015)

Source PC (2011), Chaudhuri (2015), West and Lansang (2018), World Bank (2018b)

Table 2.11 Manufacturing value added and global manufacturing and exports

S. No.	Name of the country	Manufacturing value added (% of GDP)* (2015)	Percent of global manufacturing (2015)*	Share in world exports (%)*****
1	India	16.0 (high of 16.5% in 2008***)	3	1.83
2	China	27.0 (32.5% in 2006****)	28.7	17.8
5	South Korea	29.0	4	4.3
6	Taiwan	31.0	2	–
7	Thailand	27 (2018)****	0.94**	–

Source *West and Lansang (2018); **UNIDO (2018); ***Planning Commission (2011); ****World Bank (2018b); *****WTO (2018)

Table 2.12 CAGR for manufacturing and GDP (India)

S. No.	Periods	CAGR for manufacturing	CAGR for GDP
1	1951 till 1980	5.3	3.4
2	1980–2002	5.8	5.3
3	2003–2007	9.0	8.2
4	2008–2017	6.5*	6.8**

Source PC (2011)
*World Bank (2018c); **World Bank (2018d)
CAGR compound annual growth rate

well (Planning Commission 2011). The period of 2010s is seen as the beginning of the 4th industrial revolution with advanced technologies and smart factories. During this period, the performance has not improved much in terms of manufacturing value added as a percentage of GDP (Table 2.10). Many fast-emerging economies like South Korea, Taiwan, and China took advantage of the 3rd industrial revolution at a large scale by creating a skilled workforce and quality industrial infrastructure, enhancing R&D and improving their technology base. The same trend has continued in the 4th IR (GPS 2016; UNIDO 2018; World Bank 2018b).

Exports and competitiveness. At the global level, in 2017, the exports of total merchandise and total commercial services stood at $17.73 trillion and $5.28 trillion, respectively (Table 2.9). The high-income countries dominate in terms of exports of both goods and services (WTO 2018). North America and the EU together had a share of 51.6% in global exports, while Asia had a share of 34.0%, China 13.2%, and India 1.7% (WTO 2018). As regards the exports of manufactures, in 2017, the EU (38.9%), China (17.8%), and the USA (9.4%) were the leading exporters, while India's share was 1.83%. Likewise, the per capita manufactured exports remained significantly low for India. As regards the competitiveness in ICT, the exports of ICT goods were 0.16% ($2.9 billion), a small fraction of total global exports ($1794 billion) (WTO 2016) (see Table 2.13).

Manufacturing competitiveness. While examining deeper, as regards high-skill global innovations, over a period from 2002 to 2011, China has moved to a first position, and high-income countries (HICs) (Germany, Japan, South Korea, and the USA) remain in the top ten in terms of domestic manufacturing value added in gross exports at a global level (Table 2.14). And as for capital-intensive processing, HICs are among the top ten global ranks (World Bank 2018a). The position of India is at a lower level. It further highlights the fact that the competitiveness is in favor of HICs, and China has strengthened its position considerably concerning high-skill global innovations.

Premature deindustrialization. When deindustrialization happens at a lower level of economic development, this phenomenon is referred to as 'premature deindustrialization'. Most developing countries have reached 'peak manufacturing' in terms of both total value added and employment generation at a much lower level than the

2.2 Sectoral Analysis: Notability of Policymaking

Table 2.13 Exports of manufactured products

S. No.	India	Value (2017) ($ billion) (current $)***	Share in world exports (%)***		Per capita manufactured exports (current $)*		ICT goods exports ($ billion)****
			2010	2017	2010	2015	2014
1	India	< 206 (2017)* 205 (2015)**	1.73*	1.83 (for 2015)*	152	168	2.9
2	China	2,132	14.6	17.8	1,132	1,601	595
3	EU	4,668	40.3	38.9	13,719 (Germany)	14,625 (Germany)	352
4	Japan	604	6.8	5.0	5,539	4,485	–
5	South Korea	511	4.1	4.3	9,201	10,189	–
6	USA	1,126	9.5	9.4	2,783	3,000	145

Source *UNIDO (2018); **UNIDO (2016); ***WTO (2018); ****WTO (2016)

Table 2.14 Exports ranking of countries for manufacturing

S. No.	Name of the countries	High-skill global innovations (ranking by domestic value added in gross exports)		Medium-skill global innovations (ranking by domestic value added in gross exports)		Capital-intensive processing (ranking by domestic value added in gross exports)	
		2002	2011	2002	2011	2002	2011
1	India	> 50 (for 2010)	> 50 (for 2015)	> 50 (for 2010)	> 50 (for 2015)	NA	NA
2	China	8	1	4	4	> 10	> 10
3	Germany	3	6	1	1	2	2
4	Japan	2	2	2	3	4	7
5	South Korea	4	4	9	6	> 10	> 10
6	USA	1	3	2	2	1	1

Source World Bank (2018a), UNIDO (2018), and own analysis

advanced nations. In addition, it is happening at a lower per capita GDP than in the past, as shown in Table 2.15. The interpretation of premature deindustrialization is that countries are running out of industrialization opportunities sooner and at a much lower level of income than early industrialized countries (Rodrik 2015). For India, the peak manufacturing employment share (%) and GDP per capita, when employment peaked, have been 12.5% and $700, and it reached so in 2002 (Table 2.15), and the share in GDP has been about 15.5%. It signifies that the likelihood of increasing employment is not bright in manufacturing. Also, a historical advantage of manufacturing in raising per capita income through its productivity contribution will be lower. It has a bearing on economic growth (GPS 2016 and Rodrik 2015).

Disposal income and aggregate demand. Table 2.16 reflects the per capita disposable income for a few countries. For India, it is $1,154 against much higher value for China, Japan, and the USA. It has a direct link with per capita family income. Closely linked, the report by Deloitte (2016) reflects that the hourly wages in India have been $1.7, which are $38, $24, $20.7, and $3.3 for the United States, Japan, South Korea, and China, respectively. Low wages have a direct link with the disposable income of families and leave little room for the majority of households to have enough disposable income to purchase consumer durables or industrial products, affecting aggregate demand (Table 2.16) (Deloitte 2016; World Bank 2018a).

Table 2.15 Peak manufacturing employment share and GDP per capita

S. No.	Name of the country	Peak manufacturing employment share (%) (year)[a]	GDP per capita when employment peaked (in constant 2005$)
1	India	12.5 (2002)	700
2	China	19.0 (2010)	3,000
3	France	26.0 (1974)	21,000
4	Japan	24.0 (1973)	18,000
5	South Korea	27.0 (1989)	6,500
6	Taiwan	34.0 (1987)	6,000
7	Malaysia	25.0 (1997)	5,000
8	USA	25.0 (1953)	12,000

Source
[a] GPS (2016), Rodrik (2015)
Note The figures in parenthesis represent the year in which peak manufacturing employment occurred

Table 2.16 Labor costs, labor productivity, and disposal income

S. No.	Countries	Labor wages ($ per hour) (2015)	Labor productivity (in thousands) (constant 2011 PPP$)	Per capita disposable income (2015$)
1	India	1.7	10.0	$1,154
2	China	3.3	19.0	$3,549
3	Germany	45.5	87.0	$24,110
4	Japan	24.0	70.0	$19,502
5	South Korea	20.7	60.0	$14,513
6	USA	38.0	99.3	$42,255

Source Deloitte (2016)

2.2.6 Advanced Manufacturing, General Automation, and Future of Jobs

In the new industrial era, multiple advanced technologies are converging. Convergence is driven by the interconnectivity of the physical world, speed of data flow, computing power, and artificial intelligence (AI). These have got multidisciplinary aspects in which ICT, nanotechnology, human science, biotechnology, energy, and smart materials, among other disciplines, are integrated. These have got exponential potential.

Due to gradual advancements in technologies over three centuries, the industrial revolutions are encapsulated as follows: the eighteenth–nineteenth century, the first industrial revolution, coal-fired engines; the beginning of the twentieth century, the second industrial revolution, electricity-driven machineries; the 1970s–2000s, the third industrial revolution, electronic automation; and 2010 onward, the fourth industrial revolution (industry 4.0), smart automation and exponential change. Industry 4.0 can impact exponentially business and production processes, productivity, product quality, and production cost. Thereby, it can displace the existing business models, impact the sourcing of products and services, and bring disruption in any industry (CGD 2018; WEF 2018).

Industry 4.0 provides distinct advantages in the form of automation and robotics for higher productivity and accuracy; simplification of complex operations and remote monitoring and control due to the Internet of Things (IoT), sensors, and augmented reality; data analytics and artificial intelligence for optimizing operations; and flexibility, high productivity, and customized manufacturing, bringing a trend away from high volume low variety manufacturing to wide variety low volume for meeting ever-changing customer demands (DSU 2018; Brown 2018). The combination of these advantages is prompting developed countries toward a trend for insourcing or in-house management.

R&D and innovation—drivers for the future of manufacturing and economy. With concerted research and development (R&D) investment, high-income countries (HICs), including China, have evolved a robust innovation ecosystem in their respective countries. Manufacturing in the USA has evolved a sound R&D system by actively engaging industry, National laboratories, and universities to improve competitiveness in the technology and develop manufacturing hubs. Such efforts have helped advanced research in energy, nanotechnology, and new materials for new generation devices and equipments, to name a few (DSU 2018). More specifically, for advanced manufacturing capabilities, special focus is given through advanced manufacturing partnership (AMP) programs like AMP 1.0 and AMP 2.0 to enhance competitiveness and create high-quality manufacturing jobs (MIT 2014; Bonvillian and Singer 2018).

Along similar lines, South Korea, Germany, Japan, and Taiwan are leading in innovation by providing government funding to businesses and through tax incentives. China is investing substantially in innovation infrastructure and R&D in advanced technologies. In India, low R&D expenditure at 0.8% of GDP, vis-à-vis higher value for other high-income economies, such as the USA (2.81%), Japan (3.47%), South Korea (4.15%), China (2.1%), and Taiwan (3.3%), has resulted in lower capacity for innovation in technologies and reduced technology readiness, especially for manufacturing. For developed countries, higher R&D has resulted in improved productivity, competitiveness in manufacturing, higher manufacturing base, and exports, besides high per capita GDP (Tables 2.8 and 2.13). More investment in R&D has resulted in a virtuous cycle (Deloitte 2016; UNIDO 2018; WEF 2017b).

Reshoring. In the USA and developed countries, due to low fertility and decreasing young population, their priorities are to automate their operations to overcome first the problem of shortage of labor, then to raise productivity level to remain competitive and increase the jobs in high-skilled areas suiting their population and technological environment, while producing products with higher quality and protecting their intellectual property.

Due to the increase in the pace of robotic adoption by industry relative to trends in wage costs, by 2025, it is estimated that the cost competitiveness (in manufacturing) from robotics could tilt in favor of the industrial countries (Sirkin et al. 2015; GPS 2016). Also, due to the rising demand for customized products in domestic markets, reshoring is becoming an economical option. As per the study by BCG (2011), based on the trends of changes in labor cost, besides higher transportation cost, inventory cost, quality control cost, and theft of intellectual property, the total cost advantage of manufacturing in China and other Asian countries is likely to shrink. It has prompted many producers back in USA and EU to reshore manufacturing in their respective countries (EPRS 2014). As a result, thus the labor cost arbitrage is lost not only in favor of China but also for other countries like India, Indonesia, Thailand, etc. As per the study by WEF, in the near future, most of the manufacturing units will likely shift their geographical base of operations (WEF 2018). In addition, due to automation and convergence of other technologies, as some studies reflect (EPRS 2014; MGI 2017b), the developed countries will produce superior quality products, including customized products, at lower prices. This way, the developing countries will lose further the advantage of labor cost arbitrage.

Among Asian countries, China (Deloitte 2016; UNIDO 2018; World Bank 2018a, b; Worldatlas 2019) will continue to have a significant advantage on account of a robust manufacturing base due to the manufacturing value of $3.7 trillion and exports exceeding $2.1 trillion, with a share of 17.8% (in 2015, Table 2.13) in global export. In addition, high R&D investment and promotion of innovation hubs for advanced technologies and manufacturing put China in a relatively good position. For example, by 2016, about 75% of industrial robots globally were utilized in five industrialized countries—China, Germany, Japan, Korea, and the USA (GPS 2016; World Bank 2018a).

Job losses and displacements. The studies have indicated that automation has a share in jobless growth (Brynjolfsson and McAfee 2011). Occupations (like manufacturing, transportation, etc.) that have pre-determined processes and procedures can be efficiently performed by computer algorithms, artificial intelligence (AI), and

2.2 Sectoral Analysis: Notability of Policymaking

robots (Jaimovich and Siu 2012). The current decline in manufacturing employment and the loss of routine jobs are resulting in a moderate rate of employment growth.

The research has highlighted that automation will put 47% of current US jobs at risk. Corresponding figures for other countries are 77% for China, 69% for India, and 65% for Argentina (Table 2.17). The automation of work activities does not necessarily mean that jobs are lost. There may be losses in the short term, but new jobs may be created in the future, as observed historically. On the likely job losses for India, it is predicted that about 30% of low-skilled jobs comprising pre-defined processes repetitive in nature, with less educational qualifications and skills, are likely to be at risk (GPS 2016; Business Today 2017; CGD 2018; WEF 2016).

With the advent of advanced manufacturing, some jobs are at risk in many sectors of the economy. The study by MGI (2017a) underscores that 60% of the current major occupations have more than 30% of the automatable activities that are at risk for the jobs. The maximum impact is likely in sectors such as the hotel industry, manufacturing, and agriculture (Table 2.18). The sectors that are likely to be least impacted by automation are education, management, professional services, information, health care, and administration, requiring higher analytical and cognitive skills (GPS 2016; CGD 2018). Some occupations, like office and administrative work and manufacturing and production, will likely observe the maximum decline in jobs by 4.91% and 1.63%, respectively (WEF 2016) (Table 2.19).

Table 2.17 Likely job losses due to automation

S. No.	Name of the country	Percent of jobs at risk
1	India	69
2	Argentina	65
3	China	77
4	USA	47
5	Thailand	72
6	OECD	57

Source GPS (2016), BusinessToday (2017)

Table 2.18 Technical potential for automation for select sectors

S. No.	Sectors	Technical potential for automation (% of activities)
1	Hotel industry	73
2	Manufacturing	60
3	Agriculture	58
4	Management	35
5	Educational services	27

Source MGI (2017a)

Table 2.19 Likely employment growth rate in select sectors

S. No.	Sectors	Likely employment growth rate (%)
1	Computer and computing	3.21
2	Architecture and engineering	2.71
3	Management	0.97
4	Business and financial	0.70
5	Manufacturing and production	-1.61
6	Office and administrative work	-4.91

Source WEF (2016)

Challenges for India. In light of the above discussions, India faces challenges of a low manufacturing base; low exports competitiveness in manufacturing and high technology areas, likely reduction in employment due to advanced manufacturing; and the trend toward technology-intensive and capital-intensive industries when R&D expenditure is low and investment is not matching with the requirements. Due to evolving new advanced technology scenario, it may be difficult for India to take advantage of labor cost arbitrage in the future. In the emerging scenario, advanced manufacturing will leverage nanotechnology, quantum computing, artificial intelligence, and bio-science to evolve new manufacturing processes and systems that may significantly impact production and provide disproportionate advantages to some producers within the country in new technologies. It may put many existing companies at risk and disrupt the current manufacturing industry. Or, in some other cases, due to automation and much higher productivity in developed countries, it may be difficult to set up new companies, and thus employment may be at risk.

Three distinct situations need to be appreciated. *First*, if the manufacturing base does not expand in the country, there will be a necessity for import, resulting in a loss of foreign exchange. *Second*, if high technology-based manufacturing does not improve due to rising requirements for technology-based applications, there will be a likelihood of an exponential increase in import demands for high-tech products like ICT hardware, renewable energy equipments, batteries, electric vehicles, etc. It may result in further loss of competitiveness in the technology area. *Third*, when high-tech-based products become cheaper in the medium term in developed countries, it may be difficult to sustain the existing manufacturing units for the same products in the country.

India needs to enhance the performance in the manufacturing sector if higher economic growth is to be sustained, if poverty is to be alleviated, and if the middle class is to grow to lift aggregate demand. The low research and development (R&D) expenditure is another area of concern, leading to reduced capabilities for innovation and technology applications. The lack of human capital and low technology readiness have adversely impacted labor productivity. In India, labor productivity in manufacturing is less than 15% of the advanced economies, including Germany, the USA, and South Korea, and is about 50% of China, as reflected by studies (Deloitte 2016;

2.2 Sectoral Analysis: Notability of Policymaking 67

World Bank 2018a). It has unfavorable consequences for competitiveness, manufacturing growth, exports, and economic growth. India's growth has seen the dynamism of the service sector. In contrast, the performance of manufacturing has been less robust. The contribution of manufacturing to the GDP has stagnated at 16%. It has implications for the sustainability of economic growth and for generating adequate employment. It raises issues about revisiting the manufacturing policy.

Policy issues. Firstly, broadly for the manufacturing sector, some important policy issues are: how manufacturing can be a National strategy for driving growth and enhancing income levels across the sections, and, specifically, what policy measures should be initiated for setting up new manufacturing units and expanding the existing ones. *Secondly,* in the changing technological scenario, which policies should be designed to stay competitive. It will require examining: how new technologies will impact the current manufacturing industry; for which industry, new technologies may cause disruption; what needs to be done to develop competitiveness in advanced manufacturing; and, with the automation of industrial processes, what changes are required for reskilling and upskilling for the new generation of workforce.

2.2.7 Strategic Materials

In the twenty-first century, be it clean energy, electronics, mobility, space, nuclear, defense, sustainable energy, medical devices, ICT applications, or genetics, the future of new technologies is gravitating toward strategic materials. Such technologies have significance for future advanced manufacturing, which requires applications of many strategic and advanced materials (Kenneth 1990; Lele and Bhardwaj 2014). The underlying considerations for using such materials are driven by the need for miniaturization, environmental protection; increasing demand for renewable power plants, battery storage, and fuel efficiency; and strategic importance from the points of view of competitiveness, critical applications, and significant cost advantage.

Some of the strategic materials are Chromium, Platinum, Gallium, Silicon, and Rare Earth Materials. Advanced materials refer to all new materials and modifications to existing materials to obtain superior performance, and examples of these materials include magnets, ceramics, glass, metals, composites, semiconductors, and polymers (Naumo 2008; Hatch 2012).

These materials can steer the country toward a knowledge-based economy, provide international competitiveness through technological advances, generate industry capability for job creation, have a multiplier effect, and incentivize R&D to build and strengthen value chains. For India to stay competitive, such materials will impact the capabilities for manufacturing in general and advanced and innovative products in particular. So, the country needs to look at sound policies and strategic investments to serve twin objectives, *first,* building a reserve for strategic materials, and, *second,* reducing the risk of supply disruptions of materials and building the base for future advanced manufacturing capabilities.

2.2.8 Innovation and Entrepreneurship

The world is heading toward a knowledge economy. The knowledge economy is driven by ideas, knowledge, and innovation. Specifically, innovation is for developing new solutions for critical problems, generating employment opportunities, spurring economic growth, and improving quality of life. Innovation is not only about developing new technology or product but also a business model, service, process, structure, or system. It has value for business, industry, and society. In the context of technology, innovation can be thought of in two major ways. *Firstly*, the application of existing technologies for developing new products and services, and, *secondly*, discerning local problems and then creating new technology to develop products (Hamel 2007; OECD 2016; DSU 2018).

Globally, startups are emerging as new entities creating value for the business and contributing to the economy and jobs. These are technology-linked business possibilities. Startups are spurring business growth and creating new economic prosperity, driven by a customer-centric approach. Some are disrupting big businesses. All countries—developed, emerging, developing, and in transition—have been seeking business opportunities and promoting policies for starting new businesses (McCarthy 2016; Nair 2017; INSEAD 2018; IVCA 2018). Since the 1970s, academia has played the role of catalyst. For example, the R&D work at various institutes, such as Stanford, University of California Berkley, and MIT, has provided a strong foundation for technological advances. In Silicon Valley in the USA, various companies, like Oracle, Microsoft, Intel, Apple, and Google, to name a few, benefited immensely, and they successfully converted academic ideas into big businesses. Initially, they were funded by seed money, private equity, and some venture capital (VC). Thereafter, from 1990s, the angel funding and venture capital got momentum in a big way (Sturgeon 2000; Castells 2011; Anjum 2014; Business.com 2015).

India has benefited from research labs and academia, which provided scientific manpower and an ecosystem for the industry. In India, startups grew rapidly from the 2010s onward. The cities like Bengaluru, Pune, Hyderabad, and Delhi NCR took a leading role. Subsequently, through policies, the government developed a multi-pronged strategy to support entrepreneurs (Infodev 2008; Rajaraman 2012; Dhar and Saha 2014; Sareen 2018). Table 2.20 shows how the number of Unicorns and VC investment have grown in major countries. The number of startups and VC investment in India are increasing consistently (Table 2.21).

There are some policy issues. The first is about the pattern of investment. More startups and investments are seen mainly in two sectors, software and Internet services and e-commerce, while manufacturing attracts much less investment (Table 2.22). The second issue concerns the heavy concentration of startups in Tier 1 or big cities (Nair 2017; NASSCOM 2017; IITM 2018). It requires more robust academia-industry-government tie-ups to develop an innovation ecosystem in many cities and also to promote facilities to design and develop prototypes for new products. These two aspects deserve consideration for policy interventions.

2.2 Sectoral Analysis: Notability of Policymaking

Table 2.20 Status of Unicorns and VC investment

S. No.	Name of the countries	Number of unicorns (2017)	VC investment (2012–2018) ($ billion)	Market value (2017/2018) ($ billion)
1	India	10	32	15
2	China	98	260	300
3	USA	106	300	250
4	World	252	650	679

Source Chen (2017), Jain and Jain (2017), Business Standard (2018), INSEAD (2018), KPMG (2019) (https://en.wikipedia.org/wiki/List_of_unicorn_startup_companies#History) ($b Billion$)

Table 2.21 Number of startups and VC investment in India

S. No.	Year	India	
		Venture investment ($ billion)	Number of startups
1.	2012	1.7	850
2.	2013	1.6	2,200
3.	2014	5.5	3,100
4.	2015	8.5	4,100
5.	2016	3.6	4,750
6.	2017	13.4	5,200
7.	2018	8.6	8,625

Source NASSCOM (2017), IITM (2018), IVCA (2018)

Table 2.22 Percentage of startups and investment in India (average of 2015, 2016, 2017)

S. No.	Sectors	Number[a] (%)	Investment[b] (% of total)
1	Software and Internet services	59	19
2	e-Commerce	19	20
3	Edutech	3	5
4	Fintech	5.5	9
5	Healthtech	4	15
6	Foodtech	0.5	5
7	Data analytics and AI	2	15
8	Manufacturing	4	5
9	Others	2	7

Source
[a] IITM (2018)
[b] IVCA (2018), Sareen (2018), Nair (2017)

2.2.9 Infrastructure Development and Public–Private Partnership (PPP)

Infrastructure is essential for sustained economic growth. Infrastructure in India remains an area of concern. The Global Competitiveness Index, 2017–18, reflects that in terms of infrastructure, India was ranked 66th. Within the infrastructure segment, the ranking for quality of electricity supply, quality of air transport infrastructure, and quality of roads have been 80th, 61st, and 55th (WEF 2018). Realizing the criticality of economic growth and the manufacturing sector, India is steadily improving investment in infrastructure, which rose from 5.08% in the 10th Plan to 7.21% in the 11th Plan and then to 8.18% in the 12th Plan (Planning Commission 2013). The rising investment demand has resulted in an investment gap planned through public–private partnership (PPP) projects.

Though the share of infrastructure in total investment in the country has increased from 23.3% in 2007 to 32.5% in 2015, the infrastructure spending in India currently stood at 8% of GDP. The aim should be to increase it to 10%. The extent of scaling up in infrastructure development in India is immense (ASSOCAHAM 2016; FICCI 2017; KPMG, 2018). Over two decades, China spent 11–14% of its GDP (about five times of India's GDP) on infrastructure, touching 14% in 2017 (KPMG 2018). China's economy has had a substantial investment from State-led budget spending, which is one of the factors responsible for the high competitiveness of the manufacturing sector in China.

It distinctly reflects three points, *firstly*, the need for large infrastructure spending, *secondly*, the requirement of debt financing for the investment gap, and, *thirdly*, the need for private sector investment and reliance on PPP (Planning Commission 2013; PPP Cell 2016; FICCI 2017). Of the total infrastructure investment requirement, the sectors like electricity, telecom, roads, and railways have required the maximum investment. To meet the growing need of deficit in infrastructure financing, it was felt that PPP investments could spur infrastructure development and economic growth with less fiscal burden on the government. Though efforts have been made since 1991, the PPP policy got momentum, especially since 2004, when several measures were initiated to promote private investment with the initiative of the private sector (PPP Cell 2016).

The rationale behind PPP has been to benefit from the private sector efficiency by creating more competition, economies of scale, greater operational flexibility, and expertise in the planning and execution of large projects. The Ministry of Finance created India Infrastructure Finance Company Ltd (IIFCL) to provide long-term loans for financing infrastructure projects with long gestation periods. Likewise, the viability gap funding (VGF) scheme was started to secure the financial viability of competitive bids (PPP Cell 2018).

2.2 Sectoral Analysis: Notability of Policymaking

Status of PPP Projects. Ministry of Statistics and Programme Implementation monitors major infrastructure projects. The report shows that 30% of projects were on schedule, and about 70% faced time or cost overrun (MOSPI 2017). By another report by Niti Aayog (Hans 2017), by 2016, 1,539 PPP projects were awarded in India. Out of these, about 50% were in the operational stage, while others were either scrapped or under different stages of implementation. The major factors responsible for time and cost overruns had been delays in land clearances (land acquisition), lack of supporting infrastructure facilities, change in the scope of work, law and order problems, delays in municipal permissions, difficulty in getting the equipments in time, fund constraints, force majeure, etc. Broadly, there have been constraints such as policy, regulatory, and institutional gaps; inadequate financial capacity in the private sector; and skill gaps for big infrastructure projects.

Policy issues. Various reports have estimated that India needs huge investments in various sectors. For example, India needs infrastructure investment of $4.5 trillion by 2040 to improve economic growth (Global Infrastructure Hub 2017), besides substantial investment requirements for achieving sustainable development goals (SDGs) and net-zero emission. In light of gaps in the investments and limitations of PPP, policy measures are needed to augment the investments and enhance the capacity of both the public and private sectors.

2.2.10 Labor Reforms

Realizing the need to improve job prospects and investment in manufacturing, labor market reform has been of priority for years for the governments at the Center and States. But the governments have met with less success. Over several decades, governments have passed various laws to safeguard the interest of workers and industry. There are laws pertaining to minimum wages, dispute settlements, social security, safety, health of workers, etc. These laws exist for good social or economic reasons to create a good industrial atmosphere (Monoppa 1995; Sankaran 2007; Hoda and Durgesh 2015; Mitra 2017).

There has been an expressed concern from industry groups about the rigidity in the labor market. The current labor laws in India lead firms to remain small or employ fewer workers, leading to difficulty in having a large firm size. Thus, it impacts economies of scale and competitiveness. It is cited as one of the reasons why the share of India's manufacturing sector in GDP is low. Some industry experts and representatives believe that most labor laws in India are old and create rigidity in the employment market, thus reducing competitiveness and hurting the investors' confidence (Morgan Stanley 2014; Mitra 2017; EIU 2018).

In the rigid labor market, businesses are expected to make large payments to retrench workers, give long notice periods, or even seek government approval before making layoffs. The business groups have stressed that the labor laws do not incentivize large firms and discourage businesses from scaling. Rigidity is one of the main impediments to job growth in the organized sector. But such views are strongly contested by workers' organizations, who feel that workers are paid less and their economic conditions are too vulnerable to be left to market forces in the case of no viable alternative. The level of social security is insufficient to provide meaningful protection to workers if they are retrenched. Such diametrically opposite views by industry and workers make the issue of labor reforms a challenging proposition (Morgan Stanley 2014; Hoda and Durgesh 2015).

Proposed reforms by the Labor Ministry. The labor regulations in the country are perceived to be complex. For some years, the Ministry of Labor & Employment (MoLE), Government of India, has been attempting labor market reforms and has taken certain measures (Hindu Business Line 2017; MoLE 2019, 2021). *Firstly*, by reducing the number of laws by the Ministry. It proposes to combine 44 laws related to industrial relations and the rights of workers into just four codes, viz., industrial relations; wages; social security; and safety, health, and working conditions. The proposal is a part of the draft Labor Code on the Industrial Relations Bill, 2015, prepared by combining Industrial Disputes Act, 1947, the Trade Unions Act, 1926, and the Industrial Employment (Standing Orders) Act, 1946. The aim is to simplify labor laws and benefit both businesses and workers.

Secondly, the draft code proposes to allow firms with 300 workers to retrench without prior government permission (Caravan 2019, Hindu Business Line 2015). The trade unions are against the Labor Ministry's proposal of lowering the conditions for retrenchment. Workers' organizations demand that every worker must be given social security by the statute as a matter of right. The Bill on the Labor Code on Social Security and Welfare, introduced in 2017, is not sufficient as far as social security-net to all workers—organized and unorganized—is concerned.

Labor reforms in the European Union (EU). Though one will look at the industrialized world from the point of view of technologies and sophisticated production units, the base for the growth of industrialization was created by sound human resource (HR) policies for workers and professionals, not just by R&D and technology innovation. These countries emphasized investing in human capital through education, health, skill development, and social security measures. It created a healthy industrial atmosphere. It provided a platform for leveraging technology and skills for higher productivity and staying competitive globally. By doing so, the industrialized countries put themselves ahead of others (Fraser 1984; Huberman and Lewchuk 1999; Ortiz-Ospina and Roser 2016). Table 2.23 summarizes the introduction of various social security schemes in select countries, highlighting how the industrialized countries seized the opportunities and created social-net to evolve a good industrial environment.

Developed countries from the latter part of the nineteenth century took measures to enforce minimum wages, norms for work hours, work conditions, labor market regulations, and social entitlements. In many respects, UK and Germany adopted a wide range of labor market reforms, including social insurance. France and Germany, leading industrialized countries, made initiatives to address the workers' conditions

2.2 Sectoral Analysis: Notability of Policymaking

Table 2.23 Year of introduction of various social security schemes in select countries

S. No.	Countries	Old-age pension	Unemployment insurance
1	Germany	1889	1927
2	Britain	1908	1911
3	Sweden	1913	1914
4	United States	1935	1935

Source Fraser (1984), Huberman and Lewchuk (1999), Theodoulou and Roy (2016)

by introducing health insurance in 1883, accident insurance in 1884, and old age pension in 1889 (Fraser 1984; Huberman and Lewchuk 1999; Frohlich et al. 2016; Theodoulou and Roy 2016). The USA brought measures for social security and reforms by improving the working class conditions during two periods, viz., 1933–36 and 1964–65.

In sum, the developed countries, through their proactive and generous policies, created a good foundation for workers to get social security and a healthy environment for opportunities and productive work. A look at social sector expenditure, the general government expenditure as a percentage of GDP (2016) shows that developed countries are far ahead in social spending to generate human capital (Table 2.24). While in India, the social sector expenditure as % GDP, primarily constituting health and education, has remained low compared to others (RBI 2018).

Table 2.25 summarizes the comparative study of labor laws of select countries. It highlights how developed countries have mainstreamed the concept of social security together with the need for flexibility in labor laws for engaging or retrenching workers.

Workers participation in management board. To make the corporate Board more representative, since the nineteenth century, various countries have taken steps for workers' participation in management. In corporate governance, the participation has been in the form of a work council or codetermination (co-partnership or worker participation), implying workers have the right to vote on the Board. This practice of Board-level representation has been widespread in developed countries for over a century (Herrmann et al. 2018; Frohlich et al. 2016). In India, despite many attempts,

Table 2.24 Social sector expenditure as a percentage of GDP and per capita GDP

S. No.	Countries	Social sector expenditure as % GDP (2016)**	Per capita GDP ($) (2016)***
1	India	7.5*	1,732
2	France	31.5	38,348
3	UK	21.5	41,630
4	Japan	23.0	39,411
5	USA	18.0	57,839

Source *RBI (2018), **Ortiz-Ospina and Roser (2016), Frohlich et al. (2016), ***IMF (2016)

Table 2.25 Comparative study of labor laws of select countries

S. No.	Parameters	Types of labor system				
		Rigid market	Flexible market	Rigid market with social security	Secured market (flexibility with a broad government safety net)	Special features (workers' role in management)
1	Key feature	Rigid rules for firing (countries like India, Indonesia, Sri Lanka)	Market takes care (suitable for countries like USA, Australia, Hong Kong, Singapore)	Social security (rigid system in Portugal, Luxembourg, France, and Germany, Spain)	Government/country as a whole bears the cost (countries like Denmark, Sweden, Netherlands, UK)	Workers' participation in supervisory board (Germany, France, UK)
2	Conditions of functioning	Social security is wanting and skill levels are low, so it leads to insecurity among workers, and so resistance for change	Near-perfect condition, when workers are skilled enough, or reskilling is easier and getting new jobs is easy	Rigid rules, but social security	Secured market (flexibility with a broad government safety net)	Special support to workers by laws and system of skilling, reskilling, and upskilling
3	Hiring (confidence to the business to hire)	Hiring is difficult	Hiring is easy (with less conditionality) greater flexibility in running a business makes business ownership more attractive	Hiring becomes easy, due to social security	Hiring is easy	Hiring is controlled and managed
4	System of skilling, reskilling, and upskilling	Low	High and sophisticated (about real-time information)	High	High	High
5	Firing rules (as per laws)	Firing is difficult	Firing is easy	Firing is difficult, but supported by security net	Flexible firing/dismissals are supported by social security	Rigid rules
6	Cost of firing to business/company	High	Less (market takes care of)	Medium	Very less	High

Source World Bank (2009), Allard (2017), Herrmann et al. (2018), Frohlich et al. (2016)

the workers' participation in management in industries has not met with success (Monoppa 1995, ILO 2012; Pahuja 2015).

Future strategy for labor reforms—policy issues. Governments worldwide face the challenge of finding the right balance between workers' protection and labor market flexibility. The flexible labor regulations encourage entrepreneurship. The studies suggest that flexible regulations increase the probability of startups by about 30% (World Bank 2009). Usually, labor market reforms are seen in regulations for hiring, work hours, redundancy rules, and cost, but less regarding reskilling, industry ecosystem for re-hiring, building a robust industrial ecosystem, and social security. It is essential to realize that workers contribute to the production and profitability of the company. They accumulate experience and skills on the job, which can be much more productive and valuable to a company. The skilled workforce can raise the productivity of the economy. These issues should also be considered while discussing labor market reforms.

The reforms should not be looked at from the prism of socialism versus capitalism. Why? The developed countries in Europe, which promote capitalism, have a social security system for workers on the one hand and a highly productive and advanced industrial system on the other. Social security is a generally accepted norm in developed (capitalist) countries. Likewise, instead of looking from the lens of business versus workers, it requires a broader perspective. And a win–win situation should be evolved for all concerned stakeholders—business, workers, unions, political parties, and government. It requires a confidence-building exercise and innovative solutions.

Simultaneously, it calls for a smart management information system (MIS) with a skill development program on a continuous basis. Labor reform should not just be about hiring or firing and compensation but also about the system for reskilling and upskilling, certification of the training system, availability of real-time information for jobs in different industrial locations, online registration of employment, social security, confidence-building among various stakeholders, and so on. In addition, there is a case for higher wages for workers to enhance disposable income. It can augment aggregate demand in the economy. There is a need to amend provisions regarding a call for strike with the provision of a secret ballot to determine the call for strike and subsequent advance notice to management while ensuring adequate safeguards for workers. It calls for a comprehensive review and restructuring of labor laws to make them in conformity with the present economic realities, including efficient regulatory mechanism, factoring in the concerns of social security of workers.

References

Acharya S, Ahluwalia I, Krishna KL, Patnaik I. Global research project on growth India: economic growth, 1950–2000. Indian Council for Research on International Economic Relations (ICRIER); 2003.

Adams RH. Economic growth, inequality and poverty: estimating the growth elasticity of poverty. World Dev. 2004;32(12):1989–2014.

Ali AA, Thorbecke E. The state and path of poverty in Sub-Saharan Africa: some preliminary results. J Afr Econ. 2000;9(AERC Supplement 1):9–40.

Allard G. Rigid labour markets; 2017. http://www.forbesindia.com/article/ie/rigid-labour-markets/11362/1.

Anjum Z. Startup capitals: discovering the global hotspots of innovation. Random House India; 2014.

Arthur WB. Complexity and the economy. Oxford University Press; 2014.

Aschauer D. Public capital and economic growth: issues of quantity, finance, and efficiency. Econ. Dev. Cultural Change. 2000;48:391–406. https://doi.org/10.1086/452464.

ASER. The annual status of education report (ASER); 2016. http://img.asercentre.org/docs/Publications/ASER%20Reports/ASER%202016/aser2016_nationalpressrelease.pdf.

Asian Productivity Organization (APO). Productivity databook; 2015.

ASSOCAHAM. Analysis of infrastructure investment in India; 2016.

ATKearney. Global cities 2017: leaders in a world of disruptive innovation; 2017.

Benhabib J, Spiegel MM. The role of human capital in economic development: evidence from aggregate cross-country data. J. Monetary Econ. 1994;34(2).

Birkland TA. An introduction to policy process. New Delhi: PHI Learning Pvt. Ltd.; 2011.

Bonvillian WB, Peter LS. Advanced manufacturing: the new American innovation policies. MIT Press; 2018.

Boston Consulting Group (BCG). Made in America, again: why manufacturing will return to the US; 2011. https://www.bcg.com/documents/file84471.pdf.

Brown M. Bridging the skills gap in the manufacturing industry; 2018. https://www.engineering.com/AdvancedManufacturing/ArticleID/16954/Bridging-the-Skills-Gap-in-the-Manufacturing-Industry.aspx.

Brynjolfsson E, McAfee A. Race against the machine: how the digital revolution is accelerating innovation, driving productivity, and irreversibly transforming employment and the economy. Digital Frontier Press Lexington; 2011.

Business Standard. 8625 startups recognised as on 30 March 2018; 2018. https://www.business-standard.com/article/news-cm/8-625-startups-recognised-as-on-30-march-2018-118040400743_1.html.

Business Today. Automation threatens 69 per cent jobs in India: World Bank; 2017. https://www.businesstoday.in/management/career/beware-automation-threatens-69-per-cent-jobs-in-india-world-bank/story/238164.html.

Business.com 2015. Boom or Bust? The impact of an economy driven by startups; 2015. https://www.business.com/articles/boom-or-bust-the-impact-of-an-economy-driven-by-startups/.

Business-standard. Urban population to contribute 70–75% of India's GDP by 2020, by Barclays Capital Market; 2014. https://www.business-standard.com/article/news-cm/urban-population-to-contribute-70-75-of-india-s-gdp-by-2020-barclays-114032000273_1.html.

Caravan. Trade Unions protest against pro-corporate and anti-people labour reforms; 2019. https://caravanmagazine.in/policy/trade-unions-against-modi-labour-policies.

Castells M. The rise of the network society. Wiley; 2011.

Central Pollution Control Board (CPCB). National inventory of sewage treatment plants. Government of India (GOI); 2021.

Centre for Global Development (CGD). Automation, AI, and the emerging economies, by Shahid Yusuf; 2018. https://www.cgdev.org/publication/automation-ai-and-emerging-economies.

Chakravarty B, Chand P. Public policy: concept, Theory and Practice Paperback. India: Sage Publications; 2016.

Chancel L, Piketty T. Indian income inequality, 1922–2014: from British Raj to Billionaire Raj? World inequality lab working paper series N 2017/11; 2017. https://wid.world/document/chancelpiketty2017widworld/.

Chaudhuri S. Premature deindustrialization in India and Re thinking the role of government, HAL Id: halshs-01143795; 2015. https://halshs.archives-ouvertes.fr/halshs-01143795/document.

References

Chen C. Who has the most unicorns—China or the US? 2017. https://www.scmp.com/tech/china-tech/article/2110209/who-has-most-unicorns-china-or-us.

Cochran CL, Malone EF. Public policy perspectives and choices. New York: McGraw Hill; 2005.

Deininger K, Lyn S. A new data set measuring income inequality. World Bank Econ Rev. 1996;10(3).

Deloitte and Singularity University (DSU). Exponential technologies in manufacturing: transforming the future of manufacturing through technology, talent, and the innovation ecosystem; 2018.

Deloitte. Global manufacturing competitiveness index; 2016.

Dev SM. WP-2016-009 economic reforms, poverty and inequality, Indira Gandhi Institute of Development Research, Mumbai; 2016. http://www.igidr.ac.in/pdf/publication/WP-2016-009.pdf.

DFID. Growth: building jobs and prosperity in developing countries; 2008. https://www.oecd.org/derec/unitedkingdom/40700982.pdf.

Dhar B, Saha S. An assessment of India's innovation policies, report by research and information system (RIS) for developing countries; 2014.

Duflo E. Schooling and labor market consequences of school construction in indonesia: evidence from an unusual policy experiment. Am. Econ. Rev. 2001;91(4).

Duraisamy P. Changes in return to education in India, 1983–94: by gender, age cohort and location. Econ Educ Rev. 2002;21.

Economic Survey, 2012–13. Planning commission, Government of India; 2013.

Economist Intelligence Unit (EIU). Labour reforms remain an uphill task; 2018. https://country.eiu.com/article.aspx?articleid=1086730892&Country=India&topic=Economy.

European Parliamentary Research Service (EPRS). Reshoring of EU manufacturing; 2014. http://www.eprs.ep.parl.union.eu, http://epthinktank.eu, eprs@ep.europa.eu.

Fernald JG. Roads to prosperity? Assessing the link between public capital and productivity. Am Econ Rev. 1999;89.

FFC. 14th finance commission of India; 2020.

FICCI. India PPP summit 2017, revival of PPP momentum in the transport sector; 2017.

Forrester JW. Principles of systems. Cambridge: MIT Press; 1968.

Forsyth J. Letter to the editor. Economist. 2000:6.

Fraser D. The evolution of the british welfare state. Macmillan; 1984.

Frohlich TC, Sauter MB, Comen E. Countries with the most generous welfare programs; 2016. https://finance.yahoo.com/news/countries-most-generous-welfare-programs-110004319.html.

Garg CC, Karan AK. Health and millennium development goal 1: reducing out-of-pocket expenditures to reduce income poverty—evidence from India; 2005. http://www.equitap.org/publications/docs/EquitapWP15.pdf.

Gerston LN. Public policy making: process and principles. New York: ME Sharpe Inc.; 2010.

Global Infrastructure Hub. Forecasting infrastructure investment needs and gaps; 2017. https://outlook.gihub.org/.

Global Perspectives & Solutions (GPS). Technology at work V2.0, the future is not what it used to be; 2016. https://www.oxfordmartin.ox.ac.uk/downloads/reports/Citi_GPS_Technology_Work_2.pdf.

Hamel G. Future of management. Harvard Business Review Press; 2007.

Hans A. Rebooting public private partnership in India. NITI Aayog, Government of India; 2017.

Hanushek EA, Wobmann L. Education and economic growth. In: Peterson P, Baker E, McGaw B, editors. International Encyclopedia of education, vol. 2. Elsevier; 2010. http://hanushek.stanford.edu/sites/default/files/publications/Hanushek%2BWoessmann%202010%20IntEncEduc%202.pdf.

Hanushek E, Woessmann L. The role of cognitive skills in economic development. J Econ Liter. 2008;46(3).

Hatch GP. Dynamics in the global market for rare earths. Elements. 2012;8(5):341–6. https://doi.org/10.2113/gselements.8.5.341.

Herrmann R, Hutzen P, Settekorn S, Sandmaier M. Employment & labour law in Germany. Germany: Global; 2018. https://www.lexology.com/library/detail.aspx?g=dc1738cd-23f3-43cc-b27d-62cfd8da4cf2.

High Powered Expert Committee (HPEC). Report on Indian urban infrastructure and services. Ministry of Urban Development, Govt. of India (GOI); 2011.

Hindu Business Line. Unions oppose changes to labor laws; 2015. https://www.thehindubusinessline.com/news/unions-oppose-changes-to-labour-laws/article7167432.ece.

Hindu Business Line. Ministry codifying central labor laws; 2017. https://www.thehindubusinessline.com/economy/ministry-codifying-central-labour-laws-says-dattatreya/article9559252.ece.

Hindu Businessline. 80% of engineers in India unemployable: report; 2018. https://www.thehindubusinessline.com/economy/80-of-engineers-inindia-unemployable-report/article8147656.ece.

Hindu. India had 14 out of world's 20 most polluted cities in terms of PM2.5 levels in 2016, says WHO; 2018. https://www.thehindu.com/sci-tech/energy-and-environment/14-out-of-worlds-20-most-polluted-cities-in-india-who/article23745178.ece.

Hoda A, Durgesh KR. Labour regulations and growth of manufacturing and employment in India: balancing protection and flexibility. ICRIER working paper, No. 298, New Delhi; 2015.

Hoppe R. Policy analysis, science, and politics: from speaking truth to power to making sense together. J Sci Publ Policy. 1999;26(3):201–210 (Downloads/fulltext_stamped.pdf).

Huberman M, Lewchuk W. Globalization and worker welfare in late nineteenth century Europe; 1999. https://www.researchgate.net/publication/4817331_Globalization_and_Worker_Welfare_in_Late_Nineteenth_Century_Europe.

Human Development Report (HDR). UNDP; 2016.

Indian Council for Research on International Economic Relations (ICRIER). State of municipal finances in India a study prepared for the fifteenth finance commission; 2019.

Indian Institute for Human Settlements (IIHS). Sustaining policy momentum urban water supply & sanitation in India. Bangalore: IIHS; 2014. http://iihs.co.in/knowledge-gateway/wp-content/uploads/2015/08/RF-WATSAN_reduced_sized.pdf.

Indian Institute of Technology Madras (IITM). India venture capital and private equity report; 2018. https://alumni.iitm.ac.in/wp-content/uploads/2018/10/India-Venture-Capital-and-Private-Equity-Report-2018-1.pdf.

Indian Skill Report (ISR); 2018. https://wheebox.com/static/wheebox_pdf/india-skills-report-2018.pdf.

Indian Venture Capital Association (IVCA). The fourth wheel 2018, private equity in the corporate landscape; 2018. https://www.grantthornton.in/globalassets/1.-member-firms/india/assets/pdfs/the_fourth_wheel_march-2018.pdf.

Infodev. International good practice for establishment of sustainable IT parks. Review of experiences in select countries, including three country case studies; 2008.

INSEAD. China's venture capital (VC): bigger than silicon valley's?; 2018. https://www.insead.edu/sites/default/files/assets/dept/centres/gpei/docs/insead-student-china-venture-capital-apr-2018.pdf.

International Labour Organization (ILO). Employee participation in India by Ratna Sen. Geneva: International Labour Office, Industrial and Employment Relations Department; 2012.

International Monetary Fund (IMF). GDP per capita; 2016. https://www.imf.org/external/datamapper/NGDPDPC@WEO/OEMDC/ADVEC/WEOWORLD.

International Monetary Fund (IMF). World economic outlook database (April 2019); 2019.

Jaimovich N, Siu HE. The trend is the cycle: job polarization and jobless recoveries. NBER working paper no. 18334, National Bureau of Economic Research; 2012.

Jain M, Jain PR. Venture capital: global and indian perspective. Int J Latest Trends Eng Technol. 2017;9(1):124–130. https://www.ijltet.org/journal/150667259619.%201950.pdf.

Janaagraha. Annual survey of india's city-systems 2016: shaping India's urban agenda, a publication of Janaagraha Centre for citizenship and democracy and jana USP; 2014.

References

Joumard I, Kumar A. Improving health outcomes and health care in India, OECD economics department working papers, no. 1184, OECD Publishing; 2015.

Kakwani N. Poverty and economic growth with application to Cote d'Ivoire, review of income and wealth, vol. 39; 1993.

Kaldor N. Strategic factors in economic development. Ithaca, New York: New York State School of Industrial and Labor Relations, Cornell University; 1967.

Kapsos S. Employment intensity of growth: trends and macro-determinants. ILO; 2005.

Kenneth AK. Strategic minerals: US alternatives. National Defence University Press; 1990.

Kirman A. Complex economics: individual and collective rationality. Routledge; 2011.

KPMG and FICCI. Re-engineering the skill ecosystem; 2016. http://ficci.in/spdocument/20762/Re-engineering-the-skill-ecosystem.pdf.

KPMG. China outlook 2018 (investment in infrastructure); 2018. https://assets.kpmg/content/dam/kpmg/cn/pdf/en/2018/03/china-outlook-2018.pdf.

KPMG. Venture pulse Q1 2019 global analysis of venture funding; 2019. https://assets.kpmg/content/dam/kpmg/xx/pdf/2019/04/venture-pulse-q1-2019-americas.pdf.

Lasswell HD. A pre-view of policy sciences. American Elsevier Publishing; 1971.

Lele A, Bhardwaj P. Strategic materials: a resource challenge for India. Pentagon Press; 2014.

Lopez-casasnova G, Rivera B, Currais L. Health and economic growth—findings and policy implications. MIT Press; 2007.

Lucas RE. On the mechanics of economic development. J Monet Econ. 1988;22:3–42.

Maddison A. The world economy. OECD; 2006.

Mankiw NG, Romer D, Weil D. A contribution to the empirics of economic growth. Q J Econ. 1992;107(2):407–37. https://eml.berkeley.edu/~dromer/papers/MRW_QJE1992.pdf.

McCarthy N. Which industries attract the most venture capital; 2016. https://www.statista.com/chart/5528/which-industries-attract-the-most-venture-capital/.

McKinsey Global Institute (MGI). Preparing China's urban billion; 2009. https://www.mckinsey.com/~/media/McKinsey/Featured%20Insights/Urbanization/Preparing%20for%20urban%20billion%20in%20China/MGI_Preparing_for_Chinas_Urban_Billion_full_report.ashx.

McKinsey Global Institute (MGI). India's urban awakening: building inclusive cities, sustaining economic growth; 2010.

McKinsey Global Institute (MGI). Jobs lost, jobs gained: workforce transitions in a time of automation; 2017a. https://www.mckinsey.com/~/media/BAB489A30B724BECB5DEDC41E9BB9FAC.ashx.

McKinsey Global Institute (MGI). A future that works: automation, employment, and productivity; 2017b.

Mehrotra S. The shape of the jobs crisis in Hindu newspaper; 2019a. https://www.thehindu.com/opinion/lead/the-shape-of-the-jobs-crisis/article26252357.ece.

Mehrotra S. Why an industrial policy is crucial; 2019b. https://www.thehindu.com/opinion/lead/why-an-industrial-policy-is-crucial/article27153226.ece.

Ministry of Health & Family Welfare (MHFW). Draft health policy. Government of India; 2014. https://www.nhp.gov.in/sites/default/files/pdf/draft_national_health_policy_2015.pdf.

Ministry of Health & Family Welfare (MHFW). Household health expenditures in India. Government of India; 2016. https://mohfw.gov.in/sites/default/files/38300411751489562625.pdf.

Ministry of Health. Annual report, 2015–16. Ministry of Health & Family Welfare. Government of India; 2016. https://main.mohfw.gov.in/documents-health-family-welfare-year-2015-16.

Ministry of Housing and Urban Affairs (MoUA). Atal mission for rejuvenation and urban transformation 2.0; 2021.

Ministry of Labour & Employment (MoLE). Labour reforms; 2019. https://labour.gov.in/labour-reforms.

Ministry of Labour & Employment (MoLE). Labour reforms initiatives; 2021. https://labour.gov.in/initiatives-central-government.

Ministry of Statistics and Programme Implementation (MOSPI). Project implementation status report of central sector projects costing Rs. 150 crore & above. New Delhi; 2017.

Mirvis DM, Chang CF, Cosby A. Health as an economic engine: evidence for the importance of health in economic development. J Health Human Serv Administr Summer. 2008;31(1):30–57. https://www.ncbi.nlm.nih.gov/pubmed/18575147.

MIT. MIT-Massachusetts advanced manufacturing forum; 2014. http://web.mit.edu/pie/amp/.

Mitra D. India on a jobless growth path. Bloomberg; 2017. https://www.bqprime.com/opinion/2017/01/11/india-on-a-jobless-growth-path.

Mohan R, Kapur M. Pressing the Indian growth accelerator: policy imperatives. IMF working paper, International Monetary Fund; 2015.

Mohanty PK. Financing cities in India: municipal reforms, fiscal accountability and urban infrastructure. Sage Publications; 2016.

Monoppa A. Industrial relations. New Delhi: Tata McGraw-Hill Publishing Company; 1995.

Mookerjee S, Bohra Z. Honors thesis international economics' mentor: does access lead to utilization? The case of health care in India; 2017. https://repository.library.georgetown.edu/bitstream/handle/10822/1044251/Economics%20Honors%20Thesis%20Zarine%20Bohra.pdf?sequence=1.

Morgan Stanley. 3 reasons why labour market is hindering India's growth; 2014. https://www.moneylife.in/article/3-reasons-why-labour-market-is-hindering-indias-growth/38482.html.

Muralidharan K. Forthcoming in the NCAER-brookings India policy forum 2013. Priorities for primary education policy in India's 12th five-year plan; 2013. https://pdel.ucsd.edu/_files/paper_2013_karthik.pdf.

Nair RP. The YourStory 2017 startup funding report; 2017. https://yourstory.com/2017/12/2017-startup-funding-report.

NASSCOM. Indian startup ecosystem—travelling the maturity cycle; 2017. https://smartnet.niua.org/sites/default/files/resources/nasscom-start-up-report-2017.pdf.

National Association of Manufacturers (NAM). Top 20 facts about manufacturing; 2017. http://hsvchamber.org/wp-content/uploads/2017/05/Adv-Manufacturing-Cool-Sites.pdf.

National Council of Educational Research and Training (NCERT). All India school education survey (8th round); 2016.

National Institute of Public Finance and Policy (NIPFP). Health shocks and the urban poor: a case study of slums in Delhi consultant. By Samik Chowdhury; 2011. http://www.isid.ac.in/~pu/conference/dec_09_conf/Papers/SamikChowdhury.pdf.

National Programme on Technology Enhanced Learning (NPTEL). Humanities and social sciences—Indian society: issues and problems, illiteracy, poverty, unemployment and population growth; 2017. https://nptel.ac.in/courses/109103022/pdf/mod2/lec6.pdf.

National Statistical Commission (NSC). Report of the committee on unorganised sector statistics. Government of India; 2012. http://www.lmis.gov.in/sites/default/files/NSC-report-unorg-sector-statistics.pdf.

Naumo V. Review of the world market of rare-earth metals. Russ J Non-Ferrous Metals. 2008;49(1).

Nelson RR, Phelps E. Investment in humans, technology diffusion and economic growth. Am Econ Rev. 1966;56(2).

Niti Aayog. National nutrition strategy. New Delhi: Govt of India; 2018. http://niti.gov.in/writereaddata/files/document_publication/Nutrition_Strategy_Booklet.pdf.

OECD. Background paper for the global development outlook, shifting wealth: implications for development, growth, inequality and poverty reduction in developing countries: recent global evidence, by Augustin Kwasi Fosu. OECD Development Centre; 2010.

OECD. Megatrends affecting science, technology and innovation; 2016. https://www.oecd.org/sti/Megatrends%20affecting%20science,%20technology%20and%20innovation.pdf.

References

One Goal. Fuelling Asia's footballers for the future one goal to level the playing field one goal; 2014. http://d3n8a8pro7vhmx.cloudfront.net/onegoal/pages/1/attachments/original/1398299334/Fuelling_Asias_Footballers_for_the_Future_REPORT_from_ONE_GOAL.pdf?1398299334.

ORF. Indian cities and air pollution by Ramanath Jha; 2019. https://www.orfonline.org/expert-speak/indian-cities-and-air-pollution-51628/.

Ortiz-Ospina E, Roser M. Government spending; 2016. https://ourworldindata.org/government-spending.

Oxford Poverty & Human Development Initiative (OPHI). Global multidimensional poverty index (MPI). University of Oxford; 2018. https://ophi.org.uk/multidimensional-poverty-index/global-mpi-2018/.

Pahuja H. Workers' participation management in India. Technol Manage. 2015;4(1). http://www.ijstm.com/images/short_pdf/189a.pdf.

Panagariya A, Bhagwati J. Why growth matters: how economic growth in india reduced poverty and the lessons for other developing countries. New York: Public Affairs; 2014.

Patel V. Our best investment: to improve educational outcomes, policy must address deprivations in early years of children's lives. http://indianexpress.com/article/opinion/columns/our-best-investment-right-of-children-to-free-and-compulsory-education-in-india/.

PISA Report. Do schools get their money (accountability initiative 2012), annual survey of education research (ASER); 2012. http://www.accountabilityindia.in/sites/default/files/state-report-cards/paisa_report_2012.pdf.

Planning Commission (PC). Twelfth five year plan (2012–2017) faster, more inclusive and sustainable growth, vol. I. Government of India; 2013.

Planning Commission (PC). The manufacturing plan strategies for accelerating growth of manufacturing in India in the 12th five year plan and beyond; 2011.

Planning Commission (PC). Report of the expert group to review the methodology for measurement of poverty. In: Rangarajan C, Chaired. Planning Commission, Government of India; 2014.

Planning Commission. 12th five-year plan, report of the working group on financing urban infrastructure. Steering committee on urban development & management; 2011.

Planning Commission. Skill development and training. Planning Commission; 2012. http://planningcommission.nic.in/plans/planrel/fiveyr/11th/11_v1/11v1_ch5.pdf.

PPP Cell. Public private partnership in India. A fast growing free market democracy; 2016. https://www.pppinindia.gov.in/toolkit/ports/module1-oopi-infra-wipii.php?links=oopii1a.

PPP Cell. Appraisal and approval mechanism for public private partnership (PPP). Department of Economic Affairs, Ministry of Finance, Government of India (GOI); 2018. https://www.pppinindia.gov.in/.

Rajaraman V. History of computing in India 1955–2010, Bangalore: Supercomputer Education and Research Centre. Indian Institute of Science; 2012. www.cbi.umn.edu/hostedpublications/pdf/Rajaraman_HistComputingIndia.pdf.

Rao VM. Policy making in India for rural development: the contextual limits to quantitative approaches. In: IGIDR proceedings/project reports series PP-062-07; 2009. http://www.igidr.ac.in/pdf/publication/PP-062-07.pdf.

Rao KS. Do we care: India's health system. India: Oxford University Press; 2017.

Ravallion M. Can high inequality developing countries escape absolute poverty? Econ Lett. 1997;56.

Raymond WC, Susan JB, Morgan BN. Public administration in theory and practice. Pearson; 1994.

RBI. Union budget 2018–19: an assessment. RBI Bull. 2018.

RBI. Handbook of statistics on Indian states; 2019.

Reinhardt K, Fanzo J. Addressing chronic malnutrition through multi-sectoral, sustainable approaches: a review of the causes and consequences; 2014. https://www.ncbi.nlm.nih.gov/pmc/articles/PMC4428483/pdf/fnut-01-00013.pdf.

Research in Infrastructure System (RIS) for Developing Countries. The financing of urban infrastructure issues and challenges; 2018. http://ris.org.in/pdf/aiib/19April2018/Urban%20Development%20Background%20Note.pdf.

Rodrik D. Premature deindustrialization. Working paper 20935. National Bureau of Economic Research; 2015. http://www.nber.org/papers/w20935.

Sankaran K. Labour laws in South Asia: the need for an inclusive approach. Discussion paper series. Geneva: International Institute for Labour Studies; 2007.

Sapru RK. Public policy: formulation, implementation and evaluation paperback. India: Sterling Publishers; 2012.

Sareen P. Indian tech startup funding report 2017: $13.5 Bn, 885 Deals, 1078 investors; 2018. https://inc42.com/datalab/indian-tech-startup-funding-2017/.

Shih WC. Just how important is manufacturing? Harvard Bus Rev. 2012. https://hbr.org/2012/02/just-how-important-is-manufact.

Simon HA. Models of man: social and rational. New York: Wiley; 1957.

Sirkin H, Rose J, Choraria R. Building an adaptive US manufacturing workforce; 2015. https://www.bcg.com/publications/2017/lean-manufacturing-operations-building-adaptive-us-workforce.aspx.

Spears D, Ghosh A, Cumming O. Open defecation and childhood stunting in India: an ecological analysis of new data from 112 districts. PLoS One. 2013;8(9):e73784. https://doi.org/10.1371/journal.pone.0073784.

Squire L. Fighting poverty. Am Econ Rev. 1993:377–82.

Sturgeon TJ. How silicon valley came to be. Published as chapter one. In: Kenney M, editor. Understanding silicon valley: anatomy of an entrepreneurial region. Stanford University Press; 2000.

The National Centre on Education and the Economy (NCEE); 2018a. http://ncee.org/wp-content/uploads/2018/03/RenoldVETReport032018.pdf.

The National Centre on Education and the Economy (NCEE). Comparing international vocational education and training programs; 2018b. http://ncee.org/wp-content/uploads/2018/03/RenoldVETReport032018.pdf.

Theodoulou SZ, Roy RK. Public administration: a very short introduction (very short introductions). Oxford University Press; 2016.

Tong K, Zhao Z, Feiock R, Ramaswami A. Patterns of urban infrastructure capital investment in Chinese cities and explanation through a political market; 2018. https://doi.org/10.1080/07352166.2018.1499417.

Tripathi S. Elementary education in India: focus on quality instead of quantity. Online. Sai Om J Arts Educ. 2016;3(3). www.saiompublications.com.

UNCTAD. Information economy report; 2017.

UNDP. Human development report; 1992.

UNESCO. UNESCO science report towards 2030; 2015. http://uis.unesco.org/sites/default/files/documents/unesco-science-report-towards-2030-part1.pdf.

UNICEF. Education for women and girls a lifeline to development; 2011. https://www.unicef.org/media/media_58417.html.

UNIDO. Industrial development report; 2016.

UNIDO. Industrial development report; 2018.

United Nations Development Programme (UNDP). Human development indices and indicators; 2018.

WaterAid. The water gap—the state of the world's water; 2018. http://wateraidindia.in/wp-content/uploads/2018/03/The-Water-Gap-State-of-Water-report-PAGES.pdf.

West DM, Lansang C. Global manufacturing scorecard: how the US compares to 18 other nations; 2018. https://www.brookings.edu/research/global-manufacturing-scorecard-how-the-us-compares-to-18-other-nations/.

WHO. Technical paper: the impact of health expenditure on households and options for alternative financing; 2004. http://www.who.int/health_financing/documents/emrc51-4-healthexpenditureimpact.pdf.

WHO. Air pollution, Health, environment, and sustainable development; 2018. https://www.who.int/sustainable-development/cities/health-risks/air-pollution/en/.

References

World Bank. Global monitoring report; 2006a.
World Bank. Equity and development. World development report; 2006b.
World Bank. Repositioning nutrition; 2006c. https://siteresources.worldbank.org/NUTRITION/Resources/281846-1131636806329/NutritionStrategyOverview.pdf.
World Bank. Doing business 2009 report; 2009.
World Bank. Economic costs of air pollution with special reference to India. In: Lvovsky K, editor; 1998. http://siteresources.worldbank.org/PAKISTANEXTN/Resources/UrbanAir/Economic+costs+of+air+pollution+KL.pdf.
World Bank. Policy research working paper 2972, economic growth, inequality, and poverty, findings from a new data set. In: Richard HA, editor. The world bank poverty reduction and economic management network poverty reduction group; 2003.
World Bank. Pro-poor growth in the 1990s: lessons and insights from 14 countries. Washington; 2005.
World Bank. Population health and economic growth, working paper no. 24. In: Bloom DE, Canning D, editors. The World Bank; 2008. https://siteresources.worldbank.org/EXTPREMNET/Resources/489960-1338997241035/Growth_Commission_Working_Paper_24_Population_Health_Economic_Growth.pdf.
World Bank. Trouble in the making?: The future of manufacturing-led development. In: Hallward-Driemeier M, Nayyar G, editors; 2018a. file:///C:/Users/SONY/Downloads/9781464811746.pdf.
World Bank. Manufacturing, value added (% of GDP); 2018b. https://data.worldbank.org/indicator/NV.IND.MANF.ZS?locations=CN.
World Bank. Manufacturing, value added (annual % growth); 2018c. https://data.worldbank.org/indicator/NV.IND.MANF.KD.ZG.
World Bank. GDP growth (annual %); 2018d. https://data.worldbank.org/indicator/ny.gdp.mktp.kd.zg.
World Bank. Urban development; 2018e. http://www.worldbank.org/en/topic/urbandevelopment/overview.
World Development Index (WDI). Washington DC; 2014.
World Economic Forum (WEF). The global human capital report; 2017a. www3.weforum.org/docs/WEF_Global_Human_Capital_Report_2017.pdf.
World Economic Forum (WEF). The global competitiveness report, 2016–2017; 2017b.
World Economic Forum (WEF). The future of jobs: employment, skills and workforce strategy for the fourth industrial revolution; 2016.
World Economic Forum (WEF). The future of jobs report; 2018.
World Health Organization (WHO). Macroeconomics and health: investing in health for economic development; 2001. http://www1.worldbank.org/publicsector/pe/PEAMMarch2005/CMHReport.pdf.
World Health Organization (WHO). World health Statistics; 2015.
World Literacy Foundation (WLF). The economic & social cost of illiteracy a snapshot of illiteracy in a global context; 2015. https://worldliteracyfoundation.org/wp-content/uploads/2015/02/WLF-FINAL-ECONOMIC-REPORT.pdf.
Worldatlas; 2019. https://www.worldatlas.com/articles/10-countries-with-the-highest-industrial-outputs-in-the-world.html.
WSP. The economic impacts of inadequate sanitation in India. New Delhi; 2010. https://www.wsp.org/sites/wsp/files/publications/wsp-esi-india.pdf.
WTO. World trade statistical review; 2018.
WTO. World trade report, levelling the trading field for SMEs; 2016. https://www.wto.org/english/res_e/booksp_e/world_trade_report16_e.pdf.

Chapter 3
Unraveling Complexity in Policy System, Economy, Business, and Organizations

I think the next Century will be the Century of complexity.
Stephen Hawking, Physicist and Author.

Abstract So far, the world has been dealing with certainty, orderliness, and stability in the social and economic systems. The system in question—social or economic—was taken as a single homogeneous structure. These have defined the thoughts about the method of inquiry and policy and economic theories. In contrast, social and economic systems consisting of real-world problems are complex. A system is called complex when it comprises multiple interconnected elements, parts, or subsystems, and their interactions and feedback loops determine the behavior of the system or economy. It is the interaction between elements that matters. Studying the policy system or economy as a single structure may not provide a reasoned approach. Though challenging, understanding complexity can add an advantage by realizing the hidden potential of interacting elements. For over a century, scholarly research about complexity has brought to the fore concepts that were not realized before. The research in complexity economics at Santa Fe Institute has made a significant contribution since the 1980s. The deeper understanding has added characteristics, such as the interactive nature of elements, emergence, adaptation, evolution, and path dependency, to examine a complex system. Understanding them assumes importance in exploring new approaches and strategies for better policymaking, managing the economy, and meeting the challenges of the twenty-first century.

Keywords Complexity · Interactive behavior · Emergence · Adaptation · Complex adaptive system (CAS) · Self-organization · Evolution · Path dependency · Attractor

From the historical perspective, various scholars (Prigogine and Stengers 1984; Grobman 2005; Rosenberg 2006) have examined the genesis of the approaches for scientific inquiry. They learned about the history of understanding the system and the approaches to solving scientific and social problems. From the seventeenth century till the nineteenth century, the overwhelming paradigm emphasized linear and scientifically known cause-effect relationships in the system, defined by reductionism, determinism, and Newtonian mechanistic approach. The reductionism has been defined as a concept that the whole can be broken down into its parts or complex phenomena can be reduced into their most basic parts. The parts are related through a simple cause-effect relationship and have defining characteristics of a system. The determinism concept underscores that every phenomenon has a cause and that a particular cause impacts in a unique manner under different conditions (Dafermos 2014, Ismael 2019). The Newtonian paradigm postulates that reductionism, determinism, and well-defined causality determine the behavior of a system (Fernandez et al. 2007; Ronn 2011).

Guided by the Newtonian worldview, classical mechanics was taken as a basis for scientific inquiry and research and was ingrained in scientific analysis until the middle of the twentieth century (Rosenberg 2006; Mazzocchi 2008). The mechanistic approach, synonymous with the Newtonian paradigm, has been mainly defined by technical methods, structures of control, and direction. It has been basically applicable to stable, steady, and simple environments (Zanzi 1987; Dickson et al. 2006; Liening 2013; Ehsani 2018).

From 1920s onward. As early as 1926, Smuts (1926) postulated that the opposite of reductionism is called—*holism* and suggested that any system, physical, biological, chemical, social, or economic, and its properties should be viewed as a whole, not just as a collection and sum of its constituents. The origin of the work on 'system' research is credited to Von Bertalanffy (1928), his seminal book (Von Bertalanffy 1928) titled *'Kritische Theorie der Formbildung'* (a German title) (Boulding 1962; Sieniutycz 2020). Realizing the limitations and inadequacies of the then-existing theories and approaches, during the 1940s–50s, the research on new scientific analysis got momentum (Kuhn 1962; Boulding 1962; Von Bertalanffy 1972). It emphasized a fundamental change in scientific thinking. Scholars in the field of system study began exploring new ways of understanding system problems. The scholarly work on the complex phenomenon by von Bertalanffy and Boulding in the 1950s contributed to the foundation of general systems theory (GST) (Chen and Stroup 1993; Ryan 2008; Chikere and Nwoka 2015). GST is a transdisciplinary unifying theoretical framework focusing on complexity and interdependence (Boulding 1962; Von Bertalanffy 1973). The main features of the theory include an open system, wholeness or holism, dynamics and change, and hierarchical order.

It is considered a field of inquiry rather than any specific discipline. With the emergence of general systems theory (GST), the field of research in systems got more prominence (Forrester 1961; Ryan 2008). It resulted in a family of system approaches, including complex systems, nonlinear dynamical systems, system dynamics, systems engineering, cybernetics, and soft systems, to name a few (Coyle 1977; von Foerster 1979; Checkland 1981; Morecroft 1983; Kauffman 1993; Bar-Yam 1997).

Many phenomena, such as emergent behavior; the adaptive nature of living organisms; the social, political, economic, and cultural behavior and pattern; network effects in the social systems; and the growth of computer technology, gave rise to the exploration of new approaches in living systems, social systems, and organizations (Forrester 1961; Von Bertalanffy 1972; Coyle 1977; Anderson et al. 1988;

Mitchell 2009). The rigorous research, from the 1960s onward, by scholars like Edward Lorenz, von Bertalanffy, Jay Forrester, Friedrich Hayek, Jamshid Gharajedaghi, and Brian Arthur, revealed that for the living or biological and social systems, due to the presence of a multitude of elements (individuals and variables) and their interactions, the nonlinear dynamics and emergent property need to be studied for understanding system's behavior and analyzing complex problems (Morecroft 1983; Sterman 2000; Mitchell 2009).

For a long period, the dominating perspective of scientific inquiry has been based on the lens of Newtonian principles. Especially from the middle of the twentieth century, such a proposition was found to be having limitations, and there was a felt need for a new and comprehensive approach to the study of inquiry into the world. Gradually, by the proponents of systems theory, it was increasingly realized that the behavior of the system could not always be explained merely from the knowledge of the behavior of its constituent parts or subsystems, and understanding the behavior of a whole system required systemic study, including interdependencies.

In the 1980s, Santa Fe Institute made a pioneering contribution to the field of complexity and economics (Arthur et al. 1997). It enhanced the understanding of concepts like feedback loops, emergence, self-organization, and evolution, which became the basis for complexity theory. It articulated the complexity. Complexity results from the interactions between numerous elements, parts, components, individuals, and system variables. Such interactions display nonlinearity, dynamic nature, causality, feedback, and emergence properties.

The literature reveals that the complexity in the social and economic systems is majorly a consequence of five inter-connected forms (Baetu 2012; Cairney 2012; Morcol 2012; Mueller 2020):

- *first, structural complexity*: referred to as inherent characteristic due to multiple elements, components, entities, individuals, or economic agents;
- *second, individual complexity*: on account of attitudes, cognitive understanding, and biases, and how individuals respond to complex issues, interact with each other, and manage the issues;
- *third, socio-economic and political complexity*: due to social, economic, cultural, and political environment and institutional factors;
- *fourth, interdependency (between elements) complexity*: because of interactions of elements, dynamic nature, emergence, adaptive, and self-organizing properties; and
- *fifth, operational complexity*: as a result of data, information and knowledge gathering, conceptualization, analyses, and decision-making during policymaking and implementation.

The complexity is recognized in the public policy system, economy, business, and public and business organizations. These systems are complex, interconnected, and influence one another (Nordtveit 2007; Morcol 2012; Boulton et al. 2015; Mueller 2020). These should be studied holistically. For instance, public policy is expected to advance a good economic environment and facilitate businesses to grow and meet the challenges of innovation, investment, and economic growth. Businesses are expected to leverage government policies to drive economic activities; thus, how businesses respond to policies is a matter of public policy formulation. Some business entities contribute to policymaking along with government agencies. There are numerous overlapping issues and areas of dependence, so it necessitates studying all the complex systems and underlying issues systemically.

3.1 What Constitutes Complexity: Characteristics of a Complex System

Study of complexity that took a structured and scientific approach since the 1960s is a result of insightful contributions in an incremental way by several scientists in both biological (living) science and social sciences, including philosophy. But the scholarly contribution to understanding complexity has begun much earlier (Smuts 1926; Boulding 1962; Coyle 1977; Anderson et al. 1988; Rihani 2005; Gharajedaghi 2011). In a significant departure from the reductionist approach and due to the persistent need to deal with uncertain, dynamic, and complex problems, it has been a unique and bold effort by scholars to provide a distinct lens of inquiry into various phenomena taking place in social and economic systems. Some characteristics of complexity have been identified in view of deeper analysis and nuanced scrutiny. It is done through a process of critical inquiry at the fundamental level, as it would have been difficult to discern characteristics through conventional methods of analysis. To deal with complex problems, the knowledge of the characteristics of the complex system is imperative.

For managing the twenty-first century challenges, the study of complexity opens up a new paradigm of inquiry and the possibility of solutions that are not apparent through the existing conventional approaches (Kauffman 1995; Stacey 1996; Byrne 1998; Arthur 2013). The experts have highlighted some key characteristics, viz., social networks, emergent behavior, self-organization, complex adaptive system (CAS), adaptation, evolution, coevolution, path dependency, edge of chaos, attractors, and basin of attraction, to understand better a complex system and its relation with the environment.

Though the characteristics have distinct features, there are some points of overlap. Understanding such characteristics will aid in a better appreciation of the environment in which the public policy system, economy, business, and organizations function. The characteristics of complex systems are presented in Table 3.1. It will help formulate the right policies and strategies and then better implementation. The basic characteristics are summarized as follows:

- *Networks—elements and interactions.* At the most basic level, multiple elements, individuals, or economic agents interact with each other with a common cause or motivation to undertake some tasks. Such interactions take a bigger form with time and may involve thousands or millions or more individuals or agents as members. Such a group of interacting members is referred to as a network. The study of

3.1 What Constitutes Complexity: Characteristics of a Complex System

Table 3.1 Matrix of characteristics of complex systems

S. No.	Characteristics	Systems		
		General complex system	Public policy system	Economy
1	Multiple and diverse elements	Presence of a large number of individuals, variables, and institutional issues	Numerous stakeholders; multiple sectors, policies, public institutions, socio-cultural factors, etc.	Numerous economic agents and entities, several firms, multiple policies and institutions, etc. (Multiple policies related to savings, consumption, investment, foreign investment, trade, etc.)
2	Nonlinearity, dynamic behavior	Relationships between elements are nonlinear and dynamic due to continuous interactions between elements, feedback loops, and qualitative variables	Due to behavioral issues, psychological needs, institutional factors, continuous interactive effects of individuals, and feedback, the system behavior is nonlinear and dynamic	Due to behavioral issues, psychological and institutional factors, and feedback loops, the relationships between economic agents and entities are nonlinear and keep evolving with time
3	Feedback loops	Elements keep sending feedback to others, which in turn send feedback, and thus feedback loops are formed	Individuals send feedback to each other, leading to feedback loops, which change their behavior and actions. In the structure, there may be multiple loops	Agents, economic entities, and policies send feedback to each other. Feedback impacts the behavior of agents and economy
4	Causality[a]	Causality (in precise form) is not known and not knowable due to nonlinear behavior, multiple interactions between elements, behavioral dimension, cognitive limitations, and feedback loops. (But, causality is knowable with expertise and in-depth analyses under certain assumptions)	Cause-effect relations between output and system variables cannot be determined. Bounded rationality makes the analysis difficult. Lack of perfect information or complete knowledge makes analysis difficult	Causal relations between behavior of the economy and elements (variables and agents) are not discernible
5	Uncertainty	Due to nonlinearity, dynamic behavior, feedback loops, and unknown cause-effects, the system behavior is uncertain	Behavioral issues, psychological needs, and institutional factors cannot be predicted, and the combination of these leads to uncertainty. The output cannot be defined with certainty, and a pattern can be observed as time passes	Behavior of economy is not certain due to dynamic numerous interactive economic agents and feedback loops. Economic behavior is influenced by behavioral issues and institutional factors

(continued)

Table 3.1 (continued)

S. No.	Characteristics	Systems		
		General complex system	Public policy system	Economy
6	Path dependency	History or past events matter and influence the future	Social systems and organizations depend upon culture, beliefs, processes, and practices that cannot be changed on short notice	Dependence of economic entities on past economic policies, technologies, and incentive structures
7	Network, emergence, adaptation, self-organization, and evolution	Elements are linked to each other in a network. Due to interactions, new behavior emerges over time. And then, through a process of adaptation, the system self-organizes into a new state and evolves	People interact (due to human nature) and form networks. Such interactions result in emergence, and system self-organizes	Economy emerges due to the interactive effects of economic agents, entities, and policies. It self-organizes into a new state as it adapts to new conditions and then evolves
8	Coevolution	Due to feedback from elements to environment and vice-versa, the systems in the environment coevolve to adapt to new conditions	Various policies coevolve due to feedback from stakeholders	Markets, economic institutions, complementary policies, and regulatory mechanisms coevolve
9	Disorder / non-equilibrium	System tends to settle in a stable state or an orderly state for a brief period and may be disturbed by perturbation from within or environment	System remains in a dynamic state due to changes taking place within and in the environment	Economy remains in a state of flux and dynamic state, and due to frequent changes in the environment, it remains in a non-equilibrium state

[a] It implies the relations between causes and effects on system behavior

networks can help in identifying the sources of complexity and understanding the complexity in the system. The interactions between network members are caused by the desire to exchange resources, ideas, and information through a shared purpose or cause. They work on mutual trust and are modulated by the rules as worked out and agreed upon by the members (Potts 2000; Morcol 2012; Terna and Fontana 2014; Koliba et al. 2016).

Box 3.1 Elements in a System

A system consists of subsystems, components, parts, or elements. And these are used interchangeably, depending on the context. The variables, agents, or people are within a system. In the book, the parts, variables, agents, individuals, citizens, or people in a combined form are referred to as elements. Regarding the interactions, these are between elements. In general, for a large or global system, various systems or subsystems are referred to as elements.

3.1 What Constitutes Complexity: Characteristics of a Complex System

Figures 3.1 and 3.2 represent a sample network of elements. Box 3.1 defines elements in a system. In the network, many interactions are depicted, and such a complex web of interactions makes the system complex. Such interactions influence the outputs of the system as indicated by the following equation:

Results/Outputs = Interactive effects $(e_{12}, e_{13}...; e_{123}, ..; e_{1234}; ... e_{123...n})$.

- *Emergent behavior*. The vital feature of complex systems is the presence of emergent behavior as a result of interactions between parts, variables, individuals, or elements within the system and between elements and the environment. The presence of individuals is a necessary condition. The emergent behavior reflects the property or trait of the system, which is not apparent from the property of its parts, variables, or individuals in isolation. Thus, the behavior cannot be predicted by the examination of system's parts or elements. And the behavior results from collective interaction between elements at a local level by following written or unwritten rules (Wolf and Holvoet 2004; Morcol 2012; Colander and Kupers 2016).

It signifies that the people or economic agents in the social or economic system do not act individually alone. Instead, collective action emerges due to their interactions and interrelationships. The interactions are due to agreed norms and values, shared cause, or dependencies when the elements are together in a system. The environment from outside or the government policies influence the behavior of people and then, through interactions, the system's behavior. An emergent behavior or property can appear when many simple entities (individuals or agents) interact, forming more complex behavior as a collective effect.

Emergence underscores a new macro-level phenomenon—property, behavior, and structure—results from the interactions between elements at the micro level. It is influenced by the behavioral and cognitive attributes, values, structures, and capabilities of individuals (Chan 2001; Wolf and Holvoet 2004; Hazy et al. 2007; Morcol

Fig. 3.1 Interactions of elements in a network in two subsystems

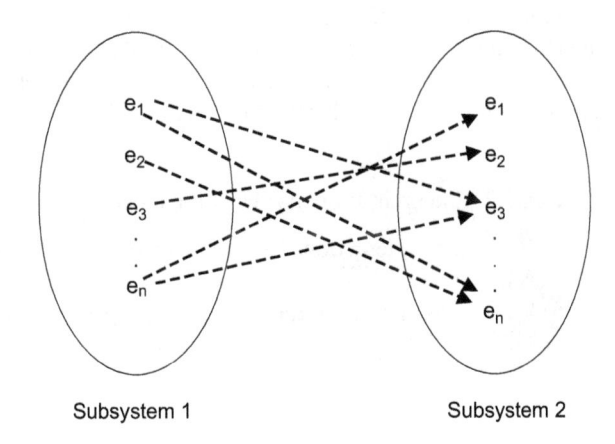

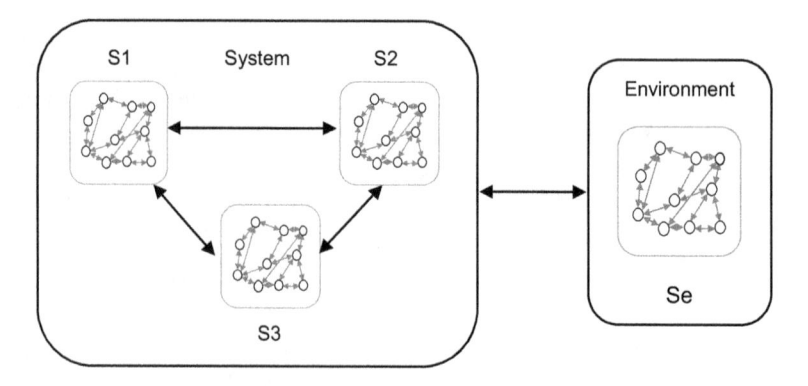

[○]: Nodes (representing elements)
[↔]: Edges
S1, S2, S3 and Se represent subsystems

Fig. 3.2 Interactions between elements and subsystems in the network

2012; Boulton et al. 2015). In addition, as regards the emergent behavior, the causality is not known and not knowable, or causality cannot be determined in a precise form due to nonlinear behavior, multiple interactions between numerous elements, behavioral dimensions, cognitive limitations, and feedback loops. Causality means the relations between causes and effects on the system output (or system behavior). The interactions occur between elements within the system and with other systems' elements in the environment. The relationships between variables in the system structure can be identified through the analysis. And causality is knowable only with a detailed examination under certain assumptions.

Key propositions. The behavior of elements can be influenced by external inputs like policies, norms, and regulations and through an exchange of resources, information, or interventions; the environment influences the elements or agents of the system; the individual elements influence the environment and also other elements; and the interactions between elements shape the behavior of the system, and then the emerging system puts influence on elements and the environment, and as a result, the system remains in a dynamic form (Box 3.2).

Box 3.2 Emergent Property: How it happens
- It is due to interactions between elements at a 'local level' based on local rules.
- The values, norms, culture, structures, capabilities, and individual attributes influence interactions and emergence.

- The environment or government policies influence the behavior of elements and then emergence.
- It results from collective behavior, which gives rise to dynamic nature.
- The new pattern emerges or is formed without any specific direction to elements or agents.
- The properties of the system that emerges are independent of the properties of each element.

The examples of emergent behavior of the stock market, business, and economy are briefly discussed. The investors (economic agents) in the stock market interact with each other at the level of the stock exchange as a group of individuals. Their interactions are governed by government policies, regulations, investment climate, international investment sentiment, and individual values, preferences, and capabilities. In addition, these investors have their own written or unwritten rules. These, in a combined form, determine their transactions and relationships. Over time, owing to collective interactions, due to decision-making and investments by the investors, the stock prices of different companies are discovered, and collectively, the behavior of the stock market emerges. With the acquisitions of more knowledge, technological devices, and capabilities, the agents enhance their performance and influence their environment and nature of interactions with other investors. So, there are dynamic interactions between investors who influence the behavior of the stock market.

In the case of business, due to collective interactions, the entrepreneurs and business units acquire ideas, knowledge, technologies, or resources. There remain dynamic interactions between elements (entrepreneurs or business units). Over time, on account of collaborations, investment in technologies, and setting up enterprises by the entrepreneurs, the overall behavior of the business system emerges (Kapur 2002; Avnimelech and Teubal 2003; Saxenian 2003; Sharma 2015).

To further illustrate, in the case of the economy, from the interactions of the individual agents, the macro-level behavior or pattern emerges, which cannot be predicted by understanding each agent. The overall behavior of the economy emerges following several decisions and interventions by millions of individual agents or entrepreneurs as a consequence of competition, conflict, or cooperation between them (Hayek 1967; Arthur et al. 1997). In other words, at the macro level, the economy emerges due to the interconnectedness of system variables, policies such as monetary policy and trade policy, the performance of the stock market, foreign investment, foreign exchange management, the ecosystem within the country, and so on.

Likewise, the health system emerges due to the impact of interacting multiple elements within the health system (like budget, health personnel, infrastructure, equipments, logistics, etc.) and with the environment (feedback from stakeholders in the environment, etc.). As a consequence of collective interactive behavior, another typical example is the development of a city as an emergent phenomenon. It results from the interactions between thousands or lakhs of individuals in the city for a shared relationship and purpose.

- *Self-organization.* It is referred to as a spontaneous order. It is a dynamic and adaptive process where some form of overall new order arises after the emergence from local interactions between elements in a decentralized manner without external control. It is the next stage of emergent behavior through adaptation. The control of a self-organizing system is distributed across elements or agents and integrated through interactions between them. It results in new structures, patterns, and properties, which are no longer correlated to the behavior of individual elements or parts. It is amplified by positive feedback. Self-organization is a regular process in complex systems, and new interactive patterns may emerge with time and cause more complexity (Goldstein 1999; Wolf and Holvoet 2004; Sammut-Bonnici 2015).

The agents are heterogeneous and independent in thinking and may possess specialized knowledge for decision-making and remain organically linked. These agents are the building blocks for a new system's behavior (Coleman 1999; Kelly and Allison 1999; Pascale 1999; Brownlee 2007; Sammut-Bonnici 2015).

In the social system, through interactions in the networks, self-organizing is the process concerning issues of common interest. Depending upon the conditions, it may facilitate building social capital, community engagement, collaboration, and cooperation. Similarly, the economy displays a self-organizing phenomenon through interactions between entrepreneurs or businesses at the local level or the marketplace. The coordination, exploration, and learning by the economic agents influence it (Hayek 1967; Holland 1995; Krugman 1996).

In self-organized systems, certain states (in the system) in 'space and time' act as a kind of attractor toward which the system settles. Such states may be created by certain conditions like cultural values, adequate incentives, or the availability of facilitating conditions. In organizations, self-organization is natural behavior when people interact freely and form a network to pursue certain objectives. It may involve crossing organizational hierarchy or boundary created by formal structures (Stacey 1996; Coleman 1999; Tominomori 2002; Allen 2007).

The lack of land use planning and management of public land leading to unorganized urban growth over time or social networking and collaboration in times of natural calamity are some examples of self-organization in which, based on shared aspirations or needs, the agents or people at the local level interact to generate macro-level order.

- *Complex adaptive system* (CAS). The CAS consists of three keywords: complex, adaptive, and system. 'Complex' word refers to complexity—numerous interacting elements, nonlinearity, dynamic nature, feedback loops, and uncertainty; 'adaptive' relates to adaptation, in a dynamic mode, to changing environments to fit to perform better or survive; and 'system' implies that elements or agents interconnected, interdependent, and interacting. It produces macro-level or macroscopic global structure or behavior that emerges from the nonlinear and dynamic

3.1 What Constitutes Complexity: Characteristics of a Complex System

interactions between elements at the local or microscopic level. The emergent behavior or property is more than the sum of the parts or elements (Kauffman 1995; Pascale 1999; Tzafestas 2018). CAS is a special case of complex system. It learns, emerges, and adapts through self-organization.

The external environment, e.g., competition, climate change, or policy change at the global level, impacts the elements. Government policies affect the behavior of elements. These influence the emergent behavior of the system and try to adapt to new conditions. CAS is self-organizing, and the property of emergence is observed without external control but due to the continuous, including competitive, interactions between elements or agents, depending on the feedback from other elements and the environment. There is distributed control over agents, and no centralized control mechanism operates to determine the system behavior. The key features of CAS are presented in Box 3.3 (Gharajedaghi 2011; Bar-Yam 1997).

CAS works far from equilibrium, thereby meaning that it remains in dynamic mode and may not sustain itself when in equilibrium. Over time, the CAS tends to move toward the edge of chaos or point of inflection when disturbed by the environment, complex problems, the changing needs of agents, or the calibrated interventions (Kauffman 1995; Pascale 1999; Chan 2001; Palmberg 2009; Ramalingam 2015; Tzafestas 2018). The emergent, self-organization, and CAS are interlinked concepts with overlap. Examples of complex adaptive systems are economies, markets, cities, industrial clusters, governments, health systems, social networks, political parties, communities, traffic flows, social media, etc.

Box 3.3 Complex Adaptive System (CAS) Features

- Dynamic nature and nonlinear behavior
- Multiple agents or elements are organically linked over space and time
- Emergent, adaptation, and self-organizing
- Adaptive nature to changes in the environment and, or behavior of agents
- System is hierarchically nested
- Learning ability and exhibiting memory
- Subject to the 2nd law of thermodynamics, exhibiting entropy, losing energy and drive over time; needs resources and innovation to sustain
- Path dependence and sensitivity to initial conditions
- Nonlinear behavior, the small inputs can produce significant effects on the system, and large inputs may have little effect.

For example, in the business system, numerous entrepreneurs meet and consult each other. Their interactions are governed by government policies, incentives, regulations, technological capabilities, and the business ecosystem, besides individual values, skills, and capabilities. Furthermore, these entrepreneurs have their working rules for business dealings, which determine their collaboration for ideas, technologies, or resources. Together with this, the acquisition of more ideas, knowledge, innovation, technologies, and higher skill sets, business units raise their performance. By virtue of that, they influence the environment and quality of interactions with other entrepreneurs or businesses.

Innovative ideas, knowledge, technologies, and skills are exchanged with the environment, which may be the immediate environment or international business environment. So, there is a dynamic interaction between elements (entrepreneurs or business units) who create dynamic behavior of the system (business system) (Kapur 2002; Avnimelech and Teubal 2003; Saxenian 2003; Sharma 2015). With time, due to collective interactions, on account of investment in technologies and setting up enterprises, the overall behavior of the business system emerges and adapts to a new state. The key message is that such interactions, emergence, self-organizing, and adaptation take place due to the inherent nature of entrepreneurs within the business ecosystem without any external control.

There is another example of emergence in the government system. It is based on the case of emergence at the local level in government agencies, as highlighted by Lipsky (2010) in his seminal book. Government agencies have the big task of delivering results on multiple objectives through many programs. Implementing departments issue guidelines to ensure compliance with specific procedures and norms. At the frontline level, the field staff members are expected to implement programs as per guidelines while dealing with challenging or sometimes competing environment due to the demand to cover more beneficiaries. The number of beneficiaries for many programs in many villages under one field member may be staggering. This ground situation is not fully captured in the guidelines. But achieving targets is expected in a time-bound manner, and following the guidelines is essential. Fulfilling these objectives of attaining targets and adhering to guidelines may not be a realistic possibility in a short time.

It leaves little room for the frontline staff members to follow government rules strictly and prompts them to work on their own rules and procedures, which are unwritten, to achieve targets. They try to make an effort to stick to guidelines. In the end, the achievement of targets is highly appreciated. Thus, it gives rise to the emergence of a new system by devising different convenient procedures to achieve targets. It results from the interactions between local staff and is a local phenomenon due to interactive effects at the local level, without any central control. The new methods adapt to the overall requirements of targets. The target-oriented monitoring from the top cannot control the emergence of such behavior.

- *Adaptation.* Adaptation is a process of acclimatizing or adjusting to new conditions. It is a characteristic or capability in complex systems—natural or social. It plays a vital role for all living organisms and social systems as elements constantly self-adjust and change their inner properties to fit better in or adapt to the environment. The experiential learning of individuals, groups, or organizations embedded in interacting subsystems or social networks plays a vital role. The self-adjusting ability of people, being a part of a social and cultural system, political system, economy, or organization, brings adaptation behavior in the system in a collective manner. Such systems respond dynamically to changes. Human beings continuously learn from their experiences, make use of their capabilities, respond to changes within the system and in their environment, make efforts to achieve certain objectives, and seek benefits or new opportunities. It is how human systems evolve and adapt to new challenges due to learning and adaptive behavior (Coleman 1999; Kauffman 1995, Miles et al. 1997; Carmichael and Hadzikadi 2019).

The development system, stock market, cities, manufacturing, businesses, and human social groups adapt to the socio-cultural and political environment in which they function. In the development system, for example, agriculture, it evolves with time to adapt to new conditions—like new farming techniques, technologies, internal market demands, exports, etc., due to the collective effort of farmers, governments, and entrepreneurs. In the context of the economic system, the economy self-organizes and adapts to an unfolding global environment. Adaptation is needed for success in a complex business system. In the context of business and industry, with the increasing customer demands and competition, entrepreneurs adapt to emerging scenario and look for innovation across the value chain and also in systems and processes, organizational design, and new product development (Hayek 1967; Tapscott and Williams 2006; Ramalingam 2015).

There are two forms of adaptation. *Firstly, adaptation at element or individual (agent) level.* It is based on the individual's values, beliefs, ability, or fitness level to modify as per the demand of the environment or other agents. It is individual attribute-centric, linked to personal and system goals. *Secondly, adaptation at system level.* It arises when a dominant or a significant group of elements or agents changes in a coordinated manner in response to changing environment, which could be due to disruptive technology, government policies, social unrest, or change in political regime. It may involve more substantial and holistic change. It may lead to changes in the rules of interactions between agents (Miles et al. 1997; Tapscott and Williams 2006; Carmichael and Hadzikadi 2019).

The primary mechanism of adaptation is through feedback or feed-forward and learning. Through interactions with the environment or people, the feedback is received by people who modify their behavior or learn new ways of working. In the case of feed-forward, some people signal certain messages to others and the environment based on their expertise. Such messages may be progressive ideas or warnings based on which people make decisions about the future course of action. In this way, a pattern of behavior or structure of the system changes. Based on feedback, such adaptation can be goal-seeking adaptation to achieve specific objectives. It can take the form of evolution in response to environmental change, and a completely new behavior or pattern may emerge, which may normally take a longer time. It can also be seen as a process to enhance fitness and to survive and thrive (Tapscott and Williams 2006; Ramalingam 2015; Tzafestas 2018).

- *Evolution.* In complex systems, evolution takes place to adapt to a new state or condition. It is due to a process of self-organization and adaptation to the internal demands and external environment. From a system perspective, all human systems, like economies, societies, or organizations, are inextricably interconnected in a complex web of mutually influential relationships. These lead to a dynamic process of evolution. The basic premise is that there is an inherent tendency in a complex system to evolve or shape into a changed behavior, (Morcol 2012; Boulton et al. 2015; Tzafestas 2018).

The emergence, adaptation, and self-organization leading to evolution are influenced by the values, norms, culture, structures, and individual attributes in the system; capabilities of individuals or agents; internal interventions through incentives, policies, and strategies; control parameters from outside; and the changes in the environment (Kauffman 1995; Pascale 1999; Chan 2001; Palmberg 2009; Colander and Kupers 2016).

- *Coevolution.* Complex systems—government, social, economic, organizations, industry, and business—manifest the occurrence of coevolution. In the socio-economic system, coevolution results from sharing culture, values, ideas, information, and resources in the environment by cooperating or competing systems. The environment constitutes social, cultural, educational, political, economic, ecological, and technological aspects (Mc Millan 2004; Sotarauta and Srinivas 2006; Morcol 2012). Through interactions, the systems influence each other and shape each other's development or evolution, depending on their attributes. Some examples are, in the environment of cooperation, innovation, and technologies, many startup companies and venture capital (VC) firms coevolve. Due to competition, many industrial units, like e-commerce ventures, real estate businesses, and ICT software companies, etc., may coevolve.

The coevolving systems have reciprocal relationships—mutual interconnectivity and interdependencies. Due to their dynamic interactions, one system can causally influence the environment or other systems in the environment, which can feed back their response to the original system. Such a process may continue for a period of time, and as a result, it can impact their evolutionary path. In a rapidly changing global environment, the actions of one company or group of companies may trigger actions and reactions in other companies whose actions may cause actions in the original companies (Kelly and Allison 1999; McKelvey 2002). Understanding the phenomenon of coevolution is essential for designing industrial policies.

Studies reflect that the coevolution or evolutionary path is a result of a combination of various effects such as (Huygens et al. 2001; Avnimelech and Teubal 2003; Benbya and McKelvey 2006; Almudi and Fatas-Villafranca 2021) (Table 3.2):

- *Multiple feedback effect.* The feedback may be positive or negative. It may be from the environment and other agents or entities within the system. The positive feedback may contribute to coevolution, while the negative feedback may control the system to a particular state.

3.1 What Constitutes Complexity: Characteristics of a Complex System

Table 3.2 Different system effects and their examples (coevolution)

S. No.	System effects	Examples
1	Multiple feedback effect	Health system gets feedback from internal health staff and patients, elected members, and outside experts
2	Circular causality	Competition, capabilities, and innovation impact each other. It implies competition may lead to enhanced capabilities and innovation, which may further lead to more competition
3	Multi-causal effect	Within a particular industry, the firms, venture capital (VC), angel investors, and financial market impact investment decisions
4	Multi-level effects	In the case of the social system, it is at the grassroots, sub-district, State, National, and international levels. In the case of industry, it is at the firm, cluster, regional, National, and international levels. Another example is the supply chain from bottom to State, National, and international levels
5	Nonlinear, dynamic interactions, and emergent effect	Relationships between agents or people and system variables are nonlinear and dynamic. These may give rise to the emergence of a new system in the environment

- *Circular causality.* The effect of the cause returns to the original cause and may change the original cause and then modifies the effect, i.e., causes and effects reinforce each other.
- *Multi-causal effect.* The output (objective) of the system is affected by linkages with multiple variables.
- *Multi-level effects.* The feedback and linkages are at various levels (micro to meso to macro) in the environment.
- *Nonlinear, dynamic interactions, and emergent effect.* The interactions are nonlinear and dynamic, and as a result, a new system emerges along with other systems in the environment.

When coevolution takes place, each system tries to reinforce the other. The examples of pair-wise coevolution are public policy and innovation; economic policy and industry clusters; innovation processes and technologies; and competition and capabilities (Huygens et al. 2001; Sotarauta and Srinivas 2006; Breslin 2014; Marks and Gerrits 2017; Mueller 2020). Organizational capabilities and technologies shape the competitive environment, and then it shapes the organizations and technologies (Huygens et al. 2001). Likewise, innovation processes evolve as new ideas and technologies emerge. In the public policy system, policy in one sector, say, industry, requires complementary policy in the energy sector due to a likely increase in demand for electricity. Or, the growth in the agro-based industry can give impetus to agriculture, e.g., the production of cotton and sugarcane crops, as a response to textiles and sugar mills and vice-versa.

Coevolution is the reason why the government should keep itself abreast of the changes in the environment or the impact of policy in one area on other areas. Or, in the global context, it needs to be examined how the innovation in technologies in other countries or climate change policies in multilateral fora may impact the social and economic systems within the country, as the country context coevolves with the changes taking place at the world level. Similarly, businesses should be aware of what is happening in other similar or different companies, learn about their strategies and products, and then take actions to be competitive (Kelly and Allison 1999; Sotarauta and Srinivas 2006; Aarset and Jakobsen 2015). The implication of coevolution is that complementary policies, businesses, industries, and standards should coevolve to support one another to achieve better results and higher growth.

- *Path dependency*. Path dependency is a phenomenon that reflects that history matters or signifies what has happened in the past is vital for future policymaking or strategy formulation. The past decisions, events, values, principles, processes, structures, and usage of technologies persist in the system or organization. Usually, path dependence is associated with the continuation of the present, lock-in state, or resistance to change. The technological, organizational, institutional, and social processes strengthen as well as weaken path dependence depending on the case. Path dependency may lead to a continuation of the current inefficient processes or technologies with negative externalities and contribute to reluctance or inability to invest in forward-thinking innovations (North 1990; Liebowitz and Margolis 1995; Pierson 2000; Cecere et el 2014).

In the context of public policy, governments successively invest time and resources in building certain internal management processes and systems and formulating policies, which create both formal and informal structures, mindsets, practices, routines, and institutions. These become committed and established in the system in certain ways. These are human-centric and become integral to the public system or organization and define the institutional path. It determines the culture and the thought process in the organization.

Long legislative processes and large investments in existing programs also contribute to lock-in state, as people want to continue with the existing state. In addition, historical institutionalism stresses how the timings and sequence of decision-making and actions affect public systems. These lead to path dependency as the decisions or outcomes follow previous development paths. The institutions—beliefs, values, norms, rules, and behavior patterns—shape the behavior of the government or social system. The institutional paths take the form of a lock-in state or resistance to intervention. Besides, the system is sensitive to the initial conditions of the system. Such features influence the future state of public policy (Boulton et al. 2015; Cairney and Geyer 2017; OECD 2017).

As regards the economy, path dependence is due to continued reliance on existing economic ecosystems and institutions, endogenous processes, production systems, technologies, set technical standards, and feedback from multiple economic agents. It occurs as it is more cost-effective to continue along an existing set path than to develop a new process, production system, or economic path (North 1990; Krugman

3.1 What Constitutes Complexity: Characteristics of a Complex System   101

1991; Liebowitz and Margolis 1995; Arthur et al. 1997; Gigante 2016). Financial implications and difficulty in taking risks contribute to the resistance to change. In addition, the current knowledge and skill sets, networks and coordination, and expectations on a predictable evolution of markets put limitations on introducing new ideas (Pierson 2000; North 1990; D'Costa 2003).

In sum, the path dependence is due to a combination of the following factors (Peters and Pierre 1998; Pollitt and Bouckaert 2004; Stuteville and Jumara 2010):

- *history*: past decisions have a bearing on how the organizations think and perform;
- *lock-in*: due to commitment to existing policies, technologies, or production systems, continuing over a long time;
- *increasing returns*: the current policies, methods, or services provide increasing returns due to positive feedback in the absence of any tested alternative, and the momentum continues for the ongoing activities;
- *institutions*: the values, norms, and behavioral patterns get ingrained and difficult to change;
- *rules*: initial decisions and choices are reinforced when the rules governing the behavior are deep-rooted and difficult to change;
- *inertia*: like social inertia, which is resistance to change the existing stable relationships in social groups or organizations; and psychological inertia, that is to maintain the status quo and avoid taking action for new ideas; and
- *inability or a reluctance to commit to change*: due to the inability to take the risk or financial implications, change becomes difficult.

Understanding path dependence can provide useful inputs for policymaking and sustainable economic growth.

- *Attractors.* An attractor is a metaphor that signifies the state toward which a dynamic system evolves or settles with time, regardless of the starting conditions in the system. There may be more than one attractor in the dynamic system. Or in other words, the attractor pulls or attracts the trajectories or paths of the initial states in the basin of attraction. These initial conditions lead in the direction of attractor with time, through a process of interactions, feedback loops, and self-organization of the system. The state may be a critical value, compelling tendency, or outcome. It attracts the system elements collectively. The state may be defined as a shared vision, behavioral trend, ideals, norms, pattern, innovation ecosystem, and economic trend toward which system approaches (Svyantek and Brown 2000; Newman 2009; Kuhmonen 2016).

In the complex dynamic system, the system reaches a stable state through feedback and self-organizing properties and provides a stable boundary for the system. It represents the stability at a given time, which may last long or be short-lived depending upon the strength of an attractor. Such a state depends upon control parameters like principles, strategies, rules, policies, processes, institutional mechanisms, capabilities and capacity, and incentives. These also determine the ecosystem within the system. It potentially remains the desired state in a dynamic system (Dolan et al 2000; Byrne 1998; Hiver 2014; Gerrits 2012).

Comments. Complex systems evolve through interactions and approach toward a state of stability in space and time. Stability is necessary for providing steadiness to elements or people to perform their tasks. But, continued stability may not be desirable in the medium and long term, as the system may not grow to meet new challenges. Also, changing external environment or internal needs may exert pressure on the system to change. So, small and calibrated changes are needed for the medium term. And for the long term, necessary changes by way of new capabilities, culture, improved processes, or innovations are to be effected. Thus, the system will move to a new attractor state. For example, in the public policy system, the economy will reach an attractor state by the combination of investment, productivity, innovation, technology adaptation, setting up new enterprises, etc.; or urbanization will evolve around an acceptable state with time after taking into account migration, housing problems, traffic management, infrastructure needs and bottlenecks, and so on.

- *Basin of attraction.* The basin of attraction is defined as the set of all the initial conditions in the phase space whose trajectories or paths go to an attractor state. A phase space or state space is referred to as a space in which all possible unique states of a system are represented. It is the space in which a system can be located during a transition period along a unique trajectory or path. The basin of attraction may be taken as an analogy to gravitational attraction in a physical three-dimensional system, in which all the objects from all the initial conditions in the space are attracted toward the ground, equivalent to an attractor state. The essence of the term basin of attraction is that all the different initial conditions in the phase space reach toward an attractor through feedback from the elements of a system. The elements in the system interact as a result of rules, values, norms, and policies and provide feedback resulting in the emergence of a new pattern or structure, which over time approaches an attractor state (Kauffman 1995; Svyantek and Brown 2000; Elhadj and Sprott 2013).

In the social system, including the economy and organizations, the elements collectively try to settle for a stable state. There may be more than one attractor state in the system during the process of settling, and also, the attractor may change to a new state during the transition (Nowak et al. 2005; Carmichael and Hadzikadi 2019).

Acceptability and robustness of attractor. The attractor states can be characterized *first* by 'width', denoting the span and limit of the reach of the attractor state, supported by a wider basin of attraction, reflecting the number of states that can be directed toward an attractor. It is a measure of the acceptability of the attractor. More width reflects that more states of the system can lead to the attractor state; thus, the attractor has more acceptability. It indicates despite differences in the initial states, the attractor attracts the system dynamics, and the path (trajectory) follows in the direction of the attractor. And *second* by the 'depth', characterizing the robustness, power, or strength of an attractor. As an analogy to a physical system, in terms of potential energy, it will reflect a low energy level. More depth means more robustness, implying that more force is required to disturb the system. It is about the ability to withstand adverse conditions and resist the perturbations in the system. The strength of the attractor can help in overcoming rigorous tests by the environment or internal disturbance. The robustness creates internal dynamic interactions and feedback between elements, which promote the path of initial conditions toward the attractor state, and the perturbations are rejected by the system (Haken 2006; Demongeot et al. 2010; Elhadj and Sprott 2013; Hiver 2014; Carmichael and Hadzikadi 2019).

For example, there may be different conditions in the system regarding the status of education and health due to certain public policies and cultural values. But due to internal dynamics, depending on the basin of attraction, from any initial state of the system, it may converge toward the attractor state. The Kerala State is a case in point. As a result of values and practices in the families over time, society converges toward achieving higher education and health standards. A large part of the system, comprising almost all the families, from rich to poor, from different regions—forward or backward, from highly educated to less educated, representing different states, will reach toward attaining high human resource development. It reflects the acceptability or width of the attractor state. Likewise, more the depth of the attractor reflects higher the stability of the attractor state to sustain disturbance. For example, in the social system, the depth may be determined by deep-rooted values and beliefs in society. These provide strength to the attractor to keep the system stable. It is like a firmly held belief or cultural trait, or impact of successful public policy, which a society or groups in the system give the highest priority or cherish as an ideal. These, in a collective manner, determine the attractor state.

- *Edge of chaos*. In a complex adaptive system, an important phenomenon or a metaphor called the edge of chaos is a transition space between disorder (also called chaos) and order and represents bounded instability. The transition space is marked by the dynamic interactions between order and disorder, and the system evolves into a new state. Normally, for a system to reach a level of transformation, it has to pass through the edge of chaos, a particular state in time and space. It is a new paradigm for the complex system. The concept of the edge of chaos is abstract and figurative. It has many applications in social systems, economy, business, and organizations. Though the word 'chaos' is mentioned, it does not necessarily mean that the system is out of control or cannot be managed. The essence of the word 'chaos' is symbolic, implying that the system is calling for a change or transformation to meet new challenges. Societies, markets, companies, or businesses represent stable states that can change rapidly at any time. Both endogenous and exogenous feedback can cause a nonlinear change in the system behavior, resulting in uncertain behavior. It requires recognizing that systems behave in a stable manner until they reach a critical threshold, called the edge of chaos (Holland 1995; Kauffman 1995; Smith and Humphries 2004).

The edge of chaos has underpinnings of theoretical concepts such as emergence, self-organization, and adaptation. It indicates a transformational effect on the system, which is irreversible. It is like a tipping point or point of inflection, the terms used in management. Such a state arises when either forces within the system or when the influences of the external environment disturb the equilibrium or stable state over time (Youngblood 1997; Smith and Humphries 2004; Houry 2012). Such disturbance or challenge to a public system may arise from social unrest or political movement. In the case of the economy or industry, the challenge may come from market volatility, competition, disruptive technologies, or structural change. For a public organization, due to demands from or changes in the expectations of citizens, the need for altering internal systems or processes may be felt. For business organizations, the need for change arises when the existing processes, structure, technology application, and management systems do not support the changes in the business environment or emerging competition (Brown and Eisenhardt 1998; Pascale 1999).

3.2 Complexity in Socio-Economic Systems: An Overview

Social systems, including social phenomena and subsystems or entities, deal with a large number of heterogeneous individuals, groups, or economic agents within the system. They interact with each other in a natural way for the exchange of ideas, information, and resource; consult each other for advice, learning, and help; and discuss issues of common interests. The system may be economic, government, business, or organization. The subsystems within a system are departments or divisions within government organizations; production centers and divisions within business groups; economic institutions and structures; public organizations, business units, and associations; or social and political groups based on specific shared interests. In general, the elements are referred to as system variables, people, or economic agents (Byrne 1998; Gilstrap 2005; Nordtveit 2007; Mason 2008).

The interactions in the system lead to the emergence of a new phenomenon, which could be urbanization, industrial cluster development, or the stock market, to name a few. They follow their defined and agreed local rules, take inputs from many sources, interact in multiple ways, and are influenced by prevailing work culture at the workplace or in society. As a result of regular interactions, a new thought process emerges, a common understanding is developed based on mutual interests, and a line of the action takes shape. For example, as a result of interactions in the economic system, choices of consumption, savings, and investment emerge; in the government system, a set of values, a pattern of behavior, and the method to undertake certain tasks related to public functions take shape; and in business, practices, processes, and areas of cooperation and competition emerge (Zimmerman et al. 2001; Capra and Luisi 2014).

Some of the basic features of a complex system are as follows (Cleveland 1994; Schneider and Somers 2006; Uhl-Bien et al. 2007):

- A system is an open system with a defined boundary and environment. It has inputs and outputs through the exchange of matter, energy, or information with its surrounding or environment.
- A system comprises distinct elements (individuals and system variables), who form networks in which they engage and interact with each other, as per their rules. The interactions may change as evolution takes place.

3.2 Complexity in Socio-Economic Systems: An Overview

- Due to multiple interactions and nonlinearity, cause-and-effect relationships are not discernible, and it is difficult to know what caused a specific change. Such change is often a combination of various causes (factors) that come together distinctively. For this reason, there is no prior knowledge of emerging behavior. The multitude of interactions results in unpredictable new patterns.
- A complex system is greater or less than the sum of its parts. The system-level (or macro-level) behavior emerges due to interactions between elements. The output is not a linear sum of the parts, but it could be more or less than the sum depending on the system. The property and purpose of the system are distinct from that of the elements, and each element has distinct nature and purpose.

The elements, actors, agents, parts, components, constituents, subsystems, and variables are within a system and are interchangeably used depending on the context. The socio-economic systems—government, economy, business, industry, and organizations—generally deal with individuals, institutions, spatial (geographical features), enabling entities, policies, management (functions), system performance, and environment. Each one of them represents a subsystem (Fig. 3.3). The system and environment can be defined depending upon the context. In the given case, the seven subsystems constitute system. The environment, which is external to system, includes environment within the country and at international level. These eight subsystems are briefly discussed below:

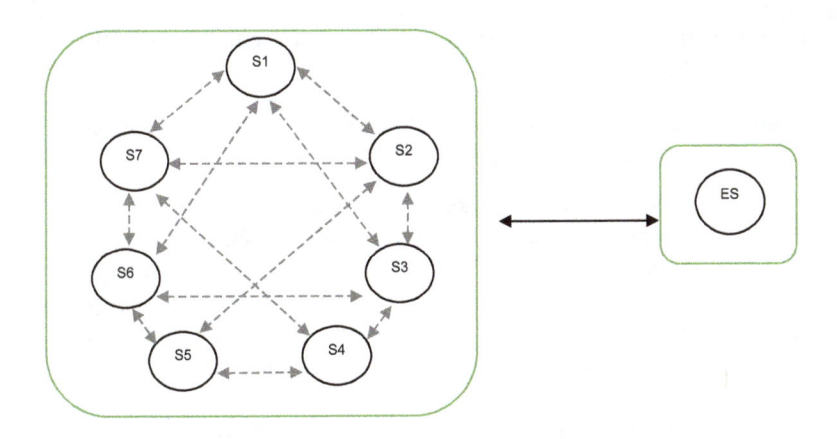

Nodes represent subsystem (s): (O)
Edges represent relationships: (←——→)
S: Subsystem
S1: Individuals; S2: Institutions; S3: Spatial; S4: Enabling entities; S5: Policies; S6: Management; S7: System performance; ES (S8): Environment.

Fig. 3.3 Subsystems' linkages

- *First, individuals.* Socio-economic systems constitute numerous individuals. The individuals directly as economic agents, citizens, officers, staff, or executives interact for the conduct of their affairs as well as the working of their respective systems or organizations. The factors such as knowledge, skills, capabilities, and local rules and norms influence their interactions. The human and social factors matter during the process of interactions.
- *Second, institutions.* Norms of governance regulations, social institutions, political institutions (both formal and informal), values, norms, and structures.
- *Third, spatial (geographical features).* Geographical features like infrastructure, transport, and local resources, including human, mineral, and natural resources.
- *Fourth, enabling entities.* Development sectors, ecosystem, business units, industries, infrastructure, technologies, projects, organizations, departments, and divisions.
- *Fifth, policies.* Various policies, including historical policies and events, strategies, and programs for various sectors, the economy, or the business.
- *Sixth, management (functions).* Functional or operational aspects, including problem solving, strategy formulation, internal management of systems and processes, decision-making, etc., for planning, policymaking, implementation of policies, or running of business and industry.
- *Seventh, system performance.* It represents performance in the form of the creation of infrastructure, industries, business units, and so on.
- *Eighth, environment.* Social and political environment in the country, social capital, international political environment, innovation culture, technological changes, competition, etc.

The system is influenced by interactions of the subsystems and, in turn, influences the subsystems through an interactive process.

Complexity cost. The complexity can add more cost due to the following reasons. *First, decision-making may be difficult.* More complexity means more difficulty in understanding the problems. So the decision-making may take more time or result in wrong decisions if the problem is not correctly analyzed. *Second, confusion in managing system.* Due to the inability to comprehend the problem and system. *Third, unpredictability,* if not managed well, may lead to unintended consequences and costs.

Unique advantages of complexity. Though apparently, the idea of complexity evokes an uncomfortable thought or the possibility of challenging conditions, it can be an advantage for the system if the complexity is understood and addressed in a correct manner (Kelly and Allison1999; Gilstrap 2005; Mckinsey 2007; Nordtveit 2007; Mason 2008; IBM 2010; HBR 2020). Some of the advantages are indicated below:

- *Synergy through multiple interactions of large elements.* Presence of a large number of elements, system variables, or individuals lead to increased complexity. But each element brings unique features and has the potential to provide benefits to the system or an organization if the right kind of enabling conditions are available at the level of interactions. Each addition of a system variable can have

a multiplier effect through interactions between variables and individuals, thus, enhancing the number of possible outcomes. It has implications for education, health, and climate change, in which complementing and converging policies and programs with the engagement of multiple individuals (stakeholders) can create conditions for higher performance and better results. What is of importance is interactions between policies, programs, and stakeholders. Such interactions may give rise to possibilities of new solutions, generate synergy, or create a cascading effect, which may lead to the emergence of success if rightly managed.
- *Leveraging diversity.* Diversity leads to complexity but can be an opportunity, as people with diverse backgrounds or capabilities may add distinct inputs or values. These may not be available to a limited number of people. For promoting innovation, divergent thinking is required, and a team with diverse skill sets can be helpful. For example, in Industry 4.0, a host of technologies are integrated, resulting in the emergence of new innovative products. It is a result of the understanding of the efficacy of technologies and their interactions and complementarities.
- *Unlocking hidden potential.* If examined critically and comprehensively, complexity can provide insights that are otherwise difficult to discern and, thus, unlock hidden potential. Through in-depth inquiry, it can lead to more scope for improvement or stimulate innovation.
- *Competitive advantage.* If the complexity is understood and solved, it may provide a competitive advantage to a business. For example, the more complex the product or IT application developed after understanding the complex issues, the more difficult it becomes for the competitors to copy. The advantage could be due to discerning insights from the customers, designing customized products with special features, or developing unique and personalized service delivery.

3.3 Complexity in Policy System

Since the 1990s, realizing the complexity in the policy system and policymaking process, policy studies brought focus on the 'system', while examining public policies in the social and economic sectors (Rihani and Geyer 2001; Jones 2011; Eppel and Rhodes 2018). Relying on the system studies, there has been growing interest in scrutinizing deeper issues in public policy—both social and economic. It was felt that various social and economic problems were not addressed systemically, and the public policies were not adequate enough to meet the challenges that people and the economy faced (Colander and Kupers 2016; OECD 2017). With the increase in scholarly work on understanding complexity in policymaking and implementation, the complexity analysis got increased recognition and acceptability (Ryan 2011; Liening 2013; Morcol 2012; Hill and Varone 2016).

The studies have reflected that the policy system is marked by emergent behavior, self-organizing property, and path dependency. In such a system, cause-effect linkages are not discernible. The system is far from equilibrium, and there are conditions of uncertainty (Arthur et al. 1997; Ryan 2011; Eppel and Rhodes 2018). Furthermore, the policymaking process has seen complexity due to numerous diverse groups leading to fuzziness in defining the boundary; behavioral complexity within the policy system as a result of interactions, conflicting interests, emotions, and variations in knowledge and competence among stakeholders and policymakers; dynamic and emerging problems; and need for introducing changes in policy decisions during policy cycle. These new findings on the properties of the policy system necessitated the application of concepts of complexity in policymaking and implementation for addressing emerging development challenges (Gerrits 2012; Subroto 2015; Mueller 2020).

Earlier, the policy system was considered predictable and controllable by the policymakers. Such understanding influenced strategies and policies that were not in alignment with the reality of uncertainty, dynamic nature, and emergence at the grassroots or implementation level. Subsequently, with enhanced research in complex systems, the complexity dimension has been recognized in policymaking, and a new perspective has been added to examine and manage the interdependent variables and stakeholders and the dynamic nature of the policy system (Osman 2002; Lipsky 2010; Jones 2011; Geyer and Cairney 2015).

Complexity in policymaking: basic issues. Social systems deal with a web of stakeholders, behavioral issues, individual attributes, initial conditions of families and communities, locational effects, history, institutional factors, economic security, and so on. At the operational level, systems consist of multiple problems, competing and conflicting interests of stakeholders, and linkages of many sectors. The multiple interactions of diverse agents, contexts, and problems characterize social systems. There are continuous nonlinear and dynamic interactions between the elements or people. Many variables in the system cannot be quantified. Due to the qualitative nature of variables, nonlinear relationships, multiple interactions, and feedback loops, causal relationships cannot be determined. The complex social system is greater or less than the sum of its parts depending upon the feedback loops. The positive feedback loop can lead to increasing returns, and system behavior is more than that of the sum of parts, while the negative feedback loop will have the opposite effect.

The interactions between elements take place at a local level, not through central control. It can result in the emergence of a new pattern of behavior or structure. With time, due to interactions, emergence, and adaptation, the system may self-organize in different states. It is the fundamental point of the complexity approach. The interactions create contingency and uncertainty about the future state of the system, and as a result, the social system is not static but dynamic and remains in a state of flux. And the state keeps changing. It is this nature that needs to be recognized.

The macro- or system-level behavior emerges from the activities and behavior of the constituent parts of the system. Against the backdrop of the emerging paradigm of complexity, the policy system needs to work with a new perspective (Gilstrap 2005; Mason 2008; Eppel and Rhodes 2018; Mueller 2020; Byrne 1998). The studies (Jones 2011; Mueller 2020) indicate that in the public system, complexity is observed in various sectors like urban management, pollution management, land use planning and management, health system, financial markets, and environment management, to

3.3 Complexity in Policy System

name a few. Policymaking is demanding in an uncertain and complex public system, as evident from a few highlighted emerging situations, such as frequent fluctuations in the production and prices of agricultural products, metals, oil, and gas, within the country and at the global level; global warming and climate change and their impact on livelihood and economy; and potential for social unrest due to jobs losses, as a consequence of the application of advanced technologies and prospective large scale automation.

The public policy system is majorly constituted of eight subsystems:

- *First, individuals.* Numerous stakeholders like citizens, groups, community-based organizations (CBOs), non-governmental organizations (NGOs), political groups, industry, and business organizations. There are diverse interests and values of stakeholders. The interests may be cooperative, competing, and conflicting.
- *Second, institutions.* Social institutions, political institutions, judicial institutions, development institutions, values, norms, etc.
- *Third, spatial (geographical features).* Locational features and local problems and resources.
- *Fourth, enabling entities.* Various sectors and departments like education, health, sanitation, environment, urban development, industry, finance, and so on at National, State, and local levels.
- *Fifth, policies*: Various policies within a sector and other interlinked sectors.
- *Sixth, management (functions).* Administrative functions; internal management systems, processes, structures, principles, and approaches; examination of problem issues; and functional or operational aspects for policymaking, policy implementation, and evaluation.
- *Seventh, system performance.* Performance of past and current policies under different sectors.
- *Eighth, environment.* Socio-economic and political factors at the local as well as macro levels (including within country and at international level).

On account of interactions between stakeholders and variables, the combination of the above subsystems impacts the behavior of the policy system.

Web of policies in policy system: While examining the system under the current policymaking approach, another aspect has been related to the examination of the system or problems in parts or by separating different constituents, or by studying policies independently but not in an integrated manner. For example, the previous approaches study the policies in isolation. There has been little appreciation for how one policy, in interaction with other policies, can make a difference. The study of one policy is not sufficient to understand its likely impact unless it is examined in the context of other policies.

For complex systems, it is necessary to understand both the integrated view of policies and interactive effects of various interlinked policies (refer to Sect. 3.2). Besides, what is to be recognized is that during the interactions between policies, the relationships cannot be discerned due to nonlinearity, feedback, and circular causality. As an illustration, the interactive effect of policies in the network is captured by equation (Fig. 3.4):

Fig. 3.4 A representative view of interactions of policies

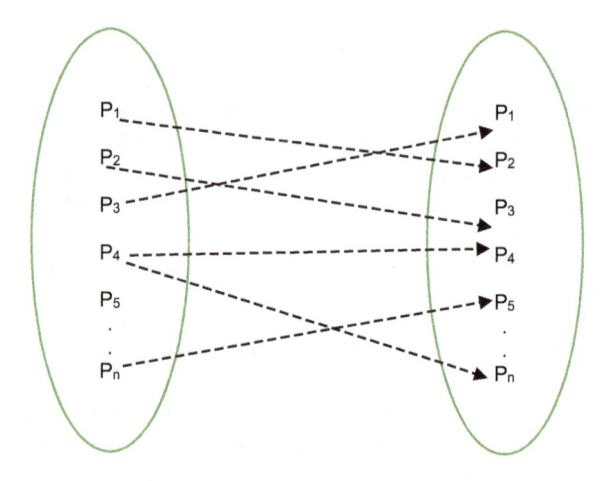

$$Y = f(P_1, P_2, P_3, \ldots P_n);$$

Y is the output and P represents the policy. The function (f) represents the interactions.

Or,

$$Y = \text{Interactive effects } (P_{12}, P_{13}, P_{14} \ldots; P_{123}, P_{124}, P_{125} \ldots;$$
$$P_{1234}, \ldots; P_{12345}, \ldots; \ldots P_{123\ldots n}).$$

For example, P_{12} reflects the interaction between policy P_1 and policy P_2.

By looking at the network of policies, a significant number of interactions are possible, and such a complex web of interactions makes the system complex and non-comprehendible. In addition, there are numerous other interactions between individuals, variables, and institutions. Understanding interactive effects is a major challenge that conventional methods have not dealt with so far.

3.4 Complexity in Economy

Complexity science emerged during the 1960s while studying complex and dynamic systems. With time, understanding of properties of complex systems encouraged the application of complexity in economics. It began with the research program at Santa Fe Institute in the 1980s, which led to the scientific inception of complexity economics under the scholarships of George Cowan, Murray Gell-Mann, Herb Anderson, and Brian Arthur, among others (Arthur et al. 1997). At the institute, based on research, a new way of thinking about the economy as an evolving and complex system was advanced.

It underscored that the economy evolves from the interactions of numerous agents and economic variables, who continually learn and adapt to changing conditions and environment. The behavior of agents coevolves with others. Likewise, many economic policies, institutions, and entities interact. Economic policies cover savings, consumption, investment, foreign investment, etc., that impact economic activities through interactive effects. Institutions are like laws, rules, norms, values, and financial and public institutions. Examples of economic entities are markets, firms, industrial ecosystem, and entrepreneurs' networks. The economic activities, through interactions, continue to change and create the structures like markets, institutions, and policies through feedback loops between agents and stakeholders at various levels—micro, meso, and macro (Kirman 2011; Arthur 2014; OECD 2017).

The existing economic theories work under many assumptions like perfect information, homogeneous nature of agents, rational choice of individuals, and equilibrium state, which are not realistic in the diverse, uncertain, and dynamic economic world. The standard economic equilibrium model has been analyzing economic systems based on rational optimizing individuals, the availability of perfect information, and the optimum role of the market in resource allocation. While examining dynamic stochastic general equilibrium (DSGE) models or mainstream economic theories, studies have highlighted that they have been short of taking into account the heterogeneous behavior of agents, dynamic interactions between agents and economic entities, the role of institutions, feedback, network effects, uncertainty, and linkages between micro-level developments and macro-level outcomes (North 2005; Kapoor 2017; OECD 2017).

Another limitation of these theories and models is that they cannot address nonlinearity resulting from interacting agents or external factors. In addition, the conventional economic policy approach has been deficient in considering three aspects—human behavior, bounded rationality, and institutional factors of a social system. It assumes importance as the economy works in a social system, which cannot be detached from the economy. Human behavior largely depends on social institutions, culture, values, and cognitive and psychological factors. It is hard to predict human behavior and quantify behavior in mathematical models. Bounded rationality makes decision-making far from perfection or rationality. In addition, public institutions and governance can create enabling conditions for enhanced economic activities. There are many behavioral and psychological variables like personal taste, emotions, family security, future needs, health needs, beliefs, cognitive biases, etc. These impact the decisions in social and economic areas, and even social activities affect economic activities. In economic theories and models, such issues and variables are not captured. Therefore, any economic theory ignoring these aspects will be unable to provide a cogent explanation for the economy (North 1990; Simon 1991; Acemoglu and Robinson 2010; Kirman 2011).

Economic complexity offers an alternative paradigm to understand problems from a different perspective by examining hidden possibilities due to the interactive effects of heterogeneous economic agents, skill sets, technologies, institutions, and entities. The underlying idea is that economic activities, development, technological change, economic growth, income pattern, and geographical advantages are a consequence of unforeseen realities (Arthur 2014; Balland et al. 2022).

So far, the approach in economics has been to aggregate data in which the information is collapsed by adding up different entries. For example, in the case of employment, the data related to employment for different sections of the population, age groups, and sectors are added up. In contrast, economic complexity appreciates the granular (micro level) or agent level data that is more than just aggregate data. Similarly, economics has not been able to provide the link between the causes of the impact of technologies on growth. It does not examine the role of the creativity of economic agents and the interactive effects of technologies on economic activities. These limit the exact understanding of the problem. It tends to explain the impact of technology as a total factor productivity parameter in an aggregate form (Wang et al. 2012; Sjotun et al. 2020).

The economic system has eight distinct subsystems, as briefly outlined below:

- *First, individuals*. Numerous economic agents as investors and millions of entrepreneurs are in industrial, business, and financial activities.
- *Second, institutions*. Central Bank, financial institutions, banking institutions, foreign exchange regulator, stock market exchange, regulatory agencies for insurance and stock market, etc.
- *Third, spatial (geographical features)*. Locational features, including distance factor, local resources, infrastructure, historical economic activities, etc.
- *Fourth, enabling entities*. Multiple sectors and economic entities locally, nationally, and globally; networks of economic activities in multiple locations; ecosystem; and several firms, could be in thousands in an industrial estate or zone and millions globally in a variety of sectors (which may run over hundred) such as automobiles, electronics, pharmaceuticals, ICT, and so on.
- *Fifth, policies*. Economic policies on savings and consumption, investment, foreign investment, trade, monetary and fiscal management, taxation, etc.
- *Sixth, management (functions)*. Economic policymaking process and policy management.
- *Seventh*, system performance. Investment, employment, industrial output, economic growth, etc.
- *Eighth, environment*. Global politics, economic environment, global competition, trade policies of major countries, climate change, multilateral trade agreements, and disruptive innovations and technologies.

These subsystems comprehensively cover underlying issues in the economic system. As a result of the interactions between subsystems, the economy evolves.

3.5 Complexity in Business

Currently, many businesses are qualitatively different from what they were a few years ago in the 2000s and entirely different from what they were in the 1960s, before the advent of the electronics era. The combined effect of factors, such as faster innovations, increasing competition, shorter product life cycles, exponential increase in the flow of data, need for higher productivity and quality, and the just-in-time product delivery, has been of little time available with the business to respond and manage the change. These made the decision-making process and operations a complex exercise for the business (IBM 2010; Ismail et al. 2014; HBR 2015).

The complexity in the business is driven by many interlinked factors such as abrupt changes in technologies and their unique efficacy, giving disproportionate advantages to some businesses; increasing needs of customers for specific features and customized products; supply chain management due to multi-country production of parts and transportation; market volatility about the demand and supply of input materials and final products; mergers and acquisitions; and multiple structures and processes. These factors have made decision-making challenging. Due to uncertainty and competition, a large number of businesses are closing down. At the same time, many tech-based startups are reaching a level of unicorn and decacorn in a short period (Kelly and Allison 1999; Ismail et al. 2014; Turner and Baker 2019).

The studies have suggested that the world in which businesses work is volatile, uncertain, and complex. Due to enhanced interconnected businesses, economies, societies, and governments, there is a rise in complexity, but many new opportunities have also surfaced. The trend toward globalization, technology disruption, shifting of industrial and business activities from both developed and developing countries, and increased standards and regulations will further add to the complexity (Mckinsey 2007; Nordtveit 2007; IBM 2010; Rees 2019; HBR 2020).

The business system constitutes the following subsystems:

- *First, individuals.* Numerous stakeholders like customers, suppliers, investors, and competitors at different locations—local, National, and international levels.
- *Second, institutions.* Corporate governance, regulations, values, and norms; regulatory institutions, etc.
- *Third, spatial (geographical features).* Country-specific features like resource endowments, infrastructure, ease of transportation, supply chain, etc.
- *Fourth, enabling entities.* Ecosystem, infrastructure, manpower availability, technologies, finance, labor market, etc.
- *Fifth, policies*: For business promotions, policies, programs, and incentives.
- *Sixth, management (functions).* Management models and practices, quality management system, performance management, supply chain management, and production and delivery of customized products at multiple locations.
- *Seventh, system performance.* Number of units, turnover, profits, exports, employment generation, etc.
- *Eighth, environment.* Socio-economic and political factors impacting the business ecosystem; country-specific policies and regulations for starting businesses;

market volatility, globalization, mergers and acquisitions; technology innovations, competition, and so on.

The above subsystems interact with each other dynamically, and their interactions result in the emergence of the system of business at different levels.

3.6 Complexity in Public and Business Organizations

All organizations—social, political, government, educational, economic, and business—comprise elements or constituents like people, structures, systems, and processes. These have external environment. The environment constitutes elements such as technology, global issues, competition, social-cultural factors, political thinking, rules, laws, government policies, climate change, etc. Due to human nature within the organization, there are organic linkages among people, leading to social bonds. These elements interact with each other and the environment based on shared values, beliefs, and concerns. The interactions lead to feedback mechanisms, which, due to need of corrections, lead to the process of change and the dynamic nature of the system. The emerging behavior or output of the organization is not predictable. As a dynamic system, it makes the organization a complex entity (Coleman 1999; Pascale 1999; Tsoukas and Hatch 2001; Uhl-Bien et al. 2007).

Globalization, information technology, local and global competition, workforce diversity, quality standards, and disruptive innovation impact organizations. It is essential in the context of when many business organizations are getting dissolved or applying for bankruptcy at a faster rate due to several factors, such as intense competition, technological disruptions, and the inability of the organizations to adapt and manage change (Stacey 1996; Ismail et al. 2014; Dobbs et al. 2015; Sapir 2020). In the case of the public system, citizen expectations are changing and putting demands on public organizations to deliver. New problems such as climate change, unemployment, or inflation keep surfacing while organizations find it hard to cope with the new expectations. The complexity dimension demands exploring new thinking and finding ways to define new theory and strategies to meet challenges in the twenty-first century.

Why public and business organizations need to learn complexity: In the light of industrial psychology dealing with behavioral issues, organizational dynamics, functional roles, and internal and external environment, organizations are complex social systems. In addition, there is complexity because of nonlinear and dynamic interactions between individuals, structures, departments and units, and the environment. Such interactions are not simple and keep on changing and evolving.

With the rising expectations and the need to reach out to distant geographical areas, the number and size of public organizations are increasing. It results in multiple stakeholders like beneficiaries, *panchayats* (local village-level bodies) and urban

3.6 Complexity in Public and Business Organizations

local bodies, and civil society organizations (CSOs) in numerous locations. In addition, it leads to the creation of multiple agencies and departments at various levels. These, in a combined form, add to the complexity.

Likewise, business organizations, with their footprints in multiple locations, are required to deal with a large customer base, suppliers, competitors, regulators, investors, and media. They have entities like divisions, business verticals, plants, logistics, infrastructure, subsidiaries, and joint ventures. The studies (Price 2004; McKinsey 2007 and 2010; EIU 2015) show that the primary sources of complexity in the business organization are structure, the pace of innovation, decision-making processes, overall size, global competition, data handling, work culture, logistics, and technology management; networks of interactions; and sharing of resources like personnel, budget, equipments, etc. in different divisions, projects, locations, or teams. Also, nonlinear and dynamic relationships between various elements or people give rise to an additional source of complexity.

Any organization, at the basic level, be it public or business, faces complexity due to three distinct factors: speed, scale, and scope. The *speed* is due to rapid changes in advanced technologies, instant communication, pressing health issues, climate change, etc. For example, the disruption in industries is a result of automation and its adverse impact on employment; the ramification of the spread of communicable diseases on the health system; the consequences of recurring fluctuations in manufacturing at the global level on the local economies, etc. All these demand calibrating strategies continuously for public organizations. Similarly, the *scale* is on account of a manifold increase in the number of beneficiaries and enhancing the reach to a bigger base of citizens and a much larger geographical region. The *scope* is due to the need to cover more issues or sectors, thus necessitating the introduction of new development programs and schemes. These tend to multiply the database and MIS requirements at multiple levels, which make the coordination, decision-making, and execution of programs a complex proposition.

Likewise, for business organizations, the *speed* is due to rapid changes in the global environment and technological innovation. For example, new advanced technologies have an impact on higher value addition of products and raising productivity level. These are likely to tilt the terms of trade in favor of developed countries, resulting in the reshoring or shifting of production units back to the country of origin. These will require calibrating the internal strategies of business organizations on a continuous and urgent basis, thus putting organizations under constant scrutiny. The *scale* is mainly due to dealing with a large customer base. The *scope* is because of introducing new products to an increased number of customers in different countries for more opportunities.

Both public and business organizations deal with the following distinct and interlinked subsystems:

- *First, individuals.* Many personnel and their interpersonal issues. Interactions in many ways at various levels, from local to National.
- *Second, institutions.* Rules, structures, values, and norms; government institutions, etc.

- *Third, spatial (geographical features).* Location of different organizations at various levels.
- *Fourth, enabling entities.* Multiple departments in the government. Business organizations at various geographical locations within the country as well as at the global level.
- *Fifth, policies.* Policies and programs for managing the organizations.
- *Sixth, management (functions).* Human resource management, financial management, logistics, functional management, and monitoring system.
- *Seventh, system performance.* Performance management system (PMS) for monitoring and managing performance.
- *Eighth, environment.* Socio-economic and political issues; competition, new business models, etc.; citizens, beneficiaries, and media in the social system, external to public organizations; customers, suppliers, regulators, investors, technological changes, competitors, and media external to business organizations.

Due to interactions of people in an organization, the above subsystems interact and result in the emergence of the organization's behavior.

References

Aarset B, Jakobsen S. Path dependency, institutionalization and co-evolution: The missing diffusion of the blue revolution in Norwegian Aquaculture. J Rural Stud. 2015;41 :37–46. https://doi.org/10.1016/j.jrurstud.2015.07.001

Acemoglu D, and Robinson J. The role of institutions in growth and development. Rev Econ Inst. 2010;1(2). http://www.rei.unipg.it/rei/article/view/14

Allen PM. Self-organization in economic systems; 2007. https://www.researchgate.net/publication/258506789

Almudi I, Fatas-Villafranca F. Coevolution in economic systems. Elem Evol Econ. 2021. https://doi.org/10.1017/9781108767798.

Anderson PW, Arrow KJ, Pines D, editors. The economy as an evolving complex system (Santa Fe Institute Series). CRC Press; 1988.

Arthur WB. Complexity and the economy. Oxford University Press; 2014.

Arthur WB. Complexity economics: a different framework for economic thought; 2013. https://www.santafe.edu/research/results/working-papers/complexity-economics-a-different-framework-for-eco

Arthur WB, Durlauf SN, Lane D, editors. The economy as an evolving complex system II (Santa Fe Institute Series). CRC Press; 1997.

Avnimelech G, Teubal M. The Indian software industry from an Israeli perspective: a systems/evolutionary and policy view. In: Anthony P. D'Costa, Sridharan E, editors. The global software industry: innovation, firm strategies and development. Palgrave Macmillan; 2003.

Baetu TM. Emergence, therefore antireductionism? Critique Emergent Antireductionism Biol Philos. 2012;27(3):433–48.

Balland PA, Broekel T, Diodato D, Giuliani E, Hausmann R, O'Clery N, Rigby D. The new paradigm of economic complexity. Res Policy. 2022;51(3):104568. https://doi.org/10.1016/j.respol.2021.104450

Bar-Yam Y. Dynamics of complex systems. Colorado: Westview Press Boulder; 1997.

References

Benbya H, McKelvey B. Using coevolutionary and complexity theories to improve IS alignment: a multi-level approach. Journal of Information Technology. 2006; 21:284–298. (file:///C:/Users/SONY/Downloads/SSRN-id1560603.pdf)

Boulding KE. Conflict and defense: a general theory. New York: Harper & Brothers; 1962.

Boulton JG, Allen PM, Bowman C. Embracing complexity: strategic perspectives for an age of turbulence. Oxford University Press; 2015.

Breslin D. What evolves in organizational co-evolution? J Manag Governance 2014. https://www.researchgate.net/publication/260266050

Brown SL, Eisenhardt KM. Competing on the edge: strategy as structured chaos. Boston: Harvard Business School Press; 1998.

Brownlee J. Complex adaptive systems technical report 070302A; 2007. http://citeseerx.ist.psu.edu/viewdoc/download?doi=10.1.1.70.7345&rep=rep1&type=pdf

Byrne DS. Complexity theory and the social sciences: an introduction. New York: Routledge; 1998.

Cairney P, Geyer R. A critical discussion of complexity theory how does complexity thinking improve our understanding of politics and policymaking? Complex Gov Netw. 2017; 3(2). https://doi.org/10.20377/cgn-56

Cairney P. Understanding public policy: theories and issues. Palgrave Macmillan: Textbooks in Policy Studies; 2012.

Capra F, Luisi P. The Newtonian world-machine. In: The systems view of life: a unifying vision. Cambridge University Press; 2014. https://doi.org/10.1017/CBO9780511895555.004

Carmichael T, Hadzikadi M. The fundamentals of complex adaptive systems; 2019. https://www.researchgate.net/publication/333780588

Cecere G, Corrocher N, Gossart C, Ozman M. Lock-in and path dependence: an evolutionary approach to eco-innovations. J Evol Econ. 2014. https://muge.wp.imt.fr/files/2014/03/lock_in.pdf

Chan S. Complex adaptive systems; 2001. https://web.mit.edu/esd.83/www/notebook/Complex%20Adaptive%20Systems.pdf

Checkland P. Systems thinking, systems practice. Chichester: John Wiley and Sons; 1981.

Chen D, Stroup W. General systems theory: toward a conceptual framework for science and technology education for all. J Sci Edu Technol. 1993;2(7).

Chikere CC, Nwoka J. The systems theory of management in modern day organizations. Int J Sci Res Publ. 2015; 5(9). ISSN 2250-3153. www.ijsrp.org

Cleveland J. Basic concepts and application to systems thinking. Innov. Netw. Commun. 1994. https://cupdf.com/document/complexity-theory-by-john-cleveland.html

Colander D, Kupers R. Complexity and the art of public policy—solving society's problems from the bottom up. Princeton University Press; 2016.

Coleman HJ. What enables self-organizing behavior in businesses. Emergence J Complex Issues Org Manag. 1999; 1(1).

Coyle RG. Management system dynamics. London: John Wiley & Sons; 1977.

D'Costa AP. Export growth and path-dependence: the locking-in of innovations in the software industry. In: D'Costa AP and Sridharan E, editors India in the global software industry: innovation, firm strategies and development. Palgrave Macmillan; 2003.

Dafermos M. In book: Encyclopedia of critical psychology. In: Teo T, editor. Reductionism. Springer, Berlin; 2014. (Downloads/ReductionismFV.pdf)

Demongeot J, Goles E, Morvan M, Noual M, Sené S. Attraction basins as gauges of robustness against boundary conditions in biological complex systems; 2010. https://doi.org/10.1371/journal.pone.0011793

Dickson M, Resick C, Hanges P. When organizational climate is unambiguous, it is also strong. J Appl Psychol. 2006;91(2):351–64. https://doi.org/10.1037/0021-9010.91.2.351.

Dobbs R, Manyika J, Woetze J. No ordinary disruption: four global forces breaking all the trends. Public Affairs; 2015.

Dolan SL, Garcia S, Diegoli S, Auerbach A. Organizational values as attractors of chaos: an emerging cultural change to manage organizational complexity. J Econ Literature Classification: D23, M14, O33; 2000. https://www.minessence.net/Articles/valuesasAttractors.pdf

Economist Intelligence Unit (EIU) Limited. Taming organisational complexity: start at the top. Economist; 2015.

Ehsani S. The challenges of purely mechanistic models in biology and the minimum need for a mechanism-plus-X framework; 2018. https://arxiv.org/ftp/arxiv/papers/1905/1905.10916.pdf

Elhadj Z, Sprott JC. About universal basins of attraction in high-dimensional systems. Int J Bifurcat Chaos. 2013;23(12):1350197. (World Scientific Publishing Company). https://doi.org/10.1142/S0218127413501976

Eppel E, Rhodes ML. Complexity theory and public management: a 'becoming' field. Public Manag Rev. 2018; 20(7):949–959. https://doi.org/10.1080/14719037.2017.1364414

Fernandez EO, de Cabo RM, Jaramillo JMV. The new complex perspective in economic analysis and business management. In: Reframing complexity—perspectives from the north and south. Mansfield, ISCE Publishing; 2007.

Forrester JW. Industrial dynamics. Pegasus Communications, Waltham; 1961.

Gerrits L. Punching clouds: an introduction to the complexity of public decision making. Litchfield Park: Emergent Publication; 2012.

Geyer R, Cairney P, editors. Handbook on complexity and public policy (handbooks of research on public policy series). Edward Elgar Publishing; 2015.

Gharajedaghi J. Systems thinking: managing chaos and complexity: a platform for designing business architecture. Morgan Kaufmann; 2011.

Gigante AA. Reviewing path dependence theory in economics: micro–foundations of endogenous change processes. MPRA Paper No. 75310; 2016. https://mpra.ub.uni-muenchen.de/75310/

Gilstrap D. Strange attractors and human interaction: leading complex organizations through the use of metaphors. Complicity Int J Complex Edu. 2005; 2(1). http://soar.wichita.edu/handle/10057/6951

Goldstein J. Emergence as a construct: history and issues. Emergence 1999; 1(1). https://doi.org/10.1207/s15327000em0101_4

Grobman GM. Complexity theory: a new way to look at organizational change. Publ Adm Q Fall. 2005; 29(3). (ABI/INFORM Global).

Haken H. Information and self-organization: a macroscopic approach to complex systems. New York: Springer; 2006.

Hayek FA. Studies in philosophy, politics and economics. Routledge; 1967.

Hazy JK, Goldstein JA, Lichtenstein BB. Complex systems leadership theory new perspectives from complexity science on social and organizational effectiveness. ISCE Publishing; 2007.

HBR. The business case for managing complexity; 2015. https://hbr.org/resources/pdfs/comm/sap/19277_HBR_SAP_Report_5.pdf

HBR. Taming complexity: make sure the benefits of any addition to an organization's systems outweigh its costs by Martin Reeves, Simon Levin, Thomas Fink, and Ania Levina; 2020. (https://hbr.org/2020/01/taming-complexity).

Hill M, Varone F. The public policy process. Routledge; 2016.

Hiver P. Attractor states. In: Dörnyei Z, MacIntyre P, Henry A, editors. Motivational dynamics in language learning (Second Language Acquisition Book 81). Multilingual Matters; 2014. https://www.researchgate.net/publication/269400183

Holland J. Hidden order: how adaptation builds complexity. Helix Books; 1995.

Houry SA. Chaos and organizational emergence: towards short term predictive modeling to navigate a way out of chaos. Syst Eng Procedia. 2012; 3:229–239. https://doi.org/10.1016/j.sepro.2011.11.025

Huygens M, Baden-Fuller C, Van Den Bosch FAJ, Volberda HW. Coevolution of firm capabilities and industry competition: investigating the music industry 1877–1997; 2001. https://doi.org/10.1177/0170840601226004

References

IBM. Capitalizing on complexity: insights from the global chief executive officer study; 2010. https://www.ibm.com/downloads/cas/1VZV5X8J

Ismael J. Determinism, counterpredictive devices, and the impossibility of Laplacean intelligences. The Monist. 2019; 102. https://doi.org/10.1093/monist/onz021

Ismail S, Malone MS, Geest YV. Exponential organizations. Diversion Books; 2014.

Jones H. Taking responsibility for complexity: how implementation can achieve results in the face of complex problems Working Paper 330. Overseas Development Institute; 2011. https://www.odi.org/sites/odi.org.uk/files/odi-assets/publications-opinion-files/6485.pdf

Kapoor S. The rising complexity of the global economy. In: Debate the issues: complexity and policy making. OECD publications; 2017. https://www.oecd.org/naec/complexity_and_policy making.pdf

Kapur K. The causes and consequences of India's IT boom. India Rev. 2002; 2. Frank Cass London. https://casi.sas.upenn.edu

Kauffman S. At home in the universe: the search for the laws of self organization and complexity. Oxford University Press; 1995.

Kauffman SA. The origins of order: self-organization and selection in evolution. Oxford University Press; 1993.

Kelly S, Allison M. The complexity advantage: how the science of complexity can help your business achieve peak performance. McGraw-Hill; 1999.

Kirman A. Complex economics: individual and collective rationality. Routledge; 2011.

Koliba C, Gerrits L, Rhodes ML, Meek JW. Complexity theory and systems analysis, Chapter 31. In: Ansell C, Torfing J, editors. Handbook on theories of governance. Edward Elgar Publishing; 2016. https://doi.org/10.4337/9781782548508

Krugman PR. The self-organizing economy. Cambridge: Blackwell Publishers; 1996.

Krugman P. Increasing returns and economic geography. J Polit Econ. 1991; 99(3).

Kuhmonen T. Exposing the attractors of evolving complex adaptive systems by utilising futures images: milestones of the food sustainability journey; 2016. https://www.researchgate.net/publication/307557847

Kuhn T. The structure of scientific revolutions. University of Chicago Press; 1962.

Liebowitz SJ, Margolis SE. Path dependence, lock-in, and history. J Law Econ Org. 1995.

Liening A. The breakdown of the traditional mechanistic worldview, the development of complexity sciences and the pretence of knowledge in economics. Modern Econ. 2013; 04(04).

Lipsky M. Street-level bureaucracy: dilemmas of the individual in public services. Russell Sage Foundation; 2010.

Marks P, Gerrits L (2017). Introduction: On the coevolution of innovation and public policy in Complexity, Governance & Networks - Special Issue: Complexity, Innovation and Policy (2017) 2–6 Introduction: On the coevolution of innovation and public policy. https://doi.org/10.20377/cgn-38

Mason M. What is complexity theory and what are its implications for educational change? In: Educational philosophy and theory, special issue: complexity theory and education, vol. 40, no 1; 2008.

Mazzocchi F. Complexity in biology: exceeding the limits of reductionism and determinism using complexity theory. EMBO Rep. 2008;9:10–4.

Mc Millan E. Complexity. Organizations and Change: Routledge Publications; 2004.

McKelvey B. Managing coevolutionary dynamics: some leverage points. In: Presented at the 18th EGOS conference, Barcelona, 4–6 July; 2002. https://www.researchgate.net/publication/228559005

Mckinsey. How do I manage the complexity in my organization? By Heywood S, Hillar R, Turnbull D; 2010.

Mckinsey (2007). Cracking the complexity code. By Heywood S, Spungin J, Turnbull D. The McKinsey Quarterly 2007.

Miles RE, Snow CC, Mathews JA, Miles G, Coleman HJ Jr. Organizing in the knowledge age: anticipating the cellular form. Acad Manag Executive. 1997; 11.

Mitchell M. Complexity: a guided tour. Oxford University Press; 2009.

Morcol G. A complexity theory for public policy Routledge research in public administration and public policy. Routledge; 2012.

Morecroft JDW. System dynamics: portraying bounded rationality. OMEGA. 1983; 11(2).

Mueller B. Why public policies fail: policymaking under complexity. EconomiA. 2020; 21(2). https://doi.org/10.1016/j.econ.2019.11.002

Newman L. Human–environment interactions: Complex systems approaches for dynamic sustainable development. In: Meyers R, editor. Encyclopedia of complexity and systems science. Springe; 2009. p. 4631–43.

Nordtveit B. Complexity theory in development, vol. 55. Center for International Education Faculty Publications. 2007. https://scholarworks.umass.edu/cie_faculty_pubs/55

North DC. Understanding the process of economic change. The Princeton economic history of the western world. Princeton University Press; 2005.

North DC. Institutions, institutional change and economic performance. Cambridge University Press; 1990.

Nowak A, Vallacher RR, Zochowski M. The emergence of personality: dynamic foundations of individual variation. Dev Rev. 2005;25:351–85.

OECD. Debate the issues: complexity and policy making. OECD Publications. (https://www.oecd.org/naec/complexity_and_policymaking.pdf).

Osman FA. Public policy making: theories and their implications in developing countries; 2002. https://www.researchgate.net/publication/253836498_public_policy_making_theories_and_their_implications_in_developing_countries

Palmberg K (2009). Complex Adaptive Systems: Properties and approaches as metaphors for organizational management The Learning Organization Vol. 16 No. 6. https://doi.org/10.1108/09696470910993954

Pascale RT. Surfing the edge of chaos; 1999. https://sloanreview.mit.edu/article/surfing-the-edge-of-chaos/

Peters BG, Pierre J. Governance without government? Rethinking public administration. J Publ Adm Res Theory. 1998;8(2):223–43.

Pierson P. Increasing returns, path dependence, and the study of politics. Am Political Sci Rev. 2000; 94(2).

Pollitt C, Bouckaert G. Public management reform: a comparative analysis. Oxford University Press; 2004.

Potts J. The new evolutionary microeconomics: complexity, competence and adaptive behavior. Edward Elgar; 2000.

Price I. Complexity, complicatedness and complexity: a new science behind organizational intervention? Emerg Complex Org ECO Spec Double Issue. 2004; 6(1–2).

Prigogine I, Stengers I. Order out of chaos: man's new dialogue with nature. London: Flamingo Edition; 1984.

Ramalingam B. Aid on the edge of chaos: rethinking international cooperation in a complex world. Oxford University Press; 2015.

Rees B. Why complexity is a good thing; 2019. https://uxplanet.org/why-complexity-is-a-good-thing-390ac180a3a6

Rihani S, Geyer R. Complexity: an appropriate framework for development? Prog Dev Stud. 2001;1:237–45.

Rihani S. Complexity theory: a new framework for development is in the offing. Progress Dev Stud. 2005; 5(1). https://doi.org/10.1191/1464993405ps101pr

Ronn H. Complexity and leadership: conceptual and competency implications; 2011. https://core.ac.uk/download/pdf/37344933.pdf

Rosenberg A. Darwinian reductionism: how to stop worrying and love molecular biology. University of Chicago Press; 2006.

References

Ryan A. Applications of complex systems to operational design; 2011. http://militaryepistem ology.com/wp-content/uploads/2011/07/Ryan_Applications-of-Complex-Systems-to-Operat ional-Design_2011.pdf

Ryan A. What is a systems approach?; 2008. https://arxiv.org/pdf/0809.1698.pdf

Sammut-Bonnici T. Complexity theory; 2015. https://www.researchgate.net/publication/272 353040

Sapir J. Thriving at the edge of chaos managing projects as complex adaptive systems. Productivity Press; 2020.

Saxenian A. The Silicon Valley connection: transnational networks and regional development in Taiwan, China and India chapter. In: D'Costa AP, Sridharan E, editors. India in the global software industry: innovation, firm strategies and development. Palgrave Macmillan; 2003.

Schneider M, Somers M. Organizations as complex adaptive systems: implications of complexity theory for leadership research. Leadersh Q. 2006; 17(4), 351–365. https://doi.org/10.1016/j.lea qua.2006.04.006

Sharma DC. The outsourcer: the story of India's IT revolution. Cambridge: MIT Press; 2015.

Sieniutycz S. Chapter 1: Systems science vs cybernetics in complexity and complex thermoeconomic systems; 2020. https://doi.org/10.1016/B978-0-12-818594-0.00001-5

Simon HA. Organizations and markets. J Econ Perspect. 1991; 5(2).

Sjotun SG, Jakobsen S, Fløysand A. Expanding analyses of path creation: interconnections between territory and technology. Econ Geogr. 2020;96:3. https://doi.org/10.1080/00130095.2020.175 6768.

Smith A, Humphries C. Complexity theory as a practical management tool: a critical evaluation. Org Manag J. 2004;1(2):91–106.

Smuts JC. Holism and evolution. MacMillan; 1926.

Sotarauta M, Srinivas S. Co-evolutionary policy processes: understanding innovative economies and future resilience. Sci Direct Futures. 2006; 38.

Stacey RD. Complexity and creativity in organizations. San Francisco: Berrett-Koehler; 1996.

Sterman JD. Business dynamics: systems thinking and modelling for a complex world. Boston: Irwin & McGraw-Hil; 2000.

Stuteville R, Jumara J. The role of path-dependency in public administration and economics and implications for the future. In: Annual conference of the national association of schools of public affairs and administration, Las Vegas, Nevada, September 30-October 2, 2010; 2010.

Subroto A. Understanding complexities in public policy making process through policy cycle model: a system dynamics approach, Universitas Indonesia, Indonesia; 2015. https://www.systemdyn amics.org/conferences/2012/proceed/papers/P1067.pdf

Svyantek DJ, Brown LL. A complex-systems approach to organizations; 2000. https://doi.org/10. 1111/1467-8721.00063

Tapscott D, Williams A. Wikinomics; how mass collaboration changes everything. Penguin Group, New York; 2006.

Terna P, Fontana M. From agent-based models to network analysis (and return): the policy-making perspective; 2014. https://doi.org/10.18278/jpcs.2.1.8

Tominomori K. Self-organization theory and its applicability to economic system. Econ J Hokkaido Univ. 2002; 31. https://eprints.lib.hokudai.ac.jp/dspace/bitstream/2115/32342/1/31_P41-62.pdf

Tsoukas H, Hatch MJ. Complex thinking, complex practice: the case for a narrative approach to organizational complexity. Hum Relat. 2001; 54(8):979–1013: 018452. (Sage Publications, London).

Turner JR, Baker RM. Complexity theory: an overview with potential applications for the social sciences. Systems. 2019;7(1):2019. https://doi.org/10.3390/systems7010004.

Tzafestas SG. Adaptation, complexity, and complex adaptive systems. In: Energy, information, feedback, adaptation, and self-organization. Intelligent systems, control and automation. Science and engineering, vol. 90. Springer; 2018. https://doi.org/10.1007/978-3-319-66999-1_8

Uhl-Bien M, Marion R, McKelvey B. Complexity leadership theory: shifting leadership from the industrial age to the knowledge era. Leadersh Q. 2007; 18(4). https://doi.org/10.1016/j.leaqua.2007.04.002

Von Bertalanffy L. General system theory. Revised. New York: George Braziller; 1973.

Von Bertalanffy L. The history and status of general systems theory Author(s): Source: Acad Manag J. 1972; 15(4); General systems theory (Dec., 1972). Academy of management stable; 1972. http://perflensburg.se/Bertalanffy.pdf

Von Bertalanffy L. Kritische Theorie der Formbildung. Berlin: Gebrüder Borntraeger (German title); 1928.

von Foerster H. Cybernetics of cybernetics. In: K. Krippendork, editor. Communication and control in society. Gordon and Breach, New York; 1979.

Wang J, Cheng S, Sukumar Ganapati S. ICT innovation: differential evolution of Zhongguancun and Bangalore. Regional Science Policy & Practice, August 2012; 2012. https://www.researchgate.net/publication/260278888

Wolf TD, Holvoet T. Emergence versus self-organization: different concepts but promising when combined; 2004. https://www.researchgate.net/publication/221456652_Emergence_Versus_Self-Organisation_Different_Concepts_but_Promising_When_Combined

Youngblood MD. Life at the edge of chaos: creating the quantum organization. Perceval Publishing; 1997.

Zanzi A. How organic is your organization? Determinants of organic/mechanistic tendencies in a public accounting firm. J Manag Stud. 1987; 24(2):AN: 4555891.

Zimmerman B, Lindberg C, Plsek P. A complexity science primer. In: Edgeware: insights from complexity science for health care leaders. Irving, VHA Inc., Texas; 2001. https://www.napcrg.org/media/1278/beginner-complexity-science-module.pdf

Chapter 4
Public Policy: Theories, Process, and Challenges

> *Science and policymaking thrive on challenge and questioning; they are vital to the health of inquiry and democracy.*
> Nicholas Stern, Economist and Author

Abstract The chapter highlights the role of institutions, values, power, structure, and contexts in the policy system. The discussion on policy theories underscores how these have shaped the thinking in the policy system. The theories provide useful insights and pointers, which can be utilized for policymaking. It covers field studies to understand the policymaking process and policy implementation. They reveal key concerns like the lack of systemic understanding of the system and problem, the mismatch between micro-level insights and macro-level concerns, the lack of rigor to carry out analyses, and the want for evidence-based decision-making. In addition, the complexity dimension in the social and economic systems is not comprehended. It underlines the deficiencies in the efficacy of the delivery system for implementation. It identifies reasons such as inadequate system capacity, lack of citizen focus, and higher transaction costs and low process efficiency in availing public services. It accentuates why implementation matters, emphasizes the need for a robust delivery mechanism, and recommends critical determinants for success.

Keywords Institutions · Culture · Politics · Policy theories · Policymaking process · Behavioral issues · Policy implementation · Decision-making · Complexity

Governments have huge responsibilities to meet numerous challenges. These range from managing basic public services for a multitude of the population to creating infrastructure and industrial clusters, managing international trade, and so on. It demands that sound policies be formulated to guide the future course of action. Right policies can make a far-reaching impact on, *first*, creating a right and predictable ecosystem for implementing policies; *second*, determining the capacity, both physical and financial, of the department or agency; and *third*, the outcomes of the policies.

How policy decisions are made is of importance. As a consequence, it lays stress on studying public policy theories and processes objectively.

4.1 Policy Environment: Understanding Fundamentals of Policymaking Process

Policy environment comprises various factors such as socio-economic and political contexts, values, culture, and structures in which the policy formulation takes place. It has a bearing on how different stakeholders interact and perform in the policy system during the policymaking process and policy implementation. It includes both internal and external environments, influencing policymaking (Huntington 1996; Acemoglu and Robinson 2010; Hodgson 2015). The following are the key aspects that affect the environment and need consideration:

External environment (factors impacting the system from outside):

- *Political culture.* A set of attitudes, beliefs, practices, and sentiments define a political process and the underlying assumptions and rules. These determine behavior in the political system. Culture impacts politics and power, affecting the functioning of the policy system.
- *Socio-cultural values in the social system.* Like the beliefs, shared values, traditions, practices, and habits that influence and shape the behavior of individuals, groups, and society. These cultural values influence how people interact and make decisions, how various practices and government programs are adopted, how economic policy decisions are taken, etc.
- *Socio-economic contexts.* Like social conditions, social inequalities, education and health conditions, social structures, economic status, state of infrastructure, etc.

Internal environment (internal factors impacting the day-to-day functioning). It affects the participation, consultations, decisions, actions, and functioning of those engaged in the policymaking process.

- *Culture of public institutions.* Norms of behavior, habits, practices, and a set of shared values and beliefs, which determine collective behavior.
- *Structures.* Like management hierarchy, distribution of functions, levels of control, coordination mechanisms, etc.
- *Values.* Norms and standards, criteria for making decisions, constitutional values such as freedom, equality, and democracy; organizational values like efficiency, transparency, and accountability; ethics and principles, and
- *Information system and tools for policy analysis.* Source of data collection, tools for data and policy analysis, internal processes, procedures, and decision-making processes.

4.1.1 Institutions

The literature on institutionalism defines institutions as the rules, norms, values, and standards that influence the behavior of individuals as well as of groups, organizations, and society (McGill 1995; DFID 2003; Paul 2017). Generally, the institutions are referred to as governmental institutions like the legislature, executive, judiciary, and bureaucratic agencies at National, State, and local levels. There may be informal institutions like social norms, family and societal values, customs, traditions, and practices in the society; and formal institutions such as rules, regulations, laws, constitution, legal systems, property rights, and enforcement mechanisms. They may perform at different levels—international (UN conventions, international trade treaties), National (laws, constitution, courts), social (norms of conduct, status of women), and family (inheritance rules). They may nest within larger institutions, e.g., village or town institutions may work with or be nested within the policy institutions of State and Central governments (IDS 2010; Joshi and Carter 2015; Majumdar and Mukand 2018).

In some cases, institutions and organizations are used interchangeably, and there is ambiguity about their usage. The difference between these two can be explained as this. The 'institutions' are defined as the 'rules' that regulate the activities, and 'organizations' are the 'structures' to perform certain tasks. An organization begins as a unit for a defined task and not necessarily as an institution, and over time, by adopting institutional characteristics and gaining credibility, it takes the form of an institution.

The institution begins as a new organization (Boin and Christensen 2008; DFID 2003; Paul 2017). The public organization takes the form of an institution as a result of a credible and effective way of working and delivering on intended objectives valued by society. Or, if an organization is contributing something especially valuable or enduring to society—like promoting health and education—it graduates to the next level and takes the shape of an 'institution'. Or, institution = 'organization' + 'value' (Moore et al. 1995; Bergstrom 2005).

Why institutions are important. The institutions embody enduring values, norms, and ideals, which act as a catalyst for a society or organization and have transformative potential. The political institutions enact, enforce, and regulate rules and laws. They make policies on various issues, resolve conflicts, and represent the people. These have a direct impact on the business environment and activities in a country (Blase 1986; Leftwich and Sen 2010). It is widely acknowledged that institutionalization enhances the effectiveness and robustness of organizations. The quality of institutions matters for a country's growth and development (Hall and Jones 1999; Acemoglu and Robinson 2010).

The uniqueness of institutions, including public institutions, lies in the combination of three distinct characteristics. *First*, the institutions provide predictability, consistency, reliability, stability, and acceptability. An institution is widely accepted and respected as it follows values, rules, and criteria, and a general perception prevails that the institution is desirable and proper (Calvert 1995; Wilson 2002; Acemoglu and

Robinson 2010). *Second*, institutions have an effective way of dealing with complex problems. It is because of experience, knowledge, understanding of issues, and the application of efforts over time. *Third*, the institutions are seen as credible and future establishments. The stakeholders develop and repose faith in them due to shared assumptions and values (March and Olsen 1984; Scartascinia et al. 2013).

How institutions play role in policymaking. From the very definition of institutions—the rules of the society or working rules of organizations, it is evident that the behavior and conduct of different stakeholders will be impacted by the institutions. It is well-acknowledged by the disciplines like economics, political science, sociology, and public administration that institutions affect social interactions and outcomes of behavior and decisions. And so, public policymaking, which works in the socio-economic and political environment, is impacted by the institutions (Ostrom 1990; Ferris and Shui-Yan 2020; Lahat 2019). The policies are embedded in political, social, administrative, and judicial institutions. They have inherent power and the capacity to mobilize resources for policy implementation. These influence behavioral and cognitive basis to understand issues, define problems, examine constraints, work on policy options, and present the likely outcomes for different policy options. By setting decision-making criteria, the institutions have a bearing on the policy process and content and influence outcomes. The central point is that institutions have a role in advancing policy ideas and affecting policy options. The individuals being a part of institutions have an important role to play, and the interactions among them determine the policy outcomes (Lowi 1971; Pierson 2004; van Heffen and Klok 2000; Peters 2016).

4.1.2 Structures, Organizational Culture, and Values

Structures

In the social system, the structures refer to the pattern of relationships between individuals or groups. They try to regulate their interactions. The structure influences individual behavior, group behavior, and attitudes within the institution or functional units. The structures evolve in multiple ways and take varied forms. Micro-structure is a pattern of relations at the basic level between individuals. It is formed by the relationships between groups, communities, or political parties. In the context of public institutions, the structure may be defined as the institutional arrangement and organizational structure based on rules, laws, and norms. In the social context, it may take the form of demographic divisions, groups based on shared values, beliefs, and attitudes, social divisions based on class, or political groups based on their ideology. Or, in the economic context, a structure may be due to tax benefits for incentivizing investment, or in the technological context, it is shaped by a pattern of skilled workforce or technology-based industries, and so on (Anderson 2003; John 2012).

In the context of public policy design and implementation, the institutional structure delineates the organizational chart, management levels, management hierarchy, distribution of functions, levels of control, coordination mechanisms, and decentralization and delegation of authority. And from the functional point of view, it defines how coordination among different units or departments is established, how responsibilities, authority, information, and resources flow, and how decisions are made.

The structures may facilitate or constrain decision-making, depending on the case. For example, certain constitutional norms or cultural factors may facilitate making policy decisions on welfare measures. Or certain rules or norms may limit the extent to which the decisions can be taken. Likewise, under a demographic structure, the young population will demand better educational facilities and job opportunities, while the aging population will look for more social security.

The socio-economic and political factors produce structures that influence the policy system and have the ability to determine outcomes. The basic premise is that the policy process is not a mere quantitative analysis or techno-rational analytical exercise and is driven by critical socio-economic conditions, including culture, beliefs, and attitudes. These set the agenda, influence decision-making, and impact implementation. More specifically, the local social structures based on class or community determine the outputs and outcomes of the policies. The dominant groups in the structure may influence results in a disproportionate manner (Hofferbert 1974; Calvert 1995).

The administrative structures and hierarchies with defined responsibilities may foster or retard decision-making. The structures may have consequences on policy options through a process of policy analysis and review. The institutional structures combined with teams, processes, procedures, and tools form a part of policymaking and have significant consequences for developing policy content. Simultaneously, the horizontal separation of power among legislative, executive, and judicial organs creates its structures, and policymaking is subject to review, modifications, and amendments. Thus, in practice, how the policy is formulated, how it is implemented, and how it is reviewed are impacted by the structures (Hofferbert 1974; John 1998; Mirakhor and Askari 2017).

Organizational culture

Policymaking is influenced by culture and values. These affect the thinking, behavior, decisions, and actions of the stakeholders within the policy system during the policy cycle. The culture corresponds to an overarching concept that defines the way personnel in public organizations or citizens in the society show their individual or collective behavior as a response to any interaction or intervention, and values represent norms, standards, or rules that shape the thinking for the work to perform certain tasks.

Two concepts, culture and values, are intertwined. For example, a group has a culture of behaving in a certain way, which is linked to what it believes in, i.e., values that constitute acceptable norms or standards of working. Culture and values influence each other and change and evolve with time in an institution. Culture is like a general behavior or way of working that provides the basis for actions by the people in an organization, and values provide the legitimacy and acceptance of actions. In the desire to utilize rationality, the culture and values should not be overshadowed. Rather, both rationality and culture should form the basis for decision-making, depending on the circumstances (Geertz 1973; Abolafia et al. 2014; Blyth et al. 2016; Muers 2017). In this section, culture and values have been examined for internal (within organizations) and external environments.

In the context of the internal environment, culture concerns people within the organization. The culture will include attitudes, beliefs, work ethics, norms of behavior, appreciation of transparency, habits, participatory approach, and way of working. The culture defines the norms of interactions and functioning and the atmosphere in a work environment. It aims to bring all on a common platform and unite the people for a common purpose. The culture determines the way of working and decision-making in the policy system.

The culture can break down the boundaries between different divisions and departments at different levels for better coordination and flow of information and efficient decision-making. A good work culture helps in better appreciation of the intents of policies, drives the process of collective action, and determines the likely outcomes. In the context of evidence-based policy, there is a need to recognize the culture of information processing, knowledge management, real-time information gathering, and application of analytical tools to analyze and rationalize that inform the discussions. It will require developing practices, habits, attitudes, and processes that can be embedded in the policymaking process. Policy formulation and implementation will be much easier when policy system follows the right culture (Kay 2006; World Bank 2017).

Social and political culture—like norms of social behavior and beliefs—in the external environment impacts policymaking. In the social context, the culture will be like the desire to participate in community work and promote a clean environment, sanitation, personal hygiene, etc. For example, stopping the habit of open defecation and promoting sanitation at the individual household level will require changes in social culture and behavior. The frontline staff faces practical difficulties during implementation due to various factors, including attitudes and beliefs of the community about the programs. For example, many communities will feel more confident to send their children to schools if they get an education in their own language during the initial formative years; or immunization and institutional delivery (in maternity cases) are resisted in remote areas, especially in tribal areas.

Particularly in the context of big projects or National-level policy reforms like economic reforms, the right kind of culture can break down the boundaries between different groups or departments at all levels from top to bottom and bring processes to improve decision-making and implementation. But the lack of the desired culture may be counterproductive. For example, it was expected that the underlying intents of economic reforms of 1991 in India would percolate from the Center to the ground level, and industrial activities would get the stimulus. But there has been a gap between intent and actual implementation. One of the reasons has been cultural issues. The necessary changes in the cultural practices for designing processes for business services and institutional mechanisms were not introduced to stimulate business and industrial activities. There has been a lack of focus on productivity. These led to low industrial competitiveness and low rank in doing business (WEF 2018a; World Bank 2019b). These were a few reasons, among others, why the economic reforms were implemented with less success in many regions of the country. Besides, it led to disparities.

The right culture and good environment can be helpful. The social culture can help create social capital, motivating people to engage in social and economic activities. Studies (Boltho 1985; Chan 1991; Claxton 1994; Granato et al. 1996; UNESCO 2010) indicate how culture impacts the process of development in a country. In some countries such as Japan, South Korea, and Thailand, socio-cultural values and social capital enabled the development process, including industrialization, for higher economic growth.

Values

The values are important in the contexts of both: *first*, public institutions or organizations responsible for policy design and implementation, and *second*, social systems in general in which citizens interact and political entities function. These represent principles, moral standards, rules of conduct, and standards of behavior, and in a generic sense, these will include family, community, and ethical values (Van der Wal et al. 2006; Muers 2017). In the organizational context, the values refer to defining the rules of conducting official business, following standards for service delivery, and norms of making decisions. Within the public institutions, the values are the consciousness for quality standards for public service delivery, sensitivity for time and cost in providing services to citizens, concerns for solving citizens' grievances, constitutional values, and ethical standards.

The values of political executives matter for political institutions. How much importance is given to the quality of public services and concerns of citizens and what is the level of trust among the citizens for institutions depend upon the value system. There is an issue of legitimacy. It depends upon the citizens' perception about: whether the process of policy formulation is rigorous, transparent, and fair, how citizens' concerns are addressed, and how they are valued (Moore 1995; Muers 2017). For policymaking, the values to be considered are: *first*, normative principles or standards for decision-making during policy analysis, and *second*, public values, which will make citizens realize the worth of public policy or action in improving their quality of life. Some of the specific values can be (Sapru 2012; Moore 1995; O'Flynn 2007):

- *constitutional values*: like equality, social justice, fundamental rights, directive principles, etc.;
- *principles*: based on which the decisions are taken, for example, financial norms or criteria, ethics in decision-making;
- *societal values*: like the need to help socially and economically disadvantaged groups and differentially-abled people, sustainable development, reducing inequality, etc.;

- *service quality standards*: quality parameters such as time, cost, reliability, etc., and
- *public values*: expected value creation while delivering on public policies like improving living standards, sustainability of the programs, transparency, accountability of decision-making, fairness, trust, and so on.

There is a need to monitor the prevailing cultural values within public organizations. Based on the value system, the personnel function. In the external environment, the values of social and political system matter. How citizens value service standards, what decides their trust in public organizations, how they value transparency and ethics in decision-making, and so on are essential. These values impact the way decisions are made by policymakers.

4.1.3 Ideas, Politics, and Power

Policymaking is a political struggle about values, ideas, ideology, beliefs, politics, and power. Though these are distinct, they are interlinked. These cannot be detached from policymaking process and influence decision-making (Stone 2012; Campbell 1998).

Ideas

The idea results from the careful articulation of thought or opinion and is a mental conception of some activity, solution, or knowledge. Good and cogent ideas can provide a germination or starting point for policymaking and influence how one approaches a problem. Good ideas are essential for both policy formulation and implementation. These can be a sound basis for debates and arguments with logic. Ideas may emerge due to one or the combination of the following: cognitive understanding of world view like emerging new technologies or paradigms; normative understanding of values or norms of society; experience; success cases in other countries or regions; expert research, which was previously unknown; motivation to improve or bring change; and, intuitive thinking (Braun and Capano 2010; Mehta 2010).

Policymakers need ideas to meet new challenges and address societal problems. The link between good 'ideas' and policy design needs to be explored. There is a need to work on the process of ideation, how to embed ideas into institutions and actions, and how to utilize ideas for policy design and change. The ideas can provide alternative opinions or expertise that can define the agenda-setting, solution, and policy content, which may have the potential to steer the direction of policy for the betterment of society (Hall 1993; Braun and Capano 2010; Cairney 2012).

The acceptance of some ideas may be constrained by institutional mechanisms like the fiscal policy of the government. Certain ideas may put a limit on the policymaking process due to the need to handle large datasets during policy analysis. The ideas may be driven by normative considerations to improve government functioning or better policy design. For example, the issues of addressing climate change fallout in vulnerable areas or social security program for workers to enhance their quality of life and confidence and, in turn, improve productivity. On the other hand, due to the influence of pressure groups and politics, some ideas may be driven by the self-interest of political groups or stakeholders. For example, in the 1980s, by certain business groups as well as political groups, the idea was perpetuated in the USA that for an economy to succeed, the market neo-liberal economy should be furthered to benefit the bottom through the trickle-down effect (Campbell 1998; Mehta 2010; Stone 2012; Stiglitz 2015).

Politics

Politics is about the activities, opinions, decisions, and resource allocations associated with public governance. Politics shapes the contours of public policy. It is central to determining which policy is pursued and how it is implemented. It involves different political parties. The development takes place in the public space and involves the political process. It is defined by politics. Political parties have high stakes in public policy. And therefore, politics influences not just the policymaking process but also implementation. Politics, among other factors, is affected by political ideology, expertise, needs of people, political discourse, and political agenda, besides social structures and power structures (Blyth et al. 2016; Matheson 2016; Muers 2017). There is a two-way relationship between public policy and politics. It influences public policy, which in turn determines politics.

For example, the Mahatma Gandhi National Rural Employment Guarantee Scheme (MNREGS) program, the Right to Education (RTE), and the disinvestment program of public sector units (PSUs) are a result of political decisions. The evidence and research findings reflect how education, health, and skill development are essential for the future of any economy. But the adoption of such ideas falls within the political domain. More specifically, politics has an impact on mainstreaming the following ideas in policies: how quality education can empower children to perform better; how better health services can lead to a healthy workforce that can enhance productivity; how immunization can help in reducing mortality or disability rate; what measures are essential for reducing malnutrition; how skill development is prerequisite for improving industrial activities; and how quality of public services is crucial, and so on. How politics can appreciate evidence-based choices and mainstream larger public interest in public policy is a challenge.

Power

Power is the capacity or ability to influence the beliefs, values, and behavior of others and change the course of action. In formal organizations, power is like decision-making processes and criteria, including rules, structures, authorities, and institutions. Informal power influences behavior through shared beliefs and ideas or coercion and pressure. The power can be exercised by an individual, a group, a social and economic structure, or a public institution. It can work at global, National, State, and local levels. The term authority is often used for power that is perceived as legitimate and formal, which derives from rules or positions. The power in the society or political system is shaped by historical, political, social, and cultural factors. Besides, certain dominant thoughts or movements like feminism, child-marriage protection, and right-based or left-based politics impact the emergence of power. These may lead to the formation of a power structure—relationships between those who hold power and who are subjected to power (Weber 1946; Junttia et al. 2009; James 2011).

There are many sources of power like political power, derived from the constitution and political institutions; bureaucratic power from the knowledge of the internal functioning of government; technical power (expertise) from knowledge and skills; financial power from control over financial resources; networks of people or organizations; and personal charisma or moral authority. The power should be seen as how legitimately it can be utilized to make a positive difference in the lives of people, how prudently it can be channeled to bring qualitative change, and how the system can be transformed through a calibrated approach (Mann 1986; Junttia et al. 2009; James 2011). In a positive and progressives sense, in the policy system, the power can be utilized to influence the behavior of individuals and groups to perform certain tasks, place systems and processes in the right way to meet the policy or organizational objectives, shape the decision-making, and determine the future action for achieving goals set by the policies.

While using the power, the leaders or team members should make an effort to examine the prevailing culture and values within the system or organization, the capabilities of personnel, and the efficacy of the delivery mechanism to achieve policy objectives. It is equally important to understand how power changes and how other individuals and groups acquire power. In the context of an organization, a power change may happen due to a lack of attention. Or some dissatisfied or ambitious individuals may form a group and exert informal power. The power groups may be formed at the frontline level in government agencies to adjust to local conditions and work as pressure groups by exercising their informal power (Lipsky 2010; Erasmus 2014).

Power, politics, culture, and public policy dynamics. In the real world, politics and power play their roles in policymaking. Power is not a static concept but dynamic. Several actors compete for political power and space. Power should be viewed in the context of political culture and ideologies. The values, culture, and ideologies impact the way different actors or individuals in the political system think, conceptualize, and make decisions and, in the process, exercise their power. Understanding this political reality surrounding the policy system is essential. Political power may not be visible. Power dynamics needs to be studied by examining the external environment. The interactions between politics, power, political culture, and public policy constantly change and evolve, and no definite outcome can be predicted. It may lead to a positive or negative impact on policymaking. It is necessary to understand the policymaking process by factoring in power, politics, and political culture to determine the control over resources and decision-making (Lipsky 2010; James 2011; Erasmus 2014).

4.1.4 Multidisciplinary Perspective

Public policies are formulated in social systems, which have numerous factors impacting the varied needs of people. These factors relate to social, economic, political, behavioral, cultural, and technological contexts. Multiple needs of so many people are required to be captured during different stages of the policy cycle—agenda-setting, policy analysis, decision-making and policy formulation, implementation, and evaluation. It makes defining the problems and the policymaking process complex. These stages require multiple perspectives.

Addressing the diverse nature of problems calls for inputs from various disciplines. No one discipline can give an exhaustive explanation of or provide solutions to the problems that arise in the social system. With the growing understanding of the complexity in the public policy system, policymaking demands interdisciplinary or transdisciplinary approaches.

For a deeper analysis, the interdisciplinary approach attempts to integrate and synthesize the concepts and knowledge of more than one discipline. In comparison, the transdisciplinary approach draws on ideas, concepts, and knowledge from the natural, social, and health sciences. It transcends traditional boundaries to create new conceptual theory and framework by integrating and advancing beyond a particular discipline to address complex societal problems. The general systems theory (GST) and complexity science are examples of transdisciplinary approaches (Forrester 1961; Sterman 2000; Senge 1990).

For example, in the social and economic systems, including economy, health, education, agriculture, and so on, the problems are complex, and their comprehension and solution transcend any single discipline and approach. It requires moving forward beyond a single discipline perspective. Complex problems require examining issues from multiple viewpoints applying concepts from various disciplines, and then synthesizing ideas, concepts, and knowledge for addressing issues.

Public policy is not just about the technical, legislative, and regulatory decision-making processes. It requires examining the problem from different lenses of inquiry. Often, these are lost sight of either due to hurry in policymaking, ignorance, or lack of capabilities to examine wide-ranging issues. Different disciplines can provide unique insights, which are not possible by a single discipline. These can help in better definition of problems, policy analysis, decision-making, designing policies, and implementation. It is more so important in the backdrop of complexity, which demands examining multiple issues in an integrated or holistic manner (Birkland 2011; Raymond et al. 1994). Though for understanding complexity in the system, the list of disciplines is quite extensive, the prominent among them are summarized as follows:

- *Sociology.* It involves issues like social processes (interactions and relationships between elements), institutions, networks, social capital, class, caste, and social inequalities. It can help in understanding the causes of social problems, examining the interactive behavior of individuals and groups, making sense of interventions, and visualizing ideas for future direction.

- *Psychology and behavioral science.* How people think, behave, and act requires examination. These deal with attitude, motivations, group dynamics, and cognitive processes for decision-making through analysis of human behavior. These have significance for designing policies and interventions by considering the need for changing behavior for better policy outcomes.
- *Political science.* How political thoughts, politics, political institutions, and political processes influence decision-making.
- *Public administration.* Role of bureaucracy in examining the problems, doing policy analysis, and making decisions for policy formulation.
- *Economics.* Examining economic status of various sections of the society, economic theories and principles, and existing economic policies.
- *Technology.* How it can bring productivity, efficiency, and transparency.
- *Management.* Tools, techniques, models, and frameworks for managing systems.
- *Natural science.* Concepts such as variation, natural selection, emergence, self-organizing property, adaptation, evolution, and coevolution have implications for social systems and organizations.
- *Philosophy.* Logic, values, principles, and ethics for decision-making.

4.1.5 Policy Contexts

The policymaking context refers to social, political, economic, institutional, and cultural factors. The context is defined by the socio-economic-political environment, historical factors, technological environment, global pressures, the structure of government, social values, political culture, and public sentiment prevalent at the time of policymaking. The contexts are mainly specific to a country. Within the country, these are State- or region-specific and are impacted by the history and dynamic nature of various factors as they change with time. The study of contexts is essential, as public policies are context-specific (Geurts 2010; Birkland 2011; Sapru 2012).

Specifically, the contexts include the influence of pressure groups during policy formulation, behavioral factors, availability of financial resources, the capacity of implementing departments or agencies, and so on. These may work as constraints or enablers in pursuit of policy objectives. Understanding such factors is vital as the policy transfer cannot take place from one country to another or from one State to another without examining the contexts. Besides, the comparative analysis of policies cannot be done without considering the context. For this reason, there cannot be a universal generalization of one-size-fits-all public policy. Examining and comprehending the specific contexts are essential for conceptualizing issues and problems. It is imperative to recognize public opinion, contemporary issues, and pressing societal concerns. The contexts exert domestic influence but are not fully insulated from evolving global trends and international negotiations (Manor 1991; Brinkerhoff and Crosby 2002; Woolcock 2017).

4.1 Policy Environment: Understanding Fundamentals of Policymaking ...

Some of the issues related to policy contexts are covered in Sect. 2.1, but a brief explanation of the contexts is presented below:

Legacy context. One needs to understand the legacy issues or history. Understanding legacy issues is essential to appreciate the prevailing socio-techno-economic conditions. In addition, many stakeholders remain a part of a particular policy regime. All sectors, be it agriculture, industry, textiles, or education, have policies that draw inputs from the past as critical sectoral issues like employment, productivity, technologies, exports, skill sets, etc., cannot be ignored. It will require requisite research and studies to facilitate proper documentation to provide inputs for future policymaking (Raymond et al. 1994; Gerston 2010; Gigante 2016).

Likewise, in the context of the constitution, the framers relied on historical facts about the socio-cultural aspects of the country. It has wider implications for public policy and has been a guiding principle to policymakers. The existing provisions in the constitution have influenced the amendments or framing of Acts such as the Right to Education, the Right to Information, the Right to Food Security, and the Right to work, to name a few. Similarly, whatever is currently done to formulate new policies will have a bearing on policymaking in the future (De 2012; Sapru 2012; Chakravarty and Chand 2016).

Institutional/structural (political) context. It is defined by political institutions, division of functions between Central or federal government and State governments; demarcations of responsibilities among the legislature, executives, and judiciary; government Ministries and agencies; implementation structure and mechanism; and citizen engagement in policymaking, transparency, and accountability. These influence the policymaking process (March and Olsen 1984; North 1990; Cairney 2012).

Social context. The social aspect of policymaking involves demographics, social structure, and development needs and priorities of various groups. The features under demographics include age, gender, caste, religion, etc. The characteristics like population growth rate, migration, and spatial locations reflect the nature of the population. The social structures include social institutions, religious groups, and groups based on class, income, social status, and caste. These structures influence individuals and groups in society. They shape public opinion on various matters and, as a result, impact the agenda for public policy.

More specifically, in the Indian context, due to diverse socio-cultural patterns, a meaningful policy shall factor in the specific needs of regions, ethnicity, class, and caste. It is supported by the Constitution of India, with provisions for addressing the interests of all groups and, especially, weaker sections. The changes in the demographics have implications for policies and budget. For example, for the younger population, the immediate needs are related to education, health, housing, basic public services, etc., which deserve early priority.

Spending on social programs is country-specific. In several countries, with the rising aspirations of citizens, public expenditure has assumed a significant role. Countries like the USA, France, Germany, Russia, and many other OECD countries gave a high priority to health, education, and social security from the 1920s onward (Cohen 1984; Leonard 2009; Gerston 2010). In India, social programs such as a family pension, health, and maternity care got a priority since the1980s.

Political context. It includes policy agenda-setting based on political requirements, advocacy for opinion building, mobilizing people, holding consultations with stakeholders, collecting feedback, and taking a stand for final decision-making. In a broader sense, it deals with determining the distribution of power and resources. Usually, public policymaking is largely driven by a political process. Together with administrative exercise and experts' inputs, political thinking, ideology, and culture play their roles. Political culture is a set of beliefs and values. It evolves in response to the changing socio-economic and political contexts. It has a role in determining legislative processes. It shapes the direction of political governance, including the principles, norms, structures of decision-making, and systems and processes of policymaking and implementation. The context is required to be aligned with constitutional values to provide legitimacy and acceptability (Birkland 2011; Sapru 2012; Chakravarty and Chand 2016).

Economic context. Due to pressure from citizens, economic issues always dominate the agenda of political parties. To ensure stability and a sense of security, governments tend to respond to economic problems on a priority. It becomes more important when the governments have to meet citizens' needs in a scenario of resource crunch. The economic issues that matter the most are economic growth, economic welfare, taxation, inflation, cost of different factors of production, debt, and trade, to name a few. In the context of financial stability, issues like fiscal policy, trade balance, current account balance, and debt-service ratio assume importance.

In a global world, the economic scenario is more complex, interdependent, dynamic, and uncertain. Together with these factors, policymaking becomes more difficult due to ever-changing factors of production and disruption by technologies, trade, and the global supply chain (Gerston 2010; Birkland 2011; De 2012).

There are two vital issues, viz., inequality and technology management, that deserve attention. *Firstly*, income inequality, social inequality, and geographical disparity have consequences for society. There is a tendency by 'haves' to augment their opportunities and take a significant share of resources. Such inequalities may lead to further inequalities and may cause disharmony. Regarding the policymaking process, disparities impact policymaking, and the regions with high growth potential tend to take significant advantage (Kapsos 2005; Piketty 2017). *Secondly*, managing technology has always been a challenge for any country. Technologies are essential for solving many societal problems, especially in health, agriculture, drinking water, etc., and raising industrial productivity and economic growth. To leverage the potential of technologies, policymaking should focus on R&D and innovation, technology standards for research and manufacturing, geographical incentives for industries, and technical standards for biotechnology, nanotechnology, new materials, and other new technologies.

Global context. Globalization is leading to an interconnected world with political, economic, and strategic significance. The issues such as trade, advanced technologies, global supply chain, oil prices, climate change, and other political issues such as terrorism and nuclear proliferation have an impact on the policies of the countries. Due to the dynamic nature of the global environment, policymakers have to calibrate the policies on a regular basis. For national governments, specific public policies require alignment with international memoranda, treaties, multilateral agreements, etc.

4.1.6 Role of Stakeholders

Public policy is a matter of concern for whom the policies are formulated or those who may be affected by the policies. There are individuals or organizations who shape and influence policymaking. A set of individuals, groups, or organizations at local, National, and global levels are referred to as stakeholders. As influencers, researchers, or experts, they have an interest in public policy. Some stakeholders could be political parties, citizens at large, special groups, subject experts, labor organizations, non-governmental organizations (NGOs), civil society groups, international organizations, aid agencies, business entities, consumers, and families.

In the complex, uncertain, and dynamic policy environment, the stakeholders' participation is increasingly felt to embrace a diversity of knowledge and values and bring transparency in decision-making. From the viewpoint of citizens, the discussion with stakeholders is particularly important as, generally, the policy formulation lacks focus on how citizens are affected by the policies or how they are benefited, while they are vital stakeholders (Chakravarty and Chand 2016; Gerston 2010; Hutahaean 2017).

There are two broad aspects. *First*, the stakeholder engagement. It assumes importance due to the need to link policy formulation and management with the needs of stakeholders (Manor 1991; Mintrom and Luetjens 2015). It requires embedding engagement into the decision-making processes. It signifies the *process* by which the stakeholders are engaged in various activities, including the following:

- informing about problems and contours of policy needs;
- eliciting feedback and insights from the perspectives of various stakeholders;
- seeking inputs during different stages of the policy cycle—agenda-setting, policy analysis, decision-making and policy formulation, implementation, and evaluation;
- understanding how public value can be created that comprises values in areas such as public services, economic issues, sustainable development, citizens' rights, societal outcomes, trust and legitimacy, and so on, and
- collaboration for participatory decision-making, co-design, and co-production by listening to stakeholders, engaging them in creative discussions, and drawing on their insights about the problems and potential solutions.

Second, stakeholder analysis. It is a methodology to add value to the policy process by incorporating the needs of those who have a 'stake' or an interest in the policy under consideration. With information about stakeholders, their interests, and their capacity to contribute, the government can choose how to accommodate them best, thus assuring policies adopted are realistic and sustainable (Brinkerhoff 1998). In this context, the stakeholder analysis (Savage et al. 1991; Fletcher et al. 2003) entails the following key steps:

- *Stakeholder identification.* Usually, in public policy, there are a large number of citizens, experts, and organizations. So categorization of different actors is important to have homogeneity in a particular category.
- *Role analysis.* The role of each stakeholder should be defined.
- *Stakeholder feedback and ranking of priorities.* The issues involved in the policies are to be explicitly explained to stakeholders, and the stakeholders should be asked to give their feedback on key issues under the policy. Based on their feedback, the ranking of the factors should be done.
- *Findings.* Based on the feedback, salient findings are to be drawn. These are to be based on: how the stakeholders view their roles and how much contribution they can make within the boundary of the policymaking, how the policy will address their concerns, and whether the policy will achieve its intended objective.

4.2 Key Challenges

Policymaking faces multiple challenges. For the benefit of stakeholders in the policy system, some of them are summarized below:

4.2.1 Complexity in Policymaking and Implementation: Operational Complexity

Policymakers work in a complex public system. The system has multiple external and internal factors or variables that keep challenging the policymaking process. Complexity results from the combination of numerous factors, nonlinearity, dynamic nature, unknown causes and effects, and uncertainty. In the public policy system, operational complexity results from interlinked issues and factors in the conceptualization of problems, policy analysis, decision-making, and implementation during the policy cycle. It is in addition to structural complexity, individual complexity, socio-political complexity, and interdependency complexity, as discussed in Chap. 3. This section describes various forms of operational complexity. From the first stage, complexity arises when stakeholders interact with differing or competing priorities and sometimes conflicting interests. It becomes difficult for the policy group to reach a common ground. During the second stage of policy analysis, complexity increases due to many questions about data and evidence, methods of analysis, and identifying policy options.

The methodology and the tools for the analyses may enhance complexity if not adequately understood by the stakeholders. The policy group is expected to have good credibility and should be able to provide cogent replies to the questions of various stakeholders. Otherwise, it might lead to confusion or distrust, adding to the complexity. The stage of discussion and decision on the policy document is important for legislatures and pressure groups, who may have differing views or competing interests. The inadequacies of evidence, policy analysis, and logic may cause concerns among the stakeholders. It may be due to limitations of cognitive skills of the decision makers or bounded rationality. The implementation stage may throw some challenges regarding the capacity of the delivery system vis-a-vis the intended objectives. More often, there is a time lag between the need for improving the delivery mechanism and the expected output.

The feedback and evaluation stage may cause unease due to gaps in achievements and outcomes if corrective measures are not taken. Non-achievement of objectives and targets may lead to questions about the credibility of policy, implementation, or both. The perception of citizens and elected members about the implementation may vary depending on their priorities. All these issues in a combined form add to the complexity during various stages of policymaking (Howlett and Ramesh 2003; Kay 2006; Jones 2011; Mueller 2020).

During the process of policymaking and implementation, different forms of complexities are discussed below (Table 4.1):

Table 4.1 Policymaking process: operational complexity

S.No.	Complexity	Issues and factors
1.	Behavioral complexity	• Values, culture, norms, attitudes, and cognitive abilities
2.	Knowledge and competence-based complexity	• Knowledge and competence to collect data and information about underlying complex issues • Capabilities to analyze data • Disparity in knowledge and skills among personnel and policymakers • Lack of specialized knowledge to address complex issues
3.	Functional complexity	• Interactions between individuals to perform tasks • Nonlinear and dynamic relationships
4.	Dynamic and emerging complexity	Emergence depends on: • The number of nodes (elements, individuals, variables) • Changes in the value and nature of variables in the system
5.	Decision-making complexity	• Influenced by the context of policymaking, interactions between requirements of performing tasks, and the nature and ability of decision makers • Numerous decisions related to tasks and the nature of information and analysis

Behavioral complexity. It pertains to behavioral issues within the organization engaged in policymaking. Values, beliefs, norms, attitudes, and cognitive abilities impact how individuals and groups interact, think, behave, function, and make decisions. In addition, due to values and cultural factors, the stakeholders have diverse and competing interests and goals. These factors in the real-world situation define behavioral complexity (Geurts 2010; Subroto 2011).

Knowledge and competence-based complexity. Complexity analysis will demand, *first*, knowledge and competence to collect data, insights, and information about underlying issues and, *second*, the competence to analyze data using requisite policy analysis tools and drawing inferences for further usage in different stages of policymaking. In a real-world situation, there are situations like a lack of adequate knowledge about the development concepts; disparity in knowledge and skills among personnel and policymakers in the departments, implying different levels of understanding; and the lack of a specialized or diverse set of technical knowledge for analysis. So the lack of ability to understand complex issues and conflicting levels of understanding among different actors may lead to many complex problems that remain hidden or unresolved. Thus complexity may continue to persist during the policymaking process.

Functional complexity. It is due to both intrinsic and extrinsic factors. The factors intrinsic to a system contribute to complexity as a result of their interactions within the policy system, several nonlinear and dynamic relationships between them, and the multiple ways in which a system interacts with its environment (Mitchell 2009; Baetu 2012; Morcol 2012). For example, the discussions, consultations, analyses, and decision-making involve multiple processes and activities and engagement with many individuals. Various factors are associated with database management, data analysis, analysis of policy options, and implementation plan.

Generally, due to uncertainty, it becomes difficult to visualize different factors and what can be the impact of the proposed policy action. There is a lack of real-time monitoring and a likelihood of delay in concurrent evaluation, and thus it becomes difficult to understand the policy impact. The systemic delay or difficulty in discerning cause-and-effect relationships is frequently observed. All these points, in a combined way, result in complexity. The higher the interdependencies between individuals and factors of a system, the greater the complexity is observed.

Major features extrinsic to a system, which make a system appear more complex, are difficulty in measuring external factors (variables), difficulty in tracking the impact of policy implementation (the way the decisions are taken and actions are implemented), and difficulty in studying causal relationships between factors. Such a lack of understanding and knowledge may have a cascading effect on the system, and so the policy analysis and formulation are affected. Furthermore, there are other features like, *first*, multiple systems (or multiple subsystems within a large system) like education, health, sanitation, drinking water, and so on; *second*, systems with many diverse actors including citizens, elected members, political groups, etc.; and *third*, multiple goals as per the preferences of different stakeholders, including a goal set by the policy documents. Due to these features, the complexity results from the invisible or unknown factors and their interactions (Rihani 2005; Eppel et al. 2011; Dunoviu et al. 2014).

Dynamic and emerging complexity. It is characterized by internal or external factors like changes in existing policy ingredients, the behavior of stakeholders, or unforeseen changes, which may be disruptive. The changes could emerge due to the introduction of new policies in other sectors, technological changes, demographic changes, industrial activities, or serious health problems. The emergence largely depends on the number of nodes (elements, individuals, variables), how much every element or variable is connected to others, and how the micro-rules guide the behavior of the nodes (Kauffman 1995; Foster and Metcalfe 2001; Fontana 2010). Emergent complexity deals with new complex patterns in the social and economic system and how new pattern emerges locally and spreads throughout the system to replace the previous pattern. For example, the emergence of industry in a region, new health or education system in a city, etc.

Decision-making complexity. It is influenced by the context of policymaking, interactions between different elements in performing tasks, and both the nature and ability of the decision makers. The complexity of decision-making is linked to the complexity of tasks to be performed. The complex tasks require more information, cognitive effort, and skills for information processing. More information may lead to increased complexity in doing analyses. Thus, the complexity of tasks, the nature of information, and analyses make decision-making complex. In addition, the decision makers may not have full knowledge of the consequences of policy options due to inherent uncertainties, and they may not have a complete understanding of the factors of past failures or successes. Together with this, the beliefs, competing multiple goals of various pressure groups, mental stress, and emotions may add to the complexity while making decisions (Bystrom and Jarvelin 1995; Meyer and Curley 1995; Van Gils and Klijn 2007).

4.2.2 Constraints

Policymaking takes place under complex conditions shaped by different social, political, economic, administrative, and legal contexts and the interactions between stakeholders and system variables. Values, norms, perceptions, understanding of micro and macro issues, and world views (like the concept of problem, surroundings, or world) of different stakeholders put limits or boundaries on how individuals and public institutions think, react, and perform. For example, it is recognized that both social and economic policies are constrained by various expediencies, including political (Kanbur and Myles 1992; Raymond et al. 1994). The policy performance depends on the institutional constraints of the political institutions and social groups or institutions, which are like structures that constrain individuals and organizations in performing their tasks. The policy outcomes are influenced and shaped by institutional rules, including accountability, transparency for the decision-making process, rights of citizens, political participation, and the rule of law. The issues such as inadequate participatory skills in the community and lack of social capital and confidence within society are constraints (Fischer and Forester 1993; Elster 1998; Do Phu 2017).

Given the emerging importance of technologies and complex issues, policy analysis requires applying specialized knowledge. Such specialized knowledge of technologies, economics, sociology, systems theory, and organizational theory is needed to design socio-economic policies and implement them effectively. The inadequacy of specialized knowledge puts constraints on the functioning of the government, which limits the set of feasible alternative options. Some of the constraints are briefly summarized below to provide an overview (Majone 1974; Kanbur and Myles 1992; Hoppe 2011):

- *Institutional*: Rules, norms, and constitutional values; work culture, processes, systems, and organizational structures; definitions, semantics, principles, and rules for policymaking; trust among political, administrative institutions, and civil society; transparency and accountability mechanism; and environment of innovation. Some of them may limit the scope of policymaking, add to rigidity in the process, and affect innovative ways of policymaking. Stakeholders, including pressure groups, may have differing priorities and competing interests.
- *Environment*: Social structures, social values, and culture; economic conditions and economic structures; physical infrastructure; globalization and international treaties; and information and communication technology (ICT), innovation, and new technologies. These may have constraining effects on the decisions on policy objectives.
- *Political*: Politics, political groups, political culture, and political institutions. The political ideas, politics, and ideologies often constrain agenda-setting and decision-making.
- *Resources*: Government resources, budget, and foreign exchange reserve. The policy objectives are dependent on resource allocations.
- *Knowledge and capabilities*: Knowledge of personnel in the government departments, subject matter specialization, and skills for data collection and policy analysis. Deficiencies in knowledge and skills may hinder policy formulation and implementation.
- *Delivery mechanism*: efficacy of delivery system for the implementation of policies. The achievement of intended objectives depends on the delivery mechanism.
- *Communication*: means of reaching out to citizens and role of social media. Debates in media. Media scrutiny of the policy objectives and outcomes.
- *Legal*: legal procedures and courts. Government decisions are subject to scrutiny, legal interpretations, and legal compliances.

Finally, the complete set of economic, social, organizational, institutional, administrative, and knowledge constraints need to be considered during policymaking.

4.2.3 Behavioral Aspect

In the traditional policymaking system, government policies are formulated based on the preconceived notion of how citizens should behave or respond to policies, with an assumption that behavioral change is rational and driven by set rules and logic. But the ground reality is generally contrary to this assumption, as the decision-making by the individuals is not always rational, and their behavior is influenced by various factors such as beliefs, social norms, attitudes, social environment, cognitive biases and limitations, and preferences. Even well-intentioned policies may not succeed for these reasons, as the policy interventions may not be compatible with how people think and make decisions. It is essential to consider and examine how human behavior deviates from the standard rational model or predetermined logic (Thaler 1981; World Bank 2015; Blyth et al. 2016; Sunstein et al. 2017).

Behavioral economists have studied that decision-making is not necessarily rational and perfect reasoning, and there is an importance of context, values, and culture in shaping decision-making (Marsh 2010; Solek 2014; Phillips 2018). The policy system dealing with human beings needs to learn what drives human behavior and factor in human behavior; how people think, make decisions, and act; how history, society, and local contexts shape individual and group thinking and behavior; and, in addition, how bounded rationality or cognitive limitations and biases impact decision-making. Specifically, behavioral science helps in identifying attributes of individuals and characteristics of the environment and examining how attributes and characteristics are causally related to behavior. Understanding human behavior can lead to better decision-making, more effective policies, and better implementation of strategies (Morecroft 1983; Simon 1955; Oliver 2013; John 2015).

The use of behavioral insights in the design and delivery of public policy has increased significantly across a number of policy domains. It can provide the inputs for informed decision-making and a citizen-centric approach. Behavioral insights in public policy involve a multidisciplinary approach involving psychology, economics, political science, sociology, and the concerned domain of interest to understand citizen behavior and decision-making. In various countries, realizing the importance, behavioral insights are being used by governments and public policy organizations in the policymaking process and interventions (OECD 2017b; World Bank 2019a).

There are some key behavioral knowledge and insights (Swanson and Bhadwal 2009; Lunn 2014; Sunstein et al. 2017) such as: effecting change in behavior is a process, not an event and, often, entails understanding the current state, incremental interventions, observations, and learning by doing. Beliefs, values, and social norms influence how people behave. The rewarding experience and incentives can impact expectations and values, bringing change.

The motivation for change can be non-monetary (social recognition) and can have a profound effect on human behavior. The economic and social environment has an impact on the way people think and react to change. Peer group pressure or influence and enhanced knowledge can prompt people to change behavior, as, by nature, they want to be a part of the process of change. Participatory leadership involving friendly consultations and supervision helps in molding attitudes toward a particular desired behavior (OECD 2017b; Sunstein et al. 2017; World Bank 2019a). In the public policy domain, these insights can help specifically to:

- understand why citizens behave in a particular way, and which factors or conditions can lead to a desired behavior,
- choose appropriate interventions from among various policy options, and
- identify ways to enhance citizens' engagement during implementation for better policy outcomes.

4.2.4 Decision-Making: Complexity and Ethical Issues

Who makes public policy decisions, how the decisions are made, and how the decisions are implemented and evaluated are of high significance for all the stakeholders, and as a consequence, lay stress on understanding the decision-making process. In the context of public policy, decision-making is regarded as a cognitive process resulting in the selection of an option from among several alternatives. The researchers have studied three separate situations about decision-making: *certainty*, where the means to achieve specific output are known; *risk*, the decisions are likely to take to different situations, each with known possibility and risk; and *uncertainty*, where outcomes are not known. The risk refers to decision-making situations under which all potential consequences and their likelihood of occurrence are known to the decision makers. The uncertainty relates to the condition under which the results and the probabilities of occurrence are unknown (Granato et al. 1996; Habtom 2017).

The decision-making can be descriptive, normative, and prescriptive. The descriptive approach of decision-making delineates how people make decisions while dealing with real problems. Generally, people are less attentive to details and rational approach. As regards complex problems, people tend to pay attention to a few issues and simplify the complex problems so that the complexity can be handled. Besides, people's ability is constrained by bounded rationality due to limited time, cognitive power, information, and tools to analyze (Simon 1955; Kahneman and Tversky 1979). The normative approach is concerned with rational standards and tries for an optimal decision through theoretical understanding, logic, and analytical tools (Byrnes 1998; Habtom 2017). In comparison, the prescriptive approach is about how people should make decisions in the real world based on specific decision rules to maximize their returns (DiMaggio 1997; Gigerenzer and Selten 2001).

Factors impacting decision-making. In the context of the descriptive approach, the decision-making process is a reasoning process based on assumptions, beliefs, values, and preferences of the decision maker(s). The research has highlighted that the psychological, cognitive, social, and cultural factors, social preferences, social networks, cultural identities, and social norms impact human behavior and decision-making (Simon 1977; World Bank 2015). The mental models of individuals reflect what they perceive. The perception and cognitive ability to reason have a bearing on the decisions they make (Claxton 1994; Granato et al. 1996; Thaler and Sunstein 2008; UNESCO 2010).

Decision-making is a challenge in policymaking, driven by politics, values, and ethics, which conflict when choosing options. Public policy takes place in the political environment, so politics has a role in influencing the policymaking process and content. The values reflect the principles and standards of behavior and conduct at the workplace. These are the underlying basis for providing a direction to the decision-making. The values determine the basis of making choices and are shaped by socio-economic-cultural and technological factors (McGill 1995; DFID 2003).

Ethical decision-making. It is a process of applying moral values and assessing their implications. It becomes the basis of accountability between citizens and the government. It helps to foster trust in the community. The values and ethics are to be rooted in the process of decision-making (Sintchenko and Coiera 2006; Van Gils and Klijn 2007). The values and ethical standards shape the direction of policies. These determine how logically correct steps are taken to meet desired standards of public values and behavior. For good decision-making, adequate alternatives should be generated, and the proper decision-making process should be followed. It should reflect a commitment to work, consistency, and competency (Thaler and Sunstein 2008; World Bank 2015). The ethical decision-making should be encouraged by designing processes in a transparent manner and by following evidence-based approach.

Complexity in decision-making. The descriptive, normative (or rational), and prescriptive approaches provide the process to arrive at decisions. But, the approaches do not specifically describe two aspects, *first*, the attributes and interactive nature of elements (variables and individuals) involved in the processes, methods, and criteria, and *second*, the uncertainty of results. The factors such as difficult or complex tasks, cognitive efforts for information processing, timely availability of information, the efficiency of processing of information, the context of work, and the interactions between attributes of various functions determine the complexity. The decision-making processes exhibit complexity due to numerous interacting actors and variables in multiple locations at different levels (Van Gils and Klijn 2007). Due to interconnected elements, the complexity should be examined in the policy cycle. The bigger the government system, organizations, or business, the decision-making is going to be a more cumbersome task and more complex.

Ethics and complexity. Ethical decision-making brings trust, confidence, efficiency, and a sense of predictability. Due to confidence and predictability of behavior, ethics will define how individuals and variables interact, and thereby the quality of conduct will be contingent upon that. On the other hand, unethical practices in decision-making bring unpredictability leading to nonlinearity and uncertainty in the thought process. Such practices percolate down and bring new structures and contribute toward complexity. Due to an unethical approach, the interacting individuals are likely to be reluctant, and interactions may get restricted or terminated (Simon 1977; Sintchenko and Coiera 2006; McBurney 2020).

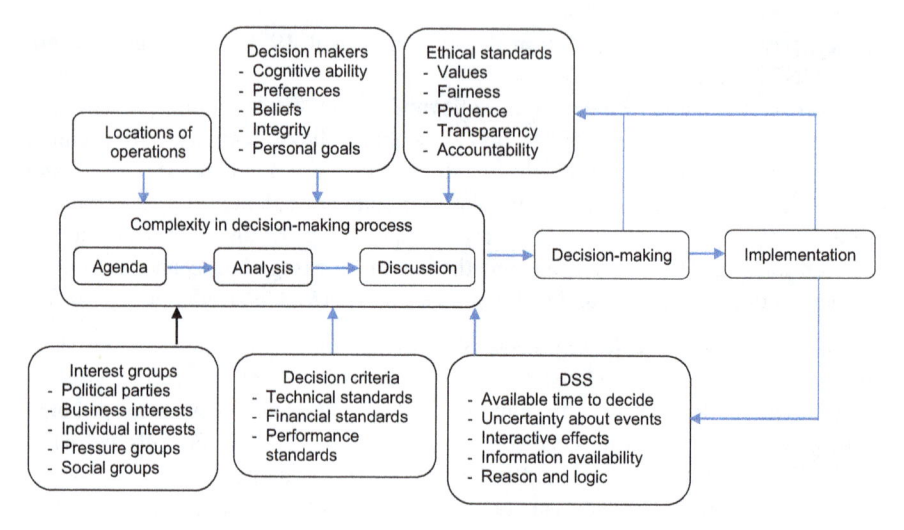

Fig. 4.1 Complexity in decision-making process

In decision-making, various components, such as decision support system (DSS), locations of operations, ethical standards, interest groups, decision criteria, and decision makers, are involved. These aspects, in combined form, bring complexity (Fig. 4.1). The elements under different components are as follows:

- *Locations of operations*: operations in different geographical locations.
- *Decision makers*: cognitive and behavioral issues, cognitive ability, beliefs, preferences, integrity, and personal goals.
- *Ethical standards*: values, fairness, prudence, transparency, and accountability.
- *Interest groups*: political parties, businesses, individuals, pressure groups, and social groups.
- *Decision criteria*: technical standards, financial standards, and performance standards.
- *Decision support system* (DSS): available time to decide, uncertainty about events, interactive effects, information availability, and reason and logic.

4.3 Theories and Models of Public Policy

Policymakers have a challenging responsibility. Persistent, often intractable problems keep questioning the efficacy of public policies. Uncertainty and dynamic changes in the environment make policymaking more complex. These changes come in many unknown forms. Advanced technologies, rising population and aspirations, and climate change are impacting in an unpredictable manner. For example, advanced technologies and their impact on manufacturing and employment are uncertain; the effects of climate change and global trade are not definite; unknown domestic and

4.3 Theories and Models of Public Policy

global factors impact businesses; and unforeseen pressure on the government for social security. These, in a combined form, are changing the setting in which the policy system works and putting pressure on the governments to respond (Sidney 2007; Swanson and Bhadwal 2009; Deloitte 2016; DSU 2018). The policy studies should cover both, *first*, what policymaking is and what its existing state is, and *second*, policy theories and their implications. There could be multi-State as well as multi-country studies covering developed and developing countries and fast emerging economies. It calls for examining the public policy approaches and theories to draw insights and lessons for better policymaking.

4.3.1 Evolution of Approaches for Public Policy

For several decades, research and studies in the public policy of various development sectors have been carried out from multidisciplinary perspectives. These have contributed to accumulating insights from the grassroots and body of knowledge. Gradually, the studies, in a combined manner, have provided the basis for the evolution of various approaches to public policy. An understanding of these approaches can help in gaining insights to conceptualize problems better and formulate policies.

A differentiation is made between approach and theory in the context of public policy. The approach is how one attempts or sets about policymaking in a general way. The theory is about a set of propositions intended to explain policymaking based on general principles. Under the current state of evolving complex problems, there are following questions that deserve to be answered:

- why good policymaking matters;
- how does the process work for policymaking;
- how complex problems, which are beyond the conventional approaches, can be understood and solved through innovative approaches; and
- how the policy process can be better developed for good policymaking.

It calls for an understanding of various approaches and how they can be better adapted for policymaking in the twenty-first century. Some of the approaches that have evolved since the twentieth century are summarized as follows:

First approach, policy diagnosis. From the beginning of the twentieth century till the 1940s, broadly, policy studies have centered around the content and evaluation of public policies and the role of government in policy formulation. It mainly focused on the diagnosis of government functioning and policies, socio-economic issues, and evaluation of the implementation of policies. The scholarly interest in public policy was felt by many social scientists since 1900 and steadily picked up momentum in the 1920s and 30s with the increase in government spending in the USA and Europe (Dunn 1981; Raymond et al. 1994; Leonard 2009). Initially, the approach concentrated on scrutiny of policy formulation (Portney 1986; Birkland 2011). During the

1920s, the focus was mainly on political philosophy and politics (Dewey 1927, 1929; Lynd 1939; Stone 2012; Goodin et al. 2013).

Second approach, policy sciences, policy analysis, and policy cycle. With the increase of the role of government in the 1930s, the importance of public policies was felt, and new approaches like policy sciences, policy analysis, and policy cycle got prominence. Lasswell (1951, 1971) contributed to the process of and knowledge in public policy formulation. It puts emphasis on a comprehensive and multidisciplinary approach to using knowledge as an essential ingredient. It included the role of individuals and behavioralism in policymaking. This approach was normative or value oriented. It laid stress on the 'policy sciences' ideal, the central role of science as a substitute for politics, and tried to establish the relationship between social sciences and policymaking. The policy sciences focused on contexts, problem solving, and multidisciplinary aspects by bringing content and technicalities from several disciplines. Its objective has been better decision-making, and a primary goal is to create a welfare society (Dunn 1981; Pielke 2004; Fischer et al. 2007).

However, despite the significant contribution of policy sciences to the growth of studies to public policy, some scholars (Kingdon 1984; Yanow 1996; de Leon and Vogenbeck 2007) had different perspectives. They highlighted that policy sciences do not deal with problem setting, problem framing, and political agenda-setting; citizen participation and creative engagement of people due to more focus on technical aspects; and complex socio-political issues, which demand context-specific perspectives. Subsequently, with a growing application of qualitative and quantitative tools, policy analysis got recognition during the 1950s (Dunn 1981; De 2012; Sapru 2012). From the 1960s onward, the policy cycle got attention (Jenkins 1978; Birkland 2011).

Third approach, economic theories as basis for public policy. Since the eighteenth century, various economic theories have played their role in shaping thoughts about public policy on the economy. Adam Smith, Thomas Malthus, and David Ricardo advanced political economy and classical theory, which became the basis of economic policies in the USA and the United Kingdom in the eighteenth century for over a century (Smith 1776; O'Sullivan and Sheffrin 2003; Mill 2009). In the twentieth century, various theories and models like Solow's growth model, Keynes's macroeconomic theory, Schumpeter's theory of innovation, dynamic stochastic general equilibrium (DSGE) model for macroeconomic, and neo-classical theory were proposed by various economists. And these became the basis for economic policies during the latter part of the last century.

Depending upon the economic theories, the focus of policies has been on analyzing issues such as capital, labor, demand, supply, consumption, employment, and market. In addition, behavioral economics, information economics, and institutional economics, to name a few, got wider acceptance due to their practical implications for the economy in the real world (Demsetz 1967; North 1990; Aron 2000; Rodrik 2000; Kahneman 2013; Stiglitz 2013; Solek 2014; Kirman 2016). These economic theories, among others, in varying degrees, had and also have an influence on public policies on the economy, firstly in developed economies and then in the developing world.

Fourth approach, system approach. Recognizing the limitations of the mental model approach in public policymaking, in the continuum of the concepts of the systems theory, the scholars proposed the system approach as a system of inquiry in policymaking. This approach deals with learning about systems (Gigch 1974; Forrester 1961; Keeney et al. 1990; Kelly 1998). The system approach puts forward systems thinking for solving problems in social systems. In furtherance of the system approach, interpretive structural modeling (ISM) and system dynamics (SD) modeling were developed for application in business, industry, and public policy.

Fifth approach, process of implementation, capacity building of institutions, and evidence-based policymaking. During the 1970s and 80s, there was a realization of the limitations of approaches for policymaking. So it gave rise to the emergence of a new set of ideas and concepts about the role of public institutions, the implementation aspect of policies, and evidence-based approach. The literature on public policy reflects that though the policy cycle recognized the role of implementation, enough attention was not paid to details, and the efficacy of the delivery mechanism was not studied in depth (Anderson 1997; Hill and Varone 2016; Camoes et al. 2017; Woolcock 2017). During policymaking, the implementation of policies did not get adequate consideration. It was assumed that the capacity of government delivery mechanism existed for implementing policies and programs, but it was not the case at the time of implementation (Birkland 2011; Brinkerhoff and Crosby 2002; Andrews et al. 2017). Mainly from the 1980s, there was a growing appreciation that public policies have not met the expectations of people. There was a felt need to understand how policies have fared in terms of delivering at the grassroots level. The focus emerged on implementation. Various policy studies were undertaken to examine the underlying implementation aspects—process and institutions (Alexander 1985; O'Toole 1986; Bates and Krueger 1993; Brinkerhoff and Crosby 2002).

Likewise, from the perspective of economic policies, economic analysts and policymakers have focused more on the allocation of resources and allocative efficiency. More emphasis has been on examining the issues from the lens of economic theories. But, little attention was paid to institutional processes, policy analyses, and implementation capacity. It has been assumed as if the implementation mechanism was available to deliver on economic policies (Israel 1989; Boin and Christensen 2008). It requires appreciating the criticality of both the policymaking process and implementation. There are issues of 'efficiency', both process as well as operational, and 'optimal' usage of resources. These have a bearing on how resources are allocated through analyses and how efficiently and effectively resources are utilized. These issues have not been dealt with by economic theories. As a result, public policy was approached from the point of view of the process of implementation. The scholarly works on policy implementation (Gunn 1978; Robichau and Lynn 2009; Woolcock

2017) sought to define the relationship between policymaking, policy implementation, and outcomes. These underscored the deficiencies in policy implementation—meeting intended objectives, providing quality services to targeted beneficiaries, and implementing projects (Potucek and Vas 2003; Hudsona et al. 2019).

How institutions are vital in the success of policy implementation received recognition from research studies (Zagha and Nankani 2005; Robichau and Lynn 2009; Acemoglu and Robinson 2010), and the causal relationship between institutions and the implementation of policies was studied. There was a call for institutional reforms for better policy outcomes (Hargrove 1975; World Bank 2000). From the point of view of shaping informed decision and objective approach, another dimension got prominence. With the increasing role of government in both social and economic sectors, rising government expenditure, demanding citizenry, and active media, the essentiality of informed decision-making and evidence-based approach in policymaking got recognition (Marston and Watts 2003; Geurts 2010; Baron 2018).

Sixth approach, network theory and agent-based modeling. While appreciating the limitations of conventional approaches, coupled with the increased understanding of the complexity in social and economic systems and, especially, the interactive behavior of individuals and economic agents, there has been a felt need for new approaches. The studies have underscored that the behavior of the system is determined by the relationships in society, communities, and markets. Social networks play their role. Due to advancements in digital technologies and connected devices, there is a rapid growth in the networked economy in the last two decades. The global markets are shaped by the interactions of economic agents and businesses in the networks at various levels—local, National, and global. Such changes are a result of complex social processes.

It is essential to understand human behavior, interactions, the structure of social networks, and group dynamics. These underlying issues have led to new approaches like social network analysis (SNA) and agent-based modeling (ABM). SNA studies the role of social relationships in the exchange of ideas, information, and knowledge. It can contribute to the understanding of various social phenomena. The study includes understanding structures, identifying local and global patterns, and comprehending network dynamics. It requires a multidisciplinary approach involving sociology, psychology, statistics, and graph theory (Freeman 2004; Will et al. 2020). The ABM is a computational model for simulating relationships, actions, and interactions of heterogeneous agents based on their attributes. The agents may be human beings dealing in economic activities, households, or economic entities. ABM can only do simulations and cannot predict the results of economic activities or system behavior (Jackson 2010; Gatti et al. 2018).

Seventh approach, complexity analysis. Since the 1990s, realizing the complexity in the public system and policymaking process, policy studies brought focus on the complex system while examining public policies (Gerrits 2010; Jones 2011; Ryan 2011). The complexity is a result of interconnected multiple global factors, nonlinearity, dynamic nature, and uncertainty. The management of climate change, quality public services in a State, transportation and power system, cyber security,

4.3 Theories and Models of Public Policy

and public institutions are examples of complex systems. They demand studying complexity (Mitchell 2009; NIC 2012; KPMG 2014). Likewise, due to an enhanced appreciation of complexity in the economic system and non-equilibrium state and evolutionary nature of the economy, there has been growing criticism of some of the economic theories, including classical theory, neo-classical theory, growth models, and dynamic stochastic general equilibrium (DSGE) model by several economists (Arthur et al. 1997; Holt et al. 2010; Solow 2010; Kocherlakota 2010). It gave recognition to complexity economics. As a response to meeting the challenge of complexity in the socio-economic system, new approaches like complexity analysis, systems theory, system approach, adaptive policies, and complexity economics are applied.

Since the 1960s, recognizing the complexity in the social system, there has been an evolution of new thinking and paradigms in the approaches of inquiry for development sectors, as reflected by Fig. 4.2 (Kelly 1998; Brinkerhoff and Crosby 2002; Ryan 2011; Jackson 2010; Morcol 2012; Gatti et al. 2018).

Eighth approach, innovative approaches to improve process of policymaking and policy design. With the increase in complexity in the system and rising demands from the citizenry, many innovative approaches have been developed to improve the process (i.e., how part) of policymaking and bring the 'design' aspect in policy formulation. Some innovative approaches are creative citizen engagement, deliberative dialogue, creating adaptive policies, policy design, and collaborative approach (co-design and co-creation). Besides, special attention has been paid to systems thinking, complexity thinking, and design thinking to explore the hidden potential and gain insights from the end-users. In addition, a few new approaches that have emerged are the behavioral approach, behavioral economics, and randomized

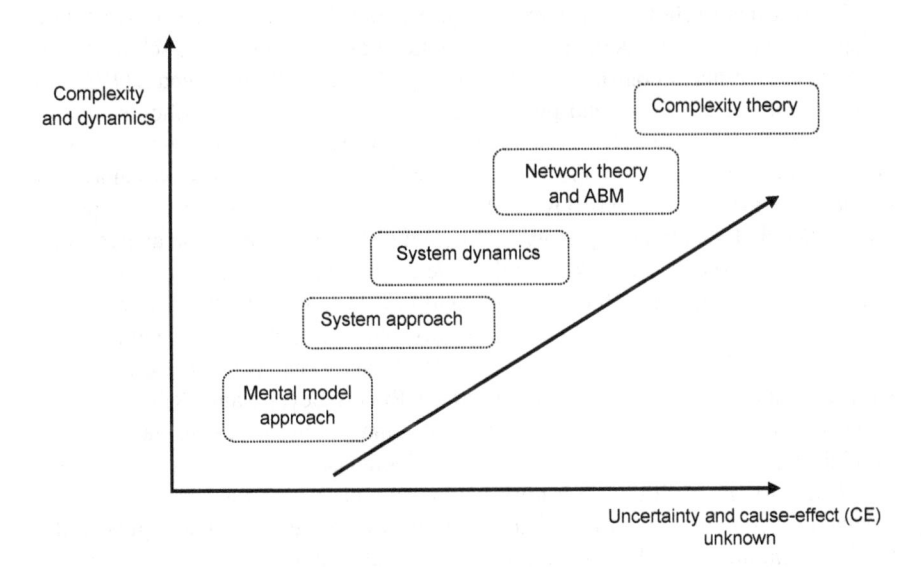

Fig. 4.2 Progression in key approaches for social and economic systems

controlled trial (RCT) for dealing with behavioral dimension in social systems. The concept of 'adaptive policies' has been recognized for dynamic and complex problems (Bankes 2002; IISD and TERI 2006; Sidney 2007; Swanson and Bhadwal 2009; Banerjee and Esther 2013).

4.3.2 Evolution of Theories and Models for Public Policy

The imperative of public policy is felt in every sphere of public life. Over the last century, public policy has attracted increasing attention due to scholarly work by many social scientists and experts in other disciplines. During this period, various theories and models of public policy have emerged. The growing interest in public policy resulted from the combination of the expansion of the power of government, the rising concerns of the people, and growing academic interest. The study of public policy was felt since the beginning of the twentieth century and got more attention in the 1920s. It mainly got a structured approach due to comprehensive work done on policy sciences by Lasswell in the 1950s to provide the basis for rational decision-making (Raymond et al. 1994; Jann and Wegrichi 2007; de Leon and Vogenbeck 2007).

Some of the key ideas, concepts, and methodologies that have helped in the evolution of theories and models for public policy are policy sciences, policy analysis, policy cycle, system approach, complexity analysis, behavioral approach in public policy and economics, innovative engagement of citizens, adaptive policies, design thinking, and policy design.

There are many scholars who have immensely contributed to the research in public policy and shaped the modern approach to policymaking. Some of the scholars who have made significant contributions are Dewey (1927, 1929) and Lynd's (1939) to political philosophy, State, and public; Lasswell (1951, 1971) to policy sciences; Easton (1957, 1965) to public systems theory; Forrester (1961) to systems theory and system dynamics; Dror (1983) to approaches of policy analysis, behavioral science, and systems analysis; Dye (1992) to politics, political science, and public policy; Dunn (1981) to policy analysis; Ostrom (1990) to institutional analysis and development (IAD) framework for collective action; Anderson et al. (1988), Gell-Mann (1995), Kauffman (1995) and Holland (1995) to complexity theory; Arthur et al. (1997) and Kirman (2011) to complexity economics; Michael Cohen, Ralph. D. Stacey, and D. J. Snowden to the complexity and organizations (Cohen 1999; Kurtz and Snowden 2003); and Morcol (2012), Robert Geyer, Samir Rihani (Rihani 2005) and Paul Cairney (2012) to complexity and public policy, to name a few. In addition, some of the Nobel laureates like Douglass C. North (for new institutionalism), Joseph E. Stiglitz (for information asymmetry), and Richard Thaler (for behavioral economics) contributed through innovative ideas and paradigms in the field of economics, which have significance for better economic public policies.

4.3.3 Public Policy Theories

Public policy has a vast canvas covering socio-economic, political, and security issues in the country. There is hardly any activity that is not touched by public policy. The actions taken by policymakers have wide implications for society. The policy actions can be in the form of development programs, legislations, executive orders, rules, regulations, etc. It may be for a specific purpose or in general and may cover part of the State or the whole State (Fischer et al. 2007; Gerston 2010; Birkland 2011). If one makes a deeper examination or searches underneath, one will find a host of aspects that matter are lengthy policymaking processes, politics, behavioral and pressing issues of multiple stakeholders, dynamic problems, institutional role, need for expert knowledge on the one hand and the necessity of collation of grassroots-level insights on the other, examination of evidence, policy analysis, dilemmas in decision-making, and so on (Anderson 1997; Marston and Watts 2003; Fischer et al. 2007; Sabatier 2007; Petridou 2014; Almeida and Gomes 2018). Therefore, if one were to consider these aspects, policymaking cannot be generalized by one policy theory.

To meet the challenge, with time, several policy scholars have put forward several theories and models after examining policy issues from different lenses. Various disciplines like political science, public administration, economics, sociology, and philosophy have played a role in shaping the evolution of public policy. Management models and systems theory have also contributed. With new learnings about evaluation studies of public policy, it has been realized that policy theories have to factor in dynamic circumstances, ever-changing environment, and complex political process (Easton 1965; Cohen et al. 1972; Sabatier and Jenkins-Smith 1993; Rihani 2005; Gerston 2010).

By learnings from the limitations of the previous theories, future theories were refined. In addition, new theories have taken shape by recognizing new dimensions or characteristics of the socio-economic system and appreciating the nuances from the feedback from various stakeholders. It has led to the broadening of knowledge horizon and contextual applicability. There have been perceptible enhanced scholarship, wisdom, and maturity in new theories.

In the backdrop of the above, the study of policy theories and models is necessitated due to the following considerations:

- which are the existing theories and models,
- what is the current state of study and analysis of established policy theories, and how they serve the public 'purpose' of sound policymaking,
- what is the evolving trend, and which are the emerging novel features,
- whether there is a need to take the theory or framework in a new direction, and
- how new study or theory should be differentiated enough to provide enhanced 'value' for policy formulation and implementation.

- *Group theory*. It says that public policy is a result of the group struggle to maximize gains. The competing groups influence public policy—process, choice, and implementation. A group may be farmer's organizations, trade unions, academic institutions, business chambers and federations, women's organizations, and so on, in which members share policy goals and strive to influence policy (Latham 1965; Anderson 1997). The theory stresses that the interest groups possess power either through resources or mass base support and have influence over the legislature and administration in making policy choices. The policy is formulated through the decision-making by the legislature or political institutions. The government provides a way to reach equilibrium through negotiations in the group struggles, and competing groups try to tilt the balance in their favor (Anderson 2003; Geurts 2010; Anyebe 2018).

Under the theory, the role of government is to determine the common ground and rules for different groups to participate. The politicians from the ruling party engage in bargaining, negotiations, and compromises with different groups. In some cases, due to overlapping memberships, the political parties are part of or coalitions of interest groups. The central point is that such groups have access to decision-making in the government, and the ability as a group to influence the policy in its favor depends on several factors such as activism and mass base support, media, influence through the use of political funding or lobbying, negotiation skills, and organizing skills. The group theory rests on the contention that interaction and struggle among groups are the central facts of political life (Latham 1965; Sharkansky and Hofferbert 1969; Isaak 1988).

Shortcomings. It is not logical to explain politics and policymaking solely through group struggle. The narrow focus that puts the process into just one group concept is not sufficient in explaining the policy process (Baumgartner and Leech 1998; Anderson 2003). It neglects many other factors such as ideas, agenda-setting, policy analysis, implementation, and the role of institutions.

Comments. It says that by design, policymaking is tilted in favor of certain groups who have influence. In the case of specific policies like the Right to Information (RTI), Right to Education (RTE), and Mahatma Gandhi National Rural Employment Guarantee Scheme (MNREGS), some individual activists and activists' organizations played their role as strong pressure or interest groups and succeeded in influencing the government through a protracted process of enactments. These pressure groups used a combination of the logic of bringing equity and accountability in society, emotional appeal, and popular support of civil society.

If it is examined closely, most development policies are directed toward serving the interests of certain groups, be it labor, farmers, or disadvantaged groups in the social sector, environmental groups, or business groups. As a result of disequilibrium due to competing interests, the government acts from time to time when any problem reaches to critical level with the support of a critical mass. It is inevitable that the policies are going to address the interest of certain groups.

The theory brings to the fore one important point, among others, that for a successful formulation of any policy, there is a need to have a critical mass of support of people in any sector. It, therefore, highlights that marginalized groups with smaller numbers have lesser chances of representation in the policymaking process and may not succeed in advancing their policy needs. Furthermore, the governments should acknowledge this limitation and, through special institutional arrangements, need to be proactive in addressing the concerns of small sections or disadvantaged groups.

- *Elite theory.* The elite theory highlights how the ruling elites influence the policy process in their favor. As a result, the policy reflects the values and preferences of elites in society. It is based on the assumption that the general citizenry or the masses are apathetic and ill-informed and do not determine or influence policy through their demands or actions (Bottomore 1993; Anderson 2003; Anyebe 2018). The basic premises of the theory are that the power is concentrated in the hands of elites, who are unified and have common interests. The power is derived from institutional position (Dye 2000; Amsden et al. 2012).

The elites may be formed based on wealth, social and religious values, and political power, depending on historical factors. Usually, wealth and political power status dominate the formation of elites. Under this theory, it is assumed that the country has two categories of people—elites with power and the common mass with little power and resources. In essence, the policy process favors the interests of elites. Due to the dominance of the elites in the political space or decision-making, it leads to a top-down approach (Dye and Zeigler 1990; Anderson 1997).

Shortcomings. The theory acknowledges the role of elites (Bottomore 1993; Amsden et al. 2012) in development policies and sharing resources of the country, but it overlooks to explain the role of political institutions, political executives, administrative departments, and other institutions like the judiciary and constitutional mechanisms.

Comments. As democracy deepens, media becomes more open, public institutions, including the judiciary, gain independent position, and citizens start exerting their rights through collective actions. It leads to more responsive policymaking. The elite theory will have less acceptance if the accountability mechanism is put in place.

- *Systems theory.* Realizing the limitation of the application of the reductionism approach in living and social systems, the systems theory was proposed by the biologist von Bertalanffy (1928, 1968). He proposed general systems theory (GST) as early as the 1920s and 30s, but it got recognition among scientists in the 1950s (Jackson 2000). It stated that the systems are open and interact with their environments and can acquire new properties through emergence, resulting in continual evolution. The theory stresses holism and relations between the parts. The system's behavior is not the sum of the properties of parts, and the system cannot be reduced to its parts for the purpose of analysis or understanding its behavior.

The changes in one part of a system may impact the behavior of other parts and the whole system. It may not be easy to predict changes in the pattern of behavior. The systems display the characteristic of adaptation depending upon the ability to learn and adapt to the environment and other constituents. It makes a distinction between dynamic and static (or mechanical) systems. Dynamic or human systems (like social systems) have structures or components that interact continuously, while static systems have structures or components that depend upon outside inputs (like mechanical machines).

GST is considered a unifying theoretical framework for studying systems based on transdisciplinary studies. It has key features like dynamics and change; linkages between the micro level and macro level, evolution, and adaptation; and integration of the natural and human world. The essential system concepts include system-environment boundary, information, input, output, process, system behavior, feedback, and hierarchy (Chen and Stroup 1993; Checkland 1999). The theory provided the basis for further research in various aspects of systems. And from the theory, new approaches, such as system approach, systems thinking, system dynamics, nonlinear dynamics, and complexity science, have emerged. The new approaches have provided robust methodologies for public policymaking (Forrester 1971; Warfield 1974; Senge 1990; Senge and Sterman 1992; Kelly 1998; Rihani 2005).

- *Political systems theory*. The work of Ludwig Von Bertalanffy on systems theory, applied in biology, inspired many social scientists from the 1920s. By applying systems theory, scholars have defined that the social and political systems have interacting parts or components, which in totality determine the behavior of a system. For example, the components, within the social system, are education, health, infrastructure, communities, families, and cultural organizations. The political system comprises a set of formal legal institutions. It will include components like public institutions, legislative bodies, administrative departments, judicial mechanisms, and political parties engaged in matters of public concern. Each component has a specific role and is indispensable and takes part in defining the system's behavior (Easton 1957, 1965).

David Easton applied the concepts of systems theory in the political system for public policymaking. The model defines the major components environment, political system, inputs, outputs, and feedback. The political system is defined as a set of institutions and processes to transform inputs from the environment into outputs as policies (Fig. 4.3).

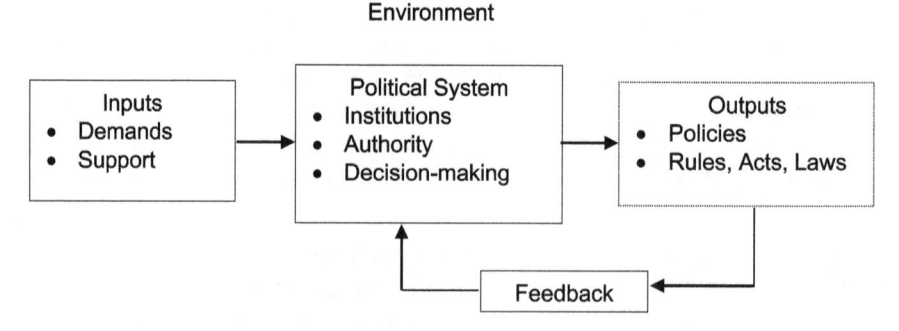

Fig. 4.3 Model of political system for policymaking

4.3 Theories and Models of Public Policy

The environment of the political system generates different demands as inputs, like the need for better education, improving the health system, etc., for example. The system gets support from the environment for its decisions. As an open system, it responds to the environment, provides feedback, and influences it. It assumes the dynamic nature of the political system and that the politics in the environment keeps changing.

Shortcomings. Some scholars believe that the usefulness of the system model for the study of public policy is too simplistic to serve as a useful model for understanding the policymaking process. And without studying the particular policy context, it cannot be generalized for different political settings. It is essential to understand issues like how the environment generates demands and impacts policies, which are the specific processes in the political system that enable it to develop public policy, and how, through feedback, the policies influence the environment (Walt 1994; Dye 1980; Osman 2002).

Comments. There may be limitations of Easton's model, but it provides contours of a system of policymaking. It analyzes various components like environment, system, inputs, outputs, and feedback. Such ideas have relevance and can be taken forward. Through more research, there may be a need to add value to the theory by understanding various social, economic, and political environmental factors and their impact on the political system as well as on inputs; values and beliefs within the environment and political system and their impact on decision-making; how the political system takes decision; and how the mechanisms work toward bringing changes in the demands and policy outputs.

To illustrate, in the context of India, the model has got implications. The policies on the green revolution in India started taking root since 1961 when India saw a stark shortage of food grains in the 1950s and 60s. Many stakeholders, like political parties, legislatures, agriculture scientists, farmers' organizations, civil society, and media, have been raising issues about the scarcity of food grains in the country. It created a demand for need for more food grains. There was the availability of technology as well as new varieties at the international level and also a conducive political and social environment for testing new varieties for raising production in the country. Some international organizations like FAO and UNDP extended support. The political system responded to such demands and made policy decisions for the import of high-yielding varieties of wheat and testing them within the country for future multiplication in the country for raising food grain production.

- *Rational choice theory.* The rational choice theory (RCT) is based on the premise that people apply the logic of cost–benefit analysis and weigh various options before making decisions. Such decisions give people maximum value and satisfaction in their self-interests. According to the theory, self-interests driven by rational decisions will result in better collective action and economy. The theory has applicability in different disciplines and areas of study in social sciences. It suggests that aggregate social behavior results from the behavior of individuals based on their rational approach. The theory has roots in rationalism and positivism by utilizing knowledge and analysis in a scientific and logical manner (Ulen 1990; Stewart 1993; Ogu 2013).

For rational decision-making, it suggests the following steps in a sequential manner: identifying the intended objectives, researching and selecting information, analyzing all possible options, weighing different options based on certain logic, selecting the option that maximizes the objectives, and then taking action based on that option. The critics of the rational choice theory say that individuals do not have access to perfect information and complete cognitive skills to analyze various options and their likely consequences. So they do not always make rational decisions. Instead, they also make decisions by considering external factors like emotions, cultural values, social norms, etc.

The Nobel laureate Simon (1955) rejected the assumption of perfect rationality in economics and proposed the concept of bounded rationality, stating that people cannot always have access to all the information to do a cost-benefit analysis and make rational decisions. Moreover, the knowledge of all the alternatives and their effects may not be known to individuals to make optimal decisions. In view of the impact of behavioral dimension, institutional factors, and politics in decision-making for public policymaking, RCT has limitations in determining policy options (Simon 1976; Neimun and Stambough 1998).

Comments. Though RCT has limitations due to difficulty in acquiring perfect information and making logical analyses and decisions, theory should not be given up because it is difficult to analyze and make rational decisions. Instead, ways should be found to enhance access to real-time and correct information and develop both qualitative (including behavioral and institutional) and quantitative models for analysis to make as rational decisions as possible.

- *Public choice theory.* The pioneering work by J. M. Buchanan, K. J. Arrow, and Duncan Black resulted in the public choice theory. It propounds the application of economic tools to deal with traditional problems of political science. It analyzes the behavior of voters, politicians, and bureaucrats as self-interested agents and states that their behavior is driven by the goal of utility maximization (Buchanan 1949; Arrow 1951).

It is similar to the economic model of rational behavior, with the assumption that people are mainly influenced by their self-interests (Black 1987; Buchanan and Musgrave 1999; Shughart 2020). These assumptions are applied to people in the political process. It states that the voters vote for a particular candidate thinking how they will be personally better off; the bureaucrats try to advance their career and self-interest; and the politicians seek election or re-election to further their interests.

The public choice recognizes that men are not angels and focus on the importance of the institutional rules under which people pursue their objectives. The bureaucrats attempt to maximize their budget through political maneuvering, and by virtue of that, they maintain their higher status. Similarly, politicians also try to maximize their

4.3 Theories and Models of Public Policy

interests. To check power and discretion by bureaucrats and politicians, the oversight committees of parliament and legislatures are required.

Comments. The public choice theory attempts to inform about the role of individual behavior in the political system and governance. It utilizes the behavioral dimension and self-interests in decision-making. The theory can be used to study further and identify specific factors that drive a particular behavior of agents or individuals and then to suggest which conditions and processes can bring desired behavior in the agents. This theory is silent on the process of public policymaking.

- *Lindblom's incrementalism approach.* For several years, since the pioneering work of Simon on bounded rationality, there has been criticism of the rational approach to decision-making on the ground of the inability to have access to perfect information and limited cognitive skills to consider all the facts to evaluate all possible alternatives to maximize the value (Simon 1955, 1976). Lindblom sought to provide an alternative approach to the rational model of decision-making. He argued that due to time, skills, and cost constraints in policymaking, it is difficult to identify policy alternatives and their likely consequences.

He put forward the idea of incrementalism (Lindblom 1959). Incrementalism tries simple incremental analyses, which consider incremental changes from the existing conditions in a step-by-step manner (Lindblom 1979). From the point of political and administrative expediency, simplicity, gradual change, and flexibility, incrementalism leads to less conflict and minimal disruption.

Limitations. If incrementalism is practiced as a policymaking approach, it will likely lead to the exanimation of limited options and short-term policy decisions. These may curtail the possibility of systemic reforms if they are needed. It may result in reduced creativity and innovation, and thereby, the possibility of new policies may get discouraged (Dror 1964; Anderson 1997).

Comments. The incrementalism approach has its utility in managing intractable social and economic problems. This approach may be applied wherever it is appropriate. For example, complex problems may require an incremental approach through a hit and trial process. Providing health services in remote areas may require a series of incremental steps by examining the situation as it evolves over time. Similarly, for developing industrial parks, many policy measures will be required for several operational issues in a continuous manner. Policymaking cannot be restricted in such a way as to use a particular type of theory. Incrementalism should not be used as a matter of routine but rather under the overall policy plan. Though rational choice theory (RCT) is criticized on the basis of some practical difficulties in having access to all information and complete cognitive skills to analyze all possible options, incrementalism has its limitations. It may not be a sufficient substitute, as explained above, for an RCT approach.

- *Garbage can model* (GCM). The garbage can model (GCM) was conceptualized for organized anarchies in organizations or decision-making due to a lack of clarity in members and their fluid participation. It applies to some organizations like public agencies dealing with many problems, educational institutions, etc. Organized anarchies provide a sense of chaos and dynamism (Cohen and March 1974). In situations of ambiguity or a lack of defined systems and processes, decision-making moves from ideas of actual problem definition, causality analysis, logic, and purpose to an unstructured approach. Cohen, March, and Olsen developed such a concept (Cohen et al. 1972).

The garbage can model (GCM) views decisions as outcomes of four independent streams within the organizations. Among the streams, the model presents three independent streams, viz., problems, solutions, and participants/decision makers, which run separately. These three streams meet only when the fourth stream of 'choice opportunity' arises. As defined by the model, these streams are (Cohen et al. 1972):

- *Problems.* These are within the organizations, affecting people and performance.
- *Solutions.* There are solutions to the problems, but they exist separately, and people do not relate solutions with problems.
- *Participants.* These people within the organizations have their perceptions and are not directly involved in problems or solutions.
- *Choice opportunities.* Due to certain factors and timings, choice opportunities arise for taking specific actions, and the decisions are taken by the combination of four streams. For example, in the case of an educational institution, the 'choice opportunities' could be due to the receipt of a grant to provide additional infrastructure or recruit manpower. Until then, the decisions are not taken.

Comments. GCM provides concepts about three streams, which are valid in real-life situations due to a lack of clarity in an organization or unsystematic approach. The stakeholders need to bear such possibilities in their minds. It could serve as an awakening call for policymakers or decision makers to be observant of the possibility of complacency or organizational inertia. In any organization or policy system, the participants are aware of problems. It could be that they are not in a position to define the problem, or due to organizational inertia, the participants tend to overlook problems. Likewise, the solutions for many problems are known to participants or authorities within the organizations, but no action is initiated. There may be some disconnect between the three streams due to either lack of attention or an unstructured approach.

GCM has been successful in terms of highlighting the reality of organizational limitations in many settings. At the same time, for many important cases, the policy process is an extensive exercise, and policymaking cannot be simplified to meeting of three streams with the 'choice opportunity'. And as such, GCM is not able to explain the policy process.

- *Multiple stream framework* (MSF). Kingdon (1984) developed a model after studying the US (United States) institutional setting for policy formulation. He laid stress on agenda-setting in policymaking and introduced the concept of policy entrepreneur. He wanted to move beyond rational and linear representations of sequence or stages in the policy process (Weible and Carter 2017; Almeida and Gomes 2018). Kingdon defined policy entrepreneurs who take the opportunity

4.3 Theories and Models of Public Policy   161

to contribute to agenda-setting as well as policy solutions. They are driven by their self-interest or professional satisfaction. Entrepreneurs are people with the knowledge, tenacity, and drive to seek the attention of policymakers. They may be elected members or leaders of interest groups and use knowledge of the process to further their policy ends. According to Kingdon, the agenda-setting process is competitive due to the participation of different actors and policy entrepreneurs.

Kingdon utilized the three streams of garbage can model (GCM) and refined them to present multiple stream framework for policymaking. He defined three steams viz., problem, policy, and politics, which show their dynamic behavior and run independently. Policy formulation takes place when these three streams come together during a brief 'window of opportunity'. These three streams influence the policy agenda and final decision-making. The three streams are briefly summarized below (Kingdon 1984; Cairney and Jones 2016):

- *Problem stream*: It highlights problems and their attributes. These seek the attention of policymakers, and only a small fraction of problems get attention. Policy entrepreneurs try various methods for attention.
- *Policy stream*: It deals with the likely ideas and solutions for the problems. Multiple actors and policy entrepreneurs play their roles in advancing their solutions through advocacy.
- *Politics stream*: The policymakers pay attention to the problems and the proposed solutions based on their beliefs, public opinions, and feedback from interest groups and political parties.

Limitations. MSF does not provide a complete policy formulation process and is more confined to opening of the window of opportunity (Sabatier 1991; Birkland 2011). It may not provide answers to policy formulation in most policy settings. At the same time, the policy process is a complex exercise, which is not explained by MSF.

Comments. Like GCM, MSF provides a practical side of policymaking in the government, in which there is a likelihood of a lack of attention paid to a systematic way of handling the policymaking process. In the context of India, the formulation of policies on the Mahatma Gandhi National Rural Employment Guarantee Scheme (MNREGS) and the Right to Information (RTI) Act are examples of MSF in which the policy activists (policy entrepreneurs) took an active part in highlighting the problems and suggesting policies, which were appreciated and accepted by the policymakers in the government.

- *Advocacy coalition framework* (ACF). From the 1980s, there was a felt need for an alternative to a policy cycle approach and other policy theories of that time. It was realized that the policy cycle is a linear or stage-based depiction of the process, including stages such as policy agenda, policy formulation, implementation, and evaluation. Under the policy cycle, there has been a dearth of causal explanations in the policy process (Sabatier and Jenkins-Smith 1988; Petridou 2014; Weible and Jenkins-Smith 2016). The advocacy coalition framework (ACF) emerged due to research efforts by Sabatier and Jekins-Smith (1988). It began as the study of policymaking in the USA, focusing on environmental issues, but subsequently, it has been applied to many policy areas and political systems.

The framework presents that the actors within the subsystem, with shared beliefs, form the coalition and compete with other coalitions. The activities take place within the subsystem and follow the policymaking process at multiple levels of government that provide constraints and opportunities to coalitions. The subsystems are issue-specific networks of people or stakeholders from multiple interests. The stakeholders may be elected members, government officials, media personnel, business organizations, labor unions, and scientists and researchers from academia. The subsystems may be formed at any level—National, State, or local. Coalitions learn from the process of policy formulation and implementation through the lens of their respective beliefs or stand on policies (Cairney and Weible 2015; Weible and Jenkins-Smith 2016).

The policy change occurs through a process of consultations, negotiations, and compromises over time (Sabatier and Jenkins-Smith 1999; Weible 2005). Policies often reflect and translate the beliefs of one or more coalitions. The policy change is due to factors such as internal policy failures or external influence from changes in socio-economic conditions, structural change in the economy, disruptions through technological advances, the impact of a court ruling, or change in the government due to some popular sentiment (Weible and Sabatier 2007; Cairney and Weible 2015).

To summarize, the ACF provides a policy process that is dynamic and is based on the premise that the interest groups are organized in policy networks within a particular policy domain. It recognizes the role of multiple stakeholders and institutional actors associated with the policy in question. Also, it appreciates the role of cultural values, social structure, and fundamental constitutional values. The framework views policymaking as an iterative process, with mechanisms for policy change that runs over a long time. It also considers the influence of coalitions, public institutions, policy implementation, and feedback to the environment (Birkland 2011; Weible and Jenkins-Smith 2016; Almeida and Gomes 2018).

Comments. ACF provides a good framework for policymaking by integrating both theory and practical understanding. It examines key elements such as stakeholders, beliefs, subsystems, political system, and the role of public institutions. But, there may be two distinct possibilities about the coalitions. *First*, it is not necessary that coalitions will be formed in all cases. The policies may be formed due to the appreciation of the problems of the stakeholders by the government. For example, the policy on export facilitation for MSMEs or on solar energy for rooftops in response to climate change. *Second*, even if the coalitions are formed, it is not necessary that there will be competitive coalitions. For example, coalitions of farmers' organizations raise their demands on higher minimum support price (MSP), while the organizations may have different priorities. In some specific cases, the coalitions may have moral support from society. For example, better working conditions for the labor class may have support from civil society.

- *Punctuated equilibrium theory* (PET). Punctuated equilibrium theory (PET), proposed by Baumgartner and Jones (1993), explains the long periods of stability in policies and then a period of sudden change or disequilibrium. The basic premise is that the continuity of policy results from institutional culture, pressure groups or vested interests, bounded rationality, selective attention by the policymakers, and policy monopolies. This model assumes that individuals operate with limited rationality. The government tries to build an image of a particular policy to continue with the policy through institutional arrangements. It helps to maintain the status quo through a negative feedback loop (balancing loop) in the system to reinforce the status quo (Baumgartner and Jones 1993; Givel 2010). At the same time, some groups try to reach out to some forums, such as the media, to highlight the critical concerns and the courts for their interventions to break the status quo or policy monopoly of the government. The system disrupts due to exogenous pressure or internal pressure from the critical mass. It causes a positive feedback loop, which results in continuous change, and the system reaches the state of disequilibrium before it settles for a new equilibrium (Cairney 2012; Petridou 2014; Almeida and Gomes 2018). The 1991 economic reforms in India are a classic example of this theory.

- *Behavioral economics*. The scholarly research by economists Herbert Simon, Daniel Kahneman, Amos Tversky, and Richard H. Thaler shaped a new paradigm of behavioral economics. It combines insights from economics and psychology to understand how and why people respond in real-world situations. Influenced by insights such as heuristic thinking, bounded rationality, bounded self-interest, bounded willpower, loss aversion, cognitive limitation, and social preferences, behavioral economics can contribute to new tools for designing public policy for bringing desired behavioral change for achieving better policy outcomes (Simon 1955; Kahneman and Tversky 1979; Thaler 1981; Sunstein et al. 2017).

It differs from neo-classical economics, which generally assumes that people have requisite information and a good understanding of preferences and make well-informed decisions based on utility maximization. Behavioral economics studies how economic decisions for purchases of assets or adoption of new policies are influenced by cognitive, emotional, social, or cultural factors.

It incorporates the ideas and concepts from psychology to understand how behavioral biases influence decision-making and how the behaviors can be changed. Behavioral economics has helped economists better appreciate human behavior in economic decision-making. The ideas like overconfidence, loss aversion, and self-control are key concepts in behavioral economics. Governments and businesses have developed policy frameworks to improve their strategies (Kahneman and Sugden 2005; Thaler and Sunstein 2008).

By improving the architecture of decision-making, behavioral economics is being increasingly used to inform and develop policy interventions for tax collection and compliance, minimizing error by interventions for prompting correct behavior. It focuses on the concept of 'nudges', which tries to provide alternative choices and guide people to adopt new and better practices. It has found application in financial education, pollution control, water and sanitation, health care, environmental protection, tax policy, poverty alleviation, and transparency and accountability.

For example, by prominently displaying ideas such as 'the public works made possible by paying taxes' and 'the moral obligation to pay taxes', it enhanced tax collection in the UK (Leicester et al. 2012; Chetty 2015; Sunstein et al. 2017). It can provide useful insights into market research and data analysis. It has laid emphasis on 'beneficial social norm', 'changing the default option (or, a tendency to return to status quo)', and 'repeated reinforcements'.

- *Behavioral approach in public policy.* As discussed in Sect. 1.1.2, the application of behavioral science in public policy is well-recognized. It postulates that understanding human behavior and subsequently promoting behavioral change has the potential to bring the desired change in individuals and society. In this context role of culture and values in the social environment matters in determining the behavior of individuals and communities (Pottenger and Martin 2014; World Bank 2019a). From the point of their applications, culture and values are interlinked. These hold importance for policy formulation and implementation (Geertz 1973; Chan 1991; Abolafia et al. 2014; World Bank 2015; Blyth et al. 2016; Muers 2017).

Comments. This approach underscores the need to have the right balance between culture and values on one hand and technical evidence and application on the other. These are to be considered during the decision-making process. Understanding values and culture should help policymakers comprehend attitudes, social norms, or habits of stakeholders. At the same time, the technical evidence cannot be overlooked and need to be considered while addressing the technical nature of problems. For example, institutional delivery in maternity cases and immunization services, especially in remote rural and tribal areas, are resisted due to cultural practices. But as a policy measure, the technical perspective of maternal health service will be better appreciated if the sensitization of beneficiaries precedes.

Likewise, in the case of practices for sanitation and personal hygiene, the technical support for modern practices should be promoted through specific behavioral changes. In India, utilizing insights to nudge people toward a desirable behavior has found application in important initiatives like '*Beti Bachao Beti Padhao* (BBBP)' and *Swachh* Bharat Mission (SBM) (Economic Survey 2020) for promoting girl child education and sanitation. So at the implementation level, the existing cultural preferences of individuals or communities for adopting new practices need to be well-examined and factored in.

In addition, the understanding of social culture and norms and family values can have significance for programs such as sending children to schools, girl child education, implications of quality education, environment management, taking modern medical prescriptions in case of serious health problems in traditional societies, household savings, promoting entrepreneurship, and so on. If proper stakeholder analysis is done to identify problems and issues from their perspectives, the socio-cultural issues and family values will become more visible.

4.3 Theories and Models of Public Policy

Note: Complexity theory and complexity in the economic system have been dealt with in detail in Chaps. 3 and 5.

Concluding remarks. The studies of various policy theories reveal that from the latter part of the nineteenth century (Fischer et al. 2007; Goodin et al. 2013), the 'what' part of policymaking got more attention. The policy theories mainly focused on different 'elements' or 'constituents' of the policy cycle—comprising both policy formulation and ex-post analysis or evaluation. But, which factors or activities would have impacted the 'how' part of policymaking or 'process of policymaking' did not get enough consideration. In addition, from the broad perspective of 'policy cycle' and 'stakeholders', the policy studies and theories have focused less on details of fundamental activities or steps in the 'policymaking process', the policy 'content' in relation to end-users needs, and the 'process' of implementation of policies (Brinkerhoff and Crosby 2002; Woolcock 2017). There has been a realization of the role of institutions and implementation (World Bank 2000; Robichau and Lynn 2009; Woolcock 2017) in achieving policy objectives. Still, the policy theories have to work more on the institutional and implementation aspects.

The discussion on different approaches and theories underscores how they have been shaped by the emerging knowledge about policy systems, policymaking, implementation, institutional aspects, and socio-economic characteristics. Various policy theories in combined form have provided an understanding of broad aspects of policymaking. The theories presented above may not address all the issues that policymaking needs or may not provide the requisite answers, but they provide useful pointers, which are complementary. As a policy analyst or policymaker, one can utilize the insights from various theories and synthesize them for further research. Yet, the policy theories do not specifically deal with the following:

- policymaking process: 'how' stakeholders' consultations, need assessment of end-users, data and information collection, evidence collection and policy analysis, and identification of policy options take place,
- causal relationships between various factors of policymaking (like how institutions influence policy choices),
- dynamics of interactions between institutions, stakeholders, ideas, values, politics, environment, and ethical issues in policymaking,
- role of decision criteria and decision-making process in selecting policy options, and
- policy implementation—process and approach of implementation, and capacity of the implementation mechanism.

4.4 Critique of Public Policy in India

4.4.1 Policymaking in India: Select Case Studies

Institutional issues

The institutions represent rules and values of functioning. The institutions influence the engagement of stakeholders, provide a way to elicit responses from them, and determine the decisions. By providing institutional structures, processes, and mechanisms, they can create an environment of credibility and develop the capacity to formulate effective policies and implement them by following norms. It can ensure self-correcting ways for effecting policy changes and the ability to sustain policies in the long run (van Heffen and Klok 2000; Anderson 2003; Spiller and Tommasi 2003).

The central argument is that institutions affect policy choices. The institutions determine the capacity of the system to formulate public policies and deliver on intended objectives. They provide the foundation for public governance and impact all spheres—education, health, public services, economy, business, etc. (Menard and Shirley 2011; Acemoglu and Robinson 2010). There is a ubiquitous influence of public policy. It requires horizontal as well as vertical integration of initiatives in all interrelated sectors for leveraging complementarities. It demands system-wide institutional development for all development sectors at macro, meso, and micro levels.

Policymaking structure. In India, the Part XI of the Indian constitution specifies the distribution of legislative, administrative, and executive powers between the Union or Central government and the States of India. There is a division of functions between Central and State governments, with specifically defined lists, viz., Union, State, and Concurrent (Table 4.2). In addition, the third tier of the local self-government has been added by way of the 73rd and 74th Amendments to the constitution with defined roles and functions. This structure broadly defines the role of governments in the public policy system.

At the Central level, the Cabinet, under the chairmanship of the Prime Minister, working on the principle of collective responsibility, is the top policymaking body in the government. The concerned Ministry brings the matter before the Cabinet for its consideration. The Cabinet may refer them to the sub-committees for a more detailed examination (Maheshwari 2000; Sharma 2004). The Cabinet approves the public policy concerning all major policy matters. With its approval, the policy proposal becomes effective. But, in some cases, the policies, depending upon the statutory requirements, are enacted by an Act of parliament. The routine matters are handled by the concerned Ministry. Similarly, the policymaking process takes place at the State level through State Legislatures and Cabinet.

In general, the stakeholders who participate in policy formulation are the Parliament, Legislatures, Cabinet, State governments, officials, media, political parties, non-governmental organizations (NGOs), and citizens (Sharma 2004; Sapru 2012).

4.4 Critique of Public Policy in India

Table 4.2 Institutional structures for public policy at various levels (India)

S.No.	Levels	Broad functions	Institutional arrangements	
			Legislative/Elected bodies	Administrative
A.	Central and State levels			
1	Central (Union government)	Under Union list and concurrent list	Parliament/Cabinet	Central Ministries and agencies
2	State	Under State list and concurrent list	State Legislatures/Cabinet	State-level departments and agencies
B.	District level			
3	District	Functions as assigned by the State government		
	District[a]	Rural: Functions assigned under Eleventh Schedule (Article 243G) of the 73rd Constitution Amendment Act	*Zilla Parishad* (local body at district level)	District Collector/CEO *Zilla Parishad*, district-level officials of departments
		Urban: Functions assigned under Twelfth Schedule (Article 243W) of the 74th Constitution Amendment Act	ULBs for urban areas (Municipal corporations/ Municipal councils/Nagar *panchayats*)	Municipal Commissioners and Chief Executives, officials of departments
	Block (sub-district)	Rural Functions assigned under Eleventh Schedule (Article 243G) of 73rd Constitution Amendment Act	*Mandal Parishad*, Block *Samiti*, or Block *panchayat* (Block level local body)	BDO and Extension officers; officials of line departments
	Gram panchayat (GP) (local bodies in rural areas)	Functions assigned by the State government (Article 243G) of the 73rd Constitution Amendment Act	*Gram panchayat* (local body) (village level)	GP level field functionaries

[a]NGOs, CBOs, and research and training institutions are engaged in some development activities
BDO Block Development Officer, *CEO* Chief Executive Officer, *ULBs* Urban Local Bodies, *NGOs* Non-Governmental Organizations, *CBOs* Community-Based Organizations

The higher judiciary intervenes if there is any infringement of laws during policy-making. Though the policy formulation takes place mainly at the Central and State levels, the policies are implemented through institutions at various levels—Central, State, district, or local bodies like municipal bodies and *panchayats*. A summary of broad functions at different levels is indicated in Table 4.2.

Contemporary trends in public policy

The policymaking process was studied during 2010–18 by consulting officials, subject matter experts, policy advisers, and citizens. The Central Ministries covered for the consultations are the Ministry of Rural Development, the Ministry of Health and Family Welfare, the Ministry of New and Renewable Energy, and the Ministry of

Human Resource Development (HRD), together with Planning Commission (before 2014). It included policymaking for Mahatma Gandhi National Rural Employment Guarantee Scheme (MNREGS), climate change, the Right to Education (RTE), economic reforms, and health.

- *Case study of Mahatma Gandhi National Rural Employment Guarantee Scheme (MNREGS).* In India, the poverty alleviation programs started with a community development (CD) program. In 1960, wage employment started with the rural manpower program (RMP) in 32 CD Blocks on a pilot basis to provide employment for 100 days per year (Planning Commission 1956, 1961). It was followed by the Crash Scheme for Rural Employment (CSRE), launched in 1971 during the 4th plan. In the 1980s, the National Rural Employment Program (NREP) and the Rural Landless Employment Guarantee Program (RLEGP) were started in 1981 and 1983, respectively. In 1989, the NREP and RLEGP were merged into a single rural employment program known as *Jawahar Rozgar Yojana* (JRY). Thereafter, The Employment Assurance Scheme (EAS) was introduced in 1993.

The State of Maharashtra passed The Maharashtra Employment Guarantee Act, 1977. In 2001, the State of Rajasthan launched an employment-based drought relief program, indicating State-level interventions. National Rural Employment Guarantee Act (NREGA) was enacted in 2005 by an Act of Parliament as an enforceable right of the citizen to demand employment. In 2009, it was renamed Mahatma Gandhi National Rural Employment Guarantee Act (MGNREGA). The wage employment program has been a result of rights-based politics and a justiciable right to work for all adults in rural India, with a promise of 100 days of work per year at the statutory minimum wage notified for the program (MGNREG Act) (Planning Commission 2002, 2007).

Comments. To understand deeper, the process of formulation of the Act has been examined, and field-level feedback was taken from beneficiaries, activist groups, and officials. Realizing the criticality of rural employment, the Act was enacted as a result of efforts of various social groups, activists, and the coalition of groups who actively mobilized the opinion in favor of assured wage employment in rural areas. The activist groups engaged with the government for the formulation of the Act. They advocated the cause by stressing that there has been rural stress and that wage employment is a better way to solve the employment problem. The Act, in principle, has a special provision to provide wage employment to people in rural areas and an elaborate system of transparency in work allocation and wage payment. This Act operates on the premise that people will get wage-employment jobs, and the unemployment problem can be mitigated substantially.

Examining from the perspective of which policy theory can explain the formulation of wage employment through the Act, the theories like advocacy coalition framework (ACF) (rights-based approach), multiple stream framework (MSF), and political systems theory (Table 4.3) can explain such an enactment.

4.4 Critique of Public Policy in India

Table 4.3 Case studies of public policies: tools, theories, thinking, and approaches

S.No.	Policies/Acts	Policy analysis tools	Policy theories	Policy process: thinking and approaches	Remarks
1	Mahatma Gandhi National Rural Employment Guarantee Scheme (MNREGS)	• Consultative process with stakeholders, especially activists and experts, and case studies of different States	Advocacy coalition framework (ACF) (rights-based approach), multiple stream framework (MSF), and political systems theory	• Consultation process • Past case studies of Maharashtra Employment Guarantee Act, Rajasthan Employment program for drought relief, *Jawahar Rozgar Yojana* (JRY), and Employment Assurance Scheme (EAS) • Opinions of some proactive activists and experts mattered. Some of them, with their groundwork, influenced the decisions in the government • Unidimensional approach: covering one dimension of solution, and not considering different possible options	• Grassroots-level consultations were needed to examine issues holistically as well as alternative options for employment • Disparities and diversity in different regions should have been considered
2	Climate change	• Experts' consultations • Commissioning studies • Case studies	Elite theory (top-down) and multiple stream framework (MSF)	• Report of Intergovernmental Panel on Climate Change (IPCC) and multilateral agreement on climate change provided the basis • Consultations with States • Top-down approach	• Grassroots-level issues of vulnerable regions were not adequately captured • Institutional mechanisms and capacity building for implementation should have been considered in detail

(continued)

Table 4.3 (continued)

S.No.	Policies/Acts	Policy analysis tools	Policy theories	Policy process: thinking and approaches	Remarks
3	Right to Education (RTE) Act	• Experts' and activists' consultations • Case studies	Multiple stream framework (MSF), political systems theory, and top-down approach (rights-based approach)	• Consultative process with stakeholders at the National and State levels • Consultations with States • Linear thinking and unidimensional approach (limited options and linear cause-effects)	• Socio-cultural issues of families need consideration • Quality of education should have been given focus (lack of integration of factors)
4	Economic reforms	• Experts' consultations • Forming experts' group, and commissioning studies • Consultative process with stakeholders • Case studies	Elite theory (top-down), political systems theory, multiple stream framework (MSF), and punctuated equilibrium theory (PET)	• Consultations, case studies, and reports on various economic issues laid the foundation of reforms • Liberalization of entry for businesses and industries, trade, and investment were the focal point • Institutional mechanism and implementation issues should have been addressed and remained wanting • Integration of human resource, skill development, technology readiness, and business service delivery not adequately considered • Top-down policy measures	• Productivity (manufacturing), per capita income, and per capita exports remained low (at global level). These factors should have been mainstreamed in the economic policies during reforms

(continued)

4.4 Critique of Public Policy in India

Table 4.3 (continued)

S.No.	Policies/Acts	Policy analysis tools	Policy theories	Policy process: thinking and approaches	Remarks
5	Health policy	• Consultative process with stakeholders • Experts' consultations • Forming experts' committees and reports • Case studies	Elite theory (top-down), multiple stream framework (MSF), and political systems theory	• Consultations with experts, health institutions at National and international levels • Consultations with States • Top-down interventions	• Grassroots-level disparities and diversity are not adequately captured • Systemic analysis of delivery mechanism is not attempted • Behavioral, economic, gender, and distance constraints are not adequately studied • Lack of integrated approach

- Linear thinking: considering the problem or system in a simple cause-effect relationship (without considering feedback and multiple causes)
- Unidimensional: covering one aspect or dimension of the solution, or not considering different possible options

Regarding the policymaking and implementation, during the discussions with the beneficiaries, they informed that the grassroots-level consultations could have been helpful in examining employment issues holistically and exploring alternative options for employment generation. During the formulation of the MNREGS Act, various other policy options for employment were not included. For example, the policy alternative could be having the program for different regions like fully or 80% irrigated, semi-irrigated, and rain-fed areas. Each could have a specific employment strategy. During consultations with people in rural areas, there were many equally pressing issues. Despite the benefits of MNREGS, many people expressed their priority for improving the quality of health services, quality education, and safe drinking water. They mentioned how they had to incur extra expenditure to get health services, how their children could not get quality education, which deprived them of future opportunities, or how the drinking water was to be fetched from distant locations. There were issues with the quality of water. The consultations suggested that the people were keen on quality infrastructure for schools, colleges, health centers, or irrigation structures. Such aspirations could have been reflected in the policy or action plan under MNREGS.

Exploring the combination of employment-cum-asset generation for irrigation and building health centers could have been a good option to try and dovetail such projects under MNREGS. Moreover, a plan for integrating with the self-employment program could be encouraged, as some families have been inclined to do their own business or run their household profession. But they needed financial support. Based on the field study, wage employment is provided to 30–40% of the people in a gram panchayat for days ranging between 30 and 50 in a year. Thus, the program has limitations in providing employment for a significant number of days (https://dashboard.rural.nic.in/dashboardnew/mgnrega.aspx).

Often, as an answer to the question of alternative ways of creating employment, it is cited that some other Ministries or departments are devoting themselves to providing employment in other sectors. This aspect has merit and deserves to be integrated for a comprehensive view. The Act provides uniform guidelines for all States, but it should consider the disparities and diversity of resources in different regions. For example, some states have a higher level of irrigation (like Punjab and Haryana). These States can provide wage employment through three crops round the year vis-à-vis other rain-fed States, which have much less irrigated areas requiring more wage employment.

Despite tangible benefits in the rural areas through MNREGS, the basic point is whether there could be a better process of policymaking to identify alternative policy options and include a broader perspective on employment to evolve a comprehensive policy for employment in rural areas.

- *Case study of climate change policy.* Climate change has been occurring due to the effects of global warming, caused by emissions of greenhouse gases such as carbon dioxide, methane, and nitrous oxide. There is a scientific consensus that climate change is happening and that human activities are the primary driver. Several adverse impacts are being observed in the form of changes in the timing

4.4 Critique of Public Policy in India

of seasonal events like the flowering of plants, decline in agricultural productivity, sea level rise, climate extremes, etc. As per reports, in India, the share of fossil fuels in electricity consumption is about 78%.

The availability of fossil energy sources is limited to sustain economic development. Climate change has been identified as one of the most significant future challenges facing nations, governments, and citizens (IPCC 2007). It will adversely impact the environment, especially the fragile coastal areas (NAPCC 2008). There are challenges of: *first*, meeting the country's energy requirement, *second*, addressing the concern of climate challenge, and *third*, finding suitable substitutes for fast-depleting fossil fuels.

The National Action Plan for Climate Change (NAPCC 2008) adopted the strategy of deploying appropriate renewable energy (RE) technologies to mitigate greenhouse gas (GHG) emissions at an accelerated pace. To meet energy needs, RE technologies are the answer even in remote areas due to the distributed nature of RE resources (IPCC 2007, 2012). RE can serve multiple policy objectives, including mitigation of the adverse impact of GHG, enhancing national energy security, economic growth, creating jobs, reducing local pollution, and providing affordable and reliable energy for all citizens. It recommended eight national missions: solar mission, energy efficiency, sustainable habitat, water mission, sustaining the Himalayan ecosystem, green India, sustainable agriculture, and strategic knowledge for climate change. Various experts and environmental activists made contributions to the policy formulation.

The proposed missions provide a comprehensive list of missions required for a climate change plan. But there remains a question about the sufficiency of missions in meeting climate change challenges. And whether other vital aspects, like the consultation process with vulnerable groups of people, institutional issues, and empowerment of communities, should have been considered in the climate action plan. The issues that deserve to be discussed with people are how a rise in atmospheric temperature could impact crop productivity; due to the rise in sea level, the submergence of low-lying areas; due to an increase in temperature, how the number of working hours might be curtailed; and how people will manage, in case of the adverse impact of climate change. How people's lives could be affected needs discussion from their perspectives.

Regarding the policymaking process, consultations with people living in coastal areas and other vulnerable regions or small farmers who could be affected were not made in a structured manner. In a way, the primary source of problem investigation or consultations with people at the grassroots is wanting. The likely consequences of adverse climatic conditions should have been discussed with people who were to be affected to sensitize them, take measures in advance, and prepare a local climate action plan.

There is a case of solar energy policy in which several elements are missing. The PLF and plant efficiency of operational plants should have been used for policymaking. Besides, for correct assessment, the estimates of solar irradiance or solar radiation flux density for a two-year-round cycle for multiple locations, say for every

100 km, covering potential geographical regions, should have been carried out. Likewise, technical data like 'cell efficiency' for operational solar power plants was not taken. At least it should have been determined for select operational plants to get up-to-date and correct information.

Similarly, for wind energy, for multiple potential locations, data on 'wind speed' and 'energy density', say for every fifty km, for a two-year-round cycle, have not been available. Besides, there are many locations, especially for wind energy, that come under protective regions or environmentally vulnerable regions, requiring environmental clearances. The data for such regions is very much needed as inputs for policymaking. Such data could have been helpful in planning for setting up windmills. Sound policymaking for renewable energy should have access to accurate scientific data for RE resources in multiple locations, the potential of RE resources, current PLF and electricity production from each plant for different RE sources, plant efficiency, land availability, environmentally vulnerable sites, district-wise grid-connectivity, and so on. The climate policy or subsequent policies should have covered such issues in detail. The policy theories that can explain the formulation of climate change policy are elite theory (top-down) and multiple stream framework (MSF) (Table 4.3).

- *Case study of Right to Education (RTE).* To provide free and compulsory education to children, the Right to Education (RTE) Act was enacted by the Parliament of India in 2009. It recognized free and compulsory education for children in the age group of 6–14 years under Article 21A of the Indian Constitution. The Act lays down some duties for governments, schools, teachers, and parents. It contains rules on pupil-teacher ratio and teacher vacancies. During the enactment process, there have been discussions in the departmental committees, legislative committees, and parliament. The activists and educationists played important roles. There were rounds of discussions with different States, which, in turn, had consultations with State-level institutes, experts, and legislatures. The members of consultative groups expressed solidarity with the cause of providing children access to primary schools as a matter of right. RTE Act was mainly driven by a combination of activism and the intent to improve access to education, following the rights-based approach. The policy theories, like multiple stream framework (MSF), political systems theory, and top-down approach, can explain the education policy (Table 4.3).

While examining the Act and the policies, it brings out that the systemic analysis of problems has been lacking. For example, the grassroots level issues that have not found adequate consideration are the distance of remote hamlets from the schools, availability and quality of school infrastructure, economic conditions of families, behavioral issues of families and community, and quality teaching culture. Understanding constraints for enrollment or reasons for absenteeism was not given enough attention in the policy. Though, every year, at the beginning of the session, a special drive ensures 100% enrollment. Thereafter, children's attendance remains a major issue, especially from disadvantaged groups. Another challenge is managing 2–3 classes in a single room with a single teacher.

From the perspective of institutions, the important issues are the number of teachers for a school, the number of pupils per teacher, the competence level of teachers, training of teachers, quality indicators, and learning outcomes. These should have been addressed by the policy. Though some studies by research experts or institutes were considered, the grassroots consultation process was not sufficient. The examination of the root causes of the inability of families to send their children to school has been lacking. There has not been institutional (social) analysis in terms of encouraging families to send their children to schools, improving the village environment to encourage communities to appreciate the need for education, and creating a good school environment. The grassroots-level consultations with families and community to understand constraints and insights from below were not reflected in the policy document.

For example, issues that required study were why families have been reluctant or were constrained to send their children to schools; what practical constraints teachers face in managing classes; why teachers are not able to provide quality teaching; why learning outcomes are not adequate; and which factors are responsible for the inadequate learning environment. In addition, based on field-level consultations, some innovative ideas that could have formed part of the policy document are how the transport facilities for girl children, through incentives, could have been included in the policy to enhance daily attendance; how teachers could be encouraged to provide extra attention for financially weak children; performance-linked scholarships for sending their children to schools; and exploration of innovative pedagogy for improving the learning outcomes of children.

- *Case study of economic reforms.* The economic reforms in India primarily focused on opening the country's economy to the world and expanding the role of private and foreign investment. The reforms were prompted by a balance of payments crisis that resulted in a recession, causing structural adjustment programs for loans from the IMF and World Bank. Some measures included reducing import tariffs, deregulating markets, reducing excise duties and taxes, removing non-tariff barriers and licensing procedures for imports, and decreasing quantitative restrictions on imports (Jadhav 1991; Mohan 2018). The policies related to economic reforms can be explained by elite theory (top-down), political systems theory, multiple stream framework (MSF), and punctuated equilibrium theory (PET) (Table 4.3).

History matters in the complex economic system. Evidence shows that the economic reforms have enabled some credible gains for the country. In the last 30 years, high level of foreign exchange reserves, sustained manufacturing contribution to GDP, increased share in global exports (from a mere 0.6% in the early 1990s to 1.8%), robust software exports, and sustained economic growth in the range of 6–8% indicate the success of the reforms. The reforms have led to an increase in foreign investment. There has been a significant poverty reduction. The economic reforms focused on the technical aspects related to the licensing system, reduction in tariffs, liberalizing norms for import, and so on. But, quite a few primary drivers of the economy—human capital, technology readiness, labor productivity, disposable income, process innovation in setting up businesses, and institutional capacity—did not get enough attention from the policy perspective. The lack of human resource capital (HRC) and low technology readiness impacted labor productivity adversely. It had unfavorable consequences for competitiveness, manufacturing growth, exports, and economic growth.

In 2019, the per capita GDP of India was $2,104 (nominal current) (145th rank globally) or $7,034 (PPP current) (131st rank) (IMF 2019). The low per capita GDP in India or low hourly wages in India have adverse on family income in comparison to the United States of America, Japan, South Korea, and China. Low income has left little room for the majority of households to have enough disposable income to purchase consumer durables or industrial products, thus affecting demand (Eugene 2007; Deloitte 2016; IMF 2019).

Due to heavy reliance on financial aspects, the economic reforms did not address issues concerning the systems, processes, and people—government institutional mechanisms, skills, culture, and processes in the organizations dealing with industrial matters. For example, when new economic reforms were initiated, adequate attention was needed to change the work culture within the government institutions to align their functioning with new intents of liberalization and facilitate setting up business and industry efficiently. Or, it required a culture of ease of doing business. Similarly, the business and industry should have paid attention to bringing a culture of innovation, enhancing R&D, upskilling and reskilling, and enhancing labor security, as all these have an impact on business expansion, productivity, and sustainability. The policy implementation lacked rigor, as it did not consider the capacity of the institutions and cultural factors to deliver on reforms in an integrated manner.

Due to a lack of skill development, people at large did not find enough opportunities to participate in the development process. It resulted in income inequality. The implementation mechanism to execute various economic policies related to infrastructure, industrial parks and zones, and business and trade facilitation was not adequately developed, resulting in low efficiency and delays. There has been some success of economic reforms, and only some regions of the country could benefit.

In contrast, to raise economic growth, many developed countries like the USA, Germany, Japan, China, Japan, South Korea, and Taiwan designed innovative policies for industrial development and manufacturing by focusing on quality education, R&D, skill development, higher wages, supply chain management, and cluster development (Hemmert 2007; DSU 2018; Gerstel and Goodman 2020; Naughton 2020). As a result, they have been successful in advancing their economies at a rapid pace.

- *Case study of health.* To understand health policies, some key policy documents like National Health Policy (NHP), 2002; National Rural Health Mission (NRHM), 2005; National Health Mission (NHM), 2013, including two Sub-Missions, the National Rural Health Mission (NRHM) and the National Urban Health Mission (NUHM); and National Health Policy (NHP), 2017 have been examined. These have many useful and comprehensive lists of recommendations and intents. The documents define goals, principles, and objectives and indicate performance indicators like 'equity', 'affordability', 'patient-centered', and

4.4 Critique of Public Policy in India

'quality of care'. These reflect targets for reducing IMR, MMR, TB, Malaria, and other Vector- and Water-borne diseases and other diseases. After the examination of the policy documents, the following observations are made:

a. *Assessment of resources.* The linkages between the current state of targets for a particular problem to a new set of targets, say, after 5 or 10 years (NHP 2002; NRHM 2005; NHM 2013; NHP 2017), as the case be, are not examined. In addition, to reduce the mortality rate or eradicate diseases, the assessment of new infrastructure, additional health manpower, new treatment facilities, logistics support, and enhanced resources are not reflected.

b. *Improving operational efficiency.* There is a need to improve the process efficiency to enhance the reach of service to patients by reducing the time to avail services. It will require improving logistics support; PHC-specific manpower planning; timely availability of equipments, medicines, vaccines, etc.; training of field staff, and reducing the administrative burden on doctors. For example, from the perspective of efficiency, the field studies reflect that as much as 30% of the time of medical doctors is occupied in administrative matters. Similarly, paramedical staff devote 20–30% of their time in traveling in the field. Reducing time in non-medical activities is a challenge.

c. *Specific requirements for a patient-centric system.* The NRHM (2005) and NHM (2013) specifically mention improving patient care, and NHP (2017) indicates 'patient-centered' and 'quality care'. But for patient-centric services, the very first requirement is to enhance the availability of doctors and nursing staff, medical equipments, and logistics support, especially during odd hours. Due to such inadequacies, there are difficulties in achieving a patient-centric quality system.

d. *Ground-level practical realities and last-mile reach.* There are practical issues. The time taken by the field staff in hilly areas is three times as much as compared to plain areas. Due to frequent disruptions in the mobile (phone) network, it becomes difficult to get timely feedback from the patients. For emergencies, timely communication and transport are essential to the successful reach of health services. Besides, in remote areas, basic amenities like housing, general transport, and educational facilities are scarcely available. These impact the living and working conditions of health staff, while the same health policy works for all areas—plain and remote. Health services during odd hours (6 P.M. to 8 A.M.) are adversely affected due to restricted movement of the field staff members, especially female staff, who live in distant locations. Such local realities of reaching out to the last mile are not recognized in the policy document.

e. *Quality health care.* The critical issues like how the reach of health services can be ensured for the last distant and remote villages; how maternity services can be made available to mothers and children in time; what are the cultural inhibitions for taking allopathic treatment and immunization; how the mobility of health personnel be increased in remote areas to enhance the reach of the health system; how the PHC can become a hub of health services for all basic health needs; how cesarean delivery can be ensured at PHC level to ensure safe delivery to reduce MMR; and how every mother from the time of pregnancy and, after birth, both mother and child can be tracked on a daily and weekly basis till 2 years after the delivery to ensure personalized care. To meet these requirements for quality health services and safe maternity services, the required policy inputs need inclusion in the policy document.

f. *Specific indicators.* For specific terms, goals, and objectives used in the policy document, the 'quality indicators' and 'performance indicators', depending on the applicability, should have been reflected in the policy documents to bring specificity and clarity for future action plans at the State and district levels.

g. *Local-specific insights.* Based on the geographical terrain and the need for local travel, how local logistics support can be better planned for efficient service delivery in remote areas and during odd hours requires examination.

The policy theories, such as elite theory (top-down), multiple stream framework (MSF), and political systems theory, can provide necessary explanations for health policies. Finally, the policy documents do not contain the implementation plan and mechanisms, except outlining some contours broadly. Having a list of policy intents and good recommendations is useful. But, these should be backed by rigorous analyses to bring the real issues from the grassroots and potential solutions to the fore.

General observations about policymaking

Usually, the discussion on policymaking begins within a group comprising top policymakers—Minister(s), elected members of Parliament, senior officials, and select technical experts. Often at the time of policymaking, instead of issue-based and problem-based discussion, the agenda-setting and policy solutions are predetermined and driven by priorities and prevailing ideas in the social and economic environment or political ideologies in some cases. The political members have their political agenda or priorities. The priorities arise from the need to address pressing citizens' concerns, deliver some results to show performance before the people and opposition parties, meet the requirement of interest groups, or meet international obligations. The members express their views, but the views and decisions of the top are taken as final.

If the process is examined closely, it will reveal that the decision makers, experts, and participants have good reasons and reasonably good knowledge. But these may not be sufficient, given the nature of specialized knowledge and the need for deeper policy analyses. They may not have access to the latest expertise or knowledge of future trends due to emerging innovations and fast-evolving technologies or may not have a full conception of the grassroots-level problems and needs. Regarding the engagement of experts from various institutes, they are consulted at short notice or may not have sufficient time to deliver quality input when engaged. Moreover, the gamut of issues concerning people living in numerous locations and diverse conditions is quite large and may not be within reach of select experts or the policymaking group.

For economic policies, there may be a battle of turf. Though the private sector is concerned about the need for professional considerations, it appreciates if the final policy aligns with their thinking and priorities. The activist experts will like to see their ideas carried forward till the final policy document and may not be favorably inclined to take others' views. The technical or economic experts, who are a part of the policy groups, are good at the technical aspects of a particular field and try to push their viewpoints forward. Besides, there are sometimes competing interests and issues related to ideologies and behavioral preferences. There may be multiple valid points—cooperating, conflicting, and competing—of different stakeholders to push forward. Officials have a difficult task of integrating the views of stakeholders and aligning them with that of political leadership. Their personal values and preferences influence decisions. Typically, past ideas and practices become the basis of decision-making for future policies, while future problems differ from past problems.

Usually, in advance, during policymaking, the field-level studies may not be available. The lack of a culture of brainstorming and informed discussion has an adverse impact during all stages of policymaking. For example, examining the state of development in different geographical regions assumes importance in the context of diversity, disparities, and cultural issues. But these issues find less time during the discussions. The need to make quick decisions keeps the discussions short. The decisions are determined by the views of the chairperson of the group. As for inputs, past case studies in a few States, some international reports, or the experts' collective ideas become the basis for discussions. These are generalized as an acceptable basis for decision-making. It eventually leads to final policymaking. Despite top policymakers working under certain constraints, they are open to good ideas and want sound policy proposals.

Specific issues about policymaking. Due to the non-availability of recent past or real-time data and analytical tools, the examination of evidence in detail and policy analyses remain wanting. Usually, the analyses do not form part of the final policy document, though some reports from experts or concerned institutions are referred to. Often, opinions or anecdotal evidence are taken as a basis for analysis. The financial or technical criteria are not adequately defined for decision-making. The policy document provides a list of good recommendations and does not contain detailed analyses or explanations for decision-making. Specifically, various analyses—stakeholders' perspectives, micro-macro linkages, system structure, institutional (including implementation mechanism), behavioral dimension, complexity, technical, and policy options—are not sufficiently attempted. For comprehending complexity, the analysis of interactive effects between elements and the evolutionary nature of the socio-economic system is not studied. The recommendations are made unanimously.

It is evident that the members of the policy group have something to contribute, but a holistic or integrated view remains a distinct possibility. It leads to a policy document with several good to excellent ideas but comprehensive and cohesive content. Overall, policymaking takes place within several constraints and leads to a narrow and short-term approach to addressing problems. Due to a lack of correct and timely information, requisite analyses, and supporting technical basis, combined with biases and lack of time, policymaking tends to become 'exercise-done-in-urgency' to achieve pre-defined objectives and addresses limited ground reality. The context-specific analyses are not carried out. Usually, the success of one region, a particular State, or another country is cited for replicating the solutions without much attention paid to the local geographical and socio-economic conditions. The success factors need examination before replication in other areas.

Public policymaking is a complex process. Often, in the government, due to the compulsion to perform quickly or deliver results in a short time, there is a tendency to oversimplify the process with less effort to examine relevant issues and undertake detailed policy analyses. There is linear thinking in policymaking, implying that the cause-and-effects are taken linearly without considering feedback and multiple causes. In contrast, there are multiple factors that work simultaneously besides feedback loops and multidimensional socio-economic issues. Without a structured approach, detailed analyses, and evidence-based decision-making, the policy document tries to include as many good ideas as possible and mainly of vocal voices who participate in the policy discussions. Thus, the inclusion of good ideas is considered a sound policy document. To understand the causality, the attempt is not made to find linkages between ideas and likely outputs.

The greatest challenge is how to balance politics, behavioral issues of stakeholders, the limitation of requisite knowledge and skills, experts' analysis, the limitation of time, and the limited capacity of the policy system. All the stakeholders have unique points to add value for policymaking, but these are to be assessed from the lens of systemic understanding, the strength of evidence, and possible alternatives. Many individuals—officials, experts, and advisers—may have good knowledge, experience, and commitment, but rigorous analysis, informed discussion, identifying alternative policy options, and informed decision-making are essential elements for sound policymaking.

Critique of policymaking from the complexity point of view. Usually, through the conventional approach, the mental model approach or mechanistic (scientific or reductionist) methods of examining issues in isolation are applied to the social and economic systems in which public policies are formulated. Policymaking has been attempted by examining different subsystems or components independently without examining the interactive effects of elements, including system variables, within the social systems. And necessary policy instruments are designed or policy contents are developed as a stand-alone exercise, away from the problem context of interactive issues and elements. There has been silos thinking, without interlinkages between different components or their integration.

The studies have reflected that there has been an increasing realization that the behavior or the performance of the whole (system) cannot be explained merely from the knowledge of the behavior of its constituent parts in isolation, as the behavior of a whole is found to be different from that of the parts or sum of the parts. And the integrated and interconnected view of the system is not captured in the policies. Usually, during policymaking, the interlinkages of factors, causal relationships, and integration of various factors are not considered for analysis. Or the policy process lacks the system-wide analysis and the examination of the interactive effects of elements. Besides, the contextual inputs—like understanding the geographical variations, cultures, and local resources—are not adequately recognized for policymaking. In combined form, as a result, there is a tendency to replicate the solutions from one region or sector to others. The underlying thought has been a one-size-fits-all approach and prescribing the same policy solutions for different contexts. For instance, one education policy or health policy has been the norm for the entire country, while there are diverse or widely differing ground situations.

As an illustration, the quality of education depends on the interactions between many factors, including quality of teaching methods, training of teachers, the motivation level of teachers, school environment, reading-writing materials, assessment methods of children, socio-cultural conditions, group behavior, etc. In the policy document, the systemic analysis of components and the factors within them are not attempted and presented. The policy document on education contains several recommendations as a summation of a list of suitable interventions. But the document lacks in providing an integrated view of underlying factors, grassroots-level problems and insights, and their interactive effects in a holistic manner. It is the interrelationship that is vital for understanding the system and then exploring the solutions while considering ground realities (based on analysis of RTE 2009; NEP 1986, 2020). Likewise, in the health policy (NRHM 2005; NHM 2013; NHP 2017), different components like infrastructure, equipments, manpower, capabilities, monitoring system, logistics, and last-mile connectivity are not addressed holistically, and also their interactive effects are not examined.

For complex systems like education, health, climate change, or manufacturing, the interactive effects of elements (including system variables) should be examined. The policymaking should explicitly and comprehensively address interlinkages of elements at the micro level, system-wide view of all the components and elements, the nonlinearity of interactions, unknown or unexplored group behavior, and likely new emergent needs of the stakeholders. These are the basic issues on which the success of the public policy depends.

Finally, in general, based on the case studies, policymaking suffers from many reasons like insufficient planning for formulating policies, the lack of patience due to constant pressure from interest groups and citizens, the need to deliver in quick time, the want of requisite knowledge and expertise, the culture deficit for informed discussions and decisions, the inadequate manpower to handle several important tasks under policy formulation, transfer of officials in key positions in the government, and insufficient time with policymakers, including top officials and internal experts, due to their preoccupations with many other matters at hand. In the age of changing needs of the citizens due to rising aspirations and sensitization by electronic and social media, rapidly evolving technologies, and the need for specialized knowledge, it is evident that the capacity of the policy system needs strengthening.

4.4.2 Policy Implementation Issues

Why implementation matters

Policy implementation is vital for the acceptability and credibility of the policy. The policy will find its acceptability among citizens if it serves the public purpose, depending upon how effective the implementation is. The credibility will depend on the norms and values of decision-making, transparency, and accountability. Formulating a policy is a starting point for the implementation. In operational terms, moving further from the enactment of the policy, implementation is a process of achieving desired policy outcomes. It is of critical importance for the success of the policy. It involves multiple steps, inputs, and actions for translating the intended objectives of a policy into outputs (Cerna 2013; Khan 2016). It will require examining how the interlinked programs and policies will converge at the implementation level, how the funds can be allocated optimally, how the infrastructure can be managed efficiently, and how quality services can be provided to citizens.

The studies have emphatically brought out the necessity of the effectiveness of the implementation of programs to achieve the desired policy objectives and to ensure that the intended benefits reach the target group. Simultaneously, it needs to be viewed in the light of how the implementing departments face operational challenges like: *first*, the delivery system has to operate and provide far-reaching and higher expected quality services with reduced resources and limited functional capacities, and *second*, being public institutions, the departments are expected to be more accountable, responsive, and effective, besides citizen-centric. The departments need to utilize the resources optimally and build capacities not only effectively but also creatively (UN 2006; Rizvi 2008; NSW 2015; Chakravarty and Chand 2016; OECD 2017a).

Case study of implementation of major programs at district level. In India, under State and Central budgets, a large number of programs are directly or indirectly implemented through district-level agencies. As an illustration, in 2016–17, at the district level, total funds amounting to about Rs. 9.5 lakh crore, i.e., $140b, or 6.4% of GDP, were allocated in the country to various socio-economic programs. These programs pertained to infrastructure, rural development, agriculture, education, health, etc. In 2016–17, it was estimated that under various programs, funds worth Rs. 4.0 lakh crore (about 27% of the total Central and State plan budget together, or about 2.7% of GDP) (Table 4.4) were allocated to district-level agencies (including urban local bodies) (approx. Rs. 700 crore per district for a population of about 20 lakh). The major portion of the funds, about 90% of the total, were related to rural areas, while urban development had a share of about 10%. For other programs, about 38% of total funds (i.e., Rs. 5.5 lakh crore, or 3.7% of GDP) were allocated. These involve inter-district or State-wide projects. The district-level agencies have limited role but provide crucial support for land acquisition, implementation of last-mile projects, and coordination. Such programs are implemented by State agencies like the public works department (PWD), irrigation, industry, etc., or by Central agencies. And the remaining amount of Rs. 5.28 lakh crore was allocated for various special State- or National-level programs related to higher education, health, irrigation, power, ports, central and State PSUs, etc.

In the backdrop of the allocation of a significant amount of funds worth Rs. 700 crore per district, the key issues that require examination are, *first*, whether the delivery mechanism at the district level has adequate capacity to implement to

Table 4.4 Implementation of central and state budgets at district level

S.No.	Items	Value (Rs. lakh crore)	Remarks
1	A. Plan budget		
1.1	Central government plan budget (implemented directly by Central ministries)	3.70 [From total Central plan (8.69 lakh crore)]	Budget at a Glance, 2016–2017 (GOI) (for ports, airports, mines, Central PSUs, etc.)
1.2	State governments plan budget, including Central government share	11.08	State finances: A Study of Budgets of States, 2016–17 (RBI)
	Sub-total	14.78	
2	B. Implementation at district level		
2.1	a. Implementation directly by districts (State government plan budget, including Central government share)	4.00	Approx. 700 crore per district for a population of about 20 lakh
2.2	b. Important indirect role of districts (i. State Govt Plan Budget, including Central Govt Share, implemented by State agencies, and ii. Central government plan budget implemented directly by Central government agencies)	5.50	For land acquisition, implementation of last-mile projects, or coordination for: • Irrigation • Highways • Industrial parks • Power projects • Electrification, etc.
3	Total of 'B'	9.50	

Source MoF (2017), RBI (2017). Analysis of budgets of States and district-level plans of select districts
PSU Public Sector Undertaking

achieve the desired objectives; *second*, which are the factors that impact the efficacy of the delivery system; *third*, how efficient implementation of programs can enhance the desired outcomes; and *fourth*, the specific interventions that can raise the efficacy of the system to achieve higher performance.

Key determinants for policy implementation

Earlier, from the beginning of the twentieth century, the studies on policy implementation have mainly focused on the evaluation of the results of the policies (Raymond et al. 1994; Jann and Wegrich 2007; Birkland 2011). The systematic study of process of policy implementation has been relatively new, while policymaking got more prominence. Subsequently, mainly from the 1980s, more attention was paid to the implementation issues (O'Toole 1986; Bates and Krueger 1993; Cerna 2013; Hudson et al. 2019).

During policy formulation, mainly due to a lack of time and resources, micro-level feedback and people's perspectives about problems and solutions do not get enough recognition. In the absence of such perspectives, the policies find it hard to address the issues that people face, and many ground-level practical difficulties are not considered (DFID 2003; IDS 2010; Mueller 2020). For example, in the health policy, the concerns of diverse stakeholders and the varied problems in the villages or towns are not reflected in the policy document. Such exclusions lead to difficulties during the implementation stage.

Generally, the agencies for implementation are not adequately consulted during the stage of policy formulation. So, as a result, there remain gaps between what is intended and what is feasible in terms of implementation. Likewise, other important factors that are not taken into consideration are the institutional capacity on which the effectiveness of implementation depends, the availability of manpower and their capabilities, the complexity issues, and the kind of approach that is to be followed for the implementation of policies (Hill and Varone 2016; Woolcock 2017; Loayza and Woolcock 2020). A good implementation strategy should take into consideration the following aspects:

- *Approach for implementation.* Based on the control of decision-making, there have been two main theories, top-down and bottom-up. From the point of view of the 'process' of implementation, two approaches, viz., rational planning and process approach, have been in practice. The process approach has practical significance as it considers the evolving nature of implementation based on local conditions. The bottom-up process approach deserves priority to cover ground realities. During implementation, the norms and standards should be adhered to.
- *Complementarity and convergence of policies and programs.* For better utilization of resources, the complementary policies of interlinked sectors and convergence of resources and services at the implementation stage are essential.
- *Why 'process' of service delivery or implementation of programs matters.* The 'process' refers to a set of activities followed to provide services to citizens or implement projects. It is more related to the management aspect. The idea of examining 'process' is to understand the activities involved, the time or cost

4.4 Critique of Public Policy in India

incurred by citizens in such activities, and the efficiency of service delivery. As regard the implementation of projects, the activities are to be planned and executed as per set standards. To add further, the 'process' (of service delivery) differs from the process used in the 'process approach' or 'process of policymaking'.

- *People's perspectives in formulating the policies.* The policies are intended to serve people's interests and achieve the objectives that the people look forward to, making it imperative to include their perspectives.
- *Micro-level feedback.* To effect timely interventions, feedback is essential to get timely information and facts from various stakeholders on various aspects of implementation. It could be through standardized reporting mechanisms, policy reviews, and opinions of stakeholders, including field-level functionaries and citizens. It will also be essential at the time of policymaking.
- *Engagement of implementing agencies in policymaking.* Implementation is an integral feature of the policy cycle. It should be thought through during policymaking. So, the frontline agencies should be consulted to get their views on the feasibility of implementability of policies.
- *Institutional capacity.* Institutional capacity is essential for the successful implementation of policies. Capacity refers to the values and norms, capable manpower, skills, resources, and support mechanisms to plan and carry out the interventions to achieve policy objectives (Rodrik 2000; Ferrini 2012).
- *Systemic approach.* The development is not merely about formulating policies but also designing the delivery system for effective implementation. The system should be robust, and the design should follow a systemic approach. It should look at the system as a whole rather than disjointed units or parts (Sushil 1993; Ryan 2008, 2014). For systemic design, the delivery system should broadly look into both hardware and software parts. The hardware includes infrastructure, human resource development, planning and monitoring units, logistics support, etc. The software involves administrative setup, organizational structure, leadership, motivation, team building, culture, and inter-group dynamics.
- *Understanding complexity.* The policy implementation takes place in a socio-political environment where a large number of stakeholders with diverse interests and cultures interact with the implementing system. Besides, the implementation involves numerous activities, managing operational and legal issues, among others. A combination of these factors creates complexity during the process of implementation.
- *Decision-making.* From the point of view of efficiency and credibility, proper decision-making assumes high importance. The norms, values, ethics, decision criteria, transparency, and accountability are essential for decision-making.

Critique of delivery system for public service delivery

To understand the implementation of development programs, field surveys were carried out for a system study in seven states during 2008–10. The States covered for the survey were Andhra Pradesh, Kerala, Madhya Pradesh, Maharashtra, Rajasthan, Tamil Nadu, and Uttar Pradesh. It covered the delivery system and public services of health, sanitation, primary education, agriculture, *Tehsil* (revenue department office), public distribution system (PDS), banks, and urban bodies. The study was conceived during the brainstorming sessions at the field level through focus group discussion (FGD) with the concerned stakeholders, viz., citizens, officers and staff, and elected members. The consultations brought out several issues to light about the service delivery and implementation of programs at the grassroots level. Broadly, the study covered the following aspects:

- Systems (of delivery of services),
- Processes (of service provisioning),
- Work culture,
- Citizen management.

The major findings of the study of the delivery system are summarized as follows:

- *State of the system* (in terms of manpower, infrastructure, equipments, logistics, etc.). As indicated in Tables 4.5 and 4.6, it reflects that there is an inadequacy in the capacity of the delivery systems under study. The average for the state of the capacity stands at 35%. The status of the system of delivery in *Tehsil* (certificate issuing office under the revenue department) is relatively low, which could be due to the non-availability of up-to-date land records and case records for service seekers and litigant parties. These have implications for many business activities for mutation and registration. Likewise, the state of systems in other services is low due to reasons like a lack of infrastructure, manpower, equipments, and logistics.
- *Process efficiency*. It measures the productive time in availing the services to the total time in the entire process. Low efficiency reflects the time utilized in non-productive activities or more waiting time in the process of availing services. For example, the process efficiency (2.5%) for availing the caste certificate remains low due to 2–3 visits that are to be made by the applicants to the office of *Patwari* (Village level functionary under the revenue department) or *Tehsil* office. Similarly, in the case of 'availing bank credit', visits are required by the farmers to agriculture, *Tehsil*, and bank or cooperatives bank offices, due to uncertainty in getting loans in time. These visits are reflected in low process efficiency (6%) for availing agriculture credit from banks. There is very little follow-up from the concerned agency or department to facilitate efficient service delivery. Thus, the unreliability of services is captured in low efficiency.
- *Focus on achieving targets*. Due to a top-down approach, the field-level agencies are given physical and financial targets and expected to achieve them. In this process, the quality of implementation does not get priority attention.
- *Cost of availing the services*. The cost of availing services is high in some cases, like availing bank credit. The farmers are required to spend about Rs. 2,200 for credit on average (for taking a loan of a high value of Rs. 50,000 or more, or a new *Kisan* Credit Card). The cost of documentation is Rs. 1,500 (though banks deny it, the beneficiaries informed that they had to spend money for documentation for

4.4 Critique of Public Policy in India 187

Table 4.5 Key indicators of survey of delivery system and public services at grassroots level

S.No.	Delivery system	State of delivery system (manpower, infrastructure, equipments, logistics, office aids, etc.) (%)	Process efficiency (%)[a]	Cost of availing the services (Rs.) (travel + wages lost + incidental expenses)	Citizen focus (concerns for citizens in terms of promptness and timely help) (on a scale of 0–100%)
1	Health	35	18% (immunization)	210 (for health check-up) (travel + wages lost + incidental expenses)	43
2	Primary education	34	–	–	45
3	Agriculture	32	15% (for seeds and fertilizer purchase)	175 per visit (for seeds and fertilizer purchase)	44
4	*Tehsil* (certificate issuing office)	29	2.5% (caste certificate by *Tehsil*)	225 (caste certificate by *Tehsil*)	35
5	Public distribution system (PDS)	38	15% (for availing the commodities from PDS shop)	175 (for availing the commodities from PDS shop)	45
6	Bank	42	6% (agriculture credit by banks)	Rs. 1,500 (documentation cost) + Rs. 700 (for new *Kisan* credit card)	35
	Average	35	–	–	41

Source Based on field survey (2008–10) (sample size: 225 beneficiaries, for field survey). *Kisan*: Farmer
[a]Process Efficiency (%) = actual time taken to avail the services/total time involved in the entire process

collateral security). Similarly, for other services, citizens have to incur expenses for travel or transportation, besides lost wages and incidental expenses.

- *Citizen focus* (concerns for citizens in terms of promptness and timely service delivery). It is linked to the ability of staff members to address the problems of citizens on a priority as well as keeping in view their convenience. As shown in

Table 4.6 Coverage of and access to delivery system

S.No.	Delivery system and services	Units	Coverage (per officer/staff)			Average distance to travel to get services (by beneficiary)	Remarks
			Population	Number of beneficiaries (active)	Number of villages		
1	Health	Medical officer at PHC	25–30,000	• 150–200 patients in a day	25–30	12 km (PHC) 25 km (CHC)	Time of 1–2 min per patient
		Nursing staff	4–500	• 90–100 patients in a day • 10–15 highly needy patients in a day in the field	5–7	4 km (sub-center)	2–5 min per patient
2	Sanitation (Block)	Engineering staff	10,000–20,000	• 500–700 cases	25–30	–	–
		Village level worker	1,000–5,000	• 10–15 in a day (together with other 20–30 works per day)	5–7	–	–
3	Agriculture	Block agriculture officer	30,000–40,000	• 5–6,000	100–120	30 km	–
		Agriculture extension worker	5–10,000	• 500–1,000	10–15	5 km	–
4	Bank credit	Bank branches (field officer)	50–60,000	• 5–7,000 active beneficiaries	50–70	25 km	–
5	Urban bodies	Health/sanitary supervisor (MSW)	1,00,000–1,50,000	• 5–6,000 households	–		–
		Field workers (MSW)	7–10,000	• 1,200–2,000 households	–		–

Source Based on field survey (2008–10)
MSW Municipal Solid Waste

4.4 Critique of Public Policy in India

Table 4.5, there is a lack of citizen focus, while delivering services. It is less than 50% (on a scale of 0–100%) in all the cases. The main reason seems to be higher targets and an inadequate support system. For example, the field staff members of health department find it difficult to address the problems of patients on a priority, either due to a lack of logistics or non-availability of health support like medicines, treatment facilities, etc. Besides, there is an excessive emphasis on physical and financial targets but less on indicators for citizen focus. It makes the system to give less priority to citizens' concerns. The official procedures, though important, come in the way of providing services in a timely manner. Disbursement of credit for farmers by banks or issue of certificates by *Tehsil* in a timely manner does not get priority over record keeping and official procedures.

- *Thinly spread of manpower.* The delivery system is expected to cover a large population, villages, and a significant number of active beneficiaries. It stretches the limit of the field officers and staff, who are supposed to address the service provisioning of a good number of beneficiaries in many villages. For example, the medical officer at PHC is required to attend to 150–200 patients in a day from 25 to 30 villages, and similarly, the nursing staff attends to 90–100 patients in a day, including 10–15 highly needy patients in the field (Table 4.6).
- *Capacity to deliver* (in time and of the desired level) (conformance to set standards). Per the feedback from the respondents, the capacity to deliver is low for the delivery system of all the services, including in the cases of health, education, and *Tehsil*. Capacity is not enough due to poor infrastructure, low number of personnel, inadequate logistics support, etc. For example, the schools lack sufficient infrastructure, the desired number of teachers, teaching aids, etc. The health system lacks adequate health staff, health equipments, and infrastructure for health centers, PHCs, and CHCs.

As highlighted by the field study, the issues related to systems, processes, and institutional capacity have not received adequate attention at the implementation stage. It has a bearing on the quality of the implementation of policies and programs.

Right to public services. Recognizing the need for timely services, the Right to Public Services legislation has been passed in many States in India, including Madhya Pradesh, Bihar, Himachal Pradesh, Karnataka, Odisha, Punjab, Rajasthan, and Jharkhand. Such legislation is meant to increase transparency and public accountability. There are good features in the Acts to provide timely services to citizens. SAKALA project in Karnataka has been successful in improving service standards (SAKALA Report Card 2012). However, to make the service delivery system robust and bring citizen focus, there is a need for measures for improving the capacity of the system, comprising the creation of infrastructure, improving manpower and logistics support, training, work culture management, raising process efficiency, and monitoring and control system.

4.4.3 Public Policymaking and Implementation: A Summary

Field surveys and case studies, discussed in Sects. 4.4.1 and 4.4.2, have amply brought out areas where the policymaking process has been deficient, and policy content and implementation have not matched the desired performance standards. The deficiencies in public policy are related to three distinct aspects: the policymaking process, policy content, and policy implementation. In addition, there are inadequacies in the capacity of policy system and research support.

- *Policymaking process*. The process is fundamental to policymaking. It entails key activities like needs assessment, insights from the grassroots, understanding end-users' concerns, the conceptualization of problems and system, systemic analyses, identification of policy options based on evidence to reach decision-making, and policy implementation. These issues have been examined through case studies and field surveys. At the basic level, examining problems, including the current state of socio-economic conditions, insights from the perspective of end-users, understanding root causes, and study of behavioral issues, is not attempted. Likewise, to conceptualize a system, the examination of components and variables, stakeholders, system structures, interlinkages, and causal relationships is not recognized. Besides, the competing and complementing interests of various stakeholders are not comprehended. It results in a lack of conceptualization of the system in which problems work.

  In addition, the local context-specific issues are not sufficiently studied. It is assumed that there is an uniformity in the problems across the country or States, and issues, such as what is the degree of problem, the extent of problem, and the variations in problems in different regions or States, are not examined. The consultation process to involve the end-users who will be affected by policies is often limited. For instance, the local realities like working during odd hours, especially for health services, and last-mile connectivity to provide public services like primary education, maternity services (health), public distribution of food, road connectivity, etc., remain pending policy issues. The major issues that get less attention are: systemic understanding of grassroots-level insights, practical realities, and last-mile reach.

  Institutional issues, like culture, values, beliefs, and structures of the social and economic institutions, matter. Mechanisms for policymaking and implementation are essential. Behavioral issues such as personal preferences, attitudes, and biases are important to understand the problems from the perspective of citizens and families and whether the policy will be adopted by the people. Such institutional and behavioral dimensions are not analyzed. For example, socio-economic conditions, including social culture, of families are not examined to identify policy inputs and design interventions to improve the attendance of children and the quality of primary education. The context-specific analysis is wanted. Likewise, the conditions of health institutions—like the status of infrastructure, equipments, manpower, logistics, and skills—at various levels are not analyzed to determine specific policy interventions.

4.4 Critique of Public Policy in India

Regarding complex problems, the issues like interlinkages between factors, feedback loops, nonlinearity in relationships, dynamic nature, uncertainty, and evolving nature, are not analyzed. For understanding complexity in a system, the systemic study of elements and their interactions and the properties like path dependence, emergence, self-organization, adaptation, evolution, etc., is not attempted, as the complexity dimension is not mainstreamed in the policy system. In addition, as regard the complexity in policymaking, it is a difficult task due to the complex nature of the process. It is not easy to understand the underlying issues during the process. The complexity is a result of many factors, including numerous activities, their interactions, nonlinearity in interactions, causality and feedback, and counterintuitive nature. Thus, the issue of complexity in both the system and policymaking process is not addressed.

There is a short-term focus in policymaking. The public system tends to react to problems, examine symptoms than analyze root causes, find solutions to address symptoms, and implement them. And then it moves to another set of problems. The long-term implications of interventions are not analyzed. The policy process tends not to consider inputs that are reflective based on deeper analysis and require long lead times, research, and evaluation. For example, in rural employment generation, the long-term perspective and inter-sectoral integration are not considered. The short-term mitigation of the employment problem remains the focus, which may be desirable under stress conditions. Besides, bounded rationality impacts decision-making and results in sub-optimal choices. It poses major constraints and needs consideration. Decision criteria and policy implementation do not get enough deliberations. The decisions suffer from the lack of analyses and are made intuitively.

There are three interlinked issues impacting policymaking are summarized below:

- *Lack of framework and deficiency in policymaking process.* The framework, in terms of process, tools, and methods to elicit insights and data collection from the ground, conceptualize problems, do analyses, take decisions, identify policy options, take decisions, and implement the policy, is not adequately developed. As a result, the process does not follow a structured way to formulate policies.
- *Lack of time for policymaking.* More often, due to impatience and lack of capacity of the policy system, there is an oversimplification of problems without examining the relevant issues and undertaking requisite analyses, as the departments or agencies have inadequate time to attempt. The planning and preparation for policymaking are not done beforehand.
- *The micro-macro linkages are not examined*: It implies how the grassroots-level concerns should be aligned with the macro-level requirements remains unexplored. Due to the top-down approach, the policies are rigid and lack flexibility.

- *Policy content.* As highlighted above, due to shortcomings in the policymaking process, the policy content is more a general prescription rather than a systemic approach to understanding issues holistically and providing sustained solutions.

Generally, the policy content is not able to reflect the ground realities and does not cover context-specific issues and last-mile reach.
- *Policy implementation.* The examination of field surveys (Sect. 4.3.2) of the delivery mechanism for primary education, health, agriculture, urban services, etc., reveals the infirmities such as a lack of infrastructure and logistics support to reach out to beneficiaries, inadequate manpower, capability deficit, and shortcoming in the monitoring system. The policy implementation is also affected due to the want of detailed analyses and disconnect between micro-level problems and macro-level perception. Moreover, it is assumed as if the policy system has the capacity to formulate policies related to socio-economic problems or that the policy management system is ready and available to deliver on every policy without examining the implementation mechanism. During policy formulation, there is another factor of the gap between the policymaking process and delivery mechanism. It acts as a barrier to involving frontline staff who are responsible for implementing policies and programs on the ground.
- *Policy system capacity.* The capacity is analyzed for the following aspects:
  - *Limited availability of information database.* At the fundamental level, there is a constraint on the availability of information that is readily usable and verifiable on a real-time basis (especially on economic issues) for analysis and decision-making. Usually, the aggregate data with time lag is available, but for different classifications, categories, or segments related to population, industry, or economic parameters. The time-series data or some problem-specific data is not available, and the scope to obtain the required datasets is limited. *For example*, time-series data of employment for different sectors, age groups, and sections of society; learning levels of children of different sections and causes for less learning outcomes; village-wise status of IMR and MMR with underlying causes are not available, etc.
  - *Lack of tools for stakeholders' engagement in policymaking.* The policy analysis tools used in the process include consultations with experts and some stakeholders and referring to reports or case studies. The tools that are currently employed have limited capabilities in eliciting insights from end-users, gaining a detailed understanding of the problem and system, and designing solutions. The tools have limitations in undertaking systemic analyses and working out policy options matching the grassroots' concerns. Due to a lack of tools, the citizens or end-users have little scope to take the initiative to make public agencies and departments aware of their concerns.
  - *Inadequate support to the policy system.* It is due to a lack of requisite manpower, infrastructure, analysis tools, capabilities, and information system to undertake policymaking exercise. Specifically, there is a dearth of knowledge and skills, especially to examine complexity. The policy steps like identification of underlying issues (including likely emerging problems), evaluation of outcomes, and research-based policy analysis are not undertaken. Often, due to a lack of analytical rigor and informed discussions, the problems are not clearly defined and conceptualized, and policies are not rightly formulated.

4.4 Critique of Public Policy in India

- *Research support.* There are broadly two issues regarding research in public policy. *First*, a lack of research about underlying reasons and systemic analysis of failures in policymaking, and *second*, a lack of sufficient application of innovative approaches and institutional support. The available literature (UN 2006; Borins 2008; Maksym and Shah 2010) on innovation in public policy highlights several successful cases and makes a good case for applying innovative approaches. But such cases are limited and mainly confined to limited sectors, problem areas, or geographical locations. Thus, they fail to make a representative case for wider acceptability. Besides, the lack of culture for innovation and institutional support puts a constraint on adopting success stories. It underscores the need for promoting innovation in government and institutional support for encouraging innovative applications.

Table 4.7 summarizes the major shortcomings in the policy system.

Other observations. Often, policymaking is considered more from the point of view of budgetary allocations rather than attempting policy analyses. There is less emphasis on comprehending problems, examining institutional mechanisms, how resources are allocated, how analyses are carried out, how criteria of resource allocations are made, and how efficiently and effectively resources can be utilized. There are a few more essential issues in the policymaking process. Usually, policymaking is agenda-driven, with pre-meditated solutions rather than a problem-driven or problem-solving approach; and relies on the select stakeholders' consultative process instead of obtaining insights from the citizens.

In addition, in the context of the economic system, at the fundamental level, the current economic models and theories have limitations. It is presumed that economic systems can be represented by mathematical models, though the value of mathematical models cannot be diminished. But in the real economic world, due to complexity, including the network of interactive effects of numerous economic variables (refer to Sect. 3.4), it will be naïve to model the economic system in the mathematical form. And as such, it will require explaining assumptions and constraints to define the boundary. The reliance on optimization (of the objective function) leads to the simplification of complex issues by eliminating non-quantifiable variables; besides, all the numerous relevant variables cannot be comprehended or factored in.

In sum, it underscores that during policymaking and implementation, the end users' concerns and ground-level realities are not adequately captured, the constraints and facilitating factors are not examined, the interrelationships between variables are not analyzed, detailed analyses are not carried out, and there remains a tendency to find quick solutions. As a result, the policy document contains intuitive solutions. There is a lack of rigor to comprehend the complexity of the problems and the dynamic environment in which the system works. The institutional mechanisms for monitoring, regulation, and implementation are not deliberated upon. And policymaking has yet to consider such vital issues explicitly.

Table 4.7 Major shortcomings in policy system

S.No.	Aspects	Issues and their status
1	Conceptual issues	• Inadequate appreciation of institutional, behavioral, and complexity issues, and assumptions and concepts (like importance of context-specific problems, diversity, etc.) for policymaking and implementation • Grassroots-level insights and practical realities are not sufficiently captured to understand problems
2	Approach and theory	• Short-term and top-down approach, usually following elite theory. These limit the scope for gaining holistic perspectives from the grassroots
3	Policymaking process	• Lack of framework for policymaking; lack of structured process; stakeholders' consultations are not adequately carried out • Policy analysis tools are not adequately developed • Study of grassroots-level difficulties, last-mile reach, and micro-macro linkages need to be adequately factored in • Conceptualization of problems and system is insufficient • Decision-making criteria are not explicitly developed, leading to subjectivity in making decisions • Political dimension: politics and the priorities of political parties tend to influence the decision-making
4	Systemic analyses	• Various analyses (stakeholders' perspectives, micro-macro linkages, system structure, institutional, including implementation mechanism, behavioral dimension, complexity, technical, and policy options) are not adequately attempted and not reflected in policy document • System analysis (causal relationships, system structure) and systemic understanding of the system are not carried out
5	Policy content	• Policy lacks the ability to match with the ground realities, cover systemic issues, and address last-mile connectivity
6	Policy implementation	• Policy implementation suffers due to inadequate capacity of the delivery mechanism due to want of infrastructure, manpower, and logistics support

(continued)

4.4 Critique of Public Policy in India

Table 4.7 (continued)

S.No.	Aspects	Issues and their status
7	Capacity of policymaking system	• Inadequate capacity of the system in terms of information infrastructure, manpower, analysis tools, capabilities to design policies, and management information system • Lack of sufficient time to undertake analyses and policymaking
8	Research support	• Lack of research about underlying reasons and systemic analysis of failures, and limited successful application of innovative approaches

System performance should be assessed at both levels, viz., micro as well as macro. In addition to micro-level issues discussed in Sects. 4.4.1 and 4.4.2, a few macro-level or aggregate-level performance indicators are presented in Tables 4.8 and 4.9. It reflects less than satisfactory values of human resource, economic, and institutional (concerning business services) indicators for India. These highlight the need for more efficacy of the public policy system. Table 4.8 presents health indicators such as IMR, MMR, and HDI. These reflect the inadequacies in the health policy and shortcomings in the implementation. And these demand that specific policy interventions need to be designed to address specific problems.

Table 4.8 Key human resource and economic indicators

S.No.	Indicators	Countries	
		India	Emerging economies (China, South Korea, Malaysia)
1	HDI (rank)	130	55 (average)
2	IMR	34	12 (average)
3	MMR	174	26 (average)
4	Per capita GDP (nominal, current) ($) (2016)[a]	1,732	15,943
5	Electricity consumption (per capita) (KWhr)[b]	947 (< 500 in rural areas)	4,546 (China), 10,654 (South Korea), 4,808 (Malaysia)
6	Crop yield (rice) (Q/Ha)[c]	34	65 (China), 43 (South Korea)

Source UNDP (2018)
[a]IMF (2016), [b]IEA (2019), [c]FAO (2013)

Table 4.9 Key institutional indicators concerning business services

S.No.	Indicators	Countries		
		India	Emerging economies (China, Taiwan)	Developed country (USA)
1	Institutions: Starting a business (rank)	137	27 (China) 20 (Taiwan)	53 (USA)
2	Institutions: Cost of starting a business (% of income per capita)	14.4	0.4 (China) 1.9 (Taiwan)	1.0 (USA)

Source World Bank (2019b)

4.5 Managing Twenty-First Century Big Trends, Challenges, and Drivers

The last few decades, since the 1990s, have seen rapid changes in the lives of all countries. Driven by technological advancements and globalization, the changes are no longer of linear nature and have become nonlinear and exponential. The speedier evolution is taking place due to the closely interconnected world. Both national and global economies are facing the challenge of changes in a significant way that cannot go unnoticed. For example, the global recession (2008–10), the fluctuations in oil prices (2019–2021), and the pandemic (2020–21) impacted globally, disrupting socio-economic lives.

Specifically, Industry 4.0, shaped by the significant reduction in the cost of computing power, storage, and internet usage, is defining the future of industrialization. The pace of change is exponential, disruptive, and nonlinear and in a complete departure from incremental improvement. Before 2010, the historical manufacturing practices were majorly linear and based on incremental change and continuous improvement. Driven by insights from data analytics, the Industrial 4.0 ecosystem is marked by multidirectional relationships between business entities, stakeholders, products, and locations. It has transformative effects, and the cycle of concept to development to value realization is much faster and shorter. How the policy can handle such transformation to provide support to the industry is a question to be examined (Brown 2018; DSU 2018; WEF 2018b).

In the dynamic and interconnected uncertain world, there is a need to understand the higher-order consequences and their cascade effect over a region due to technology disruption, pandemic, financial contagion, or climate change. For instance, due to the cascade effect, the global financial crisis impacted banking, investments, and capital market in many countries in 2008. Similarly, due to the automation of manufacturing in developed countries at a faster rate and higher productivity, there is a likelihood of shifting of industries back to the USA and European Union (EU) from many Asian countries, including India. It may result in the displacement of workers that may have consequences for employment across the region in Asia (Sirkin et al. 2015; GPS 2016).

Simultaneously, at the grassroots level, there are impending issues of quality of drinking water, scarcity of water, shortage of food for the bottom 10%, incidence of poverty, high malnutrition, high unemployment rate, and low quality of life on various parameters of human development in developing countries (FAO 2018; OPHI 2018; UNDP 2018). In addition, the increased usage of technologies is causing a rapid rise in income for a few relative to the working class resulting in inequality. Affected by complex issues and inadequate attention, these problems are a result of both deficient policies, which are not able to capture the problems faced by the citizens and infirmities in the policy implementation. Based on the gravity of the situation, certain decisions are to be taken today before the impending problems reach the citizens in a big form. For example, the issues of likely water crisis, growing need for quality urban public services, unemployment among youths, and advanced manufacturing, to name a few, need to be addressed now.

Against the backdrop of the above-highlighted policy issues, these raise questions such as: whether the present public policy system can comprehend the growing problems with the existing approaches and policy analysis tools and whether the policy system has the capacity to formulate sound policies and implement them.

References

Abolafia MY, Dodge JE, Jackson SK. Clifford Geertz and the interpretation of organisations. In: Oxford handbook of sociology, social theory and organisation studies. Oxford University Press; 2014.

Acemoglu D, Robinson J. The role of institutions in growth and development. Rev Econ Inst. 2010;1(2). https://doi.org/10.5202/rei.v1i2.1; www.rei.unipg.it; http://www.rei.unipg.it/rei/article/view/14; ISSN 2038-1379.

Alexander ER. From idea to action: notes for a contingency theory of the policy implementation process. Adm Soc. 1985;16(4).

Almeida LdeA, Gomes RC. The process of public policy: literature review, theoretical reflections and suggestions for future research. Cad EBAPE.BR. 2018;16(3). https://doi.org/10.1590/1679-395164108

Amsden AH, DiCaprio A, Robinson, JA, editors. The role of elites in economic development. Oxford University Press; 2012.

Anderson PW, Arrow KJ, Pines D, editors. The economy as an evolving complex system (Santa Fe Institute Series). CRC Press; 1988.

Anderson JE. Public policy-making: an introduction. 3rd ed. Boston: Houghton Mifflin Company; 1997.

Anderson JE. Public policymaking: an introduction. Boston: Houghton Mifflin Company; 2003. http://www.kropfpolisci.com/public.policy.anderson.pdf

Andrews M, Pritchett L, Woolcock M. Building state capability: evidence, analysis, action. Oxford University Press; 2017.

Anyebe AA. An overview of approaches to the study of public policy. Int J Polit Sci (IJPS). 2018;4(1):08–17. https://doi.org/10.20431/2454-9452.0401002; www.arcjournals.org; ISSN 2454-9452.

Aron J. Growth and institutions, a review of the evidence. In: The World Bank research observer, vol. 15:1; 2000.

Arrow KJ. Social choice and individual values. New York: Wiley; 1951.

Arthur WB, Durlauf SN, Lane D, editors. The economy as an evolving complex system II (Santa Fe Institute Series). CRC Press; 1997

Baetu TM. Emergence, therefore antireductionism? A critique of emergent antireductionism. Biol Philos. 2012;27(3). https://doi.org/10.1007/s10539-011-9290-2

Banerjee AV, Esther D. Poor economics: rethinking poverty & the ways to end it. Penguin Books; 2013.

Bankes SC. Tools and techniques for developing policies for complex and uncertain systems; 2002. https://doi.org/10.1073/pnas.092081399

Baron J. A brief history of evidence-based policy. Am Acad Polit Soc Sci. 2018;678(1).

Bates RH, Krueger AO. Political and economic interactions in economic policy reform: evidence from eight countries. Blackwell Publisher; 1993.

Baumgartner F, Jones B. Agendas and instability in American politics. University of Chicago Press; 1993.

Baumgartner FR, Leech BL. Basic interest: the importance of groups in politics and political science. Princeton University Press; 1998.

Bergstrom L. Development of institutions is created from the inside lessons, learned from consultants experiences of supporting formal and informal rules. SIDA; 2005. https://cdn.sida.se/publicati ons/files/sida23805en-development-of-institutions-is-created-from-the-inside.pdf

Birkland TA. An introduction to policy process. New Delhi: PHI Learning Pvt. Ltd.; 2011.

Black D. The theory of committees and elections. Kluwer Academic Publishers; 1987.

Blase M. Institution building: a source book. Columbia: University of Missouri Press; 1986.

Blyth M, Oddny H, Kring W. Ideas and historical institutionalism. In: Fioretos O, Felleti TG, Sheingate A, editors. The Oxford handbook of historical institutionalism. Oxford University Press; 2016.

Boin A, Christensen T. The development of public institutions reconsidering the role of leadership. Adm Soc. 2008;40(3):271–97.

Boltho A. Was Japan's industrial policy successful? Camb J Econ. 1985;9(2):187–201.

Borins S. Innovations in government. Ash Institute for Democratic Governance and Innovation, Harvard University; 2008.

Bottomore T. Elites and society. London: Rutledge; 1993.

Braun D, Capano G. Introductory paper: the missing link—policy ideas and policy instruments. Prepared for the workshop on ideas, policy design and policy instruments: casting light on the missing link. European Consortium for Political Research, Munster, Germany, 23–27 Mar 2010. https://ecpr.eu/Filestore/PaperProposal/a4357e25-a9b2-4455-89f1-0d6c2ff9f2e2.pdf

Brinkerhoff D. From design to implementation: stakeholder analysis in a PHC Project in India. Bethesda: Abt Associates Inc.; 1998.

Brinkerhoff DW, Crosby B. Managing policy reform: concepts and tools for decision-makers in developing and transitioning countries. Kumarian Press; 2002.

Brown M. Bridging the skills gap in the manufacturing industry. 2018. https://www.engineering. com/AdvancedManufacturing/ArticleID/16954/Bridging-the-Skills-Gap-in-the-Manufactu ring-Industry.aspx

Buchanan JM. The pure theory of government finance: a suggested approach. J Polit Econ. 1949;57:496–506.

Buchanan JM, Musgrave RA. Public finance and public choice: two contrasting visions of the state. MIT Press; 1999.

Byrnes JP. The nature and development of decision-making: a self-regulation model. Hillsdale: Erlbaum; 1998.

Bystrom K, Jarvelin K. Task complexity affects information seeking and use. Inf Process Manage. 1995. https://doi.org/10.1016/0306-4573(95)80035-R.

Cairney P. Understanding public policy: theories and issues. Textbooks in policy studies. Palgrave Macmillan; 2012.

Cairney P, Jones MD. Kingdon's multiple streams approach: what is the empirical impact of this universal theory. Policy Stud J. 2016;44(1).

References

Cairney P, Weible C. Comparing and contrasting Peter Hall's paradigms and ideas with the advocacy coalition framework. In: Hogan J, Howlett M, editors. Policy paradigms in theory and practice: discourses, ideas and anomalies in public policy dynamics. Palgrave Macmillan; 2015.

Calvert R. Rational actors, equilibrium and social institutions. In: Knight J, Sened I, editors. Explaining social institutions. University of Michigan Press; 1995.

Camoes MRDS, Koga NM, Fernandes CCC. State capacities and public policy implementation: a proposal for an integrated framework of analysis. In: 3rd International conference on public policy (ICPP3), Singapore, 28–30 June 2017. https://www.ippapublicpolicy.org/file/paper/593 b2a2b5453d.pdf

Campbell JL. Institutional analysis and the role of ideas in political economy. Theory Soc. 1998;27:377–409. http://webuser.bus.umich.edu/organizations/smo/protected/resources/campbell98.pdf

Cerna L. The nature of policy change and implementation: a review of different theoretical approaches. OECD; 2013.

Chakravarty B, Chand P. Public policy: concept, theory and practice paperback. Sage Publications India Private Limited; 2016.

Chan M. Economic growth in Japan cultural (Neo-Confucianism) analysis. Honors Theses, Paper 109. 1991. http://opensiuc.lib.siu.edu/uhp_theses

Checkland P. Systems thinking, systems practice: includes a 30-year retrospective. Wiley; 1999.

Chen D, Stroup W. General system theory: toward a conceptual framework for science and technology education for all. J Sci Educ Technol. 1993;2(7).

Chetty R. Behavioral economics and public policy: a pragmatic perspective. Am Econ Rev Am Econ Assoc. 2015;105(5).

Claxton M. Culture and development: a study. CLT/DEC/PRO-94/01. 1994. https://files.eric.ed.gov/fulltext/ED377116.pdf

Cohen WJ. The development of the Social Security Act of 1935: reflections some fifty years later. Minnesota Law Rev. 1984. https://core.ac.uk/download/pdf/217208529.pdf

Cohen M. Commentary on the organizational science special issue on complexity. Org Sci. 1999;10(May–June):373–6.

Cohen MD, March JG. Leadership and ambiguity: the American college president. New York: McGraw-Hill; 1974.

Cohen MD, March JG, Olsen JP. A garbage can model of organizational choice. Adm Sci Q. 1972;17(1):1–25. https://doi.org/10.2307/2392088.

De PK. Public policy and systems. Pearson; 2012.

de Leon P, Vogenbeck DM. The policy sciences at the crossroads. In: Fischer F, Miller GJ, Sidney MS, editors. Handbook of public policy analysis theory, politics, and methods, chap. 1. London: CRC Press; 2007.

Deloitte. Global manufacturing competitiveness index 2016. 2016.

Deloitte and Singularity University (DSU). Exponential technologies in manufacturing: transforming the future of manufacturing through technology, talent, and the innovation ecosystem. 2018.

Demsetz H. Toward a theory of property rights. Am Econ Rev. 1967;57(2).

Dewey J. The public and its problems. New York: Henry Holt and Company; 1927.

Dewey J. The quest for the certainty: a study of the relation of knowledge and action. New York: Putman; 1929.

DFID. Promoting institutional and organisational development. London: Department for International Development; 2003. http://www.kalidadea.org/castellano/materiales/evaluacion/DFID%20promoting%20institutional%20develpment%20guide.pdf

DiMaggio P. Culture and cognition. Ann Rev Sociol. 1997;23(1):263–87. https://doi.org/10.1146/annurev.soc.23.1.263.

Do Phu H. Do the institutional constraints on policy performance? In: 3rd International conference on public policy (ICPP3), Singapore; 2017. https://www.ippapublicpolicy.org/file/paper/593b58 79a9873.pdf

Dror Y. Muddling through—science or inertia? Publ Adm Rev. 1964;24(3):1964. https://doi.org/10.2307/973640

Dror Y. Public policy-making: re-examined. Routledge; 1983.

Dunn W. Public policy: an introduction. New Jersey: Prentice-Hall; 1981.

Dunoviu IB, Radujkoviü M, Škreba KA. Towards a new model of complexity—the case of large infrastructure projects. Procedia Soc Behav Sci. 2014;119(2014):730–8. 1877-0428. https://www.researchgate.net/publication/263527468

Dye TR. Understanding public policy. Englewood Cliffs: Prentice-Hall; 1980.

Dye TR. Understanding public policy. New Jersey: Prentice-Hall; 1992.

Dye TR. Top down policymaking. New York: Chatham House Publishers; 2000.

Dye TR, Zeigler LH. The irony of democracy. Books, Cole: Monterey, CA; 1990.

Easton D. An approach to the analysis of political systems. World Polit. 1957;9.

Easton D. A framework for political analysis. Prentice Hall; 1965.

Economic Survey. Union Finance Ministry Government of India (GOI), 2019–20. 2020.

Elster J, editor. Deliberative democracy (Cambridge studies in the theory of democracy). Cambridge University Press; 1998.

Eppel E, Matheson A, Walton M. Applying complexity theory to New Zealand public policy principles for practice. Policy Q. 2011;7(1):48–55. http://ips.ac.nz/publications/files/c6108074474.pdf

Erasmus E. The use of street-level bureaucracy theory in health policy analysis in low- and middle-income countries: a meta-ethnographic synthesis. Health Policy Plan. 2014;29(suppl 3):iii70–8. https://doi.org/10.1093/heapol/czu112

Eugene MM. An American's guide to doing business in India. 2007.

FAO. Statistical year handbook. World Food and Agriculture; 2013. https://www.fao.org/3/i3107e/i3107e.PDF

Ferrini L. The importance of institutions to economic development. 2012. https://www.e-ir.info/2012/09/19/the-importance-of-institutions-to-economic-development/

Ferris JM, Shui-Yan T. The new institutionalism and public administration: an overview. J Public Adm Res Theory J-PART. 2020;3(1), JSTOR. www.jstor.org/stable/1181566

Fischer F, Forester J, editors. The argumentative turn in policy analysis and planning. Duke University Press; 1993.

Fischer F, Miller GJ, Sidney MS. Handbook of public policy analysis theory, politics, and methods. CRC Press London; 2007.

Fletcher A, Guthrie J, Steane P, Roos G, Pike S. Mapping stakeholder perceptions for a third sector organization. J Intellect Cap. 2003;4(4):505–27.

Fontana M. Can neoclassical economics handle complexity? The fallacy of the oil spot dynamic. J Econ Behav Org. 2010. https://doi.org/10.1016/j.jebo.2010.08.010

Food and Agriculture Organization (FAO). Nations urged to accelerate efforts to wipe out hunger and malnutrition. Rome: FAO; 2018.

Forrester JW. Industrial dynamics. USA: Pegasus Communications Waltham; 1961.

Forrester JW. Counterintuitive behaviour of social systems. Technol Rev. 1971;53–68.

Foster J, Metcalfe S. Frontiers of evolutionary economics: competition, self-organization and innovation policy. Cheltenham: Edward Elgar; 2001.

Freeman L. The development of social network analysis: a study in the sociology of science. Empirical Press; 2004.

Gatti DD, Fagiolo G, Mauro G, editors. Agent-based models in economics. Cambridge University Press; 2018.

Geertz C. The interpretation of cultures selected essays. Basic Books, Inc., Publishers; 1973.

Gell-Mann M. The quark and the jaguar: adventures in the simple and the complex. St. Martin's Griffin; 1995.

Gerrits L. Public decision-making as coevolution. E:CO Issue 2010;12(1). file:///C:/Users/SONY/Downloads/Gerrits-0PublicDecisionMakingasCoevolution.pdf

Gerstel D, Goodman MP. From industrial policy to innovation strategy lessons from Japan, Europe, and the United States. Washington: Center for Strategic and International Studies (CSIS); 2020. Downloads/200901_Gerstel_InnovationStrategy_FullReport_FINAL_0(1).pdf

Gerston LN. Public policy making: process and principles. New York: M.E. Sharpe Inc.; 2010.

Geurts T. Public policy making, the 21st century perspective. 2010. http://www.lulu.com/shop/theigeurts/public-policy-making-the-21st-century-perspective/ebook/product-21759876.html

Gigante AA. Reviewing path dependence theory in economics: micro-foundations of endogenous change processes. MPRA Paper No. 75310. 2016. https://mpra.ub.uni-muenchen.de/75310/

Gigch JPV. Applied general systems theory. London: Harper and Row Publishers; 1974.

Gigerenzer G, Selten R. Rethinking rationality. In: Gigerenzer G, Selten R, editors. Bounded rationality: the adaptive toolbox. Cambridge, MA: MIT Press; 2001.

Givel M. The evolution of the theoretical foundations of punctuated equilibrium theory in public policy. Rev Policy Res. 2010;27(2).

Global Perspectives & Solutions (GPS). Technology at work V2.0, the future is not what it used to be. 2016. https://www.oxfordmartin.ox.ac.uk/downloads/reports/Citi_GPS_Technology_Work_2.pdf

Goodin RE, Rein M, Moran M. Overview of public policy: the public and its policies. In: The Oxford handbook of political science. 2013. https://doi.org/10.1093/oxfordhb/9780199604456.013.0043

Granato J, Ronald I, Leblang D. The effect of cultural values on economic development: theory, hypotheses, and some empirical tests. Am J Polit Sci. 1996;40:607. https://doi.org/10.2307/2111786.

Gunn LA. Why is implantation so difficult? Manag Serv Gov. 1978;33:169–76.

Habtom G. Factors affecting the use of maternal and child health services in eritrea. J Complement Med Altern Healthc. 2017;2. https://doi.org/10.19080/JCMAH.2017.02.555589

Hall PA. Policy paradigms, social learning, and the state: the case of economic policymaking in Britain. Comp Polit. 1993;25(3):275–96.

Hall RE, Jones CI. Why do some countries produce so much more output per worker than others? Q Q J Econ. 1999;114(1). http://www.jstor.org/stable/2586948

Hargrove EC. The missing link: the study of the implementation of social policy. Washington: The Urban Institute; 1975.

Hemmert M. The Korean innovation system: from industrial catch-up to technological leadership? In: Mahlich J, Pascha W, editors. Innovation and technology in Korea: challenges of a newly advanced economy. Heidelberg: Physica; 2007. https://doi.org/10.1007/978-3-7908-1914-4_2

Hill M, Varone F. The public policy process. Routledge; 2016.

Hodgson GM. On defining institutions: rules versus equilibria. J Inst Econ. 2015;11:3.

Hofferbert R. The study of public policy. MacMillan Publishing Company; 1974.

Holland J. Hidden order: how adaptation builds complexity. New York: Helix Books; 1995.

Holt RPF, Rosser Jr JB, Colander D. The complexity era in economics. Middlebury College Economics Discussion Paper No. 10-01. 2010. The_Complexity_Era_in_Economics.pdf

Hoppe R. Institutional constraints and practical problems in deliberative and participatory policy making. Policy Polit. 2011;39(2):163–86. https://doi.org/10.1332/030557310X519650

Howlett M, Ramesh M. Studying public policy: policy cycles and policy subsystems. Oxford University Press; 2003.

Hudsona B, Hunterb D, Peckhamc S. Policy failure and the policy-implementation gap: can policy support programs help? Policy Design Pract. 2019;2(1). https://doi.org/10.1080/25741292.2018.1540378

Huntington SP. Political order in changing societies. Yale University Press; 1996.

Hutahaean M. The importance of stakeholders approach in public policy making. In: Conference paper. Advances in social science, education and humanities research, vol. 84. 2017. https://doi.org/10.2991/iconeg-16.2017.104

IEA. Key world energy statistics, international energy agency (IEA). Paris: France; 2019.

IMF. GDP per capita. 2016. https://www.imf.org/external/datamapper/NGDPDPC@WEO/OEMDC/ADVEC/WEOWORLD
IMF. World GDP per capita. World Economic Outlook (October-2019). 2019. https://statisticstimes.com/economy/world-gdp-capita-ranking.php
Institute of Development Studies (IDS). An upside-down view of governance. Brighton: Institute of Development Studies; 2010. http://www2.ids.ac.uk/gdr/cfs/pdfs/AnUpside-downViewofGovernance.pdf
International Institute for Sustainable Development (IISD) and the Energy and Resources Institute (TERI). Designing policies in a world of uncertainty, change, and surprise. 2006. https://www.iisd.org/system/files/publications/climate_designing_policies.pdf
IPCC. Fourth assessment report of the intergovernmental panel on climate change (IPCC). Geneva: Switzerland; 2007.
IPCC. IPCC special report on renewable energy sources and climate change mitigation. Prepared by working group III, Geneva, Switzerland; 2012. http://srren.ipcc-wg3.de/report
Isaak AC. Scope and methods of political science. Chicago: Dorsey Press; 1988.
Israel A. Institutional development. John Hopkins University Press; 1989.
Jackson MC. Systems approaches to management. Springer; 2000.
Jackson MO. Social and economic networks. Princeton University Press; 2010.
Jadhav N. Rupee devaluation: real issues. Econ Pol Wkly. 1991;26(36):2119–20.
James O. Bureaucratic power. In: Dowding K, editor. Encyclopedia of power. SAGE Publications; 2011.
Jann W, Wegrich K. Theories of the policy cycle. In: Fischer F, Miller GJ, Sidney MS, editors. Handbook of public policy analysis theory, politics, and methods, chap. 4. CRC Press; 2007.
Jenkins WI. Policy-analysis. A political and organisational perspective. Martin Robertsen; 1978.
John P. Analysing public policy. London: Cassell & Co.; 1998.
John P. Analyzing public policy. Textbooks in policy studies. Routledge; 2012.
John P. Complexity and policy: behavioural approaches: how nudges lead to more intelligent policy design. In: Zittoun P, Peters BG, editors. Contemporary approaches to public policy. 2015. https://papers.ssrn.com/sol3/papers.cfm?abstract_id=2604377
Jones H. Taking responsibility for complexity How implementation can achieve results in the face of complex problems. Working Paper 330, Overseas Development Institute. 2011. https://www.odi.org/sites/odi.org.uk/files/odi-assets/publications-opinion-files/6485.pdf
Joshi A, Carter B. Public sector institutional reform: topic guide. GSDRC, University of Birmingham; 2015.
Junttia M, Russelb D, Turnpenny J. Evidence, politics and power in public policy for the environment. Environ Sci Policy. 2009;12(3).
Kahneman D. Thinking, fast and slow. Farrar, Straus and Giroux Publisher; 2013.
Kahneman D, Sugden R. Experienced utility as a standard of policy evaluation. Environ Resource Econ. 2005;32:161–81.
Kahneman D, Tversky A. Prospect theory: an analysis of decision under risk. Econometrica. 1979;47(2):263–92.
Kanbur SMR, Myles GD. Policy choice and political constraints. Eur J Polit Econ. 1992;8(1):1–29. https://doi.org/10.1016/0176-2680(92)90055-L
Kapsos S. Employment intensity of growth: trends and macro-determinants. ILO. 2005.
Kauffman S. At home in the universe: the search for the laws of self-organization and complexity. Oxford University Press; 1995.
Kay A. The dynamics of public policy: theory and evidence. Edward Elgar Publishing Limited; 2006.
Keeney RL, von Winterfeldt D, Eppel T. Eliciting public values for complex policy decisions. Manage Sci. 1990;36:1011–30.
Kelly KL. A systems approach to identifying decisive information for sustainable development. Eur J Oper Res. 1998;109:452–64.

References

Khan AR. Policy implementation: some aspects and issues. 2016. https://www.researchgate.net/publication/320549262_POLICY_IMPLEMENTATION_SOME_ASPECTS_AND_ISSUES

Kingdon JW. Agendas, alternatives, and public policies. Boston: Little Brown; 1984.

Kirman A. Complex economics: individual and collective rationality. Routledge; 2011.

Kirman A. Complexity and economic policy. In: New approaches to economic challenge: insights into complexity and policy. 2016. https://www.oecd.org/naec/Insights%20into%20Complexity%20and%20Policy.pdf

Kocherlakota N. Modern macroeconomic models as tools for economic policy. Banking and policy issues magazine. Fed Reserve Bank Minneap. 2010. https://www.minneapolisfed.org/article/2010/modern-macroeconomic-models-as-tools-for-economic-policy

KPMG. Future state 2030: the global megatrends shaping governments. 2014.

Kurtz CF, Snowden DJ. The new dynamics of strategy: sense-making in a complex and complicated world. IBM Syst J. 2003;42(3):462–83.

Lahat L. New institutionalism in public policy. In: Farazmand A, editor. Global encyclopedia of public administration, public policy, and governance. Springer; 2019. https://doi.org/10.1007/978-3-319-31816-5_3879-1.RIS

Lasswell HD. The policy orientation. In: Lerner D, Lasswell HD, editors. The policy sciences. Stanford University Press; 1951.

Lasswell HD. A pre-view of policy sciences. American Elsevier Publishing; 1971.

Latham E. The group basis of politics. New York: Octagon Books; 1965.

Leftwich A, Sen K. Beyond institutions: institutions and organizations in the politics and economics of poverty reduction—a thematic synthesis of research evidence. DFID-funded research programme consortium on improving institutions for pro-poor growth (IPPG). 2010. http://www.ippg.org.uk/8933_BeyondInstitutions.final(1).pdf

Leicester A, Levell P, Rasul I. Tax and benefit policy: insights from behavioral economics. 2012. https://www.ucl.ac.uk/~uctpimr/research/IFScomm125.pdf

Leonard TC. American economic reform in the progressive era: its foundational beliefs and their relation to eugenics. Hist Polit Econ. 2009;41:1.

Lindblom CE. The science of muddling through. Public Adm Rev. 1959;19:1959.

Lindblom CE. Still muddling, not yet through. Public Adm Rev. 1979;39(6).

Lipsky M. Street-level bureaucracy: dilemmas of the individual in public services. Russell Sage Foundation; 2010.

Loayza N, Woolcock M. Designing good policies is one thing, implementing them is another. World Bank Blogs. 2020. https://blogs.worldbank.org/developmenttalk/designing-good-policies-one-thing-implementing-them-another

Lowi TJ. Four systems of policy, politics and choice. Syracuse, Inter-University Case Program. 1971.

Lunn P. Regulatory policy and behavioural economics. Paris: OECD Publishing; 2014. https://doi.org/10.1787/9789264207851-en

Lynd RS. Knowledge for what? The place for social science in the American culture. Princeton University Press; 1939.

Maheshwari SR. Public administration in India. New Delhi: MacMillan; 2000.

Majone G. The role of constraints in policy analysis. Qual Quant. 1974;8:65–76. https://doi.org/10.1007/BF00205865

Majumdar S, Mukand SW. On institution building. 2018. https://www.isid.ac.in/~planning/ConferenceDec07/Papers/SumonMajumdar.pdf

Maksym I, Shah A. Citizen-centric governance indicators: measuring and monitoring governance by listening to the people and not the interest groups. Policy Research Working Paper 5181. Washington: World Bank; 2010.

Mann M. The sources of social power: volume 1: A history of power from the beginning to A.D. 1760. Cambridge University Press; 1986.

Manor J, editor. Rethinking third world politics. London: Longman; 1991.

March J, Olsen J. The new institutionalism: organizational factors in political life. Am Polit Sci Rev. 1984;78(3):734–49.

Marsh I. Innovation and public policy: the challenge of an emerging paradigm. AIRC Working Paper Series, WP/0710. Australian Innovation Research Centre, University of Tasmania; 2010.

Marston G, Watts R. Tampering with the evidence: a critical appraisal of evidence-based policymaking. 2003. Downloads/marston_watts.pdf

Matheson C. Politics and public policy. In: Farazmand A, editor. Global encyclopedia of public administration, public policy, and governance. Springer; 2016. https://doi.org/10.1007/978-3-319-31816-5_1407-1

McBurney P. What makes some decisions complex? 2020. https://www.gdrc.org/decision/complex-decisions.html

McGill R. Institutional development: a review of the concept. Int J Public Sect Manag. 1995;8(2):1995.

Mehta J. From whether to how: the varied roles of ideas in politics. In: Beland D, Cox B, editors. How ideas matter: reframing political research. Oxford University Press; 2010.

Menard C, Shirley MM. The contribution of Douglass North to new institutional economics, halshs-00624297. 2011. https://halshs.archives-ouvertes.fr/halshs-00624297

Meyer MH, Curley KF. The impact of knowledge and technology complexity on information system development. Expert Syst Appl. 1995;8(1). https://doi.org/10.1016/0957-4174(94)E0003-D

Mill JS. Principles of political economy: with some of their applications to social philosophy. The Project Gutenberg EBook. 2009.

Ministry of Finance (MoF). Union Budget, 2016–17. Government of India; 2017.

Mintrom M, Luetjens J. Creating public value: tightening connections between policy design and public management: Luetjens: creating public value. Policy Stud J. 2015;45(1). https://doi.org/10.1111/psj.12116

Mirakhor A, Askari H. Institutional structure of a sound economy. In: Ideal islamic economy. Political economy of Islam. Palgrave Macmillan; 2017. https://doi.org/10.1057/978-1-137-53727-0_4

Mitchell M. Complexity: a guided tour. Oxford University Press; 2009.

Mohan R. India transformed: 25 years of economic reforms. Brookings Institution; 2018.

Moore MH. Creating public value: strategic management in government. Harvard University Press; 1995.

Moore M, Stewart S, Hudock A. Institution building as a development assistance method: a review of literature and ideas. SIDA Evaluation Report 1995/1. 1995.

Morcol G. A complexity theory for public policy (Routledge research in public administration and public policy). Routledge; 2012.

Morecroft JDW. System dynamics: portraying bounded rationality. OMEGA. 1983;11(2):131–42.

Mueller B. Why public policies fail: policymaking under complexity. EconomiA. 2020;21(2):311–23. https://doi.org/10.1016/j.econ.2019.11.002

Muers S. Culture, values and public policy. 2017. https://www.bath.ac.uk/publications/culture-values-and-public-policy/attachments/culture-values-and-public-policy.pdf

NAPCC. National Action Plan on Climate Change (NAPCC). Prime Minister Council on Climate Change, Govt. of India, New Delhi; 2008.

National Education Policy (NEP). Government of India. 1986.

National Education Policy (NEP). Government of India. 2020.

National Health Mission (NHM). Ministry of Health & Family Welfare, Government of India. 2013.

National Health Policy (NHP). Ministry of Health & Family Welfare, Government of India. 2002.

National Health Policy (NHP). Ministry of Health & Family Welfare, Government of India. 2017.

National Intelligence Council (NIC). Global trends 2030: alternative worlds. 2012.

National Rural Health Mission (NRHM). Ministry of Health & Family Welfare, Government of India. 2005.

Naughton B. Industrial policy—lessons from China. Centro de Estudios China-México; 2020. Naughton2021_Industrial_Policy_in_China_CECHIMEX(1).pdf

References

Neimun M, Stambough SJ. Rational choice theory and the evaluation of public policy. Policy Stud J. 1998;26(3). https://doi.org/10.1111/j.1541-0072.1998.tb01912.x

North DC. Institutions, institutional change and economic performance. Cambridge University Press; 1990.

NSW Public Service Commission. State of the NSW public sector report 2015: to the next level. 2015. www.psc.nsw.gov.au/SOPSR/

O'Flynn J. From new public management to public value: paradigmatic change and managerial implications. Aust J Public Adm. 2007;66(3):353–66.

O'Toole LJ. Policy recommendations for multi-actor implementation: an assessment of the field. J Public Policy. 1986;6(2).

OECD. OECD observatory of public sector innovation: working with change. Systems approaches to public sector challenges. 2017a.

OECD. Behavioral insights and public policy: lessons from around the world. OECD Publishing; 2017b. https://doi.org/10.1787/9789264270480-en

Ogu MI. Rational choice theory: assumptions, strengths, and greatest weaknesses in application outside the western milieu context. Arab J Bus Manag Rev (Nigerian Chap). 2013;1(3):2013. https://doi.org/10.12816/0003628.

Oliver A, editor. Behavioural public policy. Cambridge University Press; 2013.

Osman FA. Public policy making: theories and their implications in developing countries. 2002. https://www.researchgate.net/publication/253836498_PUBLIC_POLICY_MAKING_THEORIES_AND_THEIR_IMPLICATIONS_IN_DEVELOPING_COUNTRIES

Ostrom E. Governing the commons: the evolution of institutions for collective Action. New York: Cambridge University; 1990.

O'Sullivan A, Sheffrin S. Economics: principles in action. Pearson Prentice Hall. 2003.

Oxford Poverty & Human Development Initiative (OPHI). Global multidimensional poverty index (MPI). University of Oxford; 2018. https://ophi.org.uk/multidimensional-poverty-index/global-mpi-2018/

Paul BP. Why institutions are so important for growth. 2017. http://www.ipsnews.net/2017/01/why-institutions-are-so-important-for-growth/

Peters BG. Institutionalism and public policy. In: Contemporary approaches to public policy. London: Palgrave Macmillan; 2016. p. 57–72.

Petridou E. Theories of the policy process: contemporary scholarship and future directions. Policy Stud J. 2014;42(S1):2014.

Phillips K. Applying behavioral science upstream in the policy design process. 2018. https://behavioralscientist.org/applying-behavioral-science-upstream-in-the-policy-design-process/

Pielke RA. What future for the policy sciences? J Policy Sci. 2004.

Pierson P. Politics in time, history, institutions and social analysis. Princeton University Press; 2004.

Piketty T. Capital in the twenty-first century. Harvard University Press; 2017.

Planning Commission. Second five-year plan (1956–61). Planning Commission, Government of India; 1956.

Planning Commission. Third five-year plan (1961–66). Planning Commission, Government of India; 1961.

Planning Commission. Tenth five-year plan (2002–07). Planning Commission, Government of India; 2002.

Planning Commission. Eleventh five-year plan (2007–12). Planning Commission, Government of India; 2007.

Portney K. Approaching public policy analysis: an introduction to policy and program research. Prentice-Hall; 1986.

Pottenger M, Martin A. Insights into behavioural public policy. Issues Paper Series No. 06/14. Melbourne School of Government; 2014.

Potucek M, Vas L. Dimensions of public policy: values, processes, implementation, and results. In: Potucek M, LeLoup LT, Jenei G, Várad L, editors. Public policy in central and eastern Europe:

theories, methods, practices, chap. 1. 2003. http://www.nispa.org/files/publications/ebooks/PP-in-CEE.pdf

Raymond WC, Susan JB, Morgan BN. Public administration in theory and practice. Pearson; 1994.

RBI. State finances: a study of budgets of States, 2016–17. 2017.

Right to Education (RTE). Government of India. 2009.

Rihani S. Complexity theory: a new framework for development is in the offing. Prog Dev Stud. 2005;5(1):54–61.

Rizvi G. Innovations in government, innovative governance in the 21st century. Washington: Brookings Institution Press; 2008.

Robichau R, Lynn LE. The implementation of public policy: still the missing link. Policy Stud J. 2009;37(1):21–36. https://doi.org/10.1111/j.1541-0072.2008.00293.x.

Rodrik D. Institutions for high-quality growth: what they are and how to acquire them. Stud Comp Int Dev. 2000;35(3):3–31.

Ryan A. What is a systems approach? 2008. https://arxiv.org/pdf/0809.1698.pdf

Ryan A. Applications of complex systems to operational design. 2011. http://militaryepistemology.com/wp-content/uploads/2011/07/Ryan_Applications-of-Complex-Systems-to-Operational-Design_2011.pdf

Ryan A. A framework for systemic design. 2014. https://doi.org/10.7577/formakademisk.787

Sabatier PA. Political science and public policy. PS Polit Sci Polit. 1991;24(2):138–143.

Sabatier PA, editor. Theories of the policy process. Westview Press; 2007.

Sabatier PA, Jenkins-Smith HC. An advocacy coalition framework model of policy change and the role of policy orientated learning therein. Policy Sci. 1988;21:129–68.

Sabatier PA, Jenkins-Smith HC. Policy change and learning: an advocacy coalition approach. Boulder: Westview Press; 1993.

Sabatier PA, Jenkins-Smith HC. The advocacy coalition framework: an assessment. In: Sabatier P, editor. Theories of the policy process. Westview Press; 1999. p. 117–66.

SAKALA Report Card. The Karnataka guarantee of Services to Citizens Act 2011 (SAKALA). By Dr. Shalini Rajneesh, Mission Director, SAKALA Project. 2012. https://sakala.kar.nic.in/sakala_monthly_report/June2012[ENG].pdf

Sapru RK. Public policy: formulation, implementation and evaluation paperback. India: Sterling Publishers; 2012.

Savage GT, Nix TW, Whitehead CJ, Blair JD. Strategies for assessing and managing organizational stakeholders. Acad Manag Executive. 1991;5(2).

Scartascinia C, Stein E, Tommasi M. Political institutions, intertemporal cooperation, and the quality of public policies. J Appl Econ. 2013;16(1).

Senge P. The fifth discipline: the art and practice of the learning organization. Doubleday Currency; 1990.

Senge P, Sterman JD. Systems thinking and organizational learning: acting locally and thinking globally in the organization of the future. Eur J Oper Res. 1992;59:137–50.

Sharkansky I, Hofferbert R. Dimensions of state politics, economics, and public policy. Am Polit Sci Rev. 1969;63(3):867. https://doi.org/10.2307/1954433.

Sharma M. Theory of public administration. New Delhi: Anmol Publisher; 2004.

Shughart FW. Public choice. 2020. https://www.econlib.org/library/Enc/PublicChoice.html

Sidney MS. Policy formulation: design and tools. In: Fischer F, Miller GJ, Sidney, MS, editors. Handbook of public policy analysis theory, politics, and methods, chap. 6. London: CRC Press; 2007.

Simon HA. A behavioral model of rational choice. Q J Econ. 1955;69(1):99–118.

Simon HA. Administrative behavior. 3rd ed. New York: The Free Press; 1976.

Simon HA. The new science of management decision. Prentice-Hall; 1977.

Sintchenko V, Coiera E. Decision complexity affects the extent and type of decision support use. 2006. https://www.ncbi.nlm.nih.gov/pmc/articles/PMC1839373/

References

Sirkin H, Rose J, Choraria R. Building an adaptive US manufacturing workforce. 2015. https://www.bcg.com/publications/2017/lean-manufacturing-operations-building-adaptive-us-workforce.aspx

Smith A. An inquiry into the nature and causes of the wealth of nations. Liberty Fund Inc.; 1776.

Solek A. Behavioral economics approaches to public policy. J Int Stud. 2014;7(2):33–45. https://doi.org/10.14254/2071-8330.2014/7-2/3

Solow R. Building a science of economics for the real world. Prepared statement to the house committee on science and technology, subcommittee on investigations and oversight. 2010. https://web.archive.org/web/20110204034313/http://democrats.science.house.gov/Media/file/Commdocs/hearings/2010/Oversight/20july/Solow_Testimony.pdf

Spiller PT, Tommasi M. The institutional foundations of public policy: a transactions approach with application to Argentina. J Law Econ Org. 2003;19(2):281–306, JSTOR. www.jstor.org/stable/3555106

Sterman JD. Business dynamics: systems thinking and modelling for a complex world. Boston: Irwin & McGraw-Hill; 2000.

Stewart J. Rational choice theory, public policy and the liberal state. Policy Sci. 1993;26(4).

Stiglitz JE. The price of inequality. Penguin; 2013.

Stiglitz JE. Rewriting the rules of the American economy: an agenda for shared prosperity. Roosevelt Institute; 2015. https://rentgrabbing.files.wordpress.com/2015/06/dde39-rewritingtherulesreportfullreport-singlepagefinal.pdf

Stone D. Policy paradox: the art of political decision making. W. W. Norton & Company; 2012.

Subroto A. Understanding complexities in public policy making process through policy cycle model: a system dynamics approach. Presented at II conference of WCSA-World Complexity Science Academy, Italy; 2011. https://proceedings.systemdynamics.org/2012/proceed/papers/P1067.pdf

Sunstein CR, Reisch LA, Rauber J. A worldwide consensus on nudging? Not quite, but almost. In: Regulation & governance. 2017. https://doi.org/10.1007/s10272-018-0710-2

Sushil. System dynamics: a practical approach for managerial problems. New Delhi: Wiley Eastern Limited; 1993.

Swanson D, Bhadwal S, editors. Creating adaptive policies guide for policy-making in an uncertain world. Sage Publication; 2009.

Thaler R. Some empirical evidence on dynamic inconsistency. Econ Lett. 1981;8(3):201–7.

Thaler RH, Sunstein CR. Nudge: improving decisions about health, wealth and happiness. Yale University Press; 2008.

Ulen TS. The theory of rational choice, its shortcomings, and the implications for public policy decision making. Knowledge. 1990;12(2):170–98. https://doi.org/10.1177/107554709001200204

UNESCO. Culture and development evolution and prospects by Maider Maraña. 2010. http://creativecommons.org/licenses/by-nc-nd/3.0/es/deed.es

United Nations (UN). Innovations in governance and public administration: replicating what works. Department of Economic and Social Affairs, New York; 2006.

United Nations Development Programme (UNDP). Human development indices and indicators. 2018.

Van der Wal Z, Huberts LWJC, van den Heuvel JHJ, Kolthoff EW. Values of government and business: differences, similarities, and conflicts. Public Adm Q. 2006;30(3):314–64.

Van Gils M, Klijn E. Complexity in decision making: the case of the Rotterdam harbour expansion. Connecting decisions, arenas and actors in spatial decision making. 2007. https://doi.org/10.1080/14649350701324359

van Heffen O, Klok PJ. Institutionalism: state models and policy processes. In: van Heffen O, Kickert WJM, Thomassen JJA, editors. Governance in modern society. Library of public policy and public administration, vol. 4. Springer, Dordrecht; 2000. https://doi.org/10.1007/978-94-015-9486-8_8

Von Bertalanffy L. Kritische Theorie der Formbildung. Berlin: Gebrüder Borntraeger (German title); 1928.
von Bertalanffy L. General system theory: foundations, development, applications. New York: George Braziller; 1968. ISBN 0-8076-0453-4.
Walt G. Health policy: an introduction to process and power. Witwatersrand University Press; 1994.
Warfield JW. Developing interconnected matrices in structural modelling. IEEE Transcripts Syst Man Cybern. 1974;4(1):51–81.
Weber M. From Max Weber: essays in sociology. Oxford University Press; 1946.
Weible C. Beliefs and perceived influence in a natural resource conflict: an advocacy coalition approach to policy networks. Polit Res Q. 2005;58(3):461–75.
Weible CM, Carter DP. Advancing policy process research at its overlap with public management scholarship and non-profit and voluntary action studies. Policy Stud J. 2017;45(1):2017.
Weible CM, Jenkins-Smith HC. The advocacy coalition framework: an approach for the comparative analysis of contentious policy issues. In: Peters BG, Zittoun P, editors. Contemporary approaches to public policy, theories, controversies and perspectives. Palgrave Macmillan; 2016.
Weible C, Sabatier PA. A guide to the advocacy coalition framework. In: Fischer F, Miller GJ, Sidney MS, editors. Handbook of public policy analysis theory, politics, and methods, chap. 9. CRC Press; 2007.
Will M, Groeneveld J, Frank K, Müller B. Combining social network analysis and agent-based modeling to explore dynamics of human interaction: a review. Soc Environ Syst Model. 2020;2:16325. https://doi.org/10.18174/sesmo.2020a16325
Wilson DS. Darwin's cathedral: evolution, religion, and the nature of society. Chicago: University of Chicago Press; 2002.
Woolcock M. Enhancing the quality of public service delivery: insights from recent research. World Bank research and policy briefs. 2017. https://documents.worldbank.org/en/publication/documents-reports/documentdetail/390551498836196848/enhancing-the-quality-of-public-service-delivery-insights-from-recent-research
World Bank. Reforming public institutions and strengthening governance. 2000. http://www1.worldbank.org/publicsector/Reforming.pdf
World Bank. World development report 2015: mind, society, and behavior. 2015.
World Bank. Big data in action for government big data: innovation in public services, policy and engagement. 2017.
World Economic Forum (WEF). The global competitiveness report, 2017–2018. 2018a.
World Economic Forum (WEF). The future of jobs report, 2018. 2018b.
World Bank. World Bank blogs: behavioral science in public policy: future of government? By Carolina Sánchez-Páramo, Renos Vakis, Zeina Afif. 2019a. http://blogs.worldbank.org/developmenttalk/behavioral-science-public-policy-future-government
World Bank. Doing business. World Bank report. 2019b.
Yanow D. How does a policy mean? Interpreting policy and organizational actions. Georgetown University Press; 1996.
Zagha R, Nankani GT, editors. Economic growth in the 1990s: learning from a decade of reform. World Bank Publications; 2005. https://documents.worldbank.org/en/publication/documents-reports/documentdetail/664481468315296721/economic-growth-in-the-1990s-learning-from-a-decade-of-reform

Part II
Way Ahead: Complexity Theory Framework, Policy Design Framework, and Institutional Development

Chapter 5
Complexity Theory Framework

> *Complexity is looking at interacting elements. Economists have begun exploring the economy as an evolving complex system, as a different approach—complexity economics.*
> Brian Arthur, Economist and Complexity Scientist,
> External Professor, Santa Fe Institute (SFI)

Abstract Uncertainty, dynamic nature, nonlinearity, and evolution demand a new approach to inquiry in the social and economic systems. The systems theory and dynamic systems theory from the 1960s and, subsequently, the complexity theory since the last decade of the twentieth century have shaped new thinking for dealing with complex problems. It is a clear departure from the approach of reductionism and determinism, relying on the Newtonian paradigm. Applicable to a public policy system, economy, business, and organization, the theory relies on various phenomena like emergence, self-organizing property, adaptation, coevolutionary process, and path dependency. It advances that the interactive elements and feedback loops result in system order and behavior. The theory draws on transdisciplinary knowledge and insights from multiple perspectives. It puts forward a complexity theory framework that lays out a conceptual structure for analyzing complexity and managing complex systems. Furthermore, it recommends a strategic framework to examine different contexts of systems—simple, complicated, complex, and disorder and explore strategies to manage them. It covers two case studies of the evolution of economies of silicon valleys in Bengaluru (India) and San Francisco Bay (USA). These cases highlight the essentiality of an alternative theory—a complexity theory.

Keywords Complexity theory · Evolution · Self-organization · Emergence · Adaptation · Coevolution · Path dependency · Systems thinking · Complexity thinking

5.1 New Paradigm: Complexity Theory

The twenty-first century is witnessing several changes, giving rise to diverse challenges. Globalization, climate change, new advanced technologies, automation, a digitally-connected world, cyber security, rapid urbanization, an aging population, and concerns for job losses, social security, potable water, and air pollution, to name a few, give rise to complexity in the system. These draw the attention of policymakers and businesses alike. The speed and scale of change are much higher. The interactive and dynamic nature of problems, causal loops, higher-order effects, and uncertain behavior give rise to complexity in the system (Forrester 1961; Senge 1990; Sterman 2000).

Challenge of problem definition and system conceptualization. In the backdrop of complexity in the real-world situation, it needs to be understood from the points of view of the role of stakeholders, social dimension, and technical nature. Both problem and system are intertwined. The problem and system are firstly embedded in socio-cultural and economic contexts, including history. The problems are associated with human behavior, socio-economic factors, and institutional dimension. For diverse stakeholders, the problems are defined by their respective values and interests attached to them (Conklin 2007; Head 2008; Jones 2011; Persson 2014). The personal values and beliefs of individuals matter and shape the thought process. The values and interests of individuals define the very essence of a problem. Equally important is that such values may change over time. The interests may be competing, supporting, or complementing and may shape and constrain how a particular policy problem is perceived and understood by different actors, including the policymakers. Due to competing interests and multiple differing perspectives, there is a constant struggle among the stakeholders to define the problem which represents their best interest. The perception and interpretation of reality influence the conception of the problems. Another aspect is how to interpret and define the reality to the satisfaction of a majority of the stakeholders.

From the point of view of structural complexity, the problem is hard to define as the system is open, and multiple internal issues criss-cross and interact with the external environment and vice-versa. Thus, it makes it difficult to find where the problem begins and where it ends, how the system impacts the environment, and how the environment impacts the system. In addition, the nonlinearity, dynamic nature, unpredictable behavior, the interactive nature of numerous internal elements, and the influence of several external factors add to the complexity and make it hard to define the problem (Osman 2002; Gaus 2007; Eppel and Rhodes 2018). Together with the social complexity, as a result of social-cultural and political factors, the technical complexity makes it difficult to define problems due to the limitations of doing technical analyses of complex issues in time. The traditional linear modes of problem solving and rationalist, scientific, and positivist approaches have not been enough due to bounded rationality and qualitative factors in both social and economic systems (Fischer 2003; Stone 1997; Hoppe 2011; Liedtka et al. 2017).

5.1 New Paradigm: Complexity Theory

Conventionally, as a natural tendency, a problem is defined keeping in view the symptoms associated with it and is based on an incomplete assessment of assumptions underlying the problem. In addition, there are other issues, like incorrect presumptions related to the process of development and change; solution-centric thinking without examining the details; and identification of external events or causes as justification for a problem (Mumford 1998; Head 2008; Moore 2011). The conditions, such as the pressure by top leadership to find immediate solutions and achieve quick results rather than exploring correct or long-term solution, lack of a culture of discussion, over-reliance on leadership for concurrence, and difficulty in collecting evidence and lack of evidence-based approach, obfuscate the problem definition. Thus, problem definition remains a complex matter. Some complex problems in the system are unemployment, demographic changes, climate change, global poverty, global financial management, human rights, etc.

The body of literature (Gaus 2007; Lipsky 2010; Gharajedaghi 2011; Ryan 2011; Persson 2014) on the complex system has highlighted that there is a challenge in conceptualizing the system due to difficulty in:

- *defining the problems*: in capturing the ground realities and complex features,
- *understanding interdependency of variables:* how different variables are linked and influence each other, and if one or more variables are not taken into account, how it may impact other variables and, as a result, the entire system and its behavior or output,
- *visualizing uncertainty*: the activities or interventions in a networked system may create some unintended processes—constructive or negative—whose impact is not known,
- *discerning fuzzy nature*: in the complex system, the exact features of the problems, issues, constraints, and intended goals are not clearly definable, and all these may change due to dynamic interactions, and
- *anticipating multiple possibilities*: due to the complex nature, there may be a need to consider more than one goal.

How to deal with complexity is a challenge. More specifically, the issues that need probing are: how an understanding of complexity is essential for policymaking in the public system, how the performance of the implementation of public policies is a complex matter, how economic policy has to factor in complexity, how business has to deal with a complex environment, and how the emerging complex environment impacts public policy, economy, and business.

There has been a realization that the current theories or approaches lack the ability to address issues such as the influence of multiple interacting elements, dynamic and rapid change, and uncertainty. It calls for a novel approach—complexity science. In response to complex issues in the public system, economy, and business, the essentiality of the complexity theory framework is recognized. It *first* defines the complexity theory to provide a theoretical perspective about the concepts and propositions to comprehend the underlying issues explicitly and then to respond to complexity with clear understanding, and *secondly*, it recommends a framework delineating a structure to provide a pragmatic way to approach the complex problems and manage the system.

5.1.1 Evolution of Complexity Theory

Complexity science has been researched since the 1960s and got more focused attention from 1980 onward due to growing interest in concepts like interconnectedness, uncertainty of system behavior, dynamic nature, emergence, and evolution. The theoretical, experiential, and empirical studies from various disciplines like mathematics, biology, physics, capital markets, and sociology contributed to the basis for studying complexity in public policy, economics, business, and organizational systems (Anderson et al. 1988; Mitchell 2009; Cairney 2012; Baetu 2012; Morcol 2012).

The dominating theories of the nineteenth and twentieth centuries focused on scientific management, equilibrium state, and deterministic concept have value in well-defined and predictable systems. These have been relatively short of explaining social or organizational behavior, industrial development, technology adoption, and economic development in different regions. Cartesian reductionism propounded by Descartes, mechanistic metaphor since Newtonian time, or the classical theory of economics has not been able to explain system behavior if concepts such as emergence, self-organization, and dynamic evolution were taken into consideration. Complexity science provides a useful alternative to the reductionist or mechanistic approach and classical economic theory on many counts (Grobman 2005; Dickson et al. 2006; Rosenberg 2006).

In 1984, Santa Fe Institute, the first research institute, was founded by scientists, including George Cowan, Herb Anderson, Stirling Colgate, and Murray Gell-Mann, and was dedicated to the research of complex systems, especially complex adaptive systems, and economy (Arthur et al. 1997). On account of a better appreciation of the underlying properties of the complex systems, the focus of scientific inquiry shifted toward assumptions, such as the system consists of its elements or parts; the properties of individual elements in a combined manner define the behavior of the whole system, and the properties of individual elements alone cannot define the behavior of the system; the system is more or less than the sum of parts; and concepts like dynamic and nonlinear relationships, feedback loops, interactive nature of elements, emergence, and adaptation are critical for understanding the system behavior (Coyle 1977; Morecroft 1983; Sterman 2000; Mitchell 2009). These, in a combined form, provided the fundamental basis for the complexity in the system. And the paradigms like reductionism, determinism, and Newtonian mechanistic approach have been found to be inconsistent with the research about the properties and functioning of living, social, and economic systems (Von Bertalanffy 1973; Arthur et al. 1997; Grobman 2005; Baetu 2012). These assumptions and concepts about the 'system' gave rise to systems theory and complexity theory (Forrester 1971; Sushil 1993; Morcol 2012; Boulton et al. 2015). In the backdrop of the above, while

5.1 New Paradigm: Complexity Theory

studying complexity theory, there are distinct ideas, reasonings, and deductions that can be discerned in the system studies and research in dynamical systems and deserve attention are:

- *Limits of reductionist and mechanistic approaches.* These approaches cannot be applied in the human system where interactive nature and interdependencies matter and system behavior evolves due to interactions between people or economic agents.
- *Diversity and independent nature.* The nature of individual elements (people, system variables) matters. But the overall effect is due to the interdependencies and dynamic interactions between elements, which can make a big difference.
- *Linkages between micro- and macro-level interactions.* The micro-level interactions, through feedback, impact the macro world that, in turn, influences the microworld, and both levels have a symbiotic relationship. It needs to be examined and considered while designing the policies and strategies.
- *Space–time compression.* It results from real-time and quick-time connectivity, implying that people in different locations come closer and exchange ideas and solutions. It could be due to technological breakthroughs, including communication and travel that condense spatial distances and temporal dimension. It has the potential advantage of raising economic performance by overcoming spatial or production barriers. It signifies convergence effect in quick time, network effects, and adaptability in the social systems (Harvey 1990; Decron 2001). As a result, the rate of change is faster, which increases dynamic behavior and complexity. It has implications for health, education, manufacturing units, e-commerce, etc.
- *Exploratory approach.* It is necessary to find solutions for complex problems by probing them from multiple perspectives.
- *Multiple points of influence.* They shape a system or organization through learnings, capabilities, culture, processes, structures, and innovation (Meadows 2008; Malhi et al. 2009).
- *Cascading effect and multiplier effects.* The simple efforts, knowledge, and information through interactions between numerous individuals are carried forward or transmitted throughout the system.

The above propositions have shaped the complexity theory in definite ways. From the perspective of the evolution of complexity theory, it emerged from systems theory in the 1960s, an interdisciplinary approach. From an epistemological perspective, the systems theory, fuzzy logic, chaos theory, and complex dynamic systems from bio-science have contributed significantly.

5.1.2 Complexity Theory

This theory is put forward for social and economic systems. Some of the basic features of the system are:

Subsystem networks. Complex systems are like networks comprising nodes and edges. The nodes are elements represented by individuals (people or agents) and system variables (Box 5.1), and the edges are ties or links (relationships or interactions) that connect them (Fig. 5.1). The networks are referred to as social structures, institutions, business units, knowledge networks, sectors, organizations, and so on. The network analysis examines the behavior of the elements at the micro level; interactions between the elements within the system and with the elements in the environment; and the pattern of system behavior. Depending upon the context, the system and environment can be defined. In this case, as an example in Fig. 5.1, the seven subsystems constitute a 'system'. The 'environment' is external to system. It includes country as well as international environment. Accordingly, different features of the subsystems are indicated in Box 5.1.

Box 5.1: Elements in Subsystems and Environment

Subsystems (these constitute a system)

- Individuals (economic agents, personnel, employees, stakeholders, entrepreneurs, elected members, NGOs)
- Institutions (norms of governance, rules and regulations, social and public institutions, political institutions, values, norms)
- Spatial (geographical) (locations, local resources)

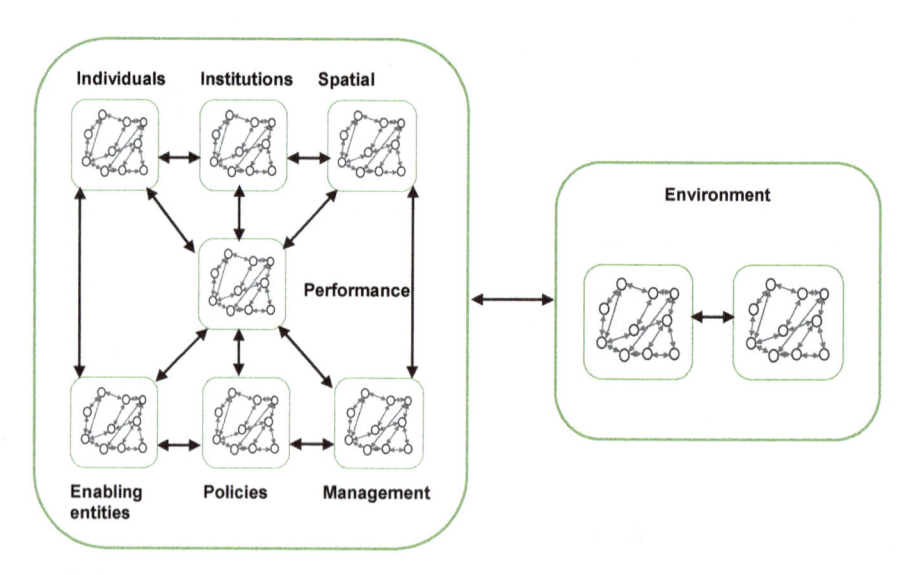

Nodes represent elements within subsystems: (O)
Edges represent relationships within subsystems: (◄──►)

Fig. 5.1 General network model for a complex system

5.1 New Paradigm: Complexity Theory

- Enabling entities (including sectors, business, industry, infrastructure, ecosystem, technologies, departments, divisions, organizations)
- Policies (government policies, strategies and programs, interventions)
- Management (administrative functions, human resource management, internal management systems, processes, structures)
- Performance (performance indicators of the system)

Environment

- Environment (social environment, policies of other countries, external technological context, external networks, international political environment)

In general, in the socio-economic system, various subsystems, viz., individuals, institutions, spatial (geographical), enabling entities, policies, management, performance, and environment (external) interact with each other. And as a result, the system emerges. These subsystems have behavioral features and qualitative variables. Their interactions have higher-order effects and are influenced by feedback loops. The relationships between them are nonlinear, dynamic, and non-determinable quantitatively and precisely in most cases due to feedback loops and uncertainty. The individuals, as citizens or economic agents, interact to exchange ideas, skills, and resources and thus make decisions for various social and economic activities. How the individuals interact in the subsystems will also be defined by the 'possibility' of interactions, which will depend upon the characteristics of elements, ecosystem, social capital, and trust level between individuals.

These subsystems and elements therein are influenced by the environment. In a combined manner, they influence the system behavior, which, in turn, impacts the environment. The system behavior could be improved education, enhanced health facilities, industrial clusters, exports, etc. This process of interactions and feedback continues in a circular flow leading to circular causality (Fig. 5.2). Social media, e-business, e-commerce, networked economy, e-education, etc., are examples of how the interactive property of elements in the system shapes the behavior and outcomes.

The key features of the system, interactions, and system behavior are summarized below:

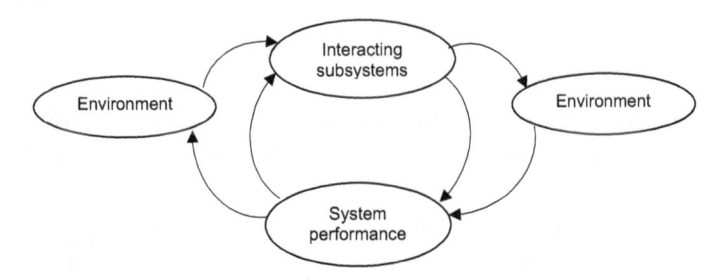

Fig. 5.2 Circular causality model

a. *System.* Every system, be it at micro level or macro level, is defined in terms of functions, subsystems, elements, boundary, and environment. Depending on the functions, context, and boundary, a subsystem may be a system or vice-versa.
b. *Elements*: Individuals and system variables.
c. *Circular causality*: Due to feedback, the causes and effects return to the original cause (Fig. 5.2).
d. *Relationships between variables:* In the networks, the relationships are nonlinear, dynamic, and uncertain.
e. *Interactions.* The elements interact in the system and with environment.
f. *Dynamics.* The interactions, relationships, and system behavior keep changing with the exchange of ideas, knowledge, resources, and internal or external influence.
g. *Mechanism of emergence.* It is due to interactions, exchange of ideas and resources, creativity, feedback, learning, and adaptation.
h. *Social capital and ethics.* They influence trust, confidence, predictability, and reliability and impact interactions between elements.
i. *Decision-making by individuals.* It depends upon knowledge, capabilities, quality of interactions, values, beliefs, ethics, and personal choices.
j. *Ecosystem.* It is determined by converging policies, institutional mechanisms, culture, infrastructure, social capital, ethics, etc.
k. *Environment.* It is external to system, and consists of external policies (could be of other countries), networks, international political environment, etc.
l. *Interactions* = f (values, trust, norms, local rules, capabilities, ecosystem, state of variables, ethics)
m. *Emergence, self-organization, and adaptability* = f (interactions between elements in the networks, path dependence, ecosystem, policies, institutions, social capital, decision-making, and actions by individuals).
n. *System performance* (behavior) = f (interactions, emergence, self-organization, and adaptation) (from the perspective of complexity phenomena).
o. *System performance* (behavior) ↔ f (interactions between: individuals, institutions, spatial features, enabling entities, policies, management, environment). It represents circular causality and is self-reinforcing. The performance is endogenized (due to circular causality as a result of feedback).

Under the umbrella of theory, firstly, the assumptions, principles, and philosophy underlying the complexity theory are defined.

Assumptions

The key assumptions of the complexity theory for the complex social and economic systems are (Grobman 2005; Richardson 2005; Boulton et al. 2015; Sjotun et al. 2020):

- system has an open boundary and is influenced by the environment,
- complex system has numerous interacting elements, and the elements are diverse in nature,

5.1 New Paradigm: Complexity Theory

- emergence in social and economic systems is due to the human nature of interactions between individuals,
- initial condition and past influence the interactions and future state,
- an absence of a master controller to control the interactions, as the elements are managed, regulated, and controlled by the local rules, values, norms, and institutional mechanisms,
- difficult to predict the system behavior, possibility of a wide range of outcomes, uncertain behavior, and end point is not determinable,
- system remains far from equilibrium in a dynamic mode, and
- generalizing a system state and data aggregation cannot provide a realistic view of the system due to the diverse nature of elements, interactive effect of elements, and context-specific system conditions that characterize complex systems.

Principles

In the light of scholarly work by various experts on complexity science and, in particular, on characteristics and system behavior, the following principles are filtered as a basis for complexity theory (Kauffman 1995; Kelly and Allison 1999; Arthur 2000; Palmberg 2009b; Gharajedaghi 2011; Morcol 2012; Colander and Kupers 2016):

- *first principle*: interactive behavior, emergence, self-organization, and adaptation are imperatives and determinants of behavior of a complex system
- *second principle*: essentiality of adaptive nature, and change is fundamental to a complex system
- *third principle*: the complex systems are constrained by path dependence
- *fourth principle*: the complex systems evolve and coevolve
- *fifth principle*: transformation occurs at the edge of chaos (equivalent of point of inflection).

The details are as follows:

First principle, interactive behavior, emergence, self-organization, and adaptation are imperatives and determinants of behavior of a complex system. For the emergent behavior in the social and economic system, the key aspects are:

a. *environment* (new technologies, external policies, etc.) like changes in the policies related to trade or regulatory mechanism of major countries, climate change policies, competition, technology disruption, etc.;
b. *government or top management interventions and policies* to bring changes in the internal processes, systems, culture, practices, structures, etc.; and
c. *interacting system variables and individuals* play a pivotal role in emergent behavior.

The complexity perspective implies that the interdependencies between elements affect macro-level behavior. Or, the output or behavior at the macro level cannot be merely a result of top-down interventions by disregarding interactive behavior at the micro level. The system structures impact the quality of interactions. It requires

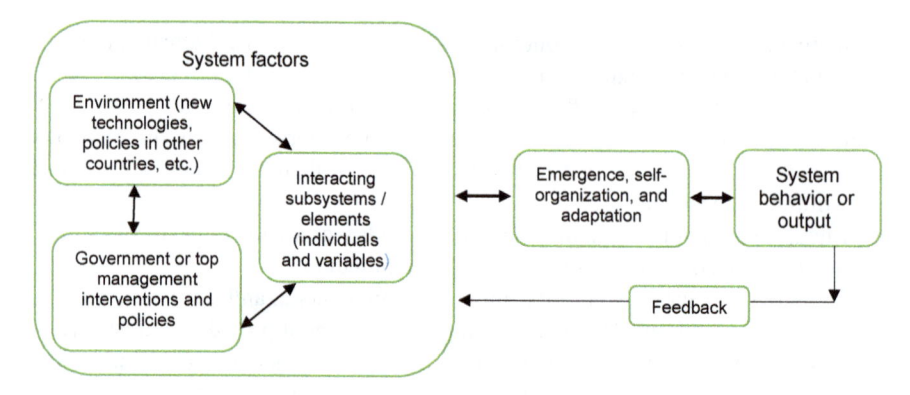

Fig. 5.3 Social system emergence model: systemic perspective

analysis of the combined effect of the environment, macro-policy interventions, and interacting elements at the micro level to understand the intricate emergent, self-organizing, and adaptation properties (Fig. 5.3).

Second principle, essentiality of adaptive nature, and change is fundamental to a complex system. Adaptation is the property that the people or economic agents use to adjust to new conditions. As a result of the influence of environment and/or policy interventions, the system adapts to new situations through a process of feedback loops and emergence. To adapt to changes, the agents of and other systems in the environment may coevolve, and then the agents of and the system under study may change. Complex adaptive systems (CASs) are characterized by high adaptive capacity. Adaptation is due to the creativity, learning ability, and adaptive power of evolutionary systems, where structure, pattern, and system emerge and change with time on account of challenges, outside influence, competition, and cooperation. For example, in the fast-emerging scenario marked by technological disruption, change is frequent, rapid, and even widespread for business entities (Brown and Eisenhardt 1997; Kelly and Allison 1999; Allen 2011; Turner and Baker 2019).

Learning is an indispensable feature. In the changing economy and technological scenario, the key ingredients in success and survival are the capacity to learn and adaptability. The economic agents in the economy or people in the organizations or social systems are influenced by others within the system or the environment. Through a learning process, they display a unique feature of adaptation to fit in the system or survive. They learn from the combined effect of the environment, policy interventions, leadership, etc. (Kelly and Allison 1999; Senge and Sterman 1992; Turner and Baker 2019).

Third principle, complex systems are constrained by path dependence. It implies that history or past events matter, and what has happened in the past continues due to a lock-in state or resistance to change.

Fourth principle, complex systems evolve and coevolve. Evolution and coevolution take place in complex systems. The public systems, economy, organizations, industry, and business manifest such phenomena. Evolution takes place to adapt to a new condition through a process of self-organization and adaptation. It is an inherent tendency in a complex system to evolve. Coevolution refers to the cases in which two or more systems reciprocally influence each other's evolution. Through interactions, the systems and processes evolve and coevolve and are determined by individuals, the environment, and other systems in the environment. The values, culture, and psychological and behavioral factors influence such evolution and coevolution. The system remains dynamic and in a changing state, and the condition of non-equilibrium persists. With time, it keeps evolving within itself and coevolving with other systems in the environment (Kelly and Allison 1999; Chan 2001; McKelvey 2002; Sotarauta and Srinivas 2006; Palmberg 2009a; Morcol 2012).

Fifth principle, transformation occurs at the edge of chaos (the point of inflection). The edge of chaos in the complex adaptive system (CAS) arises when the system is disturbed from its equilibrium or stable state by the internal factors or influence of the external environment. It can occur due to prolonged stagnation in the organization in the face of changing needs or competition from outside. Through a process of emergence, self-organization, and adaptation, the edge of chaos signifies a significant irreversible transformation in the system and is equivalent to the point of inflection. While displaying the need for stable conditions and, simultaneously, the resilience to disturbance or disorder, if the influence of the perturbation is significant, the system can exhibit critical point or disorderly condition. Under such disorder, the system may cross over the threshold limit, then begin a transition process, and finally reach a new stable state through adaptation (Brown and Eisenhardt 1997; Zimmerman et al. 2001; Carmichael and Hadzikadi 2019).

Philosophy

At the basic level, in the complex system, elements and their interactions and interdependencies matter the most. In the social system, due to nonlinear dynamic interactions and behavioral dimension, the interrelationships between elements depends on multiple factors much beyond the ability of conventional thinking to comprehend. The system behavior cannot be studied and deciphered in a precise manner by any standard rule or method. The behavior reflects the invisible or hidden role of interactions between elements. The system may be a delivery mechanism of public services, the economy, business and industrial cluster, an organization, etc.

Another key phenomenon relates to micro-macro dynamic interactions. The interactions at the micro level influence the system behavior and outputs, which influence macro-level decision-making through feedback loops. The system remains in dynamic relationships with the environment. Complex systems are complex adaptive systems (CASs), which display emergent and self-organizing behavior and adaptation property to change. These systems cannot be merely controlled or designed by the top-down approach. Fundamentally, the elements respond to the environment and top-level interventions, and in response, any new system behavior emerges due to interactions between elements at the micro level (ground level). CASs respond to and are influenced by the combined effect of, *first*, interactions within the system, *second*, changes in the environment, and *third*, the policies and strategies from the top. There is a combined effect of all three in the system through interactive effects of elements.

Theoretical Propositions

In the backdrop of characteristics, principles, and philosophy about complex systems, the theory puts forward the following underlying propositions:

- the system behavior or output is a result of the interactive role of elements at the micro level or in the networks, and the structures, values, culture, capabilities of interacting elements, and ecosystem, including social capital and ethics influence interactions;
- the environment influences the system, including elements in a positive or negative direction through feedback;
- policies and strategies from the top at the macro level can create enabling or disabling conditions for the elements to interact;
- as a result of a combination of the above three, the system emerges, self-organizes, and adapts, and thus, the behavior and performance of a system are determined; and
- due to complex nature, for any policy or strategy formulation for the social sector, economy, industry, or business, it requires understanding the system by examining the characteristics of elements, interactions between elements, interrelationships between variables, the conditions in the environment, and various complexity phenomena in the system.

The above propositions apply to all forms of socio-economic systems in which human beings are engaged, as they bring uniqueness. The uniqueness is due to the behavioral and cognitive dimensions, expertise, and creativity. It exerts influence on the system behavior or performance in an unpredictable manner. The unique feature is like hidden potential and is difficult to quantify or predict it. It needs to be factored in every step of policymaking—conceptualization of the problem, understating system, analyses, policy formulation, and implementation.

The phenomenon of organic linkage is crucial. The linkages between people or economic agents occur due to interactions based on shared values, beliefs, commitment, and resources. The people interact with and influence other people and system variables, impacting each other through feedback. Such interactions constantly occur within the system and between different systems and the external environment. In this process, due to human nature, the people adapt to each other, the system, and then the external environment. Likewise, the system adapts to people, the external environment , and other systems, and this process continues. Such linkages lead to some form of social or organic bonds, which are the underlying reasons for the emergence and adaptation and the complexity in the system.

Fundamental issues. The elements are referred to as system variables, people, or agents. The system variables are defined as elements such as policies, infrastructure, technologies, finance, poverty, income, performance indicators, individual behavior, and so on. Depending upon the system, the number of variables could be as large as a hundred, thousand, or more. The number of people or agents could be hundreds, thousands, or more. The people or agents have diverse features defined by their values, cognitive abilities, behavior, capabilities, and motivation level. The interactions between people and system variables set in motion the chain of activities in the form of ideas generation, discussions, analyses, learnings, decision-making, interventions, feedback, corrections, and so on. Such interactions are numerous and dynamic due to continuous learning, feedback, and change.

How the people influence; how they impact the system variables and outputs; and how system variables affect each other, people, and results cannot be exactly inferred. Thus, the number of interactions and the nature and quality of interactions cannot be discerned on an immediate basis, and it will take time to understand before system behavior emerges. And the relationships between variables and cause-effects remain unknown. The people or agents bring thinking, decisions, and actions, as a result, cause vibrancy to the entire system. As such, in the absence of interactions, the system variables can do little independently, and they will remain mechanical elements. The interactions in dynamic and unpredictable ways result in complexity in the system.

In the complex system, due to the interactive nature and bonds between system variables and people, the following three distinct features are essential to understand at the fundamental level:

First, organic linkages, legacy factors, and path dependence. The people, economy, business, and technologies have their past. The changes in them cannot be introduced as planned by some top-down interventions. People are organically linked to the past through their thoughts, values, beliefs, and cognitive biases. The social and personal bonds or bonds between system variables and people persist. It is purely human. Behavioral practices take time to change, adjust, and settle. Economy and business have a legacy of past practices, methods, and mechanisms that have worked over time. Likewise, the technologies and devices, which have worked under a particular ecosystem and are tied to usage by several people, cannot be changed easily unless there is a significant driving force. The future cannot be detached from the past and needs to factor in past events, policies, and programs.

Second, assumptions and causality require revisiting with time. The policies and programs are designed under specific social, political, economic, and technological contexts, which change with the passage of time (Lucas 1976; Sargent 1987). The people or agents may not respond to the same policies in the same way as they responded to in the past, as the expectations and behavior of people change and new conditions emerge. Or the interactive nature of people with policies and system variables changes. The past policies can provide some lessons but cannot be fully applied, and the new context should be appreciated. The past assumptions or causality may not work in the changed contexts. Though some assumptions, partial causal relationships, and parts of approaches may be applicable in the future, they should be redefined due to changing contexts and conditions. The assumptions and causality change with time.

Third, local context is fundamental. The problems and systems are contextual and are embedded in particular social, cultural, economic, technological, and geographical conditions. The one-size-fits-all policy cannot work. The underlying issue is the interactive role of agents with the policy variables, environment, and other system elements. The policies cannot work in isolation of people's concerns and local conditions. There is a need to examine different socio-economic and political settings in different regions or communities before credible policies and programs can be designed.

These three propositions have implications for social policies as well as economic policies.

5.1.3 Understanding Complexity Dimensions

Complexity theory offers a new way of approaching the world, a scientific paradigm. It is of importance to all areas concerning the public system—public policy and administration, health, education, urban management, economy, business, and so on. To manage complex systems, the theory emphasizes five major aspects, as presented below:

- *Underlying features of complexity.* The social systems constitute interacting people and system variables, which interact between themselves and with the environment. There is uniqueness or distinctiveness about the interactions. It comes from the presence of human beings (people) who have the tendency to interact, learn, change, and evolve. The complexity is determined mainly by the following five basic features:

  a. *A large number of interacting elements, including system variables and people or agents.* The role of people is crucial, as they bring distinct features like behavioral issues, cognitive dimension, expertise, new ideas, creativity, and innovations, which in a combined manner, bring a dynamic response. The behavior, characteristics, or capabilities of people keep evolving both within the system and in the external environment and influence other people and the system variables in a continuous manner.
  b. *Interactions with the environment.* The agents interact with the environment or vice-versa, and in the process, they influence each other.
  c. *Dynamic nature.* Due to interactions, people or agents get new and different ideas, learn new skills, use creativity, bring innovative ways of doing work, or develop new technologies. In this process, the change occurs; thus, the system remains in a dynamic mode.
  d. *Nonlinearity.* The relationships between system variables and people give rise to nonlinearity due to a combination of factors such as behavioral and institutional issues, nonlinear mathematical relations between elements, feedback loops, and higher-order effects.

5.1 New Paradigm: Complexity Theory

  e. *Uncertainty*. Due to nonlinear and dynamic interactions and feedback loops, there is uncertainty in behavior. Under such conditions, the cause-effect relationships are not discernible.

- *Conceptualization of a problem and system*. At the individual level, the values, interests, ability to interpret, and perception of reality influence the conception of a problem. In addition, due to the inadequacies in eliciting insights and extracting perspectives from the stakeholders, the problem definition is difficult. More often, it is not adequately articulated and remains fuzzy. The multiple interacting socio-economic issues and differing perspectives of diverse stakeholders put constraints on comprehending the problem and system.

The conceptualization of both problem and system is essential before making an attempt to formulate public policy and design strategy for interventions. Due to the interactive nature of elements, the system should not be examined by breaking it into constituent subsystems or elements. But it needs to be seen as a whole, together with studying the characteristics of individual subsystems or elements. The examination will entail the study of human behavior, social factors, and institutional features. To define the problem and conceptualize the system, it will call for making five distinct examinations: features of system variables, attributes of people or agents, interrelationships between system variables within the system, the relationship of the system with the environment, and characteristics of complexity, including interactive behavior. Other aspects like understanding where the problem begins and where it ends, changing nature of the problem, nonlinearity, and dynamic and unpredictable nature need to be studied (Osman 2002; Gharajedaghi 2011; Lipsky 2010; Eppel and Rhodes 2018). To understand complex systems, various characteristics need to be comprehended. These are covered in detail in Chap. 3.

In general, it requires understanding people and system variables and their features and interrelationships. Broadly, the system variables are classified into the following sets:

a. *Variables of problems, policy issues, and program design*: income level, health condition of people, infrastructure condition, technology, resources, program budget, employment, etc.;
b. *Variables of behavioral dimension in the community*: values, culture, beliefs, etc.;
c. *Variables of institutions*: values, rules, public institutions and their roles, institutional processes and mechanisms, etc.;
d. *Variables of the delivery system*: manpower, logistics, equipments, implementation mechanism, provisioning of services, quality management of projects, MIS, etc.;
e. *Variables of the organization*: like work culture, capabilities, processes, systems, structures, human resources (HR) management, decision-making, innovation, citizen management, etc.; and

f. *Variables of the environment*: social institutions, external policies, external networks and entities, international political environment, global finance, trade, etc.

Likewise, for people (or agents) in the system, it necessitates studying attributes such as values, beliefs, capabilities, decision-making abilities, etc.

There is an issue of bounded rationality or cognitive limitations, due to which people do not always make optimal decisions (Simon 1957; Morecroft 1983; Arthur et al. 1997). Different people with the same information may arrive at different decisions because of differences in their experience, knowledge, and ability to apply logic. In addition, imperfect information plays a role in limiting the ability to analyze and make correct decisions. Both lack of and timely information have a bearing on the stakeholders and policymakers in the policy system, business, and organization to analyze issues, understand, and solve problems. As a result of limitations, many complex issues are either overlooked or not studied, and there is a tendency to oversimplify the complexity to find quick answers, while underlying issues of problems remain unanswered (Jones 2011; Mueller 2020). To overcome such limitations, policymakers and strategists should purposefully keep an eye on details to discern new insights and obtain different perspectives.

- *System behavior or output—micro-level interactions and emergence.* In a web of interactions, the variables interact within the same system or with the environment. Similarly, people interact with each other and other systems in the environment. Also, people interact with the variables of systems and come in dynamic interactions with them. In this process, the attributes of people (or agents) influence that of others and get influenced by them, and likewise, the variables are impacted by the people and impact them. In this way, they create a web. It highlights how such interactions may be thousands or millions in number and that comprehending numerous interactions between people and variables will be an enormous as well as an almost impossible task.

The institutional, behavioral, and psychological factors matter during the interactions. These are influenced by the ecosystem, including institutions, culture, values, beliefs, capabilities, the capacity of institutions, and enabling policies. At the individual level, social and financial security, including emotional and trust levels within the network and in the society (environment), impact interactions. The emergence will depend upon the nature, quality, degree, and intensity of interactions. The ecosystem will influence all of them (Fig. 5.4). The nature will include informal discussions and exchange of ideas; and formal discussion forums, collaboration, agreements, and contracts. The quality parameters are trust, confidence, and reliability in exchanging ideas, knowledge, and resources. These will shape the robustness of behavior. The degree represents the extent to which the subsystems or elements will interact, and the intensity is about how quickly and frequently the interactions occur. Over time, the emergence of new behavior takes place.

To understand how elements interact within a social system, economy, or organization; how they respond to policy interventions from the top; how they interact

5.1 New Paradigm: Complexity Theory

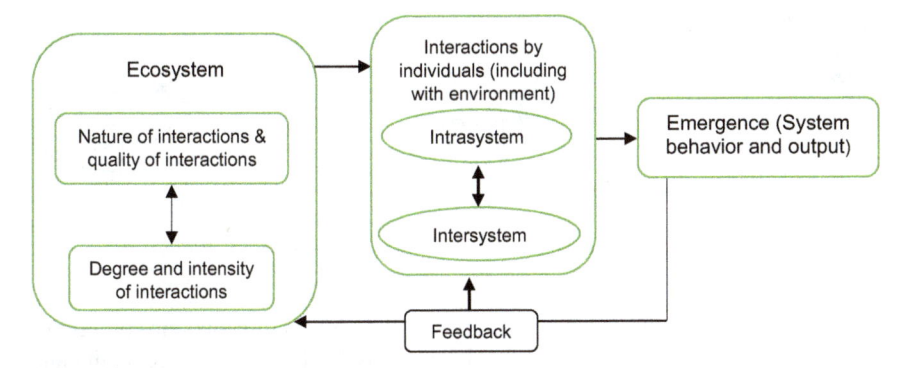

Fig. 5.4 Interactions and emergence dynamics

with other systems in the environment; and how these interactions change over time, it will require a detailed understanding of the process of interactions. In the case of the economy, the capabilities like knowledge and skills, values and culture, innovation culture, value for citizen care, etc., influence the interactions between economic agents as they try to take their positions based on their commitments and needs.

The change in one agent affects the evolution of others and may influence the system. The interactions are not controlled or influenced from the top, though the policies can affect the ecosystem in which agents interact. The interventions from the top provide opportunities for agents to accept, reject, or adapt to new conditions or regulations. For example, for promoting innovation and startups, the policy interventions and incentives provided by the government may be accepted or ignored by the startup companies, depending upon the substance of the policies and the ecosystem. When the economic agents interact with the environment, they create a web or network of relationships. They disseminate many ideas and knowledge and absorb ideas or technologies from the environment. Such adoption of technologies by agents or businesses may have cascading or ripple effects on the performance of the industry and then on the economy. The IT App-based economy and e-commerce are examples of cascading effects in which multitudes of interactions by entrepreneurs with customers, technologies, financial systems, and regulations play their roles (Beinhocker 1997; Haken 2006; Tapscott and Williams 2006).

The system-level behavior is represented by output and performance. It evolves with time due to interactions between the micro level and system level as a result of feedback (Fig. 5.5). In the context of public policy, economy, business, and organization, some of the specific output indicators are as follows. For the public system, public policies and implementation of policies are indicators; for the economic system, the financial system infrastructure, trade, industry clusters, and the emergence of the economy are indicators; for business and industry, the product development, business clusters, exports, business in different regions and countries, customer management, etc., are indicators; and for the organizations, the evolution of culture and values, systems, and processes are indicators.

Fig. 5.5 Micro-level and system-level linkage—feedback loop

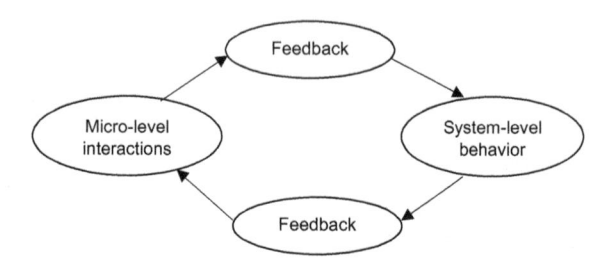

- *Environment*. It is external to the system and includes socio-economic conditions, political factors, culture, beliefs, and institutions. In the context of economy and business, the environmental factors are competition, policies of different countries, multilateral agreements, etc. The environment influences the system through interactions and feedback. It may prompt the government to effect policy changes or impact the business and industry to respond to competition and disruptive technologies. The business and economy may be susceptible to external influences or disruptions if not managed well.

- *Macro-level interventions*. Though local interactions play their roles, the governments, in the case of the public system and economy, or business management for managing enterprises are expected to respond to internal needs or the external environment. The interventions are control parameters to bring a new set of values, norms, culture, processes, systems, methods, new practices, structures, skill sets, policies, and strategies. These can create enabling conditions for the system variables and people to interact in the ecosystem and can change the basin of attraction to a new attractor state. Or, in other words, through interventions, the system can reach a new state. But, the new state will depend on the interacting elements in the system.

Finally, complexity is an inevitable reality in the social and economic systems dealing with social issues. To manage complexity, in the backdrop of details as presented above, the essential points are summarized as follows:

– *Conceptualization*. Understanding subsystems and elements and their attributes; system state in the phase space, or the system variables over time to examine the pattern of system behavior; behavioral issues; and institutional issues.
– *Emergence and self-organizing property*. Appreciating the inevitability of interactions, network effects, emergence, self-organization, and adaptation.
– *Path dependence*. Past policies, events, processes, and practices matter and need to be studied.
– *Adaptation and coevolution*. As a natural human tendency to survive, people tend to adapt to change as the system evolves, and in the process, the systems in the environment coevolve.
– *Dynamics of basin of attraction*. It should be examined whenever new policies are introduced, or the underlying socio-economic conditions change. The basin of attraction is a set of all the initial system conditions, which will gravitate toward

desired attractor state. The attractor state should be able to pull the system toward itself based on the policies and interventions.
- *Edge of chaos, adaptation, and strange attractor*: Due to external forces, internal perturbations, or the need to transform or stay competitive over time, managing the edge of chaos is a necessity and needs to be borne in mind by policymakers and management at the top level. The system may reach a new state (in phase space), which is unknown and is referred to as a strange attractor.
- *External environment*: Making sense of changes in the external environment continuously and responding appropriately. For example, the rising aspirations of people within the country, changes in the policies or political scenario of other countries, or the business landscape of industry need examination.

5.2 Complexity Theory Framework

The policy challenges are complex due to the influence of multiple interacting factors and stakeholders. It is difficult to articulate the problem and system due to a combination of difficulties: *first,* in identifying all the variables; *second*, in determining cause-effect relationships due to multidimensional and interconnected variables; and *third*, in eliciting insights from numerous stakeholders. Moreover, there are issues of identifying clear 'beginning and end points' of problems and their constantly changing nature.

So far, the complexity has been managed through an unstructured manner with short-term objectives in some cases and left unattended in most cases till some serious problem or crisis surfaces. The complexity will require managing for the short term to meet the pressing objectives of the government, economy, or organization. In the medium to long term, it will demand addressing complexity comprehensively, not just to manage but to comprehend the insights and possible hidden potential in the system and then to leverage them for higher performance through calibrated and continuous efforts. Understanding and application of concepts, philosophy, and complexity theory can unravel the possibilities that are currently unknown or unknowable through conventional approaches. The complexity may evoke inconvenient thoughts and reactions but it can be a blessing in disguise if discerned clearly. Prudence demands to appreciate, accept, and work with complexity and then analyze and address complexity. In light of the problems in the real world, the complexity theory framework is presented to manage complex systems.

The complexity theory framework has two constituents—one theory and the other framework. The complexity theory has been envisaged to give a set of acceptable assumptions, concepts, principles, and propositions that constitute a way to provide a reasoned explanation for addressing the complexity in the system in the real world. It has been dealt with at length in Sect. 5.1.

The framework lays out a conceptual structure to analyze complexity and suggest strategies to manage complex systems, and is intended to serve as a guiding map or provide general direction. The framework covers key aspects such as system diagnosis, including data collation and analysis, gaining insights into underlying issues, pattern recognition, problem analysis, and problem definition; strategy formulation; approaches of interventions; and evaluation and mid-course correction. The applicability of the theory and framework is for the public policy system, economic system, business, and organization. The framework has the following components:

- Diagnostic study: system and problem analysis, problem definition;
- Strategy formulation;
- Solution and program design;
- Implementation;
- Feedback, evaluation, adaptation, and mid-course correction.

- Diagnostic study. It entails the following steps:

Conceptualization of system and problem, and problem definition. The conceptual understanding of the system and problem is vital before attempting to formulate policies and develop strategies in order to introduce changes. The system analysis and stakeholder analysis are necessary tools for this purpose. For complex problems, the understanding of assumptions and principles spelled out in complexity theory is essential. For conceptualizing complex systems, the application of complexity thinking, systems thinking, design thinking, and critical thinking is called for. Complexity thinking stresses that a system requires systemic knowledge to obtain a complete view by examining the interactions between subsystems and elements. It analyzes interconnectedness, uncertainty, nonlinearity, and feedback loops. It emphasizes understanding patterns and different perspectives of the system. Systems thinking can help to get a system view.

Design thinking can be of use to elicit insights from end-users. Critical thinking can facilitate in analyzing causal relations. Besides, it necessitates stakeholder analysis (SA), which is a process to understand and incorporate the needs of those who have a 'stake' or an interest in the concerned policy or intervention. The analysis will entail understanding issues from multiple lenses (Savage et al. 1991; Brinkerhoff 1998; Fletcher et al. 2003).

System analysis (understanding system and problems therein). Firstly, it will include identifying subsystems and elements (including individuals and system variables) and their attributes, behavior, capabilities, values, beliefs, etc.; the context in which the system functions; internal work environment, culture, systems, processes, and practices; interrelationships between variables; interlinkages between subsystems; degree of connectivity; external environment; and goals (of different groups or segments). *Secondly,* it will involve understanding uncertainty, dynamics (of conditions, behavior, output, demands, constraints, etc.), examining interactive effects between elements, emergence, evolutionary character and patterns, and visualization of the future state.

5.2 Complexity Theory Framework

Each complex problem differs from others and may require a different way of solving. The expert knowledge and experience of the system dealing with traditional approaches may not be sufficient, and new understanding, knowledge, and approaches to handle complex problems are needed. There is no easy scientific way to examine multiple causal relationships between variables in the network in a precise manner. And deducing behavior from existing rules or knowledge may not always work. Depending upon the context, it may require empirical studies and field surveys. The grounded theory can help in gaining insights from the grassroots level. It may require pattern recognition and scenario building of system behavior.

In addition, complex problems require out-of-the-box thinking or original thinking. More specifically, to complement the critical thinking approach, 'first principles thinking' is one such approach. It is a departure from the existing methods. It requires digging deeper and searching for the root causes, analyzing different parts or elements in detail, examining their interrelationships, and then synthesizing the whole to get a complete view of the problem, system, and environment. It is like deconstructing and then reconstructing. It may call for a transdisciplinary approach to work on new ideas to get a better sense of the problems. It may require using higher-order thinking, including analyzing, reasoning, comprehending, evaluating, and synthesizing issues. It is based on reflection and an iterative process. The underlying reasons for such new approaches are to examine issues deeper, differently with diverse perspectives, and holistically.

- *Strategy formulation.* The theory puts forward that complex problems demand a novel approach, a departure from conventional approaches. The governments or top management in the public system, economic management, business, and organizations need to visualize how problems are evolving in the real world. They need to comprehend the interactive effects of multiple elements—individuals, system variables, institutions, and policies. They need to focus on institutional mechanisms, rules, values, structures, and processes that influence the interactive process in the system and its behavior.

The twentieth century paradigms for public and private management were mainly defined by the classical theory of public administration, classical scientific management, classical and neo-classical economic theories, and deterministic models based on objective functions and predictable behaviors. These were primarily based on known or knowable cause-effects and scientific and objective ways of handling a problem by applying known knowledge and expertise. Though these paradigms serve a useful purpose for known and defined systems, they have limitations for uncertain and dynamic systems dealing with heterogeneous elements, their interactive effects, and emergent and evolutionary behavior. In contrast to conventional paradigms, complexity theory has emerged as a new approach. It calls for a shift in traditional thinking, philosophy, principles, and postulates.

The theory recognizes that complex problems are unique, cause-effects are not known, the interactive network effects determine the behavior of a system in an uncertain manner, the knowledge needs to evolve by gaining insights through probing, and the solutions are to be worked out through an iterative process, based on feedback.

It emphasizes examining complex issues from new perspectives and multiple lenses of inquiry and facilitating problem solving through continuous consultations with stakeholders.

The emergent and self-organizing properties of the complex system need to be appreciated. However, these two fundamental properties don't mean that the system can live in perpetuity on its own. Instead, the reality of complexity in terms of feedback from elements and dynamics of change should be recognized. Based on that, interventions in the form of policies and strategies need to be designed. The government, business, and organization need to address and manage the complexity by understanding the properties of the complex adaptive system (CAS) (Senge 1990; Cilliers 1998; Stacey 2000; Palmberg 2009b). Over time, the enabling or disabling conditions in which people or economic agents function need revisiting regularly. It assumes importance as the system behavior is determined by the interactive role of people or economic agents. Therefore, if the changes in the system behavior are to be brought about, calibrated policy interventions are to be introduced to modify underlying conditions in which people (or economic agents) interact. These should be the prime concerns of policymakers, strategists, and experts.

The approach to addressing complex issues in public policy or economy demands a departure from traditional linear thinking, which doesn't consider the feedback and higher-order effects, or from a reductionist approach of examining parts or components in isolation. Complexity theory factors in interactive network effects, nonlinearity, feedback loops, and higher-order effects. In this backdrop, the strategy to manage the complex system will entail (Meadows 2008; Malhi et al. 2009; Fidan and Balci 2017):

- recognizing complex environment and ever-changing behavior without expecting stability and predictability;
- examining micro-level issues;
- systemic understanding of the system;
- studying evolving nature;
- identifying leverage points within the system and policy parameters, and based on that, designing pilot projects and testing;
- creating the right enabling conditions for healthy interactions (based on values, trust, ethics, learnings, collaboration) between elements, and the enabling conditions could be regulations, values, culture, ecosystem, knowledge and skills, institutional mechanisms, and structures;
- effecting calibrated changes as per the needs at the ground;
- capacity building and upgrading skills, sound performance management system (PMS), promoting decentralized approach and flexibility with close monitoring;
- establishing the mechanism of course correction; and
- observing change closely and encouraging adaptation.

Finally, for complex systems, the way forward is to take feedback from the ground, understand the end-users' insights, recognize the pattern, and visualize the possible future state. It requires transparency and trust that will facilitate the uninterrupted

5.2 Complexity Theory Framework

flow of information and bring insights into the problems on the ground. It recommends scenario planning as a tool of strategic foresight (not forecast). It entails identifying factors, both internal and external, that will shape future conditions for the policy system, economy, or business; probing the potential drivers and their likely interactions; and then visualizing the possible future states. While making scenario planning, historical analogy, past events, and the history of the system need to be considered, and the judgmental approach needs to be avoided (Meadows 2008; Malhi et al. 2009; Palmberg 2009a; Holmes et al. 2011).

- *Solution and program design.* Based on the strategy formulation and feedback from the ground and end-users, the solutions need to be worked out. Engagement with people or economic agents in the system can provide useful insights. The feedback may not provide all the required solutions but it may provide the path toward which the system needs to move. Broadly, the program design will require (Meadows 2008; Malhi et al. 2009):
  - *Identifying leverage points within the system.* These are points where action can make a significant change in the system. These points could be in the form of vision and mission; goals; processes; organizational structures; values, culture, and norms; human resource (HR) policy, and so on. The interventions are required to use leverage points to bring desired changes in the system.
  - *Identifying policy parameters.* The necessary policy parameters (e.g., range of interest rates, incentives, credit limits, etc.) need to be identified to initiate measures by the government to improve the performance. These concern public policy interventions.
  - *Identifying interventions.* Designing policies and programs based on the policy parameters.
- *Implementation.* For the implementation, it broadly entails the following steps:
  - *Firstly*, it requires an understanding of variables, both qualitative and quantitative, in the system. The qualitative variables are beliefs, social culture, social preferences, institutional issues, etc. The variables should be clearly defined. The accuracy of data should be ensured, and the data collection should be verifiable and timely.
  - *Secondly*, the interactive nature of elements needs to be appreciated and discerned at various levels—micro, meso, and macro.
  - *Thirdly*, understanding cause-effects and patterns of system behavior through consultation with stakeholders and studying system structure. It may call for a transdisciplinary approach (integrating knowledge, methodology and methods from other disciplines; and visualization, pattern recognition, and synthesization by taking researchers and experts from different areas or disciplines) to work on new ideas and innovations and explore solutions—sometimes original—that can address the problems.
  - *Fourthly*, depending on the programs and resources, introducing interventions in a calibrated manner based on feedback from the ground. The interventions

should be designed to manage the current situation and effect medium- to long-term change. Enhancing system capacity together with building capabilities of employees should be a priority. The implementation should follow a 'process approach' to have the possibility of continuous modifications based on concurrent evaluation. It should adopt a strategy that should include calibrated interventions and pilot study if needed; creating enabling conditions to perform; transparency in taking feedback from the ground; and close monitoring.

To take advantage of complexity, a different approach to organizational structure and management is required. The top management needs to acknowledge and embrace the challenge of complexity. The healthy interactions of shared vision, processes, capabilities, values and commitment, information flows, and feedback mechanism can make a difference in the organization (Gilstrap 2005; Nordtveit 2007; Mason 2008). Employees should be imparted training for innovative methods, while strengthening and upgrading existing skill sets. The government or top management should be concerned about the overall goals and strategies and then align them with the organizational structure and bottom-up emergent behavior or pattern (McKelvey 2002; Kuhmone 2016).

In summary, while implementing policies and strategies for complex problems, the key interconnected issues that need consideration are: local or ground-level interactions are to be recognized; institutional mechanisms influencing the interactions are to be studied; nonlinearity, dynamic nature, and inability to determine cause-effect relations are to be factored in; initial state of the system is to be taken into account; how the influence of the external environment can be managed, or how the system should adapt to change; and how the macro-level interventions can be designed through the feedback from elements.

'How part' is vital in the complexity theory. 'How part' deals with the process of reaching to 'emerging state'. Figure 5.6 depicts the phenomena of emergence, self-organization, and the edge of chaos, or transformation in the complex adaptive system (CAS).

- *Feedback, evaluation, adaptation, and mid-course correction.* The feedback about the interventions or outcomes is essential to monitor and regulate the system. The macro-level management needs to appreciate the value of 'regular' feedback from the micro level and then effect calibrated changes as per the needs at the ground. And simultaneously, the top management should observe change meticulously and encourage the adaptation to better processes, structures, and technology adoption through a learning process. The government or the management at the macro level should recognize the potential of people, agents, functionaries in the delivery departments, or firms at the ground level, as they have the potential to emerge and organize themselves and evolve into a new pattern of the system.

5.3 Relevance of Complexity Theory   235

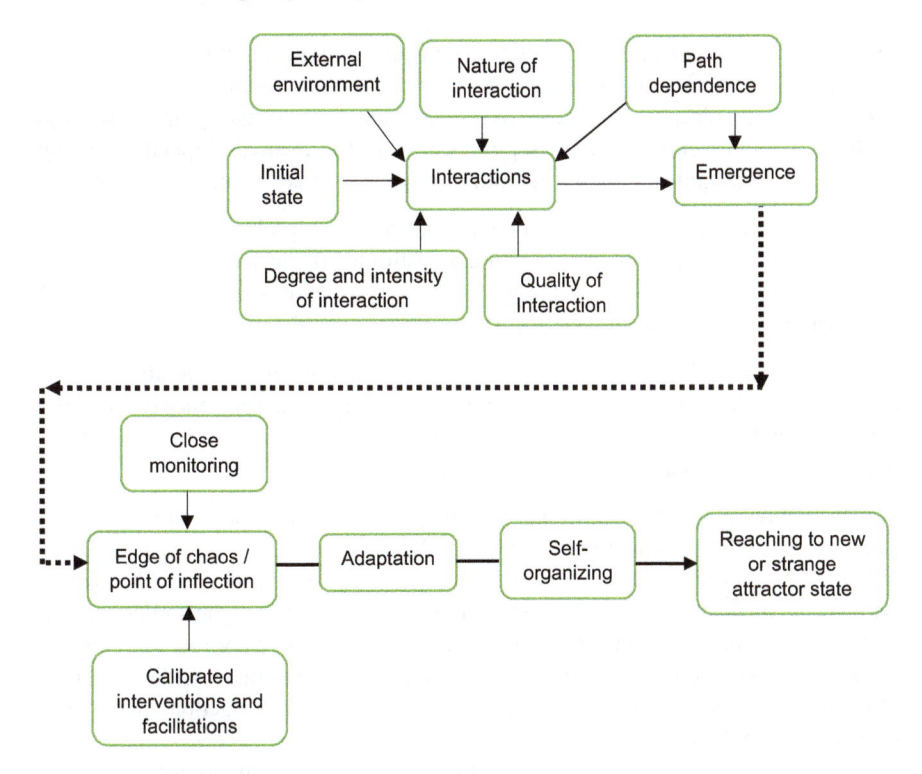

Fig. 5.6 Complex system transformation: emergence and self-organization

5.3 Relevance of Complexity Theory

Social, economic, and business systems are too large, with many issues, problems, and variables. It makes it challenging for the current economic, policy, or management theories to explain system behavior. These systems involve numerous interacting elements running into millions and many more interactions between elements. These influence the system behavior, which cannot be fully comprehended by mere aggregate behavior. It requires new approaches to inquiries that can examine the issues at the granular or micro level. Notably, a system is more complex if the number of elements (people, entities, sectors, and business entities) increases, the scope for interactions between elements increases, and the diversity of the interacting elements increases. Complex systems exhibit certain characteristics that are common across various systems like cities, health, education, economy, business, organizations, etc. It is where the complexity theory has a role to play. It is best used when the problem being studied is multidimensional, and it is difficult to identify causes.

At a conceptual level, why the complexity theory has relevance is underscored by the following fundamental features about the socio-economic systems, including policy system, economy, business, and organizations:

First, possibility of unknown variables. In the social and economic systems, there are unknown variables that, until analyzed, cannot be considered for policymaking. While such variables, due to interactive effects, may have a bearing on the success of the policy interventions. Likewise, the behavior of individuals depends on many factors, which cannot be anticipated until they surface or are brought to notice.

Second, context matters. There is a contextual basis for problems and opportunities resulting from social, physical, political, institutional, and technological factors. These can be captured only by the micro-level examination, and the macro-level approach may fail to comprehend local contexts.

Third, uncertain behavior of the system. The relationships between variables cannot be ascertained due to nonlinearity, continuous feedback, and the presence of unknown variables, and thus, it causes uncertainty about the output of the behavior. How uncertainty can be taken into account is a challenge.

Fourth, network effects of multiple interacting individuals and variables in the subsystems. In the system, due to numerous elements, including individuals (stakeholders, economic agents) and variables (which may run into hundreds or thousands) with many intricate, behavioral, and nonlinear interactions; higher-order effects; and multiple feedback loops, the number of possible responses or reactions are too numerous to be captured realistically. The networks are based on relatedness—similarity of ideas, knowledge, technology, business, etc. The interactions may cause positive feedback loops.

For example, interactions of spatial features (knowledge, technologies, manpower in a particular location) with policies, between policies, between individuals and institutions, etc., may lead to a new set of activities and to a positive feedback loop (Fig. 5.7, prepared by using system dynamics technique). The positive feedback in the networks can provide exponential effects through the spread of ideas by word-of-mouth and success. In this example, the mechanism of the positive feedback loop includes a combination of the application of diversified knowledge and skills (know-how) for working on new ideas; the relatedness of location, technology, skills, capabilities, etc.; ecosystem for smooth interactions, exchange and transactions of ideas, knowledge, and resources; the standards that provide reliability for the usage of new products and services; and value creation for users and entrepreneurs.

Fifth, limitations of mathematical model. In the context of complex systems and the scenario of fast emerging technologies and knowledge economy, the mathematical models can hardly explain how the world has changed or which factors are changing the existing social system and economy; specifically, how new knowledge and technologies emerge and impact the system or how the institutional mechanisms and structures influence the system behavior.

The qualitative variables cannot be suitably factored into the mathematical model. The quantitative variables (under socio-economic systems) have four major limitations, among others. *Firstly*, difficulty in defining the numerous socio-economic variables in a precise manner for different sections of society, sectors, and subsectors (e.g., the definition of different categories of employment for various sectors

5.3 Relevance of Complexity Theory

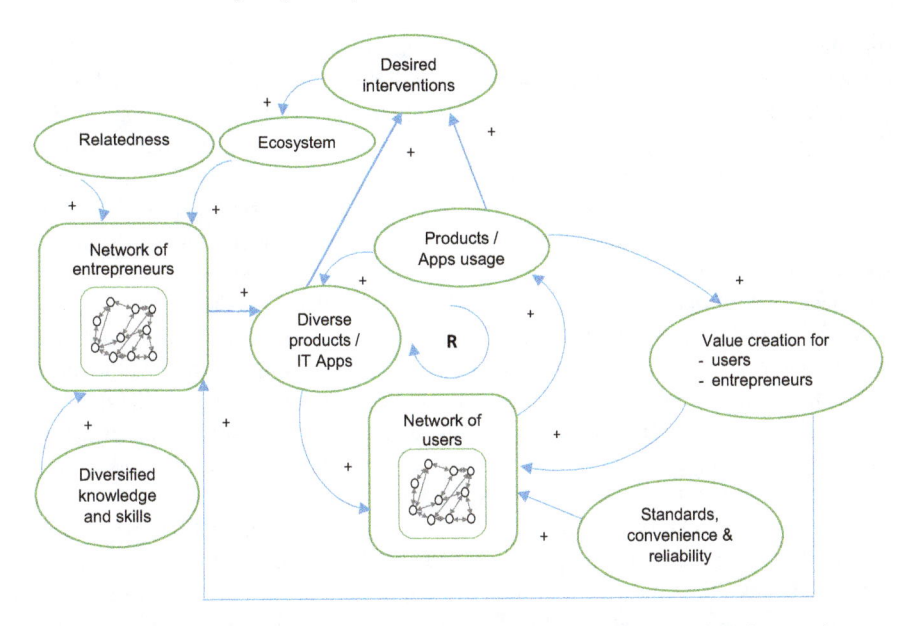

Apps applications (e.g., for social media, e-business, e-commerce, e-education, etc.)

Fig. 5.7 Sample causal loop reinforcing positive feedback model: network and interaction effects

and sub-sectors, the poverty line for different sections, etc.), *secondly*, collection of correct and verifiable data, *thirdly*, timely and real-time data collection, and *fourthly*, capturing the interactive effects of variables.

Thus, there is a limitation in identifying and using quantitative variables, and such limitations make mathematical analysis and modeling a difficult exercise for real-world problems. The attempt for any modeling is to be context-specific, as socio-economic systems are too vast to be comprehended. If it is attempted, the model should highlight the boundary conditions, constraints, and assumptions so that a realistic view is captured. At best, the mathematical model can be used for indicative purpose.

Furthermore, there is a considerable interest in the application of artificial intelligence (AI) and machine learning (ML) tools in public policy. But, there is a word of caution. In social systems, human inputs and feedback are essential and should be considered while using such tools. Similarly, the decision-making process deals with many factors, which are qualitative, behavioral, and psychological. In addition, the social, behavioral, and institutional issues, which vary from context to context and from location to location, cannot be handled by a single algorithm.

Moreover, the public systems deal with numerous sectors, which could be about fifty, and these sectors have many sub-sectors. Each sub-sector will have many policy problems, which could be more than ten. Each problem could be dealing with more than ten variables, most of which will be context- and location-specific. Besides, these sub-sectors, problems, and variables are interlinked. Such interlinkages could run into thousands or even millions. If one attempts to apply AI and ML tools for a particular sector, a huge set of variables and interlinkages need to be considered. Such interlinkages may vary over time due to internal feedback and external influence. So, it will require factoring in the time dimension. And in such a case, whether policy options can be realistically defined is a challenge.

For example, in the health sector, due to factors like diseases, personal beliefs, health infrastructure, and logistics, the system variables, problems, and stakeholders are so many that it may lead to numerous combinations. Besides, such variables will have several qualitative properties, which cannot be quantified in most cases. In addition, the variables, problems, and priorities of stakeholders are dynamic, and they frequently change over time. If one tends to disregard qualitative, behavioral, and institutional issues, either the model cannot be developed, or there will be a case of simplification of problems and variables, which will fail to represent an actual situation. Given the above reasons, mathematical models or AI and ML tools cannot be applied to big and complex problems in a realistic manner.

But these tools can be applied to a small subset of a bigger problem with well-defined boundary, assumptions, and constraints. For example, in the agriculture sector, AI and ML tools can be tried in a particular region for a particular crop in a specific season to cover a set of farmers (e.g., small or marginal) with certain assumptions. Likewise, in economic and business systems, agent-based modeling (ABM) can be applied to specific problems with defined boundaries and assumptions. 'Qualitative system dynamics modeling' can be used to conceptualize problems in complex systems. So, for complex systems, it demands qualitative analysis, pattern recognition, and an exploratory way of identifying strategies for interventions.

Sixth, evolving nature of policies is relevant. Due to the feedback mechanism, the governments at the macro level get feedback from the ground. The interactions between stakeholders like end-users, experts, and policymakers are a part of this process. Such feedback leads to the evolution of various policies, strategies, and institutional mechanisms. One-time policy prescription for all contexts or all varied geographical conditions is not practical. The policies are developed by understanding the dynamic changes in socio-economic conditions and through a regular process of interactions between stakeholders and policymakers in the government. The policies are introduced based on the existing conditions, and then as the conditions change, the policies evolve to meet new requirements.

There are a few examples to substantiate this. From the latter part of the nineteenth and early decades of the twentieth century, due to demands from industrial workers in Europe, the policies on labor reforms, including pensions, collective bargaining, and improved working conditions, evolved. These have undergone changes multiple times (Fraser 1984; Huberman and Lewchuk 1999; Theodoulou and Roy 2016). As a result of demands from civil society, institutional mechanisms and good governance were put in place in the USA and Europe in the nineteenth century to provide good law and order and social security. These helped in creating good ground conditions for social and economic activities (Acemoglu and Robinson 2010; Theodoulou and Roy 2016).

In Europe, the enhanced social spending since the latter half of the nineteenth century and its continuation in the twentieth century, and progressive era (1896–2016) (Fried 1998; Leonard 2009) and the New Deal in the 1930s (Cohen 1984; Gerston 2010) in the USA were the result of the evolving process of policymaking due to demands from people, working class, and general intelligentsia. Likewise, the complementary and converging policies have been a result of bargaining by the stakeholders with the government. For example, the automobile industry revolution in the USA from 1910 onward; the automobile and Electronics revolution in the 1960s onward in Japan; and the Hi-tech industry of a large proportion from the 1980s onward in the USA, Europe, and Japan have been a result of many enabling converging policies and standards (Hemmert 2007; Gerstel and Goodman 2020; Deloitte 2016; Deloitte and Singularity University 2018). In India, the economic reforms in 1991 have been a result of feedback from multiple sources about falling values of key economic indicators like foreign exchange reserves, exports, and so on.

Seventh, complex systems display CAS properties—emergence, adaptation, self-organization, and evolution. The system evolves due to interactive effects in networks. The interactions between elements take place at a micro level or workplace, not through direction from the top. This characteristic is at the core of the complexity approach. The emergence of the economy, stock market, health and education system, industry clusters, software companies, and IT App industry are examples of CAS (Byrne 1998; Gilstrap 2005; Mason 2008; Eppel and Rhodes 2018; Mueller 2020). The people shape the emergence by exchanging ideas, skills, creativity, and innovation. This property of CAS needs to be a fundamental basis for policymaking, and the government or top management should work on creating enabling conditions for the people, stakeholders, and economic agents to interact.

In sum, every element matters in the complex system. The aggregation of data can not capture the ground reality as information is distributed and evolves. The deterministic models and theories have limitations, and top-down approach or macro-level interventions may not work alone for complex development problems. The complex system should be visualized from the points of view of network effects, interactive effects, cascading effects (on the citizens, end-users, customers, entrepreneurs, etc., due to the process of exchange of information and knowledge), reinforcing feedback loops, and snowball effects (e.g., on business and economy).

5.3.1 Case Studies: Evolution of Silicon Valleys in Bengaluru (India) and San Francisco Bay (USA)

To understand the evolution of Silicon Valleys in Bengaluru (India) and San Francisco Bay (USA), these are analyzed from the lens of complexity theory. Under these two cases, various phenomena of complexity theory have been studied. The case studies are based on the extensive literature survey and consultations with entrepreneurs, academics, and officials. The salient features are presented below:

Case study of Silicon Valley (SV) in Bengaluru

It can be traced back to the modern education and research system in the form of the Indian Institute of Sciences (IISc), which was conceived and set up in 1909. As a legacy of Mysore State, the good educational system contributed to educated manpower. Subsequently, over time, these helped in providing a credible base for attracting many other academic and research institutions and public sector undertakings (PSUs) like Hindustan Aeronautics Limited (HAL), Bharat Electronics Limited (BEL), Bharat Heavy Electricals Limited (BHEL), Defence Research and Development Organisation (DRDO), Bharat Earth Movers Limited (BEML), and Hindustan Machine Tools (HMT), to name a few (Heitzman 2004; Rajaraman 2012; Inna et al. 2015) (Table 5.1).

Initially, entrepreneurs were attracted to Bengaluru due to the availability of a skilled workforce, power and water, and basic infrastructure. The suitable climatic conditions provided a comfort zone. The educational institutions and PSUs provided a base for technical manpower and created a conducive environment for IT software (SW) development. The city was chosen by the professional interests of entrepreneurs, not by any central direction.

Realizing the potential of software development, policy support has been provided for software development and exports since the 1970s. Some of the key policies are New Computer Policy (1984), EXIM Policy (1985), Software Policy (1986), and SEZ Policy (2000). Simultaneously, the support was extended through software technology parks of India (STPI), IT parks, and incentives for venture capital funds and angel investors (D'Costa and Sridharan 2003; Infodev 2008; Rajaraman 2012; Inna et al. 2015; Sharma 2015). All these collectively created a good ecosystem and incentives for entrepreneurs.

- *Micro-level effects.* The evolution of SV has been a gradual process without any planned interventions, and it has been due to multiple interventions and enabling conditions. There have been no specific or direct causal linkages between inputs (like policies, institutional support, etc.) and the emergence of system behavior, and no exact causal relationship can be discerned. The change has been dynamic, uncertain, and evolutionary. Fundamentally, the emergence has been due to micro-level effects with no hierarchical control. The micro-level agents (entrepreneurs, professionals, system variables, and firms) responded to socio-economic conditions, positive factors, policy interventions, and global demands and competition. The micro-level effects were determined by a culture of innovation, desire to excel, trust, knowledge- and skills-driven interactions, networks and collaborations, diversity of talents, and encouragement to attract talents from outside (Table 5.1).
- *Macro-level government policy support.* Since the middle of the 1970s and especially from the 1980s, there have been many policy interventions for software development and exports through fiscal policies, skill development policies, labor

5.3 Relevance of Complexity Theory 241

Table 5.1 Evolution of silicon valleys in Bengaluru and San Francisco Bay

S. No.	Key factors	Key issues		Analyses form complexity theory perspective
		Silicon Valley, Bengaluru (India)	Silicon Valley, San Francisco Bay (USA)	
1	Educational and research institutions	IISc and many educational and research institutions played an important role. Credible technical base by the presence of educational and research institutions and PSUs like HAL BEL, HAL, DRDO, BEML, HMT, etc	Stanford University and R&D programs played a key role. Technical base as a result of support from the US military, particularly Air Force, NASA, NIH, and NSF	• Enabling conditions – Policy interventions – Skilled manpower – Values and culture of innovation – Infrastructure for R&D – Appreciation for diversity • Micro level – Interactive effect – Dynamic and uncertain nature – No hierarchical control
2	People and firms	People with knowledge and skills formed firms to begin software business for exports	R&D, innovation, and product development encouraged starting of new firms	
3	Policy interventions and support	Policy interventions for software development and exports through fiscal policies, skill development, labor policies, investment and innovation promotion, and setting up STPI and IT parks. Skilled manpower from educational institutions at the National and State levels	Tax incentives and ease in investments, university-industry-government-military collaborations, regulations of financial capital, coevolution of technical standards, purchase of products from startup companies by government agencies	– Emergence – Self-organization – Path dependency – Adaptation – Networks • Macro level – Adaptation – Coevolution of many firms, policies, and industries – Causality of emergence is not perfectly known • Environment – Global changing demands – New and disruptive technologies – Competition
4	Infrastructure	STPI and IT parks	R&D labs and IT infrastructure support	
5	Collaborations	Collaborations among professionals and scientists in Bengaluru, other cities in India, Europe, and the USA	Collaborations among professionals, universities, and entrepreneurs, peer-to-peer groups	
6	Diversity (heterogeneity)	People with diverse talents and backgrounds joined firms	People with diverse talents and social groups were encouraged	

(continued)

Table 5.1 (continued)

S. No.	Key factors	Key issues		Analyses form complexity theory perspective
		Silicon Valley, Bengaluru (India)	Silicon Valley, San Francisco Bay (USA)	
7	Competition	Competition with other firms led to adaptation and acquiring new technologies, knowledge, and skills	Competition with other businesses or countries leading to necessity for R&D, innovation, launching new products, etc	
8	Influence by or impact of external environment	Environment of technical support and innovation. Local people welcomed talents from outside	Culture to innovate and excel. Linkages to meet high military demands initially, and subsequently driven by the market forces	

BEL Bharat Electronics Limited, *BEML* Bharat Earth Movers Limited, *BHEL* Bharat Heavy Electricals Limited, *DRDO* Defence Research and Development Organisation, *HAL* Hindustan Aeronautics Limited, *HMT* Hindustan Machine Tools, *IISc* Indian Institute of Sciences, *ICT* Information and Communication Technology, *IT* Information Technology, *NIH* National Institute of Health, *NSF* National Science Foundation, *NASA* National Aeronautics and Space Administration, *PSUs* Public Sector Undertakings, *R&D* Research & Development, *STPI* Software Technology Parks of India

policy measures, investment policies, innovation promotion policies, and setting up software technology parks of India (STPI) (Infodev 2008; Rajaraman 2012; Inna et al. 2015; Sharma 2015). Besides, from the 1980s, educational institutions at the National and State levels created a critical mass of skilled manpower for absorption in the IT industry. It created a facilitative environment for software companies. The policies coevolved with the industry as a result of feedback from the entrepreneurs. And in turn, the policies contributed to the evolution of industry at a higher pace.

- *Network effects.* For the growth of Silicon Valley, networks played their role. The networks consisted of engineers, scientists, and professionals within and abroad. Many engineers and research scholars, who had higher technical education within Bengaluru or India, and working professionals in the USA contributed by setting up enterprises, providing professional and technical support, or indirectly through the exchange of ideas, skills, and technology transfer. Many collaborations were possible through such networks of engineers, scientists, and entrepreneurs due to interactions and trust based on shared ideas and values (Kapur 2002; Saxenian 2003; Castells and Cardoso 2005; Sotarauta and Srinivas 2006; Rajaraman 2012). Another supporting factor has been social capital, including trust, local bonds, and social ties. The social capital provided a good environment to collaborate in problem solving, utilizing talents, and attracting talent and investment from different parts of the country. The local people helped and supported the IT professionals from other States, and they found welcoming gestures from the locals.
- *Adaptation and coevolution.* With the changes in technologies, the firms adapted by reskilling their workforce. Educational institutions adapted to new requirements of the curriculum. With the changes, both city development and policies coevolved as new firms were created. Likewise, there has been a coevolution of innovation culture, startups, venture capitalists, and angel investors. Together with the SW development hub, there was a coevolution of other knowledge and technology-based industries like ICT hardware and biotechnology. R&D centers were set up by Texas Instruments, INTEL, IBM, and Microsoft, to name a few. More than a hundred R&D centers of MNCs have coevolved in SV (Avnimelech and Teubal 2003; Kapur 2002; Sharma 2015).
- *Path dependency.* The entrepreneurs' focus and policy support were mainly confined to software development and exports to a few English-speaking countries in the 1970s and 80s. Hardware development has not been a priority for both entrepreneurs and the government. As a result, the phenomenon of path dependency or lock-in effect had an impact on the emergence of Valley in the 1990s and 2000s, which saw more software development and ICT service companies and exports, including overseas customer service management. There have been lesser diversification in terms of coverage of more countries, lower share in the domestic market, and less focus on high-end services and software product development. Due to lesser focus, ICT hardware manufacturing could not pick up (Kapur 2002; D'Costa 2003).

- *Organic interactions.* The organic interactions and linkages between economic agents or entrepreneurs are based on shared values, beliefs, trust, and commitment, which lead to social and professional bonds. The growth of SV has been an organic process. They shared ideas, knowledge, and resources based on trust and intellectual value. The organic interactions have helped in providing complementarities for the growth of ICT businesses and firms.

In 2021, the IT industry in Bengaluru employed about 30% of the total country's workforce in the IT and IT-enabled service sector, contributed about 40% of total exports or $45 billion, and accounted for 35% of the global in-house R&D centers in India. (https://thescalers.com/how-bangalore-became-asias-silicon-valley/, OVP 2021; Economic Times 2022). In 2019, the startups in Bengaluru raised about 45% of the total investment into the startup companies and contributed to 44% of unicorns in India (Business Standard 2019).

Finally, SV changed the economy of Bengaluru. But it has not been by any pre-meditated effort, but evolved through the interactive economic agents or entrepreneurs in the enabling ecosystem and then self-organized into a big structure through a process of adaptation. New firms and policies coevolved as the changes emerged in the system. SV in Bengaluru has been a successful case of the complex adaptive system (CAS) . The interactions in the networks or complex web of educational institutions, entrepreneurs, capabilities, social capital, enabling policies, and intuitional support contributed to the emergence of the software industry in India. Fundamentally, what played an important role has been interactive effects between entrepreneurs (agents) and other elements, resilience and agility to adapt, coevolution of policies, emergence of new technologies and opportunities, and adaptive leadership.

Case study of Silicon Valley (SV), California (USA)

The study of Silicon Valley (SV) in San Francisco Bay (USA) will require understanding the sequence of various events in the past. The literature highlights how the research initiatives by Stanford University, with the R&D support from Federal Government, sowed the seeds of innovation and entrepreneurship. From the 1930s, Stanford University and its students with entrepreneurs contributed to producing devices and equipments for the US military and Navy and, subsequently, developing a good innovation ecosystem. From the 1960s, with the need for a more scientific workforce, including research scholars, the SV attracted technical talent from all over the world. There has been a significant focus on both ICT hardware and software development (SW) industries that gradually led to the foundation for both the sectors (Sturgeon 2000; Castells 2011; Kushida 2015).

It is important to appreciate that Silicon Valley was not created by strategic government policy. It evolved organically due to the interactive network effects of innovators and entrepreneurs. There were certain government policies for R&D support; tie-ups between government, university, and industry; military-industry collaborations; and government procurement. The major support came from the US military, particularly Air Force and Navy, and, later on, from the National Aeronautics and Space

5.3 Relevance of Complexity Theory 245

Administration (NASA) for the procurement of electrical and electronics products that were the result of R&D and innovation in Stanford. The National Institute of Health (NIH) and the National Science Foundation (NSF) played their roles in R&D at a later stage. These influenced the path for scientific research, innovation, knowledge creation, technology development, and then for commercial usage at a big scale (Table 5.1).

In addition, there has been policy support for SV through venture capital and tax concessions for investments. SV benefited from innovation culture and collaborations at the local level and the network effects of peer groups and educational institutions. These have been big contributing factors. Besides, public institutions have played their roles by providing support for essential infrastructural facilities, governance of basic public services, and institutional support for property management, intellectual property rights (IPR), exports, financial capital, regulations of technical standards, bankruptcy laws, and contract management (Sturgeon 2000; Sandelin 2004; Castells 2011; Kushida 2015).

The above discussion reflects that the emergence of SV in San Francisco Bay has been without any top-down approach or deliberate and planned effort. However, the facilitating role of policies and institutional support has been there. The network effects through interactions and collaborative efforts of institutions, innovators, entrepreneurs, and firms contributed a great deal. The path dependency due to the early success of R&D, a culture of innovation, and entrepreneurship led to the evolution of technology-driven companies. The coevolution of various industries resulted from both complementing and converging effects of technologies and supporting technical standards. And organic growth contributed to the success. Social capital, including trust, shared values, and mutual respect, provided a good environment to collaborate and attract talent and investment from within the USA and abroad.

The evolution resulted in the knowledge economy. In 2020, for San Francisco Bay, the GDP amounted to $525 billion, and the public companies (in the technological area) of Silicon Valley and San Francisco had an aggregate market cap of $14 trillion. (https://www.statista.com/statistics/183843/gdp-of-the-san-francisco-bay-area/, https://www.digitalrealty.com/blog/pushing-back-on-data-gravity-in-silicon).

Learnings. Both the case studies of Silicon Valleys provide some leanings, which are summarized under:

- the phenomena of interactive effects, emergence, adaptation, and self-organization need to be considered while framing policies;
- the interventions by the government should be contingent on such phenomena of interactions and evolution, and, in turn, the interventions influence interactions;
- the economic agents or firms should be facilitated in doing their business, businesses need to be nurtured by providing enabling conditions at the micro level, and the conditions include values, norms, culture, skilled manpower, incentives, infrastructure support, and institutional support;
- institutional support should be provided for good governance and regulations, with transparency for building trust and confidence;

- policies and institutions should coevolve as the changes take place and the economy evolves, and the policymaking process should be developed to design innovative and adaptive policies; and
- for an economy to grow, business activities should grow at the ground level.

These case studies present the alternative paradigm to understand complex phenomena and draw lessons for applying concepts and principles of complexity theory to design economic policies. Also, the cases throw ideas about why economic theories should factor in complexity theory to theorize real-world economic systems.

5.3.2 Relevance for Public Policy

The characteristics of the public policy system have been well-discussed elaborately in Chap. 3 and the preceding sections of this chapter. These provide distinct concepts and ways to understand the system and design and implement the policies by factoring in complexity. The policy system is context-specific. In the real world, the system has a web of stakeholders, institutional factors, individual capabilities, behavioral factors, locational effects, history, initial conditions of families and communities, economic activities, and so on. These vary from place to place and problem to problem. Thus, every geographical problem is different from any other location. The stakeholders include individual citizens and their representatives, communities, experts, non-governmental organizations (NGOs), political groups, elected members, etc., which are interdependent and remain in the process of continuous interactions.

In the social system, there are nonlinear and dynamic interactions between elements, which define the behavior of the whole system. It results in dynamic and ever-changing behavior and becomes something different from what it was in the past. Besides, the interactions create contingency and uncertainty about the future state. As a result, the 'whole' lacks the predictability typically observed in a 'static machine system'.

The broad representation and aggregation of system behavior cannot be realistic in the face of numerous interactions of diverse stakeholders that characterize complex social systems. The interactions between elements matter and result in the emergence of performance without any direct control. Due to interactions, emergence, and adaptation, the system may self-organize and self-regulate and reach a new system state, an attractor state, or even a strange attractor. It signifies that the success of a particular sector will depend on the interactions of various policies and programs within the sector and also of other sectors that have overlaps. Policymaking needs to recognize interactive, nonlinear, and emergent behavior.

Emergence—Local-Level Interactions. In the policy system, the interactions between elements, such as the people at the grassroots and functionaries (staff members in different departments) and variables, take place in multiple ways and follow local rules without top-level direct instructions, though policies and guidelines of the programs are developed at the top. Such interactions between functionaries lead to the emergence of certain methods and practices, which define functioning at the grassroots level. To illustrate, in the health department, the field study reflects that due to the interactions (formal or informal), the functionaries evolve certain practices and procedures for actual health service delivery (e.g., for immunization and maternity services) based on specific socio-cultural values, ground working conditions, and technical norms.

The performance of a public program is a result of multiple interacting factors and programs. For example, in the case of a sanitation program, it is dependent upon behavioral change, community mobilization, financial assistance, availability of water, and an appropriate construction site for the toilet. Each factor is essential, and depending upon the local conditions, the success of the program depends. Similarly, the citizens respond to government programs through interactions in the community. The response takes into account the interactive effects of local socio-cultural values, cognitive and emotional factors, economic conditions, and potential benefits from the programs. Likewise, there are policy linkages between many sectors. For example, the health sector has linkages with sanitation, drinking water, and education. The health conditions depend upon safe drinking ware, sanitation, hygiene, and basic education about health. The policy formulation and implementation of the health sector will be contingent on such linkages and inter-sectoral overlapping. The performance of a sector is not solely determined by the policies within the sector alone but due to the interaction of policies of other sectors at the implementation level.

Example of primary education. The policies and programs of infrastructure conditions, school environment, community and family mobilization, and training and motivation level of teachers in a combined manner will determine the output and the learning outcomes rather than one individual policy or program. Simultaneously, the policies and programs in other interlinked sectors like drinking water, health, and sanitation will impact the performance in education through interconnectivity with the policies of education sectors. For instance, attendance in schools is dependent upon the health conditions of children and drinking water and sanitation facilities.

In addition, how the dropout rate in general and of a girl child can be reduced or how the learning outcomes can be improved will be determined, not by just one factor, but by the interactions of various factors such as family values, priority for the need for education, social norms, social environment, economic conditions, emotional support, quality of teaching, discipline in the schools, the distance of schools from the house, sanitation facilities, etc. The institutional capacity of the education system, among others, will depend on the interactive effects of work culture, values, training, curriculum design, teaching aids, monitoring, and supervision. And the interactions of institutional capacity with the policies and programs of the education sector, socio-economic factors, and policies of other interlinked sectors will determine the outcomes.

Another example that can be cited is the performance of the agriculture sector. It involves interactive effects of availability, quality, and cost of inputs like seeds, fertilizer, credit, and pesticides; interest on the loan from banks and money-lenders; fertility and characteristics of the soil; marketing infrastructure; transportation charges; costs of various services; network of marketing agents; enforcement of existing support price; and fixation of desired support price. Besides, local contexts like climate and geographical conditions impact the interactions of individual farmers and variables for decision-making and actions. It, therefore, underscores the need to understand the combined effect of these underlying factors.

These examples underscore that the emergence (system behavior, performance, or output) is not due to any single factor or one policy but several interconnected individuals, variables, and policies. The relationships between different variables are important. It should be recognized that system performance comes from the interactive effects of elements. For achieving higher performance, interactions and network effects play important roles.

5.3.3 Relevance for Economy and Business

The complexity theory has provided a new paradigm for understanding the economy, including business. It has underscored certain concepts—interactive effects, emergence, self-organization, and adaptation that have not been considered in mainstream economics. In addition, the knowledge economy driven by individuals, networks, information flows, innovation, and technology advancements display interactive behavior and has evolutionary features for which the mainstream economic theories have not been able to provide satisfactory answers. In this light, the complexity theory offers an alternative approach (Arthur et al. 1997; Foster 2004; LeBaron and Leigh 2008; Stiglitz 2015).

In the complex systems, the following are the fundamental realities that need appreciation and should be considered for the basis of future economic theory:

First, economic activities are determined by internal structures, behavior, and interactions. The basic property of complex systems is the interactive nature of elements. Such interactions depend on values, culture, internal structures, institutional mechanisms, and government policies. Internal structures are created by social, income, knowledge, and technological factors. Availability of resources, skills, and talent matters in determining structure and behavior. Through interactions, the agents and entrepreneurs exchange ideas, knowledge, skills, and resources, and based on that, they make decisions and initiate actions. The actions lead to the emergence of various economic activities. The interactions determine the number and speed of activities. Thus, the economy evolves over time due to the combined effects of 'interacting' economic agents.

These underlying issues demand to understand how individuals matter, how system variables are significant, and how ideas make a difference due to interactions in the structure of the system. It is essential to approach economic analysis from a network of agents and system variables, not just from the point of view of a production, profit-maximizing firms, and utility function, with an assumption of taking households, firms, and businesses as homogenous representative agents. The

5.3 Relevance of Complexity Theory

future economic theory should consider and analyze characteristics of the elements and internal structures and their interactive behavior (Foster 2004; Colander et al. 2008; OECD 2019).

Second, economy cannot be seen as a monolithic set of homogeneous economic activities; instead, it is a result of thousands or even millions of heterogeneous activities. The economy is not like a machine or a monolithic structure, which can be regulated by central control through capital and labor flow, as conceptualized in the growth model. Macroeconomics is not simply the aggregate of decisions and actions by individual agents and businesses. The aggregation of data cannot capture the interactive role and creative potential of millions of economic agents. In practice, the economy is shaped by interactions between agents, policies, and economic institutions.

The overall shape of the economy is determined by local actions, but the scale and the level of the economy can be enhanced by supporting government policies and incentives (Rodrik 2000; Foster 2004; Kirman 2011; Arthur 2014; Balland et al. 2022). The economy shows an emergent behavior due to numerous interacting elements in multiple decentralized locations. For example, the economy thrives due to progress in business and industry, representing the combination of millions of small, medium, and big units, which are diverse and not homogeneous . The efforts of thousands of entrepreneurs in the economic networks help shape the economy. The networks bring vitality to the economic system due to collective interactive efforts. The economy results from the multitude of economic activities by numerous economic agents and businesses in multiple locations. The economy is a dynamic, evolving , and complex adaptive system (CAS) . It happens without direct control, and the system self-organizes due to spontaneous order. For example, the stock market is a self-organizing system in which thousands of investors interact and determine the shape of the market within the overall government regulations.

The current approaches are not consistent with the reality of interacting heterogeneous elements and the emergent behavior of the system. The theories working on the aggregate behavior of the economy can provide a possible indicative behavior. They cannot offer a scientific basis for interactive nature, interacting disparate variables and agents, and varied economic activities. For example, all individuals may not always behave rationally and in a homogeneous manner due to behavioral reasons and bounded rationality. The decisions are influenced by personal interactions, how others react and make decisions, and personal choices, not necessarily by rational choice.

Third, possibility of hidden or invisible variables. In complex economic systems dealing with numerous elements, there are hidden or invisible variables. These could be in the form of innovative ideas which may open new possibilities; natural resources; economic incentives; innovations, technologies, strategic materials, or new products; government policies, institutional arrangements, etc. All such variables cannot be identified due to the very nature of complex systems. And in the absence of identification of such variables, the conventional economic models and theories may not provide a valid explanation for economic activities. While such invisible variables, together with other variables and agents in the economic network, may impact the economy. Some examples are: the networked economy results from the hidden potential of new technologies; the ecosystem to promote startups; social capital in business promotion; the institutional role in protecting economic rights, thus building trust, etc.

Fourth, diversity of knowledge and skills can utilize hidden potential and spur economic activities and growth. The diversity is in the form of different skill sets and specialist knowledge in the network of economic agents. These can give rise to new ideas and bring complementary skills that can enhance the possibility of diverse innovations. Thus, the hidden potential in the economic system can be tapped by insightful and innovative approaches, skills, and specialization. These are otherwise not easily feasible (Wang et al. 2012; Sjotun et al. 2020).

It can lead to the path creation for social and economic activities by harnessing creativity and novel possibility. Digital banking, networked economy, smartphones, electric vehicles, social media, customized industrial products with home delivery and assured services, and mobile Apps are some examples of path creation. These have implications for enhanced quality of life and bridging gaps between haves and have-nots. For example, at the global level, the networked economy, as a result of hidden potential and diverse skills and expertise, is growing rapidly. Specifically, e-commerce is rising rapidly (UNCTAD 2021). The global App economy reached $6.3 trillion in 2021 (Statista 2021), and artificial intelligence is projected to contribute significantly to the global economy (WEF 2021). Similarly, the Internet of Things (IoT) economic potential is likely to be $11 trillion by 2025, with 75 billion IoT devices likely to connect businesses and customers worldwide (Arif 2021). In the economic networks, these have significance for the knowledge economy and can spur economic growth by leveraging the hidden potential of creativity and specialized capabilities of entrepreneurs for innovation. Creating enabling conditions to encourage hidden potential to fructify through interactions in the network should be a priority for the government and business management. The network effect, due to the interactive nature of elements, is a unique example of a complex economic system.

Fifth, economy is context-specific. The local economic conditions regarding families' income and the existing state of business, industry, and economic infrastructure; natural resources; historical factors; social capital; and culture impact the economic ecosystem. Besides, local knowledge and skill sets of the workforce determine the shape of the type of new businesses and industries that can come up in the region. Due to complementary effects, the similarities, commonalities, and relatedness (with products, businesses, professions, and technologies) influence the setting up of new firms and business entities. The complexity theory lays stress on the interactive effects of these aspects at the local level. Future economic policies and approaches are required to take them into account. For example, in India, why industries, in general, have succeeded in Maharashtra and Tamil Nadu; how the automobile industry came up in Gurugram (Haryana), Maharashtra, and Tamil Nadu; or why the IT industry is successful in Bengaluru, Hyderabad, and Pune are a result of location-specific features.

5.3 Relevance of Complexity Theory

Sixth, aggregation of data and mathematical economic modeling have limitations. Generally, in economic theories, a common approach has been to aggregate the data of various economic performance parameters. Such an approach tends to exclude the heterogeneity in data about different economic parameters, the diverse characteristics of variables, and the interactive effects between them. Thus, a simple addition of disparate data has flaws, as heterogeneous data cannot be added to provide a correct assessment. For example, the employment data (based on skills for different societal groups) of various sub-sectors under a particular sector or consumer behavior (type of consumption pattern) and of different segments (e.g., income categories) will have heterogeneous data points. Thus, the aggregate data cannot provide a realistic view and will hide details, if added together.

Besides, a large number of variables are qualitative. Any aggregation of qualitative data is just an approximation or a rough estimate. Regarding the interactive effects, it gets excluded after data aggregation. For example, in the network, how different entrepreneurs will utilize the technologies for different economic activities through interactions between them cannot be captured by aggregate data. A realistic understanding of the system requires appreciating several interconnected issues such as: (a.) The context of qualitative behavioral insights like social culture, beliefs, and psychological satisfaction. (b.) Comprehending a holistic or systemic view of the problem and system, multiple perspectives of different stakeholders, relationships between variables, feedback loops, and conflicting and competing requirements of stakeholders. (c.) The limits of aggregation of data of heterogeneous parameters. (d.) Difficulty in obtaining determinable relationships between numerous economic variables. (e.) Consideration of the multi-criteria (including qualitative) in the decision-making. These combinedly limit the use of data and applicability of quantitative modeling for a real-world economic system.

Thus, for analysis, it is almost impossible or impractical to develop a mathematical model that can capture the reality of a complex economic system. The quantitative approach can be helpful in simulation and scenario building for an indicative purpose only under certain assumptions and boundary conditions.

Seventh, the interactive effects of institutions, public governance, and public policies play their roles in economic decision-making. The robust institutions, good governance, and sound policies create an ecosystem. They can provide enabling conditions in terms of trust, social capital, and confidence for agents to interact, make decisions, and start economic activities (Stiglitz 1989, 2015; North 1990, 2003; Simon 1991; Rodrik 2000; Kirman 2011). For example, the stock market functions keeping in view multiple factors, including institutional mechanisms and governance. It is influenced by various economic policies such as monetary policy, fiscal policy, policies on savings and consumption, investment policy, foreign investment policy, and trade policy. In the industrial sector, multiple complementing and converging policies and institutional support play their roles in a coordinated manner in shaping performance. The public governance determines the quality of various public (business) services and infrastructure management. Various economic agents or entrepreneurs utilize these enablers to interact to develop business firms.

For example, in India, the success of the software industry, automobile industry, and handloom and handicrafts sector are examples of how their emergence took place from the bottom due to the interactive effects of entrepreneurs facilitated by policy and institutional support. The specific case studies of the evolution of Silicon Valleys in Bengaluru (India) and San Francisco Bay (USA), as presented in the preceding section, bear this out. Similar are the cases of the Mobile App industry and e-commerce in many countries. Over time, the emergence of these industries provided feedback to the top, which, in turn, responded through policy interventions.

To summarize, in the complex real world, macroeconomics just cannot simply be the aggregation of actions by individuals or the mathematical sum of economic data. The locational factors, availability of the skilled workforce, entrepreneurial culture, infrastructure support, the network of entrepreneurs, global trade, investment environment, etc., through interactions between them determine the future state of the economy. The evolution cannot be pre-determined or centrally controlled. Specifically, the evolution of industrial development in any country has not been predicted before or the result of any planned effort. These industries have shaped the economy locally and globally through emergence, evolution, and coevolution. Such emergence cannot be fully explained by traditional economic theories. It differs substantially from the predictable interpretations by conventional approaches and mathematical economic models (Arthur 2014; Richardson 2008; Battiston et al. 2016; OECD 2017b; Balland et al. 2022).

5.3.4 Relevance for Public and Business Organizations

The complexity theory has relevance for any entity dealing with multiple interacting people and system variables. Organizations have a dynamic network of interactions, and their relationships are not merely an aggregation of work of individual elements. Both public and private organizations have several staff members. It necessitates that the complexity is rightly analyzed, and how it works should be comprehended. Without the appreciation of complexity, it may not be possible to visualize how the policy and management interventions will impact. In the backdrop of an emerging dynamic environment accentuated by information flow and the need for managing demanding citizens or customers, organizations need to make a departure from the twentieth century theories of scientific management and classical approach. The hierarchical, command, and control approach may not yield benefits in knowledge-based organizations. Mechanistic thinking, top-down interventions, closed system perspective, standard models, and analytical tools have limitations (Stacey 1996; Drucker 1998; Svyantek and Brown 2000; Richardson 2005; Baltaci and Balci 2017).

There is a need to revisit the assumptions and principles behind approaches and theories of the twentieth century. Their relevance needs to be studied in the context of the twenty-first century organizations requiring knowledge- and technology-driven systems. The complexity in big organizations is an inevitable phenomenon. Complexity theory is a new way of looking at how structures emerge, adapt, and change, and in the process, new behavior emerges. The theory has many implications for organizations, as summarized below:

- *First, recognizing interactions and emergence phenomena.* Organizations are complex adaptive systems. It implies that interactions and emergence are the defining concepts for designing future strategies. The employees or people within the organizations create multiple structures at the same level as well as a higher level. They should have the right conditions to interact, exchange ideas, and make decisions; and are not hierarchically controlled, but the interactions require monitoring.
- *Second, encouraging diversity and skills.* The diverse skill sets and cultural backgrounds are essential for bringing new ideas. The interactive effects for exchanging ideas, knowledge, and skills can bring dynamism and innovation. It is also essential from the point of view of the dissipation of energy over time; unless replenished with creative ideas and actions, an organization may lose its drive and standing.
- *Third, right kind of enabling conditions.* The enabling conditions need to be created to facilitate interactions and the emergence of new ideas and actions. Globalization, interconnectedness, disrupted technologies, technical and financial standards, and emerging knowledge and skills constantly demand requisite structures, processes, procedures, and rules in the workplace to meet new realities through the interactive process.
- *Fourth, decentralization with a shared vision, mission, and purpose.* While recognizing the above features, decentralization should be encouraged with a shared vision, mission, and purpose with real-time feedback. There should be a combination of hand-holding, capacity building, and sufficient working space to work innovatively.
- *Fifth, interventions should be calibrated based on feedback.* Organizations should get the opportunity to emerge and grow. In a competitive and dynamic environment, organizations cannot be taken as static entities and require a series of steps and converging strategies. The leadership should be adaptive and encourage agility and resilience.

5.4 Strategic Framework: Preparing for Future

The knowledge economy, combined with the information revolution in the age of globalization and technological advancements, will bring a new dimension to the policy system, economy, business, industry, and organization. In addition, the issues like climate change, disruptive innovations, cyber security, and demographic changes are challenging the existing paradigms. The change is uncertain, dynamic, and disruptive in many cases. There are signs of radical changes in certain areas due to the application of advanced technologies like robotics, automation, and artificial intelligence (AI) in industry.

The policy system faces the continuous challenge of providing quality public services, reaching out to the last mile, unemployment, maintaining law and order, etc. The economies face uncertainty and disruptions due to multiple forces, including technology innovations, trade disruptions, and financial volatility from the inside as well as outside the environment. In the economy, uncertainty is expected due to multiple and sometimes conflicting factors. The businesses are faced with challenges that question their business models due to market pressure, operations, sales, viability, supply chain, etc. More than before, due to dynamic socio-economic systems, there is a lack of predictability and a case for surprises or disruptions. For example, it is impossible to predict how technologies will bring a new form of industries by disrupting the current ones, how the future employment scenario will be impacted, what kind of new skill sets will be necessary, what kind of new institutional and regulatory framework will be required, how markets will evolve, etc. Some of the questions that deserve to be examined are: whether intractable persisting problems can be solved by following current approaches to public policy and governance, whether all the relevant factors are comprehended for the conceptualization of problem, and how the complexity dimension in policymaking and implementation can be addressed.

The twentieth century's rules and theories of managing social systems, economies, and organizations are being questioned and require change. The social policies, economic policies, or business strategies that were applied in the past may not work fully in the future. The economy and business in the twenty-first century will undergo changes that have not been felt before (Arthur 2014; Ismail et al. 2014; Turner and Baker 2019; HBR 2020). The changes may bring several opportunities and improvements if the future is managed well. Policymakers, leaders, experts, investors, and entrepreneurs have challenging tasks ahead. The primary issue is how to prepare for a future that cannot be predicted today.

5.4.1 VUCA, TUNA, and CYNEFIN Frameworks: An Overview

Realizing the inevitability of a dynamic environment and uncertainty and the need to manage the complex systems, three frameworks, viz., VUCA, TUNA, and CYNEFIN, have been developed by experts to provide aid to the decision makers for strategic management. Some examples, like the 9/11 strike in the USA, the financial crisis in 2008, political unrests, and disruptive business models, signify uncertainty in the world.

VUCA signifies volatility, uncertainty, complexity, and ambiguity in a system. It originated from strategy formulation by US Army College during war and arms conflicts. Subsequently, it has been applied to the business environment. It helps to understand the context in which the system's view of the current and future state is taken. It underscores the limits and scope for future planning and policy management. It facilitates how leaders and teams can make decisions, plan interventions to address problems, and manage risks. The leadership is expected to gauge the social, political, economic, market, and technological changes in the environment in which the economy, business, or organizations work. It provides a strategic framework for managing and surviving in an uncertain world (Abidi and Joshi 2015; Deaton 2018). It generally emphasizes resilient leadership, focusing on adaptability, which is vital to manage uncertainty.

Another framework, TUNA, stands for turbulence, uncertainty, novelty, and ambiguity (TUNA). In an environment marked with uncertainty and dynamic behavior, it requires examining the conditions that lead to disruptive changes and searching for new ways to address the problems. It stresses scenario planning to suggest future alternative states based on strategic foresight. It uses a dynamic way of thinking and works on strategies to deal with and plan for the uncertain future (Kahne 2013; Ramirez and Wilkinson 2016).

The CYNEFIN (pronounced as *kuh-nev-in*) framework, developed by Snowden at IBM in the USA, is a conceptual framework used to aid decision-making for managing systems under different contexts. It has been applied to different sectors in the USA. Based on conditions of cause-effects, uncertainty, and dynamic behavior, it identifies broadly four contexts, simple, complicated, complex, and chaotic, and suggests the approach to managing the system. The framework is useful for leaders to identify the current state in which their organizations work and what future interventions are required to address the problems (Snowden 2002; Kurtz and Snowden 2003).

5.4.2 Strategic Framework for Different System Contexts

In the context of the framework dealing with social contexts, it requires understanding the following concepts and approaches:

- *Behavioral dimension.* In a complex system, the behavioral dimension matters to a great extent. At the basic level, human nature influences and brings change. It is the human interactions, as a result of interactions between individuals and system variables, that impact system behavior. Due to behavioral preferences, how the groups of people in the social and political system behave or respond cannot be predicted, and their responses keep changing. As the recipients of the policies, based on their beliefs and psychological needs, the people accept or reject the policies and programs. Likewise, in the policy system, the behavioral issues affect various stakeholders like government officials, experts, citizens, entrepreneurs, and individuals in the non-governmental sectors who interact, participate, and collectively influence the decision-making (Lunn 2014; OECD 2017a; World Bank 2019).

In the economy, based on personal choices, values, and beliefs, the decisions by various economic agents, investors, entrepreneurs, innovators, etc., influence the economy. Such decisions keep evolving with the changes in the environment due to innovation, exchange of information, changes in policies, and disruptions by new technologies, products, or business models. The networks of agents operate at various levels—local, State, National, and international. They, through their knowledge and feedback, influence the system in an unpredictable manner. It results in an uncertain and dynamic nature of the economy. Among other factors, such changes are induced by human behaviors. Likewise, organizations are impacted by behavioral issues.

- *Evolving nature.* In both scientific management and the classical theories of management, economy, and organizations, the unpredictable, uncertain, and dynamic behavior of the system has not been recognized. Though theories have appreciated innovation and application of technologies, the evolving nature—as a result of interactive effects and dynamic interactions of elements—of policies, economy, or business has not got attention. The evolving nature pertains to 'emergent knowledge', 'continuous learning and adaptation', and 'emerging behavior of system'. Such evolution cannot be predicted and always remains in a state of change. Through better insights, 'new' knowledge keeps emerging. It is where the innovators have played their roles in the system. Or in other words, in the social system, knowledge is not static. Learning and adaptation are continuous and dynamic processes. And the system behavior evolves in an uncertain manner. This nature is the fundamental point of departure from the scientific management, conventional, rational, or classical theories of the twentieth century.

When it is mentioned that the system behavior evolves in an uncertain way, it does not mean that the system may go in the wrong direction or fail. The essence is that by introducing policies, one cannot determine the exact nature of change. But, by understanding the system behavior (pattern and scenarios) through a feedback mechanism, the necessary interventions in the system can be introduced to correct the trajectory. It calls for recognizing the evolving nature and the ability to cope with uncertainties. Simultaneously, the adaptive policies, complexity leadership approach , and resilient management system are the ways to deal with complex problems successfully (Uhl-Bien et al. 2007; Weberg 2012; Baltaci and Balci 2017).

- *Adaptive policies.* It is well-argued that social systems pose many complex issues and dynamic and uncertain situations. Due to the interactive nature of elements with nonlinear and unknown cause-effect relationships, the behavior of the system is uncertain and dynamic. Public policies dealing with issues related to people are formulated under certain conditions and circumstances. These change with time when the aspirations and needs of people change or ground conditions change. Besides, due to practical difficulties, all the factors and constraints cannot be factored in initially during policymaking.

In this light, the policies should not be a one-time exercise and not look at a fixed optimum solution. It requires considering the ground realities during the implementation process and a resilient approach to adapt to new emerging situations. The adaptive policies will call for a change in the approach to policymaking during the entire policy cycle—data collection and problem definition, analyses, policy formulation, implementation, and evaluation—by considering dynamic and uncertain behavior (Bankes 1999; IISD and TERI 2006; Swanson and Bhadwal 2009).

5.4 Strategic Framework: Preparing for Future

- *Complexity leadership.* The traditional leadership models have been driven by top-down, bureaucratic, and analytical concepts. These do not take into consideration the uncertainty and evolving nature of complex systems besides the human dimension of interactions. Such models are suitable for systems in which the articulation of cause-effects and problems is simpler, and the possibility of a stable environment persists for a long.

With the advent of the knowledge-based economy and exponential flow of information, besides multiple interactions between elements on a real-time basis, the environment in which the economy, business, and organizations work has been uncertain and dynamic. Moreover, the interactions between elements lead to the emergence of new ideas, innovation, and unpredictable patterns in the social system, economy, and business. Many public and business organizations are challenged by new realities and find it hard to manage. There have been spontaneous social and political unrests impacting governments. Similarly, there has been a rise in failure rates in business (Kelly and Allison 1999; Ismail et al. 2014). It has necessitated examining the system and problems from a new paradigm of complexity theory, which provides an alternative leadership approach to studying emerging phenomena like dynamic interactions, ideas, knowledge, innovation, learnings, and adaptation (Uhl-Bien et al. 2007; Baltaci and Balci 2017; Sapir 2020).

In response to a new reality, complexity leadership is needed to recognize the interactive relationships, build competence, appreciate the emergence of insights and knowledge, manage conflicting perspectives, and leverage the learning, innovation, and adaptive capacity of complex adaptive systems. The new leadership needs to shape the human cognitive capital to integrate with social capital for cohesive interactions between people to exchange ideas, knowledge, skills, and resources for a shared purpose based on trust. The trust should be built on ethical standards to enhance the confidence level of interactions.

In the knowledge economy, due to a need for a mindset of collaborative and networked approach, it is crucial that senior management facilitates rather than controls the processes that enable organizational change. Complexity leadership increases the ability of the organization to learn, adapt, and innovate (Kelly and Allison 1999; Weberg 2012; Byrne 1998).

- *Resilient management system.* To deal with conditions such as disruptions, emergencies, excessive difficulties, etc., it requires plans to minimize the adverse consequences, recover as quickly as possible, and adapt by learnings to become better-performing organizations. It calls for a resilient system with an interdisciplinary and cross-functional approach (Uhl-Bien et al. 2007; Weberg 2012; Darkow 2019).

A. *Questioning traditional thinking.* The complexity theory challenges the existing thinking in the public policy and economic systems of inquiry (Kauffman 1995; Sterman 2000; Mitchell 2009; OECD 2017b), as summarized below:

- *System works in order or equilibrium state.* Complex systems remain in a dynamic mode and evolve due to interactions between elements and feedback loops.

- *Individuals make rational choice.* Bounded rationality and behavioral preferences influence the decisions of individuals and groups, and the decisions are not determined alone by rational choices.
- *Expert knowledge and experience can manage complex problems or can be applied in most situations.* In social and economic systems, due to changing circumstances and conditions and the emerging nature of the system, the existing expert knowledge and experiences, though relevant, have limitations and require learning and updation as the system evolves. Past causal relations cannot predict the future state. Or, there is a limit to knowledge and experience when handling complex problems. Due to context-specific needs, expert knowledge has limits when dealing with complex issues that demand fresh and multiple perspectives.
- *Top management has more wisdom.* The system behavior or performance is essentially a function of interactive effects between agents and variables in the system, together with top-level interventions. Top management is vital but has limitations in terms of influencing working at the ground level.
- *Top-level interventions can bring the desired change, or change comes from the top.* The interactions between agents and variables, nonlinearity, feedback loops, and dynamic nature defy the logic of linear thinking or linear interventions from the top level. The system behavior or output is not due to linear effects or predefined cause-effect relationships. The individuals have their own beliefs, norms, and values, which cannot be changed in a short span as desired by top administration or management. However, the enabling conditions and incentives can play their roles.
- *More funding or financial resources can achieve desired results.* The resources or funds are essential but can achieve desired results only in the presence of enablers like institutional mechanisms, capabilities, and the right ecosystem for interactions between people.

B. *New thinking under the theory*: The complexity theory defines a new way of thinking, as outlined below (Bar-Yam 1997; Grobman 2005; Miles 2009; Holmes et al. 2011):

- *Individuals matter the most.* The system behavior is determined by the interactions between individuals (or economic agents) in the networks, the economy, or an organization.
- *Institutions are essential.* The interactions between individuals are influenced by institutional values, norms, culture, processes, and structures. And resulting from interactions, the system behavior emerges. Trust, confidence, and social capital are binding forces influenced by institutions.
- *History matters.* Past events have a bearing on the future shape of the system.
- *Enabling conditions and ecosystem are necessary.* The interactions between individuals or variables are influenced by the enablers in the ecosystem. Complex problems require more than the approach of simplistic linear thinking. The complexity theory perspective demands a better appreciation of interactive elements, nonlinear relationships, higher-order effects, feedback loops, and dynamic nature. Which factor or policy will impact which individual or

group cannot be predetermined. For example, one particular program may yield result in one case, while other programs may help in other cases, depending upon the needs. This perspective is to be recognized by the top management while designing the interventions.
- *Convergence and complementarity of enabling policies are necessary.* Due to interactive effects, the convergence and complementarity of policies can make a difference.
- *Complexity leadership and behavioral capabilities are essential.* The complexity leadership and the team with behavioral capabilities can better manage evolving and adaptive nature of the system.
- *Adaptive policies are needed.* As complex systems are dynamic and uncertain, the capabilities need to be improved through reskilling and upskilling, and policies need to be adaptive to the changing conditions.
- *Knowledge and experience evolve.* For different complex situations, the existing knowledge and experiences have limitations. The knowledge and capabilities need to evolve as the new system conditions evolve. The learnings should come as a result of gaining insights from the stakeholders, system conceptualization, problem analysis, and the emergence of new system order, behavior, or pattern.

C. Proposed Strategic Framework for System Management

Based on specific characteristics such as the number of elements, nature of causality, dynamic behavior, and uncertainty, the framework suggests four distinct 'contexts' for different systems in the real world (Fig. 5.8). But complicated and complex contexts are further classified, keeping the scale of the problem. Such typology is applicable to the public system, economy, business, and organizations, which are influenced by and influence the environment. The specific systems' characteristics, examples, and strategies to manage them are covered in this section. The strategic framework provides an aid for decision-making to address problems and manage the system. The system contexts that can be identified are (Table 5.2):

- Simple system
- Complicated system (with small scale)
- Complicated system (with large scale)
- Complex system (with small scale)
- Complex system (with large scale)
- Disorder (chaos) system

The system contexts are subjective. There is no quantitative way to categorize systems—simple, complicated, complex, and disorder. Depending on the context, the systems can be inferred with experience, expert knowledge, and detailed analyses. From the point of view of definition, causality means relations between causes and effects on the system behavior. The interactions are between elements and between elements and the environment. The system cannot change abruptly from one state to another, or there may be variations in degree. For example, the complicated system has different degrees of complicated nature. Similarly, the complex system has different degrees of complexity. So, the contexts with small and large

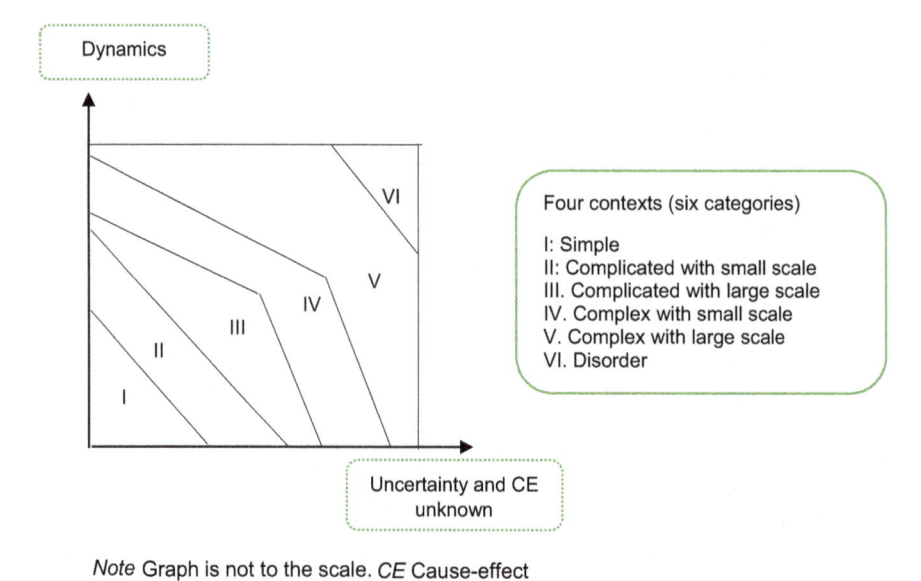

Fig. 5.8 System contexts based on uncertainty and dynamics

Four contexts (six categories)

I: Simple
II: Complicated with small scale
III: Complicated with large scale
IV. Complex with small scale
V. Complex with large scale
VI. Disorder

Note Graph is not to the scale. *CE* Cause-effect

scales for complicated and complex systems are considered. The idea is to bring categories or contexts as close to reality as possible.

Such categorization can help the government or top management first to identify the category in which the 'system under consideration' is placed and then decide about the strategy to address the problem, define the leadership role, select the interventions, and take steps for the formation of a team. The role of the leadership will vary depending upon the context of the system. Likewise, team formation will depend upon the context. Accordingly, the number of personnel with requisite capabilities needs to be placed. Complex problems will require a multidisciplinary team with higher-order thinking skills. The capabilities will include knowledge and skills in managing behavioral issues, understanding complexity, and carrying out various analyses.

To identify the context, a combination of the analytical approach and probing methods will be required. The analytical approach includes management tools like cause-effects analysis, system analysis, strategic analysis, and so on. It is more suitable for known or knowable cause-effects. The probing methods are more suited to complicated and complex problems, which will entail exploring and examining from multiple perspectives. It will demand systems thinking, complexity thinking, and design thinking, employing interpretive structural modeling (ISM), system dynamics (SD), pattern recognition, scenario building, etc.

In case there is an ambiguity in defining the context, which could be between simple and complicated, or between complicated and complex, it will require applying both analytical tools and probing. Besides, due to changes in conditions, the system may change state over time and shift from one context to another (Fig. 5.9). It

5.4 Strategic Framework: Preparing for Future   261

Table 5.2 Strategic framework: preparing for future

S. No.	System contexts	Characteristics	Environment	Examples	Tools, strategies, approaches, and theories to examine and manage systems[a]	Likely occurrence
1	Simple system	• Interacting elements are limited, and the frequency of interactions is low • Limited and known policy variables • Small-scale problems • Cause-effects are known and repeatable • System is normally steady, in a state of equilibrium, or returns to equilibrium quickly if disturbed	Stable and less impact of environment on the system	• Small organizations • Routine administrative matters, delivery of basic services like family certificates to citizens • Rule-based regulatory functions • Basic health services • Household and small businesses	• Systems thinking, system approach • Scientific management, analytical tools, best practices, SOPs, C-E analysis, BPR, QMS, PMS, etc • ISM • Leadership for scientific management, risk management • Team of personnel with hands-on knowledge • Need to keep a watch over complacency	Some cases (routine cases and known problems)
2.a	Complicated system (with small scale)	• Interacting elements are medium in number, and the frequency of interactions is low • Known policy variables • Medium-scale problems • Cause-effects are known, with an analytical approach • Reaches equilibrium after some time if disturbed	Stable, but some incremental changes, and less impact of environment on the system	• Medium organizations • Block-level (sub-district) health system • Welfare schemes • Established small businesses • Known small industrial projects with defined rules	• Systems thinking, system approach • ISM and SD (qualitative and quantitative modeling) • Scientific management, best practices, system analysis, SOPs, C-E analysis, BPR, QMS, PMS, etc • Leadership for scientific management, risk management • Team of personnel with hands-on knowledge • Analytical tools, AI, and ML tools[b]	A large number of cases

(continued)

Table 5.2 (continued)

S. No.	System contexts	Characteristics	Environment	Examples	Tools, strategies, approaches, and theories to examine and manage systems[a]	Likely occurrence
2.b	Complicated system (with large scale)	• Interacting elements are large in number, and the frequency of interactions increases • Known policy variables but in a large number • Large-scale policy matters • Cause-effect relationships are knowable, with expert knowledge • Reaches equilibrium after some time if disturbed	Stable with some incremental changes, and some impact of environment on the system	• Medium organizations with many issues • School education in the State • Health systems at district, State, and National levels • Local and regional agriculture marketing • Established big industrial projects and industries • Assured market for business • Big businesses with niche area or monopoly • Land use planning and management	As above (for complicated system with small scale) and the following: • System approach, systems thinking, and critical thinking • Innovative approaches for citizen engagement • Domain expertise • Maturity model • Collaboration: co-design and co-creation	A large number of cases

(continued)

5.4 Strategic Framework: Preparing for Future 263

Table 5.2 (continued)

S. No.	System contexts	Characteristics	Environment	Examples	Tools, strategies, approaches, and theories to examine and manage systems[a]	Likely occurrence
3.a	Complex system with small scale	• Interacting elements are large in number, and the frequency of interactions is medium • Medium number of policy variables and some unknown variables • Nonlinear and dynamic interactions • Complex problems with low scale • Causality[c]: cause-effect relationships are not known (in precise form) • System remains in a dynamic state and reaches equilibrium after a long time if disturbed	Changes from time to time, and significant impact of environment on the system	• Medium-level systems but complex • Urban management in small towns • Land acquisition with small scale • R&D, innovation, and new technologies (of small scale) • Regional agriculture marketing of diversified crops • Medium-scale businesses of multiple types • Large industrial projects • Supply chain management within a country	• Complex adaptive system management • Boundary conditions and assumptions need to be defined • Complexity theory (to understand interactive effects[d] and characteristics) • Systems thinking, complexity thinking, and design thinking • Innovative approaches for citizen engagement • Causality[c] (cause-effect relationships are knowable with analyses) (under specific assumptions)[e] • ISM and SD (qualitative modeling) • AI, ML tools, and Agent-based modeling (ABM)[b] • Collaboration: co-design and co-creation • Creating right ecosystem • Incremental and process approach (pilot study) • Promoting innovation • Introducing calibrated reforms • Leadership for emergent knowledge management, resilience, adaptive system, and risk management • Multidisciplinary team and higher-order thinking skills, QMS and PMS tools for close monitoring	A large number of cases

(continued)

Table 5.2 (continued)

S. No.	System contexts	Characteristics	Environment	Examples	Tools, strategies, approaches, and theories to examine and manage systems[a]	Likely occurrence
3.b	Complex system with large scale	• Interacting elements are in significantly large numbers, and the frequency of interactions is high, with large network effects • More policy variables and some unknown variables • Large-scale policy matters • Nonlinear and dynamic interactions, uncertainty • Causality[c]: cause-effect relationships are unknown and unknowable • Disruptive behavior with time • System remains in a dynamic state and reaches equilibrium after a long time if disturbed, and keeps changing the state of equilibrium (with possibility of transformative potential, at the edge of chaos or point of inflection)	Frequent changes in the environment, and sometimes, disruptive influence of large scale on the system	• Large systems and complex problems • Urban management and land use management in big cities • Higher education in big institutes • Land acquisition of large scale • Crop loss due to large-scale adverse climatic conditions • R&D, innovation, and new technologies (of large scale) • Development in remote, backward, tribal areas; issues of cultural diversity; socio-economic-political-cultural linkages • Climate change impact in coastal areas; air and water pollution control • Disruptive innovation, advanced manufacturing • Multi-State agriculture marketing and exports • Global supply chain management • National economy, international trade and economy; stock market • Pandemic	• As above (for complex system with small scale) and the following: • Complex adaptive system management and complexity theory (to understand interactive effects[d] and characteristics) • Causality[c] (cause-effect relationships are knowable with analyses) (under specific assumptions)[e], from the perspective of finding solutions • Strategic foresight for scenario building • Pattern recognition, experiential learning • Adaptive policies, 'design' approach for public policy	Increasing number of cases

(continued)

264   5 Complexity Theory Framework

5.4 Strategic Framework: Preparing for Future

Table 5.2 (continued)

S. No.	System contexts	Characteristics	Environment	Examples	Tools, strategies, approaches, and theories to examine and manage systems[a]	Likely occurrence
4	Disorder (or chaos)	• Interacting elements are significant in number, not necessarily large • Nonlinear and dynamic interactions • Disorganization, disarray, and confusion • Cause-effect relationships are unknowable • No possibility of pattern recognition • Disruptive behavior • Far from equilibrium for a long time	Turbulence	• Large-scale social unrest • Large-scale mismanagement in the organization • Sudden change in climatic conditions (like floods, cyclones, etc.) • Disruption due to breach of cyber security	• Crisis management • Novel approach, experiential learning, collaboration • Leadership for crisis management, management of emergent knowledge, resilience, adaptive system, and risk management • Multidisciplinary team	In a few cases

Source Own analysis, expert consultations, and literature review (Bar-Yam 1997; Snowden 2002; Kurtz and Snowden 2003; Grobman 2005; Uhl-Bien et al. 2007; Miles 2009; Swanson and Bhadwal 2009; Holmes et al. 2011; Weberg 2012; Kahne 2013; Baltaci and Balci 2017; Darkow 2019; Sapir 2020)

Note The system contexts are subjective. Different strategy teams may come out with differing categories depending on their perspectives. Such classification may change with time. Nevertheless, it provides a broad direction for formulating the strategy. It is difficult to find a quantitative way to categorize different systems—simple, complicated (small scale and large scale), complex (small scale and large scale), and disorder. Depending on the context, the systems can be classified with experience, expert knowledge, and detailed analyses using tools like system approach, system analysis, system dynamics modeling, pattern recognition, scenario building, etc.

ABM agent-based modeling, *QMS* quality management system, *AI* artificial intelligence, *BPR* business process reengineering, *C-E* cause and effect, *FMEA* failure mode and effect analysis, *ISM* interpretive structural modeling, *ML* machine learning, *PMS* performance management system, *SD* system dynamics, *SOPs* standard operating procedures, *SWOT* strength, weakness, opportunity, and threat

[a]Strategies and tools are indicative and need to be applied depending on the nature of the problem, type of context, and scale of complexity
[b]With defined boundaries and assumptions for problems
[c]Causality means relations between system output (effects) and causes
[d]Interactive effects are between elements, and the interactions lead to emergence
[e]Based on observations of addressing complex problems in tribal development, sustainable development, and managing industrial problems

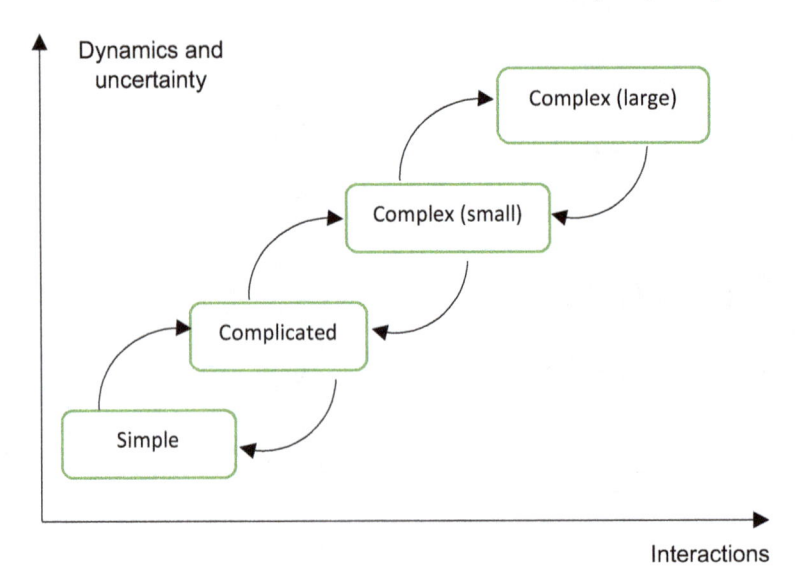

Fig. 5.9 Dynamics of system context

will necessitate a change in leadership style and strategy to match the new environment and context. Another word of caution is about complacency resulting from entrained thinking, in which the leadership and team members, working for a long time in the system, may develop a fixed mindset, and psychological inertia may develop. Also, due to their past training and experience, the experts may not appreciate the ideas of non-experts or personnel from general administration or management, resulting in delays or missed opportunities until the correction is introduced.

Broadly, the framework covers the following (Table 5.2):

- *Context of the system*: It explains in what context the system is examined. The context is determined by the nature of the problem or system. It takes into account the number of interacting elements, intensity of interacting elements, the scale of problem, nonlinearity, dynamic behavior, the possibility of discerning cause-effect relationships, and state of equilibrium.
- *Strategy to examine the problem and system*. Different contexts require distinct modes of thinking and methods of analysis for system conceptualization and problem definition. Based on known, simple and knowable, unknown but knowable, and unknowable cause-effects; the uncertainty; and dynamic nature, the strategy to comprehend the systems and problem should be worked out. Depending on the system contexts, tools may include cause-effect analysis, application of analytical tools, mathematical analyses, scenario building, pattern recognition, etc.

5.4 Strategic Framework: Preparing for Future

- *Strategy to approach solution and manage system.* Different contexts will require separate tools and approaches to manage the systems. These may include scientific management and best practices, standard operating procedures (SOPs), quality management system (QMS), business process reengineering (BPR), performance management system (PMS), process approach, systems theory, complexity theory, adaptive approach, organizational reforms, etc.

The details about the four contexts of the system are presented below:

- *Simple system.*

Context of the system. The number of interacting elements is limited, and the frequency of interactions is low. There are limited and known policy variables. The cause-effects are known due to experience and are repeatable. The system is usually steady, in a state of equilibrium, or returns to equilibrium quickly or remains there if disturbed. The environment is stable.

Examples: Routine administrative matters, delivery of basic services like family certificates, primary health services, rule-based regulatory functions, household and small businesses, food delivery to needy families, etc.

Strategy to examine the problem or system. The systems thinking and system approach can be applied. It requires a diagnostic study to examine the system variables, processes, and delivery mechanism using analytical tools like root cause analysis, process mapping, system analysis, etc.

Strategy to approach solution. Application of standard operating procedures (SOPs), quality management system (QMS), business process reengineering (BPR), and performance management system (PMS). The methods of scientific management and objective criteria are applicable. Interpretive structural modeling (ISM) and system dynamics (SD), both qualitative and quantitative, can be applied. The top-down approach with defined rules can work, as the processes are simple and access to the information to make decisions is possible. The decision-making can be delegated with a monitoring system, and functions can be automated with accuracy. The best practices for process, quality, and performance management will work successfully.

However, the management should be careful about the possibility of complacency or overconfidence. Over time, the inefficiency may settle within the system, and the forces in the external environment may dominate. The entrained thinking acquired through experience and training may start dominating over time, so the new ideas may not be accepted.

- *Complicated system (with small scale).* Initially, when any policy is formulated, a business is launched, or an organization is started, it has a small number of issues and activities. As more opportunities are felt or problems surface, the simple system gets more interactive people, and it tends to become complicated.

Context of the system. The system has a medium number of interacting elements, the frequency of interactions is low, there is a certainty of behavior, cause-effect relationships are knowable by applying analytical tools, and it reaches equilibrium after some time if disturbed. It has known policy variables and medium-scale problems. The environment remains stable, but some incremental changes, and has less impact on the system.

Examples. Medium organizations with limited problems, Block-level (sub-district) health system, well-established small businesses, known industrial projects with defined rules, etc.

Strategy to examine the problem or system. It requires using systems thinking, analytical tools like failure mode and effect analysis (FMEA), BPR, quality management tools, etc. In a complicated system, if the same problem occurs again, the same solution can be applied, as cause-effect relations are known and the system has an ordered state. The application of ISM and system dynamics (SD) will be helpful.

Strategy to approach solution. The scientific management and best practices, SOPs, BPR, QMS, PMS, etc., can be applied. The leadership needs to apply scientific management and appreciate the need for risk management. AI and ML tools can be used with defined boundaries and assumptions for problems. It requires a team with hands-on knowledge.

- *Complicated System (with large scale).*

Context of the system. As the system grows over time, the number of interacting elements becomes large, and the frequency of interactions increases, and thus the system becomes more complicated. In such a system, the cause-effect relationships are knowable, with expert knowledge, and the system reaches equilibrium after some time if disturbed. The behavior of the system is predictable. Such systems are medium organizations with many problems, known policy variables but in a large number, and large-scale policy matters. The environment remains stable, with some incremental changes, and has some impact.

Examples. School education in the State; health systems at district, State, and National levels; local and regional agriculture marketing; established large industrial projects and industries; big businesses with niche areas or monopoly; land use planning and management, etc.

Strategy to examine the problem or system. Application of systems thinking and critical thinking, analytical tools like FMEA, ISM, SD (both qualitative and quantitative modeling), etc.

Strategy to approach solution. It requires scientific management, application of system approach, best practices, strategic management, SOPs, BPR, maturity model, etc.; performance management, quality management, customer or citizen management; innovative approaches; and AI and ML tools (under defined boundaries and assumptions). The leadership for scientific management and risk management and a team of personnel with hands-on knowledge and domain expertise are necessary. The collaborative approach may be necessary.

5.4 Strategic Framework: Preparing for Future

- *Complex system (with small scale).* With the increase in the number of interacting elements and the dynamic environment, the system becomes more dynamic, and the uncertainty increases. Initially, the system may have small-scale complexity but may increase depending on the conditions.

Context of the system. In such systems, the characteristics include large numbers of interacting elements, the frequency of interactions could be medium (but increases), nonlinear, and dynamic, and the cause-effect relationships are not known (in precise form or exact form). The system remains dynamic and reaches equilibrium after a long time if disturbed. It has a medium number of policy variables and some unknown variables. The environment changes from time to time and impacts system significantly.

Examples. Urban management in small towns; land acquisition, with small scale; R&D, innovation, and new technologies (of small scale); regional agriculture marketing of diversified crops; medium-scale businesses of multiple types; large industrial projects; supply chain management within a country, etc.

Strategy to examine the problem or system. It includes the application of systems thinking, complexity thinking, and design thinking; ISM and SD (qualitative modeling); causal loop (CL) and system structures diagrams; and scenario building. To understand a complex system, boundary conditions and assumptions need to be defined. The cause-effect relationships are knowable with expertise and analyses under defined assumptions.

Strategy to approach solution. The complexity theory will be applicable to examine the interactive effects of the elements and the characteristics of complex systems. Other strategies include incremental and process approach (pilot study); innovative approaches and collaboration (co-design and co-creation); creating right ecosystem; promoting innovation; and introducing calibrated reforms. It calls for leadership for emergent knowledge management, resilience, adaptive system, and risk management; a multidisciplinary team; and higher-order thinking skills. Artificial intelligence (AI), machine learning (ML) tools, and agent-based modeling (ABM) can be applied after defining boundary of the system and assumptions. Application of QMS and PMS tools for close monitoring.

- *Complex system (with large scale).* As the number of elements (individuals and variables) increases in the system and their interactions rise, the feedback, dynamics, and uncertainty increase, causing large-scale complexity with time. Most social and economic systems dealing with a large number of individuals (or economic agents in the economy) are complex systems. The challenge is how to recognize complexity, analyze it, and manage and leverage it for better performance.

Context of the system. It involves characteristics like a large number of interacting elements, high frequency of interactions, and large network effects; nonlinear and dynamic interactions; and uncertainty of the behavior. The cause-effect relationships are unknown and unknowable due to multiple interactions between numerous elements, nonlinear behavior, and feedback loops from various sources. Or, the causality (in precise form) cannot be determined, i.e., the exact relations between outputs and causes cannot be determined. The system reaches equilibrium after a long time if disturbed and keeps changing the state of equilibrium. There is a possibility of transformative potential at the edge of chaos or point of inflection. The system has more policy variables, some unknown variables, and large-scale policy matters. The environment is dynamic and, sometimes, has disruptive influence of a large scale on the system.

Examples. It includes urban management and land use management in big cities; public services in large urban or rural areas (like primary education, health, social security, water supply, etc.); communicable disease and pandemic; land acquisition, with large scale; multi-State agriculture marketing and exports; development in remote, backward, and tribal areas; issues of cultural diversity and behavioral issues in communities; climate change impact on coastal regions; air and water pollution control; disruptive innovation, advanced manufacturing, and unemployment; socio-economic-political-cultural linkages; national economy, international trade and economy, and stock market; global supply chain, etc.

Strategy to examine the problem or system. The complexity theory can be applied to examine interactive effects, uncertainty, emergence, and evolution. The tools and strategies will include the application of systems thinking, complexity thinking, and design thinking; strategic foresight and scenario building and pattern recognition; experiential learning; complex adaptive system; and use of ISM and SD (qualitative, but not quantitative modeling), and causal loop (CL) and system structure diagrams (ISM and SD models cannot examine the interactive effects of elements).

Strategy to approach solution. Some suggested tools are the complex adaptive system approach; collaboration (co-design and co-creation); incremental and process approach (pilot study); promoting innovation; introducing calibrated reforms; adaptive policies; design approach for public policy; and creating right ecosystem. It demands leadership for emergent knowledge management, resilience, adaptive system, and risk management; forming multidisciplinary team; and using higher-order thinking skills. For complex systems, the strategy should evolve as the system evolves. The realistic way forward is a transdisciplinary approach by drawing insights from multiple lenses and stakeholder analysis for system and problem conceptualization; studying patterns and evolutionary nature; and synthesizing insights, knowledge, and patterns.

It may include applying mathematical modeling in specific cases in which variables are known, and relationships are determinable to a good extent with defined assumptions. For example, artificial intelligence (AI), machine learning (ML) tools, and Agent-based modeling (ABM) can be used for specific problems with identified system conditions and assumptions. 'Qualitative system dynamics modeling' can be applied to comprehend problems in complex systems. These tools can be suitable depending on the nature of the problem and the complexity involved in it.

Special case. The governments or managements have the responsibility to manage the system, so they have to work on finding solutions to address problems. To identify interventions, the causal relationships between variables in the system structure can be identified or are knowable with detailed study under specific assumptions. It means that, through an iterative process, the likely behavior can be explored, and future scenarios can be developed. It is so required with the objective of determining strategies. Simultaneously, the governments and business management work under demands from their respective stakeholders and are expected to deliver results in the immediate future. Pragmatism demands keeping an eye on the complexity for addressing medium- to long-term issues while addressing immediate-term to short-term problems. The measures required in the immediate term or short term will be different from medium- to long-term interventions keeping complexity into consideration.

New management paradigm. The complexly analysis is not about the application of any particular set of tools. Instead, it draws on transdisciplinary knowledge and insights from multiple perspectives, analogies from past events or cases, and problem-solving tools. Reflexive skills and pattern recognition abilities are essential, and resilience and agility are called for in the management of complex systems. There are two basic features of the social and economic systems. *First*, human nature brings the exchange of ideas and resources and then decision-making during interactions. These lead to learning, creativity, action, emergence, and evolution. *Second*, if enabling conditions persist, the virtuous cycle of creativity and innovation, actions, emergence, adaptation, and evolution continues. There are examples of the evolution of Silicon Valleys in Bengaluru (India) and San Francisco Bay (USA) and the global networked economy to substantiate the effect of the virtuous cycle. These differentiate social and economic systems from physical systems.

The system conditions and the processes are to be managed for the emergence of new ideas, insights, knowledge, and system behavior (Fig. 5.10). It will demand dynamic steering, including the following:

- gaining insights from the grassroots consultations and analyses and then generating knowledge;
- recognizing the emergence of knowledge: based on system conditions, processes, and interactions, there is an emergence of knowledge;
- managing knowledge and learnings and their application;
- emerging interventions: interventions need to be calibrated by using emerging knowledge and as per the local needs, and, simultaneously, creating the conditions for the people or agents to adapt to new ways of working; and
- adaptability to emerging conditions.

The emergent knowledge should be integrated and assimilated with the expert knowledge. Expert knowledge and analytical tools are necessary but not sufficient, and over-reliance or only reliance on them is not helpful and desirable; rather may be counterproductive in some cases. The focus should be on gaining insights through multiple lenses of inquiry, feedback from stakeholders, recognizing knowledge that

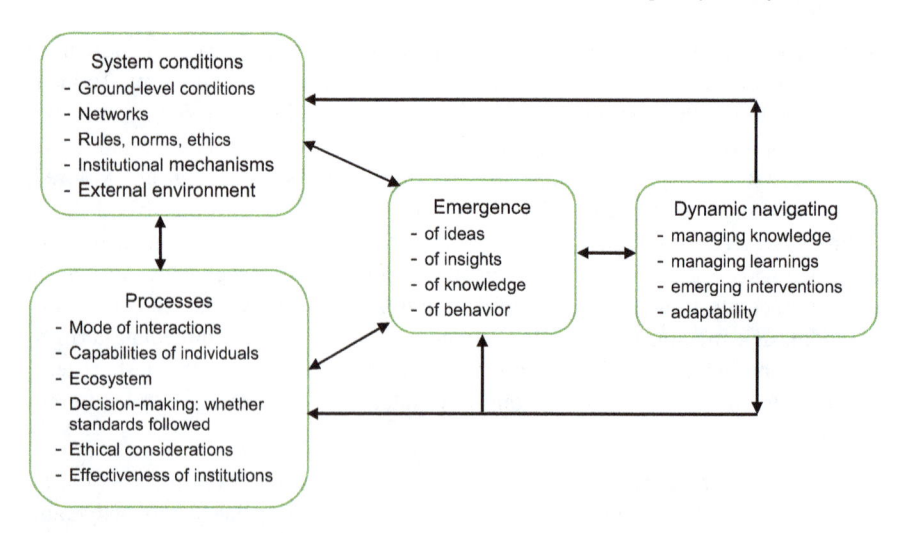

```
┌─────────────────────────────────┐
│ System conditions               │
│ - Ground-level conditions       │
│ - Networks                      │
│ - Rules, norms, ethics          │
│ - Institutional mechanisms      │
│ - External environment          │
└─────────────────────────────────┘
         ↕                    ┌──────────────────┐       ┌────────────────────────┐
                              │ Emergence        │       │ Dynamic navigating     │
┌─────────────────────────────┐│ - of ideas       │ ←→   │ - managing knowledge   │
│ Processes                   ││ - of insights    │       │ - managing learnings   │
│ - Mode of interactions      ││ - of knowledge   │       │ - emerging interventions│
│ - Capabilities of individuals││ - of behavior   │       │ - adaptability         │
│ - Ecosystem                 │└──────────────────┘       └────────────────────────┘
│ - Decision-making: whether  │
│   standards followed        │
│ - Ethical considerations    │
│ - Effectiveness of institutions│
└─────────────────────────────┘
```

Fig. 5.10 Emerging knowledge and dynamic navigation

emerges from insights, developing understanding by synthesizing insights and analysis, and then dovetailing with expert knowledge. The emergence is a result of interactions of elements at the micro level or the operational level, but interactions are constrained or enabled by the rules, institutions, and ecosystem. These are the two fundamental points—'emergence due to interactions' and 'enabling factors'—that need attention and consideration from policymakers and strategists.

Against the backdrop of the complexity theory, broadly, it will entail the following steps to manage complex systems (McKelvey 2002; Mason 2008; Meadows 2008; Miles 2009; Palmberg 2009a; Gharajedaghi 2011): *first*, scanning the problems and systems requiring multiple perspectives through systemic understanding, stakeholders' consultations, analyzing behavioral issues and group dynamics, examining interactions between elements, institutional analysis, empirical studies, and analytical approaches to understanding system boundary and assumptions; *second*, understanding complexity phenomena; *third*, developing a shared vision and values to bring people together; *fourth*, creating the right enabling conditions and the capacity to perform; and *fifth*, introducing interventions in a calibrated manner based on the feedback from the ground and close monitoring.

- *Disorder*

Context of the system. Some characteristics are: the interacting elements are significant in number, not necessarily large; disorganization, disarray, and confusion; nonlinear and dynamic interactions; cause-effect relationships are unknowable; disruptive behavior; system is far from equilibrium for a long time; and no possibility of pattern recognition. The 'disorder' in an organization may occur as a result of any or the combination of the factors such as lack of communication and rise in grievances, continuous decline in the performance of a system, blockage of decision-making, internal need for change, unforeseen circumstances, accident, or conspiracy. In the context of the economy, it represents a significant mismatch or imbalance between different factors of production or economic variables, and as for organization, it indicates disruption of functioning.

The significance of 'disorder' is that the system has to be comprehended afresh, and the long-term view of the problems is to be taken. It may be for a good reason as well, and maybe a precursor to transformation. The disorder, if managed well and analyzed *ex-post*, can throw lessons for the top management for future planning.

Examples: Large-scale social unrest, large-scale mismanagement in the organization, sudden change in climatic conditions, natural calamities, disruption in the workplace, gross IT network failure or cybersecurity problem, etc.

Strategy to examine the problem or system. Generally, there is no sufficient time to search for the causes. It calls for wider consultations to understand the problem.

Strategy to approach solution. Crisis management; collaboration; novel approach; experiential learning; collaboration; and leadership for crisis management, management of emergent knowledge, adaptive system, and risk management. In this context, the leadership and team must first act to establish order, sense where instability is likely to be present, and then work to transform the situation from chaos to a complex, complicated, or manageable situation that can be managed.

5.5 Future Research in Policy Theory

Concluding Remarks on Theory. The complexity theory is contemplated in a definite departure from the seventeenth century Newtonian paradigm, characterized by determinism and Cartesian reductionism. The theory explains that there is a need to shift the analysis from the individual parts of a system to the system as a whole, a network of elements that interact and combine to produce system behavior. It should not examine constituent parts or elements in isolation. Examining each element or system variable is essential, but what is more important is studying the interactions between elements. In the system, each element is vital. The theory defines a new paradigm and highlights the need to zoom in to examine elements, their interrelationships and interactions, and feedback, and simultaneously zoom out to view the whole system. It underscores the importance of complexity thinking in examining the system. It provides the ability to visualize the issues from the complexity perspective during the policy cycle consisting of problem analysis, policy design, implementation, feedback, and mid-course correction.

The complexity theory deals with interactive behavior, emergence, and evolution, which are unique phenomena. Still, several other underlying features, like the role of various stakeholders, insights from the grassroots, institutional and behavioral issues, interrelationships between variables, the process of multiple analyses, system structure, implementation mechanism, and their causal relations, demand further probing.

In social sciences, including economics, theorizing social, economic, cultural, institutional, behavioral, and cognitive issues is a continuing process due to the dynamics and evolving nature of problems. Public policy has multiple issues in question that are not comprehended and theorized by current policy theories.

Need for New Policy Theory—Researching Underlying Causes. The examination of policy theories in Chap. 4 has revealed that they have been short on explaining the policymaking process and causal relationships, the determinants of policy choices, and the mechanism for implementation. The 'what' part of the policy has found predominant inclusion. The future theory should cover both the 'what' part and the 'how' part, i.e., the causality aspect. To understand further details, the future theory should attempt to deal with the following aspects:

- 'how' the policy formulation takes place, or 'causality' aspect—factors that impact formulation of policies; the role of various stakeholders, including policymakers and how they define problems; holistic examination of policy system—policy variables, policy process, and structures; complexity dimension; role of social and political institutions, politics, and behavioral issues; and impact of bounded rationality on policy choices;
- how the policy choices are determined concerning 'end-users'; and
- implementation of policy—implementation theory, the issues comprising the institutional capacity, practices, culture, behavioral and complexity issues, etc.

Social systems involve numerous dimensions that are not yet covered by a single theory. Despite complexity theory, developing a new comprehensive policy theory is necessitated by synthesizing the above issues.

Issues of Application of Complexity Theory: At a conceptual level, there is an increase in complexity in social systems. But all the problems are not complex. And these may be large and complicated. In some cases, due to the vast nature of a problem, it may appear complex. In other cases, the inability to comprehend a problem, either due to bounded rationality or lack of expertise, may make the problem seem complex. Besides, the complexity may be of low or high scale, depending on the number of interacting elements, level of uncertainty, and dynamic nature.

For complex problems, government agencies and businesses have used expert knowledge and experience to manage complexity. Public as well as private organizations make an effort to handle complexity due to a combination of the competitive environment, pressure from stakeholders, and the desire to excel. For example, governments feel pressure from citizens, or companies feel pressure from customers and competition from other companies. For responsive government, businesses, or organizations, the necessity to address complex problems will lead to revising their policies and strategies to meet changing environment or evolving challenges.

Usually, managing complexity is more by intuitive methods or impulsive reaction to complex problems in various sectors such as climate challenge, urban management, or water management rather than a conscious effort. The complexity management will vary depending on the internal capabilities and commitment.

Complexity theory is an emerging theory for complex social and economic systems. It is gaining application at a slow pace, as there are a few interlinked issues. These are, *first*, at the basic level, there is a lack of awareness in the government organizations, educational institutions, and business and industry; *second*, difficulty in comprehending the concepts or terminologies in the complexity literature; and *third*, dearth of successful case studies on the application of complexity theory, despite the promise the theory holds. Thus, applying complexity theory is challenging. Presently, the literature survey (scholarly articles, books, and international reports) has underscored that in some countries like Australia, New Zealand, the UK, the USA, and Organization for Economic Cooperation and Development (OECD) countries, the policy experts and research scholars are devoting their efforts on working out strategies for the application of complexity theory in policymaking and implementation.

The complexity theory is gradually embraced for examining complex problems in economic, industrial, and business systems. A few agencies, like OECD (2017b), International Institute for Sustainable Development (IISD) (2006), and Overseas Development Agency (ODA) (UK), have applied the concepts of complexity and complex adaptive systems in some development projects and research work. The institutes that are working on complexity theory are Santa Fe Institute (USA); Institute of Public Administration Australia; New Approaches to Economic Challenges (NAEC), Critical OECD think tank; Institute for New Economic Thinking (INET), University of Oxford; and School of Government, Victoria University of Wellington, to name a few. Some consulting agencies like McKinsey (2007), IBM (2010), and KPMG (2010) are engaged in understanding complexity in business and finding solutions for complex problems. Addressing the complexity dimension requires an institutional approach by the government and academia.

References

Abidi S, Joshi M. The VUCA Company. Jaico Publishing House; 2015.
Acemoglu D, Robinson J. The role of institutions in growth and development. Rev Econ Inst. 2010;1(2). www.rei.unipg.it. https://doi.org/10.5202/rei.v1i2.1 (ISSN 2038-1379, http://www.rei.unipg.it/rei/article/view/14).
Allen PM. A complex systems approach to learning in adaptive networks. Int J Innov Manag. 2011;5(2). No Access. https://www.researchgate.net/publication/224892172.
Anderson PW, Arrow K, Pines D. The economy as an evolving complex system (Santa Fe Institute Series). CRC Press; 1988.
Arif R. With an economic potential of $11 trillion. Internet of things is here to revolutionize global economy. 2021. https://www.forbes.com/sites/raufarif/2021/06/05/with-an-economic-potential-of-11-trillion-internet-of-things-is-here-to-revolutionize-global-economy/?sh=329511a75f29.
Arthur B. Navigating complexity: the essential guide to complexity theory in business and management. Spiro Press; 2000.
Arthur WB. Complexity and the economy. USA: Oxford University Press; 2014.

Arthur WB, Durlauf SN, Lane D, editors. The economy as an evolving complex system II (Santa Fe Institute Series). CRC Press; 1997.

Avnimelech G, Teubal M. The Indian software industry from an israeli perspective: a systems/evolutionary and policy view chapter in India. In: D'Costa AP, Sridharan E, editors. The global software industry: innovation, firm strategies and development. Palgrave Macmillan; 2003.

Baetu TM. Emergence, therefore antireductionism? A critique of emergent antireductionism. Biol Philos. 2012;27(3):433–48.

Balland PA, Broekel T, Diodato D, Giuliani E, Hausmann R, O'Clery N, Rigby D. The new paradigm of economic complexity. Res Policy. 2022;51(3):104568. https://doi.org/10.1016/j.respol.2021.104450.

Baltaci A, Balci A. Complexity leadership: a theoretical perspective. Int J Educ Leaders Manag. 2017;5(1):30–58. https://doi.org/10.17583/ijelm.2017.2435.

Bankes SC. Tools and techniques for developing policies for complex and uncertain systems. 1999. https://doi.org/10.1073/pnas.092081399.

Bar-Yam Y. Dynamics of complex systems. Westview Press; 1997.

Battiston S, Farmer JD, Flache A, Garlaschelli D, Haldane AG, Heesterbeek H, Hommes C, Jaegerb C, May R, Scheffer M. Complexity theory and financial regulation. Science. 2016;351(6275):818–9.

Beinhocker ED. Strategy at the Edge of the Chaos. McKinsey Q. 1997;(1).

Boulton JG, Allen PM, Bowman C. Embracing complexity: strategic perspectives for an age of turbulence. Oxford: OUP; 2015.

Brinkerhoff D. From design to implementation: stakeholder analysis in a PHC project in India. Bethesda, MD: Abt Associates Inc.; 1998.

Brown SL, Eisenhardt KM. The art of continuous change: linking complexity theory and time-paced evolution in relentlessly shifting organizations. Admin Sci Q. 1997;42(1). http://www.jstor.org/stable/2393807.

Business Standard. Bengaluru firms claimed 45% of all investments in Indian startups in 10 Yrs. 2019. https://www.business-standard.com/article/companies/bengaluru-firms-claimed-45-of-all-investments-in-indian-startups-in-10-yrs-119121701396_1.html.

Byrne DS. Complexity theory and the social sciences: an introduction. New York: Routledge; 1998.

Cairney P. Understanding public policy: theories and issues. Palgrave Macmillan: Textbooks in Policy Studies; 2012.

Carmichael T, Hadzikadi M. The fundamentals of complex adaptive systems. 2019. https://www.researchgate.net/publication/333780588.

Castells M, Cardoso G, editors. The network society: from knowledge to policy. Washington, DC: Johns Hopkins Center for Transatlantic Relations; 2005.

Castells M. The rise of the network society. Wiley; 2011.

Chan S. Complex adaptive systems. 2001. https://web.mit.edu/esd.83/www/notebook/Complex%20Adaptive%20Systems.pdf.

Cilliers P. Complexity and postmodernism. Understanding complex systems. London: Routledge; 1998.

Cohen WJ. The development of the social security act of 1935: reflections some fifty years later, Minnesota Law Review. 1984. https://core.ac.uk/download/pdf/217208529.pdf.

Colander D, Howitt P, Kirman A, Leijonhufvud A, Perry M. The American economic review. In: Papers and proceedings of the one hundred twentieth annual meeting of the American Economic Association. 2008.

Colander D, Kupers R. Complexity and the art of public policy—solving society's problems from the bottom up. Princeton University Press; 2016.

Conklin J. Rethinking wicked problems [interview]. NextD J. 2007;10:1–30. http://nextd.org (Google Scholar).

Coyle RG. Management system dynamics. London: Wiley; 1977.

References

D'Costa AP. Export growth and path-dependence: the locking-in of innovations in the software industry, chapter in India. In: D'Costa AP, Sridharan E, editors. The global software industry: innovation, firm strategies and development. Palgrave Macmillan; 2003.

Darkow PM. Mastering adversity: resilient organizing in the age of disruption (Dissertation). Universitat Hamburg, Hamburg; 2019. https://ediss.sub.uni-hamburg.de/handle/ediss/8550.

D'Costa AP, Sridharan E, editors. India in the global software industry: innovation. Firm strategies and development. Palgrave Macmillan; 2003.

Deaton AV. Vuca tools for a Vuca world: developing leaders and teams for sustainable results. Lightning Source; 2018.

Decron C. Speed-space. In: Armitage J, editor. Virilio live. London: Sage; 2001.

Deloitte and Singularity University. Exponential technologies in manufacturing transforming the future of manufacturing through technology, talent, and the innovation ecosystem. 2018.

Deloitte. Global manufacturing competitiveness index 2016. 2016.

Dickson M, Resick C, Hanges P. When organizational climate is unambiguous, it is also strong. J Appl Psychol. 2006;91(2):351–64. https://doi.org/10.1037/0021-9010.91.2.351.

Drucker PF. Management's new paradigms. Forbes. 1998;162(7). https://www.forbes.com/global/1998/1005/0113052a.html?sh=5feec7412328.

Economic Times. Indian startups raised $42 billion in 2021. 2022. https://economictimes.indiatimes.com/tech/funding/indian-startups-raised-42-billion-in-2021-report/articleshow/88875670.cms?utm_source=contentofinterest&utm_medium=text&utm_campaign=cppst.

Eppel E, Rhodes ML. Complexity theory and public management: a 'becoming' field. Public Manag Rev. 2018;20(7):949–59. https://doi.org/10.1080/14719037.2017.1364414.

Fidan T, Balci A. Managing schools as complex adaptive systems: a strategic perspective. 2017. https://doi.org/10.26822/iejee.2017131883.

Fischer F. Reframing public policy. Discursive politics and deliberative practices. Oxford University Press; 2003.

Fletcher A, Guthrie J, Steane P, Roos G, Pike S. Mapping stakeholder perceptions for a third sector organization. J Intellect Cap. 2003;4(4):505–27.

Forrester JW. Counterintuitive behaviour of social systems. Technol. Rev. 1971:53–68.

Forrester JW. Industrial dynamics. Pegasus Communications Waltham; 1961.

Foster J. From simplistic to complex systems in economics. Discussion Paper No 335; 2004.

Fraser D. The evolution of the british welfare state. London: Macmillan; 1984.

Fried B. The progressive assault on Laissez-Faire: Robert Hale and the first law and economics movement. Harvard University Press; 1998.

Gaus G. Social complexity and evolved moral principles. In: Hunt L, McNamara P, editors. Liberalism, conservatism, and Hayek's Idea of spontaneous order. London: Palgrave Macmillan; 2007.

Gerstel D, Goodman MP. From industrial policy to innovation strategy lessons from Japan, Europe, and the United States. Washington: Center for Strategic and International Studies (CSIS); 2020. Downloads/200901_Gerstel_InnovationStrategy_FullReport_FINAL_0%20(1).pdf.

Gerston LN. Public policy making: process and principles. New York, ME: Sharpe Inc.; 2010.

Gharajedaghi, J. Systems thinking: managing chaos and complexity: a platform for designing business architecture. 3rd ed. Morgan Kaufmann; 2011.

Gilstrap DL. Strange attractors and human interaction: Leading complex organizations through the use of metaphors. Compl Int J Compl Educ. 2005;2(1). http://soar.wichita.edu/handle/10057/6951.

Grobman GM. Complexity theory: a new way to look at organizational change. Public Admin Q. 2005;29(Fall):3 (ABI/INFORM Global).

Haken H. Information and self-organization: a macroscopic approach to complex systems. New York: Springer; 2006.

Harvey D. The condition of postmodernity: an enquiry into the origins of cultural change. Cambridge MA: Blackwell; 1990.

HBR. In: Reeves M, Levin S, Fink T, Levina A, editors. Taming complexity: make sure the benefits of any addition to an organization's systems outweigh its costs. https://hbr.org/2020/01/taming-complexity.

Head BW. Wicked problems in public policy. Public Policy. 2008;3(2):101–18. https://www.researchgate.net/publication/43502862_Wicked_Problems_in_Public_Policy.

Heitzman J. Network City: planning the information society in Bangalore. New Delhi: Oxford University Press; 2004.

Hemmert M. The Korean innovation system: from industrial catch-up to technological leadership? In: Mahlich J, Pascha W, editors. Innovation and technology in Korea: challenges of a newly advanced economy. Heidelberg: Physica; 2007.

Holmes BJ, Finegood DT, Riley BL, Best A. Systems thinking in dissemination and implementation research. In Brownson R, Colditz G, Proctor E, editors. Dissemination and implementation research in health: translating science to practice. Oxford: Oxford University Press; 2011.

Hoppe R. Institutional constraints and practical problems in deliberative and participatory policy making. Policy Polit. 2011;39(2):163–86. https://doi.org/10.1332/030557310X519650.

Huberman M, Lewchuk W. Globalization and worker welfare in late nineteenth century Europe. 1999.

IBM. Capitalizing on complexity: insights from the global chief executive officer study. 2010. https://www.ibm.com/downloads/cas/1VZV5X8J.

Infodev. International good practice for establishment of sustainable IT parks. In: Review of experiences in select countries, including three country case studies: Vietnam, Russia & Jordan. Washington infoDev/World Bank; 2008. http://www.infodev.org/publications.

Inna L, Svetlana B, Svetlana R. Impact government ICT strategy on India's growth. Int J Bus Manag Stud CD-ROM. 2015;04(02):145–56 (ISSN: 2158-1479). https://www.researchgate.net/publication/308596977.

International Institute for Sustainable Development (IISD) and the Energy and Resources Institute (TERI). Designing policies in a world of uncertainty, change, and surprise. 2006. https://www.iisd.org/system/files/publications/climate_designing_policies.pdf.

Ismail S, Malone MS, Y van G. No ordinary disruption: four global forces breaking all the trends. Diversion Books; 2014.

Jones H. Taking responsibility for complexity: how implementation can achieve results in the face of complex problems. Working Paper 330, Overseas Development Institute; 2011. https://www.odi.org/sites/odi.org.uk/files/odi-assets/publications-opinion-files/6485.pdf.

Kahne A. Transformative scenario planning. Collins; 2013.

Kapur K. The causes and consequences of India's IT boom. India Rev. 2002;2. Published by Frank Cass London. https://casi.sas.upenn.edu/files/bio/uploads.

Kauffman S. At home in the universe: the search for the laws of self organization and complexity. New York: Oxford University Press; 1995.

Kelly S, Allison M. The complexity advantage: how the science of complexity can help your business achieve peak performance. New York: McGraw-Hill; 1999.

Kirman A. Complex economics: individual and collective rationality. Routledge; 2011.

KPMG. Cutting through complexity. https://assets.kpmg/content/dam/kpmg/pdf/2011/03/KPMG-International-Annual-Review-2010.pdf; 2010.

Kuhmonen T. Exposing the attractors of evolving complex adaptive systems by utilizing futures images: milestones of the food sustainability journey. 2016. https://www.researchgate.net/publication/307557847.

Kurtz CF, Snowden D. The new dynamics of strategy: sense-making in a complex and complicated world. IBM Syst J. 2003;**42**(3).

Kushida K. A strategic overview of the silicon valley ecosystem: towards effectively harnessing silicon valley. SVNJ Working Paper 2015-6. 2015. https://fsi-live.s3.us-west-1.amazonaws.com/s3fs-public/strategic_overview_of_sv_ecosystems.pdf.

References

LeBaron B, Leigh T. Modeling macroeconomics as open-ended dynamic systems of interaction agent. Am Econ Rev Papers Proc. 2008;98(2):246–50. https://www2.econ.iastate.edu/tesfatsi/AERPP2008.LeBaronTesfatsion.ACEMacro.pdf.

Leonard TC. American economic reform in the progressive era: its foundational beliefs and their relation to eugenics. History Polit Econ. 2009;41:1.

Liedtka J, Azer D, Salzman R. Design thinking for the greater good—innovation in the social sector (Columbia Business School Publishing). Columbia University Press; 2017.

Lipsky M. Street-level bureaucracy: dilemmas of the individual in public services. New York: Russell Sage Foundation; 2010.

Lucas R. Econometric policy evaluation: a critique. In: Brunner K, Meltzer A, editors. Carnegie-Rochester conference series on public policy, vol. 1, issue 1. New York: American Elsevier; 1976. pp. 19–46.

Lunn P. Regulatory policy and behavioural economics. OECD Publishing; 2014.

Malhi L, Karanfil O, Merth T, Acheson M, Palmer A, Finegood DT. Places to intervene to make complex food systems more healthy, green, fair, and affordable. J Hunger Environ Nutr. 2009;4:466–76. https://doi.org/10.1080/19320240903346448.

Mason M. What is complexity theory and what are its implications for educational change? In: Educational philosophy and theory, special issue: complexity theory and education. vol.40, no.1. 2008.

McKelvey B. Managing coevolutionary dynamics: some leverage points. In: Presented at the 18th EGOS conference, Barcelona, 4–6 July. 2002. https://www.researchgate.net/publication/228559005.

Mckinsey. Cracking the complexity code. In: Heywood S, Spungin J, Turnbull D, editors. McKinsey quarterly. 2007.

Meadows DH, Wright D, editors. Thinking in systems: a primer. Chelsea Green Publishers; 2008.

Miles A. Complexity in medicine and healthcare: people and systems, theory and practice. J Eval Clin Pract. 2009;15:409–10.

Mitchell M. Complexity: a guided tour. Oxford: Oxford University Press; 2009.

Moore T. Wicked problems, rotten outcomes and clumsy solutions: children and families in a changing world. In: Paper presented at the NIFTey/CCCH Conference, Sydney. 2011. http://www.rch.org.au/emplibrary/ccch/NIFTeY_CCCH_Conference_11_-_paper.pdf.

Morcol G. A complexity theory for public policy routledge research in public administration and public policy. Routledge; 2012.

Morecroft JDW. System dynamics: portraying bounded rationality. Omega. 1983;11(2):131–42.

Mueller B. Why public policies fail: policymaking under complexity. Economi A. 2020;21(2). https://doi.org/10.1016/j.econ.2019.11.002.

Mumford E. Problems, knowledge, solutions: solving complex problems. J Strateg Inf Syst. 1998;7(4):255–69. https://doi.org/10.1016/S0963-8687(99)00003-7.

Nordtveit B. Complexity theory in development, center for International Education Faculty Publications, vol. 55. 2007. https://scholarworks.umass.edu/cie_faculty_pubs/55.

North DC. Institutions, institutional change and economic performance. Cambridge University Press; 1990.

North DC. The role of institutions in economic development. UNECE Discussion Papers Series No. 2003.2. 2003. https://www.unece.org/fileadmin/DAM/oes/disc_papers/ECE_DP_2003-2.pdf.

OECD. Behavioural insights and public policy: lessons from around the world, OECD Publishing, Paris; 2017a. https://doi.org/10.1787/9789264270480-en.

OECD. Debate the issues: complexity and policy making. OECD publications; 2017b. https://www.oecd.org/naec/complexity_and_policymaking.pdf.

OECD. Beyond growth: towards a new economic approach. SG/NAEC (2019)3; 2019. https://www.oecd.org/officialdocuments/publicdisplaydocumentpdf/?cote=SG/NAEC(2019)3&docLanguage=En.

Orios Venture Partners (OVP). The Indian Tech Unicorn Report 2021; 2021. https://www.oriosvp.com/the-india-tech-unicorn-report.

Osman FA. Public policy making: theories and their implications in developing countries. 2002. https://www.researchgate.net/publication/253836498_public_policy_making_theories_and_their_implications_in_developing_countries.

Palmberg K. Beyond process management: exploring organizational applications and complex adaptive systems. Luleå University of Technology, Universitetstryckeriet, Luleå; 2009a. https://www.diva-portal.org/smash/get/diva2:990992/FULLTEXT01.pdf.

Palmberg K. Complex adaptive systems: properties and approaches as metaphors for organizational management. Learn Organ. 2009b;16(6). https://doi.org/10.1108/09696470910993954.

Persson M. The dynamics of policy formation—making sense of public unsafety, vol. 36. Orebro Studies in Political Science; 2014.

Rajaraman V. History of computing in India 1955–2010, Bangalore: supercomputer education and research centre. Indian Institute of Science; 2012. www.cbi.umn.edu/hostedpublications/pdf/Rajaraman_HistComputingIndia.pdf.

Ramirez R, Wilkinson A. Strategic reframing: the Oxford scenario planning approach. Oxford: OUP; 2016.

Richardson K, editor. Managing organizational complexity: philosophy, theory and application. Information Age Publishing; 2005.

Richardson KA. On the limits of bottom-up computer simulation: towards a nonlinear modeling culture. In: Dennard L, Richardson KA, Morçöl G, editors. Complexity and policy analysis. Goodyear, ISCE Publishing; 2008.

Rodrik D. Institutions for high-quality growth: what they are and how to acquire them. Stud Comp Int Dev. 2000;35(3):3–31.

Rosenberg A. Darwinian reductionism: how to stop worrying and love molecular biology. University of Chicago Press; 2006.

Ryan A. Applications of complex systems to operational design. 2011. http://militaryepistemology.com/wp-content/uploads/2011/07/Ryan_Applications-of-Complex-Systems-to-Operational-Design_2011.pdf.

Sandelin J. The story of the Stanford industrial/research park. 2004. https://web.stanford.edu/group/OTL/documents/JSstanfordpark.pdf.

Sapir J. Thriving at the edge of chaos managing projects as complex adaptive systems. Productivity Press; 2020.

Sargent T. Lucas's critique. Macroeconomic theory. Orlando: Academic Press; 1987.

Savage GT, Nix TW, Whitehead CJ, Blair JD. Strategies for assessing and managing organizational stakeholders. Acad Manag Exec. 1991;5(2).

Saxenian A. The silicon valley connection: transnational networks and regional development. Taiwan, China and India chapter in India. In: D'Costa AP, Sridharan E, editors. The global software industry: innovation, firm strategies and development. Palgrave Macmillan; 2003.

Senge P. The fifth discipline: the art and practice of the learning organization. New York: Doubleday Currency; 1990.

Senge P, Sterman JD. Systems thinking and organizational learning: acting locally and thinking globally in the organization of the future. Eur J Oper Res. 1992;59:137–50.

Sharma DC. The outsourcer: the story of India's IT revolution. Massachusetts: MIT Press; 2015.

Simon HA. Models of man: social and rational. New York: John Wiley; 1957.

Simon HA. Organizations and markets. J Econ Perspec. 1991;5(2):1991.

Sjotun SG, Jakobsen S, Fløysand A. Expanding analyses of path creation: interconnections between territory and technology. Econ Geogr. 2020;96(3):266–88. https://doi.org/10.1080/00130095.2020.1756768.

Snowden D. Complex acts of knowing—paradox and descriptive self-awareness. Special Issue J Knowl Manag. 2002;6(2).

Sotarauta M, Srinivas S. Co-evolutionary policy processes: understanding innovative economies and future resilience. Science Direct Futures. 2006;38.

Stacey RD. Complexity and creativity in organizations. San Francisco: Berrett-Koehler; 1996.

Stacey RD. Complexity and management (complexity In organizations). Routledge; 2000.

References

Statista. Global app economy market size. 2021. https://www.statista.com/statistics/267209/global-app-economy/.

Sterman JD. Business dynamics: systems thinking and modelling for a complex world. Boston: Irwin & McGraw-Hil; 2000.

Stiglitz JE. Markets, market failures, and development. Am Econ Rev. 1989;79(2) (American Economic Association. Papers and proceedings of the hundred and first annual meeting of the American economic association (May)).

Stiglitz JE. Rewriting the rules of the American economy: an agenda for shared prosperity. Roosevelt Institute; 2015. https://rentgrabbing.files.wordpress.com/2015/06/dde39-rewritingtherulesreportfullreport-singlepagefinal.pdf.

Stone DA. Policy paradox: the art of political decision making. New York: Norton; 1997.

Sturgeon TJ. How silicon valley came to be. Published as chapter one. In: Kenney M, editor. Understanding silicon valley: anatomy of an entrepreneurial region. Stanford University Press; 2000. Downloads/SturgeonHowSiliconValleyCameToBe.pdf.

Sushil. System dynamics: a practical approach for managerial problems. Wiley Eastern Limited, New Delhi; 1993.

Svyantek DJ, Brown LL. A complex-systems approach to organizations. 2000. https://doi.org/10.1111/1467-8721.00063.

Swanson D, Bhadwal S, editors. Creating adaptive policies guide for policy-making in an uncertain world. Sage Publication; 2009.

Tapscott D, Williams A. Wikinomics: how mass collaboration changes everything. New York: Penguin Group; 2006.

Theodoulou ST, Roy RK. Public administration: a very short introduction. OUP Oxford; 2016.

Turner JR, Baker RM. Complexity theory: an overview with potential applications for the social sciences. 2019 Downloads/systems-07–00004%20(3).pdf.

Uhl-Bien M, Marion R, McKelvey B. Complexity leadership theory: shifting leadership from the industrial age to the knowledge era. Leadership Institute Faculty Publications. 2007. https://digitalcommons.unl.edu/leadershipfacpub/18.

UNCTAD. COVID-19 and e-commerce: a global review. 2021. https://news.un.org/en/story/2021/05/1091182.

Von Bertalanffy L. General System theory. revised. New York: George Braziller; 1973.

Wang J, Cheng S, Ganapati S. Path dependence in regional ICT innovation: differential evolution of Zhongguancun and Bangalore. Reg Sci Policy Pract. 2012;4(3):231–45. https://www.researchgate.net/publication/260278888.

Weberg D. Complexity leadership: a healthcare imperative. 2012. https://doi.org/10.1111/j.1744-6198.2012.00276.x.

WEF. 7 views on how technology will shape geopolitics. 2021. https://www.weforum.org/agenda/2021/04/seven-business-leaders-on-how-technology-will-shape-geopolitics/.

World Bank. In: Sánchez-Páramo C, Vakis R, Afif Z, editors. World bank blogs: behavioral science in public policy: future of government? 2019. http://blogs.worldbank.org/developmenttalk/behavioral-science-public-policy-future-government.

Zimmerman B, Lindberg C, Plsek P. A complexity science primer. Edgeware: Insights from Complexity Science for Health Care Leaders. VHA Inc.; 2001.

Chapter 6
Innovation in Public Policy and Policy Design Framework

We cannot solve our problems with the same thinking we used when we created them.
Albert Einstein, Nobel Laureate in Physics

Abstract While recognizing the essentiality of public policy in the context of emerging challenges, the chapter underscores the significance of the 'process' of policymaking. The process should encourage new ideas and stimulate informed discussion and decision-making. It stresses the policy design approach for dealing with large, critical, and complex problems. A good policy system should be attentive to micro-level insights, analysis-driven processes, systemic understanding, design focus, evidence-based approach, proper decision criteria, adaptive policies, and capacity building for policy management. It requires a shift from intuitive decision-making and a top-down approach. It recommends systems thinking, design thinking, complexity thinking, and innovative approaches to deal with complex problems. It suggests a robust policy design framework and science of policymaking. Emphasizing both qualitative and quantitative methods, it stresses analyses of institutional issues, behavioral factors, complexity dimension, and implementation mechanism, to gain insights into the problems and system. It presents a case study through the comprehensive application of the system approach, specifically interpretive structural modeling (ISM) and system dynamics (SD) for policy design.

Keywords Policy design · Innovative approaches · Systems thinking · Design thinking · Complexity thinking · System approach · Interpretive structural modeling · System dynamics · Renewable energy

The twenty-first century has brought to the fore many challenges of complex problems faced by the countries. The challenges range from providing basic public services to the last mile to mitigating poverty and hunger, rising unemployment, advanced technologies and the hyper-connected world, the concentration of advanced technologies in some corporations and countries, and growing inequalities. One specific challenge is the demographic shift toward the young population in developing countries and older people in developed countries. It is resulting in the problem of unemployment in Asian countries, especially in India, and the concerns of the rising government budget for welfare measures and State pensions in developed countries.

In addition, the increasing application of advanced technologies and rapid shift toward automation will bring the concentration of future industry, business, and employment in a few developed countries. It is likely to impact developing countries in an uncertain manner and may cause disruptions in existing industries and impact employment adversely. At the global level, such change is dynamic and uncertain. These pose challenges for policymakers (Deloitte 2016; WEF 2018). There is rising inequality in the world. For instance, in the USA, in the last decade, the income of the top 1% grew manifold compared to the rest. Similarly, in India, while benefitting from globalization, income inequality has risen, and India's top 1% has 73% of the total wealth. Such trends can potentially deny opportunities to a majority of people (Chancel and Piketty 2017; Piketty 2017, https://www.oxfam.org/en/india-extreme-inequality-numbers).

India is endowed with rich resources. Over the years, there have been many achievements in areas as diverse as agriculture with sufficient food grains production, handloom, and handicraft industry with a mark on exports, ICT software exports, vibrant automobile sector, and the space program, to name a few. Despite abundant resources and achievements, however, there are many problems related to quality education, assured health services, sanitation facilities, availability of food grains at the last mile, potable drinking water to households, per capita income of people, higher incidence of poverty in northern and eastern States, the adverse impact of climate change in many States, low human development index (HDI), and inadequate institutional capacity for facilitating business and industry (UNDP 2018; WEF 2018; World Bank 2019). Lack of technology readiness and R&D are other areas of concern. Such problems impact a large percentage of the population in the country in a significant way. In turn, due to the interlinked nature of the issues, the rest of the population is affected to varying degrees. These problems have persisted for several decades. What these problems signify is the inability of public policies in terms of both—policy formulation and implementation—to meet challenges. And it leads to key interlinked questions: what should be the process of policymaking that can address the concerns at the ground level, which analyses are needed for identifying suitable policy options, and how the policy design and implementation should factor in insights from the citizens.

Some key issues that require examination are:

- how policymaking can capture comprehensively the policy variables that influence the outcomes of a particular sector;
- how the feedback, nonlinearity, dynamic nature of variables, and causal relations can be comprehended during the policymaking; and
- which policy variables can make a significant impact on the outputs.

6.1 Understanding System: Key Thinking Modes

It is realized that policymaking is a multidimensional and complex matter, as underscored in detail in Chaps. 3 and 4. In the real world, the interactions between problems and factors in the system do not follow unidimensional and linear mathematical relationships (like $y = mx + c$) and first-order effect. Rather more than one dimension or one factor at a time may impact the system behavior. There are nonlinear relationships and higher-order effects, leading to more uncertainty and unpredictability of behavior. The nonlinearity may be due to mathematical relationships, including exponential, among variables (like $Y = ax^2$, or $Y = ax_1^2 + bx_2 + cx_3^2$); or nonlinear relationships resulting from multiple feedback loops. Some of the nonlinear relationships could be because of qualitative variables, which cannot be defined as an equation. Understanding such types of relationships is essential to examining interactions between factors and analyzing the system behavior.

For problem solving and managing organizations, there are two basic approaches—linear thinking and nonlinear thinking. Linear thinking has been a predominant approach for many management and public policy problems (Gentner and Stevens 1983; Doyle and Ford 1998). Driven by data, analytical approach, and logical thinking, it follows a series of sequential steps, beginning with data analysis, identifying issues, defining problems, and working on solutions based on previous experience. The underlying premise of the thinking is 'A' results in 'B', which results in 'C', based on a structured approach. Or, to achieve an objective, one goes from event X to event Y and then to Z in a sequence.

Linear thinkers apply rules, formulae, or patterns based on past learnings from one set of problems to another to analyze and solve problems, giving the same logic of previous problem solving. From the system perspective, linear thinking is based on a reductionist approach, in which the attempt is made to break the problem into small parts or tasks, which are more understandable and manageable by using previous experience or standard practices (Senge 1990; Forrester 1971; Savigny and Adam 2009; Swanson and Bhadwal 2009). Such thinking has good value when dealing with known or pre-tested problems, where structured process-driven analysis and implementation are feasible. For example, in the health sector, once the solutions and process of addressing some health problems are known and standardized, the procedure can be applied for implementation to achieve the desired results. Similarly, in a particular industry, after the design of a product is tested, validated, and standardized, the processes can be designed and streamlined to deliver products to consumers. In the policymaking context, often based on previous experience and learning, a linear approach is applied by following a process that is objective and pre-defined, involving steps from the beginning until the final document is developed. It is focused on results and follows well-established rules and procedures (Gentner and Stevens 1983; Senge 1990; Doyle and Ford 1998; Liedtka 2013).

But, as a complex process in the social system, policymaking may find such an approach inappropriate, as many unknown issues or unexamined relationships between variables emerge while attempting policy analysis or during policy implementation. And so, it will demand revisiting the previous steps or examining other unforeseen issues. Ignoring such policy variables or issues may cause future difficulties at the implementation level.

For example, the right to education (RTE) policy in India, which relied mainly on the right to access for all children, did not adequately factor in the socio-economic and cultural issues of families and communities and the need for quality teaching. As a result, it did not yield the expected learning outcomes for the children (PISA 2012; ASER 2016). It was based on the assumption that once access to school is provided to children, learning levels will improve. Thus relying on linear thinking without examining the interrelationships between policy variables is an example of how linear thinking may not work for policymaking. Under the conditions of the complex system, the linear thinking approach with previously defined set rules or logic may not be suitable. For dealing with problems in the socio-economic systems, a different approach is necessitated.

In contrast to linear thinking, a nonlinear thinking approach uses ways to understand the problem afresh without prejudice or preconceived ideas. It tries to examine the problem from multiple directions by collecting varied ideas and studying possible relationships between factors from different perspectives. It relies on divergent possibilities rather than just one solution. It integrates the analyses and puts forth the conclusions. Nonlinear thinking is a creative process. It considers analogies and draws inferences from different, sometimes disconnected, concepts or ideas. It does not follow a structured or sequential process, and the relationships within a system cannot be arranged along a simple straight line or input–output line. It will require understanding the relationships of interacting elements and feedback loops (Senge 1990; Bankes 2002; Savigny and Adam 2009; Swanson and Bhadwal 2009; Liedtka 2013). For example, while examining the problems, many new ideas may come to the surface. By understanding these ideas, better insights can be drawn. It may require following an iterative process. It may include exploring ideas such as understanding social behavior, emotional issues, and socio-cultural values, which influence individuals to make decisions and act depending upon the context. For such an approach, every problem is original, and efforts are made to explore better insights to understand the issues and find solutions.

Complex problems or systems demand a nonlinear approach. It requires understanding problems and solving them through diverse lenses. Suppose the requisite examination is not done. In that case, many issues that citizens face may remain unnoticed, or the public services that have interlinkages with other services or programs may remain unexplored. Thus, the system may work at a sub-optimal level. It demands that the problem or system can only be understood or defined by examining them from multiple ways—different thinking modes. And some of them are: systems thinking, design thinking, critical thinking, divergent thinking, strategic thinking, and complexity thinking. The diverse forms of thinking modes have their distinct characteristics. These have unique features and need to be suitably applied

6.1 Understanding System: Key Thinking Modes

at various stages during the policymaking process to have a correct and comprehensive assessment and better insights. Each of these modes can provide perspectives for understanding problems and then analyzing and identifying the solutions. And collectively, they can complement each other.

6.1.1 Systems Thinking

Systems thinking is about understanding holistically system components and the elements therein, their characteristics, and interrelationships with cause-effects and system behavior. In the context of a larger system or macro level, it is about understanding how different systems interact, influence each other, and maintain equilibrium at a given time. For example, an ecological system in which human beings, animals, plants, water, soil, and the atmosphere work together. Likewise, the social system has social institutions, political groups, economic institutions, and political institutions that interact with each other and determine the behavior of the system. Understanding each component and the interactions between components are essential to comprehend the system.

At the philosophical level, systems thinking is about 'thinking' about the system and its constituent components or elements, the behavior of system, its impact on stakeholders, and its relationship with the environment in both space and time. For a higher level of conceptualization, systems thinking is essential. It entails examining: the results and impact of the system, the pattern of behavior over time, issues and problems, components and elements, structures and processes, and the system environment (Fig. 6.1) (Senge 1990; Savigny and Adam 2009; Richmond 2010).

Fig. 6.1 Hierarchy of system conceptualization. *Source* Senge (1990), Richardson (1996), Richmond (2010), and own analysis

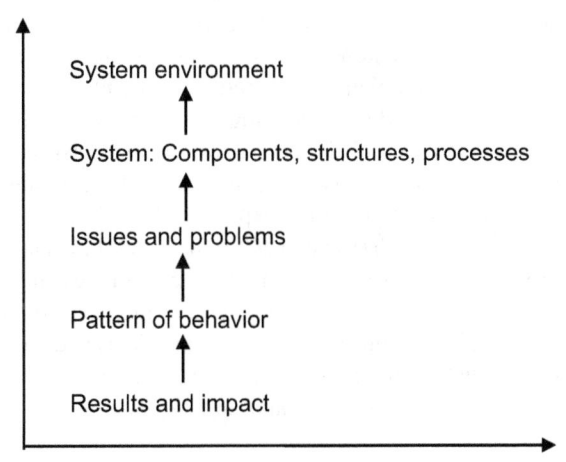

Systems thinking works to reveal the underlying characteristics of the system and relationships between components or elements within the system. It is not just about understanding individual components or elements but their features and interactions. In addition, the issues and causes involved in the system need to be examined holistically. Some challenging problems facing the world or society are essentially system failures. For example, social problems, managing economy and unemployment, environmental degradation, poverty, and climate change are a result of multiple policy or governance deficiencies, which cannot be solved by observing symptoms in isolation of many interlinked causes (Swanson and Bhadwal 2009; Richmond 2010; Ramos et al. 2019). Such systems display nonlinear, unpredictable, and dynamic behavior, and the problems require systemic understanding. It explores issues from a system perspective by examining interconnected elements and cause-and-effects by taking insights from the lens of diverse stakeholders. It encourages learning and works on system-wide planning, implementation, and evaluation.

Systems thinking is helpful where the analysis demands understanding the big picture or complete knowledge of the system; when problems keep on recurring without obvious solutions; if the system has a large number of components and numerous elements or agents therein, and when behavioral and psychological factors influence their interrelationships; if environment keeps changing or system influences the environment; or when the solutions for addressing the problems are multiple, with little clarity. In a way, systems thinking is called for when the system reaches a complicated or complex state (Checkland 1981; Gharajedaghi 2006; Ryan 2008).

6.1.2 Design Thinking

There are certain problems related to culture, behavior, or emotions that cannot be discerned by traditional methods of inquiry. For such problems, the solutions are not apparent, and the conventional approaches may not provide the desired solution. Such problems may require probing the underlying assumptions and exploring new ideas to define the problems and identify acceptable alternative solutions. For addressing such problems, design thinking is a process that involves understanding the end-users or affected stakeholders; questioning the assumptions, problems, and solutions to reach the root causes—social, cultural, economic, behavioral, or emotional—of the problems; and then exploring the solutions through iterations in a human-centered approach (Liedtka 2013). It is useful in handling poorly defined or complex problems. It is a way of thinking and practice involving steps like empathizing, defining, ideating, prototyping, and testing (Nelson and Stoiterman 2012; Liedtka et al. 2017). The purpose is to solve problems and address unmet needs by searching for alternative possibilities. It has applications for bringing behavioral practices in health and sanitation programs and introducing new teaching methods, for example.

6.1.3 Critical Thinking

For complex problem solving, critical thinking is about eliciting insights from stakeholders, doing objective analysis, and using research findings. It is based on a reasoned approach. It is to make informed decisions for defining problems and identifying options. It involves creativity, analyzing multiple dimensions from multiple perspectives, problem solving skills, and empathy for interacting with stakeholders to elicit nuanced insights. It utilizes observation, experience, reflection, and sound reasoning. It considers the depth and breadth of issues. In addition, working with an open mind, it entails examining assumptions, empirical basis, likely implications and consequences of decisions, alternative viewpoints and options, and synthesizing to provide a coherent and holistic view (Facione 1984; Chubinski 1996; Elder and Paul 1997).

6.1.4 Divergent Thinking

During policymaking, understanding problems, setting agenda, and identifying policy options require multiple perspectives from stakeholders. To achieve the objective of generating different viewpoints, divergent thinking is needed. It can help in creating varied ideas for understanding and analyzing problems. It particularly assumes importance when the problem is big, complicated, or complex and when problem definition and identification of the solution are difficult with only an analytical approach. After arriving at multiple ideas and possible solutions, convergent thinking can be applied to arrive at an appropriate solution using logic (Khandwalla 2005; Fobes and Reed 2014).

6.1.5 Strategic Thinking

Pursuing bigger opportunities and taking a competitive advantage are the primary tasks of governments, organizations, and businesses. It requires the ability to visualize the future and draw a long-term strategic plan. Strategic thinking is a process to achieve such an objective. It is an intentional and analytical process that examines critical factors, past trends, emerging trends, likely risks, external threats, and vulnerabilities in the changing environment. It clearly defines a set of goals and develops plans. It considers socio-economic conditions, innovation and technology, market forces, available resources, likely investment, and the international policy environment. It requires deep research, systems thinking, problem solving ability, and leadership skills (Bonn 2001; Wootton and Horne 2001; Abraham 2005). For the public system, it can be applied to policies on innovation and R&D, technology competitiveness, infrastructure development, energy management, climate change plans, and so on. For business and industry, strategic thinking is essential for leaders to remain competitive. But in the context of rising complexity, the strategic choices will have to factor in uncertainty and the dynamic nature of the environment.

6.1.6 Complexity Thinking

In simple terms, complexity theory is a way of understanding how a social system, an organization, or an economic entity works and behaves in the real world over time by understanding various phenomena of complexity. It attempts to understand the relationships between elements and parts through an iterative process and to synthesize ideas and knowledge from different disciplines (Rogers et al. 2013; Sherblom 2017; Hager and Beckett 2019). While recognizing the emerging, adaptive, and evolving nature of social systems, economy, and organizations, complexity thinking attempts to look beyond linear, first-order effect, bounded, logical, and analytical approaches. It prefers a process of continual engagement, learning, and Adaptation. It accentuates the evolutionary potential of the system and strives to find what can be changed in a particular direction to achieve a broad objective, but without any exact final goal or output in mind. Complexity thinking is increasingly applied in various fields, including social science, public policy, economy, organizations, business, and industry (Capra 1996; Blignaut 2013; Byrne and Callaghan 2014; Palmer et al. 2015).

Systems thinking versus complexity thinking. Both systems thinking and complexity thinking are uniquely positioned to provide scope for studying, analyzing, and exploring solutions for the twenty-first century problems. Both have the potential to contribute to an improved understanding of problems or systems and facilitate the better formulation of policies for the economy, social problems, business, and industry. At the fundamental level, both stress understanding interacting parts, nonlinearity, dynamic nature, and conceptualizing the 'whole' of the system, but subtle differences differentiate the two modes of thinking.

Systems thinking focuses on the whole picture of a problem, system, or organization. It examines the interactions and causal relationships between elements holistically, defines the objectives for the future state, and then presents the solution as a series of steps in a sequential manner. It examines the complexity and brings a certain level of simplicity to the complex problem to manage the system or problem. It works on prior expert knowledge of similar issues. Such an approach is helpful in complicated systems or systems with manageable complexity. For example, understanding solutions over time for known health problems, distributions of inputs and technology transfer for agriculture, and management of marketing of crop production, based on prior knowledge and experience of the known problems (Ryan 2008; Richmond 2010; Ramos et al. 2019).

While recognizing the uncertainty and evolutionary nature, complexity thinking views deeper into the properties of elements of the system and interactions between

6.1 Understanding System: Key Thinking Modes

Table 6.1 Summary of different modes of thinking

S. No.	Thinking mode	Attributes		
		Key attributes	Mindset to study	Application areas
1.	Systems thinking	Holistic or system-wide view	Holistic view of system and interactions with environment	Health system design, educational institutions study, industrial unit design, etc
2.	Design thinking	Understanding complex problems and solving them	Probing for gaining insights. Empathy and learning by experimenting through iteration and human-centered approach. Understanding behavioral, emotional, and psychological issues	For dealing with big and complex problems like developing industrial supply chain and agriculture marketing system. Specific problems of beneficiaries related to behavioral change (health problems, sanitation)
3.	Critical thinking	Probing the underlying causes	Rationality and deeper analysis	Problem of improving quality teaching in schools. Understanding complex problems. Analyses for climate change, unemployment, improving public service delivery, cultural dimension in health services, etc
4.	Divergent thinking	Creative problem solving	Diverse ideas for a particular problem	Establishment of industrial parks
5.	Strategic thinking	Foresight to create a competitive advantage	Unique insights about the system (or business)	Renewable energy plan, R&D, technology competitiveness, etc
6.	Complexity thinking	Holistic view of interacting elements and their evolution	Reflection on evolving nature and patterns, synthesizing different activities	Climate change problems, economy, urban management, industrial clusters, innovation and disruptions, etc

elements, in addition to the characteristics and behavior of the whole system. It attempts to identify the fuzzy context and environment, unravel hidden structures, explore invisible cultural and behavioral issues, and study patterns and evolving nature. It tends to consider uncertainty and the underlying issues that cannot be known fully. It is difficult to predict the results due to the uncertain nature. Due to uncertainty in cause-effect relationships, it requires moving back and forth multiple times before clarity emerges. It acknowledges that complexity arises due to social, political, economic, and cultural factors in the public system. It believes in the evolutionary nature and generates multiple perspectives about the system's behavior, and works through an incremental approach (Gharajedaghi 2011; Blignaut 2013; Sherblom 2017; Hager and Beckett 2019).

Finally, for sound policymaking, it underscores that during the policy cycle—policy formulation, planning, policy implementation, and evaluation—these different modes of thinking can be utilized to get a comprehensive perspective (see Table 6.1). As for policy formulation, these different modes of thinking can be suitably applied for 'understanding problem', 'policy analysis', and 'decision-making'. The problem can be better understood by gaining insights from stakeholders and by the right system conceptualization. Likewise, the policy analysis can be better attempted by examining issues and different options from multiple perspectives.

6.2 Innovative Approaches

There is growing pressure on governments to respond to emerging trends and address various National and global problems accentuated by climate change, changes in demographics, rapid usage of information technology, disruption of industries by advanced technologies, cyber security, increased pressure on urban services, etc. There are opportunities and uncertainties simultaneously. The emerging issues in the public system underscore the need to change from the present policy system dealing with the 'static state' of development to a flexible and adaptive approach of policy-making to understand dynamic problems, design policies to meet new challenges, and manage the implementation in an evolving world. As an answer to both growing problems Nationally and globally and the necessity of improving the performance of policy implementation, innovative approaches are seen as imperative in meeting challenges of understanding grassroots problems, complexity, and the twenty-first century requirements (Geurts 2010; Christiansen and Bunt 2012).

Innovative approaches are beyond conventional methods and ways of thinking. Together with different modes of thinking, covered in Sect. 6.1, these can provide insights about policymaking and implementation in social and economic sectors, and some specific application areas are as follows:

- *stakeholders' needs analysis*: for household sanitation, enrollment for primary education in remote and socio-economic backward areas; people affected by climate change; micro, small and medium enterprises (MSMEs); advanced manufacturing technology (AMT);
- *understanding problem*: by gaining insights from the stakeholders and a better understanding of the system;
- *analyzing complexity*: by examining development issues, variables including behavioral and psychological aspects, interactions between elements, uncertainty, history of previous interventions and their impact, dynamic nature, and institutional factors;

- *system conceptualization*: by studying elements, subsystems, stakeholders, causal relationships, and feedback loops (including system analysis, complexity analysis, and institutional analysis);
- *learning about special concerns*: like tribals development priorities, old-aged citizens, critical health issues, crime addicts, etc.;
- *specific purpose*: addressing behavioral and psychological issues, complicated or complex system issues in the global supply chain, etc.;
- *policy analysis, decision-making, and policy formulation*: identifying policy options from multiple perspectives; and
- *policy implementation*: complexity in implementation—behavioral, institutional, and operational issues.

6.2.1 Creative Problem Solving (CPS)

For solving difficult, challenging, and complex problems, the creative problem-solving (CPS) approach offers a process and method to find new perspectives, which are not easily perceptible. It helps in defining the problems, exploring various options for solutions, and identifying opportunities and solutions by harnessing the creative ability of people imaginatively and innovatively (Isaksen and Treffinger 1985; Basadur et al. 1999).

CPS combines both divergent and convergent thinking and can be helpful for simple, complicated, and complex problems. Divergent thinking goes beyond linear thinking and consists of exploring multiple new ideas, including novel, imaginative, and off-beat. Simultaneously, it attempts to research potential solutions and possibilities. In contrast, convergent thinking applies logic and criteria. And from a set of ideas and solutions, it selects, evaluates, revises, improves, and then provides a workable idea and solution (Khandwalla 2005; Fobes and Reed 2014). CPS tools like failure mode and effect analysis (FMEA), fishbone diagram, and business process reengineering (BPR) are mainly helpful for known problems. The brainstorming, nominal group technique (NGT), Delphi method, synectics, and scenario building can be applied to challenging and complex issues.

6.2.2 Creative Citizen Engagement

It is about how the citizens or stakeholders can be engaged in a creative manner and for creative contributions in the development process—both policymaking and implementation that can make a qualitative difference. To deal with difficult and complex problems, which are dynamic in nature and uncertain, the engagement with citizens is imperative. Besides face-to-face consultations with the citizens, they can be engaged creatively through crowdsourcing, structured feedback, social media, and social networking. Citizen engagement is context-specific, and for meaningful engagement, the service agencies need to be better listeners and develop abilities to engage citizens (Davies et al. 2012; WBG 2014; Preston et al. 2020). Their engagement can be utilized for gaining insights about the problems and development issues, understanding problems from the perspective of citizens, and taking their contribution to collaborative efforts, including co-design and co-production.

Working together can make a difference in the life of the community. It can help governments achieve improved public service delivery, better development outcomes, social inclusion, and empowerment. More specifically, the engagement can help in better grievance redressal mechanism by actionable feedback; in decision-making for policy formulation, implementation, monitoring, and evaluation through grassroots-level insights; and in taking community contributions—both financial and non-financial—in the development projects. In order to be successful in engaging citizens, government departments would be required to enhance their institutional capacity to reach out to citizens; and raise the capabilities of their personnel to be able to engage with citizens first and then provide a platform for citizens to engage and contribute in the development process.

6.2.3 Deliberative Dialogue

This approach is about a deliberate and purposive way of discussing with people in a group to share and exchange ideas and opinions on issues of public interest, especially complex cases. It is based on the premise that ordinary people have a basic understanding and wisdom to participate in reasoned discussions on issues concerning the community or country. Its objective is to inform the policymaking process from the perspective of diverse stakeholders. It has been applied in public policy for many years (Kingston 2005; Boyko et al. 2014; London 2021). By understanding diverse views and perspectives from people through interactions in a deliberative manner, it is helpful to understand the problems better, explore potential solutions, weigh options, and contribute to policymaking. It can help in knowing the priority of the stakeholders and society for a specific problem, making recommendations to policymakers on a broad range of policy options, and understanding stakeholders' values. It can help in getting a sense of priorities and ideas for informed decision-making (Culyer and Lomas 2006; Kerkhof 2006; Proden 2015).

6.2.4 Creating Adaptive Policies

It is well articulated by scholarly research work by several scholars and research institutions that the socio-economic systems are marked with nonlinear interactions between elements within the system, dynamic behavior, and uncertainty (Brinkerhoff and Crosby 2002; Swanson and Bhadwal 2009). Due to these characteristics, the system cannot be managed with static (nature of) policies. As a result of the influence

6.2 Innovative Approaches   295

of the external environment, which could be because of climate change, new technologies, or international treaties, the policies need to adjust and adapt to new conditions. Within a country, on account of internal pressure from demographic changes, rising unemployment, increasing inequality, the necessity of providing quality public services, deterioration of the environment, increased pollution, etc., the policies need to be modified to conform to the policy requirements of new conditions (IISD and TERI 2006).

In addition, during the policy implementation, there may be a positive or negative impact on the environment, socio-cultural lives of people, business environment, setting up of industrial and business units, the efficiency of transactions, and productivity of output (Holling 1978; Walker et al. 2001; Sotarauta and Srinivas 2006; Allan and Stankey 2009). For example, with the emergence of new technologies and innovation, new forms of businesses will require new investment policies and institutional support for starting new businesses. Likewise, for integrating with the global supply chain for exports, many policy changes may be needed as per trade agreements and changes in the trade policies of different countries. There is a likelihood of questions such as how the people or entrepreneurs will respond to the new interventions, how the economic lives will improve, whether there will be negative externality, whether the intended objectives can be achieved, and if not realized, what is the available remedy, and so on. Many emerging features and questions cannot be fully anticipated in advance. For these reasons, the public policies need to be adaptive, implying that the policies need to undergo change as the feedback is received from the stakeholders during the implementation process. The challenge is how the policy system can acquire knowledge, learn from the feedback, and introduce corrective measures in time.

6.2.5 Innovative Indicators

Data and evidence are critical to the success of policymaking. In this context, when used properly, the underpinning of indicators is essential during policy analysis. These add value to raw data by converting them into usable information for decision-making. But their innovative usage can add more value. Appropriate indicators could be helpful in conveying knowledge and insights about various issues. They can be utilized in all fields, from the social sector to economics to ecology to health, and can be used at the global, National, State, and local levels. Specifically, these can provide an understanding of socio-economic conditions, trends using the time-series data, and inter-indicator relationships. These can stimulate ideas and creative discussion and provide inputs for multicriteria decision-making. Another way of using indicators is to develop a composite index to provide a comprehensive view of a given state in the system and to understand the combined effect of constitutive elements (WHO 2002; Pichon et al. 2021).

Innovative indicators (InIs). The importance of indicators is well-recognized in decision-making. The indicators are required to provide new ideas and insights about the problems, process, or project implementation. Such indicators can be defined as innovative indicators (InIs). Such InIs, among others, can be useful in *first*, tracking the problem areas and identifying root causes, *second*, uncovering hidden problems or potential, and *third*, deciphering or making sense of complex issues. Some of the innovative indicators are illustrated below:

i. *For key activities within a process (for public services)*. Time and cost in availing the services for key activities; process efficiency in the delivery of services to citizens, business service transaction, or setting up of the enterprises; timelines for project cycle: time taken in finalizing the feasibility report, in sanction of projects, in the placement of work order, in releasing the money for the execution of the work, and for the completion of work; and, timelines for loan cycle—time in the collection of application, sanction of loans to beneficiaries, and the time in the disbursement of the loan.

ii. *For policymaking*. Availability of time-series data; availability of grassroots-level insights through independent research, comparative indicators for different districts, States, or countries.

iii. *For implementation*. Availability of manpower in government agencies per ten thousand, one lakh population, or hundred villages; availability of health manpower per hundred cases or within five kilometers; dominant beliefs or values within target population covered under various programs; status of implementation of projects at various stages; and the status of the frequent occurrence of certain problems during implementation.

iv. *For performance indicators for health services*. How many critical maternity cases are registered; how many such cases are attended to on a daily and weekly basis; how many referral cases for maternity cases are followed; how many critical cases are attended to in time by providing timely ambulance services and ensuring visits by health staff; how many cases are attended to in time during odd hours; and how many critical postnatal cases are followed for health check-up of babies on a daily or weekly basis.

Such is an illustrative list of specific indicators, which can be developed for many sectors and helpful in examining deeper issues and providing specific inputs for decision-making. The policymaking needs to take into account both micro- and macro-level indicators. It needs to keep an eye on the big picture or have a bird's eye view of the situation to have an overall understanding at the National and global levels. Simultaneously, it requires viewing micro-details or having a ring-side view of the situation to recognize the pattern or changes at the grassroots-level by being close to the people. It will demand working on collecting and collating data at the local, State, National, and international levels.

6.2.6 Policy Design

Policy design is an innovative way of formulating policies. It is different from the traditional policy approach mainly in three ways. *Firstly*, the policy design begins with citizens or end-users in mind and relies on the insights received from them. S*econdly*, the process involves fresh thinking without any prejudice, goes beyond what is known or what exists, and challenges all the existing assumptions and instruments of policy. And *thirdly*, what new can be explored as a solution to meet the concerns of citizens. It tries to systematically develop policies using critical inquiry, logic, and foresight in a specific context (Schneider and Ingram 1997; Howlett 2019). It weighs different alternatives and takes inputs from citizens or end-users to arrive at a conclusion. The policy is designed through a process of conscious learning and iterations (Koppenjan 2012; Peters, 2019). It is not a problem solving exercise but about the attitude to explore new ideas and nuanced differentiation and fine-tune the policy instruments to match the social, economic, technological, and emotional needs. It relies on systems thinking, design thinking, and divergent thinking.

The application areas of policy design are varied and include examples like policies for climate change in a fragile environment, cultural development issues of tribals, educational needs of vulnerable groups, household industries, agriculture in water-stress areas, setting up industrial parks for special needs of a particular sector like garments-making or startups in innovation hubs, and so on.

6.3 System Approach

In the real world, due to resource constraints, governments are in want of the requisite manpower, capabilities, and capacity to have an analytical and evidence-based approach. Moreover, public policymaking takes place under various pressure situations arising out of political expediency, demands from interest groups, social unrest, international treaties, or emerging political scenarios. Under usual and more so under pressure conditions, the policymakers rely on intuitive thinking or mental models. These models have been the main approach to policymaking and traditional management, as individuals tend to interact with problems through them.

Mental model. A mental model represents a thought process and is a representation of events or activities. Based on the intuitive perception of individuals, it can be construed as a mental image or mental frame of reference about the relationships between various issues and entities and their consequences. The mental models inform the basic understanding of the world. Models shape what one thinks and how one understands and defines constraints and opportunities. They tend to simplify big or complex situations by taking more simple and relevant issues to make problems understandable and recognizable. They can work on multiple fronts and provide broad understanding (Gentner and Stevens 1983; Senge and Sterman 1992; Mohapatra et al. 1994).

The main disadvantage of using mental data for building a model is the likelihood of errors and biases due to unreasoned information processing in mind, unjustifiable assumptions, overconfidence, and barriers to learning new ideas. The description of causation is generally represented linearly and is suitable for first-order effects. Besides, if the realistic view is taken, there can be multiple relations between system variables, but mental comprehension of them is limited. They differ from person to person, depending upon their education, skills, and experience, and thus cannot be uniformly applied. They may change with time. Due to these reasons, the models have limitations in social and economic systems (Senge and Sterman 1992; Kelly 1998; Serdar 2001).

Limitations of mental models in policymaking. The studies have highlighted the limitations of present policymaking through mental models. These fail to capture higher-order effects in the system, complex issues, and nonlinearities and feedback about relationships between factors in the system (Serdar 2001; Fuentes 2006). The linkages between factors using the mental model are based on oversimplified understanding, which is inappropriate for dealing with structures of complex systems marked with nonlinear relations, multiple loops, and feedback structures. Mental models cannot take into account all the elements of a system and capture its dynamic nature. The dependence on intuitive solutions to social and economic problems has been ineffective for development policies (Forrester 1968; Doyle and Ford 1998). The intuitive solutions may lead to erroneous results and are likely to have adverse implications for good policymaking (Gentner and Stevens 1983; Bier 2011).

System approach. Realizing the limitations of mental models and reductionist approach, a more robust approach was conceived in the 1960s for policymaking by applying the understanding based on systems theory. In response to the ever-increasing complexity in the social, economic, technical, government, and managerial systems, the system philosophy evolved, and system concepts and methodologies were developed. The system approach is a result of such a process of evolution. It provides a perspective that any problem should be examined keeping in view the whole system (Gigch 1974; Kelly 1998).

It puts forward viewpoints like *holism*, meaning that all the parts or subsystems are to be considered, and *synergy*, implying that the system's output is greater than the sum of each subsystem's output. Thus, the decisions or actions in one subsystem affect other subsystems, which in turn impact the whole system behavior. A system approach supports learning about the system and focuses on the system rather than the individual elements or subsystems (or parts). The interdependence between elements within subsystems is a vital aspect that should be considered. Such an approach can be applied to the policymaking cycle, an organization, an economic analysis, a business, and an industry.

There are some phenomena and concepts that are defined by the approach. Change is an inevitable phenomenon. It may be endogenetic, which emerges from within, and exogenetic, which flows from the outside environment. The system strives to adapt and attain equilibrium. It has a spontaneous reaction to rectify the imbalance and has a natural propensity to attain equilibrium. From the point of view of entropy, the system approach assumes dynamic equilibrium to achieve a state of negative entropy or more order, which implies integration. Entropy in the context of a system is like a degree of disorder or uncertainty. If the degree of disorder is high or entropy rises, the system lacks sustainability or an ordered state. A system that is unable to reach the state of equilibrium will result in positive entropy (Theil 1967; Bailey 1990). In addition, the system approach puts forward two concepts, *homeostasis,* which means the inclination of a system to reach a new state of equilibrium, and *equifinality,* which implies that in open systems, the end state can be reached through multiple ways. It underscores that the system tends toward homeostasis and equifinality (Bertalanffy 1968; Lindsay and Norman 1977; Stuart 2011). In sum, the system approach recognizes the following five features:

- a system consists of interacting subsystems (or parts) and elements within each subsystem, and the subsystems are interdependent, and together they represent a unified whole;
- a system has a boundary and outside environment, which interacts with the subsystems and elements therein;
- the system should be examined by studying the interrelationships between subsystems and not in isolation from each other;
- a system receives information, resources, and energy from the environment or other systems as inputs; and
- the system has a dynamic nature and responds to its environment, undergoes change and adapts to change, and maintains an equilibrium state.

From the operational point of view, for any system, the system approach envisages five components: *first,* inputs, from within and outside environment, like resources, capital, manpower, information, and knowledge; *second,* process to transform; *third,* output; *fourth,* feedback; and *fifth,* exchange of output with the environment.

6.3.1 Interpretive Structural Modeling (ISM)

During the 1960s, it was realized by scholars that unclear and poorly articulated mental models have limitations in dealing with complex problems. The studies (Warfield 1974; Sage 1977; Chidambaranathan et al. 2010) have indicated the limitations of diagnosing the factors (variables) independently without examining the interrelationship. Thus, as a result, the holistic view has been missing in the analyses. Identifying the structure of interlinked elements within a system is of great value in dealing effectively with problems and for better decision-making.

As a part of the application of the system approach, interpretive structural modeling (ISM) was evolved to depict the relationships between elements or factors that determine the system behavior. ISM is defined as a process that transforms fuzzy linkages between elements or factors as a visible structure in a large and complex system for conceptualizing the problem and system and then for policy decisions. It is helpful for large and complex systems.

ISM methodology is utilized to understand the mutual influences between different factors, in contrast with diagnosing the factors independently, as independent examination leads to a lack of system-wide understanding of the factors that influence the system. The methodology can facilitate a better understanding of the interlinkages between factors so that those driving factors, which can affect other factors, and those most influenced by driving factors, are identified. By analyzing the factors using this model, crucial factors can be extracted, which influence the success of the system (Singh et al. 2003; Luthra et al. 2011). The experts believe that ISM is about applying graph theory to construct a hierarchical model out of the complex contextual relationships between multiple factors or elements. In other words, it helps to identify structure within a system of related elements. ISM is a process that helps a group of stakeholders structure their collective knowledge (Warfield 1974; Sage, 1977). It can be used for identifying and summarizing relationships between factors that define a problem or an issue. It provides a means by which an order can be imposed on the relationships of such variables (Sushil, 2005; Saxena and Sushil 2006; Mudgal et al. 2010). It helps in getting insights about the system. Otherwise, it is difficult to comprehend (Mandal and Deshmukh 1994). ISM has been successfully applied to various contexts ranging from education to the energy sector, the computer industry, marketing, etc.

Key advantages of ISM. It is essential to employ ISM methodology that effectively captures and synthesizes stakeholders' or practitioners' viewpoints. From a practical perspective, this approach is helpful as it is context-specific or takes into account the local conditions. It can be replicated effectively by researchers in other contexts with suitable alterations. By using ISM, it has been able to focus on the concerns of stakeholders, provide real value to policymakers, and apply balanced pragmatic and academic inputs (Benbasat and Zmud, 1999). The factors may vary from system to system, but the ISM approach can be applied by considering context and local problems. The results developed using the conceptual ISM model can provide inputs for designing and implementing policies. An examination of the direct and indirect relationships between factors can give a clearer view of the problem than considering individual factors alone in isolation, without linkages. The ISM can be judiciously employed to get better insights from the system under consideration (Chidambaranathan et al. 2010; Mudgal et al. 2010; Sahney 2008).

To sum up, the ISM methodology tries to diagnose holistically the factors that are crucial for the success of the system, to understand the mutual impacts between different factors, to rank the factors of the system, to develop a hierarchy-based model of the factors, and to draw policy conclusions by identifying drivers for the improvement of the system.

Methodology of ISM. The ISM methodology is interpretive from the fact that the feedback of the group members decides whether and how the factors are related. It is structural, as on the basis of relationships between factors, an overall structure is extracted from a set of factors (Warfield 1974; Sage 1977). Broadly ISM entails three steps. *First*, it begins with the identification of a problem or an issue; *second*, it identifies the factors that reflect the specific context in which the problem lies;

and *third*, it compares pairs of factors graphically or in a relation matrix, using a contextual relationship. The steps involved in the ISM methodology are summarized as follows (Singh et al. 2003; Sushil 2005; Sahney 2008; Luthra et al. 2011; Gupta 2012):

- *Step 1*: factors affecting the system under consideration are listed, which can be objectives, actionable points, institutions, etc., and the definitions of factors are prepared.
- *Step 2*: from the factors identified in step 1, a contextual relationship is established between factors for which the pairs of factors will be examined.
- *Step 3*: a structural self-interaction matrix (SSIM) is developed for factors, which indicates pair-wise relationships between factors under consideration.
- *Step 4*: reachability matrix is developed from the SSIM, and the matrix is checked for transitivity. The transitivity of the contextual relation is a basic assumption made in ISM. It states that if a factor X is related to Y and Y is related to Z, X necessarily related to Z.
- *Step 5*: the reachability matrix obtained in step 4 is partitioned into different levels.
- *Step 6*: based on the relationships given above in the reachability matrix, an ISM model is drawn.
- *Step 7*: finally driving power and dependence graph is prepared. It provides insights into the relative importance and interdependencies between the factors. Based on the driving power and dependence, the graph classifies the factors into four groups viz., i. autonomous group (factors with low driver power and low dependency, so these factors have little impact on the system and can be ignored), ii dependent group (these factors at the top of the hierarchy are the objectives), iii. linkage group (factors that link the drivers and dependent groups), and iv. driver group (these factors drive the whole system and influence the most) (Chidambaranathan et al. 2010, and Luthra et al. 2011).
- *Step 8*: the ISM model developed in step 7 is reviewed to check for conceptual consistency.

The above is a summary of the methodology, and the details can be referred to from a standard textbook or scholarly articles. The relationships between factors may vary depending on the type of system or local conditions, so the ISM model can be developed for any system based on geographical area and by considering the local conditions through stakeholders' consultations (Chidambaranathan et al. 2010; Mudgal et al. 2010). Based on the model, policymakers can take appropriate actions for modifying or introducing new measures. The industry and entrepreneurs may benefit from the insights derived from the model.

6.3.2 System Dynamics Modeling

Change is constant. The world is marked with change, which is a universal constant. Now, the change is felt at a higher speed. It is mainly a result of the combination of issues like rapid technological advancements and exponential growth in communication systems, making communication instant and squeezing time and space; higher expectations by stakeholders; enhanced interactive effects of factors and stakeholders in the system; increased frequency of feedback; and nonlinear interactions. The change challenges the existing assumptions, values, practices, and approaches concerned with policymaking. The change enhances complexity. It demands a quick response from the top management and leadership. It engenders policymakers to learn at increasing rates while at the same time dealing with the growing complexity in the systems.

In addition, by ignoring the feedback from the stakeholders, it is difficult to comprehend the consequences. As a result, many problems arise as unanticipated side effects and interventions fail to solve the problems fully. Sometimes, actions make the problems more difficult through externalities (Richardson 1996; Coyle 2000). For example, due to inadequate attention paid to feedback in policymaking, it results in increased industrial activities, factory air pollution, untreated industrial effluent disposal, and untreated household waste. These cause many side effects on health and suffering for a large population. Similarly, the economy works in a dynamic environment and keeps changing due to the interactive effects of numerous economic agents and entities and feedback from agents and the environment. Adaptation to change is essential for such systems. It underscores the need to understand and address the change.

Approaches to problems in complex social and economic systems. In the decades before and beginning of the twentieth century, with much fewer economic activities, slower communication, and lesser mobility, the social systems and problems were relatively simple. The systems had limited interacting factors, and cause-and-effects were generally known or knowable. The comprehension of the problems was easy. The problems were addressed by practices and methods with linear thinking, and the systems were managed majorly through interventions in the known external environment.

With the rise in government expenditure from the 1930s onward, the advent of new communication technologies, and the rise in population, socio-economic activities have seen steady to exponential growth after 1990 (Cohen 1984; Curtain 2000; Gerston 2010; Gagnon 2017). It is essential to appreciate the fundamental nature of social systems. In the hierarchy of complex systems (Boulding 1956), the social systems lie at a higher level of complexity. And the level of knowledge and understanding about their structure and functioning has been comparatively limited. Due to human nature, the social systems are conscious and internally motivated and thus are self-aware and self-correcting, though it varies from individual to individual. At the same time, the seek-conscious nature makes human beings unique, and given the right conditions, they utilize the opportunities to perform simple to innovative tasks (Capra 1996; Sawyer 2005; Sherblom 2017). These issues make the social systems challenging to understand.

The relationships between variables in social systems are not as exact, linear, predictable, and measurable as in the physical system. The dynamic nature of social

6.3 System Approach

systems arises from human attitudes, behavior, and activities besides interactions with the attributes of variables of physical entities. The characteristics of these systems are discussed in Sect. 3.1 in Chap. 3.

In such a system, due to its multidimensional and interconnected nature, together with the engagement of diverse stakeholders, the identification and articulation of causal relationships between factors have been observed to be difficult or unknowable. Due to feedback loops, the relationships result in second- and third-order consequences. The interconnected nature of activities adds to uncertainty and complexity. The basic features of such systems, both social and economic, are defined by the following:

- *Nonlinearity*. The nonlinearity in the social systems is due to three sources. The first form of nonlinearity is when the relationship between variables is not a linear mathematical equation. The second type is due to behavioral reasons, as there are interactions between system variables and humans (individuals or economic agents) in different unknown ways. A third source of nonlinearity is due to simultaneous feedback from one or more than one variable or an outside source. And thus, the output of a policy is not proportional to the input variables (Warfield 1974; Forrester 1994; Stacey 2002).
- *Unknown or unknowable cause-effects during policymaking and of outcomes*. In complex social systems, the cause-effects are unknown or unknowable due to reasons like: *first*, behavioral factors, as social systems do not change as desired; *second*, likely discord between the short-term gain and the long-term implications; and, *third*, probability of conflicting interests of different stakeholders, as a result of policy interventions. The influence of one element on the behavior of the system may be different from that of the others. Thus, it becomes difficult to discern cause-effects in the system. For these reasons, during policymaking, the studies (Forrester 1971; Richardson 1996; Sterman 2000) have highlighted the difficulty in identifying leverage points for introducing interventions. And how the policy will yield results is difficult to know or not knowable, and outputs remain uncertain. As a result, it is difficult to determine or visualize the policy outcomes.
- *Dynamic nature*. Due to the interactive nature of elements, through feedback, the action and behavior of one element impact the other elements in the social system, which brings in dynamic nature. And such interactions create emergence as a natural phenomenon in a complex system.

Besides, on account of temporal (time-related) interactions and subsequent interrelationships over time, it results in dynamic complexity—implying that the complexity in the system changes with time. The factors such as delays in the availability of information and decision-making, behavioral issues, continuous feedback from multiple variables and individuals, accumulations in stock variables (like resources), and nonlinearities of interactions contribute to complexity. The dynamic complexity is often not expected or is not predicted. But it is manifested through patterns like the spread of health problems, land degradation, rise in inflation, unemployment, and growth of a city, to cite a few examples. Any future approach needs to consider these three characteristics—nonlinearity, unknown or unknowable cause-effects, and the dynamic nature—of the social and economic systems to understand better the problems and policy formulation.

To understand issues in a dynamic and complex system, certain features and concepts require examination and elaboration to get the right perspective about the system (Forrester 1961, 1968; Coyle 2000; Sterman 2000). These are summarized as follows:

- *How silo or closed-group approach leads to bounded rationality.* In traditional functioning, the policymakers in the policy system or managers in business tend to work in their respective areas and departments. Thus they think and work from their understanding, perspectives, and requirements. They try to optimize their functions. Operating in their silos or a close-knit group reduces the possibility of the right ideas and timely information, limiting their perspectives. It results in bounded rationality.
- *How feedback is critical and impacts policy adoption or resistance.* Due to a lack of structured analysis, it is difficult to elicit information from diverse stakeholders, visualize a range of options, or take feedback, so policy adoption or resistance cannot be understood easily. The policy adoption or resistance will depend upon the feedback from stakeholders as well as system variables. Human nature is to perceive and give its reaction—positive or negative, depending upon the decisions by the policymakers. The feedback from variables in the system can provide reinforcing (positive) or counterbalancing (negative) loops. The positive loop leads to policy adoption as the stakeholders respond to give positive feedback. In contrast, a negative feedback loop leads to policy resistance.

In the system, various stakeholders have different interests and perceptions about the problems. There are competing interests, so some may find a policy useful while others struggle. Besides, the resistance may be from different variables within the system. In many cases, policy resistance arises as the full range of feedback in the system is not captured during policymaking due to limitations in understanding the system. As the policy actions tend to alter the state of the system and precipitate side effects, some stakeholders react and press for restoring the original state.

For example, the software (SW) industry is able to create value due to reinforcing loops and create a virtuous cycle (Fig. 6.2a). One loop linked to networks of entrepreneurs, skills, and technologies is a positive feedback loop (clockwise). Likewise, another loop regarding turnover or earnings is also a positive feedback loop (clockwise). Thus, they mutually reinforce each other, as both loops are clockwise.

Similarly, as an illustration, after the renewable energy (RE) policy is announced, there is an initial success. Thereafter, there is a need to examine the dynamics of change as capacity increases. The changes in the availability of land for plants with reasonable prices, grid-connectivity from RE plant, operational difficulties in terms of maintaining PLF and plant efficiency, and grid management (power quality issues like voltage and frequency fluctuations, overloading of transmission lines, demand and supply matching) need examination for policy adoption. Figure 6.2b reflects one loop (RE investment) is a positive feedback loop (clockwise), and the other loop (due

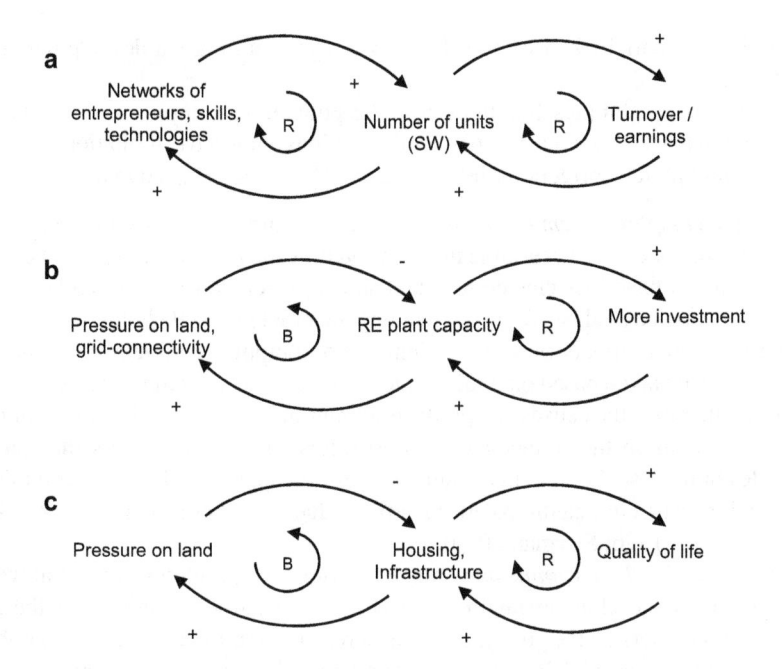

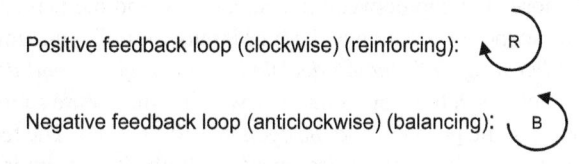

6.3 System Approach

Fig. 6.2 Feedback and reinforcing and balancing effects. **a** Software industry (reinforcing effects). **b** Renewable energy (RE) plants (reinforcing and balancing effects). **c** Urban development (reinforcing and balancing effects)

to pressure on land availability and grid-connectivity) is a negative feedback loop (anticlockwise). So they are balancing (or limiting) each other, as one is positive and the other is negative, thus limiting the growth of RE plants.

In another example, the dynamics need to be examined for urban development. Specifically, when urban activities in terms of housing, infrastructure development, and civic amenities improve, there is a rise in quality of life. These are positive effects. But as a result, these have implications for pressure on land, land price, occupation of government land for private activities in some cases, increased economic activities, rise in pollution, and then likely adverse impact on quality of life. Analysts and policymakers need to look into the dynamics of change over time (Forrester 1968, 1969). The loop related to the quality of life due to housing and infrastructure is a positive feedback loop (clockwise). And the loop related to pressure on land is a negative feedback loop (anticlockwise), thus limiting the growth in urban development (see Fig. 6.2c).

The last two examples highlight how the policies in complex systems fail to consider feedback. So even the best policy actions may have limitations as time passes unless policy corrections are introduced. Feedback brings dynamics.

- *How the complex system is counterintuitive.* In complex systems, the causes and effects are not easily discernible in space and time, thereby meaning that the decision makers have less chance to establish causal relationships. In addition, for want of detailed analysis for understanding the problems, stakeholders' concerns, and interactive effects of various elements on outputs or system behavior, the decisions are taken based on intuitive mental models. These tend to address symptoms rather than the causes and produce counterintuitive effects. Intuitive policies bring benefits in the immediate or short terms and fail to address the causes, while complex social systems require a long-term approach. The counterintuitive behavior results in unanticipated side effects due to past policy actions (Warfield 1974; Coyle 1996; Sterman 2000).
- *How micro-level viewpoints and insights matter.* The problems in the real world require micro-level understanding. It is possible only when insights from the citizens or end-users on the ground are considered. The multiple interacting variables need to be discerned. These aspects are not usually factored in during the traditional mental mapping or policymaking process. The ground-level insights impact the mental models and understanding, and change the perception about the real nature of problems. It closes the gap between the actual state and the perceived value. It can provide the scope for learning and better inputs for policymaking.
- *How feedback impacts learning, influencing decision criteria, goals, and decisions.* The results of our actions define new situations, which refine future actions. These alter the perception of the problem and the decisions to be taken. The feedback may be from internal sources, the environment, or both. It may improve understanding of delays in adoption of policy interventions, nonlinearity, time-dimension, and exogenous and endogenous factors. Through feedback, people learn, and the learning helps in bringing changes in approaches, strategies, goals, assumptions, and decisions. Figure 6.3a reflects a basic mental model. Figure 6.3b reflects how based on feedback, the individuals respond to the real world, which leads to learning and then changes in decision-making (Coyle 1996; Sterman, 2000).

Traditional approaches and scientific management. Over the years, many traditional approaches and scientific management tools have been developed. These have shown promise in certain stable and known conditions but limitations while dealing with the dynamic and uncertain social environment. Key limitations are discussed below:

- *How traditional approaches, including linear thinking, limit the understanding of problems and systems.* The traditional approaches, based on mental models, rely on linear thinking. They are apt for handling simple and linear relationships (Gentner and Stevens 1983; Kelly 1998; Serdar 2001). Linear thinking is about taking actions in a linear fashion, as represented by Fig. 6.4. It has difficulty in considering the feedback at every stage, either due to limitations of mental models

6.3 System Approach

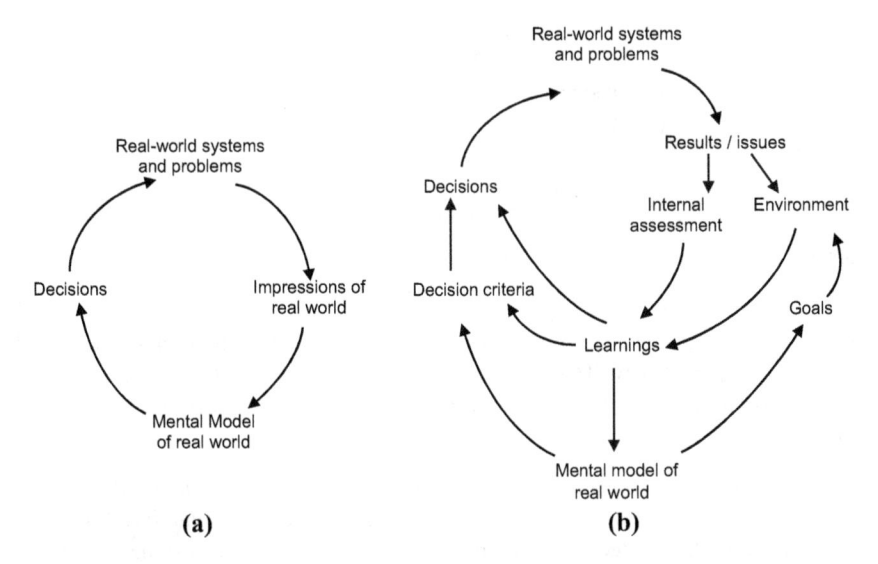

Fig. 6.3 Mental model and real-world interaction. **a** Basic mental model. **b** Improved mental model: feedback, learnings, and decisions

or lack of attention. For example, in the policymaking process, it has the inability to take feedback from stakeholders for analysis, policy options, or actions.

In the linear system, the independent variables can be written as a linear sum. It follows the superposition principle in which the variables can be added, and the outputs are proportional to the inputs. The traditional approaches using heuristic, rule-of-thumb, or simplified practical mental models have shown limitations in understanding multiple complex interconnections, feedback, causality, nonlinearity, time delays, and the dynamic nature of problems (Khalil 2001; Sterman 2000; Nicolis 1995). While in a nonlinear system, the change in the output is not proportional to the change in the inputs. The nonlinearity in the system is on three independent counts. *First*, nonlinear mathematical relationships, *second*, institutional and behavioral factors, and *third*, nonlinear interactions as a result of feedback loops, as shown by Fig. 6.5.

Due to cognitive limitations, the traditional approaches are unable to address feedback and nonlinearity and are not suitable for large and complex systems. Conventional thinking has limitations, as it is usually based on linear models, static references, and two-dimensional analysis. The mental representation of a problem has limitations due to bounded rationality, lack of informed discussion, and the likelihood of misperception about problems because of incoherence in their mental images. In the real world, the system with multidimensional, nonlinear (including exponential), dynamic nature, closed loop, and open boundary is beyond the ability of mental

Problem ⟶ Analysis ⟶ Options ⟶ Decisions ⟶ Actions

Fig. 6.4 Linear thinking approach

Problem → Analysis → Options → Decisions → Actions

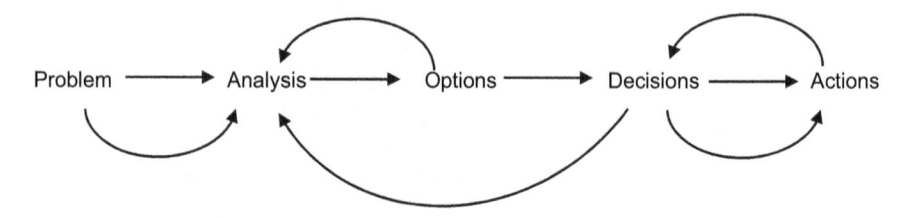

Fig. 6.5 Nonlinear thinking approach (with feedback)

models or conventional approaches. So, it is difficult for decision makers to deal with dynamic complexity. The decision-making in complex systems such as health, economy, or big businesses requires approaches that enable understanding dynamic complexity.

- *How scientific optimization and quantitative approaches have limitations: inability to capture feedback, nonlinearity, and dynamic behavior.* From the 1950s onward, for decision-making, various methods like optimization techniques, mathematical tools, and statistical models were developed for dealing with multiple and sometimes conflicting conditions. These were suitable for addressing certain problems in physical systems, which did not deal with the dynamic nature requiring Adaptation to changing conditions. The optimization methods provide algorithms for objective functions for determining optimum solutions under well-defined assumptions and boundaries. These are more suitable for physical, engineering, and business problems (without interactive effects of individuals) and easily quantifiable variables.

    The social systems dealing with people are nonlinear and complex due to behavioral and cognitive factors, so optimization tools have little relevance. The nonlinear dynamical systems which define changes in variables with time are likely to be uncertain and counterintuitive, unlike simpler linear systems. These systems with a dynamic environment call for new approaches (Forrester 1961; Khalil 2001; Guastello 2017).

Understanding the foundation of system dynamics

Since the 1940s, as a response to the limitations of mental models and traditional approaches, many scientific approaches were developed that utilized analytical tools and mathematical modeling to aid decision-making. Management science generally applies mathematical or quantitative methods, including operations research for decision-making, mainly for strategic, logistics, and tactical problems (McCulloch et al. 1998; Camm and James 2000). Some management science techniques include linear programming, dynamic programming, goal programming, transportation modeling, etc. These were utilized as decision-making models but were more like abstract mathematical models seeking to optimize problems under specific assumptions and constraints. These left the problems under consideration (in the social systems or management of businesses) away from the ground realities. Though these serve a good purpose for physical systems like running machines, simplified business operations, or logistics issues, but failed to capture behavioral, institutional, and social issues (Forrester 1968; Simon 1977; Sushil 1993). Such approaches advocated for analytical and optimum solutions for a limited purpose rather than understanding the problem from a real world perspective. They relied on the simplification of problems, considered linear relationships, and focused on forecasting rather than systemic analysis. It created gaps between what is perceived and what is reality. Such tools have been inadequate for use in nonlinear, feedback, closed loop, and dynamic complex systems.

Prior to the twentieth century, Forrester (1961) underscored that management grew more as an art than a science. It tried to simplify the problems and adjust as and when the problems emerged. Thus, it puts limitations in addressing the problems in a comprehensive manner as well as complexity. Subsequently, management relied on mathematical approaches but lacked the ability to provide a conceptual understanding and failed to present a systemic understanding and underlying system structure. Working on objectives for an optimum solution and working on solutions under assumptions lacked the realistic view of the ground reality in the social systems (including business and economy), leave alone complexity (Coyle 2000; Sterman 2000). In addition, the conventional management and analytical approaches have been more focused on the immediate concerns of the system than the long-term view. These approaches try to maximize gains or optimize the solutions under a given set of conditions and assumptions. They tend to address the symptoms or a few pressing problems. They have been short of examining the underlying reasons for the problems, systemic issues, and the behavior of the system.

In the case of an economic system, the experts (Forrester 1961, 1968; Kirman 2011; Arthur 2014) have highlighted the inability of economic models and theories to examine the interactive behavior of elements, feedback loops, and the structures that form economic systems; behavioral issues and policy acceptance and resistance; the process of change including decision-making, actions, and implementation; and flows and accumulations of information, resources, goods, money, and labor, and their associated delays. The delay is a time lag between decisions and actions or actions and results on the ground. The economic models do not provide one single interrelated model. Their overreliance on statistical models with constrained optimization, inability to define the implications of assumptions, and abstract description of mathematical coefficients have little relevance for real socio-economic problems. Earlier in the 1970s, the econometrics models and management tools provided analysis for a short-term solution by relying on established theories and referring to historical data. Such models did not examine the dynamic nature of the system, which put limitations on understanding uncertain and dynamic aspects of the system.

Likewise, the conventional mathematical approaches do not comprehend the complexity in both the environment and internal systems, the complexity in the process of policymaking, or strategy formulation in business. They do not capture real-world issues in social systems or organizational issues. To recapitulate, they lack the ability to understand interactions between factors and causal relations between them in the system structure. Such limitations lead to inadequate assessment of problems, difficulty in capturing reality, and incorrect decision-making (Byrne 1998; Mason 2008; OECD 2017b).

Besides, in reality, the mere occurrence of a few problems or events in the system does not reflect the output or behavior of a system. So, there is a need to examine all the interrelated elements or components, the interactive effects of elements, all the problems within the system but not in piecemeal, and the whole system. Through interactive effects of elements, the failure of one element may make the system dysfunctional.

Traditional mathematical and scientific methods primarily create solutions for engineering problems and non-organic or physical systems. The managerial, human, and social systems and their associated problems are more complex as compared to engineering problems and physical systems. The social and economic systems and organizations are complex due to numerous individuals, organic linkages between individuals, behavioral and institutional issues, hidden or unknown factors, and multiple internal processes involving discussions, decision-making, and actions.

The above discussion stresses how traditional approaches, including linear thinking and scientific approaches, have the inability to address problems in social systems. These underlying reasons demand an approach that considers the concepts and features of complex systems.

Evolution of new approaches. The inherently complex and multidimensional nature of social systems dealing with social and economic policies demands a comprehensive approach to policymaking. There has been a felt need to substantiate the knowledge and tools for examining information and comprehending the problems and systems. Over time, since the 1930s, with research work by scholars like Bertalanffy, Lasswell, Simon, and Forrester, to name a few, there has been a better appreciation of underlying issues in social systems, complexity, and public policy.

Modeling approach. Intuitively or as a matter of convenience, the individuals approach the problems with the help of a model. The model is a notional or theoretical description of the existing situation, observed phenomena, or a proposed idea and concept. It could be in the form of a simplified or rationalized depiction. In the social and economic systems, the models are the fundamental basis for the analysis of problems, conceptual understanding, or technical aspects. They are applied to both qualitative and quantitative studies. These can be used for issues of an individual or a family, community, or problems at National or global levels, and for a simple problem, complicated, or complex one at any level. In the increasing order of rationality, the models can be developed through a mental map using perceptions, cognitive skills, and previous experience, by applying conceptual understanding, or by using rational criteria, mathematical reasons, and scientific basis.

At every level, from micro to macro, in every stage of policymaking, due to a lack of evidence-based approach, the policymakers invariably apply mental models to understand problems, select policy options, and implement programs. And so, the effectiveness of mental models determines policymaking and policy outcomes. The mental models are a simplified version of a complicated or complex problem, as the human mind can keep track of a limited number of simultaneous interactions, which determine the behavior and outcome in the real world. The primary issue is how best models can be developed to represent and convey real-world problems and systems. The limitations of the human mind or mental models are discussed in the previous section. In reality, the elements in the systems are so interrelated they make the problems complex, which cannot be abstracted and comprehended by mental models.

Need for system perspective. Various studies (Forrester 1961; Warfield 1974; Serdar 2001) have underscored that a methodology was needed for conceptualizing the socio-economic and technological systems, including the ever-increasing complexity dimension, and, through analyses, for identifying strategies and policy options. As a response to this new requirement, the system concepts and system approach emerged from systems theory in the 1960s. It is suitable for subsystems with nonlinearity, dynamic nature, and feedback loops, which have known or knowable cause-effects. It applies to a stable and equilibrium state. It relies on stakeholders' perspectives, practitioners' views, and applied systems thinking (Gentner and Stevens 1983; Senge and Sterman 1992; Kelly 1998).

Since the 1960s, many quantitative and qualitative models and approaches have been developed for better inquiry into problems and system and for policy modeling. The prominent models and approaches are like interpretive structural modeling (ISM), institutional approach, system analysis, fuzzy logic approach, and grounded theory. To overcome the limitations of traditional management, under the umbrella of the system approach, a more scientific approach—system dynamics—was developed using both qualitative and mathematical models. Currently, new tools like big data analysis, artificial intelligence (AI), machine learning (ML), social network analysis (SNA), and agent-based modeling (ABM) are being explored.

In complex social systems, the conceptualization of a problem and system, and subsequently, the problem definition, is the first level of challenge. In addition, the synthesis of various factors and issues, defining objectives, and policy formulation are other issues confronting policymakers. The social systems deal with human beings in which values, beliefs, and behavioral and cognitive factors matter, in contrast with static and simple problems or the mechanical world of machines. So same set of approaches applied to simple problems or the mechanistic world cannot be applied to social problems. In a departure from conventional methods, it calls for a change in the mode of approaching the problems, from linear thinking to nonlinear thinking and from examining individual parts to a systemic study and examining interactive effects.

One distinction is to be made with respect to (w.r.t) known, knowable, and unknowable cause-effects. For known or knowable cause-effects, the system approach applying systems thinking is appropriate. But for unknowable cause-effects leading to uncertain behavior, the complexity theory will be a suitable approach. At the same time, for conceptualizing and addressing problems in complex systems, especially nonlinearity, unknown (due to a lack of analysis) but knowable cause-effects, and dynamic nature, the following three basic analyses can yield results:

- discerning subsystems and elements within them;
- developing the causal loop diagram by determining interlinkages of both qualitative and quantitative factors; and
- drawing structures of the system in question.

Such analyses will entail an iterative process through consultations with the concerned stakeholders. Through deep probing, systems thinking, and application of system dynamics, unknown but knowable cause-effects can be discerned. Despite the strength of the system approach, in light of the complexity in the social and economic systems, it is suitable for the equilibrium state of the system and certain behavior. It is not envisaged to handle the uncertain, emergent, and evolutionary nature of changes in the system.

Public policy, economy, and organizations are complex systems. However, for a limited complexity, when the system returns to an equilibrium state and stays there for a sufficient time despite being dynamic, and for known or unknown but knowable cause-effects through the causal loop and system structure diagrams, the methodology of system dynamics (SD) can be applied. SD is not suitable for an evolving complex system. However, the qualitative SD model can be developed for the purpose of conceptual understanding. Regarding uncertainty and the emergent nature of systems, complexity analysis using complexity theory will be necessitated, as explained in Chap. 5. Uncertainty can be unraveled with deep probing and detailed analyses.

The above discussion laid the foundation of system dynamics (Forrester 1961, 1968; Coyle 2000).

Unlike engineering problems, physical systems, or scientific matters examined and addressed by time-tested scientific theories, principles, and mathematical models, the socio-economic systems face more complex issues. There are some essential points of difference. The *first* issue concerns the lack of any accepted theory to deal with a wide variety of problems in social and economic systems. *Second*, there are inadequacies in the research methods to make sense of the complete range of variables—economic, institutional, and behavioral, and their relationships. And *third*, the sheer size and volume of the social system. Such systems are not amenable to analytical tools and mathematical modeling (Forrester 1969; Simon 1977; Senge 1990; Guastello 2017).

It has been apparent that the conventional approaches have limitations in comprehending simultaneous changes in more than one variable or understanding the dynamics of change in multiple variables at a time. As the inter-system interactions of variables increase, understanding the system becomes more difficult. The proponents of the system dynamics felt the need for an approach that deals with how the system behavior changes with time. Primarily, the main consideration has been to understand and visualize the whole structure created by the interactions between the elements or variables of the system.

What is important is to appreciate that the interactions (or interdependencies), dynamic behavior, and feedback loops are fundamental, rather than the static nature

6.3 System Approach

of elements and linear causality, to examine better the social problems. The new approach was required to:

- develop the model to examine the system as a whole—its elements and processes;
- provide insights about the conditions that impact the behavior;
- enable the model to monitor and feed back the changes in the system behavior; and
- suggest alternative options for the design of the policies.

Comprehending complex dynamic systems requires more than mathematical tools. It necessitates interdisciplinary methods of conceptualizing problems. Such a fundamental need has been the foundation of a new approach called system dynamics (SD) to deal with dynamic complex systems involving interacting elements, structures, feedback, and nonlinearity. The SD approach is credited to the scholarly work of J.W. Forrester. Forrester's (1961, 1968, 1969) work on Industrial Dynamics, Urban Dynamics, and Principles of Systems. Subsequently, the book on the Limits to Growth (Meadows et al. 1972) added value to applying system dynamics to examine the public system, business, industry, and economy.

The SD methodology is built upon the foundation laid by traditional management, systems theory, nonlinear dynamic system approach, feedback theory or cybernetics, and computer simulation. The principles, concepts, and methods of these fields have been integrated to develop a methodology for conceptualizing problems and system, visualization, scenario building, and simulation for solving social and management problems in a systemic manner. It emphasizes systems thinking, analytical tools, and an interdisciplinary approach to understanding problems, analysis, and decision-making. In contrast with other methods like fuzzy logic, calculus, matrices, econometrics, and regression analysis to study social and economic systems, the application of system dynamics entails feedback loops, internal structure, time dimension, and stocks and flows. These are essential points of difference. It helps in understanding the nonlinearity and dynamic behavior of the system (Kelly 1998; Coyle 2000).

SD philosophy and practice arise from feedback theory and various disciplines—economics, sociology, psychology, and management—to improve understanding of multiple aspects of system behavior. Fundamentally, system dynamics is a method to learn complex systems better. It helps to acquire knowledge about causal relationships and feedback, understand the reasons for policy adoption or resistance, examine dynamic behavior, and design effective policies (Senge and Sterman 1992; Richardson 1996; Sterman, 2000). SD modeling begins with an effort to elicit or externalize knowledge and insights. Despite the limitations of mental models, they provide a primary source of information in model building. The methodology considers sharing the model with the stakeholders to provide feedback and inputs based on their needs. As a result of stakeholders' engagement, it gives a scope for obtaining realities from the grassroots. Due to the interdisciplinary approach, SD modeling offers a common language for systems' problems.

Premise of system dynamics approach. System dynamics (SD) is an approach and methodology to understand the behavior of a system over time. It deals with internal structure, feedback loops, and time delays that affect the behavior and state of the entire system. It includes both qualitative and mathematical modeling for discussing and conceptualizing complex issues and problems (Senge and Sterman 1992; Saeed 1994). The system dynamics build upon the combination of an extensive knowledge base of mental models, experience, and expertise. It makes use of the system philosophy to develop the structure or model of a system, which represents the real world. The model could be qualitative or quantitative and is used to study the dynamic behavior of the system. In addition, the SD methodology has a causal philosophy to understand cause-and-effect relationships for the purpose of gaining insights into the working of a system. It emphasizes looking within the system. It stresses that the problems are inherently caused by the structure of the system, not as such, directly caused by outside factors or a few individual factors. In reality, the internal factors and structure result in feedback loops, considering the external factors. Thus, fundamentally, the SD model is characterized by endogenous, internal structure, and feedback perspectives.

Against the above backdrop, the premise of the approach contains four aspects, as captured in Fig. 6.6. *First, the real-world issues* are socio-economic systems, complex nature, limitations of mental models, and policy resistance due to feedback from stakeholders. *Second*, it is based on *assumptions* like the interacting nature of elements, feedback, dynamic response, nonlinearity, complexity in the system, bounded rationality, and counterintuitive behavior. *Third*, the *foundation* of SD includes the integration of traditional approaches (human mind or mental models), system approach, cybernetics (feedback theory of control), and computer simulations.

Fourth, philosophy and principles. The understanding behind the conceptualization of problems, model building, testing and validation, and policy design needs to be informed. These should be supported by reflecting on the philosophical background and principles. The philosophical underpinnings of a discipline require basic assumptions, concepts, and principles, which are shared by practitioners and researchers. SD relies on the philosophy of understanding the system structure derived from causal relationships between variables and feedback (Forrester 1961; Senge and Sterman 1992). It determines dynamic behavior and complexity. It has general principles—the strength of the micro world (grassroots) is crucial for deeper understanding for comprehending problems and systems; interacting elements and feedback loops bring nonlinearity and complexity; and the endogenous factors determine the dynamic behavior. Specifically, SD includes principles such as the imperative of system-wide understanding; focus on policy design; essentiality of long-term view; gaining insights from the micro world (through causality, feedback, and learning); multidimensional group knowledge for discerning feedback loops and structures; endogenous factors determine the dynamic behavior (but the exogenous policy parameters influence the model through the structure), and decision-making is a dynamic process.

The key features of system dynamics are as follows: it applies thinking modes like systems thinking and critical thinking; it relies on multiple sources of data, including qualitative and quantitative data; it follows an approach of qualitative as

6.3 System Approach

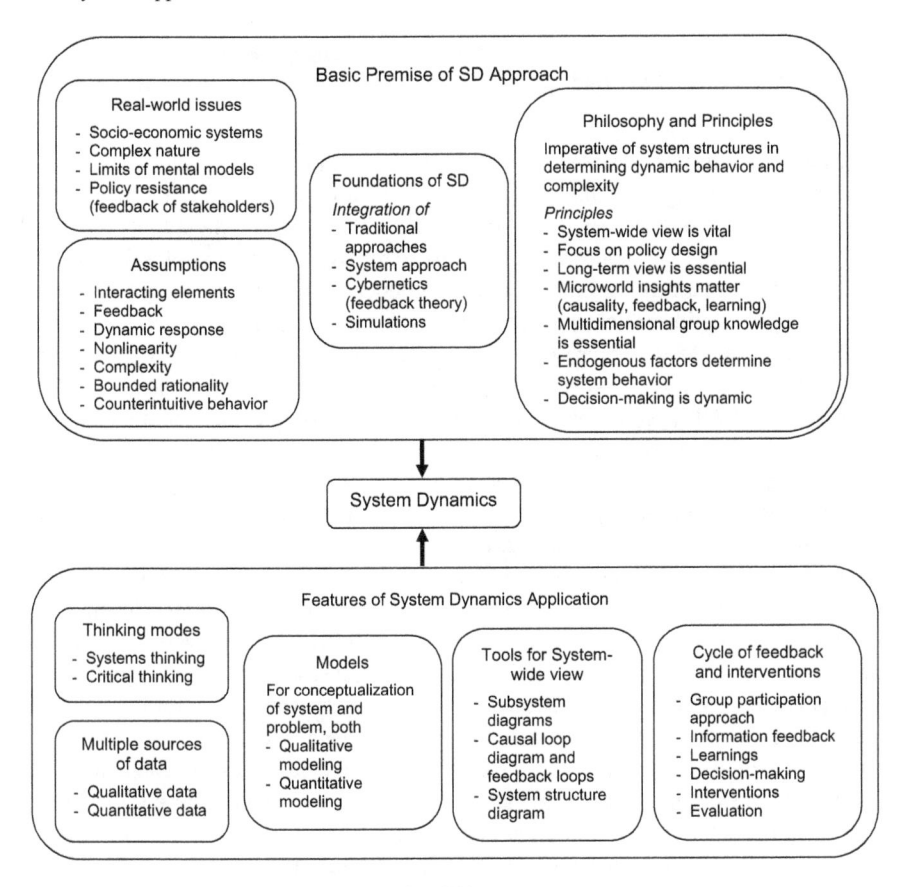

Fig. 6.6 Building blocks of system dynamics (SD)

well as quantitative modeling for the conceptualization of system and problem; and it uses tools for system-wide view, including subsystem diagram, causal loop diagram, feedback loops (both physical and information flows), and system structure diagram. Finally, it works on a cycle of feedback and interventions involving a group participation approach, information feedback, learning, decision-making, interventions, evaluation, and course correction.

Application of system dynamics. As a result of robust methodology, system dynamics have found wider acceptability. It can be effectively applied to problems in different spheres of social systems. It has applications in socio-economic sectors ranging from urban development, energy management, health to sustainable development. The socio-economic systems should be studied and piloted through times to understand the realities of the world. The notable application areas include the changes in cities, social behavior for adopting new practices, and the cycles of economic expansion and recession. The purpose of the SD model has been to make sense of complex problems in the business and development sector and to develop alternative scenarios to design new strategies for any system. It tries to overcome conceptual barriers through the usage of systems thinking and interdisciplinary study (Randers 1980; Kelly 1998; Bier 2011).

Fundamental points of system dynamics. In the real world, the system deals with the combination of stock-flow and feedback-action-control to create dynamic behavior (Forrester 1968; Mohapatra et al. 1994; Sterman 2000). It is a fundamental point that is a departure from other approaches and unique for the system dynamics. Examples of stock (accumulation) are gross domestic product (GDP) in the economy, natural resources, goods and services produced, infrastructure, etc., in the general sense. In the business, the stock is represented by capital investment, machinery, inventory, and finished goods. It will involve learning and information as stock in the knowledge system. In the R&D system, innovations and new technologies represent stock.

In the socio-economic reality, all the systems involve accumulation by some variables. This aspect needs appreciation, consideration, and mainstreaming in the system study. In the system, mainly the accumulation is a result of, *first*, net flow (inflow as a result of production minus outflow as a result of discharge or consumption) within the system and *second*, time delays. Such flow can be controlled by feedback from other variables within the system or exogenous policy parameters through the structure of the system. The feedback leads to actions by the concerned officials or managers. The stock in a system can be controlled (governed) by flows through feedback mechanism and internal structure. Basically, the dynamic behavior is produced and controlled by both, *first,* endogenous feedback mechanisms and *second*, exogenous policy interventions (or parameters) through the feedback mechanisms and structure of the system. These may have a good or bad impact on the performance, depending upon the feedback, action, and structure. Thus, the endogenous factors, internal structure, and feedback determine the behavior of the system.

Steps of methodology. With the main focus on the conceptualization of the problem and system, the methodology remains involves five steps (Vennix 1992; Sushil 1993; Forrester 1994; Coyle 2000) (Fig. 6.7 and Table 6.2):

- Problem identification and definition
- System conceptualization
- Model formulation
- Simulation, scenario building, and sensitivity analysis
- Model validation and policy analysis

The methodology of system dynamics is an iterative process. The process begins with the identification and definition of a problem. To define a problem, situation analysis is required and may involve redefinition of the problem as the analysis progresses. The cycle of analysis continues until an acceptable model of system conceptualization is obtained. The system is conceptualized in light of the problem under examination. The system analysis proceeds with three diagrams, viz., subsystem diagram, causal loop diagram, and policy structure diagram, to elicit an in-depth understanding of the

6.3 System Approach

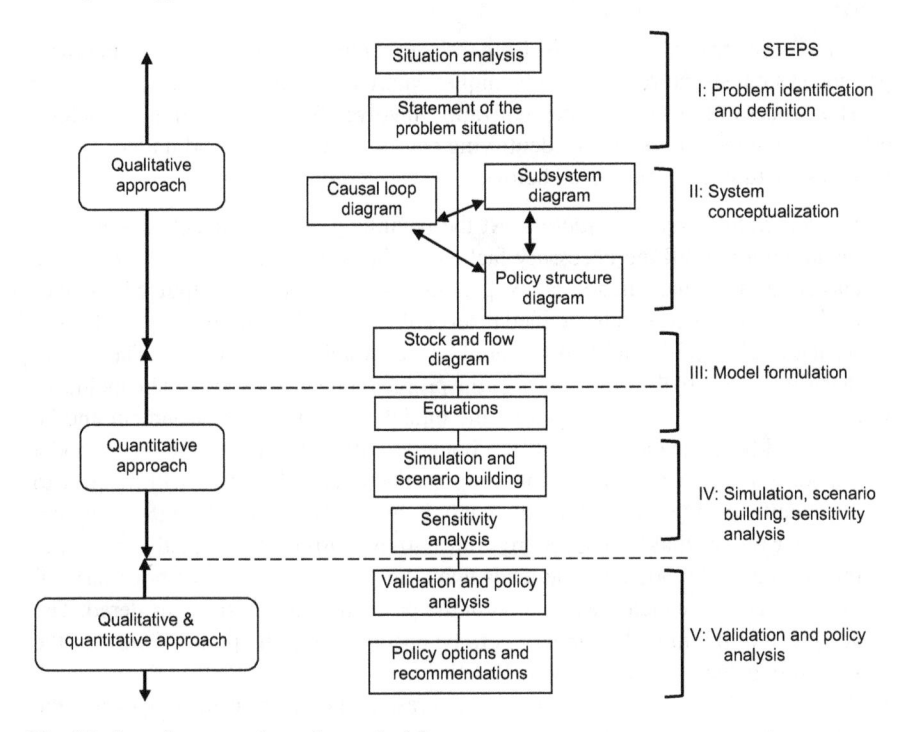

Fig. 6.7 Steps in system dynamics methodology

Table 6.2 Stages and steps in system dynamics model development

S. No.	Stages	Steps
1.	Problem definition	• Stakeholder analysis • Eliciting insights • Problem definition
2.	System conceptualization	• Identifying relevant factors (variables) • Defining system boundary • Subsystem, causal loop, and policy structure diagrams • Identifying feedback loops
3.	Model formulation	• Stock and flow diagram • Developing mathematical equations • Specifying model parameters
4.	Simulation, scenario building, and sensitivity analysis	• Simulation and scenario building • Conducting sensitivity analysis
5.	Validation and policy analysis	• Validating model • Conducting policy experiments • Evaluating policy experiments

system. These are qualitative tools. Both the causal loop and stock and flow diagrams provide system structure, which is a unique feature of the methodology.

The process of system conceptualization involves the identification of factors, establishing a model boundary, identifying causal relationships, and understanding system structure, as summarized below:

- *Identification of relevant factors.* At the beginning of the conceptual stage, the identification of all the necessary factors (variables) is required. The factors are classified into three categories: exogenous, endogenous, and output. Simultaneously, the factors should be defined in an explicit form. While selecting the factors for the model, the model builder should have an unbiased approach. The factors that are relevant to the description of the problem under study should be included.
- *Model boundary.* Like any system, the model will have an environment and be separated from the environment by a boundary. Both the environment and model boundary are conceptual. A model represents an actual system with respect to the specific problem for which the study is made. The model is built to capture behavior modes that have direct relevance to the purpose of the study. In the SD model, the model boundary depends upon the purpose. Within the boundary, all relevant factors, which are essential in the problem context, are considered. The adequacy of the model boundary is to be checked from the point of view of the structure, behavior, and policy implications.
- *Subsystem diagram.* Its purpose is to present the relationships between the interacting subsystems at an aggregate level.
- *Causal loop diagram.* The system is conceptualized regarding the components, factors, and interactions. In the model, all the interactions between elements within the structure are causal relationships.
- *Policy structure diagram.* The focus of the model is on decision-making for policymaking. This diagram depicts various policy parameters in the overall system structure.
- *System conceptualization.* Different factors are interrelated through causal relationships and feedback loops in the structure. Diagramming aids—subsystem, causal loop, and policy structure diagrams—assist in understanding and communicating the model with stakeholders.

After defining the problem and conceptualizing the system, the stock and flow diagram is developed. It may be qualitative if equations are not written due to qualitative variables. It may provide conceptual understanding. After writing mathematical equations, the model becomes quantitative. Based on the model, the following analyses are required: testing of principles, simulation, scenarios building—optimistic, normal and pessimistic, and sensitivity analysis. It is followed by validation which gives feedback on the definition of the problem and system conceptualization, and then the model refinement and reformulation are carried out. The valid model is subjected to policy analysis and improvement, and further understanding is obtained. Finally, the policies are recommended for implementation. It indicates that there is a learning aspect of the policy model.

In essence, the system dynamics model provides an advantage for the conceptualization of problems and demonstrates its ability to: *first*, include multiple factors in the structure through the causal loop diagram; *second*, address nonlinear relationships and feedback; *third*, model social and behavioral variables in a qualitative model; *fourth*, develop scenarios and validate model and different policy options; and *fifth*, present the model and explain the results and recommendations to stakeholders in a user-friendly manner. The problem identification and definition, system conceptualization, and stock and flow diagram are part of the qualitative methods; while developing equations, simulation, scenario building, and sensitivity analysis are part of the quantitative approach; and validation and policy analysis are both qualitative and quantitative. The methodology includes user-friendly and transparent methods with interactive software. Its emphasis on learning and communication with stakeholders indicates a unique role of the SD model in the policymaking process.

6.4 Policy Design Framework

Correct policies can help in providing the right path forward. Policies need to address both macro-level concerns and micro-level realities. Good policies can open new opportunities by addressing micro-level issues for various sectors, such as health care, education, green energy, natural resource management, and so on, and steer the process toward a sustainable future. Policies should lay stress on systemic issues that are essential for any sector and for shaping development. Right policies can drive the development in a defined way and instill confidence in the stakeholders.

The government has to deal with numerous problems, from simple nature to complicated to complex ones. These problems are of a wide range dealing with multiple stakeholders, diverse socio-economic issues, and varied geographical conditions. Policymaking is critical for meeting the intents of the government and realizing the aspirations of citizens. Designing different policies in diverse socio-economic contexts, and more so in a complex world, requires a structured approach. In addition, it necessitates defining underlying assumptions, concepts, methods, and policy approaches.

6.4.1 Good Policy System Imperatives

How policies are crucial and how these shape the country's development are elaborately discussed in Chaps. 1 and 2. Furthermore, Chaps. 2, 3, and 4 have amply highlighted the underlying issues in policymaking and implementation and spelled out the problems in the policy system. The need for policymaking arises from multiple sources, including unknown ones. Thus it reflects an element of uncertainty. Policy problems may emerge at the local, State, National, or international levels. These may be of economic, social, or political nature.

In the policy system, numerous individuals, political parties, experts, and interest groups participate in a competitive or cooperative way to influence policies. How they are to be engaged is both an opportunity and a challenge. In the evolving world characterized as a dynamic, uncertain, and complex system, policymaking and implementation are challenging tasks. The complexity is due to multiple issues such as nonlinearity, numerous interacting elements, rising aspirations of people, technological changes, and behavioral and institutional matters. These issues necessitate consideration during policymaking. Thus it calls for a policy system to evolve to remain relevant to the changing and complex nature of the system. The key aspects that policymaking and implementation need to address are:

a. conceptualization of problems from the perspectives of end-users and micro-level needs;
b. designing policies that match the citizens' needs;
c. developing institutional mechanisms for effective and efficient policy implementation; and,
d. building competencies of public organizations for policy management.

Due to its dynamic nature, public policymaking needs to be a continuous process by working on feedback loops. As societies change, the policy system needs to evolve to meet the changing needs. In a dynamic environment, adaptive policies are preferred and expected. Changing needs or problems demand calibrated or adaptive policy responses. Due to contextual importance, different public problems require specific policy solutions matching those problems instead of being fixed and goal-oriented or having a one-size-fits-all approach. So far, the conventional methods have dealt with linear thinking, simplified approach (without examining interlinkages between system variables) to understand problem and system, standalone problem analysis, and short-term and narrow perspectives. In addition, the management tools and mathematical tools, including econometrics models, have limitations as they do not take into account the dynamics of the system, non-equilibrium state, behavioral and institutional issues, and interactive behavior of elements in the system (Forrester 1961; Coyle 1996; Mueller 2020).

Existing complex systems, coupled with emerging problems, demand innovative approaches. Many scholars and practitioners have worked on new methods of policymaking and policy management. Design thinking, policy design, and collaborative approach together, with co-design and co-creation, are among the emerging practices. As covered in Sect. 6.2, innovative approaches like creative citizen engagement, deliberative dialogue, and creating adaptive policies are required. Against this backdrop, the future of public policy is conceived as a 'design' approach, in which insights from stakeholders and comprehending complex interacting issues get prominence.

Design thinking is a way of solving complex problems in the social system. It is useful when the problems are poorly structured or not clearly definable. It is characterized by probing-ability, curiosity, and empathy for understanding problems from the end-users' standpoint and then working on finding solutions. It is necessary for policy design, which is about gaining insights from citizens and then identifying the policy options that meet their expectations and needs.

6.4 Policy Design Framework

In a departure from conventional approaches, the policy design centers on comprehending problems from the perspective of the last mile and exploring new ideas and possibilities without any predetermined notion or conception. It then works on introducing policy interventions while observing the impact and modifying interventions as the situation evolves. It uses innovative approaches and works on continuous Adaptation through feedback. At the basic level, policy design concentrates on: *first*, the conceptualization of problems; *second*, methods of defining the solutions and interventions based on micro-level insights; and *third*, the ability to discern the changes and take corrective measures, and thereby continuous Adaptation of policy to changes taking place in the system and environment (Schneider and Ingram 1997; Liedtka et al. 2017; Howlett 2019).

Continuous Adaptation implies that when a new situation emerges or interventions fail, the necessary calibrated changes need to be introduced to adapt to new requirements. Or in case the interventions succeed, the level of policy initiatives should be enhanced. The 'policy design' looks akin to 'adaptive policies', but is different as regards the nature of the problems to be addressed. The policy design is more focused on the citizen-centric perspective to design policy. In contrast, adaptive policies are concerned with dynamic and uncertain aspects of problems due to internal or environmental factors.

In addition, due to the multidimensional nature of the problem and limited resources, the collaborative approach in public policy has assumed importance. It is based on the premise that there is wisdom and creativity outside the government. This approach is a process of operating in a multi-organizational forum. Public organizations or departments collaborate with educational institutions, communities, NGOs, and the private sector to analyze problems, develop policies, and introduce interventions collaboratively (O'Leary and Vij 2012; Chris and Gash 2008).

Co-design and co-creation are collaborative approaches that can facilitate in designing better policies. Both are creative and citizen-centric problem solving ways of collective idea generation and using understanding with citizens to gain insights that are otherwise difficult to elicit. The co-design involves engaging citizens or stakeholders to design the processes and services that represent their concerns and needs. It can be applied to public services like health and education. It examines people's needs and concerns, including emotional needs and the design of service delivery processes, considering the local constraints. The co-creation is about the engagement of citizens and other stakeholders in creating new ideas and solutions, services, and processes for service delivery that citizens would like to use. It is like collaborative innovation—ideation, sharing ideas, and developing new values (Kim et al. 2017; Abookire et al. 2020; Van der Wal 2017).

Thus, in a departure from traditional methods, by applying new approaches, the focus of future policymaking should be on the following:

- *first*, eliciting insights from the ground, end-users, and last mile;
- *second*, end-users'-centric policy analysis; and
- *third*, using 'design' principles.

At the fundamental level, in the context of the findings presented in Chaps. 2 and 4, sound policymaking will require the underpinnings of institutional support mechanisms, good capacity of the system, and decision criteria. These are captured in the institutional conceptual model (Fig. 6.8 and Table 6.3). The institutional underpinning provides legitimacy and raises confidence in the minds of people. Good capacity renders the policy system robust and contributes to credibility. Convincing decision criteria, based on technical, financial, performance, and quality standards, together with ethics, will result in enhanced acceptability and reliability.

The institutionalization of the policymaking process and implementation assumes importance. It will include defining the roles of all institutions, viz., constitutional bodies, political institutions, judicial institutions, government departments, political

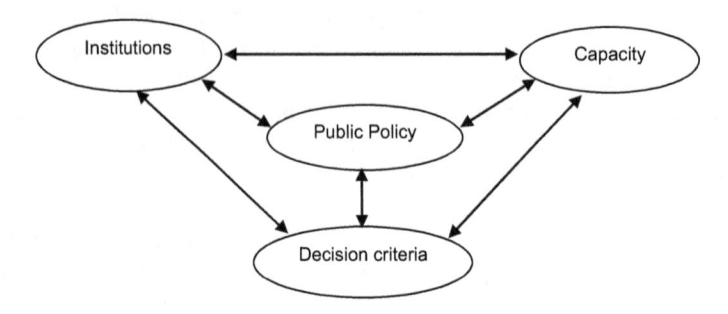

Fig. 6.8 Institutional conceptual model for public policy system

Table 6.3 Institutional dimensions for public policy system

S. No.	Dimensions	Purpose	Elements	Contribution to quality standards
1.	Institutions	Institutionalization of policymaking process and implementation	Rules, beliefs, values, and culture	Legitimacy
2.	Capacity (of public policy system)	Capacity to undertake the tasks of policy design and implementation	Principles and approaches; capacity to conceptualize, analyze, and present evidence for informed decision-making; stakeholders' engagement, capacity to implement	Robustness and credibility
3.	Decision criteria	For decision-making, and selection of right policy options and policy formulation	Technical, financial, performance, and quality standards; evidence-based approach; and ethics	Acceptability and reliability

parties, and social institutions. The capacity of the public policy system will entail the capabilities to conceptualize, analyze, and work on policy options; and implement policies effectively and efficiently. The well-defined decision criteria will contribute to the sense of predictability.

A. Science of policymaking. For the framework, policymaking is presented as a science by relying on concepts, processes, theories, and approaches evolved through scholarly research over the last century. The scientific basis is determined by a body of organized knowledge accrued through empirical studies and observations. The knowledge has been conceptualized, applied, tested, and documented by scholars in various fields like sociology, economics, engineering, management, and policy system. Such knowledge has evolved through peer-reviewed and time-tested empirical research in public policy. The ideas, observations, research hypotheses, and results have been scrutinized by experts and researchers in the concerned field to ensure academic quality. Scientific knowledge is based on published articles in recognized journals or books published by standard publishers, which have been in the public domain for years and decades. The relevant body of knowledge has provided a good foundation for a scientific basis.

Several studies in different fields have contributed to the science of public policy. The prominent fields are policy sciences (Dewey 1927; Lynd 1939; Lasswell 1951); policy analysis, behavioral science, and system analysis (Dunn 1981; Dror 1983; Dye 1992); systems theory, nonlinear dynamic theory, and ISM and system dynamics (Forrester 1961; Sage 1977; Warfield 1974; Kelly 1998; Coyle 2000); participatory approach (Brinkerhoff and Crosby 2002; Sutcliffe and Court 2005); evidence-based policy (EBP) (Randers 1980; Strauss and Corbin 1990; Marston and Watts 2003); policy tools (Glaser 1992; Raiffa 1982; Strauss and Corbin 1990; Brinkerhoff 1998; Luna-Reyes and Andersen 2003); management techniques like reflection and scenario building (Swanson and Bhadwal 2009; Kahne 2013); institutional dimension (North 1990; Burki and Perry 1998; Rodrik 1999), behavioral dimension (Thaler 1980; Lunn 2014; OECD 2017a; World Bank 2019); and complexity theory (Anderson et al. 1988; Kauffman 1995; Sanderson 2009; Morcol 2012; Arthur 2014; Geyer and Cairney 2015).

B. Key imperatives for sound public policy. Based on studies, research, and underlying assumptions (Cohen and Levinthal 1990; GoUK 1999; Curtain 2000; Geurts 2010; Hallsworth and Rutter 2011), the framework uses the following essential aspects:

- *Process-driven approach.* The process of policymaking should be a priority. The process includes eliciting ground realities, data analysis, conceptualization of problems, analyses, decision criteria, identifying policy options, and implementation plan. Policymaking is not a linear process and involves iterations.
- *Information and knowledge are fundamental to policymaking.* Data, information, and knowledge are essential for formulating a good policy. The data and information should be verifiable and reliable, and if possible, on a real-time basis (or with the least time lag).

- *Institutional and behavioral issues and complexity influence public policy.* These determine problem framing, system conceptualization, and policy adoption and need to be factored in for policy options, design, and implementation.
- *Good capacity of policy system.* Good capacity is essential for requisite analyses, design of policy, implementation, monitoring, and corrections to instill credibility, legitimacy, and salience. It is necessary for institutional learning.
- *Institutional development of policy system is necessary.* For legitimacy and credibility. From the disorganized or disjointed approach to the institutionalization of process and policy system.

C. *Principles for policymaking.* The following are the fundamental principles that should be adhered to:

- *Policymaking needs to be context specific.* Policymaking should begin with understanding the context in which the policies are to be formulated.
- *Value in micro-level detail.* Insights from the ground and knowledge about interacting variables are essential for conceptualizing problems and then determining policy options.
- *Holistic perspective and systemic analyses are essential.* To get a holistic perspective, a systemic understanding of all the parts and elements and their relationships, together with systemic analyses for conceptualizing the system, is essential.
- *Large, critical, and complex problems demand a design approach.* The design approach provides a way to gain insights from the ground and understand problems from the perspective of end-users. It is essential for large, critical, and complex problems that top-down and conventional methods cannot discern.
- *Informed decision-making based on evidence.* For sound policymaking, informed discussion and decisions are essential.
- *Implementation matters and should be mainstreamed*: Policymaking should examine the efficacy of the delivery system, be cognizant of it, and engage with implementing agencies—frontline officers and staff— to draw the proper feedback about practical issues faced by them.
- *Complexity analysis is indispensable for complex systems.* For social and economic systems, policymaking demands applying principles of complexity theory (Sect. 5.1.2). Both social policies and economic policies must factor in the complexity dimension.

D. *Evidence and quality of policymaking.* The evidence can be collected through data analysis, empirical studies, observations validated over time, field surveys, literature surveys, etc. Various analyses, viz., problem analysis, system analysis, behavioral analysis, institutional analysis, and complexity analysis, can help to provide evidence. The micro-level or grassroots-level insights are essential, and expert knowledge should be organized in usable formats (Marston and Watts 2003; Sutcliffe and Court 2005; Banks 2009). The policymaking process will get credibility by following principles, reliable evidence, and detailed analyses. The following quality dimensions are necessary for a successful policy formulation process (Table 6.4):

6.4 Policy Design Framework

Table 6.4 Quality dimensions in policymaking process

S. No.	Quality dimensions	Features	How achievable
1.	Credibility	That can be trusted, believed, or convincing	Transparency in data collection, detailed analysis, and wide-ranging consultations
2.	Legitimacy	Which is conforming to laws, rules, guidelines, logic, and facts	Government rules, Acts, guidelines, framework for policymaking; and institutionalization of policymaking process
3.	Saliency	Which is noticeable, and prominently displayed for the appreciation of the people	Framework for policymaking, wider circulation of policy document

- *credibility*: that can be trusted, believed, or convincing. For example, credible information, knowledge, etc.;
- *legitimacy*: conforming to the law, rules, and guidelines, or that can be explained with logic and justified with facts and performance; and
- *saliency*: that is noticeable due to the value creation by public policy, prominently displayed for the appreciation of the people.

6.4.2 Framework

A. *Need for a framework*. Generally, a framework is required to provide a conceptual structure and serve as a guide for defining the process to achieve a specific objective. It is a fundamental base to proceed. The policy design framework constitutes a set of assumptions, concepts, principles, approaches, tools, and practices to provide a view of real-world problems, analyze them, and provide a way to solve them. It is essential as problems can be large and complex. Without a defined set of processes and principles, it may be difficult to follow the proper steps, and policymaking may become inconsistent with the desired process. It ensures alignment among the intended purpose, policy design and implementation, and value creation. It can help evaluate the policymaking process, identify good elements for strengthening and replication, and understand gaps where corrections are required. The framework can provide the base for diagnosis and examining the shortcomings if there is any misstep or omission in the policymaking process.

Against the backdrop of issues and problems underlined in the policymaking and implementation in the previous chapters and research studies (Geurts 2010; Hallsworth and Rutter 2011; World Bank 2017; Studinka and Guenduez 2018; Loayza and Woolcock 2020), the following five distinct aspects have been holistically addressed for the policy design framework:

- *Conceptual foundation.* The conceptual understanding of underlying issues in the policy system is indispensable. The issues that matter are assumptions, concepts, approaches, and principles for policymaking; context-specific issues—diversity, local issues, and geography; systemic dimension; institutional issues; behavioral dimension; policy resistance; complexity dimension; and implementability and efficacy of delivery mechanism. The clarity of such issues will provide a good foundation for public policy.
- *Theories and approaches.* The theory and approach determine the outcomes of policies, so they deserve careful consideration and identification. For simple and complicated systems, systems theory is suitable. For complex systems—social and economic systems—complexity theory deserves priority to understand interactive behavior, emergence and evolution, uncertainty, and dynamic nature.

   Suitable approaches and strategies are needed to address specific problems, depending on their nature. For dynamic and complex systems, system approach, process approach, innovative approaches for citizen engagement, evidence-based practices, policy design approach, collaboration, co-design, co-creation, and adaptive policies are recommended. It should take into account both short-term and long-term views.
- *Capacity of policy system.* Good public policy will depend on the capacity of the policy system. The capacity building will entail robust information infrastructure (InIn); manpower with requisite capabilities; capabilities for new innovative approaches and thinking modes; policy analysis tools for system diagnosis, conceptualization of problems and system, stakeholders consultations, and policy analysis to examine different policy options; policy implementation mechanism; and monitoring and evaluation unit.
- *Policy design process.* The policy design approach focuses on insights from end-users and grassroots for system diagnosis and context-specific analyses. Based on such examination, the design of policy interventions should be done while matching the grassroots-level insights.
- *Policy implementation.* The implementation stage may throw some challenges as regards the capacity of the delivery system vis-a-vis the intended objectives. More often, there is a time lag between the available capacity of the delivery mechanism and the creation of the desired capacity. The policy implementation should take into consideration the institutional, cultural, and behavioral issues, efficacy to deliver, local contexts, and geographical conditions. The design of the delivery mechanism should factor in requisite manpower with capabilities, infrastructure, and logistics support for reaching out to citizens.

B. *Key features.* The proposed framework provides a normative approach. It includes a value-based scientific approach. The values are represented by evidence, norms, standards, and decision criteria. And the scientific basis is in the form of time-tested concepts, assumptions, postulates, and theories. It has the following features (Table 6.5):

6.4 Policy Design Framework

Table 6.5 Policy design framework

S. No.	Components	Sub-components	Elements
1.	External environment	Current policies in the sector	• Identifying key policies and their impacts (within the country and internationally)
		Current state (status) of development in the concerned sector	• Development activities and trends
		Socio-economic and technological environment (including international)	• Socio-economics trends Nationally and internationally, and their likely impact; identifying technological trends at the global level
2.	Internal support system	Conceptual foundation	• Understanding key terms: assumptions, concepts, principles, policy theories, approaches, tools, practices, value creation, behavioral issues, context-specific issues, complexity, policy resistance, and implementability
			Assumptions (in general, and for simple and complicated systems) • Both policymaking process and policy implementation are essential • Delineating ground-level insights is prerequisite • Evidence should form the basis for public policy *Assumptions for complex socio-economic systems* • Interacting behavior of elements influences the system's behavior • Social and economic systems display dynamic behavior and evolving nature
			Concepts (in general) • System structure, causal relationships, feedback, systemic analysis, and institutional and behavioral dimensions *Concepts of complex systems* • Interactive effects of elements, emergence, self-organizing property, Adaptation, evolution, and path dependency

(continued)

Table 6.5 (continued)

S. No.	Components	Sub-components	Elements
			Approaches: System approach, process approach, innovative approaches for citizen engagement, bottom-up participatory approach, evidence-based approach, policy design, collaboration, co-design, and co-creation
			Policy theories • Systems theory for a general system • Complexity theory for complex systems
			Principles • Policymaking needs to be context specific • Value in micro-level details • Holistic perspective and systemic analyses are essential • Large, critical, and complex problems demand a 'design approach' • Informed decision-making based on evidence • Implementation is critical and should be mainstreamed • Complexity analysis is indispensable for complex systems
			Policy analysis tools (*in general*) • Systems thinking, design thinking, creative citizen engagement, application of grounded theory, system diagnostic tools like causal loop and system structure diagrams, and data analytics • ISM and SD modeling for known or knowable cause-effects *For complex system*: • Complexity theory framework (Sect. 5.2), strategic foresight for scenario building, pattern recognition, and experiential learning • ISM and SD modeling (qualitative) under specific assumptions

(continued)

6.4 Policy Design Framework

Table 6.5 (continued)

S. No.	Components	Sub-components	Elements
			Work culture for • Citizen-centric approach, detailed analyses, evidence-based approach, participatory approach, and innovation
			Practices • Eliciting citizens' concerns and ground-level realities • Creating a data management system and informed decision-making • Undertaking detailed analyses • Determining the right decision criteria
			Value creation by the framework • Understanding citizens' needs and integrating them into policy instruments, consistency in policymaking, transparency, outcome-based policy, and creating public value
			Paradigms • Process-driven approach; systemic inquiry and nonlinear thinking; context-specific study; micro-level insights (end-users' needs, ground realties, and last-mile issues) driven; factoring in dynamics; systemic inquiry and nonlinear thinking; micro-level interrelationships between variables; micro-macro linkages; 'design' approach; adaptive policies for dynamic problems; and continuous engagement and improvement *From complexity perspective* • Understanding interactive effects, and emergence and evolution phenomena
		Capacity of policy system	• *Ownership*: policy group
			• *Internal structure*: for discussions and decision-making

(continued)

Table 6.5 (continued)

S. No.	Components	Sub-components	Elements
			• *Policy group*: multidisciplinary team, including data analysts and specialists • *Analysis tools* • *Manpower and capabilities*: knowledge and skills level for carrying out analyses, innovative approaches, application of systems thinking, design thinking, and complexity thinking • *Work culture management*
			• *Control*: monitoring system, concurrent evaluation mechanism, control mechanism for corrections
			• *Knowledge management*: documentation, comprehensive database system, and information infrastructure (InIn)
3.	Policy design process	Problem and system conceptualization • Basic issues	• Examining system contexts—simple, complicated, and complex (refer to Tables 5.2 and 6.6)
			• Understanding paradigms and conceptual issues in public policy and identifying approaches and theories
			Appreciating basic concerns • Grassroots-level insights, end-users' needs, practical realities, last-mile issues, and systemic issues
		Problem and system conceptualization • Systemic analyses (system diagnosis)	*Stakeholder analysis* • Understanding end-users • Gaining micro-level insights • Linking micro-macro concerns
			System analysis • Identification of factors, determining system boundary, identifying causal relationships, interrelationships between variables, and system structure • Holistic view

(continued)

6.4 Policy Design Framework

Table 6.5 (continued)

S. No.	Components	Sub-components	Elements
			Institutional analysis (for both social system and government institutions) • Political institutions, rules, laws, constitutional basis; values and culture; transparency; capacity of institutions; behavioral issues in the social institutions; and institutional mechanism for implementation
			Behavioral analysis (*community*) • Beliefs, values, culture, and preferences of individuals, families, and communities
			Complexity analysis (*of complex system*) • Identifications of stakeholders, variables, sectoral policies, and institutions; and examining interactive effects • Dynamic nature, nonlinearity, emergence, adaptation, self-organization, evolution, path dependency, etc *Complexity analysis of policy design* (*policymaking*) *cycle* • Complexity in policymaking and implementation process
			Technical analysis • Technical contexts • Technological
			Constraints analysis • Social, economic, infrastructural, institutional, and cultural
			Examination of externality • Impact of policy on environment, people, etc
			Micro-macro linkages analysis • Micro-level insights reflecting the needs of citizens • Macro-level requirements like budget, financial stability, balancing inter-sectoral priorities, etc • Linking micro-level needs and macro-level requirements

(continued)

Table 6.5 (continued)

S. No.	Components	Sub-components	Elements
		Policy analysis	Policy analysis: context-specific analysis, including trend analysis, cost–benefit analysis, scenario analysis, etc. Application of qualitative and mathematical modeling and analytical tools (ISM and SD modeling)
		Decision-making	Based on criteria: grassroots insights and end-users' needs; technical, financial, quality parameters, and ethical standards
		Policy options	Identifying different policy options based on analyses
		Policy design	Designing policies based on end-users' needs and systemic analyses
		Policy document	Intents, objectives, instruments of policies, and performance indicators
4.	Implementation	Approach for implementation	• Process approach and collaborative approach (co-design and co-creation) • Examination of institutional, behavioral, complexity, and technical issues for implementation
		Delivery system design	• Capacity to deliver: manpower, training, capabilities, logistics support, monitoring system, etc • Management practices, systems, and processes like quality management system (QMS), performance management system (PMS), citizen-centric system, key result areas (KRAs), and key performance indicators (KPIs)
5.	Outputs and outcomes	Results	• Measuring outputs in terms of set indicators (KRAs and KPIs) • Outcomes of the programs in terms of broad societal objectives • Performance management system (PMS)

(continued)

6.4 Policy Design Framework

Table 6.5 (continued)

S. No.	Components	Sub-components	Elements
		Public value	• Public value: addressing basic needs of citizens, quality of public services, efficiency of service delivery, and sustainability of the programs
6.	Evaluation	Evaluation of each policy and program	• Mechanism to carry out evaluation studies • Future course correction based on evaluation studies

Note Framework covers the policy design for simple, complicated, and complex systems
ISM interpretive structural modeling, *SD* system dynamics

- *Assumptions.* The assumptions are like premises or beliefs that underpin a framework or theory. For sound policymaking, under this framework, the basic assumptions are: both the policymaking process and policy implementation are essential; delineating ground-level insights are prerequisites; and evidence should form the basis for public policy. From the perspective of complex socio-economic systems, the assumptions are: the interacting behavior of elements needs consideration; interactions between individuals, system variables, policies, programs, institutions, and external environment influence the system's behavior; and the social and economic systems display dynamic behavior and evolving nature.
- *Concepts.* For a general system, the concepts that need appreciation are system structure, causal relationships, feedback, systemic analysis, and institutional and behavioral dimensions. For complex systems, together with these, other concepts are interactive behavior, emergence, Adaptation, self-organization, evolution, and path dependence.
- *Principles.* The principles are discussed above in Sect. 6.4.1. These should form the basis for policymaking.
- *Policy analysis tools.* There is a wide range of tools for analysis. Some of them are systems thinking, design thinking, creative citizen engagement, application of grounded theory, system diagnostic tools like causal loop and system structure diagrams, data analytics, etc. For simple and complicated problems, including nonlinear and dynamic, the ISM) and SD modeling can be applied. These can be applied to known or unknown but knowable cause-effects. These can examine the interrelationships between variables and model their causal effects. For complex systems, the suitable tools are strategic foresight for scenario building, pattern recognition, and experiential learning. ISM and SD modeling (qualitative) can be applied for conceptual understanding only under specific assumptions. These modeling approaches do not examine the interactive effects of elements. The complexity theory framework can manage complex systems.
- *Work culture and practices.* The requisite work culture and certain practices need to be ingrained in the policymaking process to create a robust ecosystem. The work culture of a citizen-centric approach, detailed analyses, evidence-based approach,

participatory approach, and innovation is required in the policy system. The recommended practices are eliciting citizens' concerns and ground-level realities, creating a data management system and informed decision-making; undertaking detailed analyses; and determining proper right decision criteria—technical, financial, performance, and quality standards, etc.
- *Value creation by the framework.* It is in terms of understanding citizens' needs and integrating them into policy instruments, consistency in policymaking, transparency, outcome-based policy, and creating public value.

C. *Paradigm shift.* For dealing with complex socio-economic issues, the policy system needs to handle issues like discerning insights from the ground, comprehending problems, examining the system through multiple analyses, and formulating policies reflecting the citizens' needs. It calls for a paradigm shift in policymaking, comprising the following:

- *Context-specific policymaking*: from one-size-fits-all policy to context-specific policymaking based on geographical and local socio-economic conditions.
- *Systemic inquiry and nonlinear thinking*: from traditional linear thinking and mental models to systemic inquiry and nonlinear thinking.
- *'Design' approach*: from identified solutions or prescriptive approach to designing policy by factoring in local realities and insights from end-users.
- *Micro-level insights driven*: from consultative process to discerning insights from end-users and concerned stakeholders through deliberate dialogue and citizen engagement.
- *Practical realities*: from a top-down approach to understanding practical realities like grassroots-level constraints and barriers (geographical, psychological, mobility, etc.).
- *Last-mile issues*: from uniform policy prescription to addressing last-mile concerns;
- *Conscious learning*: from one-time learning to conscious and structured learning from the end-users' feedback, trends, and performance parameters.
- *Local specific data:* from approach of relying on the aggregate value of variables to the segregated data of different sections based on local conditions.
- *Micro-macro linkages*: from macro-level perspective or top-down approach to linking micro-level insights with macro-level perspective.
- *Micro-level interrelationships between variables*: from an approach of assuming a single composite system to understand causal relationships between system variables and then gaining a view of interrelationships within the system.
- *Fragmented to holistic treatment*: from addressing problems in parts to approaching them holistically by considering all the parts and their interrelated problems holistically.
- *Understanding complexity*: from an aggregate level of understanding to examining interactive effects of elements (individuals and system variables) at the micro level and the phenomena of emergence and evolution. For complex systems, the interactive effects matter.

6.4 Policy Design Framework

- *Factoring in dynamics*: from assuming static conditions to examining changing conditions within the system and in environment.
- *Detailed analyses for evidence-based approach*: from a simplified approach by examining limited issues and factors to detailed analyses (like institutional, complexity, behavioral, technical, etc.) for an evidence-based approach.
- *Criteria-based decision-making*: from an intuitive or past experience to criteria-based decision-making (technical, financial, performance, quality, and ethical standards).
- *Adaptive policies*: from fixed policies to adaptive policies to adapt to changing conditions in dynamic systems.
- *Continuous engagement and improvement*: from one-time intervention to continuous engagement and improvement based on feedback.

D. Why micro-level insights. The reasons why micro-level insights in policymaking should be given priority are: micro level is represented by the people or end-users for whom the policies are designed, and so the process of consultations can provide more credence and a sense of belongingness; to tap into the hidden human potential; to enhance the acceptability of policy due to better policy design through analyses of micro-level or grassroots-level problems; to enhance the implementability of policy; and in the knowledge economy coupled with digital integration, people play vital roles, and thus, the speed, scope, and scale of adoption of economic activities can be much higher.

E. Methodological issues in policy design. In the social and economic systems, better policy design requires the process to factor in two general requirements. *Firstly*, it should delineate the ground realities and citizens' needs, and *secondly*, it needs to consider the dynamic needs of the system. In addition, in the context of uncertainty and nonlinearity, a dynamic environment, and complex problems, the application of the complexity theory is necessitated. It necessitates examining the 'heterogeneity' of contexts and 'interactions' between individuals, system variables, institutions, inter-sectoral policies, and the global environment.

At a broader level, to conceptualize the problem and system, including complexity, the process should incorporate the combination of the following, depending upon the extent of the problem: multi-level analyses at micro, meso, State, National, and global levels; an interdisciplinary approach to gain insights and discern causes of problems; understanding of multifaceted aspects like technological, institutional, organizational, behavioral, technical, and cultural issues; and comparative perspectives of both State-wise or region-wise within the country and country-wise in the global context to bring diverse viewpoints.

For dealing with different kinds of system conditions, the policy approaches are summarized in Table 6.6 (refer to Sect. 5.2 and Table 5.2, complexity theory framework in Chap. 5, and system dynamics modeling in Sect. 6.3.2).

The tools that are currently employed have limited capabilities. It calls for tools with capabilities to elicit insights from the grassroots, conceptualize problems and system, and, subsequently, design policies. For policy design, a set of tools,

Table 6.6 Different system conditions: approaches, thinking modes, and policy analysis tools

S. No.	System conditions (nature of problems/ types of system)	Approaches and theories	Thinking modes	Policy analysis tools
1.	Simple and complicated problems	• System approach • Process approach • ISM, system dynamics • Policy design	• Systems thinking • Design thinking	• Creative citizen (end-users) engagement • Deliberative dialogue • Causal loop and system structure diagrams
2.	Complex and dynamic problems, but definable cause-effects (known or unknown but knowable)	• Systems theory • Adaptive policies • System approach • ISM and system dynamics modeling • Micro-macro linkages • Policy design	• Systems thinking • Design thinking	• Creative citizen (end-users) engagement • Deliberative dialogue • Causal loop and system structure diagrams
3.	Complex problems (uncertainty, nonlinearity, dynamic environment, emergence)	• Complexity theory • Qualitative system dynamics modeling • Adaptive policies • Process approach • Micro-macro linkages • Policy design	• Complexity thinking • Systems thinking • Design thinking	• Creative citizen (end-users) engagement • Deliberative dialogue • Causal loop and system structure diagrams • Pattern recognition • Scenario building
Analyses, approaches, and tools common to all conditions		Institutional, behavioral, complexity, and technical analyses; grounded theory; evidence-based approach; analytical tools		

approaches, and modes of thinking are needed for conceptualization, policy analysis, implementation, and evaluation, as shown in Table 6.7.

F. Components of policy design framework. The governments have the ubiquitous task of managing public affairs in all the fields and levels—Central, State, district, and sub-district. They are required to address immediate to short-term and long-term pressing issues and deal with numerous problems—simple, complicated, and complex. In this light, to manage multifaceted problems holistically, a robust framework is necessitated. The proposed framework draws on the vast network of knowledge in the field of policymaking, system approach, evidence-based approach, and complexity theory. It comprehensively covers the paradigms, approaches, processes, analyses, and institutional mechanism. The framework emphasizes system perspective, evidence-based approach, robust process of policymaking and applying innovative methods, and both qualitative and quantitative modeling approaches. It suggests promoting design as an innovative approach to policymaking (and implementation).

6.4 Policy Design Framework

Table 6.7 Policy design: approaches, thinking modes, and policy analysis tools

S. No.	Stages of policy design	Approaches	Thinking modes	Policy analysis tools
1.	Problem conceptualization and definition	• Design approach • System approach • Creative citizen (end-users) engagement • Deliberative dialogue	• Design thinking (empathizing) • Systems thinking • Complexity thinking (for complex problems)	• Stakeholder analysis, probing, • Focus group discussion (FGD) • Brainstorming, • Grounded theory • Causal loop diagram • System structure diagram • Pattern recognition • Scenario building • Analytical tools • Creative citizen (end-users) engagement • Deliberative dialogue
2.	System conceptualization (institutional, behavioral, complexity, technical, delivery system analyses)	• System approach (ISM and system dynamics modeling) • Complexity theory (for complex problems) • Evidence-based approach • Micro-macro linkages		
3.	Policy analysis, policy options, and decision-making	• Design approach • Adaptive policies		
4.	Implementation (institutional, behavioral, complexity, technical analyses)	• Design approach • Process approach • Collaborative approach		
5.	Evaluation	• System approach • Process approach		

The process is set in motion with the conceptualization of problem and system and then followed through various steps for policy design.

It lays stress to examine trends and trajectories, symptoms, causes, second- and third-order effects, and the pattern of system behavior. The existing assumptions are to be revisited to understand whether the assumptions are correct, whether the assumptions are putting constraints on understanding the problem and defining the future state, and whether the assumptions need to be re-defined. For example, the studies show that socio-economic conditions put constraints on families to send their children to schools. Whether such constraints are considered while defining the assumptions for formulating the policy on primary education needs examination.

Figure 6.9 presents a policy design framework with components such as external environment, internal support system, policy design process, implementation, results, and evaluation. And the framework is outlined in Table 6.5.

F1. External environment. It includes examining issues such as the state of development, policies in the concerned sector at National and global levels, and the socio-economic and technological environment. It analyzes whether the external environment is adequately captured for making an appropriate case for policymaking.

F2. Internal support system. It defines the underlying basis for policymaking, covering assumptions, paradigms, and principles (Sect. 6.4.1). It includes application of thinking modes, analysis tools, theories, innovative approaches, and undertaking systemic analyses. It recommends complexity theory for complex social and economic problems. The policy system should have the capacity to perform various tasks of policy design. The capacity includes a policy group with a multidisciplinary team, data analysts and specialists, requisite expertise, ownership, internal structure, capabilities, control, culture, concurrent evaluation, and knowledge management. It stresses the need for information infrastructure.

Comprehensive database system. In addition to institutional and behavioral issues, the application of technology is called for handling large datasets. For evidence-based policymaking, the requirement of a comprehensive database system needs special mention. With the increase in the number of programs and beneficiaries, the development and performance indicators have increased manifold. Such a dataset is too large and complex to be dealt with by traditional methods. It requires a new way of handling, and one such approach is 'big data'. The application of big data is a way to extract information from a dataset systematically and analyze it. In addition, artificial intelligence (AI tools), Natural Language Processing (NLP), and Machine Learning (ML) techniques can be leveraged to do data analysis for various development programs (Kalil 1995; Meso et al. 2009; Giest 2017; World Bank 2017).

Realizing the potential of data, it will call for creating an institutional mechanism for information infrastructure (InIn). It comprises capacity building, including ICT hardware and software support, big data, and data analytics tools; competency building for using big data tools; real-time data collection for select indicators of high importance; data collation and storage; and user-friendly collation of data for decision-making. As an illustration, among others, the information infrastructure

6.4 Policy Design Framework

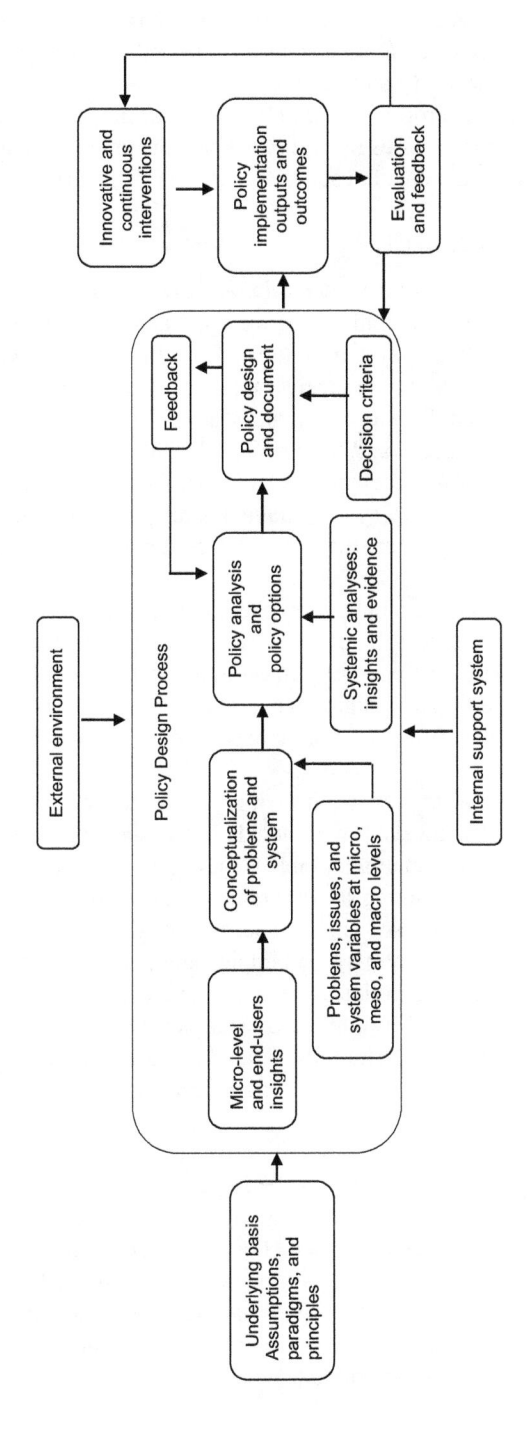

Fig. 6.9 Policy design framework

(InIn) is required for real-time data for sector-wise and subsector-wise employment; skill-wise data for the unskilled, skilled, and specialized skilled workforce; income of different professions, sections, and age groups, to give a few examples. Another example relates to real-time crop-wise agriculture production data, Block-wise and district-wise; prices of commodities in each Block and district and the international market; commodity-wise sale data in each Block and district, and so on.

F3. Policy design process. It entails the following steps:

a. Identification of system contexts and approaches. The first step is to identify the types of systems. Table 6.6 summarizes the approaches, thinking modes, and policy analysis tools for different system contexts. Four different contexts are shown in Table 5.2. Based on the contexts, strategies, approaches, and theories for different systems need to be identified. Based on that, the policy design should be undertaken. The system contexts are subjective and can be inferred with experience, expert knowledge, and detailed analyses like scenario building and pattern recognition (refer to Sect. 5.4). The schematic view of system diagnosis for policy design is presented in Fig. 6.10a. The framework covers the policy design for simple, complicated, and complex systems.

b. Alternative paradigms. It emphasizes alternative paradigms consisting of a 'design' approach and adaptive policies. These are necessitated as a result of both, *first*, increased complexity and emerging uncertainty of large scale, and *second*, generation of new knowledge and insights about characteristics of systems and problems. These innovative ways of policymaking have emerged from the research work over the years.

c. Conceptualization. The process begins with the problem and system conceptualization through system diagnosis. It will include identifying approaches, theories, thinking modes, and tools for analyses (Table 6.7). Figure 6.10b depicts the basics of policy design. It entails examining sectoral issues like development issues, development indicators, and trends; and understanding policy system—policymaking process, institutional issues, complexity, and implementation issues. It recommends an iterative process. Designing policies demands appreciating the importance of basic issues like grassroots-level insights, end-users' needs, practical realities, last-mile issues, and systemic issues. The process applies design thinking and critical inquiry for discerning insights and recommends conscious learning, designing, and iterations.

d. Systemic analyses: There is a need to make a departure from the current approach of assuming the system is static and in an equilibrium and stable environment; examining the problems and system in parts or variables independently, without a holistic consideration and studying interactions between elements; and dealing with the economy in an aggregate form, without examining interactive behavior of elements and the emergence and evolutionary nature. Such an approach limits the ability to address the issues systemically and from the standpoint of complexity. For a holistic understanding of the problem and system, the following analyses are needed:

6.4 Policy Design Framework

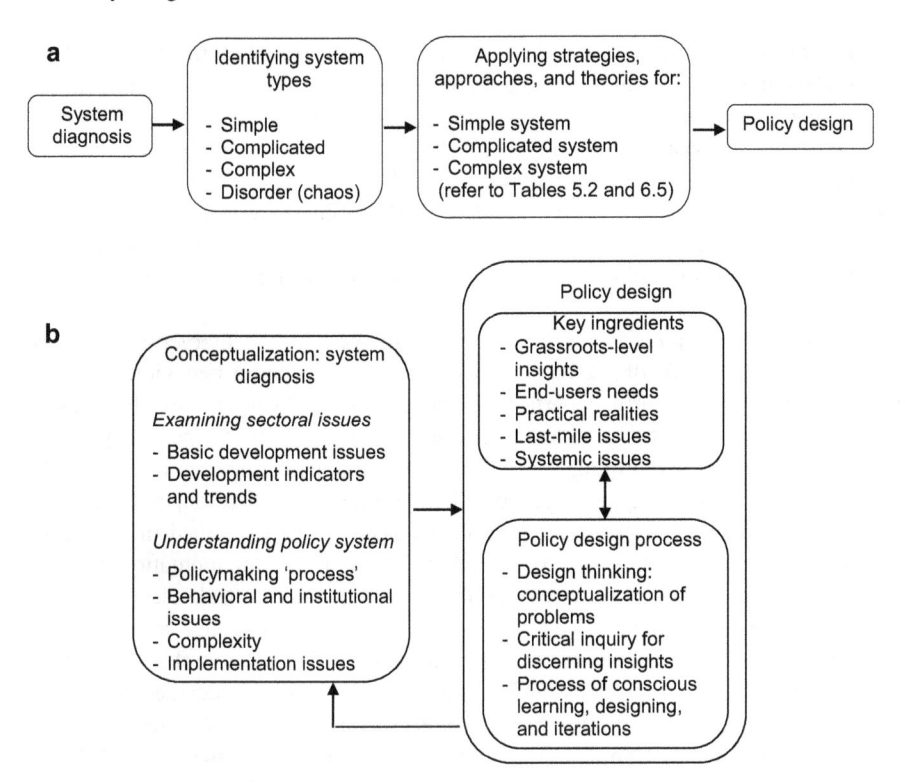

Fig. 6.10 Schematic view of policy design. **a** Schematic view of process. **b** Schematic view: basic features

- *Stakeholder analysis*. It is for the purpose of gaining micro-level insights, understanding end-users, and linking micro-level needs with macro-level requirements.
- *System analysis*. It includes identifying factors and components, determining system boundary, identifying causal relationships, and system structure. Interpretive structural modeling (ISM), system dynamics (SD) modeling, and complexity analysis (for complex problems) are recommended for system analysis (w.r.t. conditions identified in Tables 5.2 and 6.6). It will involve obtaining a holistic view. *Holistic view*. It implies understanding the characteristics of parts (or components) and their interrelationships, examining the features of system variables (of parts) and their interrelationships, and thereby obtaining a holistic view. The interrelationships are between variables. To study a system, certain assumptions should be made to understand the boundary. To illustrate an example for the health system, it will include identifying *parts*—infrastructure, logistics, medical personnel, equipments, etc.; *elements*—individuals and system variables together; *variables*—conditions of patients, cultural issues, distance, etc.; and *individuals*—health staff, doctors, patients, beneficiaries, citizens, etc. Subsequently, the interrelationships need to be examined.

- *Institutional analysis* (for both social and government institutions). It is about understanding the features of the institutions, which provide a structure in the policy system. It will entail examining political institutions, rules, laws, and constitutional basis; values, culture, attitudes, and beliefs; transparency; capacity of institutions; and institutional mechanism for implementation.
- *Behavioral analysis (of the community)*. Public policies are formulated for social systems in which the behavioral issues of people matter. It requires understanding the beliefs, values, culture, and personal preferences of individuals, families, and communities.
- *Complexity analysis (of a system)*. Complexity means large interacting elements, dynamic nature, feedback loop, nonlinearity, and uncertain behavior. Complex systems are inherently uncertain. These are generally acceptable features. It will require identifying stakeholders and system variables, sectoral policies, and institutions, examining their interactions, and analyzing characteristics like dynamics, nonlinearity, emergence, Adaptation, self-organization, evolution, and path dependence. Besides, the complexity needs to be examined in the policy design cycle, including the policymaking and policy implementation process. The interrelationships between variables are related to causal effects, and the interactive effects are related to the phenomena of emergence and evolution with time. These necessitate study. For comprehending the complexity, together with a holistic view, understanding the interactive effects, besides examining the emergence and evolutionary nature, is essential. The interactions take place between elements comprising individuals and variables, as shown in Box 6.1. The interactions influence the outputs as given in the equation below:

System outputs = Interactive effects of elements $(e_1, e_2, e_3, \ldots, e_n)$; e : element.

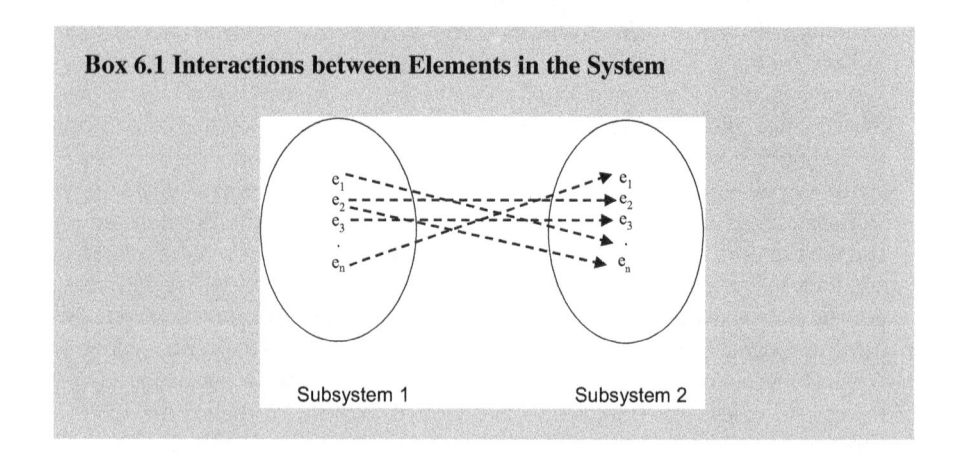

Box 6.1 Interactions between Elements in the System

Subsystem 1   Subsystem 2

6.4 Policy Design Framework

- *Technical analysis.* It includes examining technical issues and the technological environment. Issues like the evolution of technologies and their impact on the economy, employment, and competitiveness need examination.
- *Constraints analysis.* There are social, economic, infrastructure, institutional, and cultural constraints, which require examination. These constraints could be in the form of family income, skill sets, infrastructure, etc.
- *Examination of externality.* It is the likely impact of policy on the environment, community, people, etc. It may be positive or negative. For example, the impact of pollution on the environment, infrastructure creation on the income of people, etc.
- *Micro-macro linkages analysis.* The micro-level insights reflecting the needs of citizens or end-users provide a unique perspective that cannot be captured by the macro level. At the same time, macro-level requirements, like budget, financial stability, balancing inter-sectoral priorities, etc., are essential elements. It demands linking micro-level needs and macro-level requirements to get a holistic view.
- *Policy analysis.* The analysis will contain context-specific trend analysis, cost–benefit analysis, scenario analysis, etc., to provide inputs for policy options. It consists of applying qualitative and mathematical modeling (for a specific problem and after defining boundary) and may include analytical tools like ISM and SD modeling.
- *Policy option analysis.* Identification of policy option matching insights from the grassroots and end-users' needs, systemic analyses, macro-level conditions, and decision criteria.

e. *Policy document.* The policy design requires considering end-users' needs, analyses, and policy options, and accordingly, the policy instruments should be designed. The decision-making for the policy design should factor in insights and concerns from the grassroots and apply technical, financial, quality parameters, and ethical criteria. The document will comprise policy intents, objectives, instruments, and performance indicators.

F4. Implementation : Good policy implementation will determine the success of the policies. Firstly, the approaches for the implementation are to be identified. These will include the process approach, bottom-up participatory approach, and collaborative approach. Besides, co-design and co-creation methods are required for citizen-specific or local-specific problems by engaging stakeholders. Like policymaking, the implementation will necessitate examining institutional, behavioral, complexity, and technical issues. It calls for a robust delivery system to implement the policies and will entail infrastructure, requisite manpower with capabilities, equipments, logistics support, and so on, depending on the system. Good management practices, systems, and processes are necessitated. Some of them are the quality management system (QMS), performance management system (PMS), and citizen-centric system.

It involves defining key result areas (KRAs) and key performance indicators (KPIs) for a particular policy and program and establishing a monitoring and control system.

F5. Outputs and outcomes measurement: It calls for the mechanism in the form of a management information system (MIS) for measuring set indicators (KPIs). The outcomes of the programs, including broad societal outcomes, need assessment. It also demands an examination of the creation of public values like addressing the basic needs of citizens, the quality of public services, the efficiency of service delivery, and the sustainability of the programs.

F6. Evaluation: The mechanism to conduct evaluation studies should be determined and put in place. Based on evaluation studies, it calls for the introduction of future course corrections.

6.5 Case Study: Policymaking for Renewable Energy

6.5.1 Overview of Energy Scenario in the Country

India has experienced a good growth rate over several years. For the Indian economy to continue with high growth, India needs to address its energy needs, which cover all the sectors and impact both rural and urban areas in the country. Electricity—both in terms of quality and access—is a vital challenge (Planning Commission 2005; IEA 2011b). In 2009, the per capita total primary energy supply (TPES) in India stood at 0.58 tons of oil equivalents (TOE). It has been much less than the world average of 1.80 TOE (IEA 2011a) (Table 6.8). The per capita electricity consumption in the country has been 597 KWhr compared to the world average of 2730 KWhr. Providing electricity to the people while moving to low-carbon electricity generation is a social imperative. Table 6.9 reflects CO_2 emissions for India and the world. Indian electricity supply and demand would increase significantly in the coming decades (Remme et al. 2011).

Table 6.8 Comparison of key energy indicators (India vs. World) (in 2009 and 2017)

S. No.	Indicators	2009		2017	
		India	World	India	World
1.	Per capita TPES (TOE)	0.58	1.80	0.66	1.86
2.	TPES /GDP (Kgoe/$) (2000 PPP)	0.15	0.19	0.10	0.12
3.	Per capita electricity consumption (KWhr)	597	2,730	947	3,152
4.	Energy production (MTOE)	502	12,292	554.4	14,035

Source IEA (2011a) and IEA (2019)
TPES total primary energy supply, *Kgoe* kilograms of oil equivalents, *PPP* purchasing power parity, *TOE* tons of oil equivalents, *MTOE* million tons of oil equivalents

6.5 Case Study: Policymaking for Renewable Energy

Table 6.9 CO_2 emissions: comparison of key indicators (India vs. World) (in 2009 and 2017)

S. No.	Indicators*	2009 India	2009 World	2017 India	2017 World
1.	CO_2 emissions (Billion tons)	1.585	28.99	2.161	32.84
2.	Per capita CO_2 emissions (tCO_2)	1.37	4.29	1.61	4.37
3.	CO_2 emissions per GDP (tCO_2/$)(2000 PPP)	0.35	0.45	0.26	0.29

Source IEA (2011a)
* Emissions from fuel combustion only (*PPP* purchasing power parity)

As per the integrated energy policy (Planning Commission 2005), 'to deliver a sustained growth of 8% through 2031', India will, at the very least, need to grow its primary energy supply by 3–4 times and electricity supply by 5–7 times the present consumption. The installed power capacity (MW) by source in India is reflected in Table 6.10, and the installed capacity of renewable energy by source in India is presented in Table 6.11. Some energy indicators are depicted in Tables 6.22 (REN21 2018), 6.23 (REN21 2011, 2020), 6.24 (REN21 2018), and 6.25 (Arora et al. 2010; CEA 2010; MOSPI 2019) in Appendix 1. In the concerned Tables, the comparison between 2009 and 2017 (or 2018 or 2019) is made to get an idea about the change that has taken place.

Note The case study is based on the research work under the Ph.D. program during 2005–12, so data for this period is taken for analysis in the ISM and SD modeling. While the data for 2017/2018 is for comparison

Climate change results from anthropogenic activities like the combustion of fossil fuels, industrial processes, agricultural practices, deforestation, and greenhouse gases (GHGs) released into the atmosphere. Globally, relying on coal, the power sector alone contributes 40–45% of the total carbon emissions. In India, as per the report of the Ministry of Environment and Forests (MoEF 2010), coal contributes 90% of the total CO_2 emissions in electricity generation. Climate change has wider implications

Table 6.10 Installed power capacity by source in India (grid connected)

S. No.	Sources	2010 Capacity (MW)	2018 Capacity (MW)
1.	Thermal	1,15,649	2,76,124
	Coal	96,743	2,30,006
	Gas	17,706	31,112
	Oil	1199	15,156
2.	Hydro	38,106	45,363
3.	Nuclear	4,798	6,780
4.	Renewable (excluding small hydro)	18,442	70,562
	Total	1,76,990	3,99,900

Source Arora et al. (2010), CEA (2010) and MOSPI (2019)

Table 6.11 Installed capacity by renewable energy source in India (2010 and 2018)

S. No.	Sources	Capacity (MW) 2010	Capacity (MW) 2018
1.	Wind	12,717	34,986
2.	Solar	45	24,312
3.	Small hydro	2,767	4,506
4.	Biomass	2,913	9,545
5.	Total	18,442	73,349

Source CEA (2010) and REN21 (2018)

for governments, businesses, communities, and citizens in the coming decades (IPCC 2007).

India is expected to face the challenge of sustaining rapid economic growth while dealing with the global challenge of climate change (NAPCC 2008). Recognizing that climate change is a global challenge, India was actively involved in the multilateral negotiations in UN Framework Convention on Climate Change (UNFCCC). In response to the challenge of climate change and to meet international obligations, the National Action Plan for Climate Change (NAPCC) has stressed deploying appropriate renewable energy technologies to mitigate greenhouse gas emissions. Renewable energy (RE) sources provide electricity without emissions of GHGs. And these are also abundantly available resources for the future. To realize the high potential of the renewable energy (RE) sector in the country, Government has placed a policy and regulatory framework by way of the Electricity Act 2003, National Electricity Policy 2005, and National Tariff Policy 2006 (Arora et al. 2010; World Bank 2010).

6.5.2 Systems Thinking and Design Thinking Application

The problems in the real world are intricate. They consist of a network of interconnected issues and factors. Due to interlinked relationships in the web, it makes understanding the problems a difficult task. Usually, while analyzing problems, the traditional approaches tend not to take a holistic view and understand the interlinkages. In addition, they pass over behavioral, institutional, and social issues. There is a tendency to note the simple and easy parts or issues, which are easy to understand. And by overlooking intricate matters, there is an oversimplification of a difficult, big, or complex problem. In this process, some essential issues or factors are missed, understanding the influence of interconnected relationships is not discerned, and the knowledge about the 'whole of the system is disregarded. Besides, many a time, due to previous experience, limited time to reflect, or sometimes biases, there is a tendency to settle into a pattern of thinking, analysis, and working. This tendency may be counterproductive when dealing with big or complex problems. Addressing such problems demands challenging existing thought process, assumptions, and approaches and then redefining the approach of inquiry (Saeed 1994; Liedtka 2013; Howlett 2019).

For dealing with a policy of biomass power system comprising a large number of stakeholders, issues, and factors—economic, technological, logistical, behavioral, institutional, and management, it necessitated applying new ways of thinking about the problems. Based on the literature review, systems thinking and design thinking were considered for the research work (Senge 1990; Richmond 2010; Liedtka et al. 2017). Systems thinking is about understanding a system in a holistic manner. It helps to recognize various factors and their interconnections to obtain perspective about the whole system. The system could be a social sector, economy, industry, or organization.

Systems thinking was applied to provide insights about subsystems, factors, and their linkages in the case study. At the basic level, the study employed systems thinking to conceptualize the problem and system. It included studying diverse stakeholders, identifying the components or subsystems and factors therein, defining the basis for the inclusion of factors, examining the linkages between factors, understanding the feedback from stakeholders, and examining the causal relations. At the advanced level, it was utilized to prepare the system dynamics model and do technical analysis. It entailed a policy structure diagram, causal loop (CL) diagrams, stock and flow diagram, and simulations and sensitivity analysis. Design thinking is about exploring issues when the problems are not obvious and involve behavioral and intricate matters. It requires an iterative and open-ended process, challenges assumptions, redefines problems, and identifies innovative solutions from the perspective of end-users. It attempts to engage the end-users and empathize to build trust and confidence. In the case study, the end-users are plant developers and farmers. They were engaged to elicit insights into the issues and problems.

6.5.3 Research Design

Motivation for the research. Biomass has vast potential in an agrarian economy like India. The cost of generating electricity from biomass is similar to or less than that of wind (MNRE 2011a). According to the Ministry of New and Renewable Energy (MNRE) (2010), India has a good surplus biomass that can be used for electricity generation. It has been estimated that the gross potential from biomass-based electricity system is about 51,000 MW—17,000 MW from Agro-residue and 34,000 MW from energy plantations in the wasteland (MNRE 2011a). The Agro-residue (biomass) resources can be leveraged to support different options, viz., grid extension, captive power generation, and off-grid solutions for local village needs. To harness the potential of renewable energy (RE) sector in the country, several policy measures have been taken. Some measures, like the framework for quotas for renewable energy and preferential feed-in tariffs besides capital subsidy, have been provided to promote biomass power system. Despite the regulatory framework, the growth in biomass power system has not been adequate (MERC 2010). Equally important is the low utilization of installed capacity, resulting in a low plant load factor (PLF), thus indicating that whatever capacity is added is not fully utilized (UNEP 2008; World Bank 2010).

In the context of biomass (Agro-residue) for electricity plants, some of the key issues are as follows:

- It is noted by MERC (2010) that electricity generation based on renewable energy sources is 'infirm' and requires that the electricity produced be effectively dispatched as and when available. The biomass availability depends on crop residue generation and utilization patterns, seasonal weather conditions, etc. Hence, there could be significant variation in the electricity generation from biomass during the year (CERC 2009).
- Agro-residue is used in the case study and referred to as fuel or raw material for biomass electricity plants. Despite the vast potential of Agro-residue-based electricity plants and the associated benefits of improving farmers' income and providing employment in rural areas, there have been several barriers. All forms of biomass face problems like availability, price fluctuation, handling, transportation, and storage. And the realization of potential remains much less (UNEP 2008; World Bank 2010).

The above discussion highlights that, despite limitations, biomass can contribute significantly to meeting the future electricity requirement. It can be successfully utilized in mitigating the adverse impact of fossil fuels. There is a case for examining the current policies and identifying factors that are contributing to or hindering the progress of this sector and researching the policy options that can facilitate the growth of the Agro-residue plant on a sustainable basis.

Research objectives. It has come out from the literature survey that the factors hindering success have been analyzed by several studies, but these are not examined holistically, and a unified view of the problems is not available. The policy of the Government, by way of several initiatives, tries to address some issues but is not able to address all the issues comprehensively. Some of the issues that need examination in an integrated manner are collection efficiency of Agro-residue, regulation of the price of cotton Agro-residue, enhancing the plant load factor (PLF), and technological advancements.

From the perspective of the system, it requires studying multiple factors from a 'system point of view' and providing a systematic way of understanding their interdependencies and their impact on the Agro-residue power system for making better policy decisions. The focus group discussions (FGDs) with stakeholders have helped in evolving and formulating the research questions, which are as follows:

i. Which are the factors that influence setting up an Agro-residue power system?
ii. How are these factors interlinked with one another in the structure of the system, and do they facilitate system conceptualization?
iii. How can these factors be modeled to represent the real-world situation, and nonlinearity and complexity be addressed?
iv. Which are the factors that are dependents or drivers in the system?

6.5 Case Study: Policymaking for Renewable Energy

v. What are the policy options to promote Agro-residue for setting up a power system?

Research methodology. For the purpose of research, the Wardha Block in Wardha district of Maharashtra was chosen (during Ph.D. program). It applied interpretive structural modeling (ISM) and system dynamics (SD) modeling for grid-connected Agro-residue plant, with combustion technology utilizing cotton as Agro-residue. The research methodology applied both qualitative and quantitative approaches. It began with the literature review, preliminary stakeholder analysis (SA), and expert consultations. It involved steps like delineation of the problem, system conceptualization, model preparation, simulation, validation, and scenario building, and finally, the policy options were recommended. To add value to modeling, the qualitative approaches, including the soft system approach and systems thinking, were applied (Luna-Reyes and Andersen 2003; Kusmuljono et al. 2007) at all stages, viz., problem definition, system conceptualization, simulation phase, policy analysis, and recommendations (Table 6.12). Systems thinking helped in examining social and psychological, technical, financial, and institutional factors to gain a system-wide view.

The concepts of design thinking were used to understand the end-users' (farmers and plant developers) problems and the assumptions behind the policies and then explore the solutions through iterations in a human-centered problem-solving approach during policy analysis (Osborn 1963; Schon 1983). While using design thinking, the innovative approach of policy design was applied to identify solutions and policies from the perspectives of end-users during policy analysis. It worked on

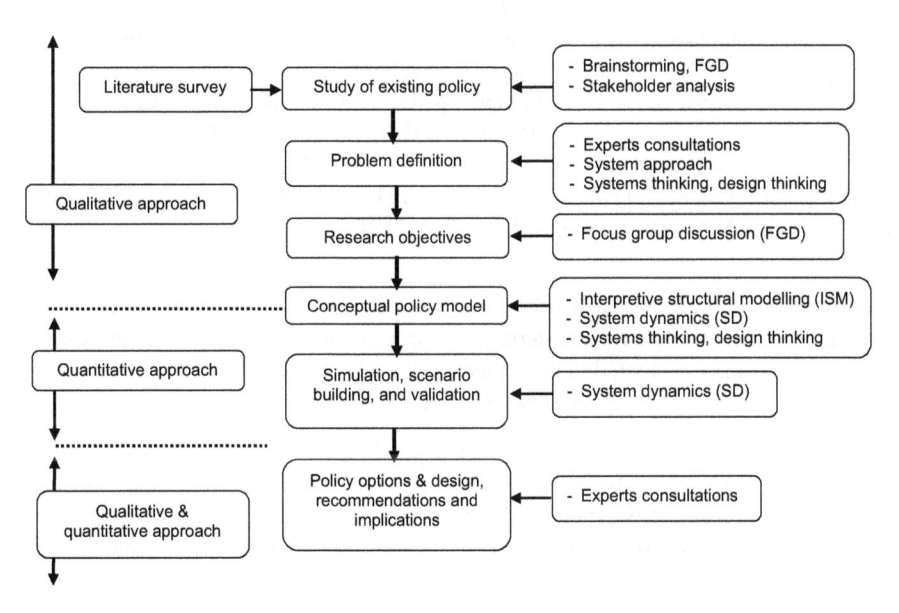

Fig. 6.11 Flow chart of research methodology

Table 6.12 Policy research tools applied in the research study for ISM and SD modeling

S. No.	Policy research tools	Purpose
1.	Systems thinking	To obtain a system-wide view and undertake a holistic analysis of problems
2.	Design thinking	To obtain insights from end-users (farmers and plant developers) and to understand their perspectives
3.	Focus group discussion (FGD)	Qualitative data collection, delineation of issues, and stakeholder analysis. For specialized knowledge for modeling and validation from experts. In both ISM and SD modeling, FGD has been applied for the purpose of understanding the nature of the problem, identification of factors, and understanding causal relationships. For system dynamics modeling, it was applied at the following stages: • conceptualization stage • the model formulation stage • the simulation and testing stage (model behavior and evaluation) • the policy analysis stage
4.	Brainstorming	For idea generation for various factors in the system
5.	Stakeholder analysis (SA)	For government policy and implementation (applied FGD, brainstorming, interviews, systems thinking)
6.	Experts consultations	With experts in educational and research institutes
7.	Interviews	Collection of data through structured formats
8.	Grounded theory	Data collection and analysis at the conceptualization and the model formulation stage (applied systems thinking and design thinking)
9.	PEST analysis	Political (P), economic (E), social (S), and technology (T) analysis for Agro-residue power system
10.	Policy design	To explore policy options based on insights from the end-users and then design the policies using feedback through an iterative process

Source Glaser (1992), Raiffa (1982), Strauss and Corbin (1990), Brinkerhoff (1998), Kahan (2001), Fletcher et al. (2003) and Luna-Reyes and Andersen (2003)

continuous feedback from end-users, who were directly affected by the policies. As presented in Fig. 6.11, different steps of research are as follows: study of an existing policy, problem statement, defining research objectives, preparing conceptual policy model, simulation, scenario building, validation, and policy design.

Tools applied in the research work. In the research, the combination of various tools like systems thinking, design thinking, focus group discussion (FGD), brainstorming, stakeholder analysis (SA), interviews, grounded theory, PEST analysis, and policy design has been applied as per the specific requirement in the research during ISM and SD modeling, as indicated in Table 6.12.

6.5 Case Study: Policymaking for Renewable Energy 351

6.5.4 Application of Interpretive Structural Modeling (ISM)

After identifying research objectives, the comprehension of the problem and system was attempted. The research made use of systems thinking and design thinking. Systems thinking helped in the systemic understanding of issues. While the design thinking, using open-ended questions to probe, helped in gaining insights from key stakeholders—entrepreneurs (plant developers) and farmers. Together with the literature survey, the tools helped in understanding the policy for Agro-residue power plants, the areas of concern, and the status of policy implementation. The research tools identified subsystems and factors. SA brought out how the policy has addressed the concerns of different stakeholders and whether it has been able to achieve its intended objectives. It reflected on the process of policy formulation and the major issues therein. It informed the very issues that were at the core of the problem of setting up biomass power plants (Appendix 2).

Observations about the process of policymaking. Based on the focus group discussions (FGDs) and the application of systems thinking and design thinking about the existing process of policymaking for Agro-residue power plants, some of the key points are summarized as follows:

- *Firstly, lack of consultations.* Key stakeholders, viz., farmers and plant developers, are not consulted sufficiently during policymaking, so their concerns are not captured in the policy document. As a result, the plant developers face practical operational difficulties, and the farmers (Agro-residue suppliers) find it hard to get a fair price for Agro-residue. These issues continue to be critical factors in determining success.
- *Secondly, the resource assessment of Agro-residue is not attempted scientifically.* There is a lack of assessment of raw material Block-wise, biomass-wise, and season-wise. The resource assessment at the Block level or within 50 km of the plant is essential, as otherwise, the transport cost becomes too prohibitive. But such assessment is not recommended by and attempted in the policy document. Though the macro-level analysis is attempted, a scientific way of data collection and analysis of the grassroots-level situation has been lacking. It reflects a lack of focus on an evidence-based approach to policy analysis.
- *Thirdly, the analysis to examine the complexity in the system is not attempted.* There are complex issues related to interactions between multiple factors and nonlinearity between different factors. These are not examined under the current policymaking. The interlinkages between factors are not studied. In the dynamic environment in which the system works, the biomass supply and its price are uncertain. The biomass supply and price and their linkages with the running of the plant, plant load factor (PLF), and plant viability are not studied. The behavioral issues like trust and confidence between plant developers and farmers about the supply and price of Agro-residue, together with the ability of the State renewable agency to find the workable mechanism for the collection of Agro-residue, are not examined.

- *Fourthly, practical constraints and facilitating factors are not assessed.* The institutional mechanisms through the State Electricity Regulatory Commission (SERC) and the State renewable agency for monitoring, regulation, and implementation of policy in general and the smooth running of plants have limitations in the absence of enforceable ways of ensuring biomass in time. The risks or uncertainty are not examined, and there is an oversimplification of complex issues. For example, the non-availability of biomass is left to the ability of plant developers, and the State renewable energy agency is expected to facilitate. To be specific, the current availability of Agro-residue, its seasonal variation, its impact on the price, and plant efficiency are not studied in detail and analyzed during policymaking, while these factors determine the very success of the policy.

  Despite the important role played by the Central Electricity Regulatory Commission (CERC) and SERC in fixation of tariffs for electricity, such tariffs don't help the cause, due to many practical issues like requisite availability of Agro-residue in time and of desired price, besides low conversion efficiency and inability to maintain desired PLF of 80% due to operational and maintenance issues from 2nd year onward. Moreover, Agro-residue is too voluminous raw material and seasonal and cannot be arranged easily. Also, the price of electricity cannot be enhanced indefinitely by SERC.
- *Fifthly, financial viability is not addressed.* There are fundamental factors on which the success of the whole policy and the financial viability of plants depend. For example, issues like R&D, assured availability of Agro-residue, and good PLF, which require long-term interventions, are not addressed. In addition, the causal relationships between R&D, plant efficiency, electricity output per unit (kg) of biomass consumption, and financial viability are not examined. As reflected by plant developers, the mathematical models and project calculations reflect viability and profit. But, when it comes to timely availability and the right price of Agro-residue and when operational problems and low PLF are taken into consideration, the balance sheet does not show financial viability.

The stakeholder analysis has brought out that in Maharashtra, the PLF has been a matter of concern. In some plants, PLF had been as low as 30% and reached 80% in only a few. The average PLF had been 50%. In addition, it came out during FGDs that the current efficiency level of the power plant has been low, at about 18–25%. The expert opinion and FGDs have been that for combustion technology, the efficiency of the biomass plant can be enhanced to 27–32% (average 30%) from the current range average of 21% (Appendix 2). As for the State policy formulation for the biomass system, the tools that have been mainly used include the study of available literature and reports of National and international agencies; and consultations with some experts, research institutions, and State departments. A few successful examples from other countries are cited. Though some case studies are considered, such studies indicate some specific cases in a particular location or district and do not provide a larger representative sample.

Based on the biomass policy (MNRE 2011a, b) and the order by Central Electricity Regulatory Commission (CERC 2009), there are some assumptions. *First*, once the

6.5 Case Study: Policymaking for Renewable Energy

plant is set up, the Agro-residue will be collected by the developers from the farmers; *second*, the farmers will get a fair price for the Agro-residue; *third*, there will be a reasonable cost of transportation; *fourth*, the plant will run at good efficiency of about 30%; and *fifth*, the PLF of the plant will be 80%. Based on such assumptions, the feed-in tariffs are fixed. As reflected in the field study, such assumptions have not held the ground.

Against the backdrop of the above, during policymaking, various basic issues, including causes of problems and viability of power plants, are not examined in detail. The study of micro-macro linkages, i.e., the link between micro-level problems with macro-level requirements, the systemic examination of issues, and the institutional analysis are not carried out. The institutional mechanisms for monitoring, regulation, and implementation in operational terms are not factored in. Thus these have resulted in incorrect assumptions about the availability and price of Agro-residue, PLF, and conversion efficiency; simplification of complex problems; and short-term perspective while making policy. It highlights that policymaking lacks ground-level detailed analysis and informed decision-making.

Findings of stakeholder analysis. The consultations with stakeholders highlighted multiple problems in setting up biomass power plants. Based on the feedback from the stakeholders, as compiled in Appendix 2, Tables 6.26 and 6.27, the salient findings are drawn.

- For key stakeholders, plant developers, and farmers, the critical factors are the availability of Agro-residue and the price of Agro-residue. But these were not given prominence by the policy, as perceived by both plant developers and farmers.
- Similarly, from the point of view of plant developers, though the purchase price of electricity by State utility, support for setting up of electricity plants, and R&D (technology) are the most important, the first two factors were addressed only partially, and the third factor was not addressed.

The policy has recognized factors such as the availability and price of Agro-residue, capital subsidy, renewable purchase obligation (RPO), conversion efficiency, fiscal incentive, and so on. But how different factors influence each other and, in turn, how they impact the viability of the power plant have not been examined. It has come out explicitly that the policy does not provide an integrated view of all the relevant issues.

Often, the most intuitive policies bring immediate benefits, only to see those benefits undermined gradually by policy resistance (Kelly 1998; Sterman 2000; Serdar 2001). As Forrester (1971) notes, because of policy resistance, systems are often insensitive to the most intuitive policies. Policy resistance often arises through the balancing feedback loops, which exist in systems. For example, initially, when the policy was announced for biomass power plants, there was momentum to take advantage of opportunities. But due to many practical problems, there was resistance due to feedback from the farmers and plant developers.

In light of the above, the existing approaches have focused on considering the factors independently, so a holistic view is hindered. Thus, to analyze the problem holistically and from the system perspective, interpretive structural modeling (ISM) and system dynamics (SD) were chosen for the research.

Preliminary interpretive structural modeling (ISM)

To apply ISM, firstly, the objective for the model was identified. The objective has been 'to enhance investment in Agro-residue power system'. It was followed by identifying relevant factors through brainstorming and FGDs (Table 6.13). The list and definitions of factors are given in Table 6.28, Appendix 2.

Following the steps in ISM methodology, a structural self-interaction matrix (SSIM) was developed for the identified factors. It was followed by the creation of the initial reachability matrix (IRM) and final reachability matrix (FRM), and then finally, the driving power and dependence graph (Fig. 6.12) was developed.

The analysis of the graph (driver power and dependence graph) is presented below:

Table 6.13 List of factors for preliminary ISM

S. No.	Factors
1.	Availability of resources
2.	Income of farmers
3.	Cotton production
4.	Agro-residue production
5.	Household consumption of Agro-residue
6.	Surplus Agro-residue
7.	Possible Agro-residue collection
8.	Feasible Agro-residue collection
9.	Price of cotton Agro-residue
10.	Distance of plant from Fields
11.	Total cost of Agro-residue
12.	Investment
13.	PLF
14.	Benefit of certified emissions reduction (CER)
15.	Cost of electricity generation
16.	Price of electricity
17.	Financial incentive
18.	Maximum acceptable cost
19.	Regulator (Agro-residue plant)
20.	Industrial parks
21.	R&D for efficiency
22.	Decentralized depots
23.	Captive plantation
24.	Efficient stoves
25.	Multi-fuel power plant

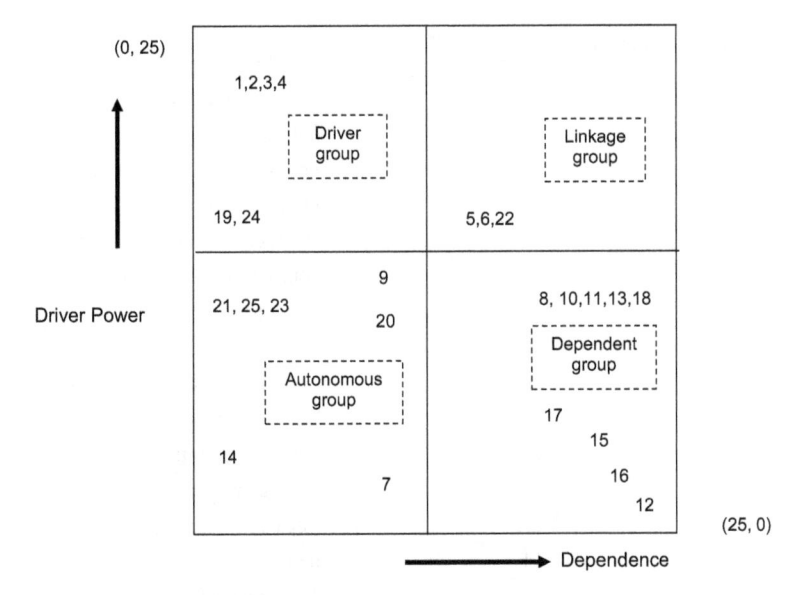

6.5 Case Study: Policymaking for Renewable Energy

Fig. 6.12 Preliminary ISM: driver power and dependence graph

- The analysis of the graph of preliminary ISM revealed that four factors, availability of resources (1), income of farmer (2), cotton production (3), and Agro-residue production (4), have identical drivers and dependent power values. Also, these factors are linked linearly to one another and thus impact the model identically. So only one factor, cotton Agro-residue production, was finally chosen, and the remaining three were excluded.
- Similarly, the factor household consumption of Agro-residue (5) is not independent vis-à-vis surplus cotton Agro-residue (6), as the value of the latter is derived after subtracting the former from cotton Agro-residue production, besides both the factors have an identical driver and dependent power values. So, the factor, household consumption of Agro-residue, was dropped.
- Two factors, benefit of CER (14) and possible cotton Agro-residue collection (7), have very low driving power as well as low dependence, so they are autonomous factors. It means that they are least affecting the other factors or affected by others in the model and thus were dropped from the list of factors. It is a standard practice to drop factors that have low driving power as well as low dependence (Chidambaranathan et al. 2010; Luthra et al. 2011).
- Two other factors, R&D for efficiency (21) and multi-fuel power plant (25), have identical values in the matrix. They are similar in nature as being R&D factors, so they were merged into one.

As discussed above, after preliminary analysis, six factors were dropped and two factors were merged into one. Thus, the final list of factors was developed as indicated by Table 6.14 (see Table 6.29, Appendix 2 for definitions).

Table 6.14 List of factors for final ISM

S. No.	Factors
1.	Agro-residue production
2.	Surplus Agro-residue
3.	Feasible Agro-residue collection
4.	Price of Agro-residue
5.	Distance of plant from fields
6.	Total cost of Agro-residue
7.	Investment
8.	PLF
9.	Cost of electricity generation
10.	Price of electricity
11.	Financial incentive
12.	Maximum acceptable cost
13.	Regulator (Agro-residue plant)
14.	Industrial parks
15.	Decentralized depots
16.	Captive plantation
17.	Efficient stoves
18.	R&D in design

Final interpretive structural modeling (ISM)

Based on the analysis of preliminary ISM, again, after applying ISM methodology, structural self-interaction matrix (SSIM) (Table 6.30 in Appendix 2), initial reachability matrix (IRM), final reachability matrix (FRM), and level partition were developed. Finally, the driving power and dependence graph was prepared, indicated in Fig. 6.13, and the final ISM model is reflected in Fig. 6.14. The model shows the factors in a hierarchical form, in which the factors at the bottom are drivers, the factor at the top is the objective of the system, and the factors in the middle are links between drivers and the objective.

The graph classified the factors into four groups, (i) autonomous group, (ii) dependent group, (iii) linkage group, and (iv) driver group. It gave valuable insights into the relative importance of the factors and their interdependencies. The brief analysis is as follows:

- *Autonomous group.* There is no factor under autonomous group. It indicates that no factor has low driving or dependent power, and so all the factors considered in final ISM influence the model.
- *Dependent group.* The dependent group contains four factors, investment, cost of electricity generation, price of electricity, and financial incentive. In the ISM model, these factors are at the top part of the model. The factor 'investment' at the top represents the objective to be achieved in the system (Fig. 6.14).

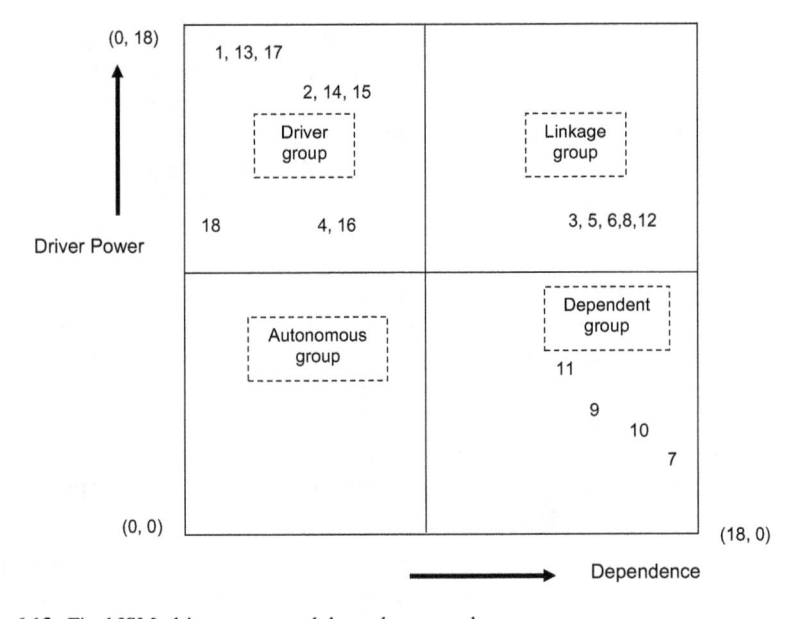

6.5 Case Study: Policymaking for Renewable Energy

Fig. 6.13 Final ISM: driver power and dependence graph

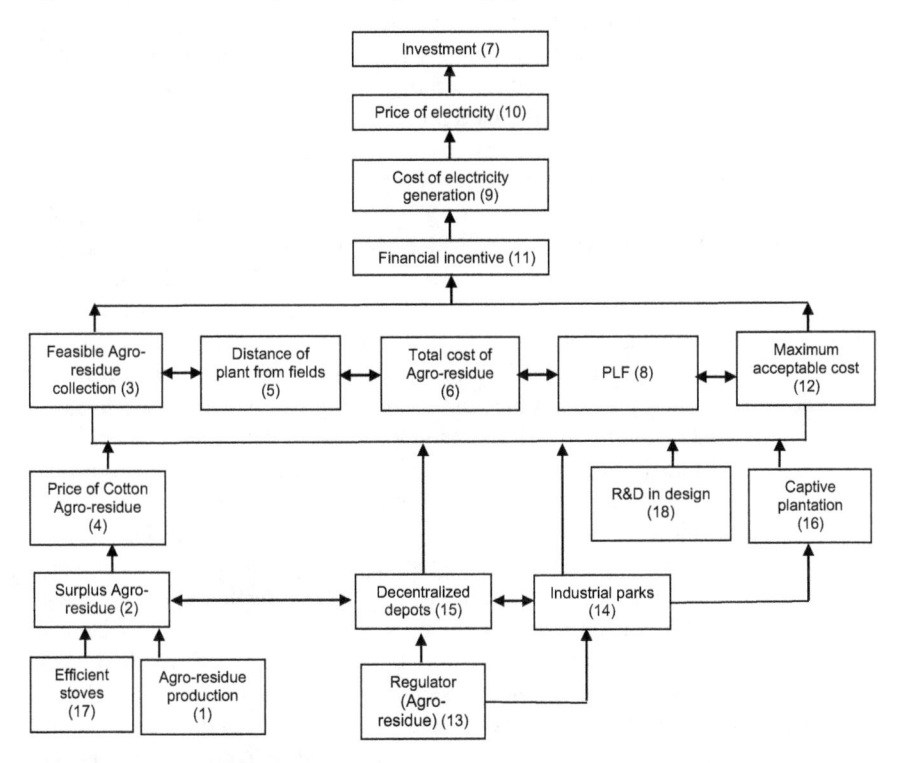

Fig. 6.14 Final ISM model

- *Linkage group.* In this group, there are five factors, feasible Agro-residue collection, distance of plant from the fields, total cost of Agro-residue, PLF, and maximum acceptable cost. They have significantly high driving power and high dependent power of fourteen. These factors provide linkages in the system and are referred to as enablers or facilitators. In the ISM model, these are in the middle of the model and are links between factors at the bottom (drivers or independent factors) and the factors at the top (dependents) (Fig. 6.14). These factors are dependent on the drivers but assist the dependents. Therefore, policymakers should closely monitor their role to achieve the objective of the system.
- *Driver group.* This group has high driving power and less dependent power, thereby meaning that these are less dependent on other factors. These factors are the root causes and should be addressed by the policymakers as a first priority and should be given priority for the success of the system. The factors that fall in this group are: Agro-residue production, surplus Agro-residue, price of Agro-residue, regulator, industrial parks, decentralized depots, captive plantation, efficient stoves, and R&D in design.

Among all the factors, Agro-residue production, efficient stoves, and regulator for Agro-residue price have the maximum driving power of fifteen and thus deserve the maximum attention from the policymakers. And closely following them are factors, decentralized depots and industrial parks, which also require priority support from policymakers so that the desired objective can be met. To manage these driving factors, a comprehensive strategic plan for the system should be initiated.

In the past, various studies on biomass power system have highlighted the problems in general. But so far, the relationships between factors, the sequence of interactions, and their potential impact on the system were not examined holistically. The present ISM has helped in filling this gap by developing an integrated model for the Agro-reside power system. It provided specific policy inputs for setting up power plants in the country. The model so developed reflects the causal relationships between numerous factors. It is not easy to comprehend linkages between many factors through traditional methods or mental models. The relationships between factors may vary somewhat depending on the biomass fuel. But the ISM model can be developed for any biomass fuel and technology, with suitable modifications incorporated based on geographical area and by considering the local context.

The stakeholder analysis (SA) and ISM highlight that the government policy does not address all the issues comprehensively. The research has raised concerns about the deficiencies in the process of policymaking. It reflects that the policy has not been able to address critical concerns like the availability of Agro-residue, price of Agro-residue, and R&D (technology). The ISM has shown how the model has facilitated a better understanding of the mutual influences between factors in the system. It has helped to evolve the hierarchical structure of factors and to identify drivers and dependents for the Agro-residue power system. The presentation of the problem in a pictorial form will help policymakers to understand better and draw conclusions. It can help in examining how the policy has impacted and addressed the concerns of different stakeholders, especially plant developers and farmers.

Though ISM provides a hierarchical model, the weightage to different factors is not given or the impact of one factor on the other is not quantified. This gap can be filled by system dynamics (SD) modeling by developing mathematical relationships between factors. It is discussed in the next section.

6.5.5 Application of System Dynamics (SD) Modeling

The necessary methodology for system dynamics (SD) modeling is discussed in Sect. 6.3.2. In this section, the application of SD modeling is presented. It includes the following steps:

- *First, problem Identification and definition.* The identification and definition of the problem and conceptualization of the system are the first steps in the SD methodology. The appropriate definition of the problem can facilitate the correct formulation of the model and then the proper interpretation. It sets the agenda for the modeling. The learning from the ISM model was taken as inputs for identifying factors and developing relationships between factors. The problem identification process began by drawing upon the stakeholders' inputs—knowledge and experience. It involved two major steps, *first*, situation analysis, providing a broader view of the system, and *second*, understanding underlying issues that define the problems. It applied both systems thinking to obtain a holistic view of the system and design thinking to collect insights from plant developers (entrepreneurs) and farmers, the supplier of the Agro-residue.

Situation analysis. The situation analysis is required to understand the internal and external situation of the system. It provides the context and knowledge for defining the problem and familiarizing the modeler with the issues concerning the system. The study used PEST analysis for the situation analysis. Under this, four categories—political, economic, social, and technology—were examined (Porter 1998; CIMA 2007). The key questions that were probed are: the government policies for biomass power plants; performance level of plants, how different stakeholders, especially entrepreneurs and farmers, responded to the policies; the support system for setting up power plants; and the key factors that worked as facilitators or impediments.

In addition, during FGDs, the socio-cultural factors were examined. Some farmers were apprehensive about the guarantee whether developers would make the payment on time on a regular basis. Some expressed the opinion that plant developers might get undue benefits, but farmers might not get benefits and be exploited in the process. Similarly, the developers were of the opinion that initially, the farmers would agree to supply Agro-residue, but subsequently, after a gap of 2–3 years when the demand would increase, they might refuse to supply Agro-residue and raise the price. One developer commented, 'in Yavatmal district (near Wardha District), initially in the year 2006–07, the price of the cotton Agro-residue was Rs. 1000 per ton. But after two years, the price went up to Rs. 2800 per ton, thereby significantly affecting the financial viability of the plants'.

Another dimension of the discussion has been an environmental concern. Though most farmers and other stakeholders appreciated the need to address climate change concerns, some of them and their representatives were critical. They mentioned that the farmers should not be burdened with the responsibility of sharing the burden of climate change and must be given a reasonable price for the Agro-residue. Some farmers during FGD commented, 'why only farmers should bear the burden of environmental problem, as they are already so much burdened'.

Examining underlying issues. For a successful model building exercise, it is essential to interpret the problems and causes thereof from the past behavior of the system. For the identification of the specific issues, there were several rounds of discussions with stakeholders, especially with the plant developers and farmers, besides an extensive literature review.

As came out during FGDs by engaging with them, the problems mainly pertained to the availability and price of Agro-residue. Both farmers and developers had their viewpoints that conflicted with each other, but they had their respective logic. The farmers expressed their problems in the collection of Agro-residue, as they did not find enough incentive to collect and expect a reasonable price from the developers. In comparison, developers expressed concerns about the difficulty in getting Agro-residue in time and the likely sudden increase in the price of Agro-residue in the future when the demand would increase. It required examining the policy options to find the optimum solution satisfying both the key stakeholders. During discussions, the developers wanted as low a price for the Agro-residue as possible.

Besides, developers had problems with the low efficiency of power plants and inefficient multi-fuel combustion, low capital subsidy, and delay in setting up power plant units. Based on the discussion about the problems, including PEST analysis, some specific questions that were examined are: how cotton Agro-residue collection could be enhanced to increase the surplus Agro-residue, how the price of cotton Agro-residue could be regulated, what steps were needed to enhance the plant load factor (PLF), how technological advancements could help in improving efficiency and thereby reducing Agro-residue usage (in terms of kg per KWhr) in the electricity plants to reduce the cost of electricity generation, and how the process of setting up Agro-residue power plant could be streamlined to minimize the time for setting up power plants.

- *Second, system conceptualization.* At the stage of system conceptualization, it required focusing on the real-world context and utilizing the knowledge of the mental model of stakeholders to describe the system. It involved identifying the factors and subsystems, defining model boundary, and determining the causal relationships between factors. For system conceptualization, the following diagramming-aids were utilized:
  – Subsystem diagram
  – Policy structure diagram
  – Causal loop diagram

6.5 Case Study: Policymaking for Renewable Energy

Subsystem diagram: Following the process of grounded theory and applying systems thinking, the subsystem diagram and analysis involved the steps like: (i) identification and definition of factors, (ii) identification of different components for various factors, (iii) identification of subsystems, and (iv) analysis of subsystems.

For the Agro-residue power system, all relevant factors were identified that represented the model structure. The factors were classified into three categories, viz., exogenous factors, endogenous factors, and output factors. The list of classified factors with their definition is indicated in Table 6.31. Further, the components of the system that form the basis for an Agro-residue power system were identified. The list of components is as follows:

- C1: Available resources
- C2: Resource deployment
- C3: Cotton production
- C4: Agro-residue surplus
- C5: Price and feasible collection of Agro-residue
- C6: Investment, capacity, and electricity generation
- C7: Cost of electricity generation
- C8: Incentive and net capital
- C9: Requirement of Agro-residue
- C10: Purchase by State utility and surplus
- C11: Income of farmers

Based on its distinct nature, three subsystems were identified. These are: the *first* subsystem, resources and cotton production (A); the *second* subsystem, Agro-residue surplus and cost (B); and the *third* subsystem, Agro-residue power system (C) (Fig. 6.15).

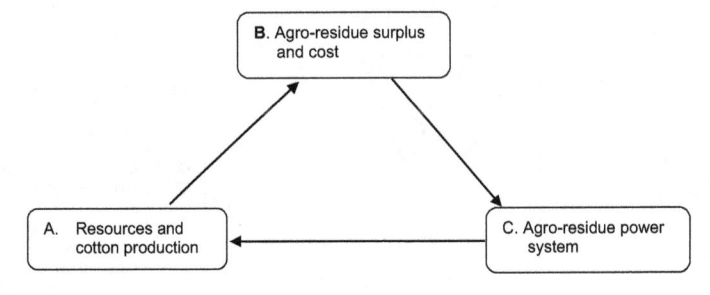

Fig. 6.15 Subsystem diagram

The components, as identified in the previous step, are classified under three subsystems, as shown below:

Subsystem A: Resources and cotton production

- C1: Available resources
- C2: Resource deployment
- C3: Cotton production
- C11: Income of farmers

SubsystemB: Agro-residue surplus and cost

- C4: Agro-residue surplus
- C5: Price and feasible collection of Agro-residue

Subsystem C: Agro-residue power system

- C6: Investment, capacity, and electricity generation
- C7: Cost of electricity generation
- C8: Incentive and net capital
- C9: Requirement of Agro-residue
- C10: Purchase by State utility and viability

The detailed analysis of subsystems is as follows:

The subsystem of 'resources and cotton production' consists of factors linked to resources (money) and cotton production. Agro-residue is a by-product of crop production. To raise the crop, bank credit, loans from private sources (LPVS), and

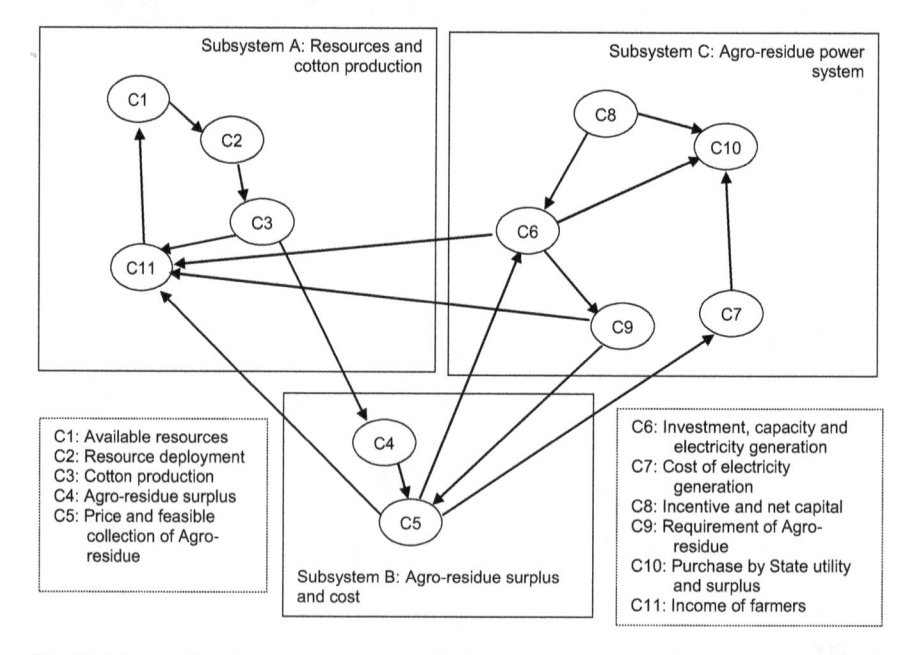

Fig. 6.16 Interactions between components of subsystems

a part of the income from their own source are mobilized by the farmers. To a greater extent, the actual deployment of resources for crop production is dependent on rainfall. Cotton Agro-residue (CTAGRPR) is a by-product of the cotton crop and mainly consists of cotton bark. Based on the survey, bark yield is 1.5–2.5 times the cotton production. The studies indicate (Lal 2005; Ramachandra and Kamakshi 2005) that the bark yield value varies between 3.5 and 4.0, and the yield may be 32–42 Q/He (average 30 Q/He). This subsystem provides input to subsystem 'Agro-residue surplus and cost', as indicated in Fig. 6.16.

Under the 'Agro-residue surplus and cost' subsystem, after the Agro-residue production, there are two important activities, viz., *first*, total collection of Agro-residue and *second*, usage of Agro-residue for household consumption. Based on their difference, the surplus is generated, which can be utilized for power plants. But the total collection and utilization of Agro-residue for household purposes are dependent on the price of Agro-residue. Based on FGDs with framers, the efficiency of the collection of Agro-residue and usage of Agro-residue for household consumption may undergo change with the increase in the price of Agro-residue. Specifically, the efficiency of collection may increase and household consumption may decrease with the rise in the price of Agro-residue.

After the procurement of surplus Agro-residue, it is transported to a power plant. It involves handling cost as well. As Agro-residue is a voluminous one, the transportation cost is significantly high. From the point of view of the power plant developer, the total cost includes the price of Agro-residue and transportation and handling cost. The transportation and handling cost are equally crucial to minimize the cost of electricity generation. To achieve this, the developer tries to procure the Agro-residue from the nearby agriculture fields. Based on the total cost, the feasible Agro-residue collection by the power plant is assessed.

For the 'Agro-residue power system' subsystem, the Agro-residue is utilized as fuel for the plant. Based on the assessment of the availability of Agro-residue, the prospective developers organize the investment. The investment will also take into account the financial incentive on capital as provided by the Ministry of New and Renewable Energy (MNRE), return on investment (ROI), carbon emissions reduction (CER), plant load factor (PLF), and the purchase price of electricity (PPREL) by State utility. Income earned from subsystem B is invested by farmers in crop production, as indicated in subsystem A.

It was followed by the identification of the model boundary. The identified factors, the delineation of subsystems, and the interactions of subsystems altogether, as indicated by Fig. 6.16, defined the model boundary of the Agro-residue power system. It contains all the relevant factors that describe the system.

Policy structure diagram. For each of these subsystems, the policy factors likely to impact subsystems are depicted in Fig. 6.17. For subsystem A (resources and cotton production), the policy on Agro-residue production, considering factors like bank credit (BCR) and the sale price of cotton (SLPCT), is essential. For subsystem B (Agro-residue surplus and cost), policy on Agro-residue price, combining factors like collection efficiency and price of Agro-residue, and policy on an industrial

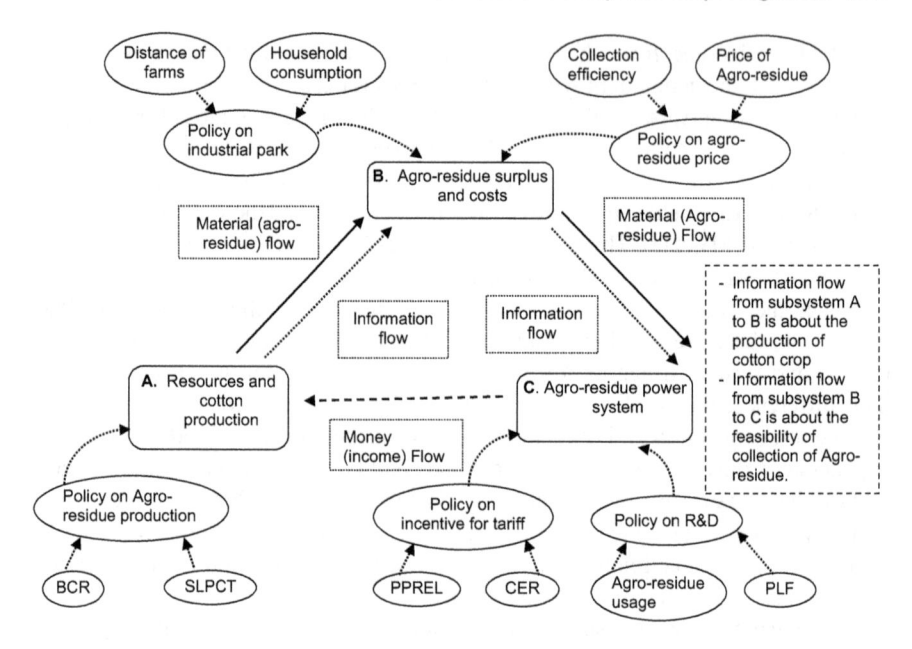

Fig. 6.17 Policy structure diagram for agro-residue power system with policy linkage

park, considering factors like the distance of farms from the power plant and household consumption, need to be examined. And for subsystem C (Agro-residue power system), policy on incentive for tariff, taking factors like purchase price of electricity (PPREL) and certified emissions reduction (CER), and policy on R&D (for improving efficiency and multi-fuel system), taking into account the amount of Agro-residue usage for generating electricity and PLF, need examination.

Causal loop diagram (CLD): The causal loop diagram was drawn, as shown in Fig. 6.18. The diagram consists of factors within three subsystems. Firstly, the starting point is the mobilization of resources for cotton production. The causal relationships show that bank credit (BCR) positively influences the resources for cotton. The rainfall affects the actual resources to be deployed for crop production, more rainfall means that more resources can be deployed. The actual resources positively impact cotton production. The causal relationships, as depicted in the figure, are self-explanatory, and these form a closed loop. It indicates how different factors in the system are linked to one another through causal relationships.

The identification of factors, construction of a model boundary, determination of causal relationships, and development of a policy structure diagram provided a sound understanding of the system. After the conceptualization of the system, the model preparation was the next step.

- *Third, model formulation.* SD model was developed for an Agro-residue power system. For developing the model, the system dynamics STELLA software (Richmond 2010) was applied. The model preparation began with a stock and flow

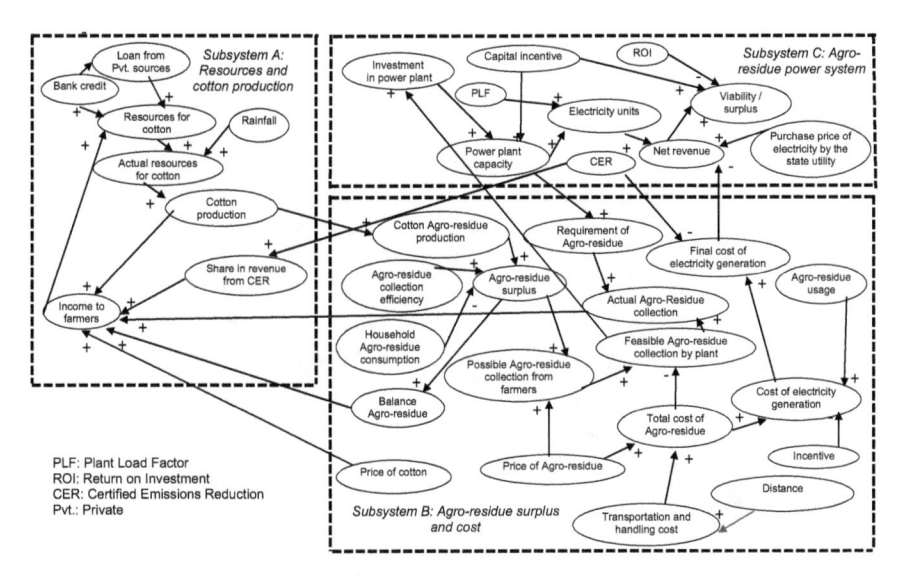

6.5 Case Study: Policymaking for Renewable Energy

Fig. 6.18 Causal loop diagram for agro-residue power system

diagram. In a step-by-step manner, the model was developed. The model was prepared component-wise, and all the components were linked to one another to give a composite view of the system structure. While formulating the SD model, the learnings from the ISM model provided useful inputs. For developing the model, the feedback from stakeholders helped in improved understanding. The relationships, as regards the key factors like Agro-residue collection, cost of Agro-residue, generation of electricity units, and cost of electricity generation, were suitably refined. And the necessary policy parameters were incorporated to match the final model close to a real-world situation.

After applying STELLA software, in Appendix 3, the component-wise diagrams are given in Figs. 6.24, 6.25, 6.26, 6.27, 6.28, 6.29, 6.30, 6.31, 6.32, 6.33 and 6.34, and the final shape of the SD model is presented in Fig. 6.19. After the preparation of the model, the equations were developed for the mathematical relationships of factors in the structure. The necessary data was collected from various government departments and plant developers and through focus group discussions (FGDs). The details of the equations are indicated in Appendix 3.

After developing the model, before it could be utilized for policymaking, it has been necessary to undertake specific analyses to ascertain its utility and acceptability. The qualitative inputs (Randers 1980; Luna-Reyes and Andersen 2003; Fuentes 2006) are essential for SD modeling analysis. The inputs were obtained from stakeholders through consultations. These have been part of modeling and helped in refining the structure, the interpretation of the results, analysis of the scenario building, and validation of policy options.

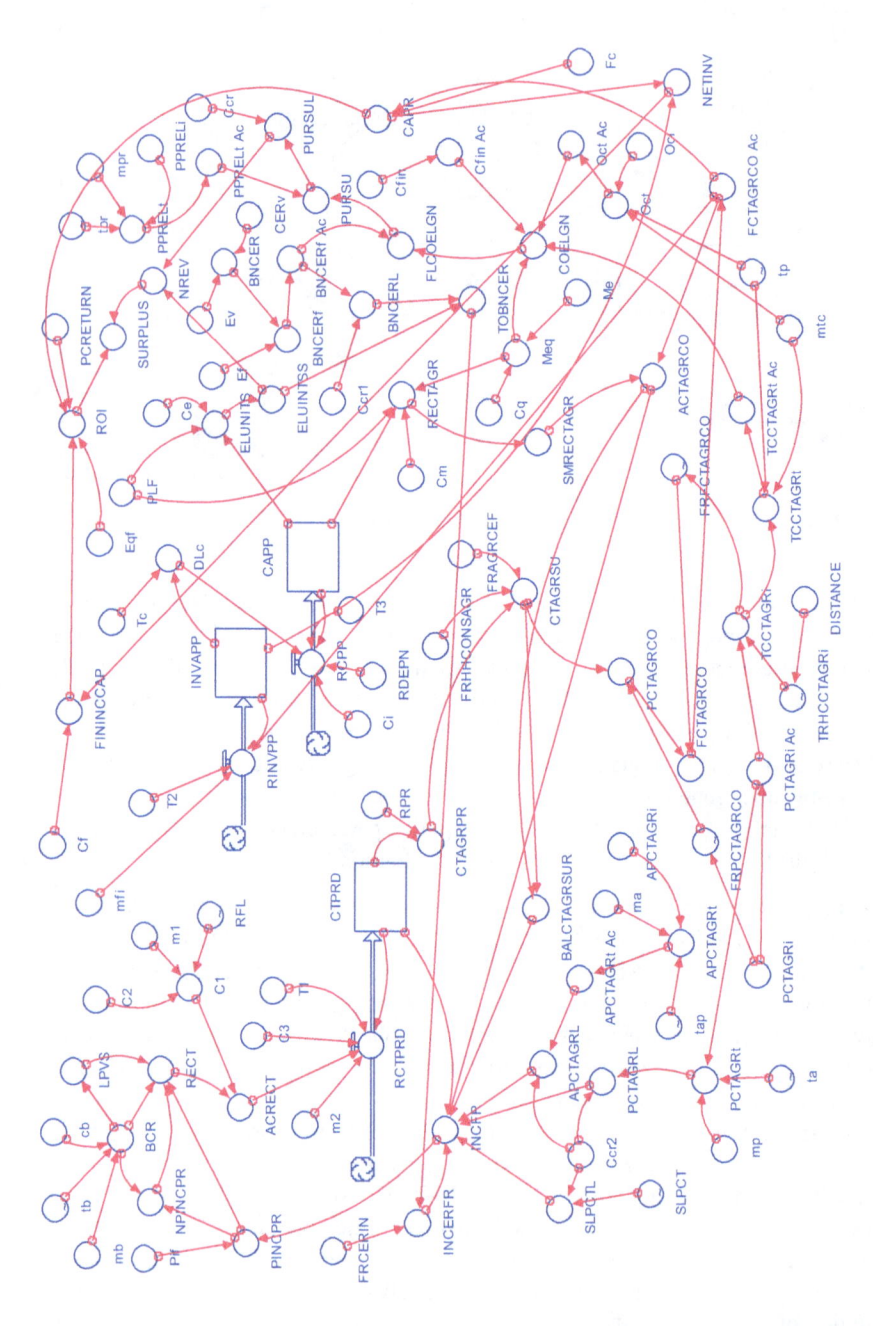

Fig. 6.19 System dynamics model with STELLA software

6.5 Case Study: Policymaking for Renewable Energy

- *Fourth, testing of principles, simulation, scenario building, and sensitivity analysis*. It included the following analyses (Coyle 2000; Sushil 1993; Sterman 2000; Mohapatra et al. 1994):
  - *testing of principles*: the principles that were checked for the system dynamics (SD) model are 'closed boundary', 'solution intervals', 'development of equations', and 'dimensional consistency',
  - *simulation*: it was for viewing the impact of different values of parameters on performance factors and their behavior,
  - *scenario building*: under the model, three types of scenarios, viz., optimistic, normal, and pessimistic, were developed, and
  - *sensitivity analysis*: it was carried out by defining the range of values of policy parameters.

Testing of principles: Under the system dynamics model, the testing of principles is a continuous process. The testing of some of the principles is briefly discussed below:

- *Principle of a closed boundary*. All the necessary interactions between factors were included in the structure, and the feedback loop was closed. Besides, in the SD model and influence diagram (causal loop diagram), from any point (factor), it has been possible to return to that point (factor) by following the influence lines in the direction of causation. Or it represents the case of circular causality. This test has been applied to all the points in the model, except in three situations in which it has been permissible not to be able to return to the starting point. These are: policy parameters like the price of cotton Agro-residue (PCTAGR), PLF, average distance of Agro-residue power plant from fields (DISTANCE), etc.; input factors like BCR, RFL, etc.; and supplementary factors like net revenue (NREV), ROI, SURPLUS, etc. (not playing a part in the control of policies of the system).
- *Solution intervals*. In the model, the solution intervention of 'one (1)' is chosen. It is half of the first-order delay in the model. Usually, in any model, the solution interval should be less than half the shortest first-order delay in the system (Forrester 1968). The duration of the first-order delay is taken as two years. This condition for analysis is fulfilled by the model.
- *Development of equations*. During the preparation of equations, the rationale behind the existing relationships between factors was scrutinized. Based on the literature, FGDs with stakeholders, and expert consultations, the equations were developed. While establishing equations, the values of inputs and output factors and parameters were checked concurrently (by the SD software) and verified for conformity with the outputs and behavior of the system.
- *Dimensional consistency*. In the SD model, the equations were found to be dimensionally consistent. The units (dimensions in which a factor is measured) on the 'right-hand side' (RHS) were checked with the units for the 'left-hand side' (LHS) of the equation. After examination, these were consistent for all the equations in the model.

For simulation, scenario building, and sensitivity analysis, seven parameters were identified. These are: fraction cotton Agro-residue collection efficiency (FRAGRCEF) (%), fraction of total cotton Agro-residue as household consumption (FRHHCONSAGR) (%), price of cotton Agro-residue (PCTAGR) (Rs./Q), plant load factor (PLF) (%), Agro-residue usage per unit of electricity generation (Me) (kg per KWhr), average distance of power plant from fields (DISTANCE) (km), and certified emissions reduction value (CERv) (Rs./kg). In addition, five performance factors (with units) that were chosen are: capacity of Agro-residue power plant (CAPP) (KW), total electricity units (ELUNITSS) (KWhr/year) (using SMOOTH function), cost of electricity generation (COELGN) (Rs./KWhr), final cost of electricity generation (FLCOELGN) (Rs./KWhr), and revenue (SURPLUS) (Rs. Lakh). The identification of parameters and performance factors was based on the extensive literature survey and consultations with experts, plant developers, and farmers. Table 6.31, 6.32, and 6.33 (Appendix 3) include necessary definitions, dimensions, and abbreviations.

Simulation. The simulation is required for visualizing the real-world condition and response over time. It is carried out after developing the model. The model represents the system, whereas the simulation represents how the system is likely to work with time. For developing simulations, the first step is to determine the most critical parameters. It is based on defining the range of values to parameters in the system and then viewing their effect on performance factors. For simulation, two sets of conditions were identified, first the most favorable and other the most unfavorable. The attempt was to visualize how the performance factors would vary under two extremities. The rest of the simulations would vary between these two extremities. As indicated, the values under two conditions are shown in Table 6.15. The results of the simulation are discussed below:

a. *Simulation for the most favorable conditions.* As per the modeling exercise, the full functional capacity of the plant would be after the 16th year. The simulation

Table 6.15 Parameter values for simulation

S. No.	Critical parameters	Values taken for parameters	
		For most favorable conditions	For most unfavorable conditions
1.	FRAGRCEF (%)	80	60
2.	FRHHCONSAGR (%)	5%	15%
3.	PCTAGR (Rs./Q)	60	100
4.	PLF (%)	85%	65%
5.	Me (kg per KWhr)	1.1	1.4
6.	DISTANCE (km)	30	50
7.	CERv (Rs./kg)	0.5	0.4

Source FGDs with plant developers and farmers

6.5 Case Study: Policymaking for Renewable Energy

has been taken from the year 17th year. The value of CAPP increased from 1.90 MW to 2.74 MW, and the corresponding percentage increase is 44.21% (Table 6.16). The ELUNITSS increased by 91.39%. The values of COELGN and FLCOELGN did not increase much (Fig. 6.20). The faster increase in the value of ELUNITSS in the later years has been due to SMOOTH function that has considered the initial delay in the SD modeling. So initially, in the 17th and 18th years, due to the delay, the generation of units was less, and in the 19th and 20th years, there was a faster addition in the number of units. There has been a maximum increase in the value of SURPLUS, which has increased by 145.68% on account of a faster rise in ELUNITSS.

Note: For developing equations, the data has been taken from 1998–99 till 2010–11 to get a wide range of databases (period of field research 2009–11). It was assumed that the investment would be from 2011–12, and the plant setting up would take two years. And from then, the full functional capacity would be after one year. Thus the total period of sixteen years (or four years after the decision for investment) was considered before the full capacity of the plant was achieved.

Table 6.16 Simulation: values of performance factors over time for most favorable conditions

S. No.	Year	CAPP (MW)	ELUNITSS (Million KWhr)	COELGN (Rs./KWhr)	FLCOELGN (Rs./KWhr)	SURPLUS (Rs. Lakh)
1.	17th	1.90	9.87	4.53	4.11	147.50
2.	18th	2.27	14.16	4.86	4.44	247.64
3.	19th	2.54	16.87	5.19	4.76	313.59
4.	20th	2.74	18.89	5.51	5.09	361.65
%age change in 20th year		44.21	91.39	21.63	23.84	145.68

Fig. 6.20 Simulation: variation in values of COELGN and FLCOELGN over years for most favorable conditions

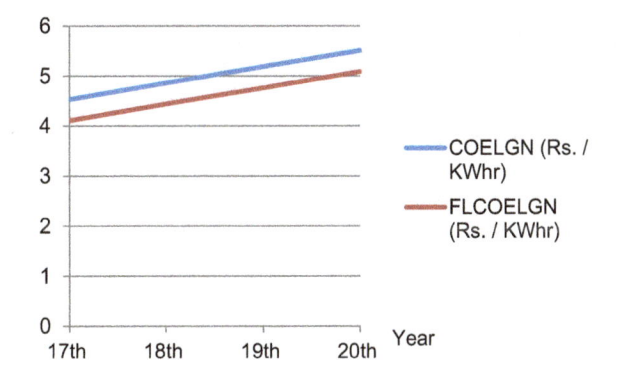

b. *Simulation for the most unfavorable conditions.* Under this condition, as indicated in Table 6.17, the value of CAPP increased by 42.86% and ELUNITSS by 91.45%. The significant increase in the 19th and 20th years is attributed to the SMOOTH function, as explained above. But the increase in this condition is less than that of favorable conditions. There has been a steady increase in COELGN and FLCOELGN (Fig. 6.21). There has been a significant decrease in the value of SURPLUS. It decreased by 96.05%. In absolute terms, the values of two performance factors, CAPP and ELUNITSS, fell sharply compared to favorable conditions. And the SURPLUS became negative, indicating a loss to the power developer.

Scenario building. To get a perspective on the future, three scenarios were developed from the point of view of the developer of the power plants. These scenarios were:

- *optimistic scenario*: it was derived assuming the most favorable conditions of the parameters;
- *pessimistic scenario*: it considered the most adverse conditions; and
- *normal scenario*: it was an expected scenario under normal conditions.

Table 6.17 Simulation: values of performance factors over time for most unfavorable conditions

S. No.	Year	CAPP (MW)	ELUNITSS (Million KWhr)	COELGN (Rs./KWhr)	FLCOELGN (Rs./KWhr)	SURPLUS (Rs. Lakh)
1.	17th	0.77	3.04	7.17	6.83	-44.35
2.	18th	0.91	4.36	7.68	7.34	-57.58
3.	19th	1.02	5.20	8.19	7.85	-71.35
4.	20th	1.10	5.82	8.71	8.37	-86.95
%age change in 20th Year		42.86	91.45	21.48	22.55	-96.05

Fig. 6.21 Simulation: variation in values of COELGN and FLCOELGN over years for most unfavorable conditions

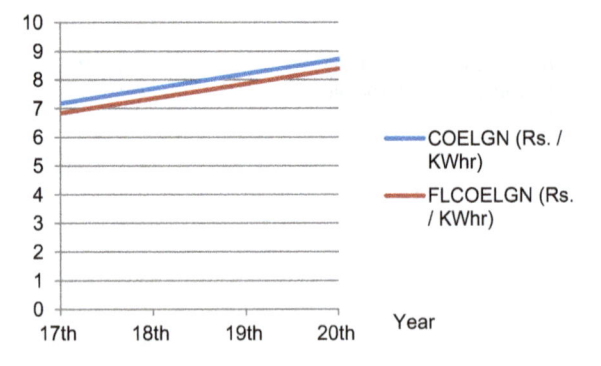

6.5 Case Study: Policymaking for Renewable Energy

Under these three scenarios, the dynamic response of the performance factors was examined to get an indication of the policy options. The values of parameters for identified scenarios with values of parameters are summarized in Table 6.18. The analysis of different scenarios is as follows:

Table 6.19 shows the values of the performance factors for the 20th year for three scenarios, viz., optimistic, normal, and pessimistic. It shows a sharp decline in the figures for the capacity (CAPP) and the number of electricity units (ELUNITSS) generated from an optimistic to a pessimistic scenario. The reduction in the generation of electricity units has been 69.19%. Both COELGN and FLCOELGN have shown an abrupt increase. As regards the final cost of electricity generation (FLCOELGN), it has increased by 64.50%, which is a significant increase. Correspondingly, there has been a decline in the SURPLUS (a measure of financial viability) from Rs. 361.65 Lakh to (-) Rs. 86.95 Lakh, mainly due to an increase in the cost of electricity generation. The values for performance factors under an optimistic scenario are depicted in Fig. 6.22. The variation in the values (for the 20th year) of COELGN and FLCOELGN under different scenarios is reflected in Fig. 6.23.

The optimistic, normal, and pessimistic scenarios are shown in Fig. 6.36a–c, respectively (Appendix 3). The variations in the values of performance factors can

Table 6.18 Parameter values for scenario building

S. No.	Parameters	Range of values for parameters	Values taken for parameters (initial value)		
			S1	S2	S3
1.	FRAGRCEF (%)	60–80%	80	70	60
2.	FRHHCONSAGR (%)	5–15%	5%	10%,	15%
3.	PCTAGR (Rs./Q)	60–100	60	80	100
4.	PLF (%)	65–85%	85%	80%	65%
5.	Me (kg per KWhr)	1.1–1.4	1.1	1.25	1.4
6.	DISTANCE (km)	30–50	30	40	50
7.	CERv (Rs./kg)	0.4–0.5	0.5	0.4	0.4

S1 Optimistic Scenario, *S2* Normal, *S3* Pessimistic Scenario

Table 6.19 Summary of results for different scenarios

S. No.	Scenarios	Performance factors (values for 20th year)				
		CAPP (MW)	ELUNITSS (MKWhr)	COELGN (Rs./KWhr)	FLCOELGN (Rs./KWhr)	SURPLUS (Rs. Lakh)
1.	S1	2.74	18.89	5.51	5.09	361.65
2.	S2	2.27	14.73	6.77	6.35	92.90
3.	S3	1.10	5.82	8.71	8.37	-86.95

S1 Optimistic Scenario, *S2* Normal, *S3* Pessimistic Scenario. *MKWhr* Million KWhr

be observed. The scenarios were developed to understand the dynamic depiction of the performance. It helps to understand what lies between the current state and the future. These scenarios can provide the plant developers with a broad view. Scenarios will enable them to examine how the changes in the values of critical parameters may

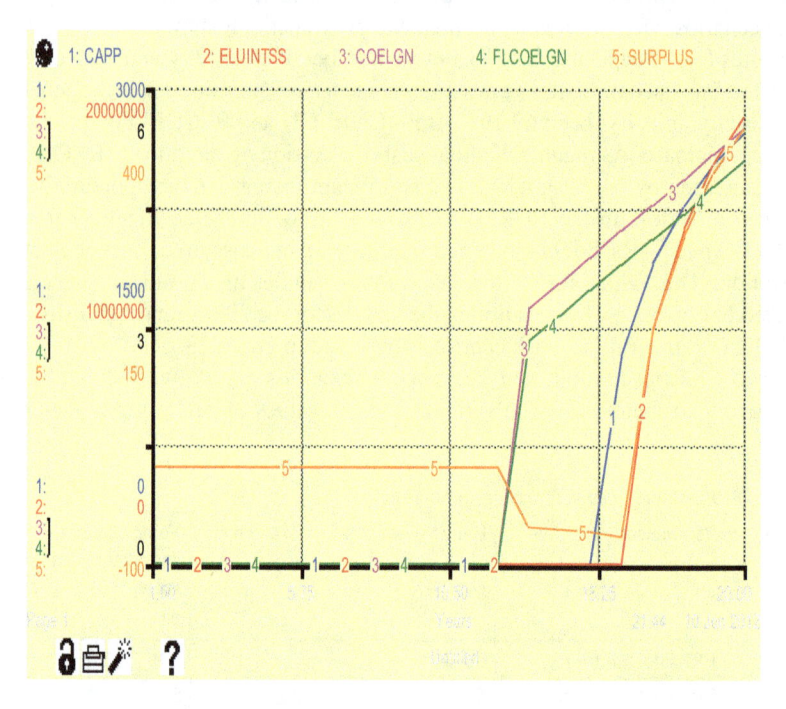

Fig. 6.22 Performance factors under optimistic Scenario (using STELLA Software)

Note Units in parenthesis CAPP (MW) (1), ELUNITSS (MKWhr) (2), COELGN (Rs./KWhr) (3), FLCOELGN (Rs./KWhr) (4), and SURPLUS (Rs. Lakh) (5)

Fig. 6.23 Variation in values of COELGN and FLCOELGN under different scenarios
Note Values are for the 20th year (S1: Optimistic Scenario; S2: Normal; S3: Pessimistic Scenario)

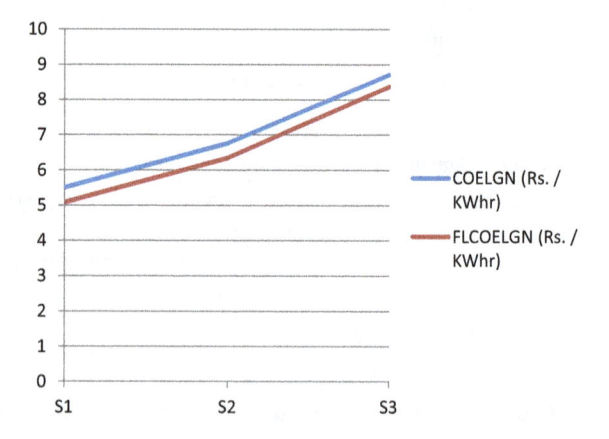

6.5 Case Study: Policymaking for Renewable Energy

impact the performance before taking steps for investment decisions. Simultaneously, the scenarios provide a basis for questions like which policy parameters need to be followed closely and which policy options to be promoted to avoid the situation of a pessimistic scenario.

Sensitivity analysis. The sensitivity analysis was carried out to understand the effect of different possible values of policy parameters from one extremity to other on the behavior of the performance factors. Specifically, the sensitivity analysis was carried out for the normal scenario to examine how sensitive this scenario is to the changes in values for policy parameters. The values of parameters were changed one at a time, and their impact was studied on the performance. Two parameters, FRHHCONSAGR and CERv, were not considered due to their relatively less impact. To understand the worst-case scenario, the following most adverse values were assigned to the parameters, one at a time for the normal scenario: FRAGRCEF: 50%; PCTAGR (Rs. 110 and Rs. 120); PLF (50%); Agro-residue usage (Me) (1.44 and 1.45 kg per KWhr); and DISTANCE (45 km).

The impact on the performance factors for the most adverse values of individual parameters is compiled in Table 6.20. Based on this, a brief explanation is presented below:

- When the value of collection efficiency (FRAGRCEF) was reduced to the most adverse level of 50%, the value of SURPLUS remained positive. It indicated that the collection efficiency alone could not alter the SURPLUS performance factor to a negative level.
- At the Agro-reside price (PCTAGR) of Rs. 120/Q, the final cost of electricity generation reached Rs. 7.20, and the SURPLUS became negative (Rs. 22.66

Table 6.20 Sensitivity analysis: impact on performance factors by the most adverse values of individual parameters

S. No.	Parameters	Values of performance factors (normal scenario)					
		CAPP (MW)	ELUNITSS (MKWhr/MUs)	COELGN (Rs./KWhr)	FLCOELGN (Rs./KWhr)	SURPLUS (Rs. Lakh)
1	FRAGRCEF (50%)	1.62	10.53	6.77	6.35	66.36
2.1	PCTAGR (110)	1.82	11.79	7.41	6.98	-0.84
2.2	PCTAGR (120)	1.59	10.32	7.62	7.20	-22.66
3	PLF (50%)	2.27	9.21	6.77	6.35	33.54
4.1	Me (1.44)	2.27	14.74	7.42	6.99	-2.31
4.2	Me (1.45)	2.27	14.74	7.45	7.03	-7.32
5	Distance (45)	1.81	11.79	7.41	6.98	-0.84

MKWhr Million KWhr. *Note* Parameters taken one at a time (for normal scenario)

Lakh). While at Rs. 110/Q, the SURPLUS became almost zero [(-) Rs. 0.84 Lakh]. It showed that the price should not exceed Rs. 110/Q under a normal scenario; otherwise, it would affect financial viability (price excludes the collection and bundling, transportation, and handling costs).
- When the result for the most adverse value of 50% for PLF was observed, the SURPLUS continued to be positive, indicating that PLF alone cannot impact adversely.
- With the most adverse value of Agro-reside usage (Me) at 1.45 kg/KWhr, the final cost of electricity generation went up significantly to Rs. 7.03/KWhr. And the SURPLUS became negative (Rs. 7.32 Lakh). Still, the SURPLUS became negative (Rs. 2.31 Lakh) even at 1.44 kg/KWhr, so the value of Me should not go beyond 1.44 kg/KWhr, under a normal scenario.
- When the value of DISTANCE was taken as 45 km, the SURPLUS became negative (0.84), or almost zero. So, beyond 45 km, the SURPLUS would be negative, or there would be an adverse impact on viability.

Besides, the sensitivity analysis for changes in values of different parameters is given in Tables 6.34, 6.35, 6.36, 6.37 and 6.38 (Appendix 3). It is evident when the policy parameters were changed to the most adverse level for individual parameters, three policy parameters, viz., PCTAGR, Me, and DISTANCE, were crucial, as they impacted the SURPLUS the most. The collection efficiency (FRAGRCEF) and PLF didn't impact the cost of electricity generation (COELGN).

- *Fifth, validation of model and policy analysis.* To instill confidence in the model, validation is an essential step in system dynamics. The analysis included three kinds of model validation. These are validation of structure and purpose, behavior, and policy implications. These are discussed below:

Structural validation and purpose. It was based on a walk-through with stakeholders for closed boundary analysis and the verification of the inclusion of relevant factors and sequencing of all the factors in the causal loop diagram and SD model. It was found to be an appropriate structure of the real system modeled for an Agro-residue power system. It tested the model's adequacy. It indicated that all the subsystems and the relevant factors therein were included. Thus, the model serves a practical purpose for the plant developers. As discussed above, it relied on testing of principles, including the correctness and dimensional consistency of equations. The knowledge of the system was used through a literature survey and expert consultations.

Behavior reproduction test and validation of policy implication. By varying policy parameters, the simulation results, as well as sensitivity analysis, indicated that the behaviors in terms of the shape of the graph or values of performance factors, viz., CAPP, COELGN, FLCOELGN, ELUNITSS, and SURPLUS have been consistent with the expected pattern and past behavior and matched with the actual system at the ground. The validation results indicated that the model was near the real-life system and could be applied to make policy decisions.

6.5 Case Study: Policymaking for Renewable Energy 375

Policy options. Finally, how the performance factors responded to the changes in the policy parameters was analyzed, and the policy options were explored. The objective of the SD modeling exercise was to evolve the policy options of the real system through model-based policy analysis. The policy analysis was carried out by changing policy parameters, which could be changed by assigning values within an acceptable range. Based on the discussion with and feedback from stakeholders, the qualitative policy analysis was undertaken. The policy design approach helped refine the policy options through feedback from plant developers and farmers and matching their concerns. Some of the policy options are listed below:

- the improvement in the collection efficiency of Agro-residue needs a priority for enhancing the capacity utilization and generating more electricity units,
- the price of Agro-residue (PCTAGR) affects all the performance factors, and so this policy parameter requires close scrutiny,
- for generating higher units of electricity, PLF should be high, and the plant should be run close to the rated capacity to generate sufficient electricity, enhance the financial viability, and make a good surplus,
- the Agro-reside usage (Me) for producing one unit of electricity has a direct effect on the cost of electricity production and also in generating a surplus, thereby improving the financial viability, and thus enhancement in the efficiency of the plant should be a significant policy option to reduce the Agro-residue consumption, and
- the power plant should be near the agricultural fields to lower the cost of electricity generation and enhance capacity utilization.

Analysis of the characteristics of the system. Against the backdrop of subsystem and policy structure diagrams (Figs. 6.15, 6.16, and 6.17), causal loop diagram (Fig. 6.18), and SD model (Fig. 6.19), the key observations about the characteristics of the Agro-residue electricity system and how the model addressed the complexity are summarized below:

The FGDs with stakeholders and the analyses unraveled many intricacies during SD modeling. The model brought a structure in which all the factors could be linked logically, and then the mathematical relationships could be developed. It is evident from the equations that relationships between Agro-residue production, household consumption, collection efficiency, and feasible collection of cotton Agro-residue (FCTAGRCO) are nonlinear. Similarly, FCTAGRCO has nonlinear relations with the price of Agro-residue, transportation cost of Agro-residue, electricity generation, and SURPLUS (revenue). In another case, the distance of agriculture farms from the plants impacts the creation of the capacity, generation of electricity units, cost of generation, or SURPLUS through nonlinear relations. Due to feedback loops, the relationships in the model reflect that there are second- and third-order consequences, due to factors like collection efficiency and distance of agriculture farms from the plants, for example.

Likewise, the cost of electricity generation (COELGN) would depend on the price of Agro-residue, the distance, the efficiency of the power plant, PLF, and financial incentives. It was not known how these factors might impact the COELGN. It could not be visualized by mental models, and as such, there was no static or directly proportional relationship. During model preparation, it used Table function and equations using statistical software. These examples indicate nonlinearity in the system. The values of factors affecting the feasible Agro-residue collection (FCTAGRCO) might change over time. The cotton production, household consumption, and collection efficiency affecting FCTAGRCO might vary year-to-year. Such factors, whose values vary without any prior indication, affect the FCTAGRCO nonlinearly. Thus, there are not only multiple factors affecting FCTAGRCO, but also the relationships have been dynamic, nonlinear, and not known. Besides, the behavioral or psychological issues related to trust and confidence impact the buying and selling relationships between plant developers and farmers, as farmers were not sure about the assured price of Agro-residue from the developers. These issues created a lack of clarity (due to insufficient analysis). In a way, the issues of nonlinearity, previously unknown issues, and dynamic nature were considered by the SD model.

In addition, there had been an issue of a lack of clarity about the underlying issues. At the beginning of the model preparation, it was not known how the Agro-residue production would vary and, in turn, how the combined effect of household consumption and collection efficiency would impact the feasible collection of Agro-residue (FCTAGRCO). There were similar questions for several other factors in the system. The literature survey and analysis indicated that there had been difficulties in tracking the impact of past policies or in understanding the likely links between policy options and outputs to determine the causal relationships. And, thus, the specific cause-effect relationships between them were not discernible in the policies. SD model brought out clarity about cause-effects for appreciation of the system behavior.

While preparing the model, the system had many factors in the causal loop diagram. They were linked to each other through causal relationships. The feedback and closed loop in the system were examined. There were two issues. *First*, which factor would provide feedback became clear, but it was not clear through the mental model. For example, how the Agro-residue price would impact its collection and decision for setting up the power plant and what would be the feedback mechanism could be understood by CLD. *Second*, the examination of the causal loop diagram (CLD) indicated that the feedback was required at several points, viz., at the stage of possible collection of Agro-residue (PCTAGRCO), which depended upon the price of Agro-residue; at the node of feasible collection of Agro-residue (FCTAGRCO), which depended upon the total cost of Agro-residue, including transportation cost; at the point of the capacity of power plant (CAPP), which was affected by the delay in investment or execution of plants; and at the time of the actual collection of Agro-residue (ACTAGRCO), which was impacted by the requirement of Agro-residue and its feasible collection. At each stage, there was a need for feedback to make appropriate decisions. The development of the CLD and SD model helped in resolving such issues. The causal relationships among factors led to a closed loop, as represented in the causal loop diagram (CLD). The diagram included the loop starting from the resource deployment to cotton production to Agro-residue collection to capacity creation of power plant to the collection of Agro-residue to income from

6.5 Case Study: Policymaking for Renewable Energy 377

the sale of Agro-reside to resource deployment, and thus it represented a circular causality. The feedback and closed loop could be understood only after the CLD and SD models were developed.

The issue of bounded rationality and counterintuitive behavior was analyzed. The analysis brought out that the current policymaking lacked to take insights from key stakeholders like farmers and entrepreneurs. The field problems were not adequately reflected in the policies. For example, the issues, like how the efficiency of cotton Agro-residue collection could be enhanced to increase the surplus Agro-residue, how the price of cotton Agro-residue can be regulated, how technological advancements might help in improving power plant efficiency, and how the process of setting up of power plants could be expedited, were not explicitly addressed in the policies. Apparently, policymaking was based on an intuitive understanding of the problems rather than objective assessment, logical approach, and ground-level insights. It reflects that the policy formulation was affected by bounded rationality and intuitive thinking.

The model underscored that all the issues and characteristics, like multiple interacting factors, nonlinearity, dynamic nature, bounded rationality, intuitive behavior, lack of clarity of relationships, unknown features or issues, behavioral issues, second- and third-order results, circular causality, and feedback loops, in a combined form added to the complexity in the system. And the CLD and SD model have successfully addressed these characteristics of the complex system through detailed analysis and multiple perspectives with the participation of stakeholders.

Implications of study. This section has presented system dynamics modeling. By following the system approach, understanding the problem and conceptualization of the system were undertaken. It was followed by the preparation of the SD model, which was developed through an iterative process by combining the knowledge and experience of stakeholders. The model comprised eleven components and was prepared component-wise. The components were linked to each other to provide an integrated view. The model incorporated the mathematical relationships between factors through equations. In a step-by-step manner, the final model was developed by applying STELLA software. The model was followed by various analyses. The model and its analyses provided a sound basis for understanding and explaining the problem situation before making recommendations for policy options.

The distinct feature of the system dynamics is that it deals with simultaneous effects of feedback, control, and policy interventions. SD model shows how the results are fed back and interpreted, how feedback is utilized for control or effecting change in policy parameters, and how the policy parameters can influence the internal interactions in the system through feedback and structure thus regulating the system for desired results.

The SD model helped in addressing basic system issues for policymaking in the following way:

- the 'nonlinearity', 'feedback', and 'closed loop' can be understood through CLD and SD model,
- the 'bounded rationality and counterintuitive behavior' can be addressed by a robust process of understanding the ground reality by capturing the perspectives of

different stakeholders using systems thinking and design thinking and by bringing an analytical approach to understanding and analyzing the problems, and
- the 'complexity' can be dealt with by a system approach, and more specifically, by subsystem analysis, examining policy structure, developing a causal loop diagram, understanding the relationships between factors, and generating both qualitative and quantitative model.

The model has made a significant contribution by examining multiple factors in a system, which is not easy with a conventional approach. The model brought out second- and third-order effects in both the causal loop diagram and the SD model. It will encourage stakeholders, especially policymakers, to avoid intuitive decision-making. In light of the above discussion, a critical examination of policy on biomass power plants is needed. The study has revealed that the biomass power policy, though well-intended, was not sufficient in terms of considering in detail many factors like the price of biomass, fluctuations in price and availability of biomass, R&D, plant efficiency, and PLF that impact the viability of the plants. There have not been enough deliberations about understanding these factors.

As envisaged in the policy, the mechanism of the regulator, SERC or CERC, has constraints in addressing all the critical problems discussed above. For example, the calculations for the cost of electricity generation by developers in their project reports or by regulators reflect calculations in a static manner, together with simplified assumptions (without considering the fluctuations in the biomass price or non-availability of Agro-residue). The assumptions may not reflect the ground reality, as there may be simultaneous changes in the values of multiple factors (or variables). The calculations do not reflect fluctuations in variables like biomass price, biomass availability, transportation cost, plant efficiency, and PLF. Such issues may even cause dysfunction in the power system. Due to multiple problems, as highlighted above, for the country, the PLF of biomass-based power plants has come down to about 20% by 2021, based on reports of MOSPI and CEA (2021a, b; MOSPI 2021, 2022).

Value addition. System dynamics has been successful in adding value by challenging existing assumptions, gaining new insights, and improving confidence level in policy analysis. Through modeling and system analysis, the study questioned the basic premise that the Agro-residue availability would ensure the establishment of power plants. While based on the study, it was not just the availability, but factors such as the price of Agro-residue and its collection efficiency and transportation and handling costs that mattered significantly, individually as well as collectively. Likewise, the PLF and plant efficiency were assumed to be about 80% and 30% (based on fuel consumption per unit of electricity generation), respectively. But these didn't hold good in reality and thus resulted in making plants financially unviable.

The grassroots-level consultations and insights provided an understanding of multiple factors and their relationships. Based on this, it analyzed how the factors impact the viability of the plants. To enhance value, the application of systems thinking and design thinking helped formulate the model matching the real-world situation. Systems thinking helped in examining factors for obtaining a holistic view

6.5 Case Study: Policymaking for Renewable Energy

of the system. The concepts of design thinking helped in a better appreciation of the problems of end-users—farmers and plant developers. Such significant aspects were not sufficiently covered or analyzed in the policy. The policy design approach has been useful in eliciting insights from end-users and exploring new workable possibilities. The understanding of causal relationships, the structure of the system, and validation by the stakeholders have significant contributions. Through the iterative process and feedback, the SD model helped in the policy design by identifying policy options that could match the requirement of end-users.

In sum, the system dynamics modeling, besides bringing clarity in understanding the problem and in system conceptualization, resulted in examining the structure of the biomass energy system, representing the real-world situation, addressing complexity, identifying the leverage points, and determining the policy options.

Synthesis of interpretive structural modeling (ISM) and system dynamics (SD) modeling. Worldwide developments have highlighted the social, economic, and human costs of relying heavily on fossil fuels (IPCC 2007; World Bank 2010). There are challenges in meeting the country's energy requirement and utilizing substitutes for fast-depleting fossil fuels. The reliance on renewable energy sources is the future of the country. Agro-residue, used in power plants, offers good promise in the renewable sector. But it was possible to realize only 5.8% of the gross potential by 2010 (MNRE 2011a). During the research, the literature review highlighted various policy issues in the biomass energy system. These issues necessitated a detailed examination of the biomass energy policy. To understand the problem holistically, it called for studying the system from a 'system point of view'. It required understanding multiple factors, their interdependencies, and their impact on the system's performance, carrying out policy analysis, and suggesting policy options.

To examine policy issues under the Agro-residue power system, the methodology utilized two modeling approaches—interpretive structural modeling (ISM) and system dynamics (SD) modeling. The ISM methodology facilitated understanding the interactions between factors in the system. Based on the learning from the ISM, the SD model was developed. Both ISM model (Fig. 6.14) and the SD model (Sect. 6.5.5) have indicated similarities about key factors, as summarized below:

i. for 'the availability of Agro-residue' in ISM, the correspondingly linked factors in the SD model are 'production of Agro-residue' and the 'Agro-residue collection efficiency';
ii. for 'price of cotton Agro-residue', the same factor is in both ISM and SD models;
iii. for 'facilities or ease of doing business through industrial parks' in ISM, the corresponding factor linked in the SD model is 'distance of power plant from fields' (in the SD model, the DISTANCE factor takes industrial park into account); and the 'purchase price of electricity' and 'financial incentive' are common in both the ISM and SD model; and
iv. for 'R&D in power plant design' in ISM, the linked factors in the SD model are 'PLF' and 'Agro-residue usage (kg per KWhr)' in the SD model. The success of R&D will impact two factors, viz., PLF and Agro-residue usage (kg per KWhr).

The above are the key policy issues that deserve priority attention from policy-makers. By using the policy design approach, the synthesis of results of ISM and SD model has helped in recommending policy options, as summarized in Table 6.21.

The policy options recommended above were compared with the existing biomass policies of the Center and State. It found that the policy lacked focus in essential areas. It lacked specificity and did not provide an integrated view to addressing the problems under the biomass power system. Some of the observations are summed up below:

Table 6.21 Synthesis of results (both ISM and SD): summary of policy options

S. No.	Issues	Policy options
1.	Availability of Agro-residue	Enhancing availability of Agro-residue will require taking multiple policy actions to improve Agro-residue collection efficiency to a recommended value of 70%. Key proposed measures are: • Improving the yield of the Agro-residue • Setting up decentralized Agro-residue collection depots • Captive plantations • Conservation of Agro-residue through the usage of efficient stoves
2.	Price of Agro-residue	• Agro-residue price should be reasonable for both farmers and plant developers. The recommended value is Rs. 80/Q. But the price should not exceed Rs. 110/Q (price excludes collection & bundling, transportation and handling costs) to avoid a negative impact on the financial viability • Establishing the mechanism of regulator for fixing the price of Agro-residue
3.	Agro-residue usage per unit of electricity generation (M_e) (kg per KWhr)	M_e should be as low as possible. The recommended value of M_e is 1.25 kg/KWhr. And the attempt should be to bring it down to 1.10 kg/KWhr, and it must not exceed 1.44 kg/KWhr
4.	Plant load factor (PLF) (%)	PLF should be high. The recommended value is 80% so that sufficient generation of electricity takes place
5.	Business facilitation (ease of doing business)	Setting up industrial parks with electricity evacuation facilities to expedite the process of setting up plants. Timely availability of financial incentives and declaration of feed-in-tariff in advance
6.	Average distance of Agro-residue power plant from fields (DISTANCE) (Km)	The power plant should be set up near the agriculture fields. The recommended value of DISTANCE is 40 km, which should not exceed 45 km
7.	R&D	Encouraging R&D for higher efficiency and multi-fuel power plant design, as higher efficiency of the system will reduce the cost of electricity generation, and the multi-fuel system will improve PLF

Source ISM analysis (refer to Sect. 6.5.4) and SD model analysis (refer to Sect. 6.5.5)

6.5 Case Study: Policymaking for Renewable Energy

- *First, enhancing the availability of Agro-residue.* There is a need for a correct assessment of all forms of Agro-residue, as presently, such analysis has not been made. Such assessment should include the district-wise data in the country. There is a need to set up collection depots and develop captive plantations. But the current policy by way of programs does not explicitly address the issues of availability of Agro-residue.
- *Second, the price of cotton Agro-residue.* By way of policy, some concrete initiatives are to be taken to regulate the price of cotton Agro-residue, which may create a win–win situation for both the farmers and plant developers.
- *Third, ease of doing business.* The ISM has brought out categorically the need to set up industrial parks for establishing plants.
- *Finally, encouraging R&D.* R&D is essential to achieve higher efficiency and a multi-fuel power plant, as higher efficiency of the system will reduce the cost of electricity generation, and the multi-fuel system will improve PLF. Both will enhance the financial viability. The power plant efficiency for the combustion technology should be improved to 30%. Similarly, the PLF should be 80% (refer to Appendix 2).

Limitations. Despite the comprehensive research through intensive modeling exercise and their several benefits in the policy analysis, there are some limitations in applying the ISM and SD. Some limitations have been due to the lack of time-series data and difficulty in quantifying qualitative and behavioral factors. On the part of the methodology, the ISM is not able to provide quantifiable relationships between factors. In the case of SD modeling, it was challenging to endogenize some factors due to a lack of an adequate database on the one hand and qualitative and behavioral factors on the other. For example, factors like financial incentives, plant load factor (PLF), transportation cost, and the purchase price of electricity by State utility could not be endogenized, as the time-series data was unavailable. Likewise, behavioral factors like confidence level and trust could not be modeled. However, qualitative SD modeling (comprising subsystem, policy structure, and causal loop diagrams) can be attempted while keeping in view the system perspective and factoring in the grassroots-level insights.

Research contribution. The synthesis of the results and the research implications have been discussed above. The essential contributions of the research are recapitulated as follows:

- The research findings strengthen the basic premise that ISM and SD modeling can address the problems in a complex system. The combined application of ISM and SD, together with research tools like systems thinking, design thinking, brainstorming, focus group discussion (FGD), grounded theory, and stakeholder analysis, provide a robust approach to dealing with complex systems. But these models apply to known cause-effects or unknown (or unclear without analysis) but knowable cause-effects.
- It provides a unique contribution by presenting the combination of a micro-level perspective based on insights from the end-users and a system-wide view.

- The ISM can help in developing an integrated hierarchical model. A significant contribution of this model lies in imposing order and direction on complex relationships between factors of a system. It helps in describing the problem in a graphical form, making it easier for the decision makers to understand.
- SD can contribute significantly in handling multiple factors in a complex structure, which otherwise is difficult to comprehend.
- The SD model highlights that various characteristics and complexity are understandable when detailed analyses are carried out, the system is conceptualized, and the model is developed and analyzed. By applying systems thinking, utilizing micro-level insights using design thinking, and developing a model, the exercise of system dynamics methodology can provide a way forward for policy design. It will help policymakers to rely on a comprehensive real-world structure presented by an easy-to-understand graphical presentation.

The application of ISM and SD can be attempted for wind and solar energy systems and other sectors such as urban management, health, and industry.

Appendix 1: Basic Renewable Energy Data

See Tables 6.22, 6.23, 6.24, and 6.25.

Table 6.22 Investment in renewable energy (RE) (in 2017)

S. No.	Country	Investment %	Value ($b)
1.	China	45	130.0
2.	USA	14	45.0
3.	Germany	5	12.8
4.	India	4	10.9
5.	EU	15	40.9
	World	100	279

Table 6.23 Global installed capacity (GW) by renewable energy source (2010 and 2019)

S. No.	Source	Capacity 2010	Capacity 2019
1.	Wind	198	651
2.	Solar PV	40	627
3.	Solar thermal	1.1	6.2
4.	Mini-hydro	1,010	1,150
5.	Biomass	62	139
6.	Others (Ocean, Geothermal)	11	14.4
7.	Total	1,322	2,588
	RE without mini-hydro	312 GW	1,438 GW

Appendix 2: Interpretive Structural Modeling (ISM)

Table 6.24 Renewable power capacity in world (2017)

S. No.	Country	Renewable power capacities (GW/1000 MW) (Non-hydro)	Solar (GW/1000 MW)	Wind (GW/1000 MW)	Biomass (Bio-electricity) (GW/1000 MW)
1.	China	334	135	189	14.9
2.	USA	161	52	89	12.5
3.	Germany	106	43	56	8.0
4.	India	61	19	32.8	9.13
5.	EU	320	–	–	6.0 (for UK)
	Japan	57	48	–	3.6
	World	1,081 (without hydro)	402	539	122

Table 6.25 Electricity generation by source in India (grid connected) (2010 and 2018)

S. No.	Source	2010 (Billion KWhr)	2018 (Billion KWhr)
1.	Thermal		
	Coal	658	1,134
	Gas	116	73
	Oil	11	10.4
2.	Hydro	115	127
3.	Nuclear	26	38
4.	Renewable (excluding small hydro)	41	102
	Total	967	1,484

Appendix 2: Interpretive Structural Modeling (ISM)

Stakeholder analysis (SA). It was carried out to understand how the government policy has addressed the concerns of different stakeholders and also to examine whether the policy has been able to achieve its intended objectives. It used tools such as brainstorming sessions, focus group discussions (FGDs), and interviews. The SA included the following steps:

Identification of stakeholders. In the public policy context, there are many citizens, stakeholders, experts, and organizations. The categorization of different actors is important to have clarity. So, the first step in the analysis was to identify the categories of stakeholders, as given under (see Table 6.26):

- Government officials
- Plant developers/entrepreneurs
- Farmers
- Local public representatives
- Experts

Table 6.26 Identification of the stakeholders and criticality

S. No.	Stakeholders	Role	Criticality[a]
1.	Government officials	In policymaking and program design	High
2.	Plant developers/entrepreneurs	In organizing the resources and installation and commissioning of plants	High
3.	Farmers	In the collection and supply of Agro-residue	High
4.	Local public representatives	In the process of facilitation	Low
5.	Experts	In providing the technical inputs to government	Medium

Source Expert consultations and FGD with stakeholders
[a]From the point of view of stakeholders' role in the successful implementation of policy and its impact on them (Criticality: High, Medium, Low)

Role Analysis. The role of each stakeholder was examined, keeping in view what stakeholders could contribute and how the policy would impact them. Though all stakeholders were important, the criticality of stakeholders was assessed in terms of their role in the success of policymaking and implementation. It is shown in Table 6.26.

Stakeholders' feedback and ranking of priorities. The FGDs were held with farmers, plant developers, local public representatives, experts, and officials engaged in policymaking. The discussions ranged from the availability and price of Agro-residue to the purchase price of electricity by State utility to support setting up power plants, and so on. After combining a literature survey, expert consultations, and FGD with stakeholders, the following critical issues were selected:

- Availability of Agro-residue
- Price of Agro-residue
- Purchase price of electricity by State utility
- Capital subsidy
- Support for setting up power plant
- Carbon credit
- R&D for higher efficiency and multi-fuel power plant (technology)

Table 6.27 summarizes the importance and to what extent the policies are implemented based on feedback about critical factors of the Agro-residue power system (as per their perception). Regarding the purchase price of electricity by State utility, it is the most important, and it has been addressed by setting up Central as well as State regulators (SERC/CERC). But the plant developers felt that the fixation of tariffs for electricity provides partial support as there are practical issues that limit the operations of plants. The practical issues are: the requisite availability of Agro-residue in time and of desired price, low conversion efficiency, and inability to maintain desired PLF of 80% due to operational and maintenance problems. Thus, though the mathematical models and project calculations reflect viability and profit, the balance sheet does not show the financial viability due to practical problems on the ground.

Appendix 2: Interpretive Structural Modeling (ISM)

Table 6.27 Feedback from stakeholders about key factors of the agro-residue electricity system

S. No.	Stakeholders	Criteria	Availability of Agro-residue	Price of Agro-residue	Purchase price of electricity	Capital subsidy	Support for setting up of electricity plants	Carbon credit	R&D (technology)
1.	Government officials	Importance	Average to most important	Average to most important	Most important	Average	Average	Average	Average
		How much addressed	Partially	Partially	Partially to fully addressed	Least addressed	Partially	Partially	Partially
2.	Plant developers/ entrepreneurs	Importance	Most important	Most important	Most important	Average	Most important	Average	Most Important
		How much addressed	Least addressed	Least Addressed	Partially	Partially	Partially	Partially	Least
3.	Farmers	Importance	Most important	Most important	Average	Average	Average	Least Important	Least Important
		How much addressed	Average	Least Addressed	NA	NA	NA	NA	NA
4.	Local public representatives	Importance	Average	Average	Average	Average	Average	Least Important	Least Important
		How much addressed	Least addressed	Least addressed	Partially to fully addressed	NA	Partially	NA	NA
5.	Experts	Importance	Average to most important	Average to most important	Average to most important	Average	Average to most important	Average	Average to Most Important
		How much addressed	Least addressed	Least addressed	Partially to fully addressed	Partially	Partially	Partially	Partially

Source FGD (based on more than 75% of respondents agreeing with the above response). *NA* Not applicable
Importance: Least Important (5), Average (2), Most Important (1)
How much addressed: Least Addressed (5), Partially (2), Fully Addressed (1)

The most important factors for the plant developers are the availability of Agro-residue, price of Agro-residue, the purchase price of electricity by State utility, support for setting up electricity plants, and R&D (for higher efficiency and multi-fuel system). But, they find that any of these factors are not adequately addressed. It indicates that in terms of implementation, the policy has not benefited them much. As for PLF, it has been a matter of concern, and the average PLF has been 50% (range 30–80%). Likewise, the average plant efficiency is about an average of 21% (range 18–25%), against the need of 30% (based on fuel consumption per unit of electricity generation). These two figures raise the issue of the viability of biomass power plants.

The plant developers want a better response from the regulator and the government for addressing the issue of purchase of electricity price, as per the changes in the market conditions, especially for the availability and price of Agro-residue. From the farmers' perspective, the price and production of Agro-residue are the most important, but they still need to be addressed for them.

Identification of Factors for Interpretive Structural Modeling (ISM). Through FGD, the relevant factors were identified for the Agro-residue power plant. The identified preliminary factors and their definitions are indicated in Table 6.28.

Table 6.28 Definitions of selected factors for preliminary ISM

S. No.	Factors	Definitions
1.	Availability of resources	It is the total resources that are available for raising the cotton crop. It is a sum of resources available from bank credit, loan from private sources (LPVS), and own income
2.	Income of farmers	In the model, the income of farmers is taken as a sum of income from cotton production and Agro-residue
3.	Cotton production	It is the production of cotton crop
4.	Agro-residue production	It is a by-product of Cotton production and mainly consists of cotton barks
5.	Household Consumption of Agro-residue	Agro-residue is used for a variety of purposes like household fencing, fuel for kitchen, and roof thatching
6.	Surplus Agro-residue	It is a difference between total Agro-residue collection and household consumption
7.	Possible Agro-residue collection	It is the collection of Agro-residue from farmers for power plant based on the price of Agro-residue that a power plant will offer to farmers
8.	Feasible Agro-residue collection	It is the feasible collection of Agro-residue from the point of view of a power plant. It will depend on the total cost, which will include both the price of cotton Agro-residue and the transportation and handling cost

(continued)

Table 6.28 (continued)

S. No.	Factors	Definitions
9.	Price of cotton Agro-residue	It is the value that the farmers will get from the power plant excluding the cost of collection from the field, bundling, handling, and transportation
10.	Distance of plant from fields	It is the average distance of power plant from the agricultural fields
11.	Total cost of Agro-residue	It is a sum of price of Agro-residue and transport and handling cost
12.	Investment	It is the investment required for setting up of Agro-residue-based power plant
13.	PLF	It is a measure of average capacity utilization, defined as the output of a power plant compared to the maximum output it could produce
14.	Benefit of certified emissions reduction (CER)	It is the value at which the carbon credits are sold in the market
15.	Cost of electricity generation	It is the cost of producing one unit of electricity by a power plant
16.	Price of electricity	It is the purchase price of electricity by State utility offered to developer. It is fixed by a regulatory commission and is also referred to as feed-in tariff
17.	Financial incentive	It is the financial incentive given to invested capital by the government
18.	Maximum acceptable cost	It is the maximum cost below which the electricity is to be produced to make the plant financially viable
19.	Regulator (Agro-residue)	Regulator is for fixing the Agro-residue price, keeping in view the factors like production. It is felt necessary to fix a price that is acceptable to different stakeholders
20.	Industrial parks	Industrial parks are required at decentralized locations in districts, which can provide basic facilities like roads, water, power supply, and evacuation of electricity produced
21.	R&D for efficiency	It indicates the R&D efforts required in Agro-residue power plants to achieve higher efficiency
22.	Decentralized depots	These are depots in different locations for the collection of Agro-reside from the farmers
23.	Captive plantation	It is the plantation in the nearby areas of the power plant for providing the timely supply of biomass to the plant
24.	Efficient stoves	The use of efficient stoves is recommended to enhance the efficiency of burning and thereby reducing the consumption of fuel
25.	Multi-fuel power plant	The Multi-fuel power plant design is essential for utilizing several locally available bio-fuels in order to enhance capacity utilization

Source Based on FGD with stakeholders

After preliminary analysis, six factors were dropped and two factors were merged. Thus, the final list of factors was developed, as indicated in Table 6.29.

Table 6.29 Definitions of factors for final ISM

S. No.	Factors	Definitions
1.	Agro-residue production	It is a by-product of cotton production and mainly consists of cotton barks
2.	Surplus Agro-residue	It is a difference between total Agro-residue collection and household consumption
3.	Feasible Agro-residue collection	It is the feasible collection of Agro-residue from the point of view of a power plant. It will depend on the total cost, which will include both the price of cotton Agro-residue and the handling and transportation cost
4.	Price of Agro-residue	It is a value that the farmers will get from the power plant excluding the cost of collection from the field, bundling, and transportation handling
5.	Distance of plant from fields	It is the average distance of a power plant from the agricultural fields
6.	Total cost of Agro-residue	It is a sum of price of Agro-residue and transportation and handling cost of Agro-residue
7.	Investment	It is an investment required for setting up of Agro-residue power plant
8.	PLF	It is a measure of average capacity utilization. It is represented as a percentage of the output of a power plant compared to the maximum output it could produce
9.	Cost of electricity generation	It is the cost of producing one unit of electricity by a power plant
10.	Price of electricity	It is the purchase price of electricity by state utility offered to developer. It is fixed by a regulatory commission and is also referred to as feed-in tariff
11.	Financial incentive	It is the financial incentive given to invested capital by the government
12.	Maximum acceptable cost	It is the maximum cost below which the electricity is to be produced to make the plant financially viable
13.	Regulator (Agro-residue plant)	Regulator is for fixing the Agro-residue price, keeping in view factors like production of Agro-residue. It is felt necessary to fix a price that is acceptable to different stakeholders
14.	Industrial parks	Industrial parks are required at decentralized locations in districts, which can provide basic facilities like roads, water, power supply, and evacuation of electricity produced
15.	Decentralized depots	These are Agro-residue depots in different locations for collection of Agro-reside from the farmers
16.	Captive plantation	It is the plantation in the nearby areas of the power plant to provide timely supply of biomass to the plant
17.	Efficient stoves	The use of efficient stoves is recommended to enhance the efficiency of burning and thereby reducing the consumption of fuel
18.	R&D in design	It indicates the R&D efforts required in Agro-residue power plants to achieve higher efficiency and multi-fuel system. The multi-fuel power plant design is essential for utilizing several locally available bio-fuels in order to enhance capacity utilization

Source Based on FGD with stakeholders

Appendix 2: Interpretive Structural Modeling (ISM)

Table 6.30 Structural self-interaction matrix (SSIM) (for final ISM)

S. No.	Factors	18	17	16	15	14	13	12	11	10	9	8	7	6	5	4	3	2	1
1.	Agro-residue production	0	0	0	0	0	0	0	0	0	0	0	V	0	0	0	0	V	X
2.	Surplus Agro-residue	0	A	0	X	0	0	0	0	0	0	0	V	0	0	0	V	X	
3.	Feasible Agro-residue collection	0	0	0	A	A	A	0	0	0	0	V	V	A	A	A	X		
4.	Price of Agro-residue	0	0	0	A	0	A	0	0	V	0	0	V	V	0	X			
5.	Distance of plant from fields	0	0	0	A	0	0	A	0	0	0	0	V	V	X				
6.	Total cost of Agro-residue	0	0	0	A	0	A	0	0	0	V	0	V	X					
7.	Investment	A	0	A	A	A	A	A	A	A	0	0	X						
8.	PLF	A	0	A	0	0	0	V	0	V	V	X							
9.	Cost of electricity generation	A	0	0	0	0	0	0	A	V	X								
10.	Price of electricity	0	0	0	0	0	0	A	A	X									
11.	Financial incentive	0	0	0	0	0	0	A	X										
12.	Maximum acceptable cost	A	0	0	0	0	0	X											
13.	Regulator	0	0	V	V	0	X												
14.	Industrial parks	0	0	V	X	X													
15.	Decentralized depots	0	0	0	X														
16.	Captive plantation	0	0	X															
17.	Efficient stoves	0	X																
18.	R&D in design	X																	
		18	17	16	15	14	13	12	11	10	9	8	7	6	5	4	3	2	1

V for the relation from element *i* to element *j* and not in both directions;
A for the relation from element *j* to element *i* but not in both directions;
X for both the direction relations from element *i* to *j* and *j* to *i*;
0 (zero), if the relation between the elements does not appear valid

Appendix 3: System Dynamics (SD) Modeling

See Tables 6.31, 6.32 and 6.33.

Table 6.31 Definitions of key factors for system dynamics (SD) modeling (component-wise)

Factors	Definitions
C1: Available resources	
Bank Credit (BCR)	The credit is provided by Banks and Cooperatives to farmers for raising cotton crop
Loan from private sources (LPVS)	The loan is taken by the farmers from local money lenders or traders. This loan is mainly used for availing seeds, fertilizers, and pesticides
Income of Farmer (INCFR)	In the model, the income of farmers is taken as a sum of income from cotton production, Agro-residue, and part of sale of carbon credit
Part of Income of Farmer for crop production (PINCPR)	The part of farmers' income from agriculture source that can be deployed for crop production
Resources for cotton (RECT)	It is the total resource that is available for raising the cotton crop. It is a sum of resources available from bank credit, loan from private sources (LPVS), and own income
C2: Resource deployment	
Rainfall (RFL)	It is rainfall during June and July months and is measured in millimeter. Farmers take decisions for sowing and for availing credit or loan or putting in own resources for crop, based on the rainfall during these months
Actual resources for cotton (ACRECT)	It is the actual resource that is deployed for the cotton crop. It is dependent on the rainfall. It means when the rainfall is less, less resources will be deployed for crop production and also vice-versa
C3: Cotton production	
Rate of cotton production (RCTPRD)	It is a rate of change of production in a year, measured in terms of Q/year/year
Cotton production (CTPRD)	It is a production of cotton crop, measured in terms of Q/year
C4: Agro-residue surplus	
Cotton agro-residue production (CTAGRPR)	It is a by-product of cotton production, and mainly consists of cotton barks. Based on survey, it is generally two times the cotton production. The studies indicate that *residue*-to-product ratio (RPR) may vary between 3.5 and 4.0, and the yield may be 32–42 Q/He (average 30 Q/He)
Fraction cotton Agro-residue collection efficiency (FRAGRCEF)	It is a ratio of collection of Agro-residue to total production of Agro-residue and is represented in decimal point. It can be used as 'collection efficiency' and represented in percentage. Presently, the collection efficiency varies between 50 and 60%, and there is a good scope for its increase if a better price for Agro-residue is offered to farmers

(continued)

Appendix 3: System Dynamics (SD) Modeling

Table 6.31 (continued)

Factors	Definitions
Fraction of total cotton agro-residue as household consumption (FRHHCONSAGR)	It is a ratio of household consumption of Agro-residue to total Agro-residue collection and is represented in decimal point. It can be indicated as a percentage. Agro-residue is used for a variety of purposes like household fencing, fuel for kitchen, and roof thatching. On average, one household utilizes about 30% of the Agro-residue from its field. But, if farmers get adequate price for Agro-residue, the household consumption can come down
Surplus cotton Agro-residue (CTAGRSU):	It is a difference between total Agro-residue collection and household consumption. The surplus Agro-residue can be utilized as a bio-fuel for electricity generation in a power plant
C5: Price and feasible collection of Agro-residue	
Price of cotton agro-residue (initial value) (PCTAGRi)	It is the price of cotton Agro-residue initially when the collection of Agro-residue will begin for supply to electricity power plant. It is the value that the farmers will get excluding the cost of collection from the field, bundling, handling, and transportation
Fraction of surplus cotton Agro-residue collection (FRPCTAGRCO)	It represents what fraction of 'surplus cotton Agro-residue' can be collected based on the price that will be offered by the power plants to the farmers. It is represented in decimal points
Possible cotton Agro-residue collection (PCTAGRCO)	The collection of Agro-residue from farmers for power plant is based on the price of Agro-residue, which a power plant will offer to farmers. The higher the price, higher the likelihood of Agro-residue collection
Average distance of Agro-residue power plant from fields (DISTANCE)	It is a distance of power plant from agricultural fields
Transport and handling cost of cotton Agro-residue (TRHCCTAGRi)	It is the cost of transport and handling (including the cost of collection from the field and bundling) of cotton Agro-residue from the Agricultural fields to the power plant. The Agro-residue being voluminous in nature, both transportation and handling involve high cost. This factor is important for the power plant. If this cost is high, the power plant will find it difficult to purchase Agro-residue as it will affect their financial viability
Total cost of Agro-residue (initial value) (TCCTAGRi)	It is a sum of initial price of cotton Agro-residue (PCTAGW) and transport and handling cost of cotton Agro-residue (TRHCCTAGW). The total cost will determine the feasible collection by the power plant
Feasible fraction of possible cotton Agro-residue collection (FRFCTAGRCO)	It reflects what fraction of 'possible Agro-residue collection' is feasible for the collection for usage in the plant. The feasible collection is cost sensitive
Feasible cotton Agro-residue collection (FCTAGRCO)	The feasible collection is from the point of view of power plant. It will depend on the total cost, which will include both the price of cotton Agro-residue and the transportation and handling cost. If the total cost is high, the feasibility of collection will come down, as at a higher cost, the plant will find it difficult to purchase the Agro-residue
C6: Investment, capacity, and electricity generation	
Rate of investment in power plant (RINVPP)	It is a rate at which the investment is made by developers for the Agro-residue power plant in a year
Delay function for capacity (DLc)	It represents a first-order delay function. It takes time for the investment to get translated into capacity generation, so the delay function is added in the model
Investment in Agro-residue power plant (INVAPP)	It is an investment required for setting up of Agro-residue power plant. It is dependent on the availability of Agro-residue

(continued)

Table 6.31 (continued)

Factors	Definitions
Rate of capacity addition of power plant (RCPP)	It is a rate at which the capacity of Agro-residue power plant is added
Capacity of Agro-residue power plant (CAPP)	It represents the capacity of the power plant that is added as per the investment. It is measured in terms of KW per year
Plant load factor (PLF)	A plant load factor is a measure of average capacity utilization. It is a measure of the output of a power plant compared to the maximum output it could produce. PLF in the model excludes consumption for auxiliaries, which would be about 7%. The PLF taken in the SD model is used for calculating the value of generation of electricity
Total electricity units (ELUNITS)	It is total electricity units generated by the power plant
C7: Cost of electricity generation	
Certified emissions reduction value (CERv)	It is the value earned by selling certified emissions reduction (CER), measured in Rs./kg CO_2
Per unit benefit of certified emissions reduction (BNCER)	It is the value at which the carbon credits are sold in the market. It is measured in Rs./KWhr
Cost of electricity generation (COELGN)	It is per unit cost of electricity generation, taking into account the cost of Agro-residue and other costs
Agro-residue usage (Me)	It is the Agro-residue consumption (in kg) for generation of one unit (KWhr) of electricity
Final cost of electricity generation (FLCOELGN)	It is the final cost of electricity generation calculated as difference between cost of electricity generation (COELGN) and benefits from CER (BNCER). It accounts for the benefits that will accrue due to trading of carbon credit
C8: Incentive and net capital	
Financial incentive on capital investment (FININCCAP)	It is capital subsidy that is provided to the developers by the Ministry of New and Renewable Energy (MNRE). It is the incentive or subsidy provided for setting up power plant
C9: Requirement of Agro-residue	
Requirement of Agro-residue (RECTAGW):	It will be determined depending on the capacity of the plant and the daily consumption. Based on the requirement, the plant will procure the Agro-residue from farmers
Actual cotton Agro-residue collection (ACTAGRCO)	The actual collection will depend on the requirement of the power plant and the feasible collection. It means that based on the requirement of the power plant, the plant will procure the Agro-residue. Such collection will be less than or equal to feasible collection (as collection cannot exceed the feasible collection)
C10: Purchase by state utility and surplus	
Return on investment (ROI):	It is a return on capital invested, which power plant developer expects. It is measured in Rs. Lakh/year
Purchase price of electricity (initial value) (PPRELi)	It is a price at which the state power utilities will purchase the power from the power plant. It is fixed by state electricity regulatory board. It is also referred as feed-in tariff
Net revenue (NREV)	It is the revenue earned by the power plant after subtracting the cost of electricity generation from the total revenue by sale of electricity to state utility

(continued)

Appendix 3: System Dynamics (SD) Modeling

Table 6.31 (continued)

Factors	Definitions
Surplus from the plant (revenue) (SURPLUS)	It represents the gap between the net revenue and expected return on investment. The surplus should be more than zero so that minimum return on investment is assured. It is a measure of financial viability, which assesses what entrepreneur will get from the plant by selling electricity vis-à-vis what minimum return on equity entrepreneur will expect
C11: Income of farmers	
Total benefit of CER (TOBNCER)	It represents the total benefit from all the units generated by the plant from the trading of CER
Actual local market price of cotton Agro-residue (initial value) (APCTAGRi)	It is the local market price of cotton Agro-residue for purchase by villagers for their household consumption
Sale price of Cotton (SLPCT):	It is the market price of cotton normally fixed by government as minimum support price
Income for farmers from CER (INCERFR)	In the model, it is the income for the farmers from the sale of certified emissions reduction (CER). It is assumed that the part of income from the earning from CER for the entrepreneur will be shared with the farmers. It will be distributed to them in proportion to their sale of Agro-residue
Balance surplus cotton Agro-residue (BALCTAGRSUR)	It is the difference between surplus cotton Agro-residue and actual cotton Agro-residue collection. This balance will be left with the farmers for sale in the local market, or it may remain for household consumption

Source FGDs with stakeholders
Note The definitions have been given for factors component-wise. Certain factors lie in two components, but the definitions of such factors are given only in one component

Table 6.32 Dimensions of factors

S. No.	Name of factors	Dimensions
	C1: Available resources	
1.	Bank Credit (BCR)	Rs. Lakh/year
2.	Loan from private sources (LPVS)	Rs. Lakh/year
3.	Income of farmer (INCFR)	Rs. Lakh/year
4.	Part of income of farmer (Pif)	Unitless
5.	Part of income of farmer for the crop production (PINCPR)	Rs. Lakh/year
6.	Net income of farmer for the crop production (NPINCPR)	Rs. Lakh/year
7.	Resources for cotton (RECT)	Rs. Lakh/year
	C2: Resource deployment	
8.	Rainfall (RFL)	mm
9.	Fraction of resources deployment (C1)	Unitless
10.	Actual resources for cotton (ACRECT)	Rs. Lakh/year

(continued)

Table 6.32 (continued)

S. No.	Name of factors	Dimensions
	C3: Cotton production	
11.	Rate of cotton production (RCTPRD)	Q/year/year
12.	Cotton production (CTPRD)	Q/year
	C4: Agro-residue surplus	
13.	Cotton Agro-residue production (CTAGRPR)	Q/year
14.	Residue to product ratio (RPR)	Unitless
15.	Fraction cotton Agro-residue collection efficiency (FRAGRCEF)	Unitless
16.	Fraction of total cotton Agro-residue as household consumption (FRHHCONSAGR)	Unitless
17.	Surplus cotton Agro-residue (CTAGRSU)	Q/year
	C5: Price and feasible collection of Agro-residue	
18.	Price of cotton Agro-residue (initial value) (PCTAGRi)	Rs./Q
19.	Price of cotton Agro-residue from the year of consideration (PCTAGRi Ac)	Rs./Q
20.	Fraction of surplus cotton Agro-residue collection (FRPCTAGRCO)	Unitless
21.	Possible cotton Agro-residue collection (PCTAGRCO)	Q/year
22.	Average distance of Agro-residue power plant from fields (DISTANCE)	km
23.	Transport and handling cost of cotton Agro-residue (initial value) (TRHCCTAGRi)	Rs./Q
24.	Total cost of Agro-residue (initial value) (TCCTAGRi)	Rs./Q
25.	Total cost of Agro-residue at time 't' (TCCTAGRt)	Rs./Q
26.	Total cost of Agro-residue (at time 't') from the year of consideration (TCCTAGRt Ac)	Rs./Q
27.	Feasible fraction of possible cotton Agro-residue collection (FRFCTAGRCO)	Unitless
28.	Feasible cotton Agro-residue collection (FCTAGRCO)	Q/year
29.	Feasible cotton Agro-residue collection from the year of procurement planning (FCTAGRCO Ac)	Q/year
	C6: Investment, capacity, and electricity generation	
30.	Rate of investment in power plant (RINVPP)	Rs. Lakh/year/year
31.	Delay function for capacity (DLc)	Rs. Lakh/year
32.	Investment in Agro-residue power plant (INVAPP)	Rs. Lakh/year
33.	Rate of capacity addition of power plant (RCPP)	Rs. Lakh/year/year
34.	Rate of depreciation (RDEPN)	Unitless
35.	Capacity of Agro-residue power plant (CAPP)	KW/year (unit)
36.	Capital requirement (CAPR)	Rs. Lakh/year

(continued)

Appendix 3: System Dynamics (SD) Modeling

Table 6.32 (continued)

S. No.	Name of factors	Dimensions
37.	Plant load factor (PLF)	Unitless
38.	Total electricity units (ELUNITS)	KWhr/year
39.	Total electricity units (smooth value) (ELUNITSS)	KWhr/year
	C7: Cost of electricity generation	
40.	Per unit benefit of certified emissions reduction (BNCER)	Rs./KWhr
41.	Effective per unit benefit of certified emissions reduction (BNCEREf)	Rs./KWhr
42.	Per unit benefit of certified emissions reduction from the year of consideration (BNCER Ac)	Rs./KWhr
43.	Cost of electricity generation (COELGN)	Rs./KWhr
44.	Agro-residue usage per unit of electricity generation (Me)	kg/KWhr
45.	Agro-residue usage in quintal (Meq)	Q/KWhr
46.	Other cost of electricity generation (initial value) (Oci)	Rs./KWhr
47.	Other cost of electricity generation at time 't' (Oct)	Rs./KWhr
48.	Other cost of electricity generation at time 't' from the year of consideration (Oct Ac)	Rs./KWhr
49.	Cost benefit of financial incentive (Cfin)	Rs./KWhr
50.	Cost benefit of financial incentive from the year of consideration (Cfn Ac)	Rs./KWhr
51.	Final cost of electricity generation (FLCOELGN)	Rs./KWhr
	C8: Incentive and net capital	
52.	Net investment (NETINV)	Rs. Lakh/year
53.	Financial incentive on capital (FININCCAP)	Rs. Lakh/year
54.	CAPR: Capital requirement	Rs. Lakh/year
	C9: Requirement of Agro-residue	
55.	Requirement of Agro-residue (RECTAGW)	Q/year
56.	Requirement of Agro-residue (SMOOTH value) (SMRECTAGW)	Q/year
57.	Actual Cotton Agro-residue collection (ACTAGRCO)	Q/year
	C10: Purchase by state utility and surplus	
58.	Purchase price of electricity (initial value) (PPRELi)	Rs./KWhr
59.	Purchase price of electricity (at time 't') (PPRELt)	Rs./KWhr
60.	Purchase price of electricity (at time 't') from the year of consideration (PPRELt Ac)	Rs./KWhr
61.	Purchase subsidy per unit of electricity (PURSU)	Rs./KWhr
62.	Purchase subsidy per unit of electricity (in Rs. Lakh) (PURSUL)	Rs. Lakh/KWhr
63.	Return on investment (ROI)	Rs. Lakh/year
64.	Net revenue (NREV)	Rs. Lakh/year
65.	Surplus from the plant (SURPLUS)	Rs. Lakh/year

(continued)

Table 6.32 (continued)

S. No.	Name of factors	Dimensions
	C11: Income of farmers	
66.	Per unit benefit of certified emissions reduction (in Rs. Lakh) (BNCERL)	Rs. Lakh/KWhr
67.	Total benefit of CER (TOBNCER)	Rs. Lakh/year
68.	Balance surplus cotton Agro-residue (BALCTAGRSUR)	Q/year
69.	Actual local market price of cotton Agro-residue (initial value) (APCTAGRi)	Rs./Q
70.	Actual local market price of cotton Agro-residue (at time 't') (APCTAGRt)	Rs./Q
71.	Actual local market price of cotton Agro-residue (at time 't') from the year of consideration (APCTAGRt Ac)	Rs./Q
72.	Actual local market price of cotton Agro-residue (in Rs. Lakh/Q) (APCTAGRL)	Rs. Lakh/Q
73.	Price of cotton Agro-residue at time 't' (PCTAGRt)	Rs./Q
74.	Price of cotton Agro-residue (in Rs. Lakh/Q) (PCTAGRL)	Rs. Lakh/Q
75.	Sale price of cotton (SLPCT)	Rs./Q
76.	Sale price of cotton (in Rs. Lakh/Q) (SLPCTL)	Rs. Lakh/Q
77.	Income for farmers from CER (INCERFR)	Rs. Lakh/year

Table 6.33 Dimensions of parameters

S. No.	Parameters	Dimensions
1.	tb	Year
2.	cb	Rs. Lakh/year
3.	mb	Rs. Lakh/year/year
4.	pif	Unitless
5.	m1	/mm
6.	C2	Unitless
7.	m2	Q/Rs. Lakh
8.	C3	Q/year
9.	T1	Year
10.	RPR	Unitless
11.	FRPCTAGRCO	Unitless
12.	FRFCTAGRCO	Unitless
13.	tp	Year
14.	mtc	/year
15.	mfi	Rs. Lakh/Q

(continued)

Appendix 3: System Dynamics (SD) Modeling

Table 6.33 (continued)

S. No.	Parameters	Dimensions
16.	T2	Year
17.	DLc	Rs. Lakh/year
18.	Tc	Year
19.	Ci	KW/Rs. Lakh
20.	T3	Year
21.	Ce	KWhr/KW
22.	Cfin	Rs./KWhr
23.	Cfin Ac	Rs./KWhr
24.	Oci	Rs./KWhr
25.	Oct	Rs./KWhr
26.	Oct Ac	Rs./KWhr
27.	Ef	kg/KWhr
28.	Ev	Unitless
29.	Cq	Q/Kg
30.	Cf	Unitless
31.	Fc	Rs. Lakh/Q
32.	Eqf	Unitless
33.	Tf	Year
34.	T3	Year
35.	Cm	KWhr/KW
36.	tpr	Year
37.	mpr	/year
38.	Ccr	Rs. Lakh/Rs.
39.	PCRETURN	Unitless
40.	Eqf	Unitless
41.	FRCERIN	Unitless
42.	Ccr1	Rs. Lakh/Rs.
43.	Ccr2	Rs. Lakh/Rs.
44.	mp	/year
45.	ta	Year
46.	tap	Year
47.	ma	/year

SD model equations

After applying STELLA software to develop the model, the component-wise diagrams are given in Figs. 6.24, 6.25, 6.26, 6.27, 6.28, 6.29, 6.30, 6.31, 6.32, 6.33 and 6.34 and the final shape of the SD model is presented in Fig. 6.35. After the model preparation, the equations were developed for all the relationships of factors in the structure. The necessary data was collected from various government departments and through focus group discussions (FGDs). For developing equations, the data has been taken from 1998–99 till 2010–11. It was assumed that the investment would start from 2011–12.

The equations for various components are as follows:

Component 1: Available resources

See Fig. 6.24.

- BCR: Bank Credit

    BCR = tb * mb + cb (* represents multiplication sign)

    The equation between BCR and time was developed using SPSS software.

    tb: It is a time factor over which the value of BCR varies.

    mb: It is a slope for the equation between time and BCR.

    cb: It is a constant for the equation between time and BCR.

    mb = 118.516

    cb = -51.231

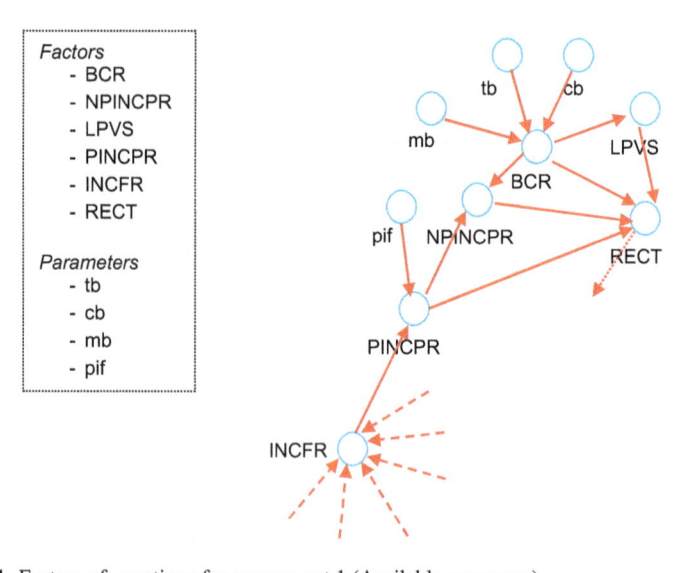

Fig. 6.24 Factors of equations for component 1 (Available resources)

Appendix 3: System Dynamics (SD) Modeling

(R^2: 0.912; Significance level: 0.1%).
- LPVS: Loan from private sources

  LPVS = 0.35 * BCR.
- PINCPR: Part of Income of farmer for the crop production

  PINCPR = INCFR * 0.35 * Pif

  The net income is taken as 35% of total income.
- Pif: Part of income of farmer

  Pif = 0.25.
- NPINCPR: Net Income of farmer for the crop production

  NPINCPR = BCR * (0.25) − PINCPR.

The contribution from own income from crop production is maximum 25% of BCR.

- RECT: Resources for cotton

  RECT = BCR + LPVS + PINCPR + NPINCPR.

Component 2: Resource deployment

See Fig. 6.25.

- RFL: Rainfall

  RFL (based on office data).
- C1: It is a parameter, and is represented in decimal point.

  C1 = m1 * RFL + C2

  The equation between C1 and RFL was developed using SPSS software.

  m1: It is a slope for the equation between C1 and RFL.

  C2: It is a constant for the equation between C1 and RFL.

  m1 = 0.0010.

Fig. 6.25 Factors of equations for component 2 (Resource deployment)

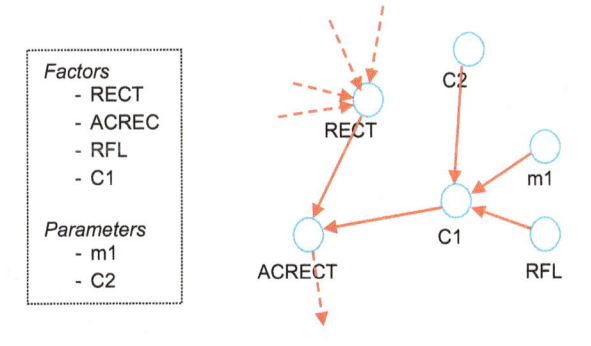

Factors
- RECT
- ACREC
- RFL
- C1

Parameters
- m1
- C2

$C2 = 0.499$

($R^2 = 0.525$; Significance level: 0.5 %).
- ACRECT: Actual resources for cotton

    ACRECT = RECT * C1.

Component 3: Cotton production

See Fig. 6.26.

- RCTPRD: Rate of cotton production

    RCTPRD = ((ACRECT * m2 + C3) − (CTPRD)) / T1

    CTPRD (T) = ACRECT * m2 + C3

    The equation between CTPRD (T) and ACRECT was developed using SPSS software.

    CTPRD (T): Value of cotton production at time t.

    m2 = 34.50.

    C3 = 79720.

    m2: It is a slope for the equation between ACRECT and CTPRD.

    C3: It is a constant for the equation between ACRECT and CTPRD.

    ($R^2 = 0.949$; Significance level: 0.1%).

    T1: Time in years.
- CTPRD: Cotton production

    CTPRD (T) = CTPRD (T-dT) + RCTPRD * dT (based on STELLA software).

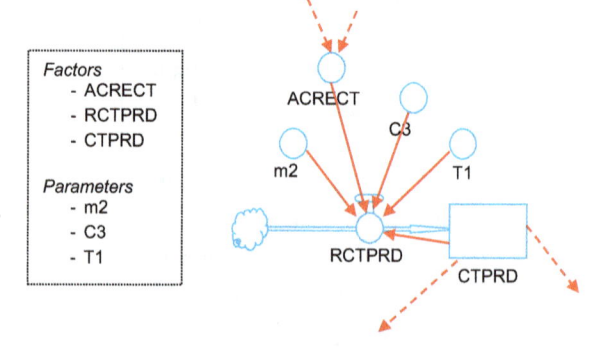

Fig. 6.26 Factors of equations for component 3 (Cotton production)

Appendix 3: System Dynamics (SD) Modeling

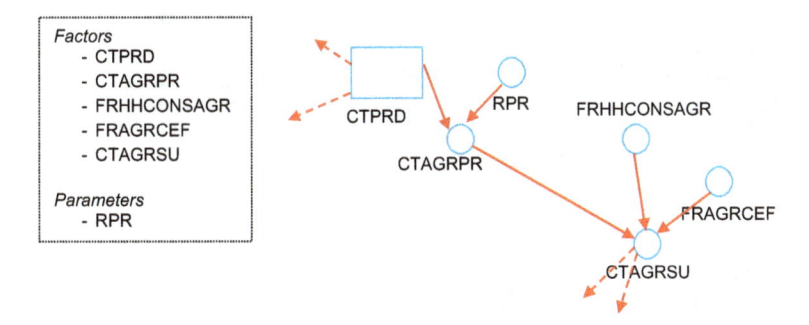

Fig. 6.27 Factors of equations for component 4 (Agro-residue surplus)

Component 4: Agro-residue surplus

See Fig. 6.27.

- CTAGRPR: Cotton Agro-residue production

  CTAGRPR = RPR * CTPRD.
- RPR: Residue to product ratio

  RPR = Parameter value (likely to vary between 1.5 and 2.5).
- FRAGRCEF: Fraction total cotton Agro-residue collection efficiency

  FRAGRCEF = Parameter Value (likely to vary between 0.60 and 0.80).
- FRHHCONSAGR: Fraction of total cotton Agro-residue as household consumption

  FRHHCONSAGR = Parameter value (likely to vary between 0.05 and 0.15).
- CTAGRSU: Surplus cotton Agro-residue

  CTAGRSU = CTAGRPR * FRAGRCEF * (1 − (FRHHCONSAGR)).

Component 5: Price and collection of Agro-residue

See Fig. 6.28.

- PCTAGRi: Price of cotton Agro-residue (initial value)

  PCTAGRi = Numerical value (likely to vary between Rs. 60-100 / Q, excluding the cost of collection and bundling, transportation and handling)

  PCTAGRi Ac = STEP (PCTAGRi, 13)

  (PCTAGRi Ac: Price of cotton Agro-residue from the year of consideration, which is 13th year).
- FRPCTAGRCO: Fraction of surplus cotton Agro-residue collection.
- PCTAGRCO: Possible cotton Agro-residue collection

  PCTAGRCO = FRPCTAGRCO * CTAGRSU.

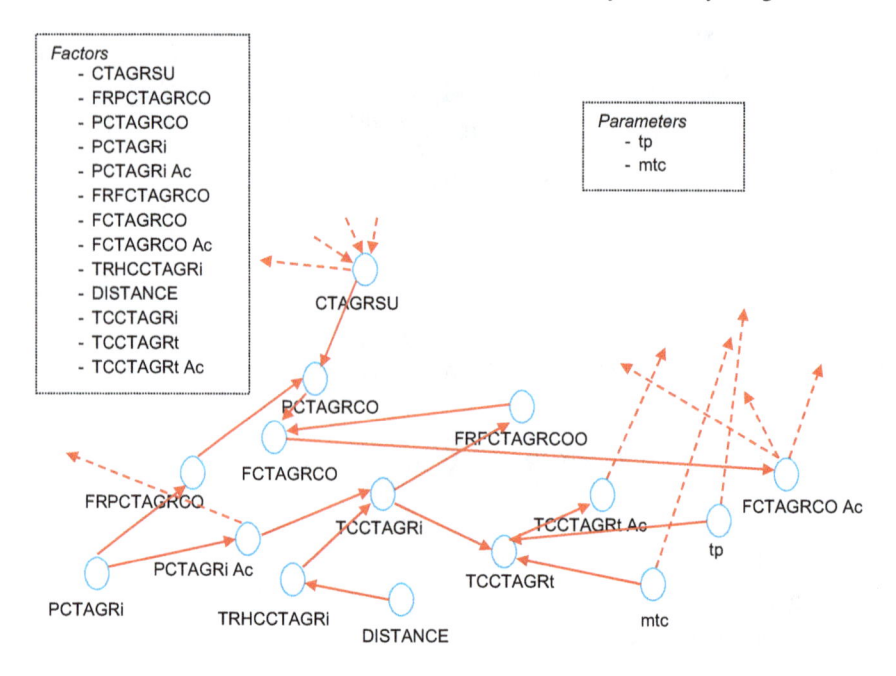

Fig. 6.28 Factors of equations for Component 5 (Price and collection of Agro-residue)

- DISTANCE: Average distance of Agro-residue power plant from fields.

  It is a numeric value ranging normally between 30 and 50 km.
- TRHCCTAGRi: Transport and handling cost of cotton Agro-residue (initial value) (the initial year is taken from 13th year for transport and handling cost).
- TCCTAGRi: Total cost of Agro-residue (initial value)

  TCCTAGRi = PCTAGRi Ac + TRHCCTAGRi.
- TCCTAGRt: Total cost of Agro-residue at time 't'

  TCCTAGRt = TCCTAGRi + TCCTAGRi * mtc * tp

  mtc: average rate of change of transport and handling cost of cotton Agro-residue over a year.

  tp: time in years, with an interval of one year.
- TCCTAGRt Ac: Total cost of Agro-residue (at time 't') from the year of consideration

  TCCTAGRt Ac = STEP (TCCTAGRt, 13).
- FRFCTAGRCO: Feasible fraction of possible cotton Agro-residue collection.
- Feasible Cotton Agro-residue collection (FCTAGRCO)

  FCTAGRCO = FRFCTAGRCO * PCTAGRCO.

- FCTAGRCO Ac: Feasible cotton Agro-residue collection from the year of procurement planning

    FCTAGRCO Ac = STEP (FCTAGRCO, 13)

    The time should be from '13th' year, i.e., from 2010–11 (that is the base year for planning for setting up the power plant). It means up-to '12th' year (2010–11), the value is 'zero', or the value is not applicable.

Component 6: Investment, capacity, and electricity generation

See Fig. 6.29.

- RINVPP: Rate of investment in power plant

    RINVPP = [(mfi*FCTAGRCO Ac) – (INVAPP)]/T2

    mfi: It represents the value that is to be multiplied to the quantity of Agro-reside to determine the investment for power plant, per 1000 KW.

    mfi = 0.0046 (Rs. Lakh per Q); mfi = (403/1000)/[365 (days) * 24 (hours) * PLF * Me].

    – Investment for one MW plant (INVAPP) = Rs. 403 Lakh/1000 KW (in 2010).

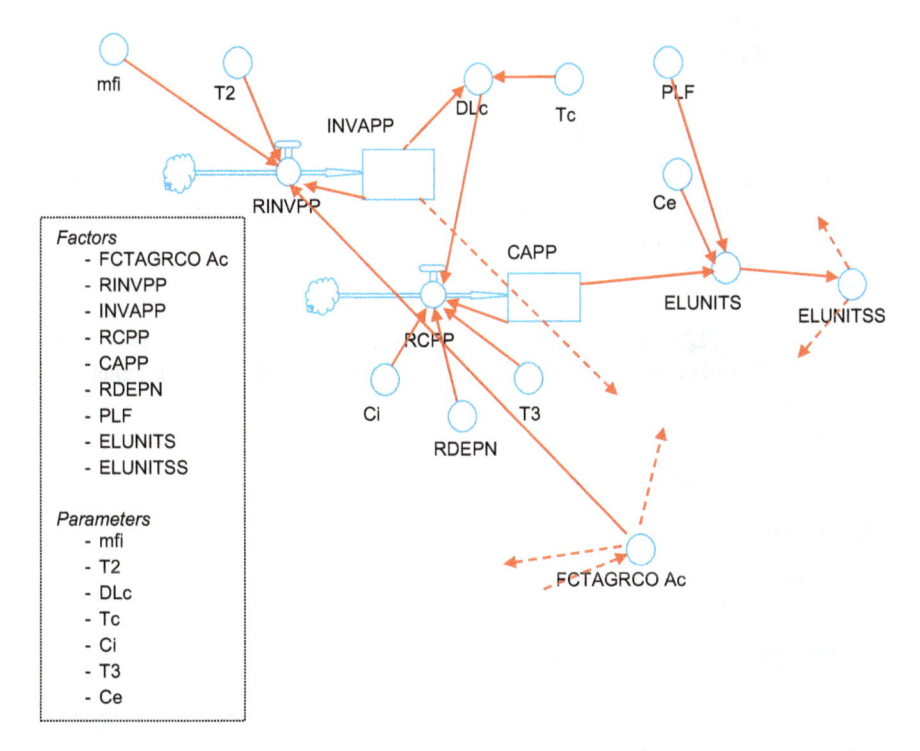

Fig. 6.29 Factors of equations for Component 6 (Investment, capacity, and electricity generation)

- PLF: 80% (average value).
- Me: the quantity of Agro-reside for generating one unit of electricity (average value 1.25 kg/KWhr = 1.25 */100 Q/KWhr).
- T2 (Time period) = 1 year.

- **INVAPP**: Investment in Agro-residue power plant

  INVAPP (T) = INVAPP (T-Dt) + RINVPP * Dt (based on STELLA software). It is calculated by the model. It is cumulative, at the end of each year.

- **DLc**: Delay function for capacity

  DLc = DELAY1 (INVAPP, Tc)

  Tc (Time period) = 2 years

  The normal likely time in setting up of plants is two years.

- **RCPP**: Rate of capacity of Addition of power plant

  RCPP = [(DLc)*Ci) / T3-(CAPP*RDEPN / T3)] - CAPP/T3

  Ci: It represents the value that is to be multiplied to investment (Rs. 403 Lakh) in Agro-residue power plant, per 1000 KW.

  Ci = 2.48 (KW/Rs. Lakh).

  T3 (Time period) = 1.

- **RDEPN**: Rate of depreciation (Constant)

  RDEPN: 0.07.

- **CAPP**: Capacity of Agro-residue power plant

  CAPP (T) = CAPP (T-Dt) + RCPP * Dt (based on STELLA software). It is calculated by the model. It is cumulative, at the end of every year.

- **PLF**: Plant load factor

  PLF is likely to vary between 65 and 85%.

  In the model, PLF excludes consumption for auxiliaries, which would be about 7%. The PLF taken in the SD model is used for calculating the value of generation of electricity.

- **ELUNITS**: Total electricity units

  ELUNITS = CAPP * Ce * PLF

  Ce: 8760 h (365 days * 24 h = 8760).

  PLF: Value varies from 65% to 85%.

- **ELUNITSS**: Total electricity units (smooth value)

  ELUNITSS = SMTH1 (ELUNITS, 1).

Appendix 3: System Dynamics (SD) Modeling 405

Component 7: Cost of electricity generation

See Fig. 6.30.

- COELGN: Cost of electricity generation

  COELGN = (TCCTAGRt Ac * Meq) + (Oct Ac) − (Cfin Ac)

  Me: Agro-residue usage (kg/KWhr)

  Me = Numerical value (likely to vary between 1.1 and 1.4).
- Meq: Agro-residue usage (in quintal) (Q/KWhr)

  Meq = Me * Cq.
- Oct: Other cost at time 't'

  Oct = Oci + Oci * tp * mtc

  Oci: Other cost of electricity generation (initial value)

  mtc: average rate of change of other cost of electricity generation over a year.

  tp: time in years, with an interval of one year.
- Oct Ac: Other cost from the year of consideration

  Oct Ac = STEP (Oct, 13).

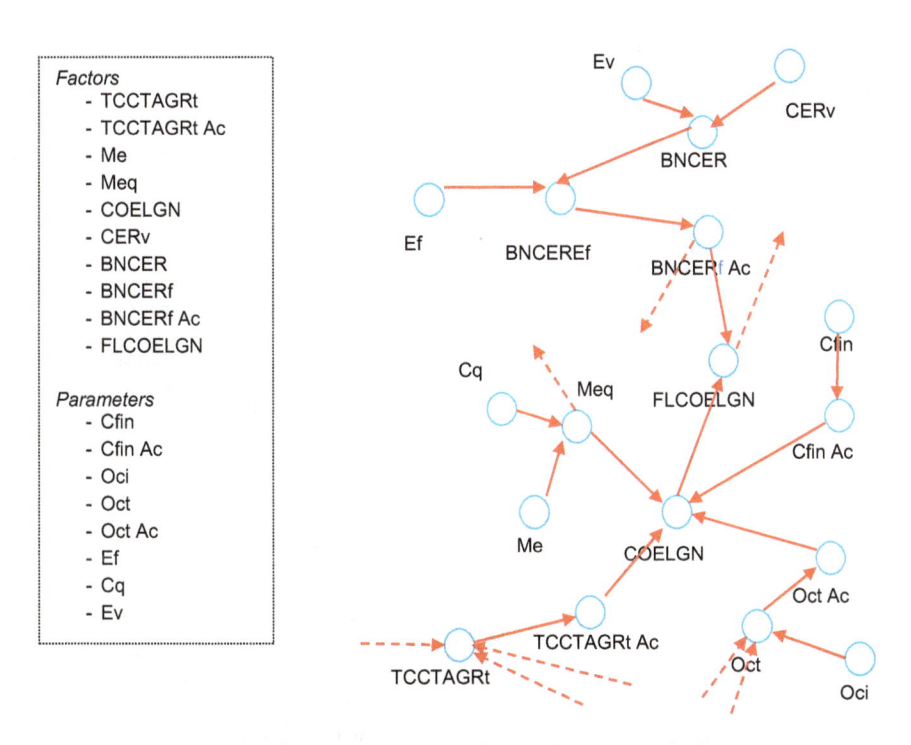

Factors
- TCCTAGRt
- TCCTAGRt Ac
- Me
- Meq
- COELGN
- CERv
- BNCER
- BNCERf
- BNCERf Ac
- FLCOELGN

Parameters
- Cfin
- Cfin Ac
- Oci
- Oct
- Oct Ac
- Ef
- Cq
- Ev

Fig. 6.30 Factors of equations for Component 7 (Cost of electricity generation)

- Cfin: Cost benefit of financial incentive

  Cfin = Rs. 14.57 Lakh (Capital subsidy)/7 MU/7 Years = Rs. 0.03/KWhr.
- Cost benefit of financial incentive from the year of consideration (Cfn Ac)

  Cfin Ac = STEP (Cfin, 13).
- FLCOELGN: Final Cost of Electricity Generation

  FLCOELGN = COELGN − BNCER Ac.
- BNCER: Per unit benefit of certified emissions reduction

  BNCER = CERv * Ev

  CERv is likely to vary between Rs. 0.40–0.50 per kg.

  Emissions Value (Ev) = 1 (as it will take into account the total emissions).
- BNCEREf: Effective per unit benefit of certified emissions reduction

  BNCEREf = BNCER * Ef

  Emissions factor (Ef) = 0.901 (kg/KWhr) (for Maharashtra State).
- BNCER Ac: Per unit benefit of certified emissions reduction from the year of consideration

  BNCERf Ac = STEP (BNCERf, 13).

Component 8: Incentive and net capital

See Fig. 6.31.

- CAPR: Capital requirement

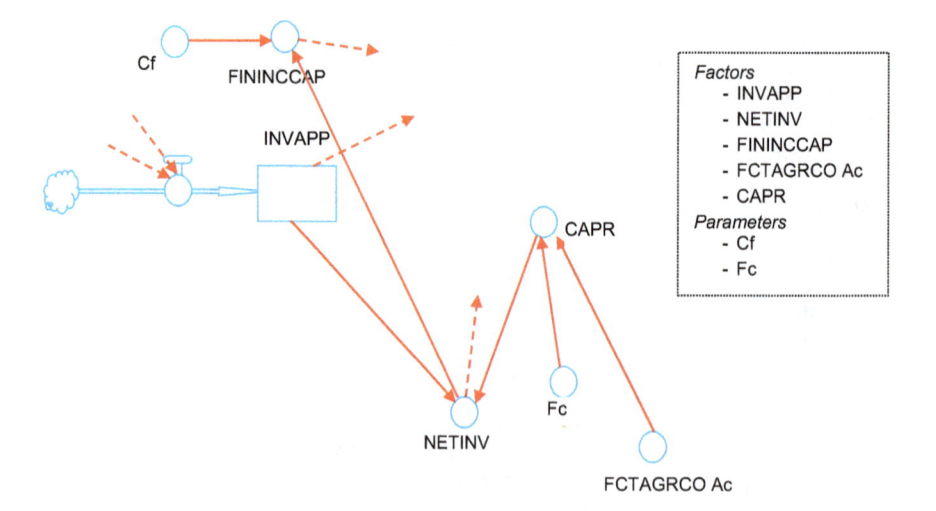

Fig. 6.31 Factors of equations for Component 8 (Incentive and net capital)

Appendix 3: System Dynamics (SD) Modeling

CAPR = FCTAGRCO Ac * Fc

Fc: It represents the value that is to be multiplied to the quantity of Agro-reside to determine the investment for power plant, per 1000 KW. Fc = 0.0046 (Rs. Lakh per Q).

- NETINV: Net investment

NETINV = CAPR − INVAPP

The Net Investment is calculated, as the capital subsidy will be calculated on the fresh investment only, not on accumulated investment.

- FININCCAP: Financial incentive on capital (Rs. Lakh/year)

FININCCAP = NETINV * Cf

Cf (Average value for 2–3 MW plant) = Rs. 14.57 Lakh (subsidy)/403 Lakh (capital cost) = 0.035.

Capital Cost: Rs. 403 Lakh/MW.

Component 9: Requirement of Agro-residue

See Fig. 6.32

- RECTAGR: Requirement of Agro-residue (Q/KW)

RECTAGR = [CAPP * Cm * PLF * Meq] * 100

Cm: 87.60 KWhr/KW.

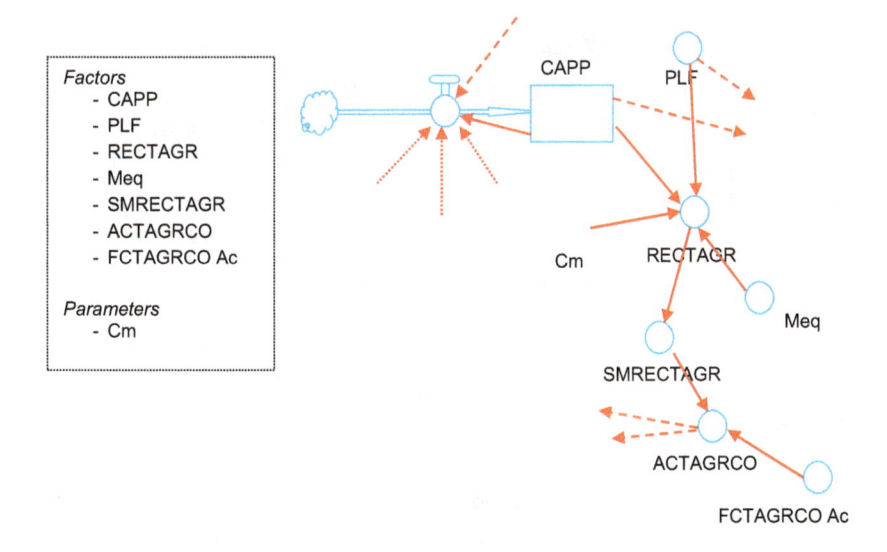

Fig. 6.32 Factors of equations for Component 9 (Requirement of Agro-residue)

- SMRECTAGR: Requirement of Agro-residue (Smooth value)

  SMRECTAGR= SMTH1 (RECTAGR, 1).
- ACTAGRCO

  ACTAGRCO = MIN (FCTAGRCO Ac, SMRECTAGR)

  Table Function 'MIN' has been utilized.

Component 10: Purchase by state utility and surplus

See Fig. 6.33.

- PPRELi: Purchase price of electricity (initial value)

  It is the price fixed by the state electricity regulatory commission.
- PPRELt: Purchase price of electricity (at time 't')

  PPRELt = PPRELi + PPRELi * mpr * tpr

  mpr: average rate of change of purchase price of electricity over a year.

  tpr: time in years, with an interval of one year.
- PPRELt Ac: Purchase price of electricity (at time 't') from the year of consideration

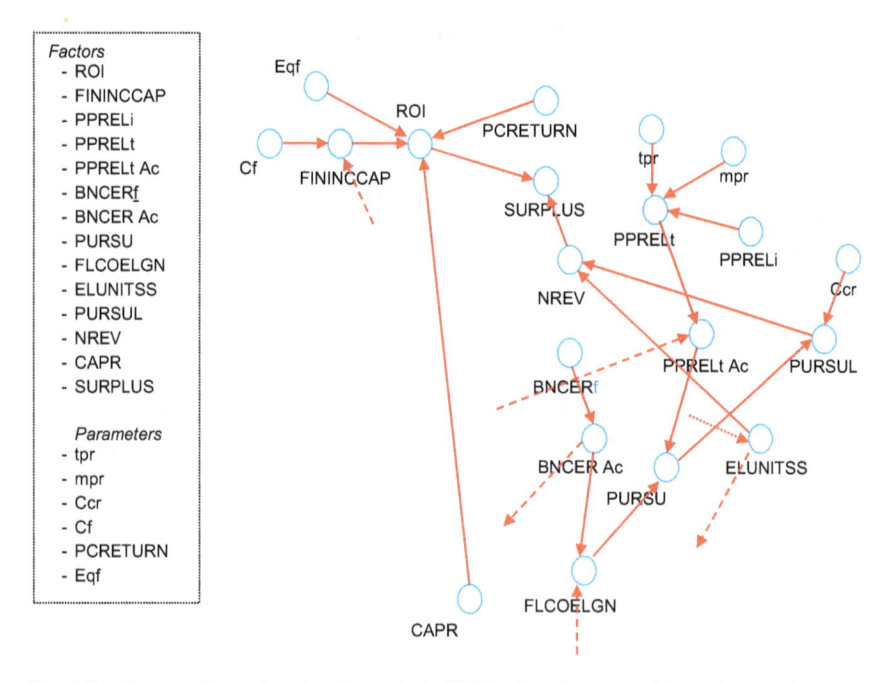

Factors
- ROI
- FININCCAP
- PPRELi
- PPRELt
- PPRELt Ac
- BNCERf
- BNCER Ac
- PURSU
- FLCOELGN
- ELUNITSS
- PURSUL
- NREV
- CAPR
- SURPLUS

Parameters
- tpr
- mpr
- Ccr
- Cf
- PCRETURN
- Eqf

Fig. 6.33 Factors of equations for Component 10 (Purchase by state utility and surplus)

Appendix 3: System Dynamics (SD) Modeling   409

PPRELt Ac = STEP (PPRELt, 13).
- PURSU: Purchase subsidy per unit of electricity

  PURSU = PPRELt Ac − FLCOELGN.
- PURSUL: Purchase subsidy per unit of electricity (value in Rs. Lakh)

  PURSUL = PURSU * Ccr

  Ccr (conversion factor) = 0.00001 (Rs. Lakh/Rs.).
- ROI: Return on investment

  ROI = [(CAPR * Eqf − FININCCAP)*PCRETURN]

  Eqf = 0.3 (30% equity).
- NERV = ELUNITSS * PURSUL.
- SURPLUS

  SURPLUS = NREV − ROI.

Component 11: Income of farmers

See Fig. 6.34.

- BNCERL: Per unit benefit of certified emissions reduction (value in Rs. Lakh)

  BNCERL = BNCERf Ac * Ccr1

  Ccr1 (conversion factor) = 0.00001 (Rs. Lakh/Rs.).
- TOBNCER: Total Benefit of CER

  TOBNCER = BNCERL * ELUINTSS.
- BALCTAGRSUR: Balance Surplus Cotton Agro-residue

  BALCTSUR = CTAGRSU − ACTAGRCO.
- PCTAGRt: Price of cotton Agro-residue at time 't'

  PCTAGRt = PCTAGRi Ac + PCTAGRi Ac * mp * ta

  mp: average rate of change of price of Agro-residue over a year

  ta: time in years, with an interval of one year.
- PCTAGRL: Price of cotton Agro-residue (value in Rs. Lakh)

  PCTAGRL = PCTAGRt * Ccr2

  Ccr2 (conversion factor) = 0.00001 (Rs. Lakh/Rs.).
- APCTAGRi: Actual local market price of cotton Agro-residue (initial value)

  APCTAGRi = Numerical Value.
- APCTAGRt: Actual local market price of cotton Agro-residue (at time 't')

  APCTAGRt = APCTAGRi + APCTAGRi * ma * tap

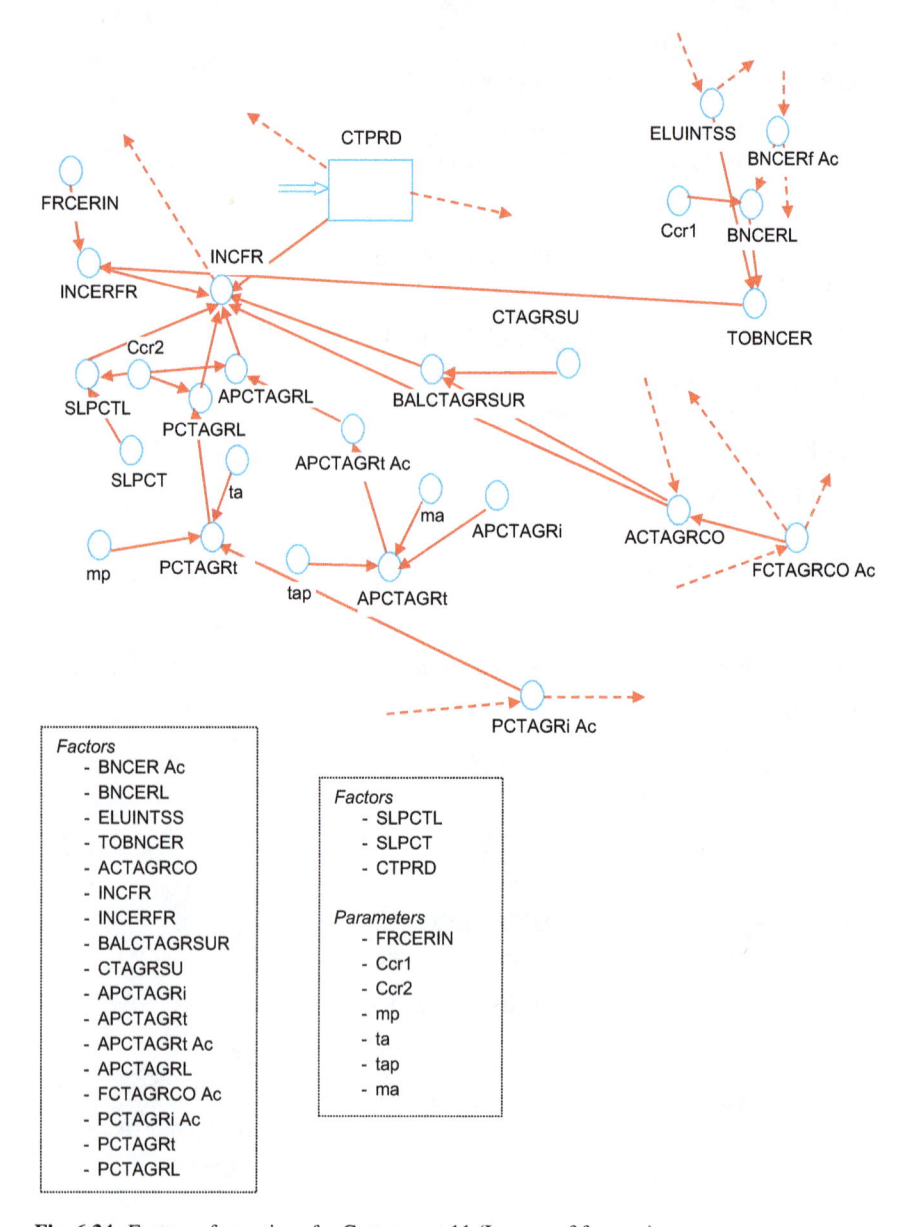

410   6 Innovation in Public Policy and Policy Design Framework

Fig. 6.34 Factors of equations for Component 11 (Income of farmers)

Appendix 3: System Dynamics (SD) Modeling   411

mp: average rate of change of actual local market price of Agro-residue over a year.

tap: time in years, with an interval of one year.

- APCTAGRt Ac: Actual local market price of cotton Agro-residue (at time 't') from the year of consideration

  APCTAGRt Ac = STEP (APCTAGRt, 13).

- APCTAGRL: Actual local market price of cotton Agro-residue (value in Rs. Lakh)

  APCTAGRL = APCTAGRt Ac * Ccr2

  Ccr2 (conversion factor) = 0.00001 (Rs. Lakh/Rs.).

- SLPCT: Sale price of cotton

  SLPCT is decided by the Government.

- SLPCTL: Sale price of cotton (value in Rs. Lakh)

  SLPCTL = SLPCT * Ccr2

  Ccr2 (conversion factor) = 0.00001 (Rs. Lakh/Rs.).

- INCERFR: Income for farmers from CER

  INCERFR = TOBNCER * FRCERIN

  FRCERN is a Numerical Value (0.25; assuming 25% of the income from CER is shared with farmers) (Fig. 6.35).

- INCFR: Income of Farmer

  INCFR = (BALCTAGRSUR * APCTAGRL + ACTAGRCO * PCTAGRL + CTPRD * SLPCTL) + INCERFR.

Scenario Building

See Fig. 6.36.

Sensitivity analysis

See Tables 6.34, 6.35, 6.36, 6.37 and 6.38.

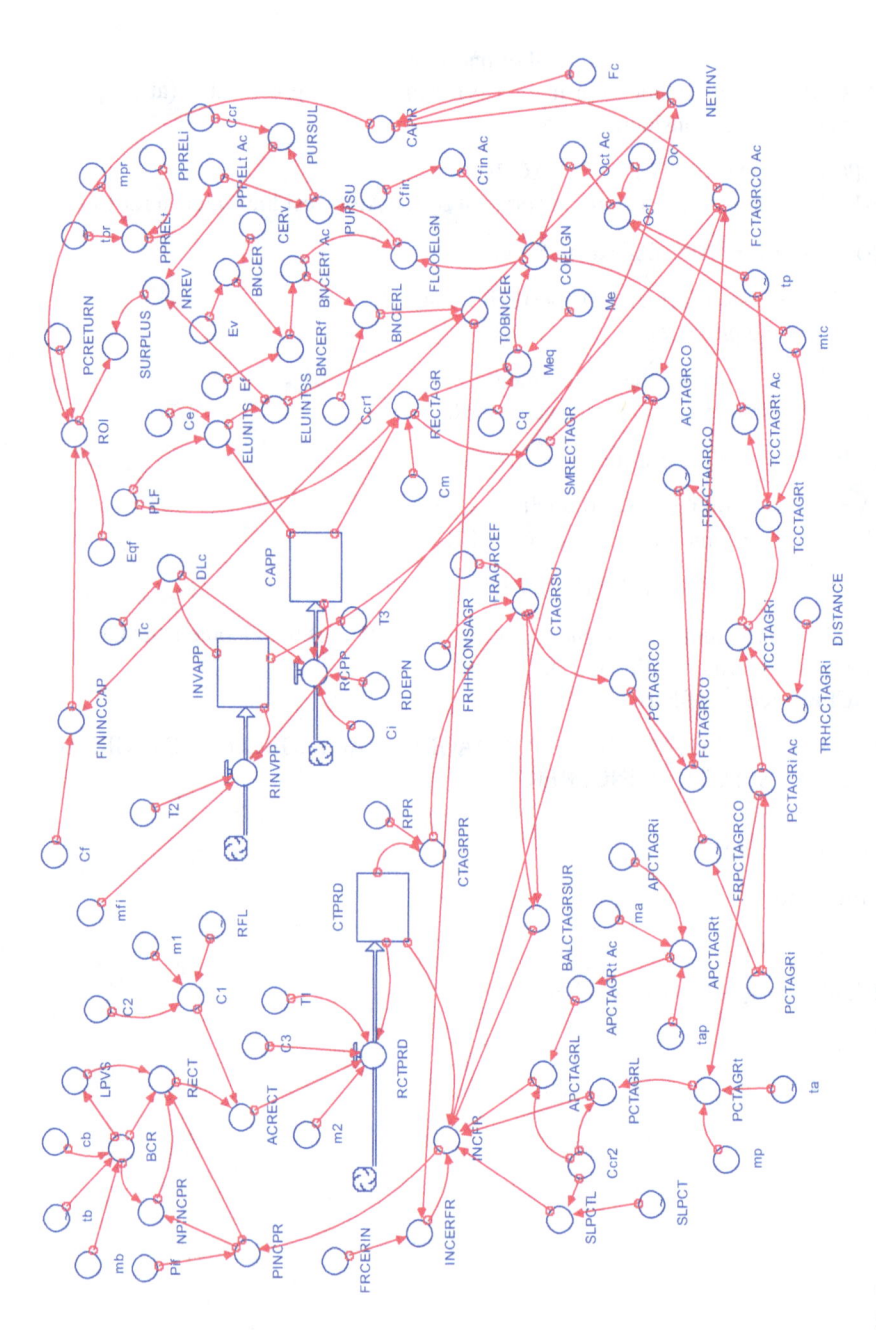

412   6 Innovation in Public Policy and Policy Design Framework

Fig. 6.35 System dynamics model with STELLA software

Appendix 3: System Dynamics (SD) Modeling

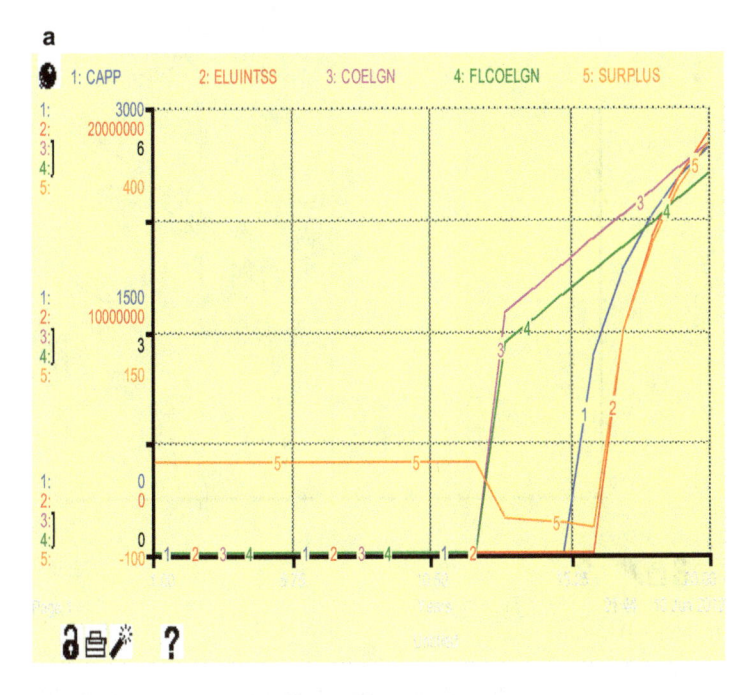

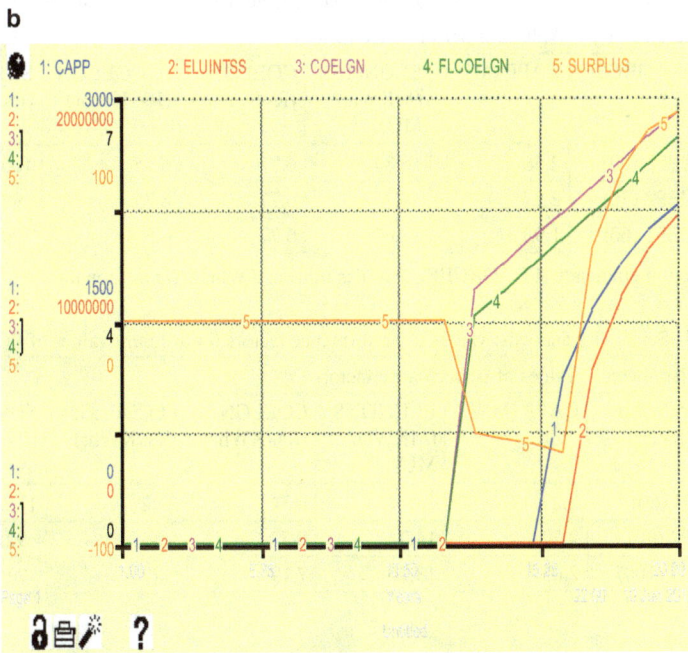

Fig. 6.36 a Performance factors under optimistic scenario. b Performance factors under normal scenario. c Performance factors under pessimistic scenario (using STELLA software)

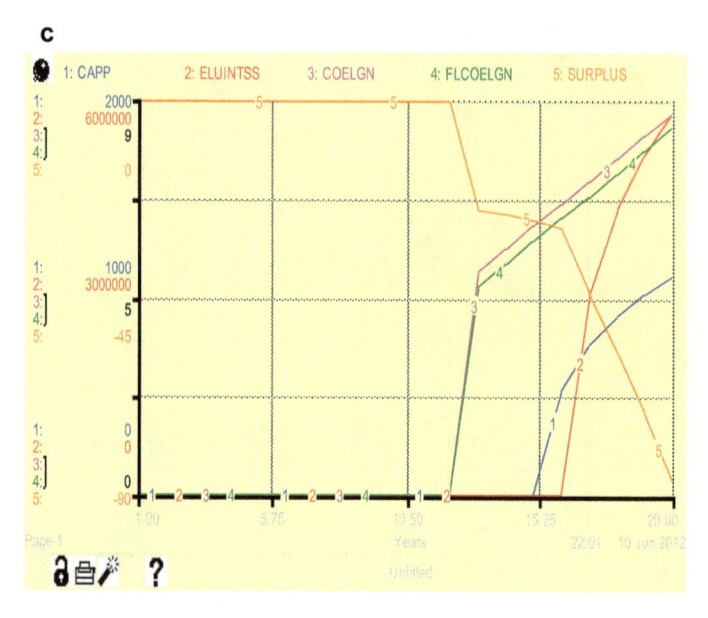

Fig. 6.36 (continued)

Table 6.34 Sensitivity analysis: values of performance factors for different values of FRAGRCEF

S. No.	Parameter	Values of performance factors				
	FRAGRCEF (%)	CAPP (MW)	ELUNITSS (MKWhr/MUs)	COELGN (Rs./KWhr)	FLCOELGN (Rs./KWhr)	SURPLUS (Rs. Lakhs)
1.	CEF3 (80)	2.56	16.84	6.77	6.35	106.17
2.	CEF2 (70)	2.27	14.74	6.77	6.35	92.90
3.	CEF1 (60)	1.95	12.63	6.77	6.35	79.63

CEF collection efficiency (FRAGRCEF), *MKWhr* million KWhr, *MUs* million units

Table 6.35 Sensitivity analysis: values of performance factors for different values of PCTAGR

S. No.	Parameter	Values of performance factors				
	PCTAGR (Rs./Q)	CAPP (MW)	ELUNITSS (MKWhr/MUs)	COELGN (Rs./KWhr)	FLCOELGN (Rs./KWhr)	SURPLUS (Rs. Lakhs)
1.	PI (60)	2.27	14.74	6.34	5.92	155.54
2.	P2 (80)	2.27	14.74	6.77	6.35	92.90
3.	P3 (100)	2.05	13.26	7.19	6.77	27.24

Table 6.36 Sensitivity analysis: values of performance factors for different values of PLF

S. No.	Parameter	Values of Performance Factors				
	PLF (%)	CAPP (MW)	ELUNITSS (MKWhr/MUs)	COELGN (Rs./KWhr)	FLCOELGN (Rs./KWhr)	SURPLUS (Rs. Lakhs)
1.	PLF1 (85%)	2.27	15.66	6.77	6.35	102.79
2.	PLF2 (80%)	2.27	14.74	6.77	6.35	92.90
3.	PLF3 (65%)	2.27	11.97	6.77	6.35	63.22

MKWhr million KWhr, *MUs* million units

Table 6.37 Sensitivity analysis: values of performance factors for different values of Me

S. No.	Parameter	Values of performance factors				
	Me (kg per KWhr)	CAPP (MW)	ELUNITSS (MKWhr/MUs)	COELGN (Rs./KWhr)	FLCOELGN (Rs./KWhr)	SURPLUS (Rs. Lakhs)
1.	Me1 (1.1)	2.27	14.74	6.26	5.84	168.06
2.	Me2 (1.25)	2.27	14.74	6.77	6.35	92.90
3.	Me3 (1.4)	2.27	14.74	7.28	6.86	17.74

Me Agro-residue usage per unit of electricity generation

Table 6.38 Sensitivity analysis: values of performance factors for different values of DISTANCE

S. No.	Parameter	Values of performance factors				
	DISTANCE (km)	CAPP (MW)	ELUNITSS (MKWhr/MUs)	COELGN (Rs./KWhr)	FLCOELGN (Rs./KWhr)	SURPLUS (Rs. Lakhs)
1.	DIST1 (30)	2.27	14.74	6.34	5.92	155.54
2.	DIST2 (40)	2.27	14.74	6.77	6.35	92.90
3.	DIST3 (50)	1.59	10.32	7.62	7.20	-22.66

Dist Distance

References

Abookire S, Plover C, Frasso R, Ku B. Health design thinking: an innovative approach in public health to defining problems and finding solutions. Front Public Health. 2020. https://doi.org/10.3389/fpubh.2020.00459.

Abraham S. Stretching strategic thinking. Strateg Leadersh. 2005;33(5):12.

Allan C, Stankey GH. Adaptive environmental management: a practitioner's guide. Berlin: Springer; 2009.

Anderson PW, Arrow KJ, Pines D, editors. The economy as an evolving complex system. Redwood City: Addison-Wesley; 1988.

Arora DS, Sarah B, Shannon C, Tobias E, Hanna J, Anelia M, Shannon W. Indian renewable energy status report background report for DIREC 2010, NREL/TP-6A20-48948. 2010.

Arthur WB. Complexity and the economy. Oxford: Oxford University Press; 2014.

ASER. The annual status of education report (ASER). 2016. http://img.asercentre.org/docs/Publications/ASER%20Reports/ASER%202016/aser2016_nationalpressrelease.pdf.

Bailey K. Social entropy theory. Albany: State University of New York Press; 1990.

Bankes SC. Tools and techniques for developing policies for complex and uncertain systems. Proc Natl Acad Sci. 2002. https://doi.org/10.1073/pnas.092081399.

Banks G. Evidence-based policy making: What is it? How do we get it? (ANU Public Lecture Series, presented by ANZSOG). Canberra: Productivity Commission; 2009.

Basadur M, Taggar S, Pringle P. Improving the measurement of divergent thinking attitudes in organizations. J Creat Behav. 1999;33(2):1999.

Benbasat I, Zmud RW. Empirical research in information systems: the practice of relevance. MIS Q. 1999;23(1):3–16.

Bertalanffy L. General systems theory: foundations, development, applications. New York: George Braziller; 1968.

Bier A. Sensitivity analysis techniques for system dynamics models of human behaviour. In: 29th International Conference of the System Dynamics Society July 24th–28th, 2011. Washington; 2011. http://www.systemdynamics.org/conferences/2011/proceed/papers/P1112.pdf.

Blignaut S. 5 differences between complexity and systems thinking, more beyond. 2013. http://sonjablignaut.wordpress.com.

Bonn I. Developing strategic thinking as a core competency. Manage Decis. 2001;39(1):63–71.

Boulding KE. General systems theory—the skeleton of science. In: Buckley W, editor. Modern systems research for the behavioral scientist. Chicago: Aldine Publishing; 1956.

Boyko JA, Lavis JN, Dobbins M. Deliberative dialogues as a strategy for system-level knowledge translation and exchange. Health Policy. 2014;9(4):122–31.

Brinkerhoff DW, Crosby BL. Managing policy reform: concepts and tools for decision-makers in developing and transitioning countries. Boulder: Kumarian Press; 2002.

Brinkerhoff D. From design to implementation: stakeholder analysis in a PHC Project in India. Bethesda: Abt Associates Inc.; 1998.

Burki SJ, Perry GE. Beyond the Washington consensus: institutions matter. The World Bank. 1998. https://documents.worldbank.org.

Byrne D, Callaghan G. Complexity theory and the social sciences. Abington: Routledge; 2014.

Byrne DS. Complexity theory and the social sciences: an introduction. New York: Routledge; 1998.

Camm DJ, James RE. Management science and decision technology. Cincinnati: South-Western Publishing; 2000.

Capra F. The web of life: a new scientific understanding of living systems. New York: Doubleday; 1996.

CEA. Monthly review of power sector, executive summary. Central Electricity Commission. 2010. http://www.cea.nic.in/power_sec_reports/executive_summary/2010_03/1-2.pdf

Central Electricity Authority (CEA). Executive summary on power sector. 2021a.

Central Electricity Authority (CEA). Monthly renewable energy generation report (for electricity generation). 2021b.

CERC. Terms and conditions for tariff determination from renewable energy sources regulations. New Delhi: Central Electricity Regulatory Commission (CERC). 2009. http://www.cercind.gov.in/Regulations/Final_SOR_RE_Tariff_Regulations.pdf.

Chancel L, Piketty T. Indian income inequality, 1922–2014: From British Raj to Billionaire Raj? World Inequality Lab Working Paper Series N° 2017/11. 2017. https://wid.world/document/chancelpiketty2017widworld/

References

Checkland P. Systems thinking, systems practice. Chichester: Wiley; 1981.
Chidambaranathan S, Muralidharan C, Deshmukh SG. Analyzing the buyer supplier relationship factors: an integrated modeling approach. Int J Manage Sci Eng Manage. 2010;5(4):292–301.
Chris A, Gash A. Collaborative governance in theory and practice. J Pub Admin Res Theory. 2008;18(4):543–57.
Christiansen J, Bunt L. Innovation in policy: allowing for creativity, social complexity and uncertainty in public governance. NESTA. 2012.
Chubinski S. Creative critical thinking strategies. Nurse Educ. 1996;21(6):23–7.
CIMA. Strategic analysis tools. Topic Gateway Series No. 34. 2007. http://www.cimaglobal.com/Documents/ImportedDocuments/cid_tg_strategic_analysis_tools_nov07.pdf.pdf.
Cohen WM, Levinthal DA. Absorptive capacity: a new perspective on learning and innovation. Adm Sci Q. 1990;35:128–52.
Cohen WJ. The development of the Social Security Act of 1935: reflections some fifty years later. Minnesota Law Review. 1984. https://core.ac.uk/download/pdf/217208529.pdf.
Coyle RG. System dynamics modelling: a practical approach. London: Chapman and Hall; 1996.
Coyle RG. Qualitative and quantitative modelling in system dynamics: some research questions. Syst Dyn Rev. 2000;16(3):225–44.
Culyer AJ, Lomas J. Deliberative process and evidence-informed decision-making in health care: do they work and how might we know? Evid Policy. 2006;12(31):357–71.
Curtain R. Good public policy making: how australia fares, agenda. J Policy Anal Reform. 2000;8(1):33–46.
Davies A, Simon J, Patrick R, Norman W. Mapping citizen engagement in the process of social innovation. In: A deliverable of the project: the theoretical, empirical and policy foundations for building social innovation in Europe (TEPSIE), European Commission—7th Framework Programme, Brussels: European Commission, DG Research. 2012.
Deloitte. Global manufacturing competitiveness index 2016. 2016.
Dewey J. The public and its problems. New York: Henry Holt and Company; 1927.
Doyle JK, Ford DN. Mental models concepts for system dynamics research. Syst Dyn Rev. 1998;14(1):3–29.
Dror Y. Public policy-making: re-examined. London: Routledge; 1983.
Dunn W. Public policy: an introduction. New Jersey: Prentice-Hall; 1981.
Dye TR. Understanding public policy. New Jersey: Prentice-Hall; 1992.
Elder L, Paul R. Critical thinking: crucial distinctions for questioning. J Dev Educ. 1997;21(2):34.
Facione PA. Toward a theory of critical thinking. Lib Educ. 1984;70(3):253–61.
Fletcher A, Guthrie J, Steane P, Roos G, Pike S. Mapping stakeholder perceptions for a third sector organization. J Intellect Cap. 2003;4(4):505–27.
Fobes R, Reed J. The creative problem solver's toolbox: a complete course in the art of creating solutions to problems of any kind. Dayton: Solutions Through Innovation Publisher; 2014.
Forrester JW. Counterintuitive behaviour of social systems. Technol Rev. 1971; 53–68.
Forrester JW. Indusrial dynamics. Massachusetts: MIT Press; 1961.
Forrester JW. Principles of systems. Massachusetts: MIT Press; 1968.
Forrester JW. Urban dynamics. Massachusetts: MIT Press; 1969.
Forrester JW. System dynamics, systems thinking, and soft operation research. Syst Dyn Rev. 1994;10:245–56.
Fuentes HCT. Systemic methodologies in regional sustainable development. Syst Res Sci. 2006;23(5):659–66.
Gagnon J. The redistributive properties of the social security act of 1935. J Undergrad Res. 2017;22(1):10.
Gentner D, Stevens AL, editors. Mental models. Elrbaum: Hillsdale; 1983.
Gerston LN. Public policy making: process and principles. New York: Sharpe Inc.; 2010.
Geurts T. Public policy making, the 21st century perspective. 2010. http://www.lulu.com/shop/theigeurts/public-policy-making-the-21st-century-perspective/ebook/product-21759876.html.

Geyer R, Cairney P. Handbook on complexity and public policy (Handbooks of research on public policy series). Cheltenham: Edward Elgar Publishing Ltd; 2015.

Gharajedaghi J. Systems thinking: managing chaos and complexity: a platform for designing business architecture, vol. 111. New York: Elsevier; 2006. p. 38–40.

Gharajedaghi J. Systems thinking, third edition: managing chaos and complexity: a platform for designing business architecture. Burlington: Morgan Kaufmann; 2011.

Giest S. Big data for policymaking: fad or fasttrack? Policy Sci. 2017;50:367–82.

Gigch JPV. Applied general systems theory. London: Harper and Row Publishers; 1974.

Glaser BG. Basics of grounded theory analysis emergence vs forcing. California: The Sociology Press; 1992.

Government of UK (GoUK). Modernising government white paper. 1999. http://www.ofmdfmni.gov.uk/practical-guide-policy-making.pdf.

Guastello SJ. Nonlinear dynamical systems for theory and research in ergonomics. New Paradig Ergon. 2020. https://doi.org/10.1080/00140139.2016.1162851.

Gupta DN. Policy options for agro-residue electricity system: a case study of Wardha Block. PhD Thesis (IIT, Delhi, India); 2012.

Hager P, Beckett D. Complex systems and complexity thinking. In: The emergence of complexity. Perspectives on rethinking and reforming education. Cham: Springer; 2019. https://doi.org/10.1007/978-3-030-31839-0_7.

Hallsworth M, Rutter J. Making policy better, improving Whitehall's core business. London: Institute for Government; 2011.

Holling CS. Adaptive environmental assessment and management. New York: Wiley; 1978.

Howlett M. Designing public policies: principles and instruments. London: Routledge; 2019.

IEA. Key world energy statistics. Paris: International Energy Agency (IEA); 2011a.

IEA. World energy outlook 2011: energy for all. Paris: International Energy Agency (IEA); 2011b.

IEA. Key world energy statistics. Paris: IEA; 2019.

International Institute for Sustainable Development (IISD) and the Energy and Resources Institute (TERI). Designing policies in a world of uncertainty, change, and surprise. 2006. https://www.iisd.org/system/files/publications/climate_designing_policies.pdf.

IPCC. Fourth assessment report of the intergovernmental panel on climate change (IPCC). Geneva: Switzerland; 2007.

Isaksen SG, Treffinger DJ. Creative problem solving: the basic course. Buffalo, NY: Bearly Limited; 1985.

Kahan JP. Focus groups as a tool for policy analysis. Analyses of Social Issues and Public Policy, 129–146; 2001. http://www.psicopolis.com/GruppoNew/focgrpol.pdf.

Kahne A. Transformative Scenario Planning Paperback. Collins; 2013.

Kalil T. Public policy and the national information infrastructure. Bus Econ. 1995;3(4):15–20.

Kauffman S. At home in the universe: the search for the laws of self-organization and complexity. New York: Oxford University Press; 1995.

Kelly KL. A systems approach to identifying decisive information for sustainable development. Eur J Oper Res. 1998;109:452–64.

Kerkhof M. Making a difference: on the constraints of consensus building and the relevance of deliberation in stakeholder dialogues. Policy Sci. 2006;39(3):279–99.

Khalil HK. Nonlinear systems. Upper Saddle River: Prentice Hall; 2001.

Khandwalla PN. Corporate creativity, the winning edge. Noida: Tata McGraw Hill; 2005.

Kim SH, Myers CG, Allen L. Health care providers can use design thinking to improve patient experiences. 2017. https://hbr.org/2017/08/health-care-providers-can-use-design-thinking-to-improve-patient-experiences.

Kingston RJ. The power of deliberative dialogue, public thought and foreign policy. Dayton: Kettering Foundation Press; 2005.

Kirman A. Complex economics: individual and collective rationality. Abingdon: Routledge; 2011.

Koppenjan J. The new public governance in public service delivery. Den Haag: Eleven International Publishing; 2012.

References

Kusmuljono BS, Eriyatno, Marimin, Arini RD. The application of soft system methodology for agro business micro financing policy. 2007. http://journals.isss.org/index.php/proceedings51st/article/view/453/246.

Lal R. World crop residues production and implications as its use as a biofuel. Environ Int. 2005;31:575–84.

Lasswell HD. The policy orientation. In: Lerner D, Lasswell HD, editors. The policy sciences. Palo Alto, CA: Stanford University Press; 1951.

Liedtka J, Azer D, Salzman R. Design thinking for the greater good—innovation in the social sector. New York, NY: Columbia University Press; 2017.

Liedtka J. Solving problems with design thinking—ten stories of what works. New York, NY: Columbia University Press; 2013.

Lindsay PH, Norman DA. Human information processing. New York: Academic Press; 1977.

Loayza N, Woolcock M. Designing good policies is one thing, implementing them is another. World Bank Blogs; 2020. https://blogs.worldbank.org/developmenttalk/designing-good-policies-one-thing-implementing-them-another.

London S. Thinking together: the power of deliberative dialogue; 2021. http://scott.london/reports/dialogue.html.

Luna-Reyes LF, Andersen DL. Collecting and analyzing qualitative data. Syst Dyn Rev. 2003;19(4):271–96.

Lunn P. Regulatory policy and behavioural economics. Berlin: OECD Publishing; 2014.

Luthra S, Kumar V, Kumar S, Haleem A. Barriers to implement green supply chain management in automobile industry using interpretive structural modeling technique: an indian perspective. J Indus Eng Manag. 2011;4(2):231–57.

Lynd RS. Knowledge for what? The place for social science in the American culture. Princeton: Princeton University Press; 1939.

Mandal A, Deshmukh SG. Vendor selection using interpretive structural modeling (ISM). Int J Oper Prod Manag. 1994;14(6):52–9.

Marston G, Watts R. Tampering with the evidence: a critical appraisal of evidence-based policymaking. 2003. Downloads/marston_watts.pdf.

Mason M. What is complexity theory and what are its implications for educational change? Educ Philos Theory. 2008;40(1):35–49.

McCulloch CE, Paal B, Ashdown SP. An optimisation approach to apparel sizing. J Oper Res Soc. 1998;49(5):492–9.

Meadows DH, Meadows DL, Randers J, Behrens WW. Limits to growth: the 30-year update. New York: University Books; 1972.

MERC. Discussion paper on development of renewable energy framework for maharashtra for new control period. Pune: Maharashtra Electricity Regulatory Commission; 2010. http://www.mercindia.org.in/pdf/Order%2058%2042/Discussion%20paper_MERC_RE%20Framework_modified_final4upload_03.03.2010.pdf.

Meso P, Musa P, Straub D, Mbarika V. Information infrastructure, governance, and socio-economic development in developing countries. Eur J Inform Syst. 2009;2009(18):52–65.

Ministry of Environment and Forests (MoEF). India: greenhouse gas emissions 2007. New Delhi: Government of India; 2010. http://moef.nic.in/downloads/public-information/Report_INCCA.pdf.

Ministry of Statistics and Programme Implementation (MOSPI). Energy statistics, 2021. Government of India; 2021.

Ministry of Statistics and Programme Implementation (MOSPI). Energy statistics, 2022. Government of India; 2022.

Ministry of Statistics and Programme Implementation (MOSPI). Energy statistics. Government of India; 2019.

MNRE. National biomass resource atlas (developed at IISc under MNRE project). New Delhi: Ministry of New and Renewable Energy (MNRE), Govt. of India; 2010. http://mnre.gov.in/mnre-2010/schemes/resource-assessment/biomass-resource-atlas/.

MNRE. Draft recommendations of sub-group on 'bioenergy mission' under the working group on new and renewable energy for 12th five year plan (2012–17). New Delhi: Ministry of New and Renewable Energy (MNRE), Govt. of India; 2011a. http://www.mnre.gov.in/pdf/plan12sg2-draft.pdf.

MNRE. Strategy on R&D activities for thermo-chemical conversion and promotion of biomass energy in the country, prepared by combustion and gasification laboratory. New Delhi: Indian Institute of Science, Bangalore for Ministry of New and Renewable Energy (MNRE), Govt. of India; 2011b. http://mnre.gov.in/pdf/national-rdbiomass.pdf.

Mohapatra PK, Mandal P, Bora MC. Introduction to system dynamics modelling. Hyderabad: Universities Press Ltd.; 1994.

Morcol G. A complexity theory for public policy routledge research in public administration and public policy. London: Routledge; 2012.

Mudgal RK, Shankar R, Talib P, Raj T. Modelling the barriers of green supply chain practices: an Indian perspective. Int J Logist Syst Manage. 2010;7(1):81–107.

Mueller B. Why public policies fail: policymaking under complexity. Economia. 2020;21(2):311–23. https://doi.org/10.1016/j.econ.2019.11.002.

NAPCC. National action plan on climate change (NAPCC). Prime Minister Council on Climate Change. New Delhi: Govt. of India; 2008.

Nelson GH, Stoiterman E. The design way: intentional change in an unpredictable world. Cambridge: MIT Press; 2012.

Nicolis G. Introduction to nonlinear science. Cambridge: Cambridge University Press; 1995.

North DC. Institutions, institutional change and economic performance. New York: Cambridge University Press; 1990.

O'Leary R, Vij N. Collaborative public management: where have we been and where are we going? Am Rev Pub Admin. 2012;42(5):507–22.

OECD. Behavioural insights and public policy: lessons from around the world. Paris: OECD Publishing; 2017a. https://doi.org/10.1787/9789264270480-en.

OECD. Debate the issues: complexity and policy making. OECD publications; 2017b. https://www.oecd.org/naec/complexity_and_policymaking.pdf

Osborn AF. Applied imagination: principles and procedures of creative thinking. New York: Scribner; 1963.

Palmer CG, Biggs R, Cumming GS. Applied research for enhancing human well-being and environmental stewardship: using complexity thinking in Southern Africa. Ecol Soc. 2015;20(1):53. https://doi.org/10.5751/ES-07087-200153.

Peters BG. Policy design: from technocracy to complexity, and beyond. 2019. https://www.ippapublicpolicy.org/file/paper/5932fa23369d0.pdf.

Pichon E, Widuto A, Dobreva A, Jensen L. Ten composite indices for policy-making. European Parliamentary Research Service (EPRS); 2021. https://epthinktank.eu/2021/09/10/ten-composite-indices-for-policy-making/.

Piketty T. Capital in the twenty-first century. Harvard University Press. 2017

PISA Report. Do schools get their money (accountability initiative 2012). Annual Survey of Education Research (ASER); 2012. http://www.accountabilityindia.in/sites/default/files/state-report-cards/paisa_report_2012.pdf.

Planning Commission. Draft report of the expert committee on integrated policy on energy. New Delhi: Yojana Bhavan, Govt. of India; 2005.

Porter ME. Competitive advantage: creating and sustaining superior performance. London: Free Press; 1998.

Preston S, Mazhar MU, Bull R. Citizen engagement for co-creating low carbon smart cities: practical lessons from Nottingham City Council in the UK. Energies. 2020;13:6615. https://doi.org/10.3390/en13246615.

Proden P. Deliberative dialogue. 2015. https://s3.wp.wsu.edu/uploads/sites/2164/2015/03/Deliberative_Dialogue_Urban_Wrkshop_PP_2_18_15.pdf.

Raiffa H. The art and science of negotiation. Cambridge, MA: Harvard University Press; 1982.

Ramachandra TV, Kamakshi G. Bioresource potential of Karnataka (talukwise inventory with management options), energy and wetlands research group, Technical Report No.: 109. Bangalore: Centre for Ecological Sciences, Indian Institute of Science; 2005.

Ramos G, Hynes W, Müller J, Lees, M. Systemic thinking for policy making—the potential of systems analysis for addressing global policy challenges in the 21st century. OECD and the International Institute for Applied Systems Analysis (IIASA); 2019.

Randers J. Guidelines for model conceptualization. In: Randers J, editor. Elements of the system dynamics method. Cambridge, MA: MIT Press; 1980. p. 117–39.

Remme U, Trudeau N, Graczyk D, Taylor P. Technology development prospects for the Indian Power Sector. Paris: International Energy Agency (IEA); 2011.

REN21. Renewables 2011 global status report, renewable energy policy networks for the twenty first century (REN21). Paris: REN21; 2011.

REN21. Renewables 2020 global status report, renewable energy policy networks for the twenty first century (REN21). Paris: REN21; 2020.

REN21. Renewables 2018 global status report, renewable energy policy networks for the twenty first century (REN21). Paris: REN21; 2018.

Richardson GP. Problems for the future of system dynamics. Syst Dyn Rev. 1996;12(3):141–57.

Richmond B. An introduction to systems thinking. ISEE Systems, Inc.; 2010 http://www.fi.muni.cz/~xpelanek/IV109/jaro07/IST.pdf.

Rodrik D. The new global economy and developing countries: making openness work: 24 (policy essay). Baltimore: Johns Hopkins University Press; 1999.

Rogers KH, Luton R, Biggs H, Biggs R, Blignaut S, Choles AG, Palmer CG, Tangwe P. Fostering complexity thinking in action research for change in social–ecological systems. Ecol Soc. 2013;18(2):31. https://doi.org/10.5751/ES-05330-180231.

Ryan A. What is a systems approach? 2008. https://ocw.tudelft.nl/wp-content/uploads/What_Is_A_Systems_Approach.pdf.

Saeed K. Development planning and policy design: a system dynamics approach. Avebury: Aldeshot; 1994.

Sage AP. Interpretive structural modelling: methodology for large-scale systems. New York: McGraw-Hill; 1977.

Sahney S. Critical success factors in online retail—an application of quality function deployment and interpretive structural modelling. Int J Bus Inf. 2008;3(1):144–63.

Sanderson I. Intelligent policy making for a complex world: pragmatism, evidence and learning. Polit Stud. 2009;57:699–719. https://doi.org/10.1111/j.1467-9248.2009.00791.x.

Savigny D, Adam T (eds). Systems thinking for health systems strengthening. Alliance for Health Policy and Systems Research, WHO; 2009.

Sawyer RK. Social emergence: societies as complex systems. Cambridge: Cambridge University; 2005.

Saxena JP, Sushil VP. Policy and strategy formulation: an application of flexible systems methodology. New Delhi: GIFT Publishing, Global Institute of Flexible Systems Management; 2006.

Schneider A, Ingram H. Policy design for democracy. Kansas: University Press of Kansas; 1997.

Schon DA. The reflective practitioner: how professionals think in action. New York: Basic; 1983.

Senge P. The fifth discipline: the art and practice of the learning organization. New York: Doubleday Currency; 1990.

Senge P, Sterman JD. Systems thinking and organizational learning: acting locally and thinking globally in the organization of the future. Eur J Oper Res. 1992;59:137–50.

Serdar DM. A system dynamics approach for technology improvement policy, analysis: the case for Turkey. Department of Science and Technology Policy Studies, Middle East Technical University (METU); 2001. http://www.stps.metu.edu.tr/sites/stps.metu.edu.tr/files/0304.pdf.

Sherblom SA. Complexity-thinking and social science: Self-organization involving human consciousness. New Ideas Psychol. 2017;47:10–5. https://doi.org/10.1016/j.newideapsych.2017.03.003.

Simon HA. The new science of management decision. Upper Saddle River: Prentice-Hall; 1977.

Singh MD, Shankar R, Narain R, Agarwal A. An interpretive structural modelling (ISM) of knowledge management in engineering industries. J Adv Manag Res. 2003;1(1):28–40.

Sotarauta M, Srinivas S. Co-evolutionary policy processes: Understanding innovative economies and future resilience. Sci Direct Fut. 2006;38(2006):312–36.

Stacey RD. Strategic management and organisational dynamics: the challenge of complexity. Upper Saddle River: Prentice Hall; 2002.

Sterman JD. Business dynamics: systems thinking and modelling for a complex world. Boston: Irwin and McGraw-Hil; 2000.

Strauss A, Corbin J. Basics of qualitative research: grounded theory procedures and techniques. Newbury Park: Sage; 1990.

Stuart IR. Human physiology. New York: McGraw-Hill; 2011.

Studinka J, Guenduez AA. The use of big data in the public policy process: paving the way for evidence-based governance. 2018. https://www.alexandria.unisg.ch/255680/1/Studinka%20and%20Guenduez.pdf.

Sushil. Interpretive matrix: a tool to aid interpretation of management and social research. Glob J Flex Syst Manag. 2005;6(2):27–30.

Sushil. System dynamics: a practical approach for managerial problems. New Delhi: Wiley Eastern Limited; 1993.

Sutcliffe S, Court J. Evidence-based policymaking: what is it? How does it work? What relevance for developing countries? London: Overseas Development Institute (ODI); 2005.

Swanson D, Bhadwal S, editors. Creating adaptive policies guide for policy-making in an uncertain world. Thaousand Oaks: Sage Publication; 2009.

Thaler R. Toward a positive theory of consumer choice. J Econ Behav Organ. 1980;1:39–60.

Theil H. Economics and information theory. Chicago: Rand McNally; 1967.

UNEP. Integrated analysis of environmental trends and policies. IEA Training Manual: Module 5, United Nations Environment Programme (UNEP); 2008.

United Nations Development Programme (UNDP). Human development indices and indicators. 2018.

Van der Wal Z. The 21st century public manager (the public management and leadership series). London: Palgrave; 2017.

Vennix JAM. Model-building for group decision support: issues and alternatives in knowledge elicitation. Eur J Oper Res. 1992;59:28–41.

Walker WE, Rahman SA, Cave J. Adaptive policies, policy analysis, and policy-making. Eur J Oper Res. 2001;128(2001):282–9.

Warfield JW. Developing interconnected matrices in structural modelling. IEEE Trans Syst Man Cybern. 1974;4(1):51–81.

Wootton S, Horne T. Strategic thinking: a step-by-step approach to strategy. London: Kogan Page; 2001.

World Bank. Unleashing the potential of renewable energy in india, south asia energy unit. Washington: Sustainable Development Department, The World Bank; 2010.

World Bank. Big data in action for government big data: innovation in public services, policy and engagement. 2017. https://openknowledge.worldbank.org/handle/10986/26391.

World Bank. World Bank blogs: behavioral science in public policy: future of government? By Carolina Sánchez-Páramo, Renos Vakis, Zeina Afif. 2019. http://blogs.worldbank.org/developmenttalk/behavioral-science-public-policy-future-government.

World Bank Group (WBG). Citizen engagement. 2014. https://www.worldbank.org/en/topic/fragilityconflictviolence/brief/citizen-engagement.

World Economic Forum (WEF). The Global Competitiveness Report, 2017–18. 2018

World Health Organization (WHO). Health in sustainable development planning: the role of indicators. By Yasmin von Schirnding. World Health Organization; 2002. https://apps.who.int/iris/handle/10665/67391.

Chapter 7
Institutional Development and Design of New Public Organizations

> *If you do not push the boundaries, you will never know where they are.*
> T. S. Eliot, Nobel Laureate in Literature, and Essayist and Literary Critic.

Abstract The chapter brings to the fore the challenges governments face. While dealing with social and economic issues, more so complexity, it stresses that there are practical limitations. There is a limit to certainty, a limit to stability, a limit to dominating approach, and a limit to growth. These limitations need to be considered for future policymaking. The traditional approaches need to be revisited to manage dynamic and complex issues. Public organizations are required to embrace new theories, systems, and practices to meet emerging challenges. They need to deliver efficiently on quality public services. It emphasizes institutional development for sustainability. New thinking is needed to manage the future. It underscores a shift from the Weberian model, advocating hierarchy and control, to systems thinking and adaptive strategy, emphasizing building human capital and skill sets. It advances the need to evolve an innovation ecosystem in public organizations to address complex problems. It culminates with the primacy of innovation in the process of designing policy and for identifying policy options. It accentuates that an alternative paradigm for policymaking is called for. The design approach, adaptive policies, and complexity theory in policymaking provide a way forward.

Keywords New thinking · Institutional development · New public organizations · Policy design · Adaptive policies · Public value · Strategic planning · Citizen-centric system · Quality management system · Performance management system · Innovation

Going by the trends in various fields, viz., social, demographics, economy, technology, finance, trade, and so on, it is becoming evident that the twenty-first century will deal with complexity more often than ever before. Governments worldwide, including in India, are facing a number of new challenges that have manifested mainly in the last three decades due to exponential advances in technologies, social media, demographic changes, globalization, and climate change. These, in the combined form, are creating a complex web of interacting problems and issues.

To illustrate, as a result of the exponential nature of interactions (between issues, technologies, etc.), rapid changes are creating both new opportunities and posing challenges. There are opportunities on account of advances in technology front in areas such as energy, manufacturing, education, health, and so on. Due to the application of advanced technologies, automation eliminates some jobs while creating others, and thus, the need for reskilling and upskilling the workforce is increasing. Climate change is another cause of serious concern. The rising expectations of citizens keep expanding demands. The governments face a resource crunch and a large institutional capacity gap (Walby 2003; NIC 2012; KPMG 2014; PWC 2016).

While dealing with public problems, the literature survey and explanations in Chaps. 3 and 4 have brought out that there are following four limitations that define, in general, the assumptions of complex socio-economic systems (Forrester 1961; Meadows et al. 1972; Sterman 2000; Christiansen and Bunt 2012):

- *Limit to certainty.* Due to nonlinear relationships, feedback loops, and dynamics, the causality cannot be determined, and the system behavior cannot be predicted.
- *Limit to stability.* On account of the hyper-connected world through communication technologies, manifold increase in mobility of individuals and socio-economic activities, and exponential flow of capital, the system remains in a dynamic state.
- *Limit to dominating approach.* As a result of multiple interacting elements and variables, the system behavior emerges in an uncertain manner, and there is no dominating approach to explain the emergence.
- *Limit to growth.* The growth cannot be in perpetuity due to likely diminishing returns after a certain period unless novel approaches are introduced, innovations take place, and productivity improves significantly.

7.1 Institutional Development: An Overview

Public institutions are expected to perform numerous small, big, difficult, and complex tasks in a public system. The system is marked by rising aspirations, demanding political parties, international influences, limited budgets, questioning media, and scrutinizing judicial processes. It is generally held view that the policies are the ways to improve the well-being of citizens, but the outcomes have been far from the intended objectives. Usually, there is a critical gap between what is intended and what is implemented. It calls for institutions to provide a link between policymaking process and outcomes. The quality of the policy process results from institutional mechanisms and affects the content of the resulting policies (Burki and Perry 1998; Jones 2011; Mueller 2020).

Institutional development (ID) is about mainstreaming the institutions—values, norms, and rules—in the organizational system and structure and enhancing the capacity of an organization to utilize human and financial resources effectively to achieve public purpose. ID constitutes a process of institution building and measures for strengthening the institutional capacity (Israel 1989; McGill 1996; Boin and Christensen 2008). It attempts to shape behavior, both internally as well as externally. The internal aspect is with regard to the environment within the organization, and the external is in the context of outside environment or society. In the context of the evolving role of public organizations for equitable and sustainable development, ID entails institutional change, which aims to promote new norms and upgrade capacity to perform new tasks. The essentiality of institutional development (ID) emerges from the need to develop institutions that can bring qualitative change in society (Moore et al. 1995; Bergstrom 2005; Joshi and Carter 2015).

It is widely recognized that public institutions are inextricably linked to the development process in general and the delivery of public services, reducing poverty and achieving growth in particular. And the vital differentiator in the level of development across different regions or countries is in the capacity of public institutions to perform. From the causal perspective, the basic premise is that the determinant of development and economic growth is the efficacy of policy institutions, including economic and governance institutions (North 1990; Hall and Jones 1999; Acemoglu 2010). There are two key interlinked fundamental issues. *First*, development and economic growth cannot be determined in isolation from public policy institutions; and *second*, there is a definitive need to understand the institutional evolution of policy institutions, as it necessitates examining the underlying factors for the evolution and seeking measures for reforms (World Bank 2000; DFID 2003).

Scholars like Daron Acemoglu, Ronald Coase, Douglass North, Elinor Ostrom, and Oliver Williamson have contributed significantly to new institutional economics (NIE) (Bardhan 2005; Menard and Shirley 2011). The literature review of NIE (North and Thomas 1973; Forss 2001; Bardhan 2005) shows that NIE is more focused on the role of property rights and transaction cost, though vital, in encouraging innovation and improving efficiency. But under the overarching role of institutions in the economy, less focus has been given to issues such as the public governance system, including the justice system, efficiency, coordination, and collaboration, or the implementation of the economic policies and development programs. The linkages among HR capital, R&D, innovation, technology, and productivity need more elaborated discourse in institutional economics. The scope of coordination and collaborations among various institutions needs to be examined to utilize them to raise the potential of the system to a higher one (Burki and Perry 1998).

The institutional approach in the context of the economy should encompass the entire social and economic ecosystem to enable people to participate in the development process and avail opportunities, exercise property rights, and access information and capital. It should provide safety and security of property and regulate jobs, wages, market, trade, exchange rate, and monetary and fiscal policy. The causal effect of institutions on development needs to be factored in. ID is central to sustainable and beneficial economic growth. The approach can spur innovation, efficiency, economies of scale, and inclusive growth. (Forss 2001; Menard and Shirley 2011; Drzeniek 2015). There is a need to examine the virtuous cycle of good institutions, efficiency, good governance, efficient social sector, economic sector activities, higher economic activities, growth, and incentives for good institutions.

7.1.1 Institutional Development of Policy System

Public policy is determined, implemented, regulated, or enforced by public institutions. The parliamentarians or legislatures, through a process of deliberations with stakeholders, provide credence to the policy process. The transparency and legal scrutiny by the judiciary enhance the public faith. Public policy impacts all citizens in the country and has wide-ranging implications. For these reasons, the robust process of institutionalizing public policy system assumes importance (van Heffen and Klok 2000; World Bank 2010; Sapru 2012; Sanchawa 2015). The institutions influence the policymaking and implementation of policies. These provide structure and mechanism to formulate policies, bring mid-course corrections, and raise the sustainability of policy interventions. While realizing the pivotal central role of institutions in undertaking any big task in the public system, the underpinning of institutional development (ID) is essential. It is about building and strengthening institutions and the creation of the capacity of an organization to perform efficiently and effectively (Israel 1989; Keeney 1999; Spiller and Tommasi 2003).

ID provides policy direction and ways to mobilize and manage the resources and deliver the desired outputs and outcomes. In the context of public policy, ID will entail technical know-how of data handling and analysis, a process to access data, informed decision-making, change management, and organizational development (OD) for change in culture and norms for evidence-based policymaking in the government. By institutionalizing the process of policymaking and implementation, ID will provide acceptability and credibility (McGill 1996; World Bank 2000). ID should focus broadly on two aspects. *First*, creating a more systematic and general understanding of how institutions are formed and change over time; and *second*, developing a vision for how institutions shape socio-economic behavior and policy outcomes in the environment (Chang and Evans 2000; Spiller and Tommasi 2003; Menard and Shirley 2011). The institutional approach should address the following:

- *first*, how the basic issues—rules, norms, personal rights, property rights, social interactions, social inequalities, secured business operations, personal security—are addressed; and,
- *second*, how public policy management and governance get mainstreamed in the institutional framework.

As a process, institutional development begins with institution building (IB). IB contains, *first*, nurturing values, rules, internal policies, and laws that will provide scope to govern social behavior, ethical decision-making, equal opportunities, and economic activities; and *second*, capacity building of institutions to deliver on intended objectives. IB can provide a basis (Burki and Perry 1998; Spiller and Tommasi 2003):

7.1 Institutional Development: An Overview

- to define values and public purpose and position itself to ensure a better fit between the organization and its environment or society;
- to build commitment to values like the quality of work, citizen focus, participation by stakeholders, and ethical decision-making;
- to put human resource management at the center in the overall context of achieving organizational objectives;
- to collaborate with other institutions to bring synergy and complementarities, and
- to improve systems and processes through which an organization raises its performance and meets the requirements of citizens or stakeholders.

Prerequisites for ID. The institution is expected to perform consistently and effectively and be valued by stakeholders. For successful institution building, there are specific prerequisites, which are as follows (Moore et al. 1995; Bergstrom 2005):

- it requires familiarity with the local context;
- it is a long-term process, and so it requires a patient and persistent approach;
- it involves a process approach, requiring flexibility and adaptiveness, rather than a blueprint or planned intervention;
- it calls for organizational 'leadership' and broader political commitment;
- it stresses commitment and a sense of ownership; and
- it requires adaptiveness to specific political, cultural, economic, and social contexts and sufficient knowledge and trust to instill confidence.

Key features. Institutional development (ID) will require placing certain fundamentals as the basis for running a public institution (Blase 1986; Israel 1989; Spiller and Tommasi 2003; Menard and Shirley 2011). The underlying fundamentals for ID are summarized below:

- *Outcome-focused approach.* The desired outcomes should drive ID. It could be improving efficiency, reliability of service delivery, or efficient implementation of programs for meeting societal needs.
- *Rules-, norms-, and value-based conduct.* The rules should be fostered and established. These are essential for defining the behavior of individuals and groups, setting norms for performance measurement and management, addressing citizens' concerns, grievance redressal, processes of service delivery, service quality, etc., and ethics and transparency in decision-making.
- *Citizen or stakeholder participation.* The institutions work for a society or community. It demands that there should be a shared understanding with the people in society. And because of this, citizen or stakeholder participation is imperative.
- *Accountability.* It is required to meet the intended objectives and desired outcomes.

Ingredients for ID. Institutionalization is the process by which a set of activities becomes an integral and sustainable part of a formal system. It can be seen as a sequence of events leading to desired practices, processes, and systems becoming a regular part of an institution with time. Innovative institutional mechanisms and processes need to be put in place to make the public system function successfully.

Institutional development (ID) is necessitated for policy system. The vital aspects of effective ID will include (Table 7.1):

- *Purpose.* It is a common purpose or vision for which an public institution aspires to succeed. It will include meeting the needs and aspirations of citizens, addressing basic concerns, engaging citizens in the development process, and instilling confidence in citizens.
- *Mission and values statement.* The mission should define how the institutions will achieve the expectations of society and stakeholders. Values will entail a culture of taking up the tasks of informed discussions, evidence-based policymaking, quality implementation, citizen-centric public system, ethical decision-making, and so on.
- *Means.* Efficient implementation of policies will require sound institutional capacity. It will entail a delivery mechanism that can match expected service delivery standards; physical, financial, and manpower resources; leadership; and legislations, rules, and standards. For the sustainability of the institutions, organizational development (OD) is necessitated to bring systematic change in the attitudes, beliefs, and values in the organizations and manage change (Blase 1986; DFID 2003; Joshi and Carter 2015). It will include establishing processes for citizen participation, innovation, policymaking, decision-making, and implementation. The institutions should bring good practices for promoting innovation, quality management system (QMS), and citizen-centric public system.

Table 7.1 Institutional determinants

S. No.	Key aspects	Elements
1	Purpose	Public purpose: meeting needs and aspirations of citizens
2	Mission and values	How to achieve desired purpose; values, norms, and culture within public institution, ethics in decision-making
3	Means: system to match values and norms	Implementing mechanism and legislations, rules and standards, capacity of delivery system matching the expected service delivery standards, leadership, information infrastructure
		Organizational development (OD) Systematic changes in the attitudes, beliefs, and values in the organizations and managing change
		Good practices for promoting innovation, quality management system (QMS), and citizen-centric system
4	Effectiveness and results	Parameters of performance measurement to match the intended objectives, and performance management system (PMS)

Information infrastructure (InIn). To meet emerging challenges, the information infrastructure is crucial to provide insights about citizens' needs and feedback, improve decision-making processes, advance evidence-based policymaking, and raise public sector outcomes. It has potential in policy areas such as health care, agriculture, economy, urban management, environment, transportation, etc. (Giest 2017; Studinka and Guenduez 2018).

It will create new challenges and opportunities. Governments need to develop strategies, data-use policies, enabling policies for evidence-based policymaking, and a platform of engagement within the government and with the citizens. To realize value from the information infrastructure, governments should enhance their institutional capacity by strengthening technical competence and legal framework to access and use data for evidence-based decision-making. Such a shift in approach will bring efficiency and more confidence in the government (World Bank 2017). A credible institutional mechanism for public policy will call for creating an institution by an Act of parliament or Cabinet approval, together with the regulation of data collection, collation, usage, and security.

- *Effectiveness and results.* Institutional development has a causal effect on performance. To measure the impact, performance parameters for determining the effectiveness of implementation need to be identified and measured. It will necessitate establishing a performance management system (PMS).

7.2 New Public Organizations

There is a growing challenge of designing the right policies that impact a large population to meet the basic needs of education, health, sanitation, water, food, and nutrition. It is more demanding if the public services have to reach the last mile. Another major challenge facing countries is how to be successful in an uncertain environment impacted by rapid technological advancements and instant communication, rising expectations, pandemic issues, and climatic change.

The emerging trends locally, nationally, and globally impact all countries to varying degrees. The likely changes will be at a far more rapid pace than in the last several decades. There will be uncertainties in the form of disruption of existing business models, service delivery mechanisms, and manufacturing systems. It may lead to disturbance in capital markets, investments, and existing industries (due to the introduction of new products). It may cause unemployment, increased cost of skilling, and the problem of change management. Despite complex issues and their uncertain consequences, there is a good potential for new economic opportunities. Through a combination of communication and advanced technologies, better and customized products, and citizen management, even for remote areas, new possibilities are emerging for business. Health, renewable energy, engineering, agriculture, and so on have unexplored potential to create value.

The new challenges call for examining the likely future expectations, uncertainties opportunities, and the assumptions behind them. Governments should build their capacity to take advantage of the opportunities while simultaneously addressing risks and uncertainties. Against the backdrop of complexity, globalization, and emerging trends, governments have pressing challenges. How the events evolve, how to discern change, and how to respond to change are vital issues. The underlying issue is that organizations should be able to enhance their capacity to conceptualize the problems and systems, including trends of change, and identify the drivers for future change. Building new public organizations requires understanding what kind of new policy interventions, strategies, standards, systems, and capabilities are necessary (NIC 2012; KPMG 2014), as summarized below:

- *Policy interventions.* The policies should be introduced for developing culture, structures, processes, and systems that are compatible with the need to comprehend and manage emerging realities. Public organizations should be designed to be resilient and adapt to change. And the organizational capacity should be built for applying innovative methods.
- *Strategies.* It requires a shift toward adaptive leadership. And adaptive approaches are needed to drive strategic change.
- *Standards.* The quality standards for service provisioning and performance management standards should be set. And correspondingly, the processes and systems are to be placed to meet the requirement of desired standards. These should consider the feedback loops, accordingly, the standards should coevolve with the new requirements.
- *Systems.* The internal systems should align with the need for new organizational policies, strategies, and standards. The system will include human resources (HR), training, logistics support, monitoring & evaluation (M&E), etc. The structures, culture, and ecosystem should promote a culture of innovation. The capabilities are required to comprehend complexity, evolving nature, trends, and their drivers.

7.2.1 Vital Public Policy Issues

For managing in the complex and evolving world, the fundamental matter is how to enhance confidence and trust in the public governance system. Among others, it will mainly require improving the capacity of the governance system, enhancing the socio-economic conditions of citizens, and raising competitiveness at the global level. In this context, among others, public organizations need to address the following:

- *First, ability to conceptualize the problems and system.* To conceptualize the problem and system correctly, the first step is to acquire a set of knowledge and skills about the tools and methods to examine various issues. And it is more so important in the complex and dynamic environment. The complex nature of socio-economic problems underscores that public decision-making involves more than technical analyses, mathematical modeling, or standard technical criteria alone. It requires examining the complex web of interactions among system variables, institutional issues, and behavioral factors. The tools that are currently employed have limited capabilities in terms of eliciting insights from stakeholders, gaining a detailed understanding of the problem and system, and designing solutions. The usual traditional approach to policy formulation serves a limited purpose.

In the context of emerging uncertainty, dynamic environment, and complex problems, new policy approaches and tools are needed. It calls for proceeding in a comprehensive manner. *Firstly*, understanding symptoms and system behavior; *secondly*, examining trends and trajectory; and *thirdly*, examining underlying causes and second- and third-order effects. It will require developing competencies within public organizations for new skills for comprehending and managing complexity. Furthermore, for difficult or complex problems, the existing assumptions about the system are to be revisited to understand the questions like: whether the assumptions are correct; whether the assumptions (if not correct or not explicitly defined) are putting constraints on understanding the problem and defining the future state; and whether there is a need to redefine the assumptions. The correct assumptions about the problems and systems can help in proceeding in the right way for the application of the method of inquiry or theory. It can then help in progressing correctly with policymaking and implementation.

For complex problems, an innovative approach like policy design is needed. The thinking modes like systems thinking, design thinking, and complexity thinking are required. There are tools and methodologies like interpretive structural modeling (ISM), system dynamics (SD), and complexity theory framework that provide ways to address the complex nature of socio-economic problems. There is a need to create innovative processes and institutional mechanisms.

- *Second, addressing basic development issues.* Table 7.2 indicates basic socio-economic indicators represented by human development index (HDI), infant mortality rate (IMR), maternal mortality rate (MMR), human resource capital (HRC), skill development, and malnutrition. These indicators, in a combined manner, represent the human resources of the country, which is one of the determinants of productivity. India has low HRC. The low crop yield is another area of concern. In addition, electricity consumption is a primary economic indicator, which indicates both the low availability of electricity and the lack of usage of electricity in day-to-day household activities. It is also a reflection of low household income.

Likewise, some key economic output indicators related to manufacturing, productivity, disposal income, and per capita GDP are presented in Table 7.3. The state of manufacturing represents the strength of the industrial sector and the ability to absorb the workforce that is displaced from the primary sector. Besides providing high-paying jobs, it contributes to exports and service (tertiary) sector jobs. And manufacturing has a significant role in raising economic growth. In addition, low productivity level reflects a lack of technology adoption and inadequate skills. And the low disposal income indicates low wages. Associated with the low income is a lower demand for industrial products from the families, and thus, lesser industrial activities.

Table 7.2 Basic socio-economic indicators

S. No.	Indicators	Countries		
		India	Emerging economies (China, South Korea, Malaysia)	Developed countries (Germany, USA, UK)
1	HDI (rank)[a]	130	55 (Average)	10 (Average)
2	IMR[a]	34	12 (Average)	4 (Average)
3	MMR[a]	174	26 (Average)	8 (Average)
4	HRC (rank)[b]	103	34 (China) 27 (South Korea)	4 (USA)
5	Skill development (% of workforce)[c,d]	2 (4.96% in 2016)	40 (China), 96 (South Korea)	80 (Japan)
6	Child malnutrition (% under age 5)[a]	37.9	8.5 (China), 2.5 (South Korea)	2.1 (USA)
7	Electricity consumption (per capita) (KWhr)[e]	947 (<500 in rural areas)	4,546 (China), 10,654 (South Korea), 4,808 (Malaysia)	6,947 (Germany), 12,573 (USA)
8	Crop Yield (Rice) (Q/He)[f]	34	65 (China), 43 (South Korea)	75 (USA)

Source [a] UNDP (2018) [b] WEF (2017), [c] Planning Commission (2012), [d] NCEE (2018), [d] KPMG and FICCI (2016), [e] IEA (2019), [f] FAO (2013)

Table 7.3 Key economic output indicators

S. No.	Indicators	Countries		
		India	Emerging economies (China, South Korea, Malaysia)	Developed countries (Germany, USA, UK)
1	Manufacturing exports share in world exports (%)[a]	1.83	17.8 (China)	38.9 (EU) 9.4 (USA)
	Manufacturing % of global manufacturing[b]	3.0	28.7 (China)	18 (USA)
2	Productivity (2011 international dollars at PPP$)[c]	10.0	19.0 (China), 60 (South Korea)	87.0 (Germany), 99.3 (USA)
3	Disposable income (2015$)[c]	1,154	3,549 (China), 14,513 (South Korea)	24,110 (Germany), 42,255 (USA)
4	Per capita GDP 2017 (PPP$)[d]	7,874	18,110 (China)	62,606 (USA)

Source [a] WTO (2018), [b] West and Lansang (2018), [c] DELOITTE (2016), [d] IMF (2019)

7.2 New Public Organizations

For India, the performance in social and economic sectors needs examination from the public policy perspective. In large measure, the low values of indicators are a reflection of both inadequacies in public policies and their implementation for sectors such as health, education, skill development, nutrition, manufacturing, technology adoption, and wages.

Despite a strong resource base, India has a host of pressing basic issues like lack of access to quality education, significant cases of IMR and MMR, a large number of malnourished children, rising inequality, low per capita GDP, low productivity level, and so on (Niti Aayog 2018; OPHI 2018; UNDP 2018). These concerns engender revisiting policymaking and implementation system and call forth the following questions: which policy changes are needed to address basic social and economic issues; how local conditions and concerns of citizens are to be considered for better policies; and what institutional mechanisms are required for efficient implementation and effective reach out to the last mile.

- *Third, enhancing the capacity of public organizations for quality public services.* The system capacity, in large measure, will determine the ability of public organizations to manage problems in the twenty-first century. The efficacy of a public organization will be determined by how successfully it can manage current problems, how quickly it can respond to changes, how efficiently the system can design new policies and programs to meet new challenges, and how effective it is in delivering services to citizens. As discussed in Chap. 4 (refer to Table 4.5, Sect. 4.4.2), it assumes importance in the light of the field study that at the ground level, the average capacity of the delivery system stands at about 35% for services in sectors such as education, health, agriculture, etc. As regards government manpower in India, the availability of manpower remains a major issue. Table 7.4 reflects a significantly low level of public sector employment. It is less than 25% in the USA and Germany and 30% in Brazil.

For example, in health and primary education, the manpower is relatively low even compared to the global average (Table 7.5). Both indicators—number of physicians and pupils per teacher—reflect this state. These have an adverse impact on the quality of services reflected in high IMR, MMR, and low human resource capital (HRC) rank (WEF 2017; UNDP 2018). The field study has reflected (in Chap. 4) that daily, health doctors and paramedical staff have to deal with a disproportionately large number

Table 7.4 Public sector employment in total population

S. No.	Name of the country	Public-sector employees to total population
1	India	1.7
2	Brazil	5.6
3	Germany	7.3
4	USA	7.4

Sources OECD (2015), Jagannathan (2018). https://en.wikipedia.org/wiki/List_of_countries_by_public_sector

of patients at public health centers (PHCs) (refer to Table 4.6). It impacts health services unfavorably.

Further, for India, the data about the manpower employed by the government in general and by urban local bodies (ULBs) in particular reflects a low number in comparison to developed as well developing countries like the USA, Germany, South Korea, China, and Brazil (Janaagraha 2014; SPC 2015; Jagannathan 2018). At a deeper level, what is equally critical is low manpower in basic public services for health, primary education, and rural and urban services (Janaagraha 2014; World Bank 2018; World Bank 2019a). In addition, Table 7.6 highlights the increase in government employment over decades in Germany, the UK, and the USA. Such investment in manpower in the public sector, mainly in public services, helped developed countries in building vital human resources and social security system, which have provided a strong underpinning for their economy and R&D (UNESCO 2015; Theodoulou and Roy 2016; UNDP 2018).

- *Fourth, improving process efficiency and minimizing the time and cost for the transaction of public services.* Process management is a crucial step. One measure of determining the efficacy of process management is process efficiency, which measures the productive time in availing the services to the total time in the entire process (see Table 7.7). Chapter four reflects the low efficiency in availing public services at the village level, which results from multiple factors such as lack of

Table 7.5 Physicians and pupils per teacher

S. No.	Name of the country	Number	
		Physicians (per 10,000 population)[a]	Pupil teacher ratio in primary school[b]
1	Brazil	23.0	20
2	China	20.0	16
3	India	9.3	33
4	Japan	25.0	16
5	Sri Lanka	12.0	22
6	USA	26.0	16
7	Global	18.0	23

Source [a] World Bank (2019a), [b] World Bank (2018)

Table 7.6 Government employment (as percentage of total employment)

S. No.	Countries	1937	1960	2000
1	Germany	4.3	9.9	14.6
2	UK	6.5	14.8	21.5
3	USA	6.8	14.7	15.4

Sources OECD (2015), Theodoulou and Roy (2016)

7.2 New Public Organizations

capacity of the delivery system, cumbersome process, lack of quality culture, and inadequacy in the monitoring system. All these lead to the unreliability of services.

Such issues are also felt in the business services to set up a business. The large time and cost for transactions to set up businesses indicate inadequacies in process management. In India, the time to start a business, register property, and enforce contracts is high in all three cases. Likewise, the cost of starting a business (% of income per capita), cost of registering property (% of property value), and cost of enforcing contracts (% of claim value) have been significantly high compared to fast-emerging economies and India's competitors—China, Taiwan, and South Korea (Table 7.8).

- *Fifth, raising competitiveness.* The competitiveness of a country is crucial to withstand global technology disruptions and stay ahead of others. The business environment, which depends on the macro-economy and infrastructure, is low for India, as reflected in Table 7.9. Likewise, the quality of electricity supply is wanting. The Global Competitiveness Index, 2017–18 (WEF 2018) states that the competitiveness ranking is on the lower side. If India has to grow in manufacturing and job creation in business, the competitiveness should rise.

Table 7.7 Process efficiency of delivery system

S. No.	Sectors/departments	Process efficiency (%)[a]
1	Health	18% (immunization in the villages)
2	Agriculture	15% (for seeds and fertilizer purchase)
3	Tehsil (Certificate issuing office)	2.5% (caste certificate by Tehsil)
4	PDS	15% (for availing the commodities from PDS shop)

Source Field Survey (Table 4.5). [a] Process Efficiency (%) = actual time taken to avail the services / total time involved in the entire process

Table 7.8 Institutional issues for business and industry

S. No.	Countries	Starting a business Days	Starting a business Rank	Registering property Days	Registering property Rank	Enforcing contracts Years	Enforcing contracts Rank	Cost of starting a business (% of income per capita)	Cost of registering property (% of property value)	Cost of enforcing contracts (% of claim value)
1	India	16.5	137	69	166	3.95	163	14.4	8.3	31.0
2	China	8.6	28	9	27	1.36	6	0.4	4.6	16.2
3	Taiwan	10	20	4	19	1.39	11	1.9	6.2	18.3
4	South Korea	4	11	5.5	40	0.8	2	14.6	5.1	12.7

Source World Bank (2019b)

Table 7.9 Global rank: infrastructure and business environment (rank)

S. No.	Countries	Competitiveness	Quality of overall infrastructure	Macro-economic environment	Quality of electricity supply
1	India	40	66	80	80
2	China	27	46	17	65
3	Malaysia	23	21	34	34
4	Taiwan	15	15	5	41
5	South Korea	26	8	2	21

Source WEF (2018)

- *Sixth, managing development concerns, government spending, and budget and tax revenue.* Table 7.10 shows that per capita government expenditure on education is much lower in India. The same is true for expenditure on health as a percentage of GDP. In combined form, these two reflect the lower ranking in human resource capital and HDI (Table 7.2). Likewise, India's R&D expenditure (as % of GDP) is low. The expenditure on R&D is taken for both human resource development and scientific research and innovation. It limits the ability of the country to develop human resource with innovative skills and to promote creativity and innovation. The low expenditure in three sectors—education, health, and R&D—has a correlation with low per capita GDP. Lower expenditure means lower per capita GDP. The fundamental of highlighting this issue is to assess the policies on human resource development (HRD) and its linkage with budgetary support by the government. The challenge is to augment the budget for education, health, and R&D.

It is crucial to examine the government budget, including tax revenue and expenditure. It sets the direction of priorities for socio-economic activities. For example, in developed countries, the social sector assumes high importance for strengthening

Table 7.10 Key budgetary indicators for human resource development (HRD)

S. No.	Indicators	Countries		
		India	Emerging economies (China, South Korea, Malaysia)	Developed country (USA)
1	Government per capita expenditure on education PPP$ (2017) (Total % of GDP)[a]	299 (3.8)	724 (4.0) (China); 2,109 (5.1) (South Korea)	3,150 (5.0) (USA)
2	Government expenditure on health as % of GDP (2012)[b]	1.15	3.14 (China) 4.10 (South Korea)	8.0 (USA)
3	R&D expenditure (% of GDP)[c]	0.82	2.08 (China) 4.15 (South Korea)	2.81 (USA)

Source [a] UNDP (2018), [b] WHO (2015), [c] UNESCO (2015)

7.2 New Public Organizations

social cohesion and providing a level-playing platform for different sections of the population. Tables 7.11 and 7.12 show high spending on the social sector by developed countries. The tax collection, general government expenditure, and social sector expenditure are significantly low for India. The ratio between India and China is about 1:3 for per capita tax collection and general government expenditure, and the figures are high for a fast-emerging economy like South Korea. And the OECD countries are far ahead. If the case of per capita social sector spending is examined, the OECD countries are far ahead compared to India, with a ratio of 15:1 (Table 7.11). The higher spending for the social sector is linked to high HRD and socially-secured life for people in OECD countries, resulting in higher per capita GDP and better quality of life.

Tax collection is strongly tied to the capacity of the government to spend. Thus, raising the tax base is a fundamental requirement for sustainability. Likewise, the expenditure in the social sector, including human resource development (education and health) and R&D, are essential for higher productivity and quality of life. It is further linked to higher family income. The sustainability of the revenue system of the

Table 7.11 Government budget: revenue and expenditure

S. No.	Countries	Per capita tax collection (PPP$) (2017)[b]	Per capita general govt. expenditure (PPP$) (2017)[c]	Per capita social sector expenditure (PPP$) (2017)	Per capita GDP (PPP$) (2017)[f]
1	India	1,276[a]	2,125	590[a]	7,874
2	China	3,622	5,614[e]	–	18,110
3	South Korea	11,125	13,357	4,259	41,351
4	OECD	15,050	17,772	8,941[d]	44,263

Source [a] RBI (2018), [b] OECD (2021), [c] Ortiz-Ospina and Roser (2016), [d] Frohlich et al. (2016), [e] STATISTA (2021), [f] IMF (2019), and own calculations

Table 7.12 General government and social sector expenditure as a percentage of GDP

S. No.	Countries	General govt. expenditure value (as % GDP) (2016)[b]	Social sector expenditure as % GDP (2016)	Per capita GDP (nominal, current) ($) (2016)[c]
1	India	27.9[a]	7.5[a]	1,732
2	France	56.5	31.5	38,348
3	Germany	46.0	25.3	42,124
4	UK	42.0	21.5	41,630
5	Japan	39.0	23.0	39,411
6	USA	36.5	18.0	57,839
7	OECD	40.9	21.0	41,787

Source [a] RBI (2018), [b] Ortiz-Ospina and Roser (2016), Frohlich et al. (2016), [c] IMF (2016)

Table 7.13 Tax revenue indicators

S. No.	Indicators	Countries		
		India	Emerging economies (China, South Korea, Malaysia)	Developed countries (Germany, USA, UK)
1	Local bodies own revenue (% of GDP)	0.49[a]	4.5% (Average)[b]	4.8% (USA)[b]
2	Property tax (% of GDP)[b]	0.16[b] (2013)	2.9% (South Korea)[c] (2018)	2.8.% (USA)[c] (2018)
3	Total tax (% of GDP) (2017)[f]	17.7[d]	20.1% (China) (2020)[e], 26.9% (South Korea) (2016)[c]	27.1% (USA)[c] (2016)
4	Per capita GDP 2017 (PPP$)[f]	7,874	18,110 (China)	62,606 (USA)

Source [a] FFC (2015), [b] Mohanty (2016), [c] OECD (2018), [d] RBI (2019) and RBI (2020), [e] OECD (2021), [f] IMF (2019)

government is essential. The amount of revenue generation enables the government to provide direction to the essential functions of the government and key enablers of the economy. For India, the lower tax collection as a percentage of GDP at the National level and low per capita GDP are challenges for providing resources for development (Table 7.13). Own tax revenue of local bodies and property tax are significantly low. It demands working on ways to formulate policies for generating more tax. Thus, there are twin challenges for public policies. *First*, the formulation of policies for augmenting the tax revenue to contribute to budgetary support for education, health, and other sectors; and *second*, the design of policies for different sectors.

Need for new public organizations. In the socio-economic environment, government organizations are reaching the limit of their capacity and find it difficult to manage emerging complex problems. As the real world grows more complex, the loss may be significant by ignoring new challenges and realities. It calls for fresh thinking and new ways of approaching problems, as summarized below:

- *New philosophy, theory, and approach.* In the backdrop of the emergence of a dynamic and uncertain environment involving challenges, opportunities, and risks, the business-as-usual (BAU) approach has limitations. The traditional approaches are defined by linear thinking, top-down control, a closed system or silo approach, rigid guidelines, and a standardized approach for varied social conditions (without considering behavioral and institutional issues). The current organizations rooted in the twentieth century have fundamental deficiencies and are anachronous with the emerging needs of the twenty-first century. However, the scientific management of the last century holds good for simple, well-defined, and stable conditions and systems. There is a need for new philosophy, theory, and approach. For complex systems, in a departure from the public administration defined by Max Weber, based on the principle of hierarchy, the new philosophy should be about learning and an adaptive approach. The new theory should factor in the networks of interactions, nonlinearity, and emergence. The approach should be context-specific, learn from multiple perspectives, and integrate insights from end-users. It should promote the ability to learn to cope with uncertainty (McCourt 2013; UNDP 2015).

It requires a culture that embraces complexity in the public system and mission-oriented functioning to develop innovative solutions for many organizational challenges. The organizations should encourage value-driven system-based perspective and collaborative approach—co-design and co-production—and design thinking for formulating policies and their implementation. Due to the complexity and challenging nature of problems, the thinking in the policy system is undergoing change as a result of scholarly research. There is a demand for new ways of policymaking. It is beyond resource allocations and about the right methods and solutions. Due to diversity in the system, during policymaking, there is a need to bring focus on the specific context and need assessment from the ground. It involves integrating innovative solutions, behavioral change, institutional mechanisms, and creative applications. It calls for a policy design approach. Efficiently performing public organizations are required to deliver quality public services, address diverse local-specific issues, respond to new challenges, and manage complex problems.

- *New framework, systems, and processes.* To understand issues like dynamics, uncertainty, and feedback loops, the system approach is called for. Comprehending time, speed, and scope of change is crucial. More understanding of second- and third-order consequences is needed by studying causal loop and system structure diagrams, as put forward by system dynamics. Relying on techniques of pattern recognition, reflection, and scenario building, both exponential change and likely discontinuity need to be examined. There is a need to comprehend how a small change may grow into exponential change, in a clear departure from generally perceived standard linear and incremental change, and to understand discontinuity for transformation possibility, which may occur over time. Specifically, it requires understanding the relationships between trends of behavior or pattern, the trajectory of change, interlinkages between variables, causalities, impending discontinuities, and the transformation process. It will comprise examining the relationships among diverse issues, problems, actors, institutions, etc.

It demands new systems and processes to understand and manage problems better. These should be designed for different contexts, viz., simple and known, complicated, and complexity, as covered in Sect. 5.4.2 of Chap. 5. It requires employing a complexity theory framework. Simultaneously, the capacity of public organizations should be raised to augment internal resources (mainly taxes), design better policies, and implement them efficiently.

7.2.2 Mainstreaming Innovative Approaches

The public systems are too vast and involve diverse problems. These cannot be handled by a fixed set of approaches. They demand multiple perspectives, divergent ways of inquiry, and wide-ranging tools to manage the system. The complexity theory is suitable for addressing complex social and economic problems. Though the theory stipulates that the system evolves and self-organizes, the system has to be managed and run while observing the complexity (Senge 1990; Stacey 1996; Gharajedaghi 2011). The simple and complicated systems, in particular, as defined in Sect. 5.4, will require different tools to deal with the problems. The tools given in Sect. 5.4 can be applied to complex systems, depending on the nature of the problem. Some of the innovative approaches that are suitable for public organizations are discussed below:

- *Public value-driven approach.* In a world of rising aspirations and increasing demands for transparency and accountability, governments should deliver matching value for public services. It is in this context the 'public value' is defined. As perceived by the citizens, public value is the value that a public organization contributes to society. In simple terms, it includes the performance of a public organization to the satisfaction of citizens. Public administrators are expected to create value through their decisions and actions (Moore 1995; Meynhardt 2009). Public organizations need to identify values, define objectives for each value, link objectives with the overall purpose and goals of the organizations, indicate specific performance indicators of the service delivery, and develop strategies, mechanisms, structures, and processes to achieve desired objectives (Keeney 1999; Mintrom and Luetjens 2015). The public value will include the following dimensions:
    - *responsive administration*: attending to problems and grievances in a responsive manner;
    - *public services*: efficient, timely, cost-effective, and reliable public services, which create citizens' satisfaction;
    - *economic benefits*: employment, housing, incentives, etc.;
    - *outcomes*: social and economic opportunities, improved human capital, and reduced poverty and inequality; and
    - *transparency, accountability, confidence, and trust*: it is about building a relationship between citizens and public organizations.
- *Strategic planning and management.* Public organizations face internal and global challenges, diverse problems of citizens, climate change, technology disruptions, and so on. To meet these challenges, organizations are required to adopt strategies that will strengthen the capacity to manage problems and raise performance. Strategic planning is one approach that can improve the performance of organizations. It is an organization's process of defining its strategy or direction and making decisions on allocating its resources to attain strategic goals (Bryson 2004; Abdul and Rahman 2019). The planning process is not new. All government departments

have experience in preparing operational plans, annual or five-year plans, and even long-term perspective plans. But strategic planning has a different approach. It is a tool that identifies medium- and long-term outcomes and works out a systematic path or a set of well-defined actions to achieve results. It is a tool that governments can use to achieve strategic goals, which can significantly impact performance and meet citizens' needs.

It focuses on the entire organization and aligns the human resource to its vision, mission, and goal. Through strategic analysis, it studies external and internal factors as well as stakeholders' concerns. It requires analysis using critical thinking (Hinţea et al. 2015; Abdul and Rahman 2019). Through detailed analysis, the strategic planning addresses five major aspects: what is the current state; what is the future state in the next five or ten years (or beyond); what is a way to achieve the desired results; what kind of system is needed to achieve results; and how to measure the change and performance.

- *Citizen-centric public system.* The citizen-centric governance is about bringing the needs and concerns of the citizens to the center of decision-making in the government and public service delivery system. The underlying reason is that, together with improving responsiveness and transparency, the time and cost of transactions should be minimized to free human resource and energy for productive work at the individual or household level. It can improve the citizens' satisfaction. Making a citizen-centric system will call for transforming public governance. It can help better understand the needs of the citizens and families and translate the needs into desired results. This approach considers citizens' problems and needs at every stage—diagnosis of the problems, public service design, design of delivery mechanism, and service delivery. All interlinked components, viz., policies, strategies, systems, and processes, should be designed around the convenience of citizens and efficient service delivery. Accordingly, the objectives and specific indicators are to be defined. There should be a link between indicators and processes. The processes are to be designed keeping in view the service quality standards based on feedback from the citizens. The processes should be such that they facilitate citizens for easy access to collect information and avail services. The service delivery should be as near to the place of citizens as possible. Toward this objective, the work culture and teams are to be built (UN 2006; Borins 2008; Maksym and Shah 2010). To provide citizen-centric services, Bills for the Right to Public Services have been passed by various States in India. The Acts comprise statutory laws which provide time-bound delivery of various public services to citizens. Though such Acts are desired, the necessary support system and work culture management need consideration.

E-governance citizen-centric system. It is widely acknowledged that E-governance can be immensely useful in raising the efficiency of government functioning, improving public service delivery, and bridging the geographical divide (UN 2016). The citizen-centricity demands a single view to the citizen within a single service architecture based on web technology. It demands building credible service delivery locations, value addition by efficiency gains (through BPR), culture management, and building trust and confidence. It requires developing a framework for a citizen-centric system by integrating elements such as 'people', 'process', and 'technology' (PPT) (Collins 2002; Peppard and Rowland 2002; Mehra 2004; Gupta 2008).

- *Quality management system* (QMS). Public services are essential to human development and are vital for the poor (World Bank 2004). The services contribute directly to basic needs—health, education, water, sanitation, and energy. Efficient, economical, and reliable services are of fundamental importance to economic development. They are vital to improving general public welfare and have a direct impact on poverty reduction (Aspin and Chapman 1994; World Bank 2004). The excellence in governance can be gauged by the 'quality' of services, among others. Quality should be a major factor in the debate on good governance. So the focus should shift to quality services. It necessitates developing systems at the cutting-edge level where citizens need services.

  World over, there has been a quest for quality in government and public services. The process of globalization is now presenting many challenges to governments, and the quality of public services is one of them. Public service providers have to bring innovative ways to improve the quality of services while working with rules, inadequate resources, and managerial limitations. They should be challenged by the demands for quality services, improved performance standards, and more responsiveness (Osborne and Gaebler 1992; Berk and Berk 1995; UN 2006). Each public service will require a robust system and processes to provide quality services. It necessitates developing a quality management system (QMS) for each public service. The issues that deserve consideration are:

  – defining quality indicators and evolving quality culture;
  – process improvement (through process reengineering) for higher efficiency at the point of delivery level and citizen satisfaction; and
  – quality management system (QMS) design and quality implementation.

- *Comprehensive performance management system (CPMS): from micro (grassroots) to macro (State or National) level on ICT Platform.* The debate on policy implementation brings the issue of performance management to the fore. The current performance management lays more stress on setting targets, both physical and financial, and then following them so as to verify whether the targets are achieved or not. Such system has limitations. The efficient implementation will call for a sound performance management system to monitor and give feedback for continuous improvement (Gianakis 2002; Russell 2003; Kroll 2015; Capelli and Tavis 2016).

In India, a performance management system (PMS) was started in 2009 by the Government of India for various Ministries and agencies, with a view to assessing the effectiveness of government departments in their mandated functions. It covered about 80 Ministries/Departments. PMS took a detailed view of departmental performance by measuring the performance of all schemes and projects and all relevant aspects of expected departmental deliverables such as: financial, physical, quantitative, and qualitative. Through the result framework document (RFD), PMS attempted to develop a matrix comprising vision and mission, objectives, functions, and targets that are to be monitored by the Ministries or agencies. It was an initiative that provided a primary document to track various indicators as per the set objectives (Trivedi 2013). Based on a detailed examination, despite several good features of PMS, it was a macro-level exercise for performance management. There has been a felt need to capture the performance at the level of implementation in the districts and municipal bodies to get a view from the ground. In addition, there has been a realization to enhance the capacity of the delivery system for better service delivery to citizens. It also requires examining special indicators—called leading indicators—which can provide future direction. The leading indicators can provide critical inputs to indicate the likely future state. These can give an idea about how to achieve goals, overall objectives, and outcomes. These can help to know what processes and skills are required to enhance performance. CPMS includes the following aspects:

- identification of the expectations of citizens while designing the matrix for objectives and functions,
- the strategic plan for critical concerns, and
- feedback mechanism from citizens.

With these issues in mind, there is a need for a comprehensive system of performance management, which comprehensively covers the functions of departments from the micro (ground level) to the macro (State or National) level to provide a real-time view of the performance. The traditional system of performance measurement fixes targets and measures them. But these targets are inadequate for measuring performance. The targets capture only a few activities, but not the issues related to stakeholders' needs, the capacity of delivery mechanism, manpower capabilities, processes of implementation, key result areas (KRAs), key performance indicators (KPIs), leading indicators, and outcomes.

The CPMS is a *management system* (not just a measurement system) that can enable public organizations to elicit the needs of stakeholders and translate them into actions. It provides a feedback mechanism about internal processes and external outcomes to improve strategic performance and results continuously. It includes six processes related to the following: stakeholder analysis; translating the vision into operational goals; communicating the vision and linking it to individual performance; delivery system design; online system of measuring indicators; and feedback, learning, and adjusting the strategy for course correction. The CPMS approach provides a clear and comprehensive roadmap to plan the activities. Broadly, the emphasis of CPMS is on the following features:

- capturing needs from the ground,
- designing systems and processes matching the intended objectives,
- competency building and knowledge management,

- linking performance indicators from village (or village *panchayat*) to Block (sub-district) to district to State to Center, or from cities to State to Center on the ICT platform, and
- continuous monitoring (KRAs, leading indicators, and KPIs).

- *Developing ecosystem for innovation*. All over the world, governments have to respond to the demands of their citizens. Governments are required to address numerous complex social and economic issues, including poverty reduction, unemployment, education, and environmental degradation, to name a few. They are also expected to reform policies to integrate effectively into the global climate change forum, multilateral agreements, and world economy (Maksym and Shah 2010; Christiansen and Bunt 2012; Ali and Ariffin 2018).

Why innovation in government (UN 2006; Borins 2008). Governments face several problems on a regular basis and are required to pay attention to several intricate issues. Some such issues are as follows:
- It is difficult to identify causal relationships between factors and system outputs. Often, the causes are multidimensional and interconnected. As a result, it is difficult to comprehend problems easily. For example, supply chain issues in industries, behavioral issues in providing health services, or marketing of perishable agriculture products to distant places.
- Many problems are highly contextual, dependent upon the ground conditions, or personalized, contingent on personal circumstances or individual behavior. To exemplify, problems specific to growing certain crops in a particular agro-climatic condition; health issues in a particular region, community, or age group; primary education in a backward region, etc.
- Some complex problems evolve without a clear 'end point'. For instance, the problem of traffic, housing, and air pollution in urban areas.

The traditional approaches cannot address these problem issues, which require a multidisciplinary, open-ended, experimental, and innovative approach.

Developing a culture for innovation in policymaking. Innovation is critical to bringing new ideas and creativity that public organizations need in addressing difficult and complex problems. The studies highlight that fear is one of the limiting factors. There is a fear of criticism, failure, and adverse impact on a career. To develop a culture of innovation, the employees should be provided with psychological support, a purpose that values innovation, and recognition. It requires a culture of looking beyond failure or uncertainty but considering innovation as a defining moment of opportunity. Understanding cultural values and processes is essential. And it is then developing an innovative culture in the public policy system.

There is a need to change the culture from a top-down approach to encouraging people in public organizations to contribute to idea generation and recognize the efforts for new solutions, from a control system to flexibility and experimenting with new ideas, and from working in silos to collaboration with other organizations. It is the environment for innovation that matters. There is a need for introducing a culture of trying new things, recognizing beliefs that things can be changed with own efforts, and giving incentives that encourage innovation. It requires adaptable leadership and a risk-taking mindset (Christiansen and Bunt 2012; Small and Schmutte 2022).

7.2.3 Human Capital and Skill Sets

So far, the governments have worked in a relatively homogeneous, predictable, and stable environment, which is markedly different from emerging heterogeneous, dynamic, multidimensional, and complex environment. Another major challenge comes from the speed and acceleration, sometimes exponential effects. The very nature of change is in the form of technology disruptions, unemployment, economic opportunities, and rising aspirations. In specific terms, the major challenges for the organizations are *first*, anticipating change and its pace and taking appropriate measures; *second*, understanding complexity dimension and unpredictability; *third*, staying competitive in the interconnected world; and *fourth*, addressing rising hopes and aspirations. Also of importance is how the diverse grassroots-level or field-level problems are captured, as many problems may require local-specific solutions. To meet such challenges, public organizations are expected to develop capabilities for designing sound policies.

To address the twenty-first century challenges and undertake the task of policy design, there is a need to develop new knowledge and skill sets. For difficult and complex problems, the basic premise is to move from 'resource allocation' to design the solutions and interventions based on a better understanding of the problems through insights from end-users and analyses. Policymaking will require multiple skill sets for conceptualizing problems and system, undertaking various analyses, and policy design and implementation. At the same time, what is crucial is how frequently the knowledge is updated as knowledge keeps evolving with time and how knowledge is applied to diverse situations.

Capabilities to design policies. For complicated problems covering large geographical problems, or complex problems, the usual conventional methods serve little purpose. Policy design requires a new thinking or approach, which is different from conventional linear thinking and a top-down approach. The capabilities for designing policies will entail applying design thinking, gaining insights from the stakeholders, examining interlinkages of factors at various levels—micro, meso, and macro, complexity analysis, exploring policy leverage points, and so on.

The policy design is required for all sectors. It is essential for the design of policies for health or primary education in rural areas, nutritional plan, tribal development, and industrial plan. In a specific example of industrial development, a complete set of activities, from setting up enterprises to facilitation for raw materials, inputs management, marketing, and supply chain management, is required. It will call for the design of a full range of policy instruments.

On the one hand, it will require community organizing skills, conducting FGDs and brainstorming sessions, and stakeholder analysis. On the other, it demands technical knowledge and skills for undertaking analyses such as system analysis, institutional analysis, behavioral analysis, complexity analysis, technical analysis, constraints analysis, and externality analysis. In addition, for policy implementation, knowledge and skills are required for strategic planning, quality management of public services, citizen-centric system, performance management system (PMS), and innovation management. The knowledge and skill sets for policy design are summarized in Table 7.14.

Table 7.14 Knowledge and skill sets for policy design

S. No.	Areas	Knowledge and skill sets
1	Conceptualization of problem and system	System approach (systems thinking, ISM, system dynamics), design thinking, innovative policy tools, complexity theory
2	Analyses	Skills for • Engaging with community • Stakeholder analysis • Problem analysis • System analysis • Institutional analysis • Behavioral analysis • Complexity analysis • Technical analysis • Constraints analysis • Externality analysis
3	Implementation system design and evaluation	• Community mobilization, design of implementation mechanism • Strategic planning • Quality management of public services • Citizen-centric system • Performance management system (PMS) • Innovation management
4	Approaches and theory	• Systems theory • Complexity theory • Design approach • System approach • Creative end-users' engagement • Deliberative dialogue • Process approach
5	Complexity leadership[a]	• Knowledge, innovation, learning, and adaptation • New leadership roles (enabling leadership, resilient leadership, and adaptive leadership)

[a] Complexity leadership is a continual learning process that stems from complexity thinking, innovation mindset, collaboration, resilient, and adaptation

7.2.4 Looking Beyond Resources: Primacy of Innovation in Process of Policy Design and for Policy Options

The resources provide critical inputs but are not sufficient by themselves. The resources alone cannot achieve the intended objectives unless they are underpinned by innovative 'process' for better 'policy design' and innovative solutions for policy 'options'.

Firstly, a close look at investment requirements for some select sectors will reveal a need for huge money. For example, for net-zero emission by 2050, the global annual investment required is $9.2 trillion (Mckinsey 2022). And by another estimate, the global annual clean energy investment requirement is $5 trillion by 2030, and then $4.5 trillion by 2050 to achieve net-zero by 2050 (IEA 2021). Globally, the renewable sector will require an investment of about $22.5 trillion by 2050 by doubling the current annual investment level (IRENA 2022). India will need investment worth $10 trillion to achieve net-zero in the next 50 years by 2070 (CEEW-CEF 2021). As a sub-component, under climate change initiatives, for the renewable energy sector, the investment worth $500–700 billion for solar power park program, power generation, and development of transmission infrastructure will be required by 2030 (IEEFA 2020). For urban infrastructure at the global level, the investment requirement is $4.5–5.4 trillion (World Bank 2020) per year. The forecast for the cost of providing infrastructure to support global economic growth is US$94 trillion by 2040, in addition to $5–7 trillion annually for the United Nations (UN) sustainable development goals (SDGs) by 2030 (Global Infrastructure Hub 2017a; UNCTAD 2014). For India, the total requirement is $4.5 trillion by 2040 for infrastructure, and for the 17 SDGs, the investment requirement is $1.3 trillion by 2030 (Economic Times 2017; (Global Infrastructure Hub 2017b).

Secondly, there is an issue of how to utilize optimally huge budget spending by the governments. Globally, during 2019–20, based on reports by IMF, OECD, and the Reserve Bank of India (RBI) (for the Indian government budget), the governments spent about $35 trillion annually. India, both the Center and States together, spent about $1 trillion (plan and non-plan) in the budget, 2019–20. Simultaneously, there is a case of a significant budget deficit. (www.imf.org) (RBI 2019). (https://en.wikipedia.org/wiki/List_of_countries_by_government_budget, retrieved as on 15.7.2022).

A special mention is made about health and education, as these two sectors have wider ramifications for the economy and quality of life. Quality education and health have direct linkages with more income and economic growth (Hanushek and Woessmann 2008; Mookerjee and Bohra 2017). For example, every $1 invested in health gives a return of $2 to $4 in developing countries (McKinsey 2021). The additional year of primary school enhances women's wages (Duflo 2001; UNICEF 2011). And there is a 9% increase in hourly earnings for every extra year of schooling (World Bank 2022). For primary education, India needs an additional $25 billion annually (1% of GDP), and the world requires $504 billion (UNESCO 2021). As for the health sector, India needs an additional $50 billion annually (about 2% of GDP).

The world economy has been moving toward a knowledge-based networked economy since 2000. The knowledge economy is driven by innovation, specialized knowledge, and skills for solving complex problems. The networked economy works in the network of individuals, groups, businesses, or countries using information and communication technologies (ICTs) through interactive and real-time connections among people, devices, and businesses. It is likely to represent an economic value of about $90 trillion by 2030 (MIT 2014). Similarly, riding on the back of innovation, artificial intelligence may add $15 trillion to the global economy by 2030, and 5G is projected to generate $13 trillion in global economic value (Kastner 2021). The Internet of Things (IoT) and global App enabled economy have immense potential. At the global level, e-commerce (eb2b + eb2c; eb2b: e-business to business; eb2c: e-business to customer), including online retail, has reached $26 trillion (UNCTAD 2021). In sum, for public policy, there are three broad challenges. *First*, spending large budgets and mobilizing resources in case of deficit. *Second*, managing huge investments. *Third*, utilizing abundant opportunities in technological sectors.

Importance of public policymaking. The idea of presenting the abovementioned figures is to underscore the phenomenal amount of investment, government budgets, and economic opportunities. These have significant scale and scope. But the success of resource allocations will depend on how good is the public policy, which will depend on understanding the end-users and their behavioral needs, the collaborations between stakeholders, addressing complexity in the system, and establishing institutional mechanisms.

For example, the food system accounts for 34% of global greenhouse gas (GHG) emissions. Within the food system, about 20% of annual GHG emissions come from agriculture and live stocks (UNFCCC 2002; OECD 2003; IPCC 2007; IPCC 2014). Thus, to achieve net-zero emissions, agriculture and allied sectors hold importance, and several initiatives are required for new practices for rice production, crop-residue management, cattle waste management, urban waste management, enhancing plantation and vegetative cover, and energy efficiency. Higher capital costs and low plant efficiency (for energy conversion) for waste treatment are major challenges.

How new practices can be introduced in the agriculture sector will require understanding behavioral issues. It will necessitate a combination of institutional capacity in a decentralized manner, regulatory framework, behavioral change, introduction of new practices, capacity building of communities, etc. By factoring in local problems, it will require R&D to design new devices or equipments for managing waste, sowing rice with less water, and harvesting crops with better agro-residue and stubble management.

The successful RE investment will require addressing various aspects such as management of land availability, solar cell production and supply, management of renewable energy plants, capital cost and plant efficiency, power transmission management, the financial viability of distribution system, skill management, incentives for various stakeholders, institutional mechanisms, local community management, and so on. It will call for a detailed analysis of underlying causes from the perspectives of developers and end-users; understanding of complexity; innovation-driven management (including technology, process, and system innovation); continuous feedback from stakeholders for improvement; and integration of RE systems with regular power systems.

For urban management, the cities, which contribute about 75% of global GDP (World Bank 2020), require policies for fostering a culture of innovation, multiple interventions for promoting innovation, efficient urban services, etc., to emerge as future cities. In the same way, the opportunities in technologies, especially ICT, are enormous. These will require underpinnings of creating an innovation ecosystem; industry-academia-government collaborations; skilling, reskilling, and upskilling; and global supply chain management. The quality of education will depend on socio-cultural issues like family culture, values and beliefs; economic conditions; teaching-learning environment; etc. The success of health programs will depend on institutional mechanisms, understanding behavioral issues of communities, enhancing the reach of health personnel to the last mile, and so on. These demand a robust policymaking system and institutional mechanisms to effectively manage problems and implement policies.

Innovative policymaking process and solutions: In the backdrop of the need for huge investments in net-zero policy for climate change, infrastructure requirements for meeting SDGs, urban development, and large government budgets, the focus needs to be placed on both—innovative policymaking process and innovative solutions for policy content (better policy options). This point needs further elaboration. There is a need to work on two fronts. *First*, innovation is necessary for the policymaking process for the 'design' of policy. It means how the process should utilize innovative methods to design policies. The process will entail eliciting insights from the ground, doing policy analyses, and informed discussion and decision-making based on evidence. The design will include working on policy options matching the end-users' needs through iterations. *Second*, simultaneously, there is a need to work on identifying new policy options. It will call for programs to promote innovation for social and economic good, as the currently available solutions or technologies may not be sufficient to solve current and ever-expanding problems due to high capital costs and low efficiency. Though desired, the investments alone may not be in a position to meet fully the challenges facing the societies, and working on innovative solutions, including economical and efficient, should be a high priority.

As Lasswell (1971) stressed, the policy sciences are concerned with knowledge *of* and *in* the decision processes of the public and civic order (Fischer et al. 2007). Knowledge *of* the decision 'process' is achieved by systematic studies of how policies are made and, while knowledge *in* the decision process draws upon the various scientific disciplines to increase knowledge relevant to the 'content' of public policy. This aspect of policy sciences by Lasswell should be considered for public policy.

It highlights that together with resources, both the process of allocation of resources and innovative technologies and solutions for many current problems are essential. For example, the success of policies under net-zero emissions and urban management will necessitate looking beyond conventional solutions. It will require innovative technology interventions to improve efficiency (for energy conversion) and reduce capital cost. Currently, the cities are handicapped by the high capital cost of waste management. It impacts the sustainability of the cities. There is a need to explore how the capital cost can be reduced for sewage treatment, wastewater treatment, stormwater drainage, and municipal solid waste (MSW) treatment for the urban sector. Similarly, under the agriculture sector, for economical usage of water and fertilizer, drip irrigation and modern greenhouses for crop production with reduced capital cost deserve priority. These have direct implications for adopting energy conservation measures and greenhouse gas (GHG) emissions.

More specifically, for renewable energy and municipal waste management, some of the R&D projects that deserve priority for developing innovative technologies are:

- How the windmills can be designed to operate at a wind speed of 3–4 m/second (less than the minimum required speed of 5 m/second) to tap larger wind resources and produce electricity costing about Rs. 4 per unit.
- How further the solar cell efficiency can be increased from the current 20% to 28% on a large scale, thereby reducing the cost of electricity generation to less than Rs. 2 per unit.
- How sewage treatment plant (STP) capital cost can be brought to less than Rs. 50 lakhs for a population of 1000 people (250 households) from the current about Rs. 150 lakhs.
- How household wastewater treatment plant capital cost can be brought to less than Rs. 20 lakhs for a population of 1000 people (250 households) (in a decentralized manner) from the current about Rs. 40 lakhs.
- How MSW treatment plant capital cost can be brought to less than Rs. 20 lakhs for 1000 population (250 households) (in a decentralized manner) from the current about Rs. 40 lakhs.
- How the efficiency of gasification technology-based power plant (from municipal waste) can be increased to 25% on a sustained basis from the current about 10–12%.

The enhanced performance through breakthrough technologies can have a far-reaching impact on reducing capital expenditure, raising efficiency, and lowering carbon footprints.

Regarding the possibility of reduction of cost, some lessons can be learned from the steep reduction in solar electricity generation cost from Rs. 10 to less than Rs. 3–3.5 per unit between 2010 and 2018; exponential reduction (about a million times reduction) in cost for processing and storage of electronic data, thereby significant reduction in the price of computers and mobile phones; or sharp reduction, by a factor of five, in health treatment cost in India in the last two decades. As another illustration, quantum computing can help in the precise simulation of structures of molecules for the purpose of doping to achieve significantly higher efficiency of solar cells, from the current 20% to 35%. Similarly, in genomics, through simulations, there is a possibility of developing microorganisms for treating industrial and household wastes more efficiently and economically, or for developing vaccines for serious health problems. Likewise, in the power and waste treatment sector, with breakthrough technologies, engineering solutions are needed for better design of plants, new materials, and efficient running of power plants for reducing capital cost and enhancing conversion efficiency.

These examples show considerable room for innovative technologies to solve problems. And therefore, there is a case for working on new technologies to provide better policy options.

Bringing nanolevel approach. The idea is that the conventional methods have limitations for many complex problems in areas such as climate change, net-zero strategy, energy efficiency, urban management, and waste treatment. Some breakthrough policy measures to promote the combination of technology innovation, social innovation, and governance innovation is needed at the nanolevel to achieve a disproportionate advantage. And therefore, the innovative interventions are to be experimented with at the nanolevel, i.e., at the individual, household, or community level, before they are implemented at a higher level. The kind of nanolevel research done in nanoscience—nanomaterials and genomics, is needed in the social and economic systems, though challenging, to understand the complexity, develop scenarios, discern patterns of system behavior, and find possible solutions through simulations.

For a better impact of policies on the ground, it will require exploring the right combination between system variables, sectoral policies, institutional mechanisms, individual and group behavior, technology efficacy and cost-effectiveness, and policy interventions. Advanced tools like artificial intelligence (AI) and Big data can be applied with suitable assumptions and by considering qualitative issues of behavioral and institutional dimensions. The agent-based modeling (ABM) and social network analysis (SNA) can be attempted. Governments need to consciously develop an ecosystem for innovators to enable them to leverage their creativity.

Public policy system—a conceptual macro model. The macro model, as depicted in Table 7.15, underscores that the utilization of resources will depend on the policy process and design, which is influenced by other components, viz., institutional issues, behavioral dimension, implementation, and complexity analysis altogether. And the entire policy system is a result of a combination of these complements, and each component influences the other (Fig. 7.1). The complexity theory underlines that each stakeholder matters. The stakeholders can play vital roles in the policymaking process. They represent diverse backgrounds and provide diverse ideas, perspectives, technological inputs, and innovative solutions. Both innovative approaches to policymaking and innovative solutions will determine the quality of policy content. There is a need to shift from the approach of resource allocations or prescription-based policy formulation to policy design.

Policymaking beyond conventional thoughts. From the policymaking perspective, the focus should come on the combination of the following:

At the basic level

- *Grassroots insights*: eliciting insights to obtain hidden potential.
- *Interlinkages*: linkages between system variables, including behavioral aspects, institutional mechanisms, and sectoral policies for better policymaking.

Table 7.15 Public policy system: components and elements

S. No.	Components	Elements
1	Resources	Investment, budgets, innovation, and technologies
2	Complexity analysis	Socio-economic issues, system variables, stakeholders, emergence, and evolution
3	Institutional issues	Values, norms, culture, structures, and processes
4	Behavioral dimension	Beliefs, attitudes, and preferences
5	Policy process and design	Innovative methods, policymaking process, and policy content
6	Policy implementation	Efficacy of implementation mechanism

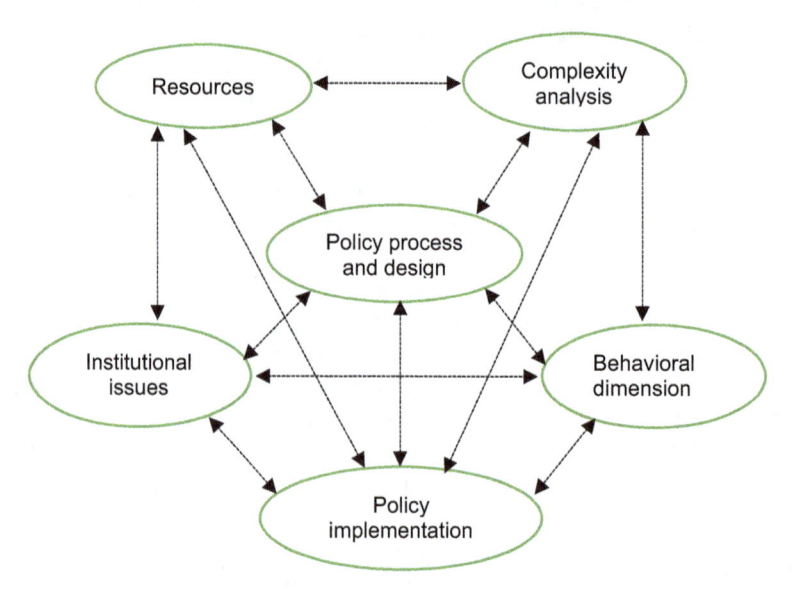

Fig. 7.1 Public policy system: a conceptual macro model

- *Social innovation*: how new ideas can be generated and how social networks can be harnessed to faster adoption of a policy and its implementation.
- *Policy design*: designing policy instruments by factoring in insights from grassroots and end-users.
- *Adaptation and continuous improvement*: considering adaptive policies as new insight is noticed or new situation emerges.

At the macro level

- Establishing robust institutional mechanisms at different levels, from macro to micro level, for policy analysis, policy design, and implementation.
- Need for an approach of macro-micro linkages—matching macro-level requirements with micro-level insights, concerns, and capacity.

The underlying issue is how policy design and implementation should consider a holistic perspective, insights from the ground, practical realities, last-mile reach, adaptive policies, and continuous improvement. Finally, the resources are essential, but innovation is vital for both the policymaking process and policy options, together with institutional underpinning.

Epilogue

The book has been written to understand basic questions like why public policy calls for rigorous study, how the policy system works to formulate policies, and how policies can be better developed to meet growing challenges. To address these questions, relying on the extensive literature survey and field-level research, it attempts to bring out insights into policy formulation and implementation. Specifically, it examines various theories and approaches to recognize their evolution and how they form the basis of policies. It entails probing the nuances of policymaking, focusing on how it can engage stakeholders, comprehend problem issues, design the right policies, and deliver intended results.

Comment on policymaking process. At the basic level, the key concern is about understanding problems from the perspectives of the recipients of policies. Usually, there is less focus on this fundamental point. Critical aspects, like eliciting insights from the end-users, systemic study, analyzing the interrelationships between system variables, studying the interactive effects between elements (system variables and individuals), and examining complementarities and convergence of policies, need more consideration. In addition, the pre-conceived ideas, existing conventions and methods, and pre-defined notions and indicators of performance are often taken without question and, when accepted, set limitations on or boundaries for new ideas.

Various problem issues, parts, or components are examined independently, not systemically. The analyses to examine problems are not carried out sufficiently to assist informed discussion and evidence-based decision-making. These inadequacies impact problem definition, conceptualization of the system, and identification of policy options, including exploring last-mile solutions. Such deficiencies are because the 'how part' or the 'process' of policymaking is not given adequate priority. Likewise, there are infirmities in the implementation, and the lack of capacity of the delivery system is the main reason. Due to the top-down approach, the grassroots conditions are not adequately captured at the execution level. The feedback for corrections is not taken into account. As a result, timely corrections are not introduced. There remains a gap between micro-level realities and macro-level appreciation.

The current approaches assume that the system is in equilibrium. They consider the environment to be stable. They tend to examine the system without a holistic perspective, isolated from the environment. Likewise, they deal with the economy in aggregate form by not studying interactive behavior. The emergence and evolutionary nature of the economy are not factored in. These put limits on the ability of the current approaches to conceptualize problems.

There is another dimension during policy formulation. The policies for education, health, agriculture, climate change, etc., are dealt with more from the standpoint of economic cost and budget, though essential, but not sufficient. Regarding the economy, more emphasis is on economic theories, while the conceptualization of problems, understanding end-users, study of complexity, and comprehension of institutional, behavioral and implementation factors do not get enough deliberations.

Despite the unique role of policies in shaping the future, the policy process has yet to get the desired recognition. In practice, the policy system suffers due to the lack of attention paid to information system, framework with tools and analyses, team with multidisciplinary perspectives, and suitable institutional mechanisms. Quite often, the process is simplified as: *first*, collection of good and intuitive ideas and prescriptions, and *second*, defining intents with prudent targets but less stress on details of analyses.

Many problems in the world are a consequence of deficient public policies. They are usually in response to short-term needs and pressures and tend to address the symptoms rather than underlying causes. Their implementation lacks a robust mechanism. These are formulated for a few specific goals or objectives rather than results and outcomes systemically.

There are issues of policy deficit, governance deficit, and institutional deficit.

Critique of current system of inquiry. So far, the traditional approaches and tools in social sciences, quantitative modeling, econometrics, and management science have offered useful inputs for stable systems and problems, equilibrium state, and steady environment. But they find it difficult to address the issues of formulating policies dealing with dynamic, uncertain, and complex systems. The main concern is that the major problems facing the world are so complex and interwoven that traditional institutions and conventional approaches cannot determine the problems and deal with them.

From the perspective of applicability, the value of quantitative data and statistical and mathematical models will continue to be of importance only under certain assumptions and boundary conditions. But, they are not suitable for comprehending socio-economic problems due to involved complex issues. Furthermore, there is a need to realize the constraints of aggregate data, usually used in examining problems in general and mathematical models in particular. It cannot capture disparate segments and diversity; real-world realities, constraints, and assumptions, including behavioral and cognitive issues; and interacting elements. In the aggregate form, many vital insights and patterns are lost. In such a scenario, the conclusions that are drawn cannot give the correct interpretations. Both current policy and economic theories have relied on such data. It is one of their significant limitations.

Complexity in policymaking—inadequacy of existing approaches. From the policy process perspective, there is a growing realization that social and economic systems are too complex to be addressed by intuition, oversimplification (considering simple issues and overlooking difficult or complex ones), and uninformed discussion and decision-making. There is a trade-off between simple and complex issues to arrive at a quick solution that may not work.

The current approaches can address simple or complicated problems with a limited number of interactions in a static environment, which is quite divergent from the dynamic and complex nature of the real world. Through current approaches, the process oversimplifies the problems by disregarding multiple interacting elements, issues, and variables, while such interactions influence the problems and system behavior. In large and complex systems, it is difficult to articulate or identify causal relationships (or mechanisms) in which the causes are multidimensional and interconnected. The absence of appreciation of concepts and phenomena of such systems and lack of analyses lead to gaps between ground reality and understanding of the problem at the macro level (policymakers' level). It limits the ability of policies to address the problems.

The social systems are complex in which policies are formulated. There are numerous interlinked issues. For example, behavioral issues, like attitudes, beliefs, values, biases, and cognitive understanding, influence problems and determine decision-making at the individual level. In addition, there are institutional and implementation aspects. These are not appreciated, analyzed, and factored in during policymaking. Besides, as these have qualitative variables, they cannot be easily fitted into mathematical models.

The complex problems demand in-depth understanding and need integrated interventions. For example, providing services for needy end-users (e.g., in health, education, agriculture, or industrial sectors) with multiple interlinked requirements. Often, the issues are context-specific or unique for a particular situation in the community or geographical region. Therefore, these cannot be addressed by one uniform policy or a single implementing agency. In addition, the problem issues keep evolving consistently or are without a clear 'endpoint' and require open-ended interventions from various agencies. For example, in health service management for poor sections or remote areas, primary education in rural areas, or supply chain management of industry (of any scale, small, medium, or large), it calls for eliciting ground-level problems from wide-ranging perspectives and then introducing multiple interventions by many agencies to address the problems on a continuous basis.

Complexity in economy—limitations of quantitative approaches. Chapter 5 has underscored the evolving nature of the economy as a result of the interactive effects of economic agents and entities in the system, influenced by institutional, behavioral, and psychological factors. In a complex economic system, the interacting elements and feedback loops result in the emergence of future economic activities that is not recognized by the existing economic theories. Such a new phenomenon in the economy cannot be mathematically modeled. These have implications for economic policies. Thus the mainstream economic theories and models cannot be a sound basis for formulating economic policies dealing with complexity.

The current policy approaches have limitations in providing the right way to policymaking in dynamic and complex systems. It is mainly valid for sectors such as health, education, agriculture, climate change, industrial development, economy, etc. It is necessary to appreciate how approaches to public policies, including economic policies, are disconnected from new knowledge about characteristics of problems, away from factoring in a dynamic environment, and anachronous with time due to increased complexity in the socio-economic systems. Often, the policy establishment does not recognize complexity, or it realizes that it means doing things with more rigor. While the appreciation for changing the approach is little, the policy system has less resources in terms of expertise, skilled personnel, policy tools, and budget to examine deeper issues. To summarize, it is required to deal with certain issues and characteristics of social and economic systems. These are encapsulated as follows:

- *emerging issues*: dynamic behavior, uncertainty, evolving nature of problems, and disruptions;
- *phenomena*: emergence, self-organization, adaptation, and evolution;
- *assumptions*: interactions between elements determine the system's behavior, and there is uncertainty, dynamics, and complexity in the system and environment; and
- *concepts*: system structure, nonlinearity, second- and third-order consequences, feedback loops, path dependency, and behavioral and institutional dimensions.

It is expected to deal with these underlying features of the systems. Disregarding them, in which social development occurs and the economy evolves, will put limits on policies to deliver and yield sub-optimal results.

The impending problems and emerging challenges require examining the assumptions, contexts, institutions, uncertainties, constraints, disruptions, expectations, and opportunities. It is more so crucial due to interconnected problems, systems, and economies at the global level having multidirectional and multi-country interactions. The provisioning of quality public services, infrastructure management, and expanding economies pose serious concerns. It is uncertain to know which factors will be dominant and which policy options will have a consequential impact in the future. In this light, it calls for revisiting questions such as:

- whether linear thinking and conventional approaches can address big and complex problems, and
- whether the policy system has the institutional capacity to manage emerging and growing local, National, and global challenges.

Future Ahead

The book is premised on fundamental issues concerning the state of development, evolving opportunities and challenges, and complexity dimension. India has a good resource base but has many recurring problems affecting a large population. These have implications for the quality of life and economic growth. Critical development concerns put questions on the capacity of the policy system. There are opportunities due to technology advancements, economic networks, improved efficiency, and enhanced productivity. Concurrently, these result in disruptions and unpredictability. In complex systems, the articulation of the problems, conceptualization of the system, and identification of cause-effects are demanding. It makes policymaking challenging.

At the country as well as global levels, there are multidimensional issues in the form of, *first*, addressing multiple concerns of citizens at various levels, from micro to macro; *second*, enormous macro problems; *third*, optimal utilization of large government budgets; *fourth*, the vast economic potential of advanced technologies and networked economy; and *fifth*, a staggering amount of investments needed for the economy.

To address challenges and opportunities, it is essential to recognize emerging assumptions, concepts, and phenomena in the real world. These merit consideration in order to obtain the right perspective about the system and problem. The persistent issues like changing behavior of problems, nonlinearities, and ever-growing concerns of stakeholders put pressure on the governments to deliver efficiently and consistently. The conventional strategies have limitations. It demands specialized and innovative methods for public policy. It should give value to distinctly different approach and theory. The new thinking is called for.

New principles for policymaking. Policy studies and understanding of complexity theory have provided a wider horizon and opened possibilities of leveraging public policies prudently for the general good of society. The findings about the inadequacies in policy formulation and implementation and the knowledge of characteristics and complexity phenomena ask for comprehensive and innovative ways. It recognizes a system of inquiry that will require the following principles:

- *Discerning correct assumptions is a primary requirement for comprehending the system.* These will include system imperatives—interactive effect between elements, linkages between variables, causality, feedback loops, and system structure.
- *Conceptualization of problem and system is critical for designing policy interventions.* It will entail a systemic examination of elements and variables, causal relationships between variables, interactions between elements and emergence thereof, and system structure. The context-specific understanding is essential, including insights from citizens and factoring in ground realities and last-mile problems. The disaggregated data is crucial.
- *Value of analyses for resource allocation.* It requires detailed analyses, like institutional, complexity, behavioral, technical, etc., for an evidence-based approach.
- *Efficiency matters.* Policymaking should examine the efficacy of the delivery system to determine its ability to implement policies and deliver services efficiently. Combined with resources, a robust implementation mechanism is essential.
- *Institutional capacity is vital.* It brings credibility. The policy system should have values, norms, and rules and a good capacity to design and implement policies efficiently.

A new system of inquiry. Generally, for problem solving, it was presumed certainty, stability, and an equilibrium state of the system. The systems were assumed as single and homogeneous structures, and the aggregate data of variables has been the basis of inquiry. For over a century, such assumptions formed the basis of thinking for examination and shaped policy and economic theories. These are divergent from the emerging knowledge about the assumptions. These lay stress on examining relationships between variables in the system, the interactive nature of elements, system structure, and the uncertainty and dynamics that affect the behavior of systems. It is requisite to recognize the constraints of applying conventional management tools and mathematical models and the deficiency of aggregate data in capturing complex social issues. The argument of examining the social system or economy as a single composite structure in equilibrium does not hold good. The disaggregated data is vital to understand underlying details, trends, and patterns for different segments. In contrast, the new thinking posits that every element, including variables, is essential. The interrelationships between variables and the interactions between elements matter and define the future state and evolution of the system or economy. It emphasizes a departure from traditional methods. Holistic inquiry is more suitable than a disjointed examination in parts.

It is central to the future of public policy, the economy, business, and organizations.

Value of 'process'. One of the vital issues facing the development is about the policymaking process, not, as such, the resources. The major challenge for public policy is integrating micro-level realities and macro-level requirements and formulating policies that concern end-users. Discerning deep understanding from the ground can bring a realistic view and add value to informed decision-making, which reflects what the citizens seek. Essentially, the policies depend on a simple term, the 'process'. How it is developed will determine the outcome. It entails how insights are drawn from the stakeholders, how these are used for analyzing the policy options and decision-making, and how these are factored into the implementation to match the expectations and realities. In a simple way, the answers to these questions will provide the right step forward to the future development path. There is a need to look beyond good ideas, budgetary allocations, and allocative efficiency to the primacy of the process. It can help identify unknown prospects and leverage points for better policy formulation. It will include interdisciplinary knowledge, rigorous analyses to allocate resources, and mechanisms to utilize them efficiently and transform intents into reality.

Public policy should be of prime concern to all stakeholders. Not just the government, the experts, intellectuals, entrepreneurs, and leaders in social, economic, business, and industry should contribute to designing policies better through their expertise and evaluating the policy impact. They can work to bring desired changes through their engagement. There are immense possibilities.

Alternative approach. In the fast-evolving complex social, economic, and environmental problems, the methods of policy formulation demand change. It necessitates system approach, systems thinking, design thinking, complexity thinking, process approach, and transdisciplinary analysis. It requires nonlinear thinking, revisiting the existing assumptions, assessing new phenomena, and examining higher-order effects. It recommends design approach and adaptive policies for dealing with complex problems. Once these are recognized, a new thought process will emerge. And then, requisite systems and practices can be developed.

For navigating dynamics, uncertainty, and disruptive changes, comprehending system behavior is vital. It involves examining the dynamics of change—the time of occurrence and speed of change, specifically the changing relations and patterns, the process of change, and the causes behind the change. It encourages a systemic study and exploring relationships between issues, actors, institutions, and the environment. These have implications for social and economic policies. In the social system, for example, the dynamic behavior of people or the community should be understood. Likewise, in the economy, the dynamics of demand, supply, economic agents' behavior, employment, and growth are to be comprehended.

Alternative theory. There is an old maxim, *God is in details*, thereby implying a hidden potential that can be realized by detailed scrutiny. It is the essence of complexity theory. It underscores the interactive role of individuals (economic agents), variables, policies, and institutions at the local level in determining the evolution of system behavior and structure by way of feedback loops. The theory stresses examining issues at the micro level (granular level). It can help gain insights from multiple viewpoints of end-users, identify problems that are not comprehendible at the macro level, and understand underlying issues. These can bring invisible possibilities to the surface.

In the physical and technological world, the analyses at the granular level have opened opportunities of the scale, which was unthinkable before the 1970s. For example, by working at the nanolevel or the atomic level in the field of electronics and nanomaterials or at the cell level for human medicines, innovative technologies are shaping the future of the world in a more definite manner and providing solutions that were not possible a few decades ago.

In a similar way, radical innovations are possible in various socio-economic sectors by utilizing the interactive behavior of people, economic agents, communities, and entities at the ground level. The challenge is how a robust ecosystem can be built to bring desired behavioral change and leverage the potential of stakeholders in the social system. Against this background, the complexity theory emphasizes developing institutions—values, culture, rules, and regulatory framework—for constructive interactions between the elements; creating enabling conditions for people and local entities to leverage their capabilities; and bringing complementarity and convergence of a set of policies for multiplier effects. It entails developing the ecosystem for creativity to explore new solutions and opportunities that may not be within sight of the macro level.

The quintessence of the complexity theory is that the grassroots (nanolevel) determines the future state of the systems. It offers a way to recognize the interactive effects and phenomenon of emergence. Grassroots is defined by what happens at the ground in a community, at the functional level in an organization, at the shop floor in the industry, or at the operational level in any business. It has implications for public services, urban management, last-mile food delivery, quality primary education, health and sanitation, climate change, industrial clusters, etc. The theory provides a way to deal with complex problems in social system, economy, and organizations.

New public organizations. The dominant traditional organizational models in the government and the private sector have evolved primarily for a stable and known system and environment. It assumed that the system behavior was predictable. It puts forward the structural hierarchy and linear thinking for planning, intervention, and control without considering nonlinearity and emergent property.

As an alternative to the twentieth century approach of hierarchy and control, the thinking in public administration is undergoing change. It necessitates the application of complexity theory. It provides insights into dealing with the unpredictable and dynamic nature of the system. The theory explains how nonlinear interactions between elements define macro behavior and patterns without direction from the top and, simultaneously, how the external environment or internal processes may impact the system behavior. In addition, it stresses the departure from the classical management theory to evolving and adaptive strategies to address complex problems. Against this backdrop, new public organizations are to be designed.

Furthermore, governments require efficiently performing organizations to deliver results with increased attention on building human capital. It emphasizes the necessity of developing an innovation ecosystem by creating structures and processes. In dealing with a dynamic environment and complex systems, the top leadership should identify the emergence of knowledge and system behavior at the micro as well as macro levels; understand how the current norms, culture, and values influence the interactions; and appreciate how the mechanisms impacting interactions need to change.

Summing Up

The last century has been more characterized by linear thinking, fragmented analysis of the system (examining in parts), and centralized control. In comparison, the problems in the twenty-first century demand different ways to navigate. The focus needs to shift toward a system-wide view, unification of ideas and concepts, resilience, and Adaptation. There has been advancement in methods of inquiry as a result of the embodiment of scholarly research over the past three decades. It is reflected in the literature on various disciplines of social sciences, system studies, and management (Anderson 1999; Cilliers 2000; Brinkerhoff and Crosby 2002; Swanson and Bhadwal 2009).

The book attempts to provide an in-depth perspective on public policy and demystify the postulates behind the complexity theory and its application. It has covered the complexity theory framework, strategic framework, and policy design framework. These frameworks complement each other and include suitable assumptions, principles, and methodologies. The policy framework puts an emphasis on the process, design, and implementation aspects and provides a way to formulate policies for systems of different types—simple, complicated, and complex.

The current policy and economic theories have yet to address the question: why different regions or countries have differing levels of human resources; poverty and family income; and technology adoption, industrialization, GDP, and prosperity? Consequently, which are the missing threads that merit exploration? The recognition of why public policy has consequential value and realization of emerging knowledge of concepts and phenomena in the social and economic systems can make a difference. And then, the thinking about policy approaches and theories will change. It will give rise to methods, practices, and tools not explored previously and, thus, will set in the process of the emergence of a new policy system. The book is an effort to realize this objective.

Policies are vital for defining the future. They touch every aspect of life, have too big a canvas, and deserve thoughtful consideration. The policies need to match the changing realities at the local, National, and global levels. Essentially, policy system should be able to design policies to meet citizens' concerns; raise process efficiency of public services, and thus release time and energy for more productive usage; encourage innovation for better policy options; and, through them, find ways to change productivity curve for higher economic growth and enhanced standard of living.

Finally, it endeavors to answer the underlying questions. *First*, what makes policy formulation a demanding and complex subject? *Second*, how can policymaking be an innovative process, and can better policies be evolved to address significant concerns of citizens and the economy? *Third*, how complexity in the system can be comprehended? *Fourth*, what policy framework is necessary to provide a comprehensive methodology? *Fifth*, which strategies are required to make public organizations more effective for policy management?

It provides the science of policymaking and accentuates that generating new knowledge for complex systems is fundamental. If the assumptions are rightly discerned, correct principles are followed, and the appropriate theory is applied, the outcomes are more likely to be achieved. An alternative paradigm—design approach, adaptive policies, complexity theory, and institutional development—is the way forward.

In essence, it is what for the book stands.

References

Abdul AA, Rahman A. The impact of strategic planning on enhancing the strategic performance of banks: evidence from Bahrain. Banks Bank Syst. 2019;14(2). https://doi.org/10.21511/bbs.14

Acemoglu D. Challenges for social sciences: institutions and economic development. American Economic Association, Ten Years and Beyond: Economists Answer NSF's Call for Long-Term Research Agendas; 2010. https://doi.org/10.2139/ssrn.1888510

Ali SS, Ariffin AS, Grassroots participation in policy formulation: gaps and challenges in the developing countries: case of Malaysia and Zanzibar grassroots. Mediterr J Soc Sci. MCSER Publishing, Rome; 2018. (Downloads/Grassroots_Participation_in_Policy_Formulation_Gap.pdf)

Anderson P. Complexity theory and organization science. Org Sci. 1999;10(May-June):217–232.

Aspin DN, Chapman JD. Quality schooling: a pragmatic approach to some current problems and issues. London: Cassell; 1994.

Bardhan P. Institutions matter, but which ones? Economics of Transition; 2005;13(3):499–532.

Bergstrom L. Development of institutions is created from the inside. Lessons Learned from Consultants' Experiences of Supporting Formal and Informal Rules. SIDA; 2005. https://cdn.sida.se/publications

Berk J, Berk S. Total quality management. New Delhi: Excel Books; 1995.

Blase M. Institution building: a source book. Columbia: University of Missouri Press; 1986.

Boin A, Christensen T. The development of public institutions reconsidering the role of leadership. Adm Soc. 2008; 40(3):271–297. (Sage Publications).

Borins S. Innovations in Government. Ash Institute for Democratic Governance and Innovation. Harvard University; 2008. https://scholar.harvard.edu/files/skelman/files/kss.pdf

Brinkerhoff DW, Crosby BL. Managing policy reform: concepts and tools for decision-makers in developing and transitioning countries. Kumarian Press; 2002.

Bryson JM. Strategic planning for public and nonprofit organizations. San Francisco: Jossey-Bass; 2004.

Burki SJ, Perry GE. Beyond the Washington consensus: institutions matter. The World Bank; 1998. https://documents.worldbank.org

Capelli P, Tavis A. The performance management revolution. Harvard Bus Rev. 2016, 58–67.

CEEW Centre for Energy Finance (CEEW-CEF). India will require investments worth over USD 10 Trillion to Achieve Net-Zero by 2070; 2021.

Chang H, Evans P (2000). The Role of Institutions in Economic Change. (https://pdfs.semanticscholar.org/2488/7a9ce7513da36f9a80b513a14056bcc92ccc.pdf).

Christiansen J, Bunt L. Innovation in policy: allowing for creativity, social complexity and uncertainty in public governance. NESTA; 2012.

Cilliers P. What can we learn from complexity, Emergence?; 2000. https://doi.org/10.1207/S15327000EM0201_03

Collins J. How great companies tame technology. Newsweek; 2002. https://www.jimcollins.com/article_topics/articles/how-great-companies.html

Deloitte. Global manufacturing competitiveness index 2016; 2016. https://www2.deloitte.com/content/dam/Deloitte/global/Documents/Manufacturing/gx-global-mfg-competitiveness-index-2016.pdf

DFID. Promoting institutional and organisational development. London: Department for International Development; 2003. http://www.kalidadea.org/castellano/materiales/evaluacion/DFID%20promoting%20institutional%20develpment%20guide.pdf

Drzeniek M. Why institutions matter for economic growth; 2015. https://www.weforum.org/agenda/2015/01/why-institutions-matter-for-economic-growth/

Duflo E. Schooling and labor market consequences of school construction in Indonesia: evidence from an unusual policy experiment. Am Econ Rev. 2001;91(4):795–813.

Economic Times (ET). India will need $4.5 trillion by 2040 for infrastructure: report; 2017. https://economictimes.indiatimes.com/news/economy/infrastructure/india-will-need-4-5-trillion-by-2040-for-infrastructure-report/articleshow/59759648.cms?from=mdr

FAO. Statistical year handbook. World Food and Agriculture; 2013. https://www.fao.org/3/i3107e/i3107e.PDF

Fischer F, Miller GJ, Sidney MS, editors. Handbook of public policy analysis theory, politics, and methods. London: CRC Press; 2007.

Forrester JW. Industrial dynamics. Massachusetts: MIT Press; 1961.

Forss K. The theory and practice of analyzing institutional development in evaluation; 2001. https://www.ecgnet.org/sites/default/files/analysing%20institutional%20development%20evaluation.pdf

Fourteenth Finance Commission (FFC). Fourteenth finance commission report, 2015. Government of India; 2015.

Frohlich TC, Sauter MB, Comen E. Countries with the most generous welfare programs; 2016. https://finance.yahoo.com/news/countries-most-generous-welfare-programs-110004319.html

Gharajedaghi J. Systems thinking: managing chaos and complexity: a platform for designing business architecture, 3rd ed. Morgan Kaufmann; 2011.

Gianakis G. The promise of public sector performance measurement: Anodyne or Placebo? Public Adm Q. 2002;26(1/2):35–64.

Giest S. Big data for policymaking: fad or fasttrack? Policy Sci. 2017; 50:367–382.

Global Infrastructure Hub. Forecasting infrastructure investment needs and gaps; 2017a. https://outlook.gihub.org/

Global Infrastructure Hub. Forecasting India infrastructure investment needs and gaps; 2017b. https://doi.org/https://outlook.gihub.org/countries/India (2017)

Gupta DN. E-governance: comprehensive framework. New Delhi: New Century Publication; 2008.

Hall R, Jones C. Why do some countries produce so much more output per worker than others? Quarterly. Q J Econ 114(1). Oxford University Press; 1999. http://www.jstor.org/stable/2586948

Hanushek E, Woessmann L. The role of cognitive skills in economic development. J Econ Lit. 2008;46(3):607–68.

Hințea CE, Profiroiu CM, Ticlau TC. Strategic planning and public management reform: the case of Romania. Transylvanian Rev Adm Sci Spec Issue. 2015;2015:30–44.

IEA. Key world energy statistics. International Energy Agency (IEA), Paris, France; 2019.

IEEFA. India's utility-scale solar parks a global success story India is home to the world's largest utility-scale solar installations; 2020. https://ieefa.org/wp-content/uploads/2020/05/Indias-Utility-Scale-Solar-Parks-Success-Story_May-2020.pdf

IMF. GDP per capita; 2016. https://www.imf.org/external/datamapper/NGDPDPC@WEO/OEMDC/ADVEC/WEOWORLD

International Energy Agency (IEA). Net Zero by 2050. A Roadmap for the Global Energy Sector; 2021. https://iea.blob.core.windows.net/assets/deebef5d-0c34-4539-9d0c-10b13d840027/NetZeroby2050-ARoadmapfortheGlobalEnergySector_CORR.pdf

International Monetary Fund (IMF) (2019). World Economic Outlook Database, April 2019.

International Renewable Energy Agency (IRENA). Investment needs for the global energy transformation; 2022. https://www.irena.org/financeinvestment/Investment-Needs

IPCC. Summary for policymakers. In: Climate change 2007: the physical science basis. Contribution of working group i to the fourth assessment report of the intergovernmental panel on climate change; 2007.

IPCC. Climate change 2014: mitigation of climate change EPA WEBSITE. Contribution of working group III to the fifth assessment report of the intergovernmental panel on climate change; 2014.

Israel A. Institutional development. John Hopkins University Press; 1989.

Jagannathan R. The jobs crisis in India. Pan Macmillan India; 2018.

Janaagraha. Annual survey of India's city-systems 2016: shaping India's Urban Agenda, a publication of Janaagraha Centre for Citizenship and Democracy and Jana USP; 2014. http://www.janaagraha.org/files/publications/Annual-Survey-of-Indias-City-Systems-2014.pdf

Jones H. Taking responsibility for complexity: how implementation can achieve results in the face of complex problems Working Paper 330, Overseas Development Institute; 2011. https://www.odi.org/sites/odi.org.uk/files/odi-assets/publications-opinion-files/6485.pdf

Joshi A, Carter B. Public sector institutional reform: topic guide. Birmingham, UK. GSDRC, University of Birmingham; 2015. https://gsdrc.org/wp-content/uploads/2015/07/PSIR_TG.pdf

Kastner A. Lead, geopolitical agenda. World Economic Forum; 2021. https://www.weforum.org/agenda/2021/04/seven-business-leaders-on-how-technology-will-shape-geopolitics/

Keeney RL. Public values and public policy. In: Shanteau J, Mellers BA, Schum DA, editors. Decision science and technology. Springer, Boston, MA; 1999. https://doi.org/10.1007/978-1-4615-5089-1_16

KPMG and FICCI. Re-engineering the skill ecosystem; 2016. http://ficci.in/spdocument/20762/Re-engineering-the-skill-ecosystem.pdf

KPMG. Future state 2030: the global megatrends shaping governments; 2014.

Kroll A. Explaining the use of performance information by public managers: a planned behavior approach. Am Rev Publ Adm. 2015;45(2):201–15.

Lasswell HD. A pre-view of policy sciences. American Elsevier Publishing; 1971.

Maksym I, Shah A. Citizen-centric governance indicators: measuring and monitoring governance by listening to the people and not the interest groups, Policy Research Working Paper 5181. World Bank, Washington; 2010.

McCourt W. Models of public service reform: a problem-solving approach. Policy research working paper, no. 6428. Washington D.C: The World Bank; 2013. http://www-wds.worldbank.org/external/default/WDSContentServer/WDSP/IB/2013/04/30/000158349_20130430082936/Rendered/PDF/wps6428.pdf

McGill R. Institutional Development (ID)—Springer; 1996. https://doi.org/10.1007/978-1-349-25071-4_1.pdf

McKinsey. Prioritizing health: a prescription for prosperity; 2021. https://www.mckinsey.com/industries/healthcare-systems-and-services/our-insights/prioritizing-health-a-prescription-for-prosperity

McKinsey. The Net-zero Transition; 2022. https://www.mckinsey.com/business-functions/sustainability/our-insights/the-net-zero-transition-what-it-would-cost-what-it-could-bring

Meadows DH, Meadows DL, Randers J, Behrens WW. Limits to growth: the 30-year update. New York: University Books; 1972.

Mehra R. Getting to transformation, a management handbook. New Delhi: Macmillan India Ltd.; 2004.

Menard C, Shirley MM. The contribution of douglass north to new institutional economics, Halshs-00624297; 2011. https://halshs.archives-ouvertes.fr/halshs-00624297

Meynhardt T. Public value inside: what is public value creation? Int J Public Adm. 2009;32(3–4):192–219.

Mintrom M, Luetjens J. Creating public value: tightening connections between policy design and public management: Luetjens: creating public value. Policy Stud J. 2015;45(1). https://doi.org/10.1111/psj.12116

MIT. Revolution in progress: the networked economy. MIT Technology Review; 2014. https://www.technologyreview.com/2014/08/27/171528/revolution-in-progress-the-networked-economy/

Mohanty PK. Financing cities in India: municipal reforms, fiscal accountability and urban infrastructure. Sage Publications; 2016.

Mookerjee S, Bohra Z. Honors thesis international economics' mentor: does access lead to utilization? The case of health care in India; 2017. https://repository.library.georgetown.edu/bitstream/handle/10822/1044251/Economics%20Honors%20Thesis%20Zarine%20Bohra.pdf?sequence=1

Moore M, Stewart S, Hudqck A. Institution building: as a development assistance method. SIDA; 1995. https://cdn.sida.se/publications/files/-institution-building-as-a-development-assistance-method---a-review-of-literature-and-ideas.pdf

Moore M. Creating public value—strategic management in government. Cambridge: Harvard University Press; 1995.

Mueller B. Why public policies fail: policymaking under complexity. Economi A. 2020;21(2):311–323. https://doi.org/10.1016/j.econ.2019.11.002

National Intelligence Council (NIC). Global trends 2030: alternative worlds; 2012

Niti Aayog. National Nutrition Strategy, New Delhi: Govt of India; 2018. http://niti.gov.in/writereaddata/files/document_publication/Nutrition_Strategy_Booklet.pdf

North DC. Institutions, institutional change and economic performance. New York: Cambridge University Press; 1990

North DC, Thomas RP. The rise of the western world. A new economic history. Cambridge University Press; 1973

OECD. OECD Environment Directorate and International Energy Agency. Policies to Reduce Greenhouse Gas Emissions in Industry; 2003

OECD. Revenue Statistics 2018: Tax Revenue Trends in the OECD; 2018. https://www.oecd.org/publications/revenue-statistics-2522770x.htm

OECD. Global Revenue Statistics Database; 2021. https://www.oecd.org/tax/tax-policy/global-revenue-statistics-database.htm

OECD. Government at a Glance 2000–2015. OECD Publishing. Paris; 2015. https://www.oecd-ilibrary.org

References

Ortiz-Ospina E, Roser M. Government Spending; 2016. https://ourworldindata.org/government-spending

Osborne D, Gaebler T. Reinventing government. Reading: Addison Wesley Publishing Company Inc.; 1992.

Oxford Poverty & Human Development Initiative (OPHI). Global Multidimensional Poverty Index (MPI), University of Oxford; 2018. https://ophi.org.uk/multidimensional-poverty-index/global-mpi-2018/

Peppard J, Rowland P. The essence of business process re-engineering. New Delhi: Prentice-Hall of India Private Limited; 2002.

Planning Commission. Skill development and training, planning commission; 2012. http://planningcommission.nic.in/plans/planrel/fiveyr/11th/11_v1/11v1_ch5.pdf

PWC. Five Megatrends and Their Implications for Global Defense & Security; 2016

RBI (2018). RBI Bulletin April 2018, Union Budget 2018–19: An Assessment.

Reserve Bank of India (RBI). State finances: a study of budgets. Government of India; 2019

Reserve Bank of India (RBI). RBI Bulletin; 2020. https://www.rbi.org.in/Scripts/BS_ViewBulletin.aspx?Id=18881

Russell D (2003). Performance Management and Evaluation: the Australian Experience. In: Jay Hyung Kim (ed). Developing a Performance Evaluation System in Korea. Korea Development Institute.

Sanchawa D. Theoretical Approaches to Public Policy; 2015. https://www.slideshare.net/denissanchawa/theoretical-approaches-to-public-policy#:~:text=Institutional%20theory(ctd)%20%E2%80%A2%20It,of%20their%20preferences%20into%20policy

Sapru RK. Public policy: formulation, implementation and evaluation paperback. India: Sterling Publishers; 2012

Senge P. The fifth discipline: the art and practice of the learning organization. New York: Doubleday Currency; 1990.

Seventh Pay Commission (SPC). The Government of India; 2015. https://doe.gov.in/sites/default/files/7cpc_report_eng.pdf

Small A, Schmutte K. Navigating ambiguity: creating opportunity in a world of unknowns. Ten Speed Press; 2022

Spiller PT, Tommasi M. The institutional foundations of public policy: a transactions approach with application to Argentina. J Law Econ Org. 2003;19(2):281–06. JSTOR. www.jstor.org/stable/3555106

Stacey RD. Complexity and creativity in organizations. San Francisco: Berrett-Koehler; 1996.

STATISTA. Public spending Ratio in China from 2010 to 2020; 2021. https://www.statista.com/statistics/236299/public-spending-ratio-in-china/

Sterman JD. Business Dynamics: Systems Thinking and Modelling for a Complex World. Boston: Irwin & McGraw-Hil; 2000.

Studinka J, Guenduez, AA. The use of big data in the public policy process: paving the way for evidence-based governance; 2018. https://www.alexandria.unisg.ch

Swanson D, Bhadwal S, editors. Creating adaptive policies guide for policy-making in an uncertain world. Sage Publication; 2009.

The National Centre on Education and the Economy (NCEE). Comparing International Vocational Education and Training Programs; 2018. http://ncee.org/wp-content/uploads/2018/03/Renold VETReport032018.pdf

Theodoulou SZ, Roy RK. Public Administration: A Very Short Introduction (Very Short Introductions). Oxford: OUP; 2016.

Trivedi P. Indian Experience with the Performance Monitoring and Evaluation System (PMES) For Government Departments. Cabinet Secretariat, Government of India; 2013.

Uhl-Bien M, Marion R, McKelvey B. Complexity leadership theory: shifting leadership from the industrial age to the knowledge era. Leadersh Q. 2007;18(4):298–18. (https://doi.org/10.1016/j.leaqua.2007.04.002).

UNCTAD. COVID-19 and e-Commerce: A Global Review; 2021. https://unctad.org/webflyer/covid-19-and-ecommerce-global-review

UNCTAD. Investing in SDGs: An action plan for promoting private sector contributions; 2014. http://unctad.org/en/PublicationChapters/wir2014ch4_en.pdf

UNDP. From Old Public Administration to the New Public Service Implications for Public Sector Reform in Developing Countries, by Mark Robinson; 2015. https://www.undp.org/sites/g/files/zskgke326/files/publications/PS-Reform_Paper.pdf

UNESCO. Education 2030 Framework for Action; 2021. https://www.education-progress.org/en/articles/finance

UNESCO. UNESCO Science Report Towards 2030; 2015. http://uis.unesco.org/sites/default/files/documents/unesco-science-report-towards-2030-part1.pdf

UNFCCC. Good Practices in Policies and Measures Among Parties; 2002.

UNICEF. Education for women and girls a lifeline to development; 2011. https://www.unicef.org/media/media_58417.html

United Nations (UN). Innovations in governance and public administration: replicating what works. New York: Department of Economic and Social Affairs; 2006.

United Nations (UN). E-Government Survey'; 2016. (https://publicadministration.un.org/egovkb/Portals/egovkb/Documents/un/2016-Survey/Executive%20Summary.pdf).

United Nations Development Programme (UNDP). Human Development Indices and Indicators; 2018.

van Heffen O, Klok PJ. Institutionalism: state models and policy processes. In: van Heffen O, Kickert WJM, Thomassen JJA, editors. Governance in modern society. Library of public policy and public administration, vol. 4. Dordrecht: Springer; 2000. https://doi.org/10.1007/978-94-015-9486-8_8

Walby S. Complexity Theory, Globalisation and Diversity School of Sociology and Social Policy University of Leeds, Leeds LS2 9JT, UK; 2003. http://www.leeds.ac.uk/sociology/people/swdocs/Complexity%20Theory%20realism%20and%20path%20dependency.pdf

WEF. The Global Competitiveness Index, 2017–18; 2018.

West and Lansang. Global manufacturing scorecard: How the US compares to 18 other nations; 2018. https://www.brookings.edu/research/global-manufacturing-scorecard-how-the-us-compares-to-18-other-nations/

World Bank. Reforming Public Institutions and Strengthening Governance; 2000. http://www1.worldbank.org/publicsector/Reforming.pdf

World Bank. World Development Report (WDR): Making Services Work for Future (WDR); 2004.

World Bank. Promoting the institutionalization of national health accounts: a global strategic action plan; 2010. https://documents1.worldbank.org/curated/ar/410301468323088938/pdf/689660PUB0publ07926B009780821394694.pdf

World Bank. Big Data in Action for Government Big Data: Innovation in Public Services, Policy and Engagement; 2017. https://documents1.worldbank.org/curated/en/176511491287380986/pdf/114011-BRI-3-4-2017-11-49-44-WGSBigDataGovernmentFinal.pdf

World Bank. Pupil-teacher ratio, primary; 2018. https://data.worldbank.org/indicator/SE.PRM.ENRL.TC.ZS

World Bank. Physicians (per 1000 people); 2019a. https://data.worldbank.org/indicator/SH.MED.PHYS.ZS?locations=IN

World Bank. Ending Learning Poverty and Building Skills: Investing in Education from Early Childhood to Lifelong Learning; 2022. https://www.worldbank.org/en/topic/education

World Bank. Doing Business Report; 2019b.

World Bank. Urban Development; 2020. https://www.worldbank.org/en/topic/urbandevelopment/overview#1

World Economic Forum (WEF).The Global Human Capital Report; 2017. www3.weforum.org/docs/WEF_Global_Human_Capital_Report_2017.pdf

World Health Organization (WHO). World health Statistics; 2015.

WTO. World Trade Statistical Review; 2018. https://www.wto.org/english/res_e/statis_e/wts2018_e/wts18_toc_e.htm

Glossary

Aggregate data
It presents data in a summary form and is for an overall presentation of trends and patterns. It combines data from various parts or segments into a consolidated form. It is also referred to as integrated or composite data.

Aggregate system
The aggregate system means treating all the parts, components, or elements combinedly as one unit. (It differs from the holistic view, which comprises understanding all the components or parts and then comprehending the whole).

Analytical tools
These use qualitative and quantitative data to draw findings about a given problem. Some of these tools are business process reengineering (BPR); failure mode and effect analysis (FMEA); strength, weakness, opportunity, and threat (SWOT) analysis; statistical analysis, etc.

Block
It is an administrative unit for development within a district of a State in India.

Circular causality
It is a result of successive causes and effects that return to the original cause due to feedback in the system, and this causality continues.

Complexity analysis
To comprehend complexity, the analysis will essentially include examining the interactive effects between elements (individuals and system variables) and the emergence and evolutionary nature together with a holistic view of the system. There is a difference between the interrelationships between variables and the interactive effects of

elements. Interrelationships reflect causal effects between variables, and the interactive effects are related to the phenomena of emergence and evolution with time. In complex systems, the interactions influence the outputs as given in the equation: System outputs = Interactive effects of elements (e_1, e_2, e_3, ... e_n); e: element.

Disaggregate data
It is to break down aggregated data into components or smaller segments like gender, community, class, regions, sub-sectors, etc., to obtain finer details, patterns, and trends for different segments.

Economic system
It is a set of processes and activities dealing with the factors of production, including land, capital, labor, and natural and physical resources, together with economic institutions. Social groups influence the economic system, and economic activities work within an overarching social system. In a general sense, there is an overlap between an economic system and a social system.

Elements in a system
A system consists of subsystems, components, parts, or elements. The terms like subsystems, parts, or elements are used interchangeably, depending upon the context. The variables, agents, or people are within a system. The parts, variables, economic agents, individuals, citizens, or people in a combined form are referred to as elements. As regard the interactions, these are between elements. In general, various systems or subsystems can be referred to as elements of a large or global system.

End-users
They are the recipients of the policies. They may be citizens; communities; students; patients; farmers; households, small, medium, or large businesses; industry clusters, etc.

Feedback
It is information received or a reaction from elements within a system due to certain causes or interventions introduced.

First-order thinking
It examines or solves the immediate problem or result of an action, without considering further consequences.

First-order effects or consequences
It is the most immediate result of a decision. It can be inferred by the reaction or feedback.

Grassroots
It is defined by what happens at the ground in a community, at the functional level in an organization, at the shop floor in the industry, or at the operational level in any business.

Glossary

Holistic view or systemic understanding
It implies understanding the characteristics of parts and their interrelationships, examining the features of system variables (within parts) and their interrelationships, and thereby obtaining a holistic view.

Insight
It is about a deep understanding of issues. It includes grassroots-level problems, ground realities, and last-mile issues. The insight may be obtained from citizens, end-users, communities, industry, etc.

Interactions or interactive effects on the social and economic systems
The elements (individuals and system variables) within the system interact with each other by observing certain rules and exchanging ideas and resources through feedback from elements and different sources. Individuals make decisions and take actions. As a result, the system emerges and takes a new form over time. The presence of individuals or human beings is a prerequisite for emergence through interactions or interactive effects.

Leverage points
These are points in the system that can have a significant or consequential impact on the performance.

Linear thinking
It deals with a simple cause-effect relationship about a problem or system without considering feedback loops. It follows a step-by-step method and applies the learning from one situation to the other, applying a reductionist approach to break a big or complex problem into manageable parts. The underlying premise of the thinking is: A results in B, which results in C, based on a structured approach. Or, to achieve an objective, one goes from event X to event Y and then to Z sequentially.

Mental model
It is a thought process and represents events or activities about problems and systems. Based on the intuitive perception of individuals, it can be construed as a mental image of the relationships between various issues and entities. The mental models inform the basic understanding of the world.

New approaches to system inquiry
From the 1960s onward, the new approaches include the system approach, system dynamics, innovative approaches, design approach, and complexity theory. Depending on the theory and approach, these consider the interrelationships between variables, interactions between elements, multiple feedbacks, dynamics, behavioral and institutional issues, and the structures that form social and economic systems.

Nonlinear thinking
In contrast to linear thinking, a nonlinear thinking approach uses ways to understand the problem afresh without prejudice or preconceived idea. It considers feedback

loops. It examines the problem from multiple directions using divergent thinking to obtain different perspectives. It is a creative process. It involves analogies and draws inferences from diverse, sometimes disconnected, concepts or ideas. It does not follow a structured or sequential process.

Nonlinearity
It is due to nonlinear mathematical relationships among variables, which could be exponential (like $Y = ax^2$, or $Y = ax_1^2 + bx_2 + cx_3^2$), and/or multiple feedback loops. It could be due to qualitative variables, which cannot be defined as a mathematical equation.

Panchayat (local body)
Panchayat is referred to as the local elected body in a District. *Gram panchayat* is a local body and administrative unit at the village level within a Block of a district. Likewise, the Block *panchayat* is at the Block level, and the *Zilla parishad* is at the district level.

Phase space
It is a space with all possible states of a system. In a multidimensional space, each axis uniquely corresponds to one of the coordinates of a particular variable of a system.

Policy/control parameters
Based on criteria and rules, these parameters set the limits within which the interventions can be made to change the performance of the system.

Policy subsystem
It is defined by a geographical region, substantive issues, and a set of stakeholders, including officials, at different levels, social and political groups, and academic institutions. These are within the policy system.

Policy system
It deals with processes and activities of policymaking and policy implementation for various sectors. It works within a public system.

Public system
It includes the role and functions of government departments concerned with public services and programs besides internal management. It consists of a policy system.

Second-order thinking
It is a process of understanding the implications of the initial decision and then analyzing the further consequences of the result of the initial decision. It may be advantageous when seeing things with the future in mind.

Glossary

Second- and third- or higher-order effects or consequences
These are longer-term or next-level effects, as every action has a result, which has a further impact. Or, a single decision can initiate a series of causes and effects that are not known initially.

Social system
It constitutes networks of individuals and groups, their interactions, and processes. These result in various activities. It includes government, economy, industry, business, and organizations.

Spatio-temporal (space and time)
It refers to both space and time or space–time. In the context of social and economic systems, a state represents a unique point in space and time. For example, infrastructure, transportation, economic entities, etc., at a particular point in space and time. (Refer to the definition of *Phase space*).

Traditional methods or conventional approaches
These include mental model approach, optimization techniques, econometrics, statistical tools, mathematical models, scientific management approach of the 20th Century, and classical theories of management and economics. They are more suitable for engineering problems and physical systems and can be applied to social and economic problems under defined boundary and specific assumptions. They mainly use linear thinking and are appropriate for learning first-order effects. They do not factor in feedback loops, interactive behavior of elements, and dynamics. They cannot adequately consider qualitative social and economic variables, including behavioral issues.

Types of the system
Broadly, there are four types of social and economic systems. *First, simple systems.* They have a small number of parts or elements and follow simple rules. The cause-effects are fully known. *Second, complicated systems.* They have many parts or elements. The behavior cannot be discerned easily, but is knowable. The cause-effects are knowable through analysis. *Third, complex systems.* They have a large number of interacting parts or elements. The dynamic interactions of elements result in the emergence of behavior. The cause-effects are not fully knowable. They display nonlinear, dynamic, and uncertain behavior. These have given rise to concepts like emergent behavior, self-organization, complex adaptive system (CAS), adaptation, evolution, coevolution, path dependency, etc. *Fourth, chaotic systems.* These have interacting elements that produce intricate dynamics and disorder. The behavior appears random.

Unidimensional analysis
It covers one dimension or a single aspect of a problem and solution and does not consider different possible options during problem-solving exercise.

Index

A

Adapt, 90, 95–97, 111, 114, 155, 220–222, 227, 228, 234, 244, 252, 256, 257, 271, 295, 298, 299, 321, 335, 430

Adaptation, 85, 88, 90, 94–98, 102, 103, 108, 134, 155, 156, 191, 211, 218–222, 228–230, 232, 234, 239, 241–246, 248, 256, 257, 271, 290, 308, 321, 327, 331, 333, 342, 446, 452, 460

Adaptive, 11, 13, 20, 87, 94, 97, 220, 244, 253, 257, 259, 263, 265, 267, 269, 270, 273, 290, 292, 295, 423, 430, 439, 446, 460

Adaptive nature, 86, 95, 219, 220, 259

Adaptive policies, 19, 151, 152, 246, 256, 259, 264, 270, 283, 294, 320, 321, 326, 329, 335–337, 340, 423, 452, 453, 458, 461

Advanced manufacturing, 6, 37, 63, 65–67, 197, 264, 270, 292

Advanced materials, 37, 67

Advocacy coalition framework (ACF), 15, 161, 162, 169

Agent-based modeling (ABM), 7, 150, 238, 263, 265, 269, 270, 311, 451

Aggregate behaviour, 157, 235, 249

Aggregate data, 112, 192, 251, 454, 457, 458, 467

Analyses, 6, 8–11, 18, 19, 25, 26, 38, 41, 42, 45, 54, 61, 86–89, 92, 123, 127, 133, 134, 138–141, 149, 152, 153, 155, 157–160, 164, 165, 175, 178–181, 183, 190–195, 216, 220, 222, 223, 230, 237, 238, 241, 242, 248, 256, 259–261, 263–273, 283–289, 291–293, 298, 299, 304, 306, 307, 309–313, 316–318, 320, 323–326, 329–338, 340–343, 345–347, 349–356, 358–362, 365, 367, 371, 374–378, 380–384, 388, 426, 430, 441, 443, 445, 446, 448, 453–455, 457–460, 467, 471

Analysis tools, 330, 338

Applications, 439

Approach, 292

Artificial intelligence, 7, 63, 64, 66, 237, 250, 253, 265, 270, 311, 338, 448, 451

ASER, 46, 286

Assumptions, 5, 11–13, 89, 92, 111, 124, 126, 143, 144, 155, 158, 193, 194, 213, 214, 218, 223, 229, 230, 237, 238, 248, 251, 252, 263–265, 268–272, 286, 288, 289, 297, 298, 301, 302, 306, 308, 309, 314, 319, 323, 325–328, 333, 338, 341, 347, 349, 352, 353, 378, 424, 429, 431, 451, 454, 456–458, 460, 461, 471

Attitudes, 14, 87, 124, 126–128, 134, 139, 140, 143, 144, 164, 190, 297, 303, 342, 428, 452, 455

Attractors, 88, 94, 101–103, 228, 229, 246

B

Basin of attraction, 88, 101–103, 228

Behavioral, 6, 13, 14, 16, 17, 21, 41, 89, 91, 92, 101, 108, 111, 114, 126, 133, 134, 140, 143, 146, 152, 153, 158, 159, 163, 164, 171, 174, 179, 180, 190, 194, 217, 221–226, 228,

© The Editor(s) (if applicable) and The Author(s), under exclusive license to Springer Nature Singapore Pte Ltd. 2024
D. N. Gupta and Sushil, *Innovation and Institutional Development for Public Policy*, https://doi.org/10.1007/978-981-97-3663-8

236–238, 246, 247, 249, 251, 255, 256, 258–260, 270, 272–274, 283, 288, 291–293, 303, 307–312, 319, 320, 323, 324, 326, 327, 331–333, 335–338, 342, 343, 346, 347, 351, 376, 377, 381, 430, 438, 439, 444, 446, 448, 449, 451, 452, 454–457, 459, 469, 471
Behavioral approach, 3, 7, 8, 14, 17, 151, 152, 164
Behavioral complexity, 108, 139, 140
Behavioral economics, 7, 148, 151, 152, 163
Behavioral knowledge, 143
Behavioral science, 9, 10, 14, 134, 143, 152, 164, 323
Beliefs, 14, 41, 90, 97, 100, 103, 111, 114, 124, 126–128, 130, 131, 136, 140, 141, 143, 144, 146, 157, 161, 162, 190, 212, 218, 222, 223, 225, 226, 228, 230, 233, 238, 244, 251, 255, 258, 296, 311, 322, 331, 333, 342, 428, 445, 449, 452, 455
Bounded rationality, 13, 18, 89, 111, 139, 143, 144, 158, 159, 163, 191, 212, 226, 249, 258, 274, 304, 307, 314, 377
Budget, 4, 51, 53, 70, 93, 115, 135, 142, 158, 182, 183, 225, 284, 331, 343, 424, 436, 437, 447–449, 452, 454, 456, 457
Business, 5, 8, 17, 21, 25, 50, 53, 63, 65, 66, 68, 69, 71, 72, 74, 75, 87, 88, 93–98, 100, 103–107, 112–116, 125, 128, 129, 131, 137, 145, 147, 149, 150, 154, 163, 166, 170, 172, 176, 186, 195, 196, 211–214, 216, 217, 220–224, 226–233, 235, 236, 238, 239, 241, 242, 244–246, 248–251, 253–257, 259, 261–263, 265, 267–269, 271, 274, 275, 284, 289–291, 293, 295, 296, 298, 304, 308, 309, 313, 315, 316, 346, 379–381, 426, 429, 435, 436, 438, 448, 458, 459, 467, 468, 471
Business organizations, 4, 87, 104, 109, 114–116, 162, 252, 257

C

Capacity, 18–20, 23–25, 28, 45, 46, 48, 52, 53, 64, 71, 101, 123, 126, 131, 134, 138, 139, 149, 165, 166, 169, 176, 180, 182–186, 189–192, 194, 195, 197, 220, 226, 247, 253, 257, 272, 274, 283, 284, 294, 297, 304, 322–324, 326, 329, 331, 332, 338, 342, 345, 346, 348, 361, 362, 368, 369, 371, 375, 376, 382, 383, 387, 388, 391, 392, 394, 403, 404, 424–426, 428–430, 433, 435, 437–440, 443, 448, 452, 453, 456, 457
Capital expenditure, 51, 450
Causal, 8, 10, 17, 89, 99, 161, 212, 230, 237, 240, 258, 269, 270, 273, 284, 309, 312, 314, 317, 318, 328, 333, 336, 337, 342, 347, 425, 429, 439, 468
Causality, 17, 28, 40, 87, 89, 92, 160, 180, 191, 241, 259, 263–265, 270, 274, 307, 313, 314, 424, 439, 457, 467
Causal loop diagram, 312, 315, 316, 318, 319, 360, 364, 365, 367, 374–376, 378
Causal relationships, 17, 108, 150, 165, 181, 190, 194, 231, 240, 271, 274, 290, 293, 303, 306, 313, 314, 318, 327, 333, 334, 352, 358, 360, 364, 376, 379, 444, 455, 457
Cause-effect relationships, 17, 20, 86, 171, 225, 229, 256, 258, 262–269, 272, 291, 376, 469
Cause-effects, 20, 89, 107, 170, 223, 231, 233, 234, 255, 257, 260, 261, 266–268, 287, 303, 304, 311, 312, 328, 333, 336, 381, 456, 471
21st Century, 3, 22, 26, 52, 67, 147, 212, 252, 254, 283, 290, 292, 423, 433, 438, 460
21st Century challenges, 3, 20, 25, 85, 88, 114, 196, 283, 292, 445
Change, 3–6, 10, 11, 13, 14, 17, 19–22, 24, 41, 43, 63, 64, 67, 71, 74, 86, 89, 90, 95–106, 108, 111, 113–116, 127, 128, 130–132, 134, 135, 139, 141, 143, 146, 150, 155–157, 159, 162–164, 166, 172, 174, 176, 196, 212, 213, 215, 219, 220, 222–224, 227–230, 232–234, 238, 240, 243, 244, 246, 247, 253–266, 268, 269, 273, 284, 291, 292, 295, 296, 298, 299, 301–309, 311–313, 315, 320, 321, 345, 363, 369, 370, 372–378, 386, 390, 402, 405, 408, 411, 424–426, 428–430, 433, 439, 441, 444, 445, 448, 458–461, 470

Index

Characteristics, 8, 13, 17, 18, 26, 28, 85–90, 96, 125, 135, 143, 153, 155, 165, 217, 219, 222, 224, 225, 235, 239, 246, 247, 249, 251, 259, 261–265, 269, 272, 286–288, 291, 294, 303, 304, 340–342, 375, 377, 382, 455–457, 469
Circular causality, 99, 109, 217, 218, 367, 377, 467
Cities, 23, 38–40, 50–54, 68, 93–95, 97, 141, 235, 240, 243, 264, 270, 303, 315, 444, 449, 450
Citizen-centric, 16, 143, 182, 321, 332, 333, 343, 428, 441, 442, 446
Citizen-centric public system, 428, 441
Citizen engagement, 135, 262, 263, 293, 326, 328, 334
Classical approach, 252
Classical theory, 12, 148, 151, 214, 231, 256, 471
Climate change, 3, 4, 12, 19, 22, 23, 25, 26, 95, 100, 107, 109, 112, 114, 115, 131, 137, 146, 150, 162, 168, 169, 172, 173, 181, 196, 212, 213, 219, 253, 264, 270, 284, 288, 289, 291, 292, 295, 297, 345, 346, 360, 424, 440, 447, 449, 451, 454, 455, 459
Coevolution, 88, 90, 98–100, 134, 220, 221, 228, 241, 243, 245, 252, 471
Cognitive, 7, 14, 16, 45, 47, 48, 50, 65, 87, 89, 91, 92, 111, 126, 130, 134, 139–141, 143–146, 158, 159, 163, 222–224, 226, 247, 257, 274, 307, 308, 310, 311, 454, 455
Collaborative approach, 151, 268, 320, 321, 332, 337, 343, 439
Competitiveness, 25–27, 56, 57, 60, 63, 64, 66, 67, 70, 71, 129, 176, 289, 291, 343, 430, 435, 436
Complex, 3, 7, 8, 11–13, 16–21, 24, 28, 42, 63, 72, 85–87, 91, 94, 97, 98, 101, 107–110, 113–115, 133, 136–142, 145, 146, 148, 150, 153, 161, 175, 180, 191, 193, 197, 211, 213, 215, 218, 222, 226, 229, 232, 235, 244, 246, 249–252, 255, 256, 258–260, 263, 265, 273–275, 285, 288, 289, 293, 294, 296–298, 300, 302, 303, 306–308, 310–314, 319, 320, 325, 327, 330, 333, 334, 336, 338, 351–353, 382, 423, 424, 429–431, 438, 440, 444, 454, 455, 458, 460, 461, 471
Complex adaptive systems (CAS), 7, 88, 94, 95, 103, 214, 220, 221, 232, 234, 239, 244, 249, 253, 257, 263, 264, 270, 275, 471
Complex environment, 213, 232, 445
Complexity, 3, 6, 7, 10–12, 16–22, 26, 28, 41, 85–88, 90, 94, 104, 106–108, 110, 113–115, 133, 138–141, 144–146, 150–152, 165, 179, 180, 184, 185, 191–194, 211–215, 218, 219, 222–226, 228, 229, 232, 234, 239, 246, 252, 254, 259, 260, 265, 269–275, 283, 290–293, 298, 302, 303, 309, 310, 312, 314, 320, 326, 327, 329, 331, 332, 334–337, 340, 342, 343, 348, 351, 375, 377–379, 382, 423, 430, 431, 439, 440, 448, 449, 451, 454–457, 461, 467
Complexity analysis, 107, 140, 150–152, 293, 312, 324, 328, 331, 341, 342, 445, 446, 451, 452, 467
Complexity dimension, 4, 20, 21, 108, 114, 123, 191, 224, 254, 274, 275, 311, 324, 445, 456
Complexity economics, 12, 13, 85, 110, 151, 152, 211
Complexity leadership, 257, 259, 446
Complexity leadership approach, 256
Complexity science, 13, 110, 133, 156, 213, 214, 219
Complexity theory, 3, 7, 9, 11, 14, 87, 152, 165, 211–215, 218, 219, 224, 229–232, 234, 235, 239, 241, 242, 246, 248, 250, 252, 257, 258, 263, 264, 267, 269, 270, 272–275, 290, 311, 312, 323, 324, 326, 328, 335–338, 423, 440, 446, 451, 457, 459–461, 469
Complexity theory framework, 28, 211, 213, 229, 328, 333, 335, 431, 439, 460
Complexity thinking, 19, 151, 230, 260, 263, 269, 270, 273, 283, 286, 290, 291, 330, 336, 337, 431, 446, 458
Complex problems, 16, 18, 87, 88, 95, 126, 133, 140, 144, 147, 152, 159, 191, 211, 213–215, 230, 231, 234, 256, 258, 260, 263–265, 274, 275, 283, 286, 288–291, 293, 299, 310, 315, 320, 324, 328, 335–337, 341, 346, 423, 431, 438, 439, 444, 445, 448, 451, 455, 456, 458–460, 469

Complex system, 7, 11, 13, 19–21, 28, 85, 86, 88–91, 94, 96–98, 102–105, 108–110, 150, 151, 181, 211, 213, 214, 216, 218–225, 229, 230, 232, 235, 236, 238, 239, 248, 249, 254, 255, 257, 259, 260, 263, 264, 269–272, 286, 293, 298, 299, 302–304, 306–313, 320, 324, 326–328, 331, 333, 334, 340, 342, 377, 381, 438, 440, 454–456, 460, 461, 468

Complicated, 8, 13, 19, 20, 211, 255, 259–262, 265, 267, 268, 273, 274, 288–290, 293, 310, 319, 326, 327, 330, 333, 336, 340, 439, 440, 445, 455, 460, 471

Constitution, 23, 125, 132, 135, 166, 167, 174

Constraints, 12, 26, 71, 126, 134, 141, 142, 159, 162, 171, 174, 175, 179, 180, 191–193, 213, 225, 230, 237, 238, 256, 297, 308, 321, 331, 334, 338, 343, 352, 378, 431, 446, 454, 456, 458

Contexts, 5, 12, 15, 16, 26, 37, 40–42, 45, 50, 54, 68, 90, 97, 100, 105, 108, 109, 114, 123, 124, 126–129, 132–139, 141, 143–145, 147, 148, 157, 161, 164, 179–181, 190, 192–194, 211, 212, 218, 219, 223, 224, 227, 228, 230, 231, 236–238, 246, 248, 250–252, 254, 255, 258–269, 272, 273, 283, 285–287, 290, 291, 293, 295, 297, 299, 300, 318, 319, 322, 324, 326–332, 334, 335, 340, 343, 348, 358–360, 383, 425–427, 430, 431, 439, 440, 456, 457, 468, 471

Context-specific, 134, 148, 250, 300, 326, 334, 343, 457

Coordination, 94, 101, 115, 124, 127, 128, 183, 425

Counterintuitive, 18, 191, 306, 308, 314, 377

Creative citizen engagement, 19, 151, 293, 320, 328, 333

Creative problem solving (CPS), 293

Critical thinking, 19, 230, 231, 262, 268, 286, 289, 291, 314, 441

Culture, 41, 53, 90, 92, 98, 100, 102, 111, 124, 127–129, 132, 136, 139, 142, 143, 163, 164, 174, 176, 179, 181, 185, 190, 193, 213, 215, 218, 221, 222, 225–228, 230, 232, 233, 240–243, 245, 248, 250–252, 258, 274, 288, 322, 331, 338, 342, 426, 428, 430, 435, 439, 441, 442, 444, 449, 452, 459, 460

D

Decision-making, 5, 6, 8–10, 12–14, 19, 26–28, 39, 40, 87, 93, 94, 100, 106, 111, 113, 115, 123, 124, 126–134, 136–138, 140–146, 148, 150, 152–155, 157–161, 163–165, 179, 180, 182, 184, 185, 190–192, 194, 218, 221, 223, 237, 248, 251, 255, 259, 267, 271, 272, 283, 292–296, 299, 303, 306, 308–310, 313–315, 318, 322, 324, 328, 329, 334, 335, 337, 338, 343, 353, 378, 426–430, 441, 449, 453–455, 458

Deliberative dialogue, 19, 151, 294, 320, 336, 337, 446

Depth of the attractor, 103

Design thinking, 20, 151, 152, 230, 260, 263, 269, 270, 283, 286, 288, 291, 297, 320, 328, 330, 333, 336, 337, 340, 346, 347, 349–351, 359, 378, 379, 381, 382, 431, 439, 445, 446, 458

Determinism, 86, 211, 214, 273

Disruptions, 4, 21, 22, 63, 67, 113–115, 136, 159, 162, 177, 196, 220, 228, 254, 255, 257, 265, 273, 284, 291, 292, 429, 435, 440, 445, 456

Divergent thinking, 19, 107, 286, 289, 291, 293, 297, 470

Dynamic complexity, 303, 308

Dynamic environment, 193, 252–254, 269, 302, 308, 320, 335, 336, 351, 430, 431, 455, 460

Dynamic evolution, 214

Dynamic interactions, 17, 20, 93, 95, 96, 98, 99, 103, 108, 111, 114, 213, 215, 221, 225, 226, 246, 256, 257, 263–265, 269, 272, 471

Dynamic nature, 10, 13, 17, 28, 87, 93–95, 108, 114, 134, 137, 138, 150, 157, 191, 211, 212, 214, 224, 234, 256, 258, 266, 274, 284, 290, 292, 298, 299, 302–304, 307–309, 311, 320, 326, 331, 342, 376, 377, 460

Dynamics, 7, 11, 13, 17, 18, 20, 86–90, 92, 94–96, 98, 99, 101, 103, 108, 110, 111, 114, 115, 132, 134, 136, 137,

Index
477

139–141, 146, 150, 152, 153, 155, 156, 161, 162, 165, 185, 196, 211, 213–215, 217–219, 221, 223–225, 228, 230–232, 238, 240, 241, 246, 249, 252–257, 259, 263, 264, 266, 269–272, 274, 284, 288, 292–294, 299, 304–306, 308, 309, 312–314, 316, 320, 321, 323, 326, 327, 329, 333, 335, 336, 342, 371, 372, 376, 423, 424, 438, 439, 445, 454–456, 458, 459, 469, 471

Dynamic stochastic general equilibrium (DSGE), 12, 13, 111, 148, 151

E

Economic agents, 13, 16, 18, 41, 87–91, 93, 94, 100, 104, 106, 111, 112, 150, 215–217, 220, 222, 227, 232, 233, 236, 239, 244, 245, 248–251, 255, 258, 269, 302, 303, 455, 459, 468

Economic complexity, 111, 112

Economic growth, 11, 12, 19, 21, 24, 26–28, 37, 40, 42, 43, 45, 46, 48, 50, 52–56, 62, 66–68, 70, 71, 87, 101, 112, 129, 136, 173, 175, 176, 250, 346, 425, 431, 447, 456, 461

Economic reforms, 128, 129, 163, 168, 170, 175, 176, 239

Economic theories, 12, 85, 111, 134, 148, 149, 151, 231, 246, 248, 249, 251, 252, 454, 455, 458, 460

Economy, 3–6, 9, 11–13, 15–18, 20–22, 24, 40, 45, 46, 48, 54–56, 58, 60, 63–68, 70, 71, 75, 85, 87–90, 93–95, 97, 98, 100, 102–107, 109–113, 115, 131, 133, 147–149, 151, 157, 162, 166, 175, 176, 195, 196, 211, 213, 214, 217, 220–224, 226–229, 232, 233, 235, 236, 239, 244, 246, 248–250, 252–259, 264, 269, 270, 273, 288, 290, 291, 302, 308, 309, 312, 313, 316, 340, 343, 344, 347, 423, 425, 429, 432, 434–438, 444, 447, 448, 453–459, 461, 471

Ecosystem, 6, 20, 47, 63, 68, 75, 95, 96, 100, 101, 113, 123, 173, 196, 217, 218, 222, 223, 226–228, 232, 236, 240, 244, 250, 251, 258, 263, 269, 270, 272, 333, 423, 425, 430, 444, 449, 451, 459, 460

Edge of chaos, 88, 95, 103, 219, 221, 229, 234, 264, 270

Education, 4–6, 8, 16, 17, 23, 25–27, 37, 39–41, 44–50, 56, 57, 65, 72, 73, 103, 107, 109, 124, 125, 128, 131, 133, 135, 136, 140, 141, 156, 157, 164, 166, 170, 172, 174–176, 181, 182, 189, 215, 217, 224, 235, 239, 240, 243, 247, 262, 268, 284, 298, 300, 319, 321, 424, 429, 433, 436–438, 442, 444, 447, 449, 454, 455

Elements, 3, 11, 14–18, 20, 21, 41, 85, 87–97, 101–106, 108, 114, 115, 133, 139, 141, 145, 146, 162, 165, 173, 179–181, 191, 211–226, 228, 230–236, 239, 244, 246, 248–250, 252, 256–259, 261–270, 272–274, 286–288, 290–295, 298–300, 303, 306, 309–314, 318–320, 322, 324, 325, 327–334, 340–343, 389, 424, 428, 442, 452–460, 467–469, 471

Elite theory, 155, 169–171, 174, 175, 178, 194

Emergence, 8, 10, 13, 14, 85–87, 90–96, 98, 99, 102–104, 107, 108, 114, 116, 132, 134, 139, 141, 149, 155, 191, 211, 214, 218–222, 226–228, 230, 234, 239–241, 243–248, 252, 253, 257, 259, 265, 270–273, 295, 303, 326, 327, 329, 331, 333, 334, 336, 340, 342, 424, 438, 439, 452, 453, 455–457, 459–461, 467, 468, 471

Emergent, 13, 20, 91, 93, 95, 99, 107, 141, 181, 219–221, 231, 232, 256, 263, 265, 269–271, 273, 312, 460

Emergent behaviour, 11, 18, 20, 28, 86, 88, 91–95, 219, 234, 246, 249, 471

Emerging trends, 289, 292, 429, 430

Employment, 3, 6, 39, 40, 42, 43, 46, 55, 56, 58–62, 65–68, 71, 72, 75, 112, 113, 115, 135, 146, 148, 154, 168, 169, 172, 191, 192, 196, 225, 236, 251, 254, 283, 284, 340, 343, 348, 433, 434, 440, 459

Environment, 4, 13, 19, 20, 47, 50, 64, 72, 73, 86–88, 90–100, 103–106, 108, 109, 111–116, 124–126, 128, 129, 134, 137, 140, 142, 143, 145, 146, 153, 155–157, 162, 164–166, 173, 175, 178, 181, 185, 212, 216–222, 224–228, 230, 231, 240–243, 245, 247, 252, 254, 255, 257, 259, 261–270, 274, 287–291, 295, 297–299, 302, 306, 309, 318, 321,

327, 331, 335, 338, 340, 343, 345, 425–427, 429, 435, 436, 438, 444, 445, 449, 453–456, 459, 460
Equilibrium, 11, 13, 15, 20, 95, 103, 107, 111, 154, 163, 214, 219, 221, 257, 261–270, 272, 287, 298, 299, 311, 312, 340, 453, 454, 457, 458
Evidence-based, 3, 7, 11, 12, 26, 42, 123, 131, 145, 149, 150, 180, 213, 283, 297, 310, 322, 326, 328, 329, 333, 335–338, 351, 426, 428, 429, 453, 457
Evidence-based policy (EBP), 12, 40, 128, 323
Evolution, 3, 4, 6, 7, 14, 28, 85, 87, 88, 90, 97, 98, 101, 104, 134, 147, 151–153, 155, 156, 191, 196, 211, 214, 215, 220, 221, 227, 238–241, 243, 245, 252, 256, 270, 271, 273, 291, 298, 310, 326, 327, 329, 331, 333, 334, 342, 343, 425, 452, 453, 456, 458, 459, 468, 471
Evolved, 7, 8, 11, 12, 15, 63, 75, 147, 238, 244, 298, 299, 323, 459, 461
Evolves, 13, 23, 90, 97, 101, 103, 111, 112, 136, 159, 215, 227, 228, 239, 246, 248, 256, 258, 270, 321, 440, 456
Evolving, 4, 13, 19, 66, 89, 110, 114, 134, 147, 153, 178, 182, 211, 221, 224, 231, 239, 249, 255, 259, 274, 292, 312, 320, 348, 425, 430, 442, 445, 455, 456, 458, 460
Evolving nature, 184, 191, 232, 238, 256, 257, 274, 290, 291, 327, 333, 430, 455, 456
Expenditure on education and health, 43
Exports, 58–61, 64, 66, 67, 97, 113, 135, 162, 170, 175, 176, 217, 227, 239–241, 243–245, 264, 270, 284, 295, 431, 432
External environment, 95, 103, 114, 124, 128, 130, 132, 212, 221, 222, 224, 228–230, 234, 242, 267, 295, 302, 327, 333, 338, 460

F
Feedback, 10, 17, 20, 28, 38, 87, 89, 90, 93–95, 97–103, 109, 111, 114, 136–139, 153, 156, 157, 161, 162, 168, 171, 177, 180, 184, 185, 189, 191, 215, 217, 218, 222, 223, 227, 228, 230–234, 236–239, 243, 252, 253, 256, 269, 271–273, 284, 293–295, 298–300, 302–309, 313–316, 318–321, 324, 327, 333–335, 347, 350, 353, 365, 375–377, 379, 384, 385, 429, 441–443, 449, 453, 467–469
Feedback loops, 3, 11, 17, 18, 20, 41, 85, 87, 89, 92, 94, 101, 108, 111, 163, 180, 191, 211, 214, 217, 220, 221, 224, 225, 228, 232, 236, 239, 251, 257, 258, 270, 285, 286, 293, 303–307, 309, 311–315, 317, 318, 342, 353, 367, 375, 377, 424, 430, 439, 455–457, 459, 469–471
Flexibility, 63, 70, 73–75, 159, 191, 232, 427, 444
Focus group discussion (FGD), 337, 348, 350–352, 354, 359, 360, 363, 365, 367, 368, 375, 381, 383–388, 393, 398, 445
Foreign investment, 21, 58, 89, 93, 111, 112, 175, 251
Framework, 6, 10, 24–27, 86, 133, 134, 152, 153, 156, 162, 191, 194, 213, 229, 230, 254, 255, 259, 266, 323, 325, 326, 329, 333, 334, 336, 338, 340, 346, 347, 426, 429, 439, 442, 443, 448, 454, 459, 460

G
Garbage can model (GCM), 159–161
General systems theory (GST), 7, 86, 133, 155, 156
Globalization, 3, 21, 25, 43, 113, 114, 137, 142, 196, 212, 253, 284, 424, 430, 442
Gross domestic product (GDP), 8, 40, 41, 43–45, 48–63, 67, 70, 71, 73, 175, 182, 183, 245, 316, 344, 345, 436–438, 447, 449, 460
Group theory, 15, 153, 154

H
Health, 4, 5, 14, 16, 17, 19, 23, 25–27, 37, 39–41, 46, 48–50, 52, 56, 71–73, 93, 95, 99, 103, 107–109, 111, 115, 123–125, 131, 133, 135, 136, 140, 141, 156, 157, 159, 164, 166–168, 171, 172, 176–178, 181–184, 186–190, 192, 195, 215, 217, 224, 225, 235, 238, 239, 242, 245, 247, 261, 262, 267, 268, 270, 284, 285, 288, 290, 291, 293, 295, 296, 302,

Index 479

303, 308, 315, 319, 321, 341, 382, 424, 429, 433–438, 442, 444, 445, 447, 449, 450, 454, 455, 459
Heterogeneity, 241, 251, 249, 335
Heterogeneous elements, 231, 249
Higher education, 47, 103, 183, 264
Higher incomes, 42, 48, 50
Higher-order effects, 212, 217, 224, 232, 236, 258, 285, 298, 458, 471
Homogeneous, 85, 111, 249, 445, 457
Human behavior, 14, 111, 134, 143, 144, 150, 163, 164, 212, 223, 225, 256
Human capital, 16, 24, 46, 48, 56, 57, 66, 72, 73, 175, 423, 440, 445, 460
Human development, 24, 39, 43, 44, 197, 442
Human development index (HDI), 25, 39, 43, 44, 195, 284, 431, 432, 436
Human resource capital (HRC), 50, 176, 431–433, 436

I

Ideas, 14, 19, 24, 26, 38, 42, 68, 90, 93, 96–99, 101, 104, 106, 111, 126, 130, 131, 133, 142, 149, 150, 152, 154, 157, 159–161, 163–165, 175, 178–180, 184, 215, 217, 218, 223, 224, 226, 227, 231, 233, 236, 239, 243, 244, 246, 248–250, 253, 257, 260, 266, 267, 271, 283, 286, 288–291, 293–298, 304, 310, 321, 323, 345, 350, 443, 444, 448, 451–454, 458, 460, 469, 470
Illiteracy, 45
Implementation, 3, 5, 6, 10, 14, 16, 17, 20, 23–26, 28, 38, 40–42, 71, 87, 88, 106–108, 123, 127–131, 133, 135–140, 142–144, 147, 149, 150, 153, 154, 161, 162, 164, 165, 169, 170, 172, 176, 178, 179, 182–186, 189, 190, 192–195, 213, 222, 225, 227, 230, 233, 234, 247, 254, 256, 273–275, 283–286, 288, 292–296, 309, 318–320, 322–326, 328, 331, 332, 336–338, 340, 342, 343, 350, 352, 353, 384, 386, 425–429, 431, 433, 439, 442, 443, 445, 446, 451–455, 457, 458, 460
Incremental, 15, 88, 143, 159, 196, 261–263, 268–270, 292, 439
Indian Institute of Sciences (IISc), 240
2ndnd industrial revolution (IR), 59
3rd industrial revolution, 59, 60, 63

4th industrial revolution, 60, 63
Industry 4.0, 63, 107, 196
Infant mortality rate (IMR), 14, 23, 25, 39, 43, 44, 177, 192, 195, 431–433
Information infrastructure, 12, 26, 195, 326, 330, 338, 428, 429
Infrastructure, 4, 15, 16, 19, 20, 24, 25, 27, 37, 42, 46, 47, 51–54, 60, 63, 70, 71, 93, 102, 106, 112, 113, 115, 123, 124, 142, 156, 160, 172, 174, 176, 177, 181, 182, 185–187, 189, 190, 192, 194, 217, 218, 222, 225, 227, 238, 240, 241, 245, 247, 250–252, 289, 305, 316, 326, 341, 343, 435, 436, 447, 449, 456, 471
Innovation, 3, 4, 6, 10, 13, 16, 18, 19, 21, 26–28, 37, 48, 52, 53, 55, 56, 58–61, 63, 64, 66, 68, 72, 87, 95–102, 107, 112–115, 136, 142, 148, 159, 176, 178, 193, 215, 224, 225, 227, 233, 239–245, 248–250, 253–257, 263, 264, 269–271, 289, 291, 295, 297, 316, 321, 329, 334, 423–425, 428, 430, 436, 444–449, 451–453, 459–461
Innovative, 447
Innovative approaches, 7, 19, 147, 151, 193, 195, 250, 262, 263, 283, 292, 320, 321, 326, 328, 330, 336, 338, 349, 431, 439, 440, 444, 451, 469
Innovative indicators, 295, 296
Innovative processes, 431, 461
Innovative solutions, 75, 347, 439, 449, 451
Insourcing, 63
Institution, 4, 6, 9, 16, 17, 23–25, 89, 90, 100, 101, 105, 106, 109–113, 115, 123, 125–127, 129–135, 141, 142, 149, 150, 154–156, 160, 165–167, 171, 175, 176, 179, 190, 196, 216–218, 225, 226, 228, 231, 236, 240, 241, 243–246, 249, 251, 258, 272, 274, 275, 287, 291, 294, 301, 321–323, 331, 333, 335, 342, 352, 424–429, 439, 454, 456, 459, 468, 470
Institutional, 3, 4, 7, 16, 21, 23–26, 28, 41, 71, 87, 89, 100, 108, 111, 125, 126, 128, 134, 135, 141, 142, 148–150, 152, 153, 155, 158, 160, 162–167, 173, 175, 176, 179, 184, 185, 189, 190, 193–196, 212, 225, 226, 228, 236–238, 240, 245–247, 249–252, 254, 258, 272–275, 283, 284,

292–295, 307, 309–312, 320, 322–324, 326, 327, 331–333, 335–338, 340, 342, 343, 349, 353, 423–430, 435, 438, 446, 448, 451–457, 461, 469
Institutional development (ID), 23, 25, 28, 423–428
Institutional mechanisms, 101, 129, 130, 169, 170, 176, 193, 218, 219, 231, 232, 234, 236, 238, 248, 251, 258, 320, 331, 336, 338, 342, 352, 353, 424, 427, 429, 431, 433, 439, 448, 449, 451, 452, 454
Institutional structures, 127, 166, 167
Institution building (IB), 425–427
Interactions, 11, 14, 15, 17, 18, 20, 21, 28, 85, 87–99, 101, 102, 104–112, 114–116, 126–128, 132, 133, 139–141, 145, 150, 154, 165, 181, 191, 215–219, 221–224, 226–228, 230, 232–240, 243–253, 255, 257–259, 261–265, 267–269, 271–273, 285, 287, 288, 290–292, 294, 301–303, 306, 307, 309, 311, 312, 318, 333, 335, 340, 342, 351, 354, 356, 358, 362, 363, 367, 377, 379, 389, 424, 426, 430, 439, 455–460, 468, 469, 471
Interactive, 18, 85, 89, 90, 93, 94, 96, 106, 109–112, 133, 145, 146, 150, 179–181, 193, 211, 212, 214, 215, 217, 219, 222–225, 230–233, 236, 237, 239, 241, 244–253, 256–259, 263–265, 267, 269, 270, 273, 302, 303, 306, 308–311, 319, 320, 326, 327, 329, 331, 333, 334, 340, 342, 448, 453, 455, 457–459, 467–469, 471
Interconnected, 3, 4, 17, 18, 20, 85, 87, 94, 98, 113, 137, 145, 150, 181, 196, 229, 234, 248, 251, 288, 303, 346, 444, 445, 455, 456
Interpretive structural modeling (ISM), 11, 28, 54, 149, 260, 261, 263, 265, 267–270, 283, 299–301, 311, 323, 328, 332, 333, 336, 337, 341, 343, 345, 349–351, 354–359, 365, 379–383, 386, 388, 389, 431, 446
Intervention, 303
Investment, 12, 21, 25, 27, 40, 46, 51–56, 58, 63, 64, 66–71, 87, 89, 93, 96, 99, 100, 102, 104, 111, 112, 126, 170, 196, 241, 243–245, 251, 252, 289, 295, 304, 316, 354, 356, 361–363, 369, 373, 376, 382, 387–389, 391–395, 398, 403, 404, 407, 409, 429, 434, 447–449, 452, 457

K
Knowledge economy, 45–47, 68, 236, 245, 248, 250, 253, 257, 335, 448

L
Labor laws, 21, 37, 71–75
Labor market, 71, 72, 75
Labor productivity, 46, 48, 55, 56, 62, 66, 175, 176
Learn, 28, 39, 48, 97, 100, 111, 114, 143, 155, 162, 220, 224, 257, 295, 302, 306, 313, 439
Learning, 10, 27, 37, 40, 42, 43, 45–47, 50, 94–97, 104, 143, 149, 153, 175, 192, 215, 218, 220, 223, 234, 237, 245, 247, 256–259, 264, 265, 270, 271, 273, 285, 286, 288, 290, 291, 293, 297, 298, 306, 307, 311, 314–316, 318, 319, 324, 328, 333, 334, 338, 340, 359, 365, 379, 439, 443, 446, 449, 469, 471
Leverage points, 232, 233, 303, 379, 445, 458, 469
Lindblom, 159
Linear models, 307
Linear thinking, 18, 170, 171, 180, 232, 258, 285, 286, 293, 302, 306, 307, 310, 311, 320, 334, 438, 445, 456, 460, 469, 471
Local actions, 249

M
Mahatma Gandhi National Rural Employment Guarantee Scheme (MNREGS), 131, 154, 161, 168, 169, 172
Malnourished, 25, 50, 433
Malnutrition, 19, 47–50, 131, 197, 431, 432
Management information system (MIS), 16, 75, 115, 225, 344
Manufacturing, 6, 21, 22, 26, 27, 37, 56, 58–71, 97, 115, 136, 146, 170, 175, 176, 181, 196, 215, 243, 424, 429, 431–433, 435
Maternal mortality rate (MMR), 14, 23, 25, 39, 177, 178, 192, 195, 431–433

Index

Mechanistic, 11, 86, 180, 214, 215, 252, 311
Mental models, 10, 19, 144, 149, 180, 297–299, 306–308, 310, 311, 313, 314, 334, 358, 360, 376, 469, 471
Multiple stream framework (MSF), 160, 161, 168–171, 174, 175, 178
Municipal solid waste, 51, 52, 188, 450

N

Neo-classical economics, 13
Neo-classical theory, 12, 13, 148, 151
Network, 7, 11, 13, 16, 52, 88, 90–92, 94–96, 101, 104, 109–112, 115, 132, 133, 144, 150, 162, 177, 193, 216, 218, 222, 226, 227, 231, 236, 237, 239–241, 243, 244, 248–252, 255, 258, 273, 304, 336, 346, 439, 448, 452, 456, 471
Networked economy, 150, 250, 271, 448, 457
Network effects, 86, 111, 215, 228, 231, 232, 236, 239, 243–245, 248, 250, 264, 269
New public organizations, 28, 423, 429, 430, 438, 459, 460
Newtonian, 11, 86, 87, 211, 214, 273
Nodes, 16, 139, 141, 216, 376
Non-equilibrium, 13, 90, 151, 221, 320
Nonlinear, 10, 11, 13, 17, 20, 86, 87, 89, 92, 94, 95, 99, 103, 108, 114, 115, 139, 140, 156, 196, 217, 218, 221, 224, 225, 236, 246, 256, 263–265, 269, 270, 272, 285, 286, 288, 294, 298, 302, 307–309, 313, 323, 333, 375, 376, 460, 470, 471
Nonlinearity, 3, 10, 11, 17, 18, 28, 41, 87, 89, 94, 105, 109, 111, 138, 145, 181, 191, 211, 212, 224, 225, 230, 232, 234, 236, 258, 266, 284, 285, 290, 298, 303, 304, 306–308, 311, 313, 314, 320, 331, 335, 336, 342, 348, 351, 376, 377, 439, 456, 457, 460, 470
Nonlinear relationships, 108, 214, 258, 285, 319, 424
Nonlinear system, 307
Nonlinear thinking, 285, 286, 308, 311, 329, 334, 458, 469
Normal, 16, 318, 367, 370, 371, 373, 374, 404, 413
Nutrition, 22, 23, 37, 39, 48–50, 429, 433

O

Operational complexity, 87, 138, 139
Operation expenditure, 51
Optimistic, 318, 367, 370–372, 413
Organic linkage, 114, 222, 223, 310
Organizations, 4, 5, 15, 16, 18, 20, 23, 25, 58, 72, 86, 88, 90, 94, 96–106, 109, 114–116, 125, 126, 128, 129, 131, 132, 134, 137, 138, 140, 141, 143, 145, 152, 154, 156, 157, 159, 160, 162, 166, 167, 176, 211, 215, 216, 220, 221, 225–227, 229–232, 235, 246, 252–259, 261, 262, 265, 267, 268, 272–275, 285, 289, 290, 298, 310, 312, 347, 383, 424–428, 430, 438–441, 444, 445, 458–460, 468, 471
Outcome, 5, 11, 13, 19, 22–28, 37, 38, 40, 45–47, 100, 101, 107, 111, 123, 126–128, 132, 134, 137, 139, 141, 142, 144, 150, 160, 163, 175, 182, 184, 192, 217, 219, 234, 247, 284, 286, 294, 303, 310, 311, 326, 329, 332, 334, 344, 424, 426, 427, 429, 440, 441, 443, 454, 458, 461

P

Path creation, 250
Path dependency, 18, 20, 85, 88, 90, 100, 107, 211, 241, 243, 245, 327, 331, 456, 471
Pattern recognition, 6, 230, 231, 238, 260, 264–266, 270–272, 328, 333, 336, 337, 340, 439
Patterns, 14, 43, 68, 86, 89, 93, 94, 97, 100–102, 104, 105, 108, 112, 126, 135, 141, 150, 155, 216, 220, 228, 230, 232–234, 251, 256, 257, 259, 270, 285, 287, 291, 296, 303, 338, 346, 348, 374, 439, 451, 454, 458–460, 467, 468
Peak manufacturing employment, 61, 62
Per capita GDP, 42–44, 55–57, 61, 64, 73, 176, 195, 431–433, 436–438
Performance management system, 16, 116, 265, 267, 332, 343, 428, 429, 442, 446
Pessimistic scenarios, 370, 371, 373, 413
PISA, 46, 47, 50, 286
Policies coevolved, 243, 244
Policy analysis, 3, 7–10, 38, 40–42, 124, 127, 129, 130, 133, 134, 137–140, 142, 148, 149, 152–154, 165,

178–180, 192, 193, 286, 292, 293, 295, 316–319, 321, 326, 332, 336, 337, 343, 349–351, 374, 375, 378, 379, 381, 449, 452
Policy analysis tools, 326, 333, 336, 337, 340
Policy content, 38, 127, 130, 180, 190–192, 194, 449, 451, 452
Policy cycle, 6, 7, 9, 10, 108, 127, 133, 137, 138, 145, 148, 149, 152, 161, 165, 185, 256, 273, 292
Policy design, 15, 26, 28, 129–131, 151, 152, 273, 283, 284, 297, 314, 320–322, 325, 326, 328, 330–333, 335–338, 340–343, 349, 350, 375, 379, 380, 382, 431, 439, 445–447, 451–453
Policy design framework, 28, 283, 319, 325, 327, 336, 338, 339, 460
Policy framework, 6, 42, 163, 460, 461
Policy implementation, 16, 17, 19, 23–26, 109, 123, 124, 126, 140, 149, 150, 162, 165, 176, 182, 184, 185, 190–192, 194, 197, 286, 292, 293, 295, 320, 326, 327, 333, 342, 343, 351, 442, 446, 452, 470
Policymakers, 3, 9, 12, 14, 19, 24, 25, 38, 39, 42, 108, 130, 135, 137–140, 146, 149, 153, 160, 161, 163–165, 178, 179, 181, 212, 226, 229, 238, 254, 272, 274, 284, 294, 297, 300–302, 304, 305, 310, 311, 358, 380, 382, 455
Policymaking, 3–5, 7–12, 14, 16–19, 21, 23, 25–28, 38, 40–42, 45, 47, 53, 85, 87, 88, 100, 101, 106–109, 123, 124, 126–130, 132–143, 145–154, 156–162, 165–168, 172–174, 178–181, 184, 185, 190–195, 213, 222, 236, 239, 246, 254, 256, 275, 283–286, 289, 292–298, 302–304, 306, 309, 310, 318–326, 328, 329, 331, 333–336, 338, 340, 342–344, 351–353, 358, 365, 377, 384, 423, 426, 428, 429, 431, 433, 439, 444, 445, 448, 449, 451, 453–457, 461, 470
Policymaking process, 3, 12, 26, 28, 41, 42, 107, 108, 112, 123, 124, 128, 130–133, 135, 136, 138–140, 143, 145, 149, 150, 153, 155, 157, 161, 162, 165–167, 173, 190–194, 246, 274, 287, 294, 306, 307, 319, 322, 324, 325, 327, 333, 340, 424, 449, 451–453, 458
Policy options, 9, 41, 42, 126, 127, 139–141, 144, 158, 165, 172, 179, 180, 190–192, 194, 238, 284, 289, 293, 294, 307, 310, 311, 319, 320, 322–324, 326, 332, 337, 343, 348–350, 360, 365, 371, 373, 375–377, 379, 380, 423, 447, 449, 451, 453, 456, 458, 461
Policy process, 5, 6, 10, 12, 28, 38, 42, 126, 127, 138, 147, 154, 155, 160–162, 169–171, 181, 191, 274, 424, 426, 451, 452, 454
Policy research tools, 350
Policy sciences, 3, 7, 9, 148, 152, 323, 449
Policy system, 4, 12, 14, 17, 27, 28, 85, 107–109, 123, 124, 127, 128, 132, 138, 140, 147, 160, 165, 180, 182, 190–194, 197, 226, 233, 235, 246, 253, 255, 274, 283, 292, 295, 304, 319, 320, 322–324, 326, 329, 334, 338, 340, 342, 426, 428, 439, 451, 453, 454, 456, 457, 461, 470
Policy theory, 3, 28, 41, 123, 124, 153, 161, 165, 168–171, 174, 178, 273, 274, 327, 328
Policy tools, 42, 323, 328, 333, 446, 456
Political culture, 124, 128, 132, 134, 136, 142
Political system, 96, 130, 132, 156, 157, 159, 162, 255
Political systems theory, 156, 168–171, 174, 175, 178
Politics, 7–9, 112, 124, 130–132, 134, 142, 145, 148, 152–154, 157, 158, 161, 165, 168, 180, 194, 274
Pollution, 26, 27, 38–40, 52, 108, 164, 173, 212, 264, 270, 295, 302, 305, 343, 444
Poverty, 3, 13, 24, 27, 40–44, 46, 48, 50, 55, 56, 66, 164, 168, 175, 197, 213, 222, 237, 283, 284, 288, 425, 440, 442, 444, 460
Power, 18, 20, 23, 63, 67, 102, 123, 124, 126, 127, 130–132, 136, 144, 150, 152, 154, 155, 159, 166, 174, 183, 196, 220, 240, 301, 304, 344, 345, 347–365, 367, 368, 370, 374–381, 383, 384, 386–388, 391, 392, 394, 402–404, 407, 447–451
Premature deindustrialization, 60, 61

Index

Primary education, 26, 39, 46, 47, 186, 187, 190, 192, 247, 270, 292, 338, 433, 434, 444, 445, 447, 455, 459
Primary school, 45, 174, 434, 447
Principles, 5, 6, 100, 101, 109, 124, 129, 134–136, 142, 145, 147, 166, 168, 176, 218–222, 229–231, 246, 252, 307, 312–314, 318, 321, 322, 324–328, 333, 338, 367, 374, 439, 457, 460, 461
Process, 3, 5, 6, 9–11, 13, 16, 19, 25, 26, 38, 41–43, 46, 58, 63–68, 88, 90, 94, 96–102, 104, 106, 109, 113–115, 123, 124, 127–134, 136, 137, 139–151, 153, 154, 156–162, 164–166, 168–176, 178, 180, 182, 184–187, 189–194, 211–213, 215, 217, 220–222, 224–228, 230, 231, 233, 234, 237–240, 244, 246, 253, 256–258, 263, 265, 267, 269–271, 273, 274, 283–290, 293–300, 309, 310, 312–314, 316, 318–321, 323–326, 328–332, 334–338, 340–343, 345–347, 350, 351, 358–361, 367, 377, 379, 380, 384, 423–430, 434, 435, 439–444, 446, 447, 449, 452–455, 458–461, 467–471
Process efficiency, 123, 177, 186, 187, 189, 296, 434, 435, 461
Process management, 434, 435
Psychological, 16, 47, 89, 101, 111, 144, 221, 226, 237, 251, 255, 266, 288, 291–293, 334, 349, 376, 444, 455
Public choice theory, 158, 159
Public governance, 6, 16, 21, 131, 166, 251, 425, 430, 441
Public institutions, 8, 19, 21, 42, 89, 111, 124–126, 129, 131, 141, 149, 151, 155, 156, 162, 182, 245, 424–427
Public organizations, 21, 23, 28, 104, 114–116, 125, 127, 130, 320, 321, 423, 425, 430, 431, 433, 439, 440, 443–445, 461
Public policies, 3–11, 13–15, 17–20, 22, 25–28, 37–40, 54, 87–90, 99, 100, 102, 103, 107, 109, 123, 124, 127, 129–135, 137, 138, 143–150, 152, 153, 157, 163, 164, 166, 167, 169, 180, 181, 190, 193, 195, 197, 211, 213, 214, 224, 227, 230, 232, 233, 237, 246, 251, 254, 256, 257, 264, 270, 283–285, 290, 294, 310, 312, 320–327, 330, 333, 342, 383, 425, 426, 429, 430, 433, 438, 444, 448, 449, 451–455, 457, 458, 460, 461
Public-private partnership (PPP), 70
Public system, 4, 11, 12, 17–21, 26, 41, 42, 100, 104, 108, 109, 114, 138, 152, 191, 213, 220, 224, 227, 228, 231, 237, 289, 291, 292, 313, 424, 426, 427, 439, 440, 470
Public value, 26, 129, 130, 137, 145, 329, 333, 334, 344, 440
Punctuated equilibrium theory (PET), 163, 170, 175

Q

Quality, 4, 5, 14–16, 19, 22, 23, 25, 26, 39–41, 45–48, 50, 52–54, 60, 63, 64, 70, 96, 113, 114, 125, 129–131, 150, 164, 170, 172, 174–178, 181, 182, 186, 189, 190, 197, 218, 219, 223, 225, 226, 247, 251, 253, 265, 267, 268, 284, 286, 291, 295, 304, 322–325, 332–335, 343, 344, 423, 424, 427, 428, 430, 433, 435, 436, 439, 441, 442, 446, 447, 449, 451, 456, 459
Quality management system (QMS), 16, 261, 265, 267, 268, 332, 343, 428, 442
Quality of life, 13, 27, 37, 38, 40, 42, 45, 52, 53, 56, 68, 129, 131, 197, 250, 305, 437, 447, 456

R

Rational choice theory (RCT), 13, 157–159
Reductionism, 11, 86, 155, 211, 214, 273
Reductionist, 11, 88, 180, 214, 215, 232, 285, 298, 469
Renewable energy, 66, 167, 173, 174, 291, 304, 305, 344–348, 352, 363, 379, 382, 392, 429, 447, 448, 450
Research and development (R&D), 21, 26, 27, 55–58, 60, 63, 64, 66–68, 72, 136, 176, 240–245, 263, 264, 269, 284, 289, 291, 316, 352–356, 358, 364, 378–381, 384–389, 425, 434, 436, 437, 448
Resilient management, 256, 257
Resilient system, 257
Revenue collection, 51
Right to education (RTE), 46, 131, 135, 154, 168, 170, 174, 181, 286

Right to public services, 189, 441
Rigidity, 71, 142
Rules, 9, 11, 13, 15, 23, 25, 37, 41, 74, 75, 90–93, 96, 97, 100–102, 104, 106, 114, 124–127, 129, 131, 132, 141–144, 153, 154, 158, 166, 174, 218, 219, 221, 225, 231, 246, 253, 254, 261, 267, 268, 272, 285, 286, 307, 322, 325, 331, 342, 424, 426–428, 442, 457, 459, 469–471
Rural, 22, 23, 26, 40, 41, 47, 50, 51, 154, 164, 167, 168, 172, 176, 182, 191, 195, 270, 344, 348, 432, 434, 445, 455

S

San Francisco Bay (USA), 211, 239, 241, 242, 244, 252, 271
Scenario building, 6, 231, 251, 260, 264–266, 269, 270, 293, 313, 316, 317, 319, 323, 328, 333, 336, 337, 340, 349, 350, 365, 367, 368, 370, 371, 411, 439
Science labs, 46, 47
Scientific management, 214, 231, 252, 256, 261, 267, 268, 306, 438, 471
Scientific management tools, 306
SD model, 270, 312, 314, 315, 318, 319, 364, 365, 367, 374–380, 382, 392, 398, 404
Self-organization, 11, 28, 87, 88, 90, 94, 95, 97, 98, 101, 103, 191, 214, 218, 219, 221, 228, 234, 239, 245, 248, 331, 333, 342, 456, 471
Self-organized, 94, 244
Self-organizing, 18, 20, 87, 94–96, 101, 107, 211, 219–221, 228, 232, 249
Self-organizing property, 134, 327
Sensitivity analysis, 316–319, 347, 367, 368, 373, 374, 411, 414, 415
Sewage treatment plant, 52, 450
Silicon valley in Bengaluru, 211, 239, 241, 252, 271
Silicon valley (SV), 68, 240–245
Simulation, 150, 251, 313, 314, 316–319, 347, 349, 350, 367–370, 374, 450, 451
Skill development, 16, 25–27, 47, 50, 56, 57, 72, 75, 131, 170, 176, 240, 241, 431–433
Skill sets, 21, 28, 96, 101, 107, 111, 135, 228, 250, 253, 254, 343, 423, 445, 446

Slum population, 50
Social capital, 94, 106, 129, 133, 142, 217, 218, 222, 243–245, 250, 251, 257, 258
Social network analysis (SNA), 150, 311, 451
Social sector spending, 437
Social security, 8, 16, 26, 71–75, 127, 131, 136, 147, 212, 238, 270, 434
Social system, 459
Space and time, 94, 95, 102, 287, 306, 471
Stakeholders, 3, 5, 9, 13, 16–20, 23, 26, 39, 41, 42, 75, 89, 90, 93, 107–109, 111, 113, 114, 124, 126, 127, 131, 135–142, 144, 153, 157, 160, 162, 164–166, 169–171, 179–181, 184–186, 190, 192–194, 196, 212, 216, 225, 226, 229, 232, 233, 236, 238, 239, 246, 251, 255, 259, 271–274, 287–289, 292–295, 300–304, 306, 307, 311–314, 317–322, 326, 330, 331, 334, 337, 341–343, 347, 348–353, 358–360, 365, 367, 374, 375, 377–379, 381, 383–385, 387, 388, 393, 426–428, 431, 441, 443, 445, 446, 448, 449, 451–453, 457–459, 470
Startups, 68, 69, 227, 241, 243, 244, 250
Strategic framework, 211, 253, 255, 259, 261, 460
Strategic materials, 67, 249
Strategic planning, 440, 441, 446
Strategic thinking, 19, 286, 289–291
Structures, 6, 13, 15, 17, 23, 25, 68, 85, 86, 89–92, 94, 97, 98, 100, 102, 104, 106, 108, 109, 111, 113–115, 123–127, 131, 132, 134–136, 141, 142, 145, 150, 156, 162, 166, 172, 185, 190, 211, 214–217, 220, 222, 228, 229, 231–234, 236, 244, 248, 249, 253, 258, 274, 287, 291, 298–300, 302, 309, 312–314, 316–319, 325, 329, 338, 342, 347, 348, 358, 360, 361, 363–365, 367, 374, 375, 377–379, 381, 382, 398, 424, 426, 430, 440, 450, 452, 457–460, 469
Structures emerge, 252
Subsystems, 15, 16, 20, 85, 87, 90–92, 104–106, 109, 112–116, 140, 162, 180, 216–218, 225, 226, 228, 230, 236, 293, 298, 299, 311, 312,

Index

315–318, 347, 351, 360–364, 374, 375, 378, 381, 468, 470
System, 3–7, 9–13, 15–26, 28, 41, 51–53, 63, 66, 68, 74, 75, 85–116, 123–126, 129, 130, 132–134, 136, 138–143, 145, 146, 149–152, 155–157, 160, 163, 165, 166, 168, 171, 175–177, 179–182, 184–195, 197, 211–240, 244, 246–252, 254–275, 283, 285–288, 290–295, 298–304, 306–324, 326–338, 340–344, 346–354, 356, 358–365, 367, 368, 374–382, 384–386, 388, 423–425, 427–431, 433–435, 437–446, 448, 449, 451–461, 467–471
System approach, 3, 7, 10, 15, 28, 86, 101, 149, 151, 152, 156, 261, 262, 265, 267, 268, 283, 297–299, 311–314, 326, 328, 336, 337, 349, 377, 378, 439, 446, 458, 469
System conceptualization, 318
System dynamics (SD), 11, 15, 28, 86, 102, 149, 152, 156, 236, 238, 260, 265, 267, 268, 270, 283, 301, 308, 311–317, 319, 323, 335–337, 341, 347, 349, 350, 354, 359, 364, 366, 367, 374, 377–379, 382, 390, 412, 431, 439, 446, 469
System dynamics (SD) modelling, 390
Systemic, 11, 15, 19, 22, 26, 40, 87, 123, 140, 159, 180, 185, 190, 191, 194, 220, 230, 232, 251, 272, 283, 288, 309, 311, 313, 319, 324, 326, 329, 330, 334, 340, 351, 353, 453, 459, 469
Systemically, 4, 15, 16, 88, 107, 340, 453, 454
Systemic analysis, 171, 174, 181, 190, 192–195, 309, 324, 327, 328, 330, 332, 333, 338, 340, 343, 457
Systems theory, 7, 9–11, 14, 87, 142, 149, 151–153, 155, 156, 211, 214, 215, 267, 298, 311, 313, 323, 326, 328, 336, 446
Systems thinking, 19, 149, 151, 156, 230, 260–263, 267–270, 283, 286–291, 297, 311–314, 316, 328, 330, 333, 336, 337, 346, 347, 349–351, 359, 361, 378, 381, 382, 423, 431, 446, 458
System structures, 92, 179, 190, 194, 219, 233, 269–271, 273, 309, 310, 312, 314, 315, 318, 327, 328, 330, 333, 336, 337, 341, 365, 439, 456–458
System variables, 87, 89, 93, 104, 106, 141, 180, 181, 215, 216, 218, 219, 222–225, 228, 230, 231, 238, 240, 248, 252, 255, 267, 273, 298, 303, 304, 320, 333–335, 341, 342, 430, 451–453, 467, 469

T

Tax collection, 42, 163, 164, 437, 438
Theories, 7, 8, 10, 12, 13, 15, 28, 86, 111, 114, 123, 133, 142, 146–148, 150, 152–159, 162, 163, 165, 168, 169, 184, 193, 194, 211, 213–215, 218, 222–224, 229–231, 235, 249, 252–254, 256, 258, 261–265, 273–275, 300, 309, 311–314, 323, 326, 328, 330, 333, 336–338, 340, 350, 361, 381, 423, 431, 438–440, 446, 453, 457, 459–461, 469
Tools, 340
Total factor productivity (TFP), 55, 56, 112
Traditional approaches, 14, 22, 231, 306–308, 310, 314, 346, 423, 431, 438, 444, 454

U

Uncertain, 11, 12, 18–20, 41, 88, 89, 103, 109, 111, 113, 136, 137, 146, 196, 212, 219, 231, 236, 240, 241, 253, 255–257, 284, 291, 293, 303, 306, 308, 309, 311, 312, 320, 321, 342, 351, 424, 429, 438, 454, 456, 471
Uncertainty, 3, 9, 11, 13, 18, 89, 94, 108, 111, 113, 138, 140, 141, 144–146, 150, 186, 191, 211, 213, 214, 225, 230, 236, 246, 254–257, 259, 264, 266, 269, 270, 274, 285, 290–292, 294, 299, 303, 312, 319, 326, 335, 336, 340, 352, 429–431, 439, 444, 456, 458, 459
Unemployment, 4, 73, 114, 168, 197, 213, 253, 270, 284, 288, 291, 295, 303, 429, 444, 445
Unicorns, 68, 69, 113, 244
University, 244
    Stanford, 244
Urban, 8, 15, 16, 19, 26, 27, 37, 40, 47, 50–54, 94, 108, 109, 114, 167, 176, 182, 186, 188, 192, 197, 224, 263, 264, 269, 270, 274, 291, 292, 305,

306, 313, 315, 344, 382, 429, 434, 444, 448, 449, 451, 459
Urban infrastructure, 51–53, 447
Urban local bodies, 23, 51, 52, 167, 182, 434
Urban population, 50
Urban sector, 50, 51, 54, 450

V
Values, 5, 6, 12, 14, 15, 17, 23–25, 28, 37, 39, 49, 55, 58–64, 67–69, 91–95, 97, 98, 100–104, 106, 107, 109, 111, 113–115, 123–132, 134, 136–146, 153, 155, 157–159, 162, 164–166, 179, 180, 182, 183, 185, 186, 190, 193, 195, 196, 212, 214, 216, 218, 219, 221–223, 225–228, 230–234, 236, 239, 241, 243–245, 247, 248, 255, 258, 272, 285, 286, 294–296, 299, 300, 302, 304, 306, 311, 313, 321, 322, 324–329, 331, 334, 342, 349, 355, 363, 367–376, 378, 380, 382, 387, 388, 391–396, 398, 400–409, 411, 414, 415, 424, 426–429, 433, 435, 437, 439–441, 444, 448, 449, 452, 454, 455, 457–461
VC investment, 68, 69
Venture capital (VC), 68, 69, 98, 99

W
Whole, 11, 15, 74, 86, 87, 153, 155, 181, 185, 214, 225, 231, 246, 273, 290, 291, 298, 299, 301, 310, 312, 313, 346, 347, 352, 467
Width of the attractor state, 103
Work culture, 16, 104, 115, 128, 142, 176, 186, 189, 225, 247, 329, 330, 333, 441

Printed in the USA
CPSIA information can be obtained
at www.ICGtesting.com
CBHW050224211024
16148CB00003B/88

9 789819 736621